A Study on the *Ratnagotravibhāga*

A Study on the *Ratnagotravibhāga* (*Uttaratantra*)

Being a Treatise on the *Tathāgatagarbha* Theory of Mahāyāna Buddhism

Including a Critical Introduction, a Synopsis of the Text, a Translation from the Original Sanskrit Text, in Comparision with its Tibetan & Chinese Versions, Critical Notes, Appendixes and Indexes

JIKIDO TAKASAKI

MOTILAL BANARSIDASS PUBLISHERS
PRIVATE LIMITED • DELHI (INDIA)

Reprint : Delhi, 2018
First Indian Edition: Delhi, 2014
Earlier published by CESMEO, 1966

ISBN: 978-81-208-3642-6

Also available at

MOTILAL BANARSIDASS

41 U.A. Bungalow Road, Jawahar Nagar, Delhi 110 007
1B, Jyoti Studio Compound, Kennedy Bridge, Nana Chowk, Mumbai 400 007
203 Royapettah High Road, Mylapore, Chennai 600 004
236, 9th Main III Block, Jayanagar, Bengaluru 560 011
8 Camac Street, Kolkata 700 017
Ashok Rajpath, Patna 800 004
Chowk, Varanasi 221 001

MLBD Cataloging-in-Publication Data
A Study on the Ratnagotravibhāga (Uttaratantra)
Being a Treatise on the *Tathāgatagarbha*
Theory of Mahāyāna Buddhism by
Jikido Takasaki
Includes Critical Introduction, a Synopsis of the Text,
a Translation from the Original Sanskrit Text,
in Comparision with its Tibetan & Chinese Versions,
Critical Notes, Appendixes and Indexes
ISBN : 978-81-208-3642-6
I. Buddhism II. Mahāyāna III. Tathāgatagarbha
IV. Takasaki, Jikido

Printed in India

by RP Jain at NAB Printing Unit,
A-44, Naraina Industrial Area, Phase I, New Delhi–110028
and published by JP Jain for Motilal Banarsidass Publishers (P) Ltd,
41 U.A. Bungalow Road, Jawahar Nagar, Delhi-110007

Publisher's Note

The Study on the **Ratnagotravibhaga**, which is also known as **Uttaratanta**, wss the subject of special study by Prof. Jikido Takasaki for which he received Ph. D. Degree from University of Poona. First this was published by Istituto Italiano Per II Medio Ed Estremo Oriente, Under the SERIE ORIENTALE ROMA in 1966. Long out of print the work is being republished by MLBD to make his masterpiece more accessible to the scholars/readers. Unfortunately Prof. Takasaki passed away before he could see his work in Indian reprint.

GENERAL TABLE OF CONTENTS

GENERAL TABLE OF CONTENTS

LIST OF ABBREVIATIONS

(for Synopsis and Notes on the Translation)

S = Sanskrit text of the *Ratnagotravibhāga* ed. by E. H. Johnston
Sanskrit term
T = Tibetan translation of the *Ratnagotravibhāga* (Sde-dge Edition, *Tohoku*, No. 4025)
Tibetan term
C = Chinese translation of the *Ratnagotravibhāga* (*Taisho Daizokyo Edition* No. 1611)
Chinese term
O = *Sublime Science of the Great Vehicle to Salvation*, by E. Obermiller (*Acta Orientalia*, XI, ii, iii, & iv)
J = E. H. Johnston's Preface & Notes on the *Ratnagotravibhāga*
K. = Kārikā
v. = verse
Taisho = *Taisho Edition of the Chinese Tripiṭaka*
Tohoku = *A Complete Catalogue of the Tibetan Buddhist Canons*, ed. by Tohoku University, Japan (1934).
BHS = *Buddhist Hybrid Sanskrit*
BHS Dic. = *Buddhist Hybrid Sanskrit Dictionary*, ed. by F. Edgerton (1953)
M. W. = M. Monier-William's *Sanskrit-English Dictionary*
PTS = Pāli Text Society's Edition of the Pāli Tipiṭaka

AA = *Abhisamayâlaṅkāra of Maitreya*, ed. by G. Tucci (Gaekward's Oriental Series No. 62)
AAĀ = *Abhisamayâlaṅkārâloka of Haribhadra*, ed. by G. Tucci (*ibid.*)
AAN = *Anūnatvâpūrṇatvanirdeśaparivarta* (*Taisho*, XVI, No. 668)
AĀS = * *Anuttarâśrayasūtra* (*Taisho*, XVI, No. 669)
AbhidhS = *Mahāyānâbhidharmasūtra*
AcintA = *Tathāgataguṇajñānâcintyaviṣayâvatāranirdeśa* (*Taisho*, X, No. 302)
AkṣP = *Akṣayamatiparipṛcchā* (*Taisho*, XIII, No. 397 (12))
AN = *Aṅguttara Nikāya* (Pāli, PTS Edition)
ASP = *Aṣṭasāhasrikā-prajñāpāramitā* (Wogihara's Edition of the *Abhisamayâlaṅkārâloka*)
AvatS = *Avataṃsakaśūtra* (*Taisho*, IX, No. 278)
BBh = *Bodhisattvabhūmi*, ed. by U. Wogihara
BGŚ = * *Buddhagotraśāstra* (*Taisho*, XXXI, No. 1610)
DAŚ = * *Mahāyānadharmadhātviśeṣaśāstra* (*Taisho*, XXXI, No. 1627)
DBS = *Daśabhūmikasūtra*, ed. by J. Rahder

DDV = *Dharmadharmatāvibhāga* (Skt. Fragment, ed. by S. Lévi; Tib. ed. by J. Nozawa, Prof. Yamaguchi's commemoration Volume)
DṛḍhP = *Dṛḍhâdhyāśayaparivarta* (Tibetan KG, Sde–dge Edition *Tohoku* No. 224)
DRS = *Dhāraṇīśvararājasūtra* (*Taisho*, XIII, No. 397 (1–2))
GagS = *Gaganagañjāsūtra* (*Taisho*, XIII, No. 397 (8))
JĀA = *Jñānâlokâlaṅkārasūtra* (*Taisho*, XII, No. 357)
KāśP = *Kāśyapaparivarta* (*Ratnakūṭasūtra*) ed. by Staël-Holstein; (*Taisho*, XI, No. 310 (23))
Laṅk = *Laṅkāvatārasūtra*, ed. by B. Nanjio
MK = *Madhyamakakārikā of Nāgārjuna* (ed. by Poussin)
MN = *Majjhima Nikāya* (Pāli, PTS Edition)
MPS = *Mahāparinirvāṇasūtra* (Mahāyāna) (*Taisho*, XII, No. 374)
MSA = *Mahāyānasūtrâlaṅkāra* (ed. by Sylvain Lévi)
MSbh(P) = *Mahāyānasaṃgraha–bhāṣya*, tr. by Paramārtha (*Taisho*, XXXI, No. 1595)
Mvyut = *Mahāvyutpatti* (Wogihara's Edition)
PP = *Prajñāpāramitā*
RCS = *Ratnacūḍasūtra* (*Taisho*, XIII, No. 397 (11))
RDS = *Ratnadhārikāsūtra* (*Taisho*, XIII, No. 397 (3))
RGV = *Ratnagotravibhāga*
ṢaḍS = * *Ṣaḍāyātanasūtra* (or *Ṣaḍindriyarāśisūtra*)
SāgP = *Sāgaramatiparipṛcchā* (*Taisho*, XIII, No. 397 (5))
ŚMS = *Āryaśrīmālāsūtra* (*Taisho*, XII, No. 353)
SN = *Saṃyutta Nikāya* (Pāli, PTS Edition)
SNS = *Sandhinirmocanasūtra* (Tib. ed. by E. Lamotte)
SPS = *Saddharmapuṇḍarīkasūtra*, ed. by E. Kern & B. Nanjio
TGS = *Tathāgatagarbhasūtra* (*Taisho*, XVI, No. 666)
YBh = *Yogācārabhūmi* (Skt. Part I, ed. by V. Bhattacharya; C. *Taisho*, XXX, No. 1579)
VajC = *Vajracchedikāsūtra*, ed. by M. Müller (*Taisho*, VIII, No. 235)
VimN = *Vimalakīrtinirdeśa* (*Taisho*, XIV, No. 475)
VMT = *Vijñaptimâtratā–triṃśikā*, ed. by S. Lévi
unk. = Source unknown

(*) Sanskrit titles with the sign * are restored from the Chinese materials.

PREFACE

The present volume was originally prepared under the guidance of Prof. V. V. Gokhale of the Fergusson College (presently of the University of Delhi) during my stay at the Bhandarkar Oriental Research Institute, Poona, from August 1954 to January 1957, under the auspices of the Indian Government, and was submitted to the University of Poona as a doctoral dissertation. I wish to express my gratitude to Prof. V. V. Gokhale who instructed me in reading the Sanskrit and Tibetan versions of the text throughout the two and half years of my stay in India and to Prof. R.D. Karmarkar of the Bhandarkar Institute from whom I received much guidance on Indian philosophy and the Sanskrit language in general.

When I was awarded the degree in September 1958, Prof. G. Tucci, who was one of the examiners of my dissertation, kindly suggested that I publish my work in the Serie Orientale Roma. I felt it a great honour, but I could not immediately respond to this kind proposal, since I felt my work inadequate and the presentation of it in English imperfect. Fortunately, Dr. Alex Wayman of Berkeley, U.S.A., kindly made suggestions. I also must acknowledge the helpful suggestions given to me by Dr. Wayman, Prof. H. Nakamura of the University of Tokyo (my faculty adviser in the Post-Graduate Course), Dr. H. Ui, and other Japanese scholars too numerous to mention in the matter of doctrinal interpretation.

Dr. Ui, an eminent Japanese Indologist, published the « *Hōshōron Kenkyū* » (A study of the Ratnagotravibhāga) in 1959. It consists of two parts. The first part consists of a critical and detailed studies on the text, author, Chinese translator, doctrinal and canonical references, etc., while the second consists of a Japanese translation of the Sanskrit text. I owe much to his interpretation in modifying my translation, although points on which I disagreed with him are kept intact. It is indeed with deep regret that I must note the passing away of Dr. Ui on July 14, 1963.

Ten years have passed since I started work on this volume. In the meanwhile I wrote several articles related to the text. Some are involved with the present work, but others, especially those written after sending the manuscript to Rome for printing, are not touched upon in this volume. Therefore, I would like to give a list of my articles so far published in order to cover the shortcomings of the present volume. If the reader has further interest on the subject, I hope that they will consult these articles.

1. « *AMUKTAJÑA no Gogi ni tsuite* » (in Jap.) (On the Meaning of the Term *amuktajña*), *JIBS*, Vol. VI–1, Jan. 1958, pp. 186–190. (Cf. Translation, p. 144, n. 23, etc.).

2. « *Kugyōichijōhōshōron no Kōzō to Genkei* » (in Jap.) (The Texual Structure of the Ratnagotravibhāga and the Supposed Form of Its Original Text), *The Journal of Religious Studies*, No. 155, Mar. 1958, pp. 14–33 (cf. Introduction, Chap. II and Appendix I).

3. « The Tathāgatôtpattisaṃbhavanirdeśa of the Avataṃsaka and the Ratnagotravibhāga — with special Reference to the Term '*tathāgatagotrasaṃbhava*' — », *JIBS*, Vol. VII–1, Dec. 1958, pp. 48–53. (cf. Introduction, Chap. IV, § 3,4).

4. « *Kegon-kyōgaku to Nyoraizō-shisō* » (in Jap.) (The Hua-yen Philosophy and the Tathāgatagarbha Theory — Development of the Idea of *gotrasaṃbhava* in India —), « *Kegon Shisō* », compiled by H. Nakamura and K. Kawada, Kyoto, 1960, pp. 275–332.

(a detailed investigation of the same subject as No. 3 mentioned above).

5. « *Tenne* » (in Jap.) (*Āśrayaparivṛtti* and *āśrayaparāvṛtti*), *Nihon Bukkyōgakkai Nempō*, No. 25, Mar. 1960, pp. 89–110. (cf. Introduction, Chap. IV, § 7)

6. « Structure of the Anuttarâśrayasūtra (*Wu-shang-i-ching*) », *JIBS*, Vol. VIII–2, Mar. 1960, pp. 30–37. (cf. Introduction, Chap. V, § 7).

7. « Description of the Ultimate Reality by means of the Six Categories in Mahāyāna Buddhism », *JIBS*, Vol. IX–2, Mar. 1961, pp. 24–33. (see Appendix III).

8. « A Comment on the Term *Ārambaṇa* in the Ratnagotravibhāga, I, 9 », *JIBS*, Vol. X–2, Mar. 1962, pp. 26–33. (cf. Translation, Chap. III, pp. 163, 168–171).

9. « Nyoraizō-setsu ni okeru Shin no Kōzō » (in Jap.) (The Structure of Faith in the Tathāgatagarbha Theory), *Komazawadaigaku-Kenkyūkiyō* (Fac. of. Buddhism), Vol. 22, Mar. 1964, pp. 86–109.

(This is an article in which the structure and significance of a set of three terms on faith, viz. *astitva*, *guṇavattva*, and *śaktatva* [cf. Translation, p. 382, n. 20] in relation to *śraddhā*, *adhimukti*, *chanda*, *abhisaṃpratyaya*, *prasāda*, and *abhilāṣa* are traced back to Abhidharma Buddhism, including works of the Vijñānavāda such as the Mahāyānasaṃgraha-bhāṣya, the Vijñaptimātratā-triṃśikā-bhāṣya, the Abhidharmasamuccaya-vyākhyā, etc., as well as those of the Tathāgatagarbha Theory such as the Ratnagotravighāga, the Buddhagotraśāstra and Paramārtha's translation of the Mahāyāna saṃgraha-bhāṣya.)

10. « *Shintai-yaku Shōdaijōron-Seshin-shaku ni okeru Nyoraizō Setsu* » Jap.) (The Tathāgatagarbha Theory Appearing in Paramārtha's Translation of the Mahāyānasaṃgraha-bhāṣya of Vasubandhu), " *Bukkyō Shisō Ronshū* " — Commemoration Volume for Prof. R. Yūki for his Sixtieth Birthday, Tokyo, 1964, pp. 241-264.

(In this article, the close relationship between the Ratnagotravibhāga and Paramārtha's said translation is made clear after picking up the parallel passages in both texts, and the Buddhagotraśāstra and the Anuttarâśrayasūtra as well. In conclusion, the author suggested that the additional parts of the Mahāyānasaṃgrahabhāṣya unique to Paramārtha's translation are probably written by Paramārtha himself on the knowledge of the Ratnagotrabvibhāga as he might have done the same with the Buddhagotraśāstra and the Anuttarāśrâyasūtra, and that Vasubandhu, consequently deprived of his authorship on the said parts as well as on the Buddhagotraśāstra, might have contributed little to the development of the Tathāgatagarbha theory. cf. Introduction, Chap. V, § 2,3). (*JIBS* = Journal of Indian and Buddhist Studies).

In conclusion I would like to express my sincere gratitude to all the professors mentioned above for their valuable assistance and encouragement without which I could never have brought the book to completion. However, the responsibility of the final result rests solely with the author. I also wish to acknowledge with many thanks the troubles taken in the past three years by the people at Is. M.E.O., especially Prof. Antonio Gargano, who set my rather complicated manuscript into print and gave it a nice arrangement.

Tokyo, 25 th August 1964.

J. TAKASAKI.

INTRODUCTION

INTRODUCTION

CONTENTS

I.

THE RATNAGOTRAVIBHĀGA, ITS TEXT, TRANSLATION, AND TRADITIONS CONCERNING THE AUTHOR

§ 1. – *Text.*

The *Ratnagotravibhāga Mahāyānôttaratantraśāstra*, on which this present study is made, is one of the treatises on the Mahāyāna doctrine written in Sanskrit. It was, however, quite recently that the Sanskrit manuscripts were discovered and critically edited [1]. Before then, it was known only through the Tibetan and Chinese versions. The first introducer of this text to the world of modern study was Dr. E. Obermiller who translated the Tibetan version into English and made this text famous under the title of "*Uttaratantra*" according to the Tibetan tradition [2]. In China, however, they used the name "*Ratnagotra–śāstra*" as its title, and this title was justified by the discovery of a Sanskrit fragment in Saka script in which we find the title "*Ratnagotravibhāga*". [3] Dr. E. H. Johnston, the discoverer of this fact and the editor of the Sanskrit edition of this text, suggested the use of "*Ratnagotravibhāga*" as the proper title showing the main subject of this text [4]. This seems quite reasonable and I followed him in this study. The reason for this will be made clear afterwards.

1) *The Ratnagotravibhāga Mahāyānottaratantraśāstra*, ed. by E. H. Johnston, D. Litt., and seen through the press and furnished with indexes by T. Chowdhury, M. A., Ph. D., Patna, 1950.

This edition is based upon two Mss. found by Rev. Rāhula Sāṅkṛtyāyana in Tibet. About the Mss., see *JBORS*, XXI, p. 31 (III. Ṣalu monastery, vol. XI–5, No. 43) and XXIII, p. 34 (VII. Ṣalu monastery, vol. XIII–5, No. 242).

2) "*The Sublime Science of the Great Vehicle to Salvation, being a Manual of Buddhist Monism, the work of Ārya Maitreya with a commentary by Āryâsaṅga*". *Acta Orientalia*, Vol. IX, parts ii, iii & iv, 1931.

3) "*A Fragment of the Uttaratantra in Sanskrit*", by H. W. Bailey & E. H. Johnston. *Bull. S.O.S.*, Vol. VIII, Part 1, 1935. The reference is to pp. 86 & 87.

4) E. H. Johnston, *op. cit.* (hereafter the abbreviation 'J.' will be used for this work) p. v, fn. 2.

About the manuscripts, I have nothing to add here to Johnston's description as I have had no chance to examine them. Some notable points for the present study are: 1) they belong to a considerably later period in comparison with the date of the Chinese translation, and consequently the latter, though it differs from the Sanskrit edition in several passages, has its importance because of its antiquity; 2) they are identified almost completely with the Tibetan version; and 3) no mention of the name of the author leaves room for taking the Chinese tradition into consideration.

Johnston's critical edition, the basic text of my English translation, shows his remarkable skill in editing Sanskrit manuscripts and is an excellent contribution to Buddhist scholarship. Nevertheless, I have found some words and passages to be corrected in the light of the Tibetan and Chinese translations, especially of the latter. Buddhist scholars should regret that Dr. Johnston passed away before completing his learned analysis of this text, and should continue to give it critical study. I believe my work, however faulty, will cast some new light on the implications of this text in Mahāyāna Buddhism.

§ 2. – *Translation and Traditions concerning the Author.*

Prior to describing the contents of the *Ratna.*, it will be necessary to refer to the translations in Tibetan and Chinese, sub-sources of the present work. Besides this, references will be made to traditions about the author in Tibet and China, so that we can further consider the authorship and date of the *Ratna.* in the absence of any material in the Sanskrit manuscripts.

There are two versions of the *Ratna.* in Tibetan Tanjur:

1. *Theg-pa-chen-po rgyud-bla-maḥi bstan-bcos* (*Mahāyāna-uttaratantra-śāstra*), Tohoku Catalogue No. 4024.
2. *Theg-pa-chen-po rgyud-bla-maḥi bstan-bcos rnam-par-bśad-pa* (*Mahāyāna-uttaratantra-śāstra-vyākhyā*), Tohoku Catalogue No. 4025.

The second one is a full translation of the Sanskrit text, probably of the same source as the present manuscripts, although it is called *vyākhyā*. On the other hand, the first one consists merely of verses in the *Ratna.* Both were translated, according to the colophon of these translations, by Blo-ldan-śes-rab (Matiprajna) at Srinagar in Kashmir under the guidance of Kashmirian pandits, Ratnavajra and Sajjana, about the end of the 11th cent. A.D.[5]. This name Sajjana reminds us of the author of the *Mahāyānôttaratantraśāstrôpadeśa*, given as Satyajñāna by Johnston from the Patna manuscript[6]. If we can identify both names, the *Mahāyānôttaratantraśāstrôpadeśa*, of which nothing is known except what Johnston tells us, will be assured of its date in the same century[7].

Tibetan tradition attributes the first one, i.e. the verse section of the *Ratna.* to Ārya Maitreya (Ḥphags-pa Mgon-po byams-pa) and the prose commentary (*vyākhyā* in the second), to Ācārya Asaṅga (Slob-dpon Thogs-med)[8], and regards the *Ratna.* as one of "five treatises written by Bodhisattva Maitreya, being his ultimate doctrine based upon the *Prajñāpāramitā*"[9]. This attribution to Maitreya of the verse section is traced in the Saka script fragment referred to above, which quotes the opening verse and the first few verses of Chapter III in the *Ratna.* as the work of Bodhisattva Maitreya[10]. This shows that Maitreya was regarded as the author of the *Ratna.* not only in Tibet but also in Central Asia, and probably in India, too, in the period between the 8th and 12th cent. A.D. About the authorship of Asaṅga on the commentary, however, nothing is mentioned anywhere else, and the point is undecided.

Chinese tradition offers a different name as to the author. The present Chinese Tripiṭaka retains one translation of the *Ratna.* entitled "*Chiu-ching yi-ch'eng pao-sing-lun*" (究竟一乘寶性論, lit. *Uttara-ekayāna-ratnagotra-śāstra*) (*Taisho*, Vol. 31, No. 1611). It was translated by Ratnamati (勒那摩提) in c. 511 A.D. at Lo-yang, the capital of the Northern Wei dynasty.

According to the *K'ai-yuan che-chiao mo-lu* (開元釋教目錄), an ancient Chinese catalogue of the Tripiṭaka (730 A.D.), there are said to be two translations, one by Ratnamati and the other by Bodhiruci,

5) Sde-dge Edition, MDO XLIV, p. 129 *a* 5 ff. (Tohoku University Copy). Hereafter, the references to the Tibetan version are made according to this edition with the abbreviation, 'Tib.' or 'T'. For the date and personage of Blo-ldan śes-rab, see George N. Roerich, *The Blue Annals*, Part I, pp. 325-6, 328, 347-350, Calcutta 1949. (This is an English translation of a history of Tibetan Buddhism called Deb-ther sṅon-po. According to the translator's calculation, his date is 1059-1109 A.D.).

6) This work was reported by Rāhula Sāṃkṛtyāyana as one of three Mss. of the Ratna. See *JBORS*, XXI, p. 33 (IV. Ngor monastery, Vol. VIII-6, No. 68).

7) I have intention to edit this work and have already asked for permission to the authority of the Jayaswar Research Institute, Patna and to Prof. G. Tucci who has got another photographic copy of the same Ms.

8) Tib. p. 129 *a* 5.

9) See, Obermiller, *op. cit.* (hereafter the abbreviation 'O'. will be used for this work) p. 81 f.

10) "*A Fragment of the Uttaratantra*", pp. 86-89.

which is lost now[11]. Furthermore it is said that both translators collaborated at the beginning, but later on, because of the differences of opinions between them, Bodhiruci made his own translation separately[12]. This record seems reliable at a glance since it is said to be taken from the *Pao–ch'ung–lu* (寶唱錄), a missing catalogue compiled in c. 518 A.D., a few years after the date of translation of the *Ratna*. However, as the result of critical examination of this record, it is clarified that the catalogue was not directly based upon the Pao–ch'ung–lu, but upon the preceding catalogues such as the *Li–tai–san–pao–chi* (歷代三寶紀, 597 A.D.), the *Ta–t'ang nei–t'en–lu* (大唐内典錄, 664 A.D.), where the record mentioned above concerned two other works, the *Daśabhūmikasūtra–śāstra* and the *Ratnakūṭasūtra–śāstra*, and there is no evidence of Bodhiruci's translation of the *Ratna*. at all.[13]. The record of the *K'ai–yuan–lu* is perhaps created by misreading of these catalogues, and there might be room for such misreading in the circumstances of Chinese Buddhism in those days. Namely, the Ti–lun (地論) school based upon the *Daśabhūmikasūtra–śāstra* of Vasubandhu divided into two branches, proclaiming Bodhiruci and Ratnamati as the nominal founder of each branch, and this division is said to have had its root in the differences of opinions due to the interpretation of the relation between '*ālayavijñāna*' and '*tathāgatagarbha*' or '*tathatā*'[14]. The branch of Southern Path of the Ti–lun school, founded by a pupil of Ratnamati, caused in later days the rise of the Hua–yen (華嚴, Avataṃsaka) school which emphasizes '*cittamātra*' theory of the *Avataṃsaka–sūtra* along with '*dharmadhātu*', '*tathāgatagarbha*' against '*vijñaptimātratā*' and '*ālayavijñāna*' of the Fa–hsiang (法相) school founded by a disciple of Hsüang–chuang (玄奘). Thus Ratnamati and Bodhiruci were standing opposite to each other, and

11) *Taisho*, Vol. 55, No. 2154, pp. 541 *a–b*, 540 *b*, 608 *c*–609 *a*, 637 *b*, 690 *b*, 714 *a*.

12) *Ibid.*, 540 *b*.

13) H. Ui, *Hōshōron–kenkyū* (in Japanese), Tokyo, 1959, pp. 3–16. Cf. *Li–tai san–pao–chi*, *Taisho*, Vol. 49, No. 2034, p. 866 *b–c*: 十地經論十二卷 (*Daśabhūmikasūtraśāstra*, 12 vols.); 寶積經論四卷 (*Ratnakūṭasūtraśāstra* 已上二論菩提流支並譯 (two treatises mentioned above are also translated by Bodhiruci). *Nai–t'en–lu*, *Taisho*, Vol. 55, No. 2149, 269 *b*: 十地經論; 究竟一乘寶性論, 四卷 (*Ratnagotra–śāstra*, 4 vols.); 寶積經論, 四卷, 與十地二論菩提流支並譯 (this and the *Daśabhūmika*, these two are also translated by Bodhiruci).

14) J. Takakusu, *The Essentials of Buddhist Philosophy* (First Indian Edition, 1956), p. 114.

this conflict between them led people to imagine that Bodhiruci could translate the *Ratna.* on the line of the Vijñānavāda. Actually however, he did not do it, and since then the *Ratna.* was not recognized as the authority for the Chinese Vijñānavādins, probably due to the fact that the author of the *Ratna.* was thought not to be an orthodox Vijñānavādin such as Asaṅga and Vasubandhu.

As will be made clear afterwards, the *Ratna.* takes the theory of the *tathāgatagarbha* as its basic standpoint and is highly estimated by Fa-tsang (法藏), the 3rd patriarch of the Hua-yen school. And it was he who left the record on the authorship of the *Ratna.* He said in his commentary on the *Mahāyānadharmadhātviśeṣa-śāstra* (大乘法界無差別論)[15] that Bodhisattva Kien-huei (堅慧), *Sāramati* (沙羅末底), *in Sanskrit*, was 'a Bodhisattva on the first stage' (地上菩薩), born in Central India 7 centuries after the Buddha's Mahāparinirvāṇa as a member of a Kṣatriya clan who after learning Buddhism, wrote *the Ratnagotravibhāga uttaratantraśāstra, the Dharmadhātviśeṣaśāstra and others*[16]. This report, heard by Fa-tsang from Devaprajña (提雲般若) the translator of the *Dharmadhātviśeṣaśāstra* and a monk come from Khotan, is reliable to some extent. At least, we may say Sāramati was believed to be the author of the *Ratna.* till the end of the 7th cent. A.D. in Central Asia. And we cannot find any other tradition concerning the author of the *Ratna.* in China.

As far as the Chinese tradition is concerned, the authorship of Sāramati on the *Ratna.* seems to be unchangeable. Still, there remains some doubt. The reason is that there is no name of the author in the Chinese translation nor in any of the old catalogues, and this translation consists actually of two parts, namely: 1) the Kārikā text, an extract of certain verses in the *Ratna.*, and 2) the whole work including the prose section but excluding certain number of verses in the Kārikā text. This Kārikā text is quite different from that of the Tibetan version, in that it omits those verses which seem to be supplementary to the basic verses. From this fact we feel the need of assuming the existence of, at least, two authors on the *Ratna.*, one heing that of the basic verses and the other the commentator on it. Here one may naturally call to mind the Tibetan tradition. But, to settle this problem, we should examine the whole contents and characteristics of this *Ratna.* We shall now proceed to the next stage.

[15] *Taisho*, Nos. 1626 and 1627.

[16] *Ta-ch'eng-fa-chieh-wu-ch'a-pieh-lun-chu* (大乘法界無差別論疏) *Taisho*, No. 1838, Vol. 44, p. 63 *c*.

II.

THE STRUCTURE OF THE TEXT

§ 1. – *Basic Text and Commentary.*

From the structural point of view, the present text of the *Ratna.* is a combination of the basic text and a commentary thereon. That much is regular in Buddhist literatures. The peculiarity of the *Ratna.* lies in the fact that it consists of two parts, in verse and in prose, while the verse section consists again of two parts, one basic, and the other supplementary. In other words, the basic part of this text is merely of verses, while another part, the commentary, is in verse and in prose and the prose section of the commentary which follows the commentary verse or verses explaining their meaning with quotations from various *sūtras* is quite detailed in Chapter I, but quite scanty for other chapters.

To clarify this characteristic, let us take an example from the text. The verse I, 4 which expresses devotion to the '*buddharatna*' as the refuge (*śaraṇa*) is followed by v. I, 5 with a prose explanation of it and the latter is again explained in detail by the following three verses and a prose commentary which continues up to p. 10, l. 14. Then the text proceeds to the next subject, the '*dharma-ratna*', beginning with v. I, 9 followed by commentary verses and a prose commentary with a structure similar to that of v. I, 4. If we take such verses as I, 4 & 9 to be typical, we may be able to compile the Kārikā-text of the *Ratna.*, and for this, we find that the Chinese Kārikā text gives a fairly good account of those verses which are basic or original.

More precisely, the Chinese Kārikā text is one of the aids for determining them. In most cases, including the example given above, it offers us a fairly good account of the basic verses. But we cannot accept the whole text as basic. For example, the first 18 verses in that text are to be omitted from this line as they are not available in either Sanskrit or Tibetan versions. They seem to be written by the Chinese translator. Besides these 18, we have another additional verse in the Chinese Kārikā text in the last chapter maintaining the respect for the teacher of the Doctrine (*dharmabhāṇaka*). As its idea matches that of the 18 introductory verses, this verse, too, seems to be composed by the translator [17]. There are also a

[17] C. p. 820 *c*. Emphasis on the respect for the '*dharmabhāṇaka*' was probably a reflection of the historical circumstances in those days, e.g. persecution of the Buddhists by the Huns, or something like that. The fact that Paramārtha's translation of the

certain number of verses whose originality is doubtful to judge from the contents. Only one thing we can say definitely: those verses which are omitted from the Chinese Kārikā-text are by no means the original ones. This is no doubt a kind of selection, but to go beyond this, we should seek for other grounds.

Prior to v. I, 4, in the heading to that verse, it is said:

Uktaḥ śāstra-saṃbandhaḥ //

Idānīṃ ślokānām artho vaktavyaḥ / — / *atas tat-prathamato buddha-ratnam adhikṛtya ślokaḥ* /

And, as the heading to v. 1,9, it is said:

Ato buddha-ratnād dharma-ratna-prabhāvanêti tad-anantaraṃ tad-adhikṛtya ślokaḥ /

This word '*śloka*' is not used for the supplementary verses in these cases, and v. I, 4 is the first verse for which the word '*śloka*' is applied; furthermore, this selection of v. I, 4 as the first basic verse is identical with that in the Chinese Kārikā text (except the 18 verses referred to above). It shows the fact that the passage up to '*uktaḥ śāstra-saṃbandhaḥ* /' is the introduction by the commentator who thereafter begins to explain the meaning of the '*ślokas*', i. e. the basic verses. Being the explanation of the meaning of *śloka*, the commentary seems to be called the '*Ślokârthasaṃgrahavyākhyāna*' as appeared in the colophons of Chapters I, IV, and V.

This limited usage of the word '*śloka*' becomes, however, confused after vv. I, 156–157 where the prose commentary disappears except for headings, and the word '*śloka*' is used for both basic and supplementary verses. How to interpret this confusion seems not so simple. Can we ascribe it to the commentator's caprice or forgetfulness of the rule ? Shall we assume another commentator in order to explain this change of style ? Again, can '*śloka*' be construed as one kind of metre, i. e. *Anuṣṭubh*, when it is used for the commentary verses?[18] One of these three possibilities must be in point, and I feel no necessity to change my former supposition.

Neither the Chinese Kārikā text nor the use of the word '*śloka*' can give the final account of the basic verses, but these two are certainly the

Mahāyānasaṃgraha-bhāṣya, which retains *Ratna*. V, 16–28 at the end of the work (*Taisho*. XXX, p. 270 a–b), omits this verse is another powerful proof in support of this supposition.

[18]) All the commentary verses in Chapters II–V, which are called '*śloka*' in the text, have the *Anuṣṭubh* metre except for v. II, 73, which is, in turn, missing in the Chinese version. And, because of a unique terminology used in this verse (e.g. '*maharṣi*' is used for the Bodhisattva), it seems to be a quotation from some old canonical work. So the third assumption has no inconsistency.

most powerful bases for the selection, and those verses which are found in the Chinese Kārikā text and called '*śloka*' will be accepted as basic. In this way, we shall evaluate all verses in the Chinese Kārikā-text.

§ 2. – *Chinese Account on the Basic Verses.*

Except for the 19 verses referred to above, all the verses in the Chinese Kārikā text are found in the Sanskrit text. Not all of them are, however, of the same character. Through their classification into certain groups, we shall try to reconstruct the original text of the *Ratna.*

First of all, let us pick up those verses which are called '*śloka*' in the Sanskrit text. The result is as follows:

Chapter I. vv. 4, 9, 13, 23, 30, 35, 42, 45, 47, 49, 52–63, 66, 79, 84, 156–157. (27)
Chapter II. vv. 1*, 3, 8, 9*, 18–20, 29, 38–41, 62, 69. (14)
Chapter III. vv. 1. (1)
Chapter IV. vv. 1–2, 13* 41*. (4)
Chapter V. vv. 1–6, 16–25*. (16)

In this table, except for verses with the sign '*', all are doubtless of genuine character in their contents as well as their style. They express the fundamental doctrine of this text and maintain a fairly archaic metre. Furthermore, they are followed by the supplementary verses, they have independent meaning and are understandable by themselves[19]. On these points, there will be no objection if we regard them as the 'basic verses.' The verses with the sign '*', however, require some more careful examination.

1) v. II, 1. This verse is of doubtful originality for the following reason. It shows, according to the commentator, 8 categories in regard to the '*nirmalā tathatā*' i. e. the '*dharmakāya*' and without other supplementary and explanatory verses, itself has no independent meaning. Formally, this verse is followed by the commentary in prose and verse. And in this commentary verse called '*uddāna*' (summary), the same categories are repeated in different terminology. The structure presents no doubt as to its originality; the point at issue is whether or not the author of the original text tried such categorization.

This question is posed regarding v. I, 29, mentioned in the Chinese Kārikā text but called merely '*uddāna*' in the Sanskrit text, and whose ter-

19) Sometimes, a series of verses expresses a united meaning under one subject word. e.g. vv. I, 30, 35, 42 & 45. For them, the subject word is '*jinagarbho 'yaṃ*' in v. 45.

minology is exactly the same as v. II, 2, i. e. the commentary verse on v. II, 1, in showing 10 categories of the '*tathāgatagarbha*.' In comparison with v. II, 2, this v. I, 29 seems clearly to be a commentary verse. Furthermore, the commentary sentence preceding this verse says:

pūrvataraṃ tu yenârthena sarvatrâviśeṣeṇa pravacane sarvâkāraṃ tadarthasūcanaṃ bhavati, tad apy adhikṛtya nirdekṣyāmi /

This '*nirdekṣyāmi*' (I will explain) is immediately followed by '*uddānaṃ*', and hence, against the Chinese tradition, there is no scope to treat this as original.

As a consequence of denying the originality of v. I, 29, the categorization of the *tathāgatagarbha* into 10 aspects also will be denied of originality. Hence, we incline to omit v. II, 1 from the line of original verses, although it retains a comparatively old terminology [20].

2) v. II, 9. This verse is composed with a view to succeeding detailed explanations of 9 examples of defilements which cover the *tathāgatagarbha*, illustrated in the *Tathāgatagarbhasūtra* and utilized in Chapter I. Without a knowledge of those explanations, it cannot be understood independently. And those verses explaining the 9 examples are, as will be set forth below, of rather doubtful originality. The omission of that verse therefore, depends on the originality of the latter verses. About its structural character, however, there is no doubtful point.

3) v. IV, 13. This verse, like v. II, 9, expects the existence of detailed explanation which follows this verse. It is called, by the commentator, '*sūtrasthānīya-śloka*' (a stanza based upon the scripture) and the following verses illustrating the examples in detail are called '*vistaravibhāganirdeśa*', and are actually taken from the *Jñānâlokâlaṅkārasūtra*. A further discussion will be made below along with examination of these illustrations.

In the same way, verses to be similarly considered are v. III, 4 and vv. I, 96–98. Of them, v. III, 4 is called '*uddāna*' according to the Tibetan and Chinese versions though not mentioned in the Sanskrit text [21]. In fact, all of these, including v. IV, 13, are '*uddāna*' – verses on the

[20] See note on my translation, XII-11. Of the terms used for such categorization in vv. I, 29 and II, 2, the first six, viz. *svabhāva*, *hetu*, *phala*, *karman*, *yoga*, *and vṛtti*, are identical with those used in the *Sūtrâlaṅkāra* (commentary on vv. IX, 59–60) and in the *Yogācārabhūmi* (on '*śabda-vidyā*', *Taisho*, 30, p. 361 *a*). This seems to show that such categorization was commonly held for any subject, regardless of the author. Therefore the question is to be limited to the categorization itself. See Appendix III.

[21] T. '*sdom-ni*', C. 略說二偈.

illustrations taken from certain scriptures. In this sense, the possibility of their being original depends on the originality of the illustrating verses which follow them.

4) v. IV, 41. The Sanskrit text shows '*śloka*' before this verse, but the Tibetan and the Chinese texts do not. Actually, this one is in the series of verses illustrating 9 examples on the acts of the Buddha, and we have no need to discuss its originality separately.

5) vv. V, 16–25. The headings for these verses are missing in the Sanskrit text but the Tibetan and Chinese versions retain them well. As far as the structure is concerned, they are no doubt basic.

There is one verse to be taken as basic, even though it was kept out of the table. It is v. I, 27. It expresses the fundamental idea of the *Ratna.* and is so important that we cannot imagine the contents of this text without this verse. Both the Chinese and Tibetan versions have confusion in arranging this passage, but the Chinese commentary says in the heading: "as it is said in the Kārikā text (*yathôktam śloka– or kārikā–granthe*)." On the other hand, v. I, 28, though it follows immediately after v. I, 27, is clearly a commentary verse and possibly the original Sanskrit text had a heading between these two verses.

As the result of examination, I will divide these verses discussed above into two groups: 'pure'–*śloka* and '*uddāna–śloka*'. In the first group, those verses mentioned in the table without the sign '*' except for vv. V, 16–25, and v. I, 27 are included. On the other hand, the second group includes vv. I, 96–98; III, 4; IV, 13 as being '*sūtrasthānīya–uddāna*.' Verses II, 9 remain of doubtful position, and v. I, 29 and, with some hesitation, v. II, 1 are also to be cancelled.

There is another kind of verses among the Chinese Kārikā text. This is the three series of verses to be called '*udāharaṇa*' taken from certain scriptural passages, namely: 1) vv. I, 99–126, 9 *udāharaṇas* on the Essence of Buddhahood covered with defilements, taken from the *Tathāgatagarbhasūtra*, 2) vv. III, 5–26, explanations on the 64 *buddhaguṇas*, based upon the *Ratnadārikāparipṛcchā*, and 3) vv. 27–30, 34–35, 41, 44–52 (with an additional one which is not found in Sanskrit), 55–57, 64–67 (with an additional one which is not found in Sanskrit), 67–68, 71–76, 88, & 89–91, 9 *udāharaṇas* on the Buddha's Acts, taken from the *Jñānâlokâlaṅkārasūtra*.

In general, these verses differ from those in the first group in their being taken from a scriptural passage; and because of this characteristic, we cannot call them 'genuine' to this text in the same degree. They have no original idea of the author but are merely 'newly composed verses' by the author out of the basic scripture. In this sense, they are to be termed '*sūtrasthānīya–udāharaṇa*'–verses. From the structural point of view, however, they seem not to be the commentator's work, as they are followed by a certain number of verses showing '*udāharaṇānāṃ piṇḍārthaḥ*'. The question is whether the same author of the 'pure'-*ślokas* had a share in composing this group of verses or not. And, if not, we shall be obliged to suppose the existence of a second author between the author of 'pure'-*ślokas* and that of the commentary. In this connection, one thing to be noted is the counting of the 32 '*mahāpuruṣalakṣaṇa*' in Chap. III. It contains actually more than 32 marks and some of them are not available in works such as the *Abhisamayâlaṅkāra*, attributed to Maitreya, and the *Prajñāpāramitāśāstra* attributed to Nāgārjuna, although it agrees with the *Ratnadārikāsūtra* [22]. It seems to show that even the *Ratnadārikāsūtra* is composed after Maitreya and as far as this part is concerned, Maitreya was not the author, against Tibetan tradition. As this part is among the series of '*udāharaṇa*', all the *udāharaṇa* groups and hence the *uddāna* group as well, seem to belong to somewhat later days in comparison with the 'pure'-*śloka* group.

We have another kind of question for Chapter IV. The Chinese Kārikā text omits a fairly large number of verses which are kept among the *udāharaṇa*-verses in the Sanskrit text and, furthermore, sometimes it also changes the order. Of these omissions, the verses 36–40 along with the passage between p. 102, l. 20 and p. 104, l. 12, and verses 59–62 along with a heading are clearly the later additions because of their contents and style. The second case concerns vv. 14–26 in the first *udāharaṇa*, vv. 31–33 in the 2nd, vv. 42–43 in the 3rd, vv. 53–54 in the 4th, v. 63 in the 5th, and vv. 69–70 in the 6th *udāharaṇa*. In each example these verses have the same contents as those kept in the Chinese Kārikā text. In the first case, it is difficult to decide whether the verses were added after the Chinese translation was made or whether the Chinese translator omitted them intentionally [23]. It depends more or less on the reliability of the Chinese Kārikā text as showing the original form of the text. This last point will be proved by the examination of the third case.

The third case is less simple than the previous ones. It is in the passage between p. 112, l. 1 and p. 113, l. 4. Of those verses contained in this passage, v. 88 is placed in the Chinese version immediately after v. 76, and vv. 89–91, at the end of the first *udāharaṇa* with a heading saying: *anutpādânirodhas tathāgata iti*. The first one is, according to the Sanskrit

[22] Detailed comparison on each 'mark' among various scriptures is given in my note on the equivalent passage in the English translation.

[23] Note that such repetition of the same idea is seen in the *udāharaṇa* verses in Chapter I.

text, one of 4 *ślokas* which show the *udāharaṇa-saṃgraha*. As a whole, this '*udāharaṇa-saṃgraha* seems to be a later addition since its terminology is never seen in other passages and this part is situated after the *udāharaṇa-piṇḍârtha* of 9 examples. But why was only one of the four kept in the Chinese version ? V. 88 is a verse which shows the significance of the three *udāharaṇas* beginning with the 7th. Such a kind of verse is observed in every *udāharaṇa* up to the 6th with a special heading like '*atatprahitānām ātmâparādhe*' before v. 41 (2nd *ud.*), '*bhājana-vimātratāyām*' before v. 46 (3rd *ud.*), etc. Verses as such are lacking from the 7th to 9th *udāharaṇa* in the present Sanskrit text, v. 88 must have represented them in the basic text for the Chinese translation. Addition of vv. 85–87 with the heading must be the result of misundertanding of the role of v. 88 as simple summarization of the three *udāharaṇas* by a certain Sanskrit copyist of later days. Difference of metre between vv. 85–87 and v. 88 yields another proof for this supposition [24]. However, it poses another question about the omission of v. 70 in the Chinese Kārikā text. This verse occupies the same position for the 6th *udāharaṇa* as v. 88 for the 7th–9th. If we admit such an omission by the Chinese translator himself, the omission in the second case in general will also be ascribed to the Chinese translator and the reliability of the Chinese version will decrease. There must have taken place an artificial selection by the Chinese translator, and as a result, those omissions in the second case may be added to the *Udāharaṇa* group.

As for the next ones, i. e. vv. 89–91, the problem is not of their genuine character but of their place in the text, i. e. whether they belong to the Kārikā text as the Chinese version does, or to the commentary as in the case of the Sanskrit text. The Chinese treatment is acceptable for the following reasons: 1) These verses show the significance of the 1st *udāharaṇa* as v. 41 does for the 2nd: 2) The *Jñānâlokâlaṅkārasūtra*, the basic scripture for the 9 *udāharaṇas*, has a similar verse between the *udāharaṇas*; [25] and con-

[24] I have previously expressed my opinion that the whole of this passage is a later interpolation, but is kept in the basic text of C. tr.: and C omitted the three verses by mistake. ("The textual structure of the Ratnagotravibhāga and the supposed form of its original text", *in Jap.*, *The Journal of Religious Studies*, No. 155). Here I have corrected it according to Dr. Ui's opinion. See H. Ui, *op. cit.*, p. 265.

[25] In the said sūtra, the *anutpādânirodhatā* of the Buddha is repeated at the end of every *udāharaṇa* up to the 4th, and at the end of the 4th *ud.* the sūtra has a summarized verse on this point. In the oldest version of the sūtra, i.e. the second Chinese translation, in the absence of the illustrations of *dundubhi* and the following two, this summarized verse comes immediately after the 1st *ud.* The verse in the said sūtra is as follows:

1. 如來常不生 諸法亦復然 世間無實法 愚癡

tinuity between v. 84 and v. 92 as given by the Chinese version seems to be consistent. At the same time, however, there remain some difficulties in accepting it. Namely, 1) the subject '*anutpādânirodhatā*' of the Tathāgata is the basic point throughout Chap. IV as well as the *Jñānâlokâlaṅkārasūtra* [26]; 2) their contents and wording are quite like to the commentary verses, especially the term '*darśanâdi*' in v. 91 is akin to '*navadhā darśanâdikam*' in v. 84 which expects the existence of v. 81 [27]. Thus the Sanskrit text also can claim its reasonability of their treatment. In view of the antiquity of the Chinese version, however, the case was most probably as follows: vv. 89–91 along with an additional verse in the Chinese Kārikā text were originally kept at the end of the 1st *udāharaṇa* but with slightly different terms in the second *pāda* of v. 91; but afterwards, in the thought that the subject is not exclusive to the 1st *udāharaṇa* but common to the whole passage, the Sanskrit copyist shifted them to the commentary, changing some words as seen in the present text and adding an explanatory heading (p. 112, ll. 18–20). As far as this point is concerned, the Chinese version recovers its reliability to some extent, but unless we could reconstruct the original form of v. 91 [28], we should treat vv. 89–91 as the commentary verses, being a part of the *udāharaṇa–piṇḍârtha*.

妄取相 無漏善法中 無如及如來 依彼善法力 現世如鏡像

(*Taisho*. Vol. 12, p. 242 *b*)

2. 如來常住 示生不滅 非心非色 非有非無
如琉璃地 見宮殿影 此影非有 亦復非無
衆生心淨 見如來身 非有非無 亦復如是

(*ibid*. p. 251 *a*)

26) See above (n. 25); The *Ratna*., p. 9, 1.7 (= *Taisho*, *ibid*., p. 240 *b*).

27) v. 91: *ayatnāt kṛtyam ity evaṃ darśanâdi pravartate* /
dharmakāyād anutpādânirodhād ā bhavasthiteḥ //
v. 84: *ayaṃ ca prakṛto 'trârtho navadhā darśanâdikam* /
janmântardhim ṛte śāstur anābhogāt pravartate //
v. 81: *darśanādeśanā vyāptir vikṛtir jñānaniḥsṛtiḥ* /
mano–vāk–kāyaguhyāni prāptiś ca karuṇâtmānām //

28) For v. 91, C.

此業自然有 見是等現前 法身不生滅 盡諸際常住

It can be otherwise translated into the following way:

This action takes place without effort, and one perceives this and that appearance (although) the *dharmakāya* has neither origination nor destruction and is eternal as long as the world exists.

§ 3. – *Supposed Form of the Original Text.*

As the result of examination of the Chinese Karikā text, we have arrived at the conclusion that 1) the Chinese Kārikā text does not stand for the original text; even the existence of the Kārikā text of such form at the time when the Chinese translation was made is doubtful, but 2) it keeps a fairly good account of those verses which are 'not the commentary verses', and 3) those verses retained in the Chinese Kārikā text are to be divided into 3 groups: A. 'pure'–*śloka*–group, B. '*uddāna*'–group, and C. *udāharaṇa*'–group; 4) in Chapter IV some verses among the Sanskrit text are to be added to the C–group, and 5) of these 3 groups, B. & C. are somewhat of later days.

The problems remaining after this examination are the treatment of v. II, 9, and the form of the original text. One way to solve these problems is to treat v. II, 9 as an insertion made simultaneously with the B.—and the C.–group by the second author, and regard the A.–group as consisting of the original form of text. By this, we can get 59 verses as original. This seems consistent in its form, as it matches the use of the title of the commentary, '*ślokârthasaṃgrahavyākhyāna*'. Strictly speaking, however, it leaves us in some doubt regarding the inconsistency of numbers in each chapter or subject [29].

Another way is to cut out all verses, starting with those in Chapter II as well as v. 23 of Chapter I from the line of the original verses, and regard them along with v. II, 9 and verses in the B. & the C.–groups as the secondary addition. In this way only 27 verses in Chapter I remain as original. The reasons are 1) vv. I, 156–157, which express the '*deśanā-prayojana*', can stand for a kind of conclusion and by this passage, i. e. in Chapter I, the *tathāgatagarbha* being the *ratnagotra* is sufficiently explained, 2) the last verse of Chapter V. (v. 25) which expresses the faith in the Buddha Amitāyus is not essentially connected with the contents of Chapter I. Denial of the originality of chapters other than Chapter I consequently means the denial of the idea of the 4 aspects of the *ratnagotra*. That is why I omitted v. I, 23 from the line of original verses. Thereby, all kinds of 'classification' are deprived of this text. There is no possibility of abridging the original form of the text more than this. This supposition, however, increases the importance of the supposed second author with regard to establishing the system of the *tathāgatagarbha* theory as appearing in the present Sanskrit text. And even if the Chapters after II were the later

[29]) It is, of course, not necessary to presume the existence of a text with 3 chapters.

addition, they had been no doubt composed before the commentary was made. In this sense, I shall treat in my translation all the verses in the A. B. C. groups, including v. II, 9 as the 'basic verses' for commenting (it means neither original verses nor '*śloka*'s) under the name of '*kārikā*'[30].

§ 4. – *The Commentary and Later Additions.*

There seems to be no difficult point to discuss about the commentary. Its style is consistent throughout the text except for the fact that the prose commentary disappears after Chapter II. This fact is construed as indicating that the commentator attached the main importance to Chapter I, and felt no necessity for detailed comment on other Chapters.

One thing to be noticed here are the omissions and additions in the Sanskrit text as compared with the Chinese version. Besides small differences between them, which will be referred to in the notes on my English translation, the passages to be added to the commentary as missing in the Sanskrit text and subtracted from it as additions in later days, are as follows:

A. *Omissions*

1) one commentary verse and its prose explanation on p. 16, l. 15 (before *na hi jātu*...) (C. p. 825 *b*)

2) one commentary verse and its prose explanation on p. 31, l. 16 (before *saṃsāraduḥkha*–) (C. p. 829 *c*–830 *a*)

3) a quotation on the parable of a castle taken from the *Ratnacūḍasūtra* after '*nagarôdāharaṇam*/' on p. 50, l. 16 (C. p. 843 *c*)

4) two commentary verses before v. I, 64 (p. 46, C. p. 832 *c*)

B. *Additions*

1) p. 51, l. 10 – p. 53, l. 8 (with a heading '*aparaḥ ślokârthaḥ*') — 10 verses and prose commentary.

2) p. 102, l. 20 – p. 104, l. 12

3) p. 108, l. 3–12.

probably 4) p. 112, ll. 1–13,18–20.

Most of these passages were already noticed by the editor of the Sanskrit text, and no explanation will be necessary for the present. Other minor points with respect to the structure of the text will be noticed in each passage of the translation.

[30] 27 verses, being the supposed form of the original text, will be mentioned in Appendix I.

III.

KEYPOINT OF THE DISCOURSE

§ 1. – *Ratnagotra, the Germ of the 3 Jewels.*

Mahāyāna Buddhism, in its philosophical approach, may generally be characterized as Monism (or Absolutism) which admits the unique Absolute [31] or Ultimate Entity, proved through the essential identification (*advayatā*) of various phenomena. And each phenomenon, just because of its being merely an aspect (or face, feature, or form) of the Absolute, cannot be the Entity different from other phenomena, and itself has no reality. But, through its being 'identical' with the Absolute, every phenomenon has the characteristics of being 'real' and is 'identical' with each other as they stand for the Absolute in one of its various 'aspects' [32].

This work, being a treatise on Mahāyāna Buddhism, is to be characterized as monistic in its philosophical approach. Though monism is one, there is a variety of forms, and this variety of forms is due to the different emphasis in each text, and this difference of standpoint gradually causes the division of various schools within Mahāyāna Buddhism. In other words, the difference of standpoint means: "to which aspect of the Absolute, is the emphasis given in the text ?" In this sense, we may define the characteristics of this text as a treatise, analyzing (*vibhāga*) the Absolute, or Ultimate Entity from its aspect of '*ratnagotra*'. This

31) Having come with connotations of Western philosophy, the word 'Absolute' contains an idea somewhat different from that in Indian philosophy and hence it is not perfectly proper to use this word for expressing the idea which is to be discussed here. In the case of the Vedānta Philosophy, the *Brahman* (or *Ātman*) is nearer to the Absolute in Western philosophy in its character than what is corresponding to it in Buddhism.

But since Buddhism denies the existence of such an eternal substance as *Brahman*, the use of the word 'Absolute' seems quite improper. Still Buddhism has its own idea of something immutable (*asaṃskṛta*), though its character is quite different from that of *Brahman* and there is no fixed term like *Brahman* to express it. In this respect, I dared adopt the word 'Absolute' as a general term for what is immutable in Buddhism. See H. v. Glasenapp, *Buddhismus und Gottesidee*, S. 99 (*Abhandlungen der Akademie der Wissenschaften und der Literatur, Geistes und Sozialwissenschaftliche Klasse, Jahrgang* 1954, Nr. 8).

32) On the other hand, the so-called Hīnayāna Buddhism whose representative is the doctrine of the Sarvāstivādin may be characterized as Realism declaring each element (*dharma*) as real. See Th. Stcherbatsky, *The Conception of Buddhist Nirvāṇa*, p. 40.

is the significance of the title '*ratnagotravibhāga*', and by this the contents of the text is fully expressed.

Then, what is '*ratnagotra*'? This word is interpreted by the commentator as '*gotraṃ ratnatrayasya*' (v. I, 24), the Germ of the 3 jewels, and explained in the *śloka* (v. I, 23) as '*viṣayaḥ paramârthadarśināṃ śubharatnasargako yataḥ*', the sphere of those who have the highest perception from which the pure 3 jewels rise. Here, '*gotra*' means something original, while '*ratnatraya*', its result. The word '*gotra*' is one of the special terms difficult to be conveyed by any other language, but the basic line of interpretation for this word among the Buddhist literatures is '*gotra*' = '*dhātu*' = '*hetu*', or '*gotra*' = '*bīja*'[33], and hence it may be translated into English by 'element', 'cause', 'source', 'origin', 'basis', 'ground', 'essence', or 'nature'. In India, however, by a common use, this word means 'family', 'clan' or 'lineage'[34], and analogically, it is used in the sense of 'germ', 'mine' or 'matrix'[35]. Actually, in the word '*gotra*', all of these senses are included, and besides '*dhātu*', '*hetu*' and '*bīja*', as synonyms of '*gotra*' with the range of senses, we can get various words such as '*pada*', '*āśraya*', '*mūla*', '*sthāna*' (for 'basis' or 'ground'); '*nidāna*' (for 'cause'); '*svabhāva*', '*prakṛti*', '*dharma*' (for 'nature'); '*sāra*' (for 'essence'); '*nidhi*', '*nidhāna*', '*ākara*' (for 'mine'), '*yoni*', '*garbha*' (for 'matrix'); '*vaṃśa*' (for lineage);

33) *Abhidharmakośakārikā*, 1, 20 (*dhātu* means *gotra*); The *Ratna.* p. 72.10 (*hetvartho'tra dhātvarthaḥ*); *Yogācārabhūmi.* Part 1, (ed. by Vidhushekhara Bhattacharva, Calcutta, 1957), p. 26, ll. 18–19: *bījaparyāyāḥ punar dhātur gotraṃ prakṛtir hetuḥ satkāya prapañca ālaya upādānaṃ duḥkhaṃ satkāyadṛṣṭyadhiṣṭhānam asmimānâdhiṣṭhānaṃ cêty evaṃ bhāgīyāḥ paryāyā veditavyâḥ*, *Bodhisattvabhūmi* (ed. by U. Wogihara), p. 3, l. 6: *gotraṃ bījam ity apy ucyate.* See Edgerton, BHS Dic., *gotra* s.v.

As for the development of the idea of '*gotra*' within Buddhist thought, see Obermiller's introduction to the *Uttaratantra.* It gives a good summary of the development of the idea from the Vinaya to the Yogācāra system through the Sarvāstivāda and the Sautrāntika, but as it is merely based upon Tibetan information (the *Gser-phreṅ*, a commentary on the *Abhisamayâlaṅkāra* by Tsoṅ-kha-pa, and the *Phar-phyin skabs brgyad-ka*, Eight Chapters on the *Pāramitā*, of Jam-yaṅ-shad-pa), a more detailed and thorough investigation on this subject based upon the Pāli, Sanskrit, and Chinese sources will be required.

34) '*Gotra*' is originally a term used in the Indo-Aryan society since the pre-Vedic age, and signifies usually an exogamous unit of families of the same lineage within the Brahmin clan. Significance of '*gotra*' in the Brahmanical system was sought for by J. Brough in his work, "*The Early Brahmanical System of Gotra and Pravara, a Translation of the Gotra-pravara-mañjali of Puruṣottama-Paṇḍita with an Introduction*", Cambridge, 1953.

35) Edgerton regards the sense of 'a mine' as uniquely belonging to Buddhist texts. In his opinion, an objection is raised by V. Raghavan ("*Buddhist Hybrid Sanskrit*", Indian Linguistics, Chatterjee Jubilee Volume, *Journal of the Linguistic Society of India*, Vol. 16, p. 322).

'*parigraha*' (for 'family') etc.[36]. On the other hand, '*ratna*' or '*ratnatraya*' is a name for the Absolute when it is regarded as the '*śaraṇa*' (refuge), or the object of worship. *Par excellence*, it is the '*buddharatna*', and the other two, i. e. the '*dharmaratna*' and '*saṅgharatna*' are merely the 'natural outflow' (*dharmatāniṣyanda*) of the former[37] (p. 7). In this sense, '*ratnatraya*' is synonymous with '*buddha*', '*tathāgata*', or '*jina*'. And combining these terms of both sides, we can get those terms like '*tathāgatagarbha*', '*buddhagarbha*', '*jinagarbha*'; '*tathāgatadhātu*', '*buddhadhatu*'; '*tathāgatagotra*', '*buddhgotra*', etc. as synonyms of '*ratnagotra*'. Thus we know the word '*ratnagotra*' used in the title indicates what is called '*tathāgatagarbha*' and this text is a treatise on the *Tathāgatagarbha* theory.

Then again, how are these terms '*tathāgatagarbha*' or '*tathāgatagotra*' employed ? The *tathāgatagarbha* is, in a concrete way, a name for '*sattvadhātu*', the multitude of the living beings. This '*sattvadhātu*', or '*sattvarāśi*' (in other words, *sarvasattvāḥ*, *sarva–dehinaḥ*, all living beings) is, according to the text, called '*tathagatagarbhāḥ*', those who have the Matrix of the Tathāgata, just because 1) the Wisdom of the Buddha penetrates it, 2) it is by nature identical with purity, i. e. the Absolute, and 3) it is the '*gotra*', through which the result, i. e. '*ratnatraya*' or, *par excellence*, the Tathāgata makes its appearance (v. I, 27).

The point of its identity with the Absolute lies in its 'essential purity' (*prakṛty-asaṃkliṣṭatā*) (v. I, 30) which is found in the 'innate mind' (*cittaprakṛti*) of living beings (v. I, 49). Through the purity of the innate mind, all living beings, irrespective of their conditions or appearances, are identical with each other. The existence of this purity, common to all living beings, is proved by the all-pervadingness of the Wisdom of the Buddha, in other words, by that of the Body of the Absolute (*dharmakāya*) (v. I, 28). At the same time, despite the existence of purity, the living beings differ from each other owing to their appearances, namely the different degrees with regard to the 'impurity' on the pure innate mind, and have various names, viz. 'the ordinary beings', 'the Saints', or 'the Buddha' (v. I, 47)[38]. This 'impurity' is, however, not essentially connected with them, but merely temporally associated with them as the accidental defilement (*āgantukakleśa*) and itself has no reality because

[36] All of these terms are taken from this text.

[37] This point is taken from the *Śrīmālāsūtra* and is called the '*ekayāna*' theory being one of the characteristics of Mahāyāna Buddhism.

[38] In another place, (v. I, 47) they are classified into '*sattvadhātu*, *bodhisattva*, and *tathāgata*', but essentially there is no difference between the two kinds of classification (the Saints are *par excellence* '*bodhisattvas*' in the Mahāyāna Buddhism).

it is constructed by the 'irregular thought' (*ayoniśomanasikāra*) (v. I, 60–63). Therefore, it is removable from them and when they remove it by realizing its accidental nature, i. e. when they accomplish the purification, they become the Buddha. Because of this possibility, the *sattvadhātu* is the '*gotra*' of the Buddha, and its pure innate mind is regarded as the Buddhahood (*buddhatva*) or the Essence of the Buddha (*buddhadhātu*).

Those are the essential characteristics of the *tathāgatagarbha*, which at the same time constitute the core of the doctrine described in this text [39].

§ 2. – 4 *Aspects of the Germ.*

On the basis of the essential characteristics of the *tathāgatagarbha* referred to above, the text explicates the doctrine in five chapters [40], under the titles: 1) *Tathāgatagarbha*, 2) *Bodhi*, 3) *Guṇa*, 4) *Tathāgatakṛtyakriyā*, and 5) *Anuśaṃsa*, respectively. Of these five, the last chapter is the conclusion in which the merits of having faith in this doctrine of the *tathāgatagarbha* are described. The other four stand for the 4 aspects of the *gotra*, which are mentioned in v. I, 23 and which show its inconceivability in each respect (v. I, 24) while Chapter I includes 3 *ślokas* on the *ratnatraya* and the commentary thereon, along with the commentator's introduction [41].

Thus, these 4 aspects of the *gotra* form the basic frame of this text and the authors refer to them in various places with various denominations. It would be better to pick up such denominations before analysing their characteristics and significance.

1) *dhātu*, *bodhi*, *guṇa*, *karman*. (v. I, 1)

2) *garbha* (*jñānadhātu–āptiniṣṭha*), *agrabodhi* (*jñānâpti*), *dharmāḥ*, *sattvârthakṛt*. (v. I, 3).

3) *samalā tathatā*, *nirmalā tathatā*, *vimalā buddhaguṇāḥ*, *jinakriyā*. (v. I, 23)

39) The whole account of this passage on the fundamental characteristics of the '*ratnagotra*' was taken from what I considered as the original text.

40) The Chinese version gives 11 chapters, dividing the Chapter on the Tathāgatagarbha into 7. But this division has probably no source in the basic text for the Chinese translation.

41) The commentary mentions the 3 Jewels along with 4 aspects of the Germ in its open verse and calls them the 7 *vajrapadas*. But this categorization does not have as much significance as the 4 aspects of the *gotra*.

4) *bodhya, bodhi, bodhyaṅgāni, bodhana.* (v. I, 26)
5) *buddhadhātu, buddhabodhi, buddhadharmāḥ, buddhakṛtya.* (v. V, 1)
6) *vyavadānadhātu, amalā bodhi, guṇāḥ, karman* (v. V, 25)
7) *āśraya, tadparāvṛtti, tadguṇāḥ, arthasādhana.* (v. V, 7)

Of these four, the first aspect represents the *tathāgatagarbha* or the *gotra*, and the second, what is to be called the Absolute. The interrelation between these two is that of 'cause' and 'result'. On the other hand, the third aspect signifies the attributes or the qualities of the Buddha, being inseparable from him; the fourth, the acts of the Buddha, being the natural outflow of the Buddhahood. Because the Buddha is one aspect of the Absolute, the latter two are said to relate to the Absolute as being 'attribute' and 'function' inseparable from the Absolute or 'substance', so to say [42]. At the same time, because of its identity with the Absolute, the *tathāgatagarbha* is said to be endowed with the same qualities and acts as those of the Buddha. [43]. In this respect, these two are regarded as 'aspects' of the *gotra.* Therefore, these two latter aspects are less independent and less important than the former two and can be included in one of them.

Thus, the 4 aspects of *gotra* are fundamentally reducible to two aspects, 'cause' and 'result'. Taking an example from the table mentioned above, they are to be termed as '*bodhya*' and '*bodhi*'. *Gotra* is different from the Absolute in its being actually not enlightened (*abudha*) (v. I, 4), but it has a relation to the latter in its being '*bodhya*', i. e. 'to be enlightened' or 'capable of getting *bodhi*'. Because of this capability, *gotra* has obtained its name of 'cause', and this capability is sought for in the fact (or postulate) that *gotra* is (or is to be) essentially identical with the Absolute (*tathatâvyatireka*). This relationship is expressed in another couple of terms, *samalā tathatā* and *nirmalā tathatā*. Here, the difference between two aspects is shown by each attribute, *samalā* and *nirmalā*, while the identity of both is expressed by the term *tathatā*. *Tathatā*, the Absolute, is characterized as *nirmalā* in comparison with *gotra*, though it is common to both. Here we may notice that there are two aspects of the Absolute, and for the 'result'-aspect, the Absolute as in common with the

[42] The relationship between the Absolute and attributes is often expressed by the term '*avinirbhāga, amuktajña (avinirmuktajñāna)* (p. 3.4 ff. &c.) and similes of lantern and ocean are used for its explanation (v. I, 42). For the acts of the Buddha, they are ragarded somehow as the natural outflow of the Buddha's Compassion (*karuṇā*) towards living beings (v. I, 4 *c d*).

[43] V. I, 49; I, 155 and v. I, 42 and commentary thereon (on *yogârtha*). (*guṇaprakṛtiyogataḥ*), p. 66.19 (*anādicittavyavadānadharmasahajâvinirbhāgatā*), etc.

gotra is the 'ground'. In other words, the Absolute can be established as 'result' because it is in common with the *gotra*.

This Absolute, as common to both cause and result, is therefore to be regarded as the third aspect which is necessary to establish the relationship of cause and result. It may be termed 'ground'-aspect or 'medium'-aspect, and including this aspect, we know, 3 aspects are often used for analyzing the *tathāgatagarbha* in this text.

The first application of the 3 aspects theory is v. I, 26 where the Absolute is on the one hand regarded as *phala* under the name of *ratnatraya* and on the other hand as *pratyaya* for establishing *ratnatraya* (i. e. *buddha*) under the name of *bodhi* in comparison with the *gotra*'s being *hetu*. Here the third aspect is characterized as 'medium' (*pratyaya*) and on the basis of *bodhi* as medium, cause and result are called *bodhya* and *buddha*, respectively. Another kind of, and more important, division of the 3 aspects is what is called *svabhāvatraya* of *gotra* (p. 69. 17 ff) by the commentator based upon v. I, 27. The names of the 3 aspects are *dharmakāya*, *tathatā*, and *tathāgatagotra*. If we apply the same idea of 'medium' in this case, *tathatā* will be regarded as 'medium', and *dharmakāya* as 'result' since the word *dharmakāya* stands for one aspect of *buddha* showing his essential nature. According to the commentator, however, *dharmakāya* is interpreted as the Absolute itself, being the 'ground' which renders *gotra* as 'cause', while *tathatā* is explained as *tathāgata* in the sense '*tathatā śuddhim āgatā*', and regarded as 'result'. Here, the third aspect is preferably called 'ground', and 'result' is considered 'to become one with the ground, i. e. the Absolute'. For 'ground' of 'cause', if we restrict the observation only to the relationship between *dharmakāya* and *tathāgatagotra*, the former is to be regarded as 'cause' and the latter, as 'result'. In this case, *tathatā* stands again for 'medium'-aspect.

By examining in this way, we come to know that these aspects are interchangeable according to the respective standpoint. From the stand point of '*gotra*', *dharmakāya* and *tathatā* are either 'result' or 'ground', while from the standpoint of the Absolute, *gotra* is 'result' as well as 'cause'.[44] Such is the fundamental structure of the Absolute and its aspects in this text. Next, let us examine the characteristics of the Absolute, taking this structure into consideration and subsequently clarifying the process from 'cause' to 'result'.

[44] The word *tathāgatagarbha* is interpreted in the *Ratna*. in three ways, namely: 1) *tathāgatasya ime garbhāḥ sarvasattvāḥ*, (p. 70.17); 2) *tathāgatas tathataiṣāṃ garbhaḥ sarvasattvānām*, and 3) *tathāgatadhātur eṣāṃ garbhaḥ sarvasattvānām*. They correspond to *dharmakāya*, *tathatā*, and *tathāgatagotra*, respectively. See my translation of each passage.

§ 3. – *The Absolute.*

The Absolute is expressed in various terms in this text. But in its fundamental characteristics, these terms can be divided into two groups: to one group belong those expressing the Absolute from the 'ground'-aspect, to the other those doing the same from the 'result'-aspect. Of course both aspects are interchangeable as has been seen in the case of '*dharmakāya*' and '*tathatā*' in the preceding passage. From the standpoint of the development of the idea or from the literal meaning of each term, however, such a division seems possible.

Originally and basically the Absolute in Buddhism is *dharma*, the universal law, or the highest truth (*paramârthasatya*), which is unchangeable and immutable (*asaṃskṛta*) and whose contents are expressed by the 4 *āryasatya* of *duḥkha*, *samudaya*, *nirodha* and *mārga*, or by the terms, *pratītyasamutpāda*, *śūnyatā*, etc. This truth is to be realized by oneself ('*pratyātmavedanīya*') as the Buddha did for the first time, and hence, is characterized as '*adhigamadharma*'. Thus the Buddhist Absolute, being the truth, is 'impersonal' and 'attainable'; in those two points we can find the peculiarity of the Buddhist Absolute, and based upon these two characteristics, the Buddhist Absolute expands its contents in two directions [45].

Firstly, as this 'impersonal' truth shows the real nature of 'things', this nature is also regarded as the Absolute under the names of '*dharmatā*' (= *dharmasvabhāva*), '*tathatā*' or '*tattva*' (suchness). Being the nature of things, it penetrates all things or phenomena including the living beings, and hence the universe is called '*dharmadhātu*', the realm of truth which is the essence of the nature (*tattvasya lakṣaṇam*) and is regarded as the Absolute itself in the sense of 'reality'. Thus the all-pervadingness, and hence the oneness of the Absolute, is introduced into the conception of Buddhist Absolute. This is nothing but the 'ground'-aspect of the Absolute.

On the other hand, the character of being 'attainable' introduces the 'result'-aspect and is shown by the absolutization of the Buddha caused by veneration and glorification of the Buddha as the founder among Buddhist followers. This is a kind of 'personification' of the Absolute,

[45] The following description does not exactly follow a historical development of the idea but is made with a logical approach. Sanskrit terms mentioned with quotation marks in the following passage are the technical terms on the Absolute used in the *Ratna*.

but even in this case, if one may discuss the matter apart from the religious feeling, the Buddha is regarded as 'impersonal', the manifestation of the truth, since he realized the truth and his essence or nature as being '*buddha*' lies in his realization ('*bodhi*') of the truth. Thus the absolutization of the Buddha consists in making the Buddha impersonal and this Buddha as the Absolute is called '*dharmakāya*'. At the same time, the term '*buddha*' is originally applicable to any person as an adjetive. Namely, anybody can become '*buddha*' if he experiences and practises what the Gautama Buddha did; in other words, the state of '*buddha*' is attainable as the result of practice. In this sense, the existence of an innumerable number of Buddhas is possible and even ordinary beings, though they are actually not the Buddha, are postulated to have the same nature as the Buddha. This same nature is called '*gotra*' or '*dhātu*' and the existence of this nature is explained by the expression '*dharmakāyaparispharaṇatā*' or '*buddhajñānântargama*'-*tva*.

Besides '*buddha*' and '*bodhi*', there is another important term for the Buddhist Absolute. It is '*nirvāṇa*'. This term was absolutized even in the Pāli and in the Adhidharma Buddhism as an idea contrary to *saṃsāra* and is stated to be the realm of peace ('*śāntipatha*'). Mahāyāna Buddhism rebelled against the dualistic conception of *Nirvāṇa* and *Saṃsāra* and emphasized the oneness of both in the sense that Nirvāṇa is the only reality; and Nirvāṇa was regarded as synonymous with '*dharmatā*', '*dharmadhātu*', or '*dharmakāya*'. Originally, however, by '*nirvāṇa*' is meant a state 'attained' by the Buddha and hence, like '*bodhi*', it shows the 'result'-aspect of the Absolute. In the case of '*bodhi*', the intuition (*prajñā*) or wisdom (*jñāna*) by which the Buddha attained the enlightenment occupies an important place and is elevated to identity with the Absolute under the name of '*prajñāpāramitā*' or '*buddhajñāna*' as the essential nature of the Buddha. On the other hand, in the case of '*nirvāṇa*', the emphasis is on the disappearance or extinction (*kṣaya*, *nirodha*) of defilements (*kleśa*) and hence the term *nirvāṇa* is much related to the purification of mind (*cittavyavadāna*). Both of these attainments of '*jñāna*' and '*vyavadāna*', are, however, combined in one as the *sine qua non* for the realization of the Absolute, and consequently there is no strict distinction of use between both terms, '*nirvāṇa*' and 'bodhi'.

Introduction of the 'result'-aspect into the Absolute thus effected the absolutization of Buddha, of the attained state, and even of the medium or instrument for such an acquisition. For the introduction of such a conception, we cannot overlook a rather primitive and magical idea that to know something is to become itself, which is believed commonly in India since the Vedic Age [46]. It was also the basic idea for the theory of the oneness of Brahman and Ātman in the philosophy of the Upaniṣads as well as of the later Vedāntavāda [47]. Rather, it is an inevitable character for all systems which declare their philosophical standpoint as Monism. And when Buddhism developed itself into Mahāyāna Buddhism, it could not but take the appearance of Monism as a result of Absolutization of the Buddha, and approach the Upaniṣadic thinking in its philosophy.

On the other hand absolutization of the Buddha made Mahāyāna Buddhism more religious than Abhidharma Buddhism. Emphasis was placed on the Buddha rather than the Dharma and effected the '*ekayāna*' theory of the Buddha. Among the 3 jewels, the jewel of the Buddha came to be regarded as the only ultimate refuge. At the same time, the purpose of religious practices was made to be the acquisition of the Buddhahood rather than the Arhatship of Abhidharma Buddhism. And for explaining the possibility of anyone's acquiring the Buddhahood, the Monistic philosophy was used as the background.

In this last point lies the significance of the *tathāgatagarbha* theory of this text. This theory is in one sense an inevitable result of the development of Mahāyānistic Monism in its religious expression. In relation to the term *tathāgatagarbha*, the Absolute is often spoken of as the *dharmakāya* of the *tathāgata*, which is characterized as '*āśrayaparivṛtti*' (Revolution of the basis, i. e. of the *tathāgatagarbha*) or *jñānâpti*. In this characterization the process from cause to result is observed, and this process is understood as the removal ('*visaṃyoga*') of two kinds of obscuration, viz. of knowable things (*jñeya-āvaraṇa*) and of defilements (*kleśa-ā.*). Basically, however, the stress lies on the purification of mind from the defilements, observed in the use of terms such as '*samalā tathatā*' and '*nirmalā tathatā*', '*vaimalyadhātu*', '*viśuddhicittaprakṛti*' or by the definition of *tathāgata* as '*tathatā śuddhim āgatā*', and of *tathāgatagarbha* as '*sarva kleśakośakoṭigūḍhas tathāgatagarbhaḥ*'. Such terminology is characteristic of this *tathāgatagarbha* theory compared with stress on *jñānâpti* in the *vijñānavāda* as the ultimate goal [48].

In relation to the conception of the Absolute in 'ground' and 'result' aspect, one thing to be noted here is the development of Buddhology. Establishment of the Buddha as the Absolute under the name of *dharma-*

[46] e.g. *Bṛhad. Up.* vi-1-1: *yo ha vai jyeṣṭhaṃ ca śreṣṭhaṃ ca veda, jyeṣṭhaś ca-śreṣṭhaś ca svānāṃ bhavati*, etc.

[47] '*sa yo ha vai tatparamaṃ brahma veda brahmaiva bhavati*'. (*Muṇḍaka Up.* iii-2-9) is regarded as one of the important authority for the Vedāntavāda.

[48] See VI, § 2. (The Ratna. and the Vijñānavāda).

kāya subsequently caused another aspect of the Buddha to rise besides the *dharmakāya*. This was originally a problem of how to treat the historical Buddha in the Buddhist doctrine. In comparison with the *dharmakāya*, this second body is called '*rūpakāya*' (v. II, 61). This division of two bodies corresponds to the two aspects of the Absolute, namely, the *rūpakāya* is 'result' and the *dharmakāya* is 'ground' for the second body. Also, it corresponds to the division of two *satyas*, *paramārtha* and *saṃvṛti*, the former being *lokottara* and the latter being *laukika*, and called '*paramārthakāya*' and '*saṃvṛtikāya*, (v. III, 1). Furthermore these two are said to represent '*svârthasaṃpatti*' and '*parârthasaṃpatti*', respectively (v. III, 1).

This double *kāya* theory is, however, immediately followed by the triple *kāya* theory, by dividing the second one into two. An usual nomination for the three is '*svābhāvika*', '*sāṃbhogika*' and '*nairmāṇika*', respectively (vv. I, 151–2; II, 43 ff.). Of them, '*svābhāvika*' is for the *dharmakāya*, the fact of being the Buddha's own nature. Here, the Buddha's own nature means, as has been observed above, '*bodhi*' or '*buddhajñāna*,' and hence the *dharmakāya*'s original character as 'result' is still retained. That is why, in this text, '*buddhajñāna*' is replaced by *dharmakāya* without interpretation (v. I, 27 and 28), and *dharmakāya* is called *svârthasaṃpatti* because of its including *jñānâpti* within itself. On the other hand, '*sāṃbogika*' and '*nairmāṇika*' are of conventional character, referring respectively to the body for the assembly of Bodhisattvas and to the body for common people in order to lead them towards the Enlightenment. Therefore, these latter two are called *parârthasaṃpatti*. Here, *sāṃbhogika* means *para–sāṃbhogika*, i. e. the Body for other's enjoyment. Literally *saṃbhoga* means enjoyment or bliss of the *dharma* by the Buddha himself as the 'result' of realization of *dharma*, but by this term all the Buddhas in ten directions and in three divisions of time, i. e. past, future and present are signified, and the manifestation of these Buddhas is regarded as for the sake of people, and is hence included under *parârthasaṃpatti*. In turn, the historical Buddha is defined as '*nairmāṇika*', the Apparitional Body.

This triple *kāya* theory seems to be basic for the *Ratna*. However, the interpretation of *sāṃbhogika* leaves some doubt with us. Why is its function limited to *para–saṃbhoga*? If the *dharmakāya* is regarded as *svârthasaṃpatti*, it is to be called '*svasāṃbhogika*' in contrast with the *sāṃbhogika* which represents *parârthasaṃpatti*. It may be more logical to include the *dharmakāya*'s character of *jñānâpti* or *svârthasaṃpatti* into the second body of *saṃbhoga*, and by it, to leave the *dharmakāya* in its pure character of truth or reality.

In this respect, attention should be paid to the division of *dharmakāya* by the commentator into ' *muktikāya* ' and ' *dharmakāya* ' in regard to its function (v. II, 21). These two *kāyas* correspond to ' *prakṛtiviśuddhi* ' and ' *vaimalyaviśuddhi* ' (p. 80), or to ' *prakṛtisthagotra* ' and ' *samudānītagotra* ' (v. I, 149), respectively. Here, the *muktikāya* is to be identified with the Absolute Essence characterized as ' *dharmadhātu* ', ' *cittaprakṛti* ' or ' *prakṛtisthagotra* ', in the sense 'the Body which represents the innate liberation '. Being ' innate ', it stands for the ' ground' aspect of the *dharmakāya*. In turn, the *dharmakāya* stands for the ' result ' aspect, since it is nothing but the *samudānītagotra* being the result produced by the *prakṛtisthagotra* (v. I, 150). Shall we then consider that the *svârthasampatti* is represented by this second body, the *dharmakāya*, and the first body, the *muktikāya* remains without *arthasampatti*? An answer is not clearly given in the text, but it is apparently ' no '. Namely, the said twofold Body is referred to as the substratum of *sva-parârthasampatti*, which is caused by means of ' *avikalpajñāna* ' and ' *tatpṛṣṭhalabdha-jñāna* ' (v. II, 30). In this description, the correspondence between each of the 3 couples of terms is not clearly observed, but it may be proven in the light of another commentary passage.

Commenting on the *dharmakāya* as one of the *svabhāvatraya* of the *tathāgatagarbha* (p. 70), the commentator divides the *dharmakāya* into (1) *dharmadhātu* which, being the realm of *avikalpajñāna*, represents ' *adhigamadharma* ', and (2) ' *tadniṣyanda* ', i. e. the natural outflow of *dharmadhātu*, which constitutes ' *deśanādharma* ' characterized as ' *parasattveṣu vijñaptiprabhavaḥ* '. Here the text does not call the latter the realm of *pṛṣṭhalabdha-jñāna*, but it might well have done so, in contrast with the former, which it calls ' the realm of *avikalpajñāna* '; and in the same way, the former might be said to represent *svârthasampatti*, in comparison with the latter, which is characterized as ' *parasattveṣu vijñaptiprabhavaḥ* '. Thus being the case, *svârthasampatti* is to be regarded as inherent to the *muktikāya* or *dharmadhātu*, and we may conclude that the complete separation of the ' result ' aspect from the *dharmakāya* is not observed in the *Ratna.*, even in the commentary [49].

[49] In Mahāyāna Buddhism, Buddhology occupies an important part among its doctrines. The development had taken place from the double *kāya* theory in Nāgārjuna's philosophy to the triple *kāya* theory as in the *Ratna.*, and lastly resulted in another kind of the triple *kāya* theory, whose characteristic lies in the division of the *dharmakāya* into two *kāyas*, or separation of the *jñāna* from the attributes of the *dharmakāya*. In Chinese Buddhism reference is often made to these two kinds of the triple *kāya* theory calling the former ' K'ai-ying-ho-chên (開應合真) ' and the latter ' K'ai-chên-ho-ying (開真合應) ', respectively. It is one of keynotes to decide the date of Mahā-

There is another thing to be noticed here with reference to the aspects of the *dharmakāya*. Up to now I have often referred to the 'result' aspect without distinction. But in regard to its contents or its relation to 'cause' or 'ground', there is a certain variety. The terms which show this variety and which are used in the *Ratna.* are '*visaṃyoga*', '*niṣyanda*' and '*vipāka*'. Of them, the first one, *visaṃyoga-phala* is used for characterizing *āśrayaparivṛtti*, or *dharmakāya* as the result of purification or attainment of Enlightenment (p. 80, 82). This is nothing but what I called the 'result' aspect of the *dharmakāya* whose 'cause' is *gotra* or *dhātu*, i. e. the *tathāgatagarbha*. On the other hand, the term *niṣyanda* is used for indicating the relation of *dharmaratna* and *saṃgharatna* to *buddharatna* (*dharmatā-niṣyanda*, p. 7) or the relation of *deśanādharma* to *adhigamadharma* as mentioned above (*dharmadhātu-niṣyanda*). This last usage actually refers to the relation of the *rūpakāya* to the *dharmakāya* in the sense that the *rūpakāya* is merely an aspect of the *dharmakāya* when it works for *parârtha*. The same relation must be observed between *samudānītagotra* and the twofold *rūpakāya* (v. I, 150), and between *avikalpajñāna* and *tatpṛṣṭha-labdha-jñāna*. In this case, the *dharmakāya* appears in its 'ground' aspect.

Now the third one, *vipāka-phala* is an entirely different one from the other two in its original character. Namely, in the case of *visaṃyoga*, cause and result are exactly the same, and in the case of *niṣyanda*, result is the same as cause or is involved within the cause, while in the case of *vipāka*, cause and result are dissimilar from each other. In the *Ratna*, however, this term is used along with *visaṃyoga* in the same context as *dharmakāya* and *rūpakāya* (v. II, 1). Namely, *saṃvṛtikāya*, representing *parârtha*, is said to be *vipāka-phala*, in contrast with *paramārthakāya* as *visaṃyoga-phala* which represents *svârtha*. This usage seems to relate to the character of *sambhogakāya* as the 'reward' of infinite practice (*bhāvanā*) before Enlightenment. If it were so, Enlightenment or *jñānâpti* may also be termed *vipākaphala* because of its character of *svasaṃbhoga*, while to include the *nirmāṇakāya* within *vipākaphala* is improper; what is proper to the *nirmāṇakāya* is the term *niṣyanda*, because this *kāya* is said to be the incarnation of the *dharmakāya* [50].

yāna Sūtras and Śāstras. About Buddhology of the triple *kāya*, see D.T. Suzuki, *Studies in the Laṅkāvatāra Sūtra*, pp. 308 ff.

50) In the *Laṅkāvatārasūtra* (p. 283, 1.4 & 11), the term *vaipākika* is used for *sāṃbhogika*, in contrast with *nairmāṇika* (see BHS Dic.) (c. 報相佛). At the same time, however, the term *niṣyanda-buddha* is mentioned as indicating the second Body (p. 56, l. 8 & 18, 57, l. 8), which, curiously enough, is rendered into the Chinese '報佛'.

IV.

GENEALOGY OF THE TATHĀGATAGARBHA THEORY

§ 1. – *Sources of the Ratnagotravibhāga.*

In the preceding chapter, we have examined the fundamental character of the *tathāgatagarbha* theory in the *Ratna.* which seems to be the first treatise exposing this theory systematically and in its pure form. For its explanation, however, the *Ratna.* has been much aided by various scriptures which expound the same theory. Sometimes it presents the whole passage by quotations without its own words, sometimes it uses the scriptural passage as if it were its own words without any sign of quotation. The number of Scriptures utilized in the *Ratna.* is more than 20 and quotations or altered scriptural passages seem to occupy more than one third of the whole text. In one sense, the *Ratna.* seems merely a collection of scriptural passages concerning the *tathāgatagarbha* theory.

Among the scriptures utilized in the *Ratna.*[51], those relating to the Kārikā text and hence assuming important roles in the arrangement of the text are, according to the commentator, following ones:

1) *Dhāraṇīśvararājasūtra* (or *Tathāgatamahākaruṇāsūtra*), from which the 7 *Vajrapadas* are derived as the body of the treatise. (v. 1, 2 *dhāraṇīrājasūtra*).

2) *Tathāgatagarbhasūtra*, from which the 9 examples illustrating how the Germ is covered with defilements are derived (p. 66.18. *tathāgatagarbhasūtrôdāharaṇanirdeśa*) (Chapter I).

3) *Ratnadārikāsūtra*, from which the 64 Attributes of the Buddha are derived (v. III, 27. *ratnasūtra*) (Chap. III).

4) *Jñānâlokâlaṅkārasūtra*, from which the 9 examples illustrating the Buddha's Acts are derived (v. IV, 79).

Of them, the *Tathāgatagarbhasūtra* is the most important one as it expounds mainly the *tathāgatagarbha* theory, and its essential doctrine constitutes the core of this text.

Besides the *Tathāgatagarbhasūtra*, the main sources of the *Ratna.* and those frequently quoted are 5) *Āryaśrīmālāsūtra* and 6) *Anūnatvâpūrṇatvanirdeśaparivarta*. Also, 7) *Avataṃsakasūtra* (*Tathāgatôtpattisaṃbhava–*

[51] Bibliographical information of these scriptures is given in my notes on the English translation under the first occurrence of quotations or name of each scripture.

parivarta), 8) *Mahāparinirvāṇasūtra* (*Mahāyāna*) (*Tathāgatadhātuparivarta*), 9) *Sāgaramatiparipṛcchā*, 10) *Gaganagañjābodhisattvaparipṛcchā*, and 11) *Ratnacūḍasūtra* are quoted, not often but with long passages. They expound more or less the same theory of *tathāgatagarbha*, and especially nos. 5) 6) and 8) are the representative scriptures on this theory.

There are two works, among the quotations, which occupy a unique position in comparison with the former group of Scriptures. They are 12) *Mahāyānâbhidharmasūtra* and 13) *Mahāyānasūtrâlaṅkāra*, both of which are regarded as the main authorities on the *Vijñānavāda*. However, the *Ratna.* utilized them only along the lines of the *tathāgatagarbha* theory and never referred to the *Vijñānavāda*. These two seem to hold a key for solving the problems of the relationship between the *tathāgatagarbha* theory and the Vijñānavāda, as well as of the authorship of the *Ratna.*

One remarkable point is that all scriptures or parts of scriptures mentioned above are unknown to Nāgārjuna or, at least, not used in the works of Nāgārjuna. They seem to have appeared after Nāgārjuna, and the *tathāgatagarbha* theory, like the Vijñānavāda, is an entirely new and later theory of Mahāyāna Buddhism.

Besides these scriptures on the *tathāgatagarbha* theory, the names *Prajñāpāramitāsūtra* and *Saddharmapuṇḍarīka*, two main and basic scriptures of Mahāyāna Buddhism, are mentioned in the *Ratna.* There is no quotation from the *Saddharmapuṇḍarīka*, but it is clear that this scripture had influenced the *Ratna.* much with its *ekayāna* theory and the doctrine of the eternal Buddha. As for the *Prajñāpāramitā*, besides its indirect influences on the *Tathāgatagarbha* theory, the *Ratna.* quotes once from 14) *Vajracchedikā* and once from 15) *Aṣṭasāhasrikā* altering the sentences into the commentary's own form. This last one is significant in its exposition of how phenomena are originated from one essence (*ekadhātu*), as well as in its ascription of the cause to irregular thought (*ayoniśo-manasikāra*) [52], which corresponds to the passage, v. 1, 52 onwards, in the *Ratna.*

Other quotations are from 16) *Dṛdhâdhyāśayaparivarta*, 17) *Tathāgataguṇajñānâcintyaviṣayâvatāranirdeśa*, 18) *Kāśyapaparivarta* (*Ratnakūṭasūtra*), 19) *Ṣaḍāyatanasūtra* (*or Ṣaḍindriyarāsi-sūtra*) and from more than eight unknown sources, of which one is in Prakrit.

To discuss and examine the character of all the scriptures mentioned above is beyond our present purpose, but it is necessary and possible for clarifying the *tathāgatagarbha* theory to trace its genealogy back to its origin by examining these sources. For this purpose, we will pick up some important ones and will refer to their historical order.

52) See my note on the Engl. tr. (III–53).

§ 2. – *Cittaprakṛti* and *Āgantukakleśa*

As has been said above, the most important and principal point of the *tathāgatagarbha* theory is to purify the mind. This is not an exclusive facture of this theory, but was also the principle of practice from the outset of Buddhism. The peculiarity of the *tathāgatagarbha* theory lies in its emphasis on this point in association with the fundamental identification of living beings with the Buddha under the name of *tathāgatagarbha*, etc. The term *tathāgatagarbha* was an entirely new usage but its basic idea is found in the expression "*prakṛtiprabhāsvaraṃ cittam āgantukair upakleśair upakliśyate.*", for which the same corresponding expression, or similar ones, are used sometimes in the Pāli canons [53]. Another expression of this same idea of purification of mind, "*cittasaṃkleśāt sattvāḥ saṃkliśyante, cittavyavadānād viśuddhyante*", seems also to be old and to have its origin in the Pāli canons [54]. This purity of the innate mind is often compared to that of gold [55]. A Prakrit verse quoted in the *Ratna.* (p. 6) seems to belong to the same line of doctrine found in the Pali canons, though it is not traced in the present Tripiṭaka. The *Dhāraṇīśvararājasūtra* together with the *Sāgaramatiparipṛcchā*, the *Ratnadārikā*, the *Ratnacūḍa*, the *Gaganagañjā*, the *Akṣayamati–paripṛcchā*, etc., which form parts of the *Mahāsaṃghātasūtra* [56], are also standing fundamentally on the theory of the *cittaprakṛti*, and they are probably written by one and the same group who later developed the *tathāgatagarbha* theory.

Characterization of defilements or phenomena in general as 'accidental' attachment on the mind is, however, not found among those scriptures belonging to the oldest group in the Pāli canon and there was a controversy about this characterization among schools of the Abhidharma Buddhism [57].

[53] e.g. AN, I, 5, 9–10 (PTS, vol. 1, p. 10).

[54] e.g. SN (PTS, vol. 3, p. 151).

[55] e.g. AN (*ibid.*, vol. 1, p. 257); SN (vol. 5, p. 92).

[56] 大方等大集經. *Taisho*, No. 397 (Vol. 13). Compilation of this big collection of *sūtras* in the present form has probably taken place after the composition of the *Ratna*.

[57] The Sarvāstivāda did not accept this theory of *cittaprakṛti*. Among other sects of the Abhidharma Buddhism, the following four are known for their acceptance of this theory:

1) the Theravāda of Ceylon—*Dhammapadâtthakathā*, 1: 2; 3; *Milindapanhā* iv–7–2.

2) the Vaibhāṣika—*Mahāvibhāṣāśāstra* (*Taisho*, 27, p. 140 *b*).

3) the Vātsīputrīya—* *Śāriputrâbhidharmaśāstra* (*Taisho*, 28, p. 697 *b*).

4) the Mahāsaṃghika—* *Lakṣaṇânusāraśāstra* (隨相論) (*Taisho*, 32, p. 163 *b*), etc.

See C. Akanuma: *Bukkyō–kyōri no Kenkyū* (*Japanese*) (Studies in the Buddhist Doctrine), p. 210 ff.

This idea had been fully accepted by the Mahāyāna Buddhism, and we can find a frequent use of the above two expressions among the Mahāyānistic scriptures. Furthermore, this characterization of defilements led to the idea of non-reality of all the phenomena and resulted in the *cittamātra* theory, whose first exposition is found in the *Daśabhūmikasūtra* [58]. This *Ratna.*, though it makes no use of the term *cittamātra*, is no doubt based upon this theory, which will be observed in the passage expounding the origination of phenomena from the *cittaprakṛti*.

Questions which arise pursuant to the idea of *cittaprakṛti* and *āgantukakleśa* are (1) why and how the phenomena of unreal character are originated and (2) how the *cittaprakṛti* is pure and identical with the Buddha or the immutable Absolute being. The *tathāgatagarbha* theory seems to put the accent on the latter of the two, and, as for the former it has not sufficient explanation to resolve the problem even in the *Ratna.* It describes only how the defilements come to cover the pure innate mind and how they are to be removed. The first exposition of these two points (consequently the first establishment of the *tathāgatagarbha* theory) is seen in the *Tathāgatagarbhasūtra*.

§ 3. – "*Buddhajñāna*" *in the Avataṃsaka.*

Prior to the establishment of the *tathāgatagarbha* theory by the *Tathāgatagarbhasūtra*, there is a stage of development with respect to the identification of living beings with the Buddha. It is the idea of the penetration of the Buddha's Wisdom into the living beings described in the *Avataṃsakasūtra* and quoted in the *Ratna.* (pp. 22–24). The *Avataṃsakasūtra* as is seen in the present form is a collection of minor scriptures among which the *Daśabhūmika*, the *Gaṇḍavyūha* are important and of early origin. The passage containing the description of the *buddhajñāna* (*Tathāgatôtpattisaṃbhavanirdeśa*) also seems old, and was translated early in the 3rd cent. A.D. into Chinese by Dharmarakṣa as an independent Sūtra [59]. The term *buddhajñāna* is a synonym of *buddhatva* or *buddhatā*,

58) The source of the *citta–mātra* theory is often sought for in the following passage: *tasyaîvam bhavati / cittamātram idam yad idaṃ traidhātukam / yāny apîmāni dvādaśāṅgāni tathāgatena prabhedaśo vyākhyātāni tāny api sarvāṇy eva cittasamāśritāni* // (Rahder's ed. p. 49 *c*, *Taisho* 9, p. 558 *b*).

Strictly speaking, however, this passage teaches only the dependence of the phenomena on the *citta*. Still there is no doubt that the *citta–mātra* theory and the Vijñānavāda have their starting point in this passage.

59) 'Ju–lai–hsing–hsien–ching (如來興顯經)', *Taisho*, no. 291.

because the Buddha's nature is represented by his Enlightenment, for which the acquisition of *jñāna* is indispensable. This *buddhajñāna* is often compared to the sun, as it appears from the *Ratna.* or the *Jñānâlokâlaṅkāra.* In their emphasis of *buddhajñāna*, the *Jñānâlokâlaṅkāra* and the *Tathāgataguṇajñānâcintyaviṣayâvatāra* seem to be consistent with the *Tathāgatôtpatisaṃbhavanirdeśa.* These scriptures expound on one hand the eternity of the Buddha and his acts which corresponds to the all-pervadingness of the *buddhajñāna* and form the basic idea of the Absolute [60].

§ 4. – *The Tathāgatagarbhasūtra.*

The *Tathāgatagarbhasūtra* is a small scripture whose main part consists merely of the 9 examples illustrating the covering of defilements over the *tathāgatagarbha.* The core of its doctrine is stated in the following four sentences in the first example, a Buddha sitting in the interior of every lotus flower:

1) I (the Buddha) observe, with the *buddhacakṣus*, that all living beings, though they are among the defilements of hatred, anger and ignorance, have the *buddhajñāna*, *buddhacakṣus*, and *buddhakāya* sitting motionless.

2) [Thus] all living beings, though they are abiding in various worlds with bodies full of defilements, are possessed of the *tathāgatagarbha* which is always unpolluted and, being endowed with the virtuous properties, they are not different from myself.

3) Having thus observed, the Buddha preached the doctrine in order to remove the defilements and manifest the Buddha nature [within the living beings].

4) *eṣā dharmānāṃ dharmatā. utpādād vā tathāgatānām anutpādād vā sadaîvaîte sattvās tathāgatagarbhāḥ* [61].

60) On the relationship between the *Tathāgatôtpattisaṃbhavanirdeśa* and the *Ratna.* with respect to the *Tathāgatgarbhasūtra*, with special reference to this idea of the penetration of *buddhajñāna*, I wrote an article in the *Journal of Indian and Buddhist Studies:* "*The Tathāgatôtpattisaṃbhavanirdeśa of the Avataṃsaka and the Ratnagotravibhāga, with special reference to the term* '*tathāgatagotra-saṃbhava*' (如来性起)", *JIBS*, Vol. 7, No. 1, Tokyo, 1958, pp. (48)-(53). This article stresses the development of the idea of '*gotrasaṃbhava*', one of the important terms in the Hua-yen philosophy and locates the first use of this compound in the *Ratna.* (p. 26, ll. 8-9). In relation to this, one thing to be noticed here is that a scriptural passage of unknown source quoted in the *Ratna.* (p. 72, ll. 10-11) seems to belong to the same group as the two said scriptures in the use of terms: *tathāgatadhātur utpanno garbhagataḥ.*

61) These four passages are in *Taisho*, 16, p. 457 *b-c*. The last one is quoted in the *Ratna.* (p. 73).

The first three of those statements are based upon the *Avantaṃsaka-sūtra*. but deepened the idea by the phrase "*sarvasattvās tathāgatagarbhāḥ*" which probably was declared for the first time in this Sūtra, and they represent, respectively, what is called the three meanings of the *tathāgata-garbha* by the *Ratna.*, viz. *dharmakāya-parispharaṇârtha*, *tathatâvyatirekârtha*, and *gotrasaṃbhavârtha* (p. 26, vv. I, 27, 28, & ll. 7–11). In the fourth sentence, it is expounded how this *tathāgatagarbha* theory is an eternal truth.

That, in short, is the whole contents of this Sūtra. However, all of these points form the basic idea of the *tathāgatagarbha* theory and are deepened by the subsequent scriptures.

§ 5. – *The Āryaśrīmālāsūtra.*

A Sūtra which deeply investigates the characters of the *tathāgatagarbha* in a more developed form than the *Tathāgatagarbhasūtra* and has a significant role for establishing the *tathāgatagarbha* theory is the *Āryaśrīmālā-sūtra.* It is quoted more often in the *Ratna.* than any other scripture, and as far as the philosophical approach is concerned, it occupies a much more important position in the *Ratna.* than does the *Tathāgatagarbhasūtra.* The original points of thought of the *tathāgatagarbha* expounded in this Sūtra are as follows:

1) Two faces of the mind: *prakṛtipariśuddhicitta* and *upakliṣṭacitta.* (quotations in pp. 15 & 22) It is another expression of the same idea of '*cittaprakṛti* and *āgantukakleśa*', and because of this co-existence of purity and impurity on the mind, the *tathāgatagarbha* has got its name and is characterized, in the *Ratna.*, as '*samalā tathatā*'.

2) In relation to those faces, the so-called '5 meanings of *garbha*' (clarified in the *Buddhagotraśāstra*), i. e. *tathāgatagarbha*, *dharmadhātu-garbha*, *dharkāyagarbha*, *lokottaradharmagarbha*, & *prakṛtipariśuddha-garbha* give the full characteristic of *garbha* on its pure side.

3) Union of the *tathāgatagarbha* with innumerable attributes of the Buddha, which identifies the *garbha* with the *dharmakāya*, and in relation to this,

4) the *aśūnya* and *śūnya* character of the *garbha* (Q in pp. 59 & 76). The explanation for this is that *garbha* is *śūnya* since it is devoid of *kleśas* which are of unreal nature, while *garbha* is *aśūnya* since it is endowed with *buddhadharmas* which are inseparable from the *dharmakāya* which is the reality.

Moreover, such an observation is regarded as the real conception of *śūnyatā*, and to know the *tathāgatagarbha* is said to be the same as to know *śūnyatā.* Here is seen the criticism on the *sarva-śūnya-vāda*, and those adhering to the *śūnya-vāda* are criticized by being called '*śūnyatāvikṣipta-cittā*' *sattvāḥ*. [62]

5) Such criticism of the *śūnyavāda* naturally leads the Sūtra to describe the *dharmakāya*, as well as the *garbha*, with positive expressions and thereby the character of the *dharmakāya* or *garbha* approaches the *Ātman* of the Vedāntavāda. One of such expressions is the *tathāgata*'s possession of 4 *guṇapāramitās* of *nitya*, *sukha*, *ātman* and *śubha*. Also 4 attributes of *nitya*, *dhruva*, *śiva* and *śāśvata* are used for the *dharmakāya*. (Q. in pp. 12, 55 & 84). At the same time, the Sūtra contends that the *garbha* identical with the *dharmakāya* of such characters is not the Ātman mentioned by the *tirthās* [63].

6) Another expression of the idea of the *śūnya* and *aśūnya* of the *garbha* is its being the support (*ādhāra*) of both the *saṃkliṣṭa*– and *vyavadāna–dharmas*, or of *saṃsāra* and *nirvāṇa* (Q. in p. 72). The latter point, i. e. the *garbha*'s being *ādhāra* of pure *dharmas*, is proved by its being endowed with *buddhadarmas* and its being considered the ground of having intention towards the Nirvāṇa (Q. in pp. 35 & 73); while the former has the simple explanation that the *saṃsāra* exists owing to the existence of the *garbha* which is beginningless (*anādikālika*). (cf. the *Ratna*. p. 72) But it does not give any account of how and why such *saṃsāra* or unreal defilements come out and cover over the *garbha*. In another place, the Sūtra seeks for the basis of origination of defilements in *avidyāvāsabhūmi* (Q. in p. 33) which is also regarded as being *anādikālika*; but its research never goes beyond this, and the problem remains unsolved.

7) Lastly, the fundamental standpoint throughout this Sūtra is the *ekayāna theory*, i. e. the acceptance of One Vehicle of the Buddha, i. e. the Mahāyāna inclusive of the other two Vehicles of Śrāvaka and Pratyekabuddha. It consequently admits the Nirvāṇa only to the Buddha (Q. in p. 57), accepts the *buddharatna* as the ultimate refuge among 3 jewels, (Q. in pp. 7, 9, & 20), and declares that the *tathāgatagarbha* is only accessible to the Buddha or those who believe in the *buddhayāna*. And to realize this *ekayāna* is said to acquire the *anuttarasamyaksaṃbodhi*, that, is *nirvāṇadhātu*, or to become *tathāgata*, in another word, to realize the *dharmakāya*, which is nothing but the 'extreme of the ekayāna' [64]. Thus we

62) Cf. Introduction, VI, § 1.

63) *Taisho*, 12, p. 222 *b*.

64) *Ibid*., p. 220 *c*. This 'extreme of the *ekayāna*' is translated into Chinese by terms 'Chiu-ching-i-ch'eng (究竟一乘)' which is identical with the Chinese title of the *Ratna*. According to the Tibetan translation, its original word seems to be '*ekayānaniṣṭhā*'. (T. *theg-pa-gcig-gi mthaḥ*). However the idea of the Chinese title of the *Ratna*. is probably taken from this term.

know that the *Ratna.* depends to a great extent on this Sūtra for its fundamental standpoints and that quite a little of its original development is added to this Sūtra.

§ 6. – *The Anūnatvâpūrṇatvanirdeśa and the Mahāparinirvāṇasūtra.*

There is a small Sūtra contemporary with the *Śrīmālāsūtra* named *Anūnatvâpūrṇatvanirdeśa* [65]. The main point of its doctrine is the non-increase and non-decrease of the *dharmadhātu*, the Universe, and consequently the full identification of the *sattvadhātu* with the *dharmakāya* of the Buddha. In most passages, it has similar terms as the *Śrīmālāsūtra* with respect to the *dharmakāya*, to its possession of innumerous *dharmas* or *guṇas*, to the *tathāgatagarbha's* being covered with *kleśas* and to its accessibility only to the Buddha. Special contributions of this Sūtra to the *Ratna.* are 1) inseparability of the *dharmakāya* and the Buddha's *dharmas* explained by similes of lantern and gems (cf. Q. in p. 39), 2) fixation of 4 terms of *nitya*, *dhruva*, *śiva* and *śāśvata* as the 4 attributes of the *dharmakāya* (Q. in pp. 12 & 54), and 3) three divisions of the *dharmakāya* under the names of *sattvadhātu*, *bodhisattva* and *tathāgata* (Q. in p. 41) [66].

About the perception of the *garbha* as identical with the *dharmadhātu*, the Sūtra ascribes it to the removal of dualistic views of various kinds, esp. of increase and decrease with respect to the *sattvadhātu* as well as the *dharmadhātu* or *nirvāṇadhātu*, and those who have such dual-conception are called, in the Sūtra, '*icchantika*' (Q. in p. 28). There is however no description of the non-possibility of acquiring Buddhahood on the part of the *icchantikas* as discussed in the *Mahāparinirvāṇasūtra* (of Mahāyāna) [67].

The *Mahāparinirvāṇasūtra*, which exposes the eternity of the *dharmakāya* of the Buddha from the standpoint of the Mahāyāna and borrows

[65] In one point this Sūtra seems older than the *Śrīmālāsūtra*, namely in the use of a term '*avinirmuktajñāna*', which is abbreviated in the latter to '*amuktajñāna*' or '*amuktajña*'. See my note on the Engl. tr., I–23.

[66] In addition, the following fact is to be noted here. The Sūtra has a passage explaining the characteristics of *tathāgatagarbha* in three points (AAN, p. 476 *b*), namely: 1) *anādisāṃnidhya–saṃbaddhasvabhāva–śubhadharmatā* (本際相應體及淸淨法), 2) *anādisāṃnidhyâsaṃbaddhasvabhāva–kleśakośatā* (本際不相應體及煩惱纏不淸淨法), and 3) *aparântakoṭisama–dhruvadharmatā–saṃvidyamānatā* (未來際平等恒及有法). Referring to them, the *Ratna.* says that no. 3 is explained thruogh the 10 meanings of *tathāgatagarbha*, whille nos. 1 & 2 are to be explained by the 9 illustrations on the defilements covering the *garbha* (S. p. 59 11–14).

[67] This work is quite a different one from the *Mahāparinirvaṇasūtra* ed. by E. Waldschmidt which is a Sanskrit equivalent for the Pāli *Mahāparinibbānasuttanta*.

its style of structure from the *Mahāparinibbānasuttanta* of Primitive Buddhism, seems to have completed its present form in days a little later than those of the *Śrīmālā* and the *Anūnatvâpūrṇatvanirdeśa*[68]. As for its *tathāgatagarbha* theory, there can hardly be found any new and advanced doctrine, but its description is detailed in several points. It describes the eternity of the *dharmakāya* by attributing the 4 *guṇapāramitās* of *nitya*, *sukha*, *ātman* and *śubba* as the result of the double negation of misconception (*viparyāsa*) as the *Śrīmālā* did but, is enriched by detail with similes (Q. in p. 74) and applies to the *tathāgatagarbha* the term *ātman*[69], which was a sort of taboo among early Buddhists. It may be called a unique point of this Sūtra.

Another point to be noted here is the doctrine of the *icchantikas*. The sūtra, as one exposition of the *garbha* theory, emphasizes the innate possession of the *buddhadhātu* in every living being, but on the other hand, it refers often to the *icchantikas* who being *agotra* have absolutely no possibility of attaining Buddhahood. Such descriptions are sometimes contradicted in various passages, but the final solution of this problem seems to be the denial of the existence of such people from the ultimate point of view through introducing the idea of the Bodhisattva's compassion or the idea of the long time needed before their achieving Buddhahood. The *Ratna*. utilizes this second idea and construes the theory of *icchantikas* as a conventional teaching to convert people (p. 37). Some Mahāyānists, however, attributed the final *agotratva* to those *icchantikas* who abuse the Mahāyāna doctrine. Such an opinion is often found in the works belonging to the Vijñānavāda. The *Sūtrâlaṅkāra*, and the *Laṅkāvatāra*, while exposing the doctrine of *tathāgatagarbha* on one hand, have on the other the same opinion on this problem as the Vijñānavāda. It is one of key points for distinguishing the pure *tathāgatagarbha* theory from the Vijñānavāda.

§ 7. – *The Mahāyānasūtrâlaṅkāra*.

The *Sūtrâlaṅkāra* is the only Śāstra quoted in the *Ratna*.. It is said to be a work of Maitreya with a commentary by Vasubandhu; consisting of

[68]) It is at least sure that the *Tathāgatagarbhasūtra* is known to the author of the Mahāparinirvāṇasūtra. See, for example, *Taisho*, Vol. 12, p. 881 *b*: 如來藏經言·一切衆生皆有佛性在於身中.... (Tib. *de-bshin-gśegs-paḥi sñiṅ-poḥi mdo-sde chen-po*, Peking Ed. KJ. Mdo. Tu. 97 *a* 6 (Photo. repr. Vol. 31, p. 185). This version (*Taisho*, No. 367), tr. by Fa-hien in 418 A. D., is regarded as the oldest version of the MPS.

[69]) *Taisho*, 12, p. 407 *b*. where the simile of gold hidden under the ground (Cf. The *Ratna*. vv. I, 112–114) is spoken of.

21 chapters, it describes the practices of the Mahāyānistic Bodhisattvas. The division of chapters has a resemblance to the chapters of the *Bodhisattvabhūmi* in the *Yogâcārabhūmiśāstra*, attributed, according to the Chinese tradition, to the same author. It expounds mainly the theory of the Vijñānavāda, but at the same time has passages referring to the *tathāgatagarbha* as seen in the quotations in the *Ratna*.

Including one verse preserved only in the Chinese version [70], all of the three verses of this Śāstra quoted in the *Ratna*. are found in Chapter IX, the chapter on '*bodhi*'. This chapter, treating the subject of *buddhatva* has a doctrine quite similar to the *Ratna*. In this chapter we come across such terms and subjects as '*buddhatvasya śaraṇatva*', '*āśrayaparāvṛtti*', '*āśrayaparivṛtti*', '*anābhogâpraśrabdhakriyā*' with the simile of the Divine drum, '*anạsravadhātu*', '*dharmadhātuviśuddhi*', '*tathatā*', '*tathāgatagarbha*', and the '*trikāya*'–theory of '*svābhāvika*', '*sāṃbhogya*', and '*nairmāṇika*', with all of which we are acquainted in the *Ratna*. As for the *garbha* theory, however, this Śāstra has no development to compare with the Sūtras referred to above, nor has any systematization on it. The term *tathāgatagarbha* is used only once throughout the passages, although this Śāstra seems to accept basically the theory of the *prakṛtiprabhāsvaratā* of *citta* and *āgantukakleśa*. Rather, it is inclined to approach the *trisvabhāva* theory in its interpretation of *cittaprakṛti*, which it regards as the same as *pariniṣpaṇṇa–svabhāva*. This point may be called unique in this Śāstra as showing a germ of reciprocal influence between the *garbha* theory and the *Vijñānavāda*.

In relation to this, one notable thing is the use of the term '*āśrayaparāvṛtti*' or '*–parivṛtti*' and its meaning. In the orthodox Vijñānavāda, the term *āśrayaparāvṛtti* or *āśrayasya parāvṛtti* is used for denoting the *anāsravadhātu*, and *āśraya* means *ālayavijñāna*, while in the *Ratna*., the term *āśrayaparivṛtti* is used for characterizing *dharmakāya* or *bodhi*, and *āśraya* means *tathāgatagarbha* or *gotra* [71]. What is meant by *āśrayaparāvṛtti* and what is meant by *āśrayaparivṛtti* are finally the same Absolute, and the difference lies in what is meant by *āśraya*. This much is clear in regard to the difference between the two theories. But whether *parāvṛtti* and *parivṛtti* differ from each other in their sense is somehow questionable. As if to answer this question, the *Sūtrâlaṅkāra* has various relevant passages.

1) 6 verses beginning with v. 12 in Chap. IX are said to be referring to '*āśrayaparāvṛtti*'. Of them, in v. 12 we have '*buddhatvaṃ* — *āśraya-*

[70] After p. 31, l. 15 *nairātmyameva ātmani kṛtvā*. See note on the Engl. tr. VIII–(III & IV)–32.

[71] An exception is found once in v. V, 7, where, instead of '*parivṛtti*', '*parāvṛtti*' is used.

syânyathāptiḥ '. Here '*anyathāpti*' seems to be an interpretation of '*parāvṛtti*', in the sense, 'change of basis from A to B'.

2) The commentary says that by this v. 12, '*āśrayaparivṛtti*' is explained.

3) Commenting on v. 13, the commentator says that by this second verse the superiority of the *tathāgata* abiding in that state (*sthitaś ca tasmin sa tathāgato*, v. 13) over other kinds of *āśrayaparāvṛtti* is explained.

4) V. 14 refers to the 10 meanings or characters of *āśrayaparāvṛtti* and says '*āśrayo... tathāgatānāṃ parivṛttir iṣyate*'. It is interpreted by the commentator as '*āśraya iti yo sau parivṛtty āśrayas taṃ darśayati*' (that which is *parivṛtti* is that which is *āśraya*.) Here the term *āśraya* seems to be synonymous with *buddhatva* as '*sarvagatâtmaka*' (v. 14). This last point is shown in v. 15 with a simile of sky, which is quoted in the *Ratna*. (p. 71)

5) Verses IX, 41–48, referring to '*vibhutva*', speak to the effect that, due to *parāvṛtti* of 5 *indriyas* and others, one obtains '*vibhutva*' (power) and enters upon the *amalâśraya* of the Buddhas.

6) The same *amalâśraya* is explained in v. IX, 77 to be the *dharmakāya*, which is, in turn, defined as '*āśrayaparāvṛtti–lakṣaṇa*' in the commentary on v. IX, 60.

7) In the commentary on vv. XI, 32–33, which refer to the investigation of *saṃkleśa* and *vyavadāna*, the commentator says that what is taught in v. 33 is the acquisition of *ālambanaviśeṣa* (special basis), i. e. *dharmâlambana*, which causes the disappearance of the manifestation of *dvaya*, i. e. *grāhya* and *grāhaka*, as the result of fixation(*yoga*) of mind on *svadhātu*, i. e. *tathatā*; and that the one who has acquired this state is called '*parāvṛttâśraya*' (one whose *āśraya* has been changed).

8) In the commentary on v. 42 of the same chapter, which refers to the '*yogabhūmi*' of Bodhisattvas, the commentator mentions '*āśraya*' as the last of the 5 *yogabhūmis* and explains that '*āśraya*' means here '*āśrayaparāvṛtti*'. But v. 42 mentions only the first 4 and the 5th *bhūmi*, i. e. *āśraya* is shown in the next verse where it is referred to by the term *āryagotra* characterized as *vimala*, *sama*, *viśiṣṭa*, and *anyūnânadhika*.

9) v. XI, 44 runs as follows:

padārtha–deha–nirbhāsa–parāvṛttir anāsravaḥ /
dhātur, bījaparāvṛtteḥ sa ca sarvatragâśrayaḥ //

and thereon the commentary says that '*bījaparāvṛtti*' means '*ālayavijñānaparāvṛtti*'; '*parāvṛtti*' of '*padârtha–deha–nirbhāsa*', i. e. of *vijñānas* (other than *ālayavijñāna*) is the '*anāsravadhātu*', i. e. the '*vimukti*'. It (= *anāsravadhātu*) is also '*sarvatragâśraya*', i. e. existing also in the *śrāvaka* and the *pratyekabuddha*.

10) The same *parāvṛtti* of *vijñānas* are referred to in the next verse (v. 45) with another expression, ' *āvṛtti* ' of *manas*, *udgraha* and *vikalpa*, and this ' *āvṛtti* ' is explained in the commentary to mean *parāvṛtti*.

11) In chapter XIV, v. 29 says that *āśrayaparāvṛtti* takes place for the first time in the first Stage of Bodhisattva, and vv. 45 & 46 say that the final *āśrayaparāvṛtti*, i. e. the acquisition of *anuttarapada* and *sarvâkarajñatā* takes place with those Bodhisattvas who practised the *vajropama–samādhi*.

12) v. IX, 49 runs as follows:

pratiṣṭhā–bhoga–bījaṃ hi nimittaṃ bandhanasya hi /
sāśrayāś cittacaitās tu badhyante 'tra sabījakāḥ //

For the second line, the commentary says: on these three *nimittas* are bound *citta–caittā* accompanied by *āśrayas*. Furthermore the ' *āśrayas* ' are here to be understood as *cakṣurvijñāna*, etc., i. e. the 5 outer-sense-based *vijñānas*.

13) v. XIX, 54 runs as follows:

akhyāna–khyānatā jñeyā asadartha–sadarthayoḥ /
āśrayasya parāvṛttir mokṣo ' sau kāmacārataḥ //

Here *āśrayaparāvṛtti* is defined as the non-manifestation of the unreal objects (*asadartha* = *nimitta*, in v. 49) and the manifestation of the reality (*sadartha* = *tathatā*).

That is the description of *āśrayaparāvṛtti* in the *Sūtrâlaṅkāra*. In conclusion, we may say, though it is not brought out clearly by the author, that there is a variety in usage of the term *āśraya*:

1) *āśraya* (in pl.) = *cakṣurvijñāna*, etc.

2) *āśraya* = *bīja* = *ālayavijñāna* (whose *parāvṛtti*, i. e. *anyathâpti* is *buddhatva*), and

3) *āśraya* = *āśrayaparāvṛtti* = *tathāgatānāṃ parivṛtti* = *sarvatragâśraya* = *amalâśraya* = *anāsravadhātu* = *dharmakāya* = *buddhatva* = = *āryagotra* = *svadhātu*.

This use of the term *āśraya* relates to the characterization of *svābhāvika* or *dharmakāya* as the *āśraya* of the other two *kāyas* (IX, 60, 66). In this third meaning, *āśraya* should be compounded only with *parivṛtti*, and not with *parāvṛtti*, because *parāvṛtti* means 'change of basis (from A to B)'; and as the result of *parāvṛtti*, the former basis, being the substratum of unreal things or phenomena, is annihilated or no more exists (*akhyāna* of *asadartha*), while at the same time there takes place the manifestation of the reality (*khyāna* of *sadartha*, i. e. *tathatā*) which is a new *āśraya*, and it is this 'manifestation' of the reality that is meant by *parivṛtti* [72].

This last interpretation of *āśraya* and its combination with *parivṛtti* is supported by the usage of these terms in the *Yogācārabhūmi*, including the *Bodhisattvabhūmi*, and the *Dharmadharmatāvibhāga* attributed to Maitreya. In these two Śāstras, we find *āśraya* in combination with *parivṛt*, but not with *parāvṛt*, with such expressions as '*— dauṣṭhulyasya prahāṇad āśrayo* '*sya bodhisattvasya parivartate*', '*asyâśyayaḥ parivṛtto bhavati, sā câsya niruttarā āśrayaparivṛttiḥ*' (*Bodhisattvabhāmi*); '*— yogināṃ parivṛttâśrayānāṃ sarvakliṣṭadharma-nirbīja āśrayaḥ parivartate*' (*Yogācārabhūmi*, II *Manobhūmi*); '(*āśrayaparivṛtter*) *svabhāvapraveśas tathatāvaimalyam āgantukamala-tathatâprakhyāna-prakhyānāya*', '*tathatā-parivṛtti*', etc. (*Dharmadh*) [73]. On the other hand, not only is the term *āśrayaparāvṛtti* found in the *Sūtrâlaṃkāra*, but also in the *Vijñaptimātratā-triṃśikā*, Sthiramati's commentary on the *Madhyântavibhāga*, the *Laṅkāvatārasūtra*, etc.; and the *Mahāyānasaṃgraha* of Asaṅga has probably the same use of *āśrayaparāvṛtti* along with its definition [74].

These facts seem to show that the term *āśrayaparāvṛtti* was used for the first time in the *Sūtrâlaṃkāra* (kārikā) and has gradually been fixed as a technical term of the Vijñānavāda by Asaṅga and Vasubandhu, defining *āśraya* as *ālayavijñāna*, and that before that term was introduced, the term *āśrayaparivṛtti* was commonly used by the Vijñānavādins and in the Tathāgatagarbha theory.

The commentator of the *Ratna.* was no doubt acquainted with both expressions—*parivṛtti* and *parāvṛtti*—but the *Ratna.* could not employ the latter expression, because *gotra*, being *āśraya*, could remain before and after the enlightenment without changing its nature.

This supposition bears upon the authorship of the *Ratna.*, and due

[72] '*Parāvṛtti*' is interpreted in three ways in the *Sūtrâlaṅkāra*. Namely, 1) *anyathâpti* (in literal sense); 2) *akhyāna, astaṃ prayātaṃ, nirasyate*, etc., disappearance, to disappear (phenomenal sense); 3) *āvṛtti*, returning (doctrinal sense). The most important one is the third interpretation, that is to say, the disappearance of the *asad-artha* (inclusive of *bīja*) signifies its returning to the reality. In this sense, '*āśrayaparāvṛtti*' means *āśrayasya bījasya tathatāyām amalâśraye parāvṛttiḥ*'. And as the result of the '*parāvṛtti*' into '*tathatā*', '*tathatā*' alone manifests itself fully without obscuration, that is to say, '*tathatāyāḥ parivṛttiḥ*' takes place.

[73] *Bodhisattvabhūmi*, Wogihara's edition, p. 368, l. 6; p. 405, ll. 25–26; *Yogācārabhūmi*, ed. by V. Bhattacharya, Part 1, p. 27, ll. 1–2; *Dharmadharmatāvibhāga*, fragments, Appendix to the *Mahāyāyasūtrâlaṅkāra*, ed. by S. Lévi, p. 190, ll. 6 & 9, respectively.

[74] *Mahāyānasaṃgraha*, Tib. Sde-dge edition, Ri 36 *b* 2: *gshan-gyur-pa ni, gaṅ gshan-gyi dbaṅ-gi ṅo-bo-ñid de-ñid-kyi gñen-po skyes-na, gaṅ kun-nas ñon-moṅs-paḥi chal dog ciṅ, rnam-par byaṅ-baḥi char gyur-paḥo*. (*gshan-gyur-pa* = *parāvṛtti*).

to the specialized use of the term *āśrayaparivṛtti*, the commentator of the *Ratna.* must be someone other than Asaṅga or Vasubaṇdhu [75].

V.

THE WONKS ON THE TATHĀGATAGARBHA THEORY CONTEMPORARY WITH OR SUCCEEDING THE RATNAGOTRAVIBHĀGA

There are many other works on the *garbha* theory which are never reffered to in the *Ratna.* though regarded as of Indian origin and preserved in the Chinese and the Tibetan Tripiṭakas. Among them those to be referred to here are (1) *Dharmadhātvaviśeṣaśāstra*, (2) *Buddhagotraśāstra*, (3) *Anuttarâśrayasūtra*, (4) *Laṅkāvatārasūtra* and (5) *Mahāyānaśraddhôtpādaśātra.* Except (4), all these are known only through the Chinese sources, that casts various problems about their authorship, date, and even their originality, and these problems are relating to the date and author of the *Ratna.* Especially, the first three are in close relation to the *Ratna.* in their contents, and hence discussions will be mainly devoted to them in this chapter.

§ 1. – *The Mahāyānadharmadhātvaviśeṣaśāstra.*

As has been referred to above, this small Śāstra is attributed to Sāramati in the Chinese Tripiṭaka. From its contents, this work seems quite consistent with the *Ratna.* The main point of doctrine in this work is the '*bodhicitta*' which is synonymous with '*cittaprakṛti*' in the *Ratna.* and hence is nothing but the *tathāgatagarbha.* The text describes this *bodhicitta* under 12 divisions, namely: 1) *phala*, 2) *hetu*, 3) *svabhāva*, 4) *paryāya*, 5) *abheda*, 6) *avasthāprabheda*, 7) *asaṃkliṣṭa*, 8) *nitya*, 9) *yoga*, 10) *anarthakriyā*, 11) *arthakriyā*, and 12) *ekatva* (or *ekadhātu*), and is mainly based upon two Sūtras, the *Āryaśrīmālā* and the *Anūnatvāpūrṇatvanirdeśa* [76].

[75] The Chinese insertion of one verse from the *Sūtrâl.* referred to above is accompanied by a prose commentary whose explanation is exactly the same as Vasubandhu's commentary on this very verse. This fact cannot be a fully reliable proof for the present problem but suggests the point to some extent. There is another point which shows the close relationship between the *Mahāyānasūtrālaṅkāra* and the *Ratna.* It is the use of the six categories (*ṣaṭ-padârtha*) beginning with *svabhāva.* As for this, see Appendix III, The Description of the Ultimate Reality.

[76] These terms are reconstructed from the Chinese translation which gives the following terms: 1) 果, 2) 因, 3) 自性, 4) 異名, 5) 無差別, 6) 分住(位), 7) 無染, 8) 常恒, 9) 相應, 10) 不作義利, 11) 作義利, 12) 一性·

This division has a resemblance not only in its terminology but also in its contents to the 10 meanings of the *gotra* described in Chap. I of the *Ratna.* (pp. 26 ff.). In particular, 6) *avasthāprabheda* is fully identical with that in the *Ratna.* in its classification of living beings into '*sattvadhātu*', '*bodhisattva*', and '*tathāgata*' seeking for its authority in the *Anūnatvâpūrṇatvanirdeśa.* Besides, under 1) *phala*, the text says *phala* means *nirvāṇadhātu* which is nothing but the *dharmakāya* characterized as *āśrayaparivṛtti*, and explains it in the same way as the *Ratna.* did in its explanation on the '*śuddhâvasthāyām avikārârtha* ([IX]–*c*). Under 2) *hetu*, it explains 4 causes, i. e. *dharmâdhimukti*, *prajñā*, *samādhi* and *karuṇā*, with a verse containing the same idea as v. 1, 34 of the *Ratna.* Under 3) *svabhāva*, *prakṛtyasaṃkliṣṭatva* is said to be the own nature of *bodhicitta.* In 4) *paryāya*, a synonym of *bodhicitta* in its *phala* state, is called *śubhâtmasukhanityapāramitā* and so authorized by a quotation from the *Śrīmālāsūtra.* The verse in 8) *nitya*, is identical with verses I, 53 & 54 of the *Ratna.* in its contents, explaining that *dharmadhātu* is, like *ākāśadhātu*, of neither origination nor destruction (*anutpādânirodha*). Under 9) *yoga*, the text has two verses, of which the first one is identical with v. 1, 42–*c d* of the *Ratna.*, the second, with I, 155, a verse referring to the *śūnya* and *aśūnya* of the *gotra.* And lastly, the contents of 12) *ekatva* are the same as those under '*asaṃbheda*' (X) in the *Ratna.*, saying that the *bodhicitta* is nothing but the *dharmakāya*, the *tathāgata*, the *āryasatya* or the Nirvāṇa, and emphasizing oneness of *nirvāṇa* with *buddhatva.*

The remaining parts not described above seem to be taken mostly from Chapters II & IV of the *Ratna.* Namely, a reference to the 2 sides of *bodhicitta* under 3) *svabhāva*, saying '*śukladharmamayalakṣaṇa* and *vaimalyapariśuddhilakṣaṇa* reminds us of the characterization of *dharmakāya* with *prakṛtiviśudhi* and *vaimalyaviśuddhi* (p. 80) or the distinction of *prakṛtisthagotra* and *samudānītagotra* in the *Ratna.*; a verse under 7) *asaṃkliṣta* resembles v. II, 3 in the *Ratna.*; similes used under 10) *anarthakriyā* and II) *arthakriyā* are the same as those in Chapters 1 (among 9 illustrations), II, and IV of the *Ratna.*; and the 10 characteristics of *asaṃbheda* under 5) can be traced one by one in various passages in the *Ratna.*

Thus examining the contents, we may say that the author of this text composed it on the basis of the *Ratna.*, compressing and revising the form according to his own view. In this case, as this text, unlike the *Sūtralaṅkāra*, seems to have been written from the same standpoint as the commentator of the *Ratna.*, it is possible that the latter is identical with the author of this text, and Sāramati to whom this work is attributed may have been the author of the commentary of the *Ratna.*

§ 2. – *The Buddhagotraśāstra.*

The *Buddhagotraśāstra* is another work which, like the *Dharmadhātvaviśeṣaśāstra*, expounds the 10 meanings of the *gotra* described in the *Ratna.* but with the same terminology and with explanations much similar to those of the *Dharmadhātvaviśeṣaśāstra.* It is translated into Chinese by Paramârtha, is attributed, according to the Chinese tradition, to Vasubandhu [77] and highly esteemed among Chinese Buddhists throughout the centuries as a representative work on the *garbha* theory. This attribution is rather doubtful, but this work poses interesting problems for us because of its very close similarity to the *Ratna.* in most parts of the text.

The whole text consists of 4 chapters, of which the last one treats the subject of the 10 meanings of the *gotra* under the title: Analysis of the characteristics (*lakṣaṇa*) (of the *Tathāgatagarbha*). Explanations under each '*lakṣaṇa*' are in most cases quite equivalent to those in the *Ratna.* even in their wording, but sometimes doctrines based upon the Vijñānavāda are interwoven among passages, and sometimes those passages which are in other chapters or other parts of Chap. I in the *Ratna.* are inserted between lines.

The main differences between the two works as mentioned in the previous paragraph are as follows: 1) 9 illustrations of the *garbha* taken from the *Tathāgatagarbhasūtra* along with the explanations of the 9 kinds of defilements and of the 3 *svabhāvas* of the *gotra* (*Ratna.* pp. 66–72) are inserted under (IX) *avikāra*, 2) (V) *yoga* includes explanations of '*dharmaratna*' and '*saṅgharatna*' which appeared in Chap. I of the *Ratna.*, 3) descriptions regarding Buddhology of the *trikāya*–theory which is taught in two places in the *Ratna.*, viz. in Chap. II (under (VI) *vṛtti*) and in Chap. I (among explanations on the 3 *svabhāvas* of the *gotra*, p. 72), are inserted under (IX) *avikāra*; 4) explanations of (VII) *nitya* and (VIII) *acintya* in Chap. II of the *Ratna.* are inserted under (IX) *avikāra* as characteristics of the *dharmakāya*; 5) descriptions of the '*śūnya* and *aśūnya*' of the *garbha* along with the 4 kinds of *sattvas*, *satkāyadṛṣṭipatitā*, etc. are inserted in (X) *asaṃbheda*.

Besides those insertions in the passages on the 10 *lakṣaṇas* of the *garbha*, important changes of arrangement in this work are 6) shift of the '*deśanāprayojana*' which is at the end of Chap. I in the *Ratna.* to the beginning of the work forming the *nidānaparivarta*' (Chap. I), and 7)

77) *Taisho*, No. 1610, '佛性論', by '天親', tr. by '真諦'.

shift of the explanation of the 3 meanings of the term *tathāgatagarbha* to Chapter III with detailed explanation. These two points show that the purpose of this text is to describe the *buddhagotra* only from its *gotra* aspect but not from 4 aspects as in the *Ratna.* This relates to the fact that the text is lacking those passages on the 4 aspects of *gotra* (*Ratna.* pp. 21–23) and Chaps. III–V of the *Ratna.*

Throughout these passages, the text is written in prose except for a few verses which are quotations. An interesting fact is that among these quoted verses, we have 3 which are identical with vv. I, 51, 154 & 155 of the *Ratna.* and one identical with v. IX, 23 of the *Sūtrâlaṅkāra* which is preserved in the parallel passage in the Chinese version of the *Ratna.* For these, except for the first one, the name of the source is not mentioned, and the first one is said to be taken from the *Sandhinirmocanasūtra*, though the verse is not found in any edition of that Sūtra. Why such a statement is made is not clear [78], but there is no doubt about their being taken from the *Ratna.* along with its prose commentary. Another point of interest is the use of the *Anuttarâśrayasūtra* in the *Buddhagotraśāstra*, as an authority, which is never quoted in the *Ratna.* It also indicates that this work was composed after the *Ratna.*

Thus examining, we are led to imagine that, as far as the *garbha* theory is concerned, this work was composed by borrowing many sentences from the *Ratna.* but arranging them more systematically by adding the author's own opinion. This author's opinion appears in descriptions of the '5 *doṣas*' and the '5 *guṇas*' in relation to the purpose of the teaching; of the 5 meanings of the *garbha* taken from the *Śrīmālāsūtra*; of the 3 natures of the *garbha* taught in (I) *svabhāva*; of the attainment of the Buddhahood by the *icchantikas* (in [IV] *karman*); of the *āśrayaparivṛtti*, *dharmakāya*, and *nirvāṇa* (in [V] *yoga*); of the 6 meanings of *avikāra*; of the '5 *lakṣaṇas* and 5 *guṇas*' of *dharmakāya* as one of *trikāya* (in [IX] *avikāra*), etc. These passages show the more developed doctrines, some of which are based upon the Vijñānavāda. Furthermore, in passages other than those referred to above, the text expresses the doctrines of the Vijñānavāda such as '3–fold *niḥsvabhāva*' '3–fold *svabhāva*' and '5–*dharmas*', for which the source is probably the *Yogācārabhūmiśāstra*.

Thus the *Buddhagotraśāstra* is based upon two works, the *Ratna.* and

[78] The *Ratna.* has a similar character of being '*sandhi–nirmocana*' in its position among the Mahāyāna Buddhism. (See Introduction, VI § 1 & 2). So it is not impossible to imagine that the *Ratna.* is also called '*Sandhinirmocana*'. According to Prof. Tsukinowa's information, one Tibetan version of the *Ratna.* has a subtitle: *Sandhimocana Mahāyāna–uttara–śāstra.* (K. Tsukinowa, "On the Uttaratantra", *Japanese, Annals of the Nihon Bukkyogaku–kyōkai*, vol. 7, 1935).

the *Yogācārabhūmiśāstra*, being a work on the *garbha* theory and the Vijñānavāda, respectively, and trying to combine both theories. This standpoint is somewhat similar to that of the *Sūtrâlaṅkāra* and hence the author was probably a Vijñānavādin who had a tendency similar to that of Vasubandhu. As far as this point is concerned, the Chinese attribution of this text to Vasubandhu seems quite reasonable, but a doubt arises about its date because of its being later than the *Ratna*. which quotes the *Sūtrâlaṅkāra*. Furthermore we have to put the *Anūttarâśrayasūtra* between the *Ratna*. and the *Buddhagotraśāstra*. To solve this problem, we should next examine the *Anuttarâśrayasūtra* [79].

§ 3. – *The Anuttarâśrayasūtra.*

At a glance, one may notice in this Sūtra, a similarity of its chapter divisions to those of the *Ratna*. Leaving aside the first and the last two chapters which form its introduction and conclusion, respectively [80], the central part of this Sūtra consists of 4 chapters whose titles are II. *Tathāgatadhātu-parivarta*, III. *Tathāgatabodhi-p.*, IV. *Tathāgataguṇa-p.* and V. *Tathāgatakriyā-p.*, respectively [81]. These are quite identical with the 4 aspects of *gotra* described in the *Ratna*. The term *anuttarâśraya* [82] seems to mean the *Tathāgata* that possesses these 4 aspects. Furthermore, at the end of each chapter, the Sūtra emphasizes the inconceivability of these 4 subjects, but their description can be traced word by word in the

79) For these problems on the *Buddhagotraśāstra* discussed above, see M. Hattori, "*Busshoron no Ichi-kosatsu*" (*Japanese*), *Bukkyoshigaku*, vol. IV, p. 160 ff. 1955.

80) The original of Chap. I. is the *Adbhutasūtra* whose versions are available in Tibetan and Chinese as well (Tib. *Tohoku*. No. 319; *Taisho*, Nos. 688, 689), and whose main subject is the admiration of merits of the Stūpa worship as the highest observance of Buddhists, while Chap. VII is a kind of eulogy on the Buddha (*buddhastotra*) and Chap. VIII *Parīndana-parivarta* is an enlargement of the conclusion of the *Adbhutasūtra* in accordance with enlargement of the central part. The connection of the *tathāgatagarbha* theory with the Stūpa worship and the eulogy on the Buddha is not a merely mechanical and accidental connection at all, but it shows the existence of an essential interrelation among them. Namely, the Stūpa worship and the eulogy on the Buddha had originally taken place among a group of Buddhist from which the Mahāyānist community came into existence, and the core of the *tathāgatagarbha* theory lies in its *ekayāna* theory, i.e. the 'pure' faith in the Buddha as often referred to in the *Ratna*.

81) In Chinese, 如來界品, 菩提品, 如來功德品, & 如來事品, respectively.

82) This term is restored from the Chinese '無上依'.

Ratna. in its prose commentary on v. I, 23 & 24 [83]. This fact does not show that the *Ratna.* imitated the structure of this Sūtra or borrowed such an idea from this Sūtra, but quite to the contrary, it seems to show that this Sūtra was composed after the *Ratna.* as a kind of sutralization of the latter. This hypothesis will be proven upon examining the contents of the Sūtra.

This Sūtra uses a categorization with respect to the characteristics of *gotra* or *dhātu*, similar to that in the *Ratna.*, but under the chapter on '*bodhi*'. Its ten divisions are (1) *svabhāva*, (2) *hetu*, (3) *paripantha*, (4) *phala*, (5) *karman*, (6) *yoga*, (7) *vṛtti*, (8) *nitya*, (9) *āveṇika* and (10) *acintya*. This is actually a mixture of the 10 meanings of '*gotra*' and the 8 meanings of '*bodhi*' in the *Ratna.* Namely, (2)–(4) are identical with (II) *hetu* and (III) *phala* among the 10 meanings of '*gotra*' in the *Ratna.*, of which (3) *paripantha* is included under (III) *phala* in case of the *Ratna.*, while the last six (nos. 5–10), except for (9) *āveṇika*, are identical with the last five subjects among the 8 meanings of '*bodhi*' in the *Ratna.* Although (9) *āveṇika* has no equivalent passage in the *Ratna.*, its idea is taught here and there. However, in the explanation of (1) *svabhāva*, whose idea is fundamentally identical with (I) *svabhāva* of '*bodhi*' in the *Ratna*, the Sūtra refers to '*āśrayaparivṛitti*' with its 4 characteristics which are not in the *Ratna.* but utilized in the *Buddhagotra* [84]. On the other hand, the six subjects starting with (V) *yoga* among the 10 meanings of '*gotra*' in the *Ratna.*, are included in the chapter on *tathāgatadhātu* in this Sūtra but with a slight difference in arrangement and wording. As to Chap. IV. *Tathāgataguṇa–parivarta*, the Sūtra mentions the 180 *āveṇikadharmas* including the 80 *anuvyañjanas* which are not in the *Ratna.*, but names for the 32 *mahāpuruṣalaksaṇas* are identical with those mentioned in the *Ratna.* It is only the chapter on *Tathāgatakriyā* that differs entirely from the *Ratna.* in its contents.

Besides these similarities with the *Ratna.*, a stronger factor which shows that this Sūtra is an imitation of the *Ratna.* is that this Sūtra refers to certain passages which are quotations from other Sūtras in the *Ratna.* as if they were its own sentences. For instance:

(Chap. II)

1. A passage on the meaning of *gotra* being *ṣaḍāyatanaviśeṣa* taken from the *Ṣaḍāyatanasūtra* (*Taisho* 16 p. 469 *b*, RGV, p. 55, 16–17);

2. a passage on *anutpādānirodhatā* of the Tathāgata taken from the *Jñānālokālaṅkārasūtra* (p. 469 *c*, RGV. p. 12, 6–10);

83) *Ratna.* 21.17–18, 22.5, 22.8–9, 24.9–25.3, = *Anuttarâśraya Taisho* 16, 470 *c*, 473 *c*, 475 *c*, 476 *b–c*, respectively.

84) 無上依經, *Taisho*, 16, p. 470 *c*; 佛性論, *Taisho*, 31, p. 801 *b*,

3. a passage on *dharmakāya* endowed with the Buddha's properties which are *avinirbhāga*, *amuktajña*, *acintya*, etc. taken from the *Śrīmālāsūtra* (p. 469 *b*, RGV. p. 12, 10–14);

4. a simile of the Vaiḍūrya stone taken from the *Sāgaramatiparipṛcchā* (p. 469 *b*, RGV. p. 49, 5–9);

5. a passage on *cittaprakṛti* and *āgantukakleśa* taken from the same Sūtra (p. 469*b–c*; RGV. pp. 49, 9–50,7);

6. a passage on the 3 states of *dhātu* (*avasthāprabheda*) taken from the *Anūnatvâpūrṇatvanirdeśa* (p. 469 *c*; RGV. pp. 40, 16–41,5);

7. a passage on the penetration of *tathāgatajñāna* into the living beings taken from the *Tathāgatôpattisaṃbhavanirdeśa* of the *Avataṃsaka* (p. 470 *a*; RGV. p. 24, 2–6, 1–2);

8. a description of the Buddha, his teaching and disciples, being an authority for the Triple Jewel taken from the *Dhāraṇīśvararājasūtra* (p. 470 *a*; RGV. p. 3, 18);

9. a parable of a householder with respect to the Bodhisattva's compassion taken from the *Sāgaramatiparipṛcchā* (p. 470 *a–b*; RGV. pp. 47, 7–48, 13);

10. a passage on *dhātu* being *āśraya* of all *dharmas*, real and unreal, taken from the *Śrīmālāsūtra* (p. 470 *b*; RGV. p. 73,2–5);

11. a passage on the inconceivability of *dhātu* taken from the same Sūtra (p. 470 *c*; RGV. p. 22,1–4);

(Chap. III)

12. a passage on *tathāgatagarbha* covered with millions of defilements taken from the *Śrīmālāsūtra* (p. 470 *c*; RGV. p. 79, 10);

13. a passage on the Icchantikas taken from the *Anūnatvâpūrṇatvanirdeśa* (p. 471 *a*; RGV. p. 28,3–4);

14. a passage on those who are proud of their conception of *śūnyatā* taken from the *Kāśyapaparivarta* (p. 471 *b*; RGV. p. 28, 11–12);

15. a passage on the 4 *guṇapāramitās* (*śubha*, *ātma*, *sukha*, *nitya*) taken from the *Śrīmālāsūtra* (p. 471 *c*, 472 *a*; RGV. pp. 30,19–31,16);

16. a passage on the 3 epithets of the Tathāgata, viz. *dharmadhātuparama*, *ākāśadhātuparyavasāna*, *and aparāntakoṭiniṣṭha* taken from the *Daśabhūmikasūtra* (p. 472 *a*; RGV. p. 32,8–9);

(Chap. V)

17. a passage on the inconceivability of *tathāgatakriyā* taken from the *Dhāraṇīśvararājasūtra* (p. 476 *b*; RGV. pp. 26,16–27,3).

Thus, the *Anuttarâśrayasūtra* is clearly a composition based upon the *Ratna*. reshaping its contents into the frame of *sūtra* style and keeping its stress on the *bodhi* aspect, which is the highest basis (*anuttarâśraya*).

But what was the intention of the author in composing this 'Sūtra'? This Sūtra is quoted only in the *Buddhagotra*, and both are translated into Chinese by Paramârtha [85]. A key to solve this question as well as the question of the author of the *Buddhagotra* seems to lie in the hands of Paramârtha. If we may surmise so, it was probably some one in the circle to which Paramârtha had belonged or rather Paramârtha himself who composed these Sūtra and Śāstra as authorities for the propagation of his unique doctrine, a combination of the *garbha* theory and the Vijñānavāda. This supposition will be supported by the fact that among Chinese translations of the *Mahāyānasaṃgrahabhāṣya* of Vasubandhu, the *garbha* theory is inserted only in Paramârtha's translation [86]. Attribution of the *Buddhagotra* to Vasubandhu will be a subsidiary proof of the fact that the *Ratna.* was not written by Asaṅga or Vasubandhu; the latter was a great and respected scholar of the Vijñānavāda, and hence it was not desirable for the Vijñānavādins to use the *Ratna.* as an authority.

Of course, the combination of both theories was already traced in the *Sūtrâlaṅkāra* to some extent, but it was not intentional nor as clear, and the *Ratna.* seems to have tried to purify its standpoint on the *garbha* theory, while the orthodox Vijñānavādins like Vasubandhu have gradually deepened their theory on the side of pure Vijñānavāda. It was after Vasubandhu that the combination again took place, but intentionally. As

[85] Quotations of the *Anuttarâśraya* in the *Buddhagotraśāstra* are as follows:

1) p. 801 *c* (如無上依經中說...) = AĀS, p. 469 *b* = RGV, p. 12,6 (a part of a quotation from the *Jñānālokālaṅkārasūtra*);

2) p. 806 *b* (故無上依經說...) = AĀS, p. 469 *c* = RGV, pp. 40, 16–41.5 (a quotation from the *Anūnatvāpūrṇatvanirdeśa*);

3) p. 806 *b* (如無上依經說...) = AĀS, p. 469 *c* = RGV, p. 41, 13–15 (a commentary passage);

4) p. 812 (如無上依經說...) = AĀS, p. 469 *b* = RGV, p. 55, 16–17 (a quotation from the *Ṣaḍāyatanasūtra*).

Paramārtha's translation of the *Mahāyānasaṃgraha-bhāṣya* of Vasubandhu (*Taisho*, No. 1595) also quotes the AĀS (Vol. 31, pp. 259 *c*–260 *a* = AĀS, p. 469 *b-c* = RGV, pp. 49, 11–50, 7, a quotation from the *Sāgaramati-paripṛcchā*). But the quotation is found neither in the Tibetan version nor in Hsüan-chuang's translation of the same text. More interesting is the fact that the quotation is much more similar to the *Ratna.* than to the *Anuttarâśraya*, which has, in turn, some insertion between lines.

[86] For example, while interpreting a verse from the *Mahāyāna-abhidharmasūtra* (*Anādikāliko dhātuḥ*) which is quoted also in the *Ratna.*, Paramârtha's translation gives two meanings for '*dhātu*'. One is '*ālayavijñāna*' and the other is '*gotra*', i.e. *tathāgatagarbha* (*Taisho*, 31, p. 156 *c*). The latter interpretation is identical with the *Ratna.* (77.13–73.8).

other examples of this combination we have two works, the *Laṅkāvatārasūtra* and the *Mahāyānaśraddhôtpādaśāstra*.

§ 4. – *The Laṅkāvatāra and the Mahāyānaśraddhôtpāda–śāstra.*

The unique point of these two works with respect to the *garbha* theory is their identification of the *tathāgatagarbha* with the *ālayavijñāna*— an identification which has never been seen in previous works, even in those of Vasubandhu. That is why the *Laṅkāvatāra* is regarded by modern scholars as a work produced after Vasubandhu. The *Laṅkāvatāra* is actually a collection of various theories among Mahāyāna Buddhism, among which the *garbha* theory, and the Vijñānavāda are prominent, and these two are combined under the theory of *cittamātra* taught in the *Avataṃsaka*. Later Vijñānavādins regarded the *Laṅkāvatāra* as one of the authorities, but in China it was respected by the followers of the Avataṃsaka school as well, because of its exposition of the *cittamātra* and *garbha* theory. This is quite significant for determing the fate of the *garbha* theory, to which we will refer at the end of this introduction.

This is another Sūtra not known to the *Ratna.*, and it was translated for the first time into Chinese in 433 A.D.[87]. Therefore, the date of the *Ratna.* cannot be placed after that year and probably lies in the 4th cent. A.D.

As for the *Śraddhôtpādaśāstra*, its doctrine is purely of the *garbha* theory in spite of its use of the term *ālayavijñāna*, and it is in one sense the most systematic exposition of its kind. One point of similarity to the *Ratna.* is the expression of faith in the Buddha Amitāyus towards the end of the treatise. Another point which seems to be under the influence of the *Ratna.* is its establishment of *tathatā* as the ultimate principle that is the basis of both *kliṣṭa* and *akliṣṭa* elements. It reminds us of the *samalā tathatā* and *nirmalā tathatā* of the *Ratna.*

However, there is some doubt about its authorship. It is attributed to Aśvaghoṣa, the famous poet contemporary with the King Kaniṣka. It is impossible that such an old poet is the author of this work containing such a new theory. Some scholars wanted to solve this contradiction by regarding the author as another Aśvaghoṣa different from the famous poet, but some are trying to prove that this work is of Chinese origin in the absence of Sanskrit and Tibetan versions. This latter opinion is not

[87] According to old Chinese Catalogues on the Tripiṭaka, (prior to this translation) there was said to have been another translation done by Dharmakṣema (曇無讖) between 412–433 A.D. but now missing. As far as the present problem is concerned, there is no difference even if we accept this tradition.

untenable since, being translated by Paramârtha, this work is in the same position as the *Buddhagotra*. There is no work which refers to this treatise in Indian literature. But one difficulty in accepting this opinion is how to explain the existence of two versions of this treatise in China. The second translation was made by Śikṣānanda who is said to have come from Khotan. The problem is still under consideration, but it is at least sure that this work shows the final development of the *garbha* theory [88].

VI.

THE POSITION OF THE RATNA. IN MAHĀYĀNA BUDDHISM

§ 1. – *The Ratna. as a Criticism on the Prajñāpāramitā.*

At the end of Chapter I., the *Ratna.* expresses its purpose of discourse, saying that the text was exposed in order to establish the existence (*astitva*) of *buddhadhātu* so that one could avoid the faults created by the theory of '*śūnyaṃ sarvam*' described in the 'previous' Sūtras (I, 158–9).

It is clear that the Sūtras which expose the theory of '*śūnyaṃ sarvam*' with similes of *megha*, *svapna*, etc. signify the *Prajñāpāramitā* and the like, and that, in contrast with the *Prajñāpāramitā* taken as the '*pūrva*' exposition, this *Ratna.* calls itself the '*uttara–tantra*', the later exposition. Namely, the subtitle: *Uttaratantra* denotes the position of the *Ratna.* in the history of Mahāyāna Buddhism in the sense "one that comes after the Prajñāpāramitā, criticizing the latter."

On what point does then the *Ratna.* criticize the *Prajñāpāramitā*? As a matter of terminology, the *Ratna.* emphasizes '*asti*' in contrast with the '*śūnya*' of the *Prajñāpāramitā*. But this '*asti–vāda*' does not mean the negation of '*śūnya–vāda*'. Rather, the *Ratna.* regards itself as the real successor to the '*śūnya–vāda*' of the *Prajñāpāramitā* declaring that the real meaning of '*śūnyatā*' is to know the '*astitva*' of the Germ having within itself both the '*śūnya*' of defilements and the '*aśūnya*' of

88) There is another Sūtra which exposes the *garbha* theory and bears a resemblance to the *Ratna.* in its contents. Its name, according to the Tibetan version, is *Ārya–candrôttaradārikā–vyākaraṇa* (Tohoku no. 191) and it was translated into Chinese in 591 A.D. (*Taisho*, 14, no. 480) Its composition seems to be later in date than the *Ratna.* and there were probably a great deal of influences from the *Ratna.* See N. Takata, *On the Āryacandrottaradārikāvyākaraṇa–nāma–mahāyāna–sūtra* (*Japanese*). *Journal of Indian and Buddhist Studies* (*Indogaku Bukkyōgaku Kenkyū*) Vol. V, No. 1, 1957 (pp. 83–86). As I received this information only recently, detailed examination of this Sūtra could not be pursued up to now.

the Buddha's Qualities. (I, 154-5). We may take this statement as an explanation of '*śūnyaṃ sarvam*', defining '*sarvam*' as '*sarvakleśa*' from which all phenomena arise and which excludes the Germ inseparably associated with the Buddha's Qualities, that is to say, identical with the Absolute; and hence the word '*śūnya*' implies '*aśūnya*' of this Germ. As the *Prajñāpāramitā* was lacking in a clear explanation of such a kind, the *Ratna.* assumes for that reason many faults among the followers of the *Prajñāpāramitā*, and, therefore, the aim of the *Ratna.* is to remove such faults in order to make known the real meaning of '*śūnya-vāda*'.

Thus the criticism is directed not to the doctrine of the *Prajñāpāramitā* itself, but to its short or unclear explanation. This point becomes clear after examining the 5 faults described in the *Ratna.*, especially the last three of them. Namely, the 3rd fault: '*abhūtagrāha*' denotes the '*Ātmavāda*' of Heretics or the '*sarvâstivāda*' of the Abhidharma and is said to be removed by '*prajñā*'. This is exactly what is aimed at by the *Prajñāpāramitā*. However, when this '*prajñā*' is stated to be the intuition of '*śūnyaṃ sarvam*', many people are likely to misunderstand the meaning of '*śūnya*': on the one hand, some regard '*śūnya*' as something substantial, on the other hand, some become the '*nāstika*' and never believe in the existence of the *dharmakāya* but rather abuse such a reality. The text calls both kind of people those of '*śūnyatāvikṣiptacitta*' (P. 75). The former have a kind of '*abhūtagrāha*'; the latter have the fault of '*bhūtadharmâpavāda*', which forms the 4th of the 5 faults. As the remedy against this fault, the commentary mentions '*jñāna*'. Here '*jñāna*' has the character of criticizing '*prajñā*' in the sense of affirming the existence of the reality undone by '*prajñā*'. But the text seems to regard this '*jñāna*' as one side of '*prajñā*', as a natural outflow of '*prajñā*'. In other words, '*prajñā*' has two functions, to negate the '*abhūtagrāha*', and to establish the '*bhūtadharma*', as represented by '*prajñā*' and '*jñāna*', respectively.

These two sides of '*prajñā*' are shown in another passage by the terms *avikalpajñāna* and *tatpṛṣṭhalabdha* (*jñāna*), and characterized as *lokottara* and *laukika*, respectively. Here the term '*laukika*' signifies the function of *jñāna* to make known the reality to the 'worldly' beings. This is nothing but a function of providing benefits for others, i. e. for the world, and hence is based upon the Compassion, *karuṇā* or *maitrī*. Unless this function of *jñāna* operates, man will have the fault of '*ātmasneha*'. This seems to be the reason for maintaining '*ātmasneha*' as the last of the 5 faults and '*maitrī*' as the remedy for it.

Thus the *Ratna.* emphasizes *karuṇā* along with *prajñā* as associating inseparably with each other for the acquisition of the Buddhahood. This point is also mentioned in the explanation of the process from cause to effect with respect to the Germ. (pp. 27–35) Namely, the text mentions four kinds of practice, viz. *adhimukti*, *prajñāpāramitā*, *samādhi*, and *mahākaruṇā*, as the cause for attaining the *dharmakāya*. Of them, *prajñāpāramitā* and *mahākaruṇā* are relevant to the present discussion. The practice of *prajñāpāramitā* is said to be the remedy for all kinds of substantial views, the *ātmavāda* of heretics and the like, while the practice of *mahākaruṇā* is said to be the remedy for any selfishness whose typical form is found in the Pratyekabuddha. Also, it is said that the result of the former practice is the establishment of the *dharmakāya* to be the '*ātmapāramitā*' extending as far as the limit of space (*ākāśadhātu–paryavasāna*), while that of the latter is the establishment of the *dharmakāya* to be the '*nityapāramitā*' continuing as far as the limit of time (*aparântakoṭiniṣṭha*). And the Bodhisattva is said to be the only one who practises both *prajñāpāramitā* and *mahākaruṇā* and who, owing to the practice of *prajñā*, never afflicts the world, but, owing to the practice of *karuṇā*, never remains in the Nirvāṇa (*apratiṣṭhitanirvāṇa*). Here we see the stress lies more on the *karuṇā* than on the *prajñā* and this standpoint relates to the *ekayāna* theory whose origin is in the *Saddharmapuṇḍarīka*, which declares the eternity of the Buddha [89].

Another important point to be noted here is the positive expression of the *dharmakāya* to be the *śubha–ātma–sukha–nityaguṇapāramitā*. These four terms, viz. *nitya*, *sukha*, *ātman* and *śubha* are usually regarded as wrong notions with respect to the phenomena, and most scriptures, including the *Prajñāpāramitā*, teach the notions of *anitya*, *duḥkha*, *anātman* and *aśubha* as the correct view (*aviparyāsa*) with respect to the *dharmas*, i. e. the phenomena. In contrast, in this *Ratna.* or in the *garbha* theory in general, these prohibited terms are used as attributes of the *dharmakāya* but in the reverse order. This is a kind of revolution in Buddhist thought, but it is, as has been examined above, another expression of the same idea of '*dhātvastitva*' being explained through the characters of the *gotra* as '*śūnya*' and '*aśūnya*'. Special attention is to be paid to the point that the *ātmapāramitā* is said to be the result of the practice of '*prajñāpāramitā*. In the *Prajñāpāramitā*, the function of *prajñā* (or *prajñāpāramitā*) is to establish the correct notions of *anitya*, etc., while here the same term is used for the function of establishing the *dharmakāya* expressed in the positive way. It seems to show that the *Ratna.* understands the *prajñā*-

[89] e.g. Saddh. P. XV–1: *Acintyā kalpasahasrakoṭyo yāsāṃ pramāṇaṃ na kadāci vidyate / prāptā mayā eṣa tadagrabodhir dharmaṃca deśemy ahu nityakālam //* (Bibl. Buddh. ed. p. 323).

paramitā in its two aspects, negation of the wrong view and manifestation of the reality, in other words, *prajñāpāramitā* as consisting of *prajñā* and *jñāna* or of *prajñā* and *karuṇā*. In clarifying such a structure of *prajñāpāramitā*, the *Ratna.* deserves to be called the successor to the *Prajñāpāramitā*. What is criticized is '*prajñā*, not accompanied by *karuṇā*', or '*prajñā* which does not work out in the world as *jñāna*'. [90].

§ 2. – *The Ratna. and the Vijñānavāda.*

There is another system in Mahāyāna Buddhism that criticizes the *Prajñāpāramitā* in a manner similar to the way done by the *Ratna.* This is the Vijñānavāda whose authority is sought for in the *Sandhinirmocana-sūtra.* The Sūtra says [91]: By the first Turning of the Wheel of Doctrine, there was taught the doctrine of the *āryasatya* and on its basis the *astivāda* of the Abhidharma has been developed. This *astivāda* was negated by the *Prajñāpāramitā* and there has been established the *śūnyavāda* of the Mahā-

[90] Both terms, *prajñā* and *jñāna* are of a great significance in Buddhism since its beginning. Literally and originally, the former has a somewhat functional character, while the latter signifies what is attained by the former. Concretely speaking, *prajñā* is the intellect or intuition by means of which the Buddha attained the *bodhi*, while *jñāna* is the knowledge which forms the contents of *bodhi*. However, such an analysis was made for the first time by Pāli Abhidhamma Buddhism, and in primitive Buddhism there seems to have been no strict distinction in the use of these terms. This distinction is of fundamental character throughout the history of Buddhism, but there was a variant in each school in the usage of both terms. Diagramatically speaking, the Sarvāstivāda laid stress on *jñāna* in which the function of *prajñā* is implied, while the *Prajñāpāramitā* emphasized *prajñā* as the highest 'practice', but this *prajñā* included both aspects of *jñāna* and *prajñā*. In contrast with the logical approach of Abhidharma Buddhism, that of Mahāyāna Buddhism may be characterized as 'practical'. This *prajñā* of the *Prajñāpāramitā* and consequently of Nāgārjuna was again analyzed by the Vijñānavāda, as mentioned above, which, in turn, sought for its basic term in *jñāna* as the Sarvāstivāda did. But a revolutionary point of Mahāyāna Buddhism in comparison with Abhidharma Buddhism is in the emphasis laid on '*parārthasampatti*', and hence on *karuṇā*; and the Vijñānavāda, in spite of its similarity to the Sarvāstivāda in its analytical method, is a successor of the *Prajñāpāramitā* in its introduction of the idea of *parārthasampatti* into *jñāna*, which changed the character of *jñāna* to its ground. A critical approach to this subject will be one of the big themes in future studies of Buddhist thought. Cf. G. Sasaki, "*Prajñā* and *Jñāna*", (*Japanese*) *Journal of Indian & Buddhist Studies*, Vol. II, No. 2. Tokyo, pp. 437–439.

[91] *Sandhinirmocanasūtra* tr. by Hsüan-Chuang (*Taisho*, No. 676) Chap. V. *Niḥsvabhāvalakṣaṇaparivarta*, *Taisho*, 16, pp. 693 *c*–697 *c*. This statement is placed towards the end of the chapter. Tib. ed. by E. Lamotte (1935), p. 85 f. (Chapitre VII, 30–31). '*Sandhinirmocana*' on account of '*niḥsvabhāva*' is the main topic of this chapter, which opens with a question by Paramārthasamudayagata Bodhisattva (Tib. Don dam yaṅ–dag–ḥphags) on this point. (Lamotte, *op. cit.*, p. 65 f.).

yāna. The amalgamation of both *asti–* and *śūnya–vāda* is now done by the *Sandhinirmocana*, and it is the last and the highest Turning of the Wheel of Doctrine. As the justification for this statement, the Sūtra continues: The ultimate doctrine of the Mahāyāna is no doubt taught in the *Prajñāpāramitā*, but its way of exposition is 'with an esoteric meaning, or 'with a hidden intention' [92]. For example the *Prajñāpāramitā* teaches the *niḥsvabhāvatā* in regard to the *sarvadharma*, but what is meant by this *niḥsvabhāvatā* is not so clear. The purpose of the *Sandhinirmocana* is to explain this meaning of *niḥsvabhāva* 'in a clear manner', that is to say, to analyze and clarify the significance of the *śūnya–vada*. Just because of this standpoint, the Sūtra is called '*sandhi–nirmocana*', i. e. the Disclosure of the Knot or Secret Doctrine. Along this line, the Sūtra establishes the doctrine of the 3 meanings with res ect to the *niḥsvabhāvatā* as the basis of the *trisvabhāva* theory [93].

This standpoint is precisely held in common with the *Ratna.* in its criticism of the *Prajñāpāramitā*. Indeed, the *Ratna.* is in one sense a *sandhinirmocana* on account of *prajñā* [94] and the *Sāndhinirmocana* may be termed the *uttaratantra* as the ultimate exposition of the *śūnyavāda* described from the two sides, of *śūnya* and *aśūnya*.

Such a community of historical background brought the *garbha* theory and the Vijñānavāda to assume a similar appearance of '*astivāda*' and to have common doctrines to a great extent, and lastly resulted in the amalgamation of both theories. *Avikalpajñāna* and *tatpṛṣṭhalabdha (jñāna)*, or *āśrayaparivṛtti* and the six categories beginning with *svabhāva* for describing the ultimate reality, are, as has been referred to above, terms borrowed by the *Ratna.* from the Vijñānavāda. The quotation of a verse from the *Mahāyāna–abhidharmasūtra* (*anādikāliko dhātuḥ*—) also shows the influence of the Vijñānavāda on the *Ratna.*, at least on the commentary. Also, we have already observed in the *Sūtrâlaṅkāra* the co-existence of the *garbha* theory and the doctrine of *trisvabhāva* and *ālayavijñāna*.

In spite of such interrelations of both theories, the unique standpoint of the *Ratna.* may be observed in the fact that there is no quotation from the *Sandhinirmocana*, nor any use of terms like *trisvabhāva* or *ālayavijñāna:* hence, the *Ratna.* cannot be regarded as a work of the *Vijñānavada*. Furthermore the *Ratna.* has many authorities for its doctrine that are, in turn, not acquainted with the Vijñānavāda at all. These facts seem to tell us that the *garbha* theory, although it criticizes the *Prajñā-*

[92] Cf. Edgerton BHS Dic. s. v. *saṃdhāya*, & *saṃdhā*, *saṃdhi*.

[93] Lamotte, *op. cit.*, Chap. VII, 3 (p. 67). He refers to the source of this *trisvabhāva* in the *Prajñāpāramitā* (*op. cit.*, Préface, pp. 14–16).

[94] See Note on Introduction, V, 3.

pāramitā, is a completely different system from the Vijñānavāda by origin, and, in its possession of many Sūtras, somewhat precedes the Vijñānavāda.

The starting point of the *garbha* theory lies in the doctrine of '*citta-prakṛti* and *āgantukakleśa*' and the stress is laid on the purification of the mind which is regarded as the attainment of the Enlightenment. This *cittaprakṛti* is unconditionally identified with *bodhi* or *dharmakāya* and is called '*dhātu*' or '*gotra*'. From such a theory of *cittaprakṛti*, we may expect the development of the *cittamātra* theory as exposed in the *Avataṃsaka* or the *Laṅkâvatāra*. In fact, we find a germ of such a theory in the *Ratna.* in the passage where the origination of the 3 impurities (*saṃkleśa*) of *kleśa*, *karman* and *janman* from *cittaprakṛti* by the force of '*ayoniśo-manasikāra*' is set forth. Nevertheless, the *Ratna.* never uses the expression of *cittamātra*. The passage referred to above is used for explaining how the *cittaprakṛti* is real and how the *āgantukakleśa* is unreal, but there is no explanation of the reason why such unreal *kleśas* are originated from the *cittaprakṛti*. In other words, the emphasis lies on the identification of *gotra* or *garbha* with the *dharmakāya* and any difference of the *garbha* or the *sattvadhātu* from the *dharmakāya* is rather neglected. This is a weak point of the *garbha* theory.

On the other hand, what is done by the Vijñānavāda is the investigation of this very point of difference between *sattvadhātu* and the Buddha. When the *Sandhinirmocana* established the theory of *trisvabhāva* as the result of the analysis of *niḥsvabhāvatā* taught in the *Prajñāparamitā*, its analytical method found the origin of the nature of *sattvadhātu* covered with *kleśas* in *vijñāna* as the function of distinguishing object from subject. The term *cittamātra* is replaced by and explained more concretely as '*vijñaptimātra*', and '*citta*', not as pure *cittaprakṛti*, but as something that manifests *kleśa*, or as the basis (*āśraya*) of phenomena, is named '*ālayavijñāna*'. In its methodology, the Vijñānavāda was really a successor of the Abhidharma Buddhism, but it was the Abhidharma based upon the *śūnyavāda* of the *Prajñāpāramitā*, and hence deserves to be called '*mahāyānâbhidharma*', as shown in the title of one scripture.

Thus the standpoint of the Vijñānavāda is the analysis of phenomena from the viewpoint of the *sattvadhātu* and thereby it stands in a clear contrast with the *garbha* theory which, in turn, exposes its doctrine always from the viewpoint of the *dharmakāya* or *bodhi*. Of course, even for the Vijñānavāda, the ultimate purpose is the realization of *bodhi*, or manifestation of the real meaning of *śūnyatā*. As regards *bodhi*, the Vijñānāvada seeks for the process towards its realization in the acquisition of '*jñāna*' as a result of the conversion of *ālayavijñāna*, and with this '*jñāna*' acquired, it is said, the '*vijñaptimātratā*' can be understood, otherwise it cannot. Thus this '*jñāna*' is characterized as '*laukika*' '*pṛṣṭhalabdha*', owing to which function the basic *prajñā*, i. e. '*avikalpajñāna*' can realize itself in the world. This point is accepted in the *Ratna*. The only difference, but of an essential character, is that the *gotra*, being '*anādikāliko dhātuḥ*' and the '*āśraya* of *sarvadharma*', is regarded as fully identical with *bodhi* or *dharmakāya*, and '*jñānâpti*' is said to be the perfect manifestation (*pari–vṛtti*) of such '*āśraya*', while in the Vijñānavāda, *ālayavijñāna*, though being *anādikāliko dhātuḥ* and being *āśraya* of *sarvadharma*, always remains as a principle of '*saṃkliṣṭadharma*' and is never regarded as identical with *dharmakāya*[95], and '*jñānâpti*' is said to be the result of the revolution (*parāvṛtti*) of *āśraya*, i. e. change of basis from *ālayavijñāna* to *jñāna*. In other words, *gotra* involves two sides, namely '*prakṛtiṣṭha*' and '*samudānīta*', and hence has the same structure as '*avikalpajñāna*' and '*tatpṛṣṭhalabdha*', while *ālayavijñāna* can never be identical with '*avikalpajñāna*' and in '*jñānâpti*', it no longer remains. This is the reason why the *Ratna*., in spite of its acceptance of the Vijñānavāda in its interpretation of '*jñāna*' and others, never introduced the doctrine of *ālayavijñāna*, and why the *Ratna*. could remain thereby, in the field of the pure *garbha* theory.

At the same time, failure to introduce the *ālayavijñāna* made the *garbha* theory weak in its explanation of the *gotra* as the substratum (*ādhāra*) of Saṃsāra or the phenomenal world. Because of this weak point, the *garbha* theory in its later development could not but introduce the doctrine of *ālayavijñāna*, and there was an attempt at identification, of *garbha* with *ālayavijñāna*, as seen in the *Laṅkāvatāra* and the *Mahāyānaśraddhôtpāda*. Furthermore, such an innovation of the Vijñānavāda resulted in the absorption of the *garbha* theory into the Vijñānavāda, preventing the former from establishing an independent school of its own. This absorption seems to have taken place not so long after the *Ratna*. in the period when the Vijñānavāda had formed an independent school as the rival of the Mādhyamika. At its starting point, however, the *garbha* theory was no doubt of an independent character, different from the Vijñānavāda, and the *Ratna*. was the first systematized and at the same time the last independent and pure exposition of the *garbha* theory.

One thing to be added here is the similarity of the *Ratna*. (and the Vijñānavāda, too) to the Upaniṣadic philosophy in the expression of

95) According to Paramārtha, however, *ālayavijñāna* is said to have a mixed character of real and unreal (真妄和合). This characterization seems to be his unique interpretation of that term, probably influenced by the *tathāgatagarbha* theory.

the Absolute with positive terms [96]. In its essence, it is clear, the Absolute taught in the *Ratna.*, being the manifestation of *śūnyatā*, is of a quite different character from the substantial Absolute of the Upaniṣad. Still it is not impossible to suppose that there was an influence from the Upaniṣadic thought for the *astivāda* of the *Ratna.* to establish its monistic doctrine. At the same time, many scholars have already remarked the influence of the Vijñanavāda on the Vedāntavāda in its change of character from the realistic philosophy of the *Brahmasūtra* to the idealistic philosophy of the Advaita-vedānta which is established by Śaṅkara through the philosophy of Gauḍapāda. To clarify the historical and social background of the *garbha* theory and the Vijñānavāda, it seems quite necessary to investigate such mutual influences and interrelations between the Brahmanical thought and Mahāyāna Buddhism. This subject is, however, too wide to cover here, and I cannot but reserve its investigation for my future studies [97].

§ 3. – *Consideration on the Date and Authorship of the Ratna.*

As a result of investigations throughout the previous passage, it may not be useless here to have in conclusion a summarized consideration of the date and authorship of the *Ratna.*

As for its date:

1) The upper limit is the date of Nāgārjuna and Āryadeva, i. e. the middle of the 3rd cent. A.D. It is common to the *garbha* theory and the Vijñānavāda in general.

2) The lower limit is 433 A.D. when the *Laṅkāvatāra* is translated into Chinese for the first time.

3) Completion of the present form of the *Ratna.*, i. e. the text consisting of the basic Kārikās and a commentary on it in verse and prose, came probably after Asaṅga and Vasubandhu but not so far from their time, and hence at early 5th cent. A.D.

96) A verse of the *Ratna.* quite similar to one of the *Bhagavadgītā* is pointed out by Prof. V. V. Gokhale (*A Note on Ratnagotravibhāga I.* 52 = *Bhagavadgītā XIII*, 32, Prof. S. Yamaguchi's Commemoration Volume, Kyoto, 1955, pp. 90–91).

97) Recently, a great work by Prof. T. R. V. Murti has appeared on this field of comparative study. (*The Central Philosophy of Buddhism*, London, 1955) Especially, Chap. XIII of his work is devoted to the subject of the Absolute seen by three systems, viz. Mādhyamika, Vijñānavāda and Vedānta. As far as the historical approach is concerned, however, so far no work has been done systematically.

4) As for the Kārikā text, especially those verses called '*śloka*' and kept in Chapter I. seem fairly old in both their style and contents; hence its date is no doubt earlier than Asaṅga's.

As for the author:

1) The author of the commentary must be Sāramati. This is certain through comparison of the *Ratna.* with the *Dharmadhātuviśeṣaśāstra*

2) Most probably the authorship of the original '*śloka*' is to be attributed to Maitreya, taking the Tibetan tradition into consideration. In the case of the *Sūtrâlaṅkāra*, the *garbha* theory and the Vijñānavāda are taught side by side, while the *Abhisamayâlaṅkāra* expresses no Vijñānavāda. Thus it is not impossible that the same author of the above two works composed the original '*śloka*' of the *Ratna.* But against the Tibetan tradition, the *Ratna.* seems to have been composed next to the *Abhisamayâlaṅkāra* but before the *Sūtrâlaṅkāra.* This is because the *garbha* theory precedes Maitreya, but the Vijñānavāda is likely to have started with Maitreya.

3) The Vijñānavāda had probably been established in its pure form by Vasubandhu. He was no doubt acquainted with the *garbha* theory but devoted himself to the systematization of the Vijñānavāda. Therefore, it is quite doubtful to attribute the *Buddhagotraśāstra* to him.

4) In the same way, Sāramati was the systematizer of the *garbha* theory in its pure form. Because of this similar position, Sāramati may have been almost contemporary with Vasubandhu. Amalgamation of both theories may consequently have taken place after Vasubandhu and Sāramati, since the *Laṅkāvatāra* was unknown to either of them.

This seems to be the most reasonable assumption on the date and author of the *Ratna.* after the present investigation. For certainty of Maitreya's authorship of the *Ratna.*, however, pieces of evidence are still not enough, and we shall be required to engage in further and detailed examination of all the works attributed to Maitreya.

SYNOPSIS
OF THE RATNAGOTRAVIBHĀGA

ANALYSIS OF THE GERM OF THE THREE JEWELS BEING A TREATISE ON THE ULTIMATE DOCTRINE OF THE GREAT VEHICLE

S. Ratnagotravibhāgo (nāma) Mahāyānottaratantraśāstram.
T. Theg-pa-chen-po rgyud-bla-maḥi bstan-bcos rnam-par bśad-pa.
C. Chiu-ching-i-ch'eng-pao-hsing-lun (究竟一乘寶性論).

SYNOPSIS

CONTENTS

1. **Topic** (abbreviations)

   a. **Divisions of chapters in the English translation (I～XVIII) and their subdivisions.**

   b. **Divisions of chapters in the Sanskrit text.**

   c. **Main topics in each division. (Mentions are made in Sanskrit for the technical terms and in English for explanations).**

2. **Number of verses**

   a. **Kārikās (those verses picked up as being basic, including *ślokas*, *uddānas* and *udāharaṇas*. See Introduction, II).** (K.)

   b. **Verses in the Sanskrit text. Number is according to Johnston's edition.** (v.)

3. **Number of pages in the three versions**

   a. **in Sanskrit (Johnston's edition)** (S.)

   b. **in Tibetan (Sde–dge edition)** (T.)

   c. **in Chinese (*Taisho* No. 1611)** (C.)

4. **Quotations & References (Authorities for the Ratna.)** (Q. & R.)

   a. **Name of sources**

   b. **Number of pages in the Chinese translation (*Taisho* edition). (in case the Sanskrit text is available, number of pages or verses in its Sanskrit edition)**

   c. **those with 'Cf' show references but not quotations. (About abbreviations for the names of texts. see List of Abbreviations)**

5. **Comparison with the 3 similar works**

   a. **The Buddhagotraśāstra** (BGŚ)

   b. **The Mahāyānadharmadhātvaviśeṣaśāstra** (DAŚ)

   c. **The Anuttarāśrayasūtra. (number of pages in *Taisho* edition)** (AĀS)

Synopsis

	K	v	S
Chapter I – The Tathāgatagarbha			
(Salutation)			1.1
(Introduction by the Commentator)			
I. Introduction			1.1–7.5
7 Adamantine Subjects (vajrapadāni sapta)			
§ 1. The Meaning of the Adamantine Subjects			
vajrapada: artha & vyañjana		1	1.1–2.3
§ 2. Authorities on the 7 Subjects			2.4–3.10
1) buddha, 2) dharma, 3) saṃgha			
4) dhātu			
5) bodhi			
6) guṇa			
7) karman			
§ 3. The Essential Character of the 7 Subjects (taken from DRS)		2	3.11–6.18
1)–3) buddha, dharma, & saṃgha			
" sarvadharmasamatā' bhisaṃbuddha " (buddha)			
" supravartitadharmacakra " (dharma)			
" anantaśiṣyagaṇasuvinīta " (saṅgha)			
" mahatā bhikṣusaṃghena sārdhaṃ..... bodhisattvagaṇena sārdham "			
" evaṃguṇasamanvāgataiḥ "			
1. buddharatnaguṇavibhāga			
2. dharmaratnaguṇavibhāga			
3. saṃgharatnaguṇavibhāga			
4) buddhadhātu			5.5
Illustration of ' vaiḍūryamaṇi ' (Q)			5.9–6.7
a verse on ' viśuddhigotra ' (Q) " yathā pattharacuṇṇamhi ... "			6.9
ṣaṣṭyākāra–viśuddhiparikarmaguṇa			6.11
4 bodhisattvâlaṃkārāḥ			
8 bodhisattv'ābhāsaḥ			
16 bodhisattvamahākaruṇā			
32 bodhisattvakarmā			
5) bodhi 16 mahābodhikaruṇā			6.14
6) guṇa 10 balāḥ, 4 vaiśāradyāḥ, & 18 āveṇikadharmāḥ			
7) karman 32 niruttaratathāgatakarmā			

T	C	Q. & R.	BGŚ	DAŚ	AĀS
74 *b* 1	om. instead, 18 verses. 813 *a–b*				
74 *b* 1–77 *b* 2	820 *c*–822 *b*				
74 *b* 1–6	820 *c*	(C) AkṣP 197 *b*			
74 *b* 6–75 *b* 2	821 *a–b*	DṛdhP 172 *b* 2–3 AAN 467 *a* ŚMS 220 *c* AAN 467 *a* Acint A 915 *b*			
75 *b* 2–77 *b* 1	821 *b*–822 *b*	DRS 1 *a* DRS 1 *a–b* (1 *c*–3 *c*) (3 *c*–4 *b*) (4 *c*–5 *b*) DRS 21 *c*			
77 *a* 4	822 *a*	unk (Prakrit) cf. DRS (cf. 5 *b*–8 *b*) (cf. 9 *a*–10 *a*) (cf. 10 *a*–10 *c*) (cf. 10 *c*–11 *b*)			
77 *a* 5	822 *b*	(cf. 11 *b*–14 *a*) (cf. 14 *c*–21 *c*) (cf. 26 –*b*27 *c*)			

	K	V	S
§ 4. The Inherent Connection among the 7 Subjects (śāstrasaṃbandha)		3	7.1–5
budha ⟶ dharma ⟶ saṅgha = garbha, jñānadhātu			
(dharmakāya =) agra-bodhi, jñānāpti ⟵			
---------- dharmāḥ (guṇāḥ)			
---------- sarvasattvārthakṛt (karman)			
(A. Ratnatraya)			
II. THE JEWEL OF THE BUDDHA			7.6–10.14
(buddharatna) (*VP. 1.)			
General statement on 'śaraṇatraya'			
(Kārikā)	1	(= 4)	
		5	
§ 1. The 8-fold Quality of the Buddhahood		6–8	7.13–9.4
1) asaṃskṛtatva (anādimadhyanidhanaṃ)			8.7
2) anābhogatā (śāntaṃ)			
3) aparapratyayābhisaṃbodhi (vibuddhaḥ svayam)			
4) jñāna, 5) karuṇā & 6) śakti			
(svayaṃ buddhvā mārgaṃ dideśa)			
(jñānakṛpāsivajravaradhṛk)			
§ 2. Reference to the Jñānālokālaṅkārasūtra (on the former 6 guṇas)			9.5–10.11
1) on 'asaṃskṛta' – anutpādānirodha			
2) on 'upaśānta' – anābhoga			
3) on 'abhisaṃbodhi'			
4) on 'jñāna' & 'karuṇā' as 'śakti'			
3 kinds of 'sattva'			
'aśuddha', 'avimala', 'sāṅgana' – perceived by 'jñāna'			
'vikrīḍitā' – 'karuṇā'			
'dharmacakrapravarta' – 'śakti' – 'parārtha'			
§ 1' 7) svārthasaṃpad & 8) parārthasaṃpad			10.11
two kinds of interpretation			
a) svārthasaṃpad – asaṃskṛta, anābhoga, abhisaṃbuddha			
parārthasaṃpatti – jñāna, karuṇā, śakti			
b) svār. – jñāna, including the former 3			
parār. – karuṇā & śakti			

* VP. vajrapada

T	C	Q. & R.	BGŚ	DAŚ	AĀS
77 *b* 1	822 *b*				
77 *b* 2–79 *b* 5	822 *b*–823 *b*	(ŚMS 221 *a*)			
77 *b* 3–4	813 *b* 822 *b*				
77 *b* 4–78 *b* 3	822 *c*–823 *a*	cf M N 1, 171			
78 *b* 3–79 *b* 3	823 *a*–823 *b*	JĀA cf. 240 *b* cf. 240 *c* cf. 247 *b* cf. 247 *b*			
79 *b* 3– 5	823 *b*				

	K	V	S
III. THE JEWEL OF THE DOCTRINE (dharmaratna) (VP 2)			10.15–13.20
(Kārikā)	2	(= 9)	
§ 1. The 8-fold Quality of the Doctrine		10	11.3
1) acintyatva, 2) advayatā, 3) nirvikalpatā, 4) śuddhi, 5) abhivyaktikaraṇa, 6) pratipakṣatā, 7) virāga, 8) virāgahetu			
§ 2. Nirodhasatya & Mārgasatya (virāgitā)		11	11.9
virāgadharma = vyavadānasatyadvayalakṣaṇa of two aspects – 'yo yena ca virāgaḥ'			
§ 3 The Doctrine as the Truth of Extinction (nirodhasatya)		12	11.16
1) 'acintyatva'			
a. tarkâgocara, b. anabhilāpya, c. pratyātmavedanīya			
2) 'advayatā' & 3) 'nirvikalpatā'			
'dvaya' = karman & kleśa, 'vikalpa' = ayoniśomanasikāra			
(Q. 1)			12.2
(Q. 2) 'ajāti' – non-origination of phenomena			12.6–10
(Q. 3) 'duḥkhanirodha' means 'dharmakāya'			12.10–14
§ 4 The Doctrine as the Truth of Path (mārgasatya)			12.16–13.20
1) Similarity to the sun (dharmadivākara) in three ways – 4. śudhi, 5. abhivyaktikaraṇa, 6. pratipakṣa			12.16
2) Origination of bondage (vibandha) and its removal by jñāna			13.1
A. 'abhūtavastunimittârambaṇa' – 'ayoniśomanasikāra'			
by 'śubhâkāra – coming forth of 'rāga' from 'anuśaya' by 'pratighâkāra – coming forth of 'dveśa' from 'anuśaya' by 'avidyâkāra – coming forth of 'moha' from 'anuśaya' 'ayoniśomanasikāra'→'kleśa'→'karman'→'janman(duḥkha)' saṃkleśa all these are caused by the lack of knowledge on 'ekadhātu'			
B. Removal of bondage – perception of 'dhātu' as it is = tattvadarśana = avikalpajñāna, being 'dharmakāyaprāptihetu'			

T	C	Q. & R.	BGŚ	DAŚ	AĀS
79 *b* 6–81 *b* 6	823 *b*–824 *b*				
79 *b* 6–7	813 *b*–*c* 823 *b*–*c*				
79 *b* 7–80 *a* 2	823 *c*		801 *a* ff. (IV, 5 yoga) 801 *a*		
80 *a* 2–5	823 *c*				
80 *a* 5–81 *a* 2	823 *c*–824 *a*				
		AAN 467 *b* JĀA 247 *a* ŚMS 221 *c*	 Q. fr. AĀS Q. fr. ŚMS		 496 *b* 496 *b*
81 *a*.2–81 *b*.6	824 *a*		virāgahetu		
81 *a* 4	824 *b*	PP cf. AAĀ 230 ff. cf. ASP VI 332.9–12 ------ 354.5–9 370.5–16	(as the Comm. by Paramārtha		

	K	v	S
IV. THE JEWEL OF THE COMMUNITY			13.21–17.13
(saṃgharatna) (VP 3) (especially, saṃgha of 'avaivartikabodhisattva') (Kārikā)	3	(= 13)	13.21–15.14
§ 1. Manner and Extent of Perception 'yathāvadbhāvikatā' & 'yāvadbhāvikatā'		14	
a) Right Manner of Perception (yathāvadbhāvikatā) perception of 'pudgaladharmâkhyasya jagato nairātmyakoṭi', as well as of 'pudgaladharmâvināśatva' caused by 'darśana' of 'cittasya prakṛtiprabhāsvaratā' and 'tadupakleśasya ādikṣayanirodha[tā]'.		15	14.11
(Q)			15.3–7
b) Unlimited Extent of Perception (yāvadbhāvikatā) perception of 'tathāgatagarbhâstitva in all sattvas', 'prativedha of dharmadhātu', by means of 'lokottarajñāna'		16 (C. in prose)	15.9–14
§ 2. Introspective Character of Bodhisattva's Perception 'avabodha' = 'pratyātmalokottarajñānadarśana' 'suviśuddha' { asaṅga → yathāvadbhāvikatā apratihata → yāvadbhāvikatā		17 (C. in prose)	16.1–8
§ 3. Superiority of Bodhisattva's Community 1. jñānadarśanaśuddhi & 2. anuttaratathāgatajñāna (–sama) these belong exclusively to 'avaivartika-bodhisattva'		18	16.9–14
(10 points of superiority of bodhisattvasaṃgha – daśaviśeṣa)		v. (in C.)	om.
§ 3'. Inferiority of Śrāvaka-saṅgha (probably a quotation) bodhisattva – gaṇasantānâvabhāsa, navacandravat, possessed of 'jñāna & karuṇā' śrāvaka – svasantānâvabhāsa, tārārūpa, possessed of 'prādeśikajñāna'			16.15–17.13
(Q) "yaḥ śīlam ātmârthakaraṃ bibharti . . ."			17.6–13
V. THE 3 JEWELS AS REFUGES (from śaraṇatraya to buddhaśaraṇa – 'ekayāna' theory)			17.14–20.18
§ 1. 3 Refuges from the Empirical Standpoint (saṃvṛtipadasthāna) 1. buddhaśaraṇa – (śāstṛ) for boddhisattvayānika & buddhakārakriyā 2. dharma-ś. – (śāsana) for pratyekabuddha-y. & dharma-k. 3. saṃgha-ś. – (śiṣya) for śrāvaka-y. & saṃgha-k.		19	17.15–18.11

T	C	Q. & R.	BGŚ	DAŚ	AĀS
81 *b* 6–83 *b* 3	824 *b*–825 *c*				
81 *b* 7–82 *a* 1	813 *c* 824 *c*				
82 *a* 2–82 *b* 5	824 *c*		(cf. 802 (IV-6 vṛtti) for. 1) 2), (5.		
82 *a* 3			yoga)		
		ŚMS 222 *b*			
82 *b* 3	825 *a*		*ibid*. (5 yoga)		
82 *b* 5–83 *a* 1	825 *a*				
			(5 yoga)		
83 *a* 1–3	825 *a*				
om.	825 *b*				
83 *a* 3–83 *b* 3	825 *c*	unk.			
		2 verses (unk)			
83 *b* 3–85 *a* 5	825 *c*–826 *c*				
83 *b* 3–84 *a* 1	825 *c*				

	K	V	S
§ 2. The Doctrine and the Community are not the Ultimate Refuge		20	18.12-20.3
reasons: 1. tyājya 2. moṣadharma 3. abhāva 4. sabhaya			
a) ' dharma '			
1. deśanā-dharma – mārga, being ' abhisamayaparyavasāna ' kolôpama – (1) tyājya			
2. adhigama-dharma			
1. mārgasatya – saṃskṛta – asatya, anitya – (2) mṛṣāmoṣadharmin			
2. nirodhasatya (of śrāvakanaya) – kleśaduḥkhâbhāva – (3) abhāva being ' abhāva ', it can be neither ' śaraṇa ' nor ' aśaraṇa '			
b) ' saṃgha ' (esp., that of śrāvaka) – (4) sabhaya			19.6
1. ' saṃgha ' means ' traiyānika-gaṇa '			
2. they are ' sabhaya ', ' tathāgataśaraṇagata ', niḥsaraṇaparyeṣin, śaikṣa, sakaraṇīya, and ' pratipannaka ' towards bodhi			
3. they have ' bhaya-saṃjñā ', on ' saṃskāra ' because of their still being possessed of ' vāsanā ', and hence they are seeking for ' śanaṇa ' in Tathāgata			
4. therefore, ' saṃgha ' is merely ' prādeśikaśaraṇa '			
5. thus, dharma & saṃgha are called ' paryantakālaśaraṇa '			
§ 3. Only the Buddha is the Refuge from the Highest Standpoint		21	20.4–10
1. ' muni ' is ' anutpādânirodha ', of the body of ' vyavadānasatyadvayalakṣaṇa-virāgadharma (= dharmakāya)			
2. Saṃgha puts its goal of acquisition on this ' dharmakāya '			
3. therefore, buddha is ' ekaṃ pāramārthikaṃ śaraṇam ', which is ' aparântakoṭisama, akṣaya, nitya, dhruva, śiva, śāśvata			
§ 4. The Meaning of the 3 Jewels – the reason why they are called ' ratna '		22	20.11–18
1. durlabhôtpāda, 2. nirmala, 3. prabhā, 4. lokâlaṃkāra, 5. agra, 6. avikāra			
(B. Ratnagotra)			
VI. The Germ of the 3 Jewels in four aspects			21.1-25.17
(Karikā)	4	(= 23)	
The 4 aspects (catvāri padāni)		24	
I) Samalā tathatā dhātu, being 'avinirmuktakleśakośa'; tathāgatagarbha			

T	C	Q. & R.	BGŚ	DAŚ	AĀS
84 *a* 2–84 *b* 5	826 *a*–*b*				
	826 *b*				
84 *a* 6		cf. ŚMS (221 *a*)			
		(221 *a*)			
		(C Quotation) (219 *b*) (221 *a*) (221 *a*)			
84 *b* 5–85 *a* 2	826 *b*–*c*				
	826 *c*	cf. (ŚMS) cf. ŚMS 221 *a*			
85 *a* 2–6	826 *c*		808 (IX avikāra, similarity to prakṛtisthagotra)		
85 *a* 6–88 *a* 4	826 *c*–828 *a*				
85 *a* 6–7	{ 813 *c* 826 *c* 828 *a*				
85 *a* 7–85 *b* 4	827 *a*				469 *b* (II tathāgatadhātu-p.) 4 *dharmas*

	K	v	S
II) Nirmalā tathatā tathāgatadharmakāya characterized as 'āśrayaparivṛtti' III) Vimalā buddhaguṇāḥ lokottarabuddhadharmāḥ, daśabala, etc. IV) Jinakriyā anuttaraṃ karma, which is 'aniṣṭhita, avirata, apratipraśrabdha'			
§ 1. Inconceivability (acintyatā) of the 4 Aspects (gotra = 'sarvadarśināṃ viṣayaḥ)		25	21.13–25.3
I) samalā tathatā – 'viśuddhā' & 'saṃkliṣṭā', at the same time			
(Q) difficulty of understanding the two aspects of citta			22.1–4
II) nirmalā tathatā – niḥsaṃkleśa-viśuddhi			
(Q) prakṛticittajñāna is 'prajñā' by which bodhi is attained			22.6–7
III) buddhaguṇa – existence of 'avinirbhāgadharmatā' in all sattvas			22.8
(Q) analogue of a big painting cloth (tathāgatajñānaṃ sattvakāye sakalam anupraviṣṭam, api tu saṃjñāgrāhataḥ sattvas taṃ na jānāti)			22.10–24.8
IV) jinakriyā – yugapat, sarvatra, anābhogena, avikalpataḥ, yathāśayeṣu, yathāvaineyikeṣu, akṣūṇam, anuguṇaṃ pravartate			24.9
(Q 1) tathāgatakarman is innumerable, nirmāṇākaraṇa being dharmadhātukriyā			24.11–15
(Q 2) tathāgatakarman acts everywhere, at every time, equally, in order to teach sattvas			24.16–25.3
§ 2. The Germ as Cause and Conditions of the 3 Jewels in its 4 Aspects (gotra = śubharatnatrayasargakaḥ = ratnagotra)		26	25.4–25.17
I) S. Tathatā – bodhya – 'hetu' II) N. Tathatā – bodhi } III) Buddhaguṇa – bodhyaṅga } 'pratyaya.' IV) Jinakriyā – bodhana }			
'hetu' – being based upon 'pratyātma' knowledge – gotra 'pratyaya' – being based upon 'parataḥ' instruction – tathāgata			25.11

T	C	Q. & R.	BGŚ	DAŚ	AĀS
85 *b* 4–87 *b* 6	827 *a*–*c*				
	827 *a*				470 *c* (end of chap. II)
		ŚMS 222 *c*			470 *c*
					473 *c* (end of chap. III)
		DRS 20 *b*			
86 *a* 3	827 *a*				475 *c* (end of chap. IV)
	827 *b*	AvatS 623 *c*–624 *c*			
87 *a* 6	827 *c*				476 *b* (end of chap. V)
		DRS 21 *c*			
		DRS 21 *c*			476 *b*
87 *b* 6–88 *a* 4	827 *c*–828 *a*				
	828 *a*				
88 *a* 2–					

	K	V	S
(I. Samalā Tathatā) (VP 4) (RG * 1) = dhātu, gotra, tathāgatagarbha, sattvadhātu			
VII. THE SERMON: ALL LIVING BEINGS ARE POSSESSED OF THE MATRIX OF THE TATHĀGATA			25.16–26.11
("sarvasattvāḥ tathāgatagarbhāḥ")			
(Kārikā)	5	(= 27)	
3 Meanings of 'tathāgatagarbhâstitva'		28	
1) "buddhajñānântargamāt sattvarāśeḥ" – tathāgatadharmakāyaparispharaṇârtha – 'dharmakāya' (TG ** a)			26.7
2) "tannairmalyasyâdvayatvāt prakṛtyā" – tathāgatatathatâvyatibhedârtha – 'tathatā' (TG b) 3) "bauddhe gotre tatphalasyôpacārāt" – tathāgatagotrasaṃbhavârtha – 'gotra' (TG c) (See S p. 69, l.17 ff.)			
VIII. ANALYSIS OF THE GERM FROM 10 POINTS OF VIEW			26.11–59.8
Summary (uddāna)	K. (acc.to C)	29	
10 points: I. svabhāva, II. hetu, III. phala, IV. karman, V. yoga, VI. (pra-)vṛtti, VII. avasthāprabheda, VIII. sarvatraga, IX. avikāra, & X. abheda			
(I) Svabhāva & (II) Hetu			26.19–30.2
(Kārikā)	6	(= 30)	
§ 1. The Nature of the Essence of the Tathāgata (svabhāva) – Similarity of 'dhātu' to jewel, sky and water in 3 aspects		31	27.1–11
(aspect) (simile) (svalakṣaṇa) (sāmānyalakṣaṇa) 1. dharmakāya – cintāmaṇi – prabhāva 2. tathatā – nabhas – ananyatābhāva } prakṛtipariśuddhi 3. gotra – vāri – snigdha			
§ 2. Obscurations and Causes for Purification (hetu)			27.12–30.2
(4 āvaraṇas, 4 kinds of sattvas, 4 hetus of purification)		32	
1) Classification of sattvas		33	

* RG = ratnagotra ** TG = tathāgatagarbha

T	C	Q. & R.	BGŚ	DAŚ	AĀS
88 *a* 5–88 *b* 2	828 *a*				
		TGS 457 *c*			
	813 *c* 828 *b*				
	828 *a*				
(both T. & C. interchange the order of v. 27 & 28)			808 *a*		
		cf MSA IX 37			
88 *b* 2–106 *a* 7	828 *b*–836 *c*				
	814 *a* 828 *b*				
88 *b* 4–90 *b* 1	828 *b*		796 *b* (10 arthas) 796 *b*	892 *a* (12 arthas) 892 *b*	10 arthas (for bodhi)
88 *b* 4–5	814 *a* 828 *b*		IV–1 (svabhāva) IV–2 (*hetu*)	III svabhāva II hetu	
88 *b* 5–89 *a* 3	828 *b*				
			796 *b* (IV–1	892 *b* (v. 4) III svabhāva	869 *b* (on cintāmaṇi)
89 *a* 3–90 *b* 1	828 *c*–829 *b*		797 *b*	892 *b* II hetu	
			797 *b* f.		471 *a*–*b* (III–2. hetu)

	K	v	S
A. 1) bhavâbhilāṣin – (1) Icchantika			27.17–28.18
a) aparinirvāṇagotraka (of mokṣamārgapratihatâśa)			
b) ihadhārmika (= bauddha), but same as a)			
(Q) – on 'icchantika'			28.3–4
2) vibhavâbhilāṣin			
a) anupāyapatita – (2) Tīrthya			
i) itobāhyā tīrthyāḥ			
ii) ihadhārmika, of pudgaladṛṣṭi (Q)			28.9
iii) ihadhārmika, of śūnyatā-dṛṣṭi (Q)			28.11–12
b) upāyapatita			
i) śrāvakayānika – (3) Śrāvaka			
ii) pratyekabuddhayānika – (4) Pratyekabuddha			
3) tadubhayânabhilāṣin (= bodhisattvayānika)			
mahāyānasaṃpraṣṭhita, of apratiṣṭhitanirvāṇa, of dṛḍhakaruṇā-adhyāśaya, mūlapariśuddha			
B. (trividha-sattvarāśi)			29.1–5
I) mithyātvaniyataḥ sattvarāśiḥ – 1) bhavâbhilāṣin (*a*) & (*b*)			
II) aniyataḥ sattvarāśiḥ – 2)-*a* (Tīrthya)			
III) samyaktva-niyataḥ sattvarāśiḥ – 2)-*b* (Śr. & Pr.)			
3) (Bodhisattva)			
C. (those who are outside of Mahāyāna)			29.5
(1) Icchantikāḥ – 1)-*a*, *b*)			
(2) Tīrthyāḥ – 2)-*a*)			
(3) Śrāvakāḥ – 2)-*b*)-*i*)			
(4) Pratyekabuddhāḥ – 2)-*b*)-ii)			
2) Obstructions (āvaraṇa) for the 4 kinds of sattvas and their antidotes (pratipakṣa)			29.7–14
(1) Ic. – mahāyānadharmapratigha – mahāyānadharmâdhimuktibhāvanā			
(2) Tī. – ātmadarśana – prajñāpāramitā-bh.			
(3) Śr. – duḥkhabhīrutva – samādhi-bh.			
(4) Pr. – sattvârthavimukhatā – mahākaruṇā-bh.			
(sattvas) (āvaraṇa) (pratipakṣa)			
3) Simile to the 4 pratipakṣas, being 'hetu' of purification (bodhisattvas are 'dharmarājaputra', or 'anujāta in the tathāgatakula' as being endowed with the 4 pratipakṣas)			29.15–30.2
(1) adhimukti is 'bīja', (2) prajñā is 'mātṛ', (3) samadhi is 'garbhasthāna', and (4) karuṇā is 'dhātrī'		34	

T	C	Q. & R.	BGŚ	DAŚ	AĀS
89 a 4–89 b 7					
		AAN 467 c			471 a
	829 a	unk.			
		KāśP 634 a (cf. Laṅk 146. 11–13)	797 b (Q. from AĀS)		471 a
89 b 7–90 a 2	829 a		797 c		471 b
90 a 2	829 a		797 c		471 b
90 a 3–90 a 7	829 a		797 c		471 b
90 a 7	829 b				
		probably a quotation. Cf. MSA. IV. 11	798 a	892 b (v. 3)	

	K	v	S
(III) Phala & (IV) Karman			30.3–37.9
(Kārikā)	7	(= 35)	
§ 1. The 4 Supreme Virtues as the Result of Purification (śubhātmasukhanityatvaguṇapāramitā)		36	30.6–31.6
(viparyāsa) (viparyāsaviparyaya) (guṇapāramitā) 1. nitya-saṃjñā anitya-saṃjñā nityapāramitā 2. sukha-s. duḥkha-s. sukhapāramitā 3. ātma-s. anātma-s. ātmapāramitā 4. śubha-s. aśubha-s. śubhapāramitā			
(Q)			30.19–31.6
§ 2. Concordance between the 4 Supreme Virtues and the 4 Causes for Purification			31.7–32.13
A. (1) Ic. – aśuci-saṃsārâbhirati – adhimukti-bhāvanā – śubha-p. (2) Ti. – asadātmagrahâbhirati – prajñā-bh. – ātma-p. (3) Sr. – saṃsāraduḥkhôpaśamamātrâbhirati – samādhi-bh. sukha-p. (4) Pr. – asaṃsargavihārâbhirati – karuṇā-bh. – nitya-p.			
(Reference) on the difference between 'ātman' of Heretics and 'ātmapāramitā' of the Tathāgata			31.16
B. (Concordance between the 4 Virtues and the 3 epithets of the Tathāgata spoken in a scriptural passage)			32.7–13
1. "dharmadhātu-parama" – śubhapāramitā 2. "ākāśadhātu-paryavasāna" – ātmapāramitā & sukhapāramitā 3. "aparântakoṭi-niṣṭha" – nityapāramitā			
§ 3. 4 Impediments to the Attainment of the Supreme Virtues (paripanthas retained in Arhats, Pratyekabuddha & Vaśitāprāpta-bodhisattvas)			32.14–34.7

	(paripantha)		(equivalent in bāla)	(saṃkleśa)
A.	(1) pratyaya-lakṣaṇa	avidyāvāsabhumi	avidyā	kleśa-saṃkleśa
	(2) hetulakṣaṇa	anāsravakarman	(sāsravakarman) saṃskāra to upādāna	karma-saṃkleśa
	(3) saṃbhava-lakṣaṇa	manomayâtmabhāva	tribhava, jāti	janma-saṃkleśa
	(4) vibhava-lakṣaṇa	acintyā pāriṇāmikīcyuti	jarā-maraṇa	

T	C	Q. & R.	BGŚ	DAŚ	AĀS
90 *b* 1–94 *b* 5	829 *b*–831 *b* 814 *a* 829 *b*		IV–3 (phala) & IV–4 (karman)	4 paryāya (for *phala*)	III–3 paripantha & III–4 phala
90 *b* 2–91 *a* 6	829 *b*		798 *a*		471 *c*
		cf. MPS 617& c			
		ŚMS 222 *a*			471 *c*
91 *a* 6–92 *a* 3	829 *c*–830 *a*		798 *b* f.		471 *c*f.
	om. adds one verse & comm. thereon with comm.	unk cf. MSA IX 23 & IX 24	798 *a* (Q. from MSA ?)		
	829 *c*–830 *a*				
91 *b* 7–92 *a* 3	830 *a*	cf. DBS p 14			
92 *a* 3–93 *a* 2	830 *b*–830 *c*		799 *a*		472 *b* (3 paripantha)

			K	v	S
(paripantha)	(reason)	(against)			
B. (1) avidyāvāsabhūmi	sarvôpakleśa-saṃniśrayabhūta	śubhapāramitā			33.4–12
(2) anāsravakarman	sūkṣmanimitta-prapañca-samudācāra-samutthāpita	ātma-p.			
(3) manomaya-ātmabhāva	manomayaskandha-yogāt	sukha-p.			
(4) acintyā pāriṇāmikī cyuti	saṃkleśanirodha-avigamāt	nitya-p.			
(Q 1)					33.15–34.4
(Q 2)					34.6
§ 4. Motives of the 4 Supreme Virtues					34.8-35.16
(Tathāgata is)	(because of)				
(1) śubha(śuci)	*a*) prakṛtiśuddhi			37	
	b) vaimalyapariśuddhi			38	
(2) paramâtma	*a*) ātmaprapañcavigamāt				
	b) nairātmyaprapañcavigamāt				
(3) sukha	*a*) duḥkhanirodhasākṣātkaraṇataḥ				
	b) manomayaskandhanirodha-sākṣ.				
(4) nitya	*a*) anityasaṃsārânapakarṣaṇataḥ				
	b) nityanirvāṇâsamāropaṇataḥ				
(Q)					34.20–35.2
§ 4′. The Unstable Nirvāṇa (apratiṣṭhitanirvāṇa) – Bodhisattva's ideal state					35.3–16
saṃsāra = nirvāṇa					
in seeking for 'nirvāṇa', – (svârtha), by 'prajñā'	Bodhisattva is not like 'aparinirvāṇagotraka'				
in abiding in 'saṃsāra', – (parārtha), by 'karuṇā'	Bodhisattva is not like 'śamaikayānagotra'			39	(probably a quotation)
§ 5. Function of the Germ for its Purification (IV. Karman) (duḥkhanirvicchamaprāpticchandapraṇidhikarmakaḥ) (K 7, *cd*)					35.17–37.9
A. karman 1) 'nirvid' of duḥkha				40	
2) 'icchā', 'prârthanā', 'praṇidhi' of nirvāṇa					
(Q)					36.1–2
B. motive of this karman is the existence of 'gotra' purification of gotra by 'adhimukti' & 'catuḥśukla'				41	36.8–37.1

T	C	Q. & R.	BGŚ	DAŚ	AĀS
				892 *c* (Q ŚMS.)	
		ŚMS 220 *a* ŚMS 222 *a*			
93 *a* 2–93 *b* 7	830 *c*–831 *a* (in prose)		799 *b*	892 *c*	472 *b*
		ŚMS 222 *a*			
93 *b* 2–93 *b* 7	om. most of the passages		799 *c*		
	has another verse instead				
93 *b* 7–94 *b* 4	831 *a*–831 *b*		799 c–800 *c*		
		ŚMS 222 *b*			

			K	v	S
§ 5′. The Saying: "the Icchantikas are of no Nirvāṇa" is only conventional					36.16–37.9
everybody that lives has the gotra of nirvāṇa					
(Q 1) simile of sunshine					36.16–37.1
(Q 2) "anādibhūto 'pi câvasānikaḥ. . . ."					37.6–9 (in verse)
(V) Yoga					37.10–39.8
(Kārikā)			8	(= 42)	
§ 1. The 'Union' of the Germ with the Factors of its Purification (yoga = hetusamanvāgama) (on K 8 *a*, *b*)					37.13–38.8
samanvāgama = saṃbandha				43	
(tathāgatadhātu is 'endowed with')	(functions)	(similarity to an ocean)			
1. dharmakāya-viśuddhihetu	(1) adhimukti	ākara			
2. buddhajñāna-samudāgamahetu	(2) prajñā & (3) samādhi	ratna			
3. tathāgatamahākaruṇāvṛttihetu	(4) karuṇā	vāri			
§ 2. The 'Union' of the Germ with the Result of Purification (yoga = phalasamanvāgama) (on K 8 *c d*)					38.9–39.8
samanvāgama = avinirbhāga, apṛthag, dharmadhatusamanvāgama					
(tathāgatadhātu is 'endowed with')	(characteristics)	(similarity to a lantern)		44	
1. abhijñā	ajñānândhakāravidhamana	āloka			
2. āsravakṣaya-jñāna	kleśa-indhanadahana	uṣṇa			
3. āsravakṣaya	vimala, viśuddhi, prabhāsvara	varṇa			
(Q)					39.5–8
(VI) Vṛtti					39.9–40.4
(Kārikā)			9	(= 45)	
'manifestation' of the Germ in 3 ways				46	
(A) pṛthagjana – viparyasta					
(B) ārya – aviparyasta					
(C) saṃbuddha – samyagaviparyasta					

T	C	Q. & R.	BGŚ	DAŚ	AĀS
94 *b* 1–4	831 *b*		800 *c*; cf. 788 *c* (II on Hīna-yāna graha)		
		JĀA 242 (cf. Avat S. 616 *b*) unk.			
94 *b* 4–95 *b* 4	831 *b*–831 *c*		801 *a* ff. (IV-5)		
	814 *a* / 831 *b*			893*b* (9) yoga	
94 *b* 4–95 *a* 4	831 *b*				
95 *a* 4–95 *b* 4	831 *c*			893 *b* (v. 13)	
95 *b* 3–4	om. (cf. 821 *b*)	AAN 467 *a*		893 *b* (Q. AAN)	
95 *b* 5–96 *a* 3	831 *c*–832 *a*		805 *c* ff. (IV-6)		
	814 *a* / 831 *c*				

	K	V	S
(VII) Avasthāprabheda			40.5–41.5
(Kārikā)	10	(= 47)	
Different States of Manifestation		48	
(A) sattvadhātu (= pṛthagjana) – aśuddhāvasthā			
(B) bodhisattva (= ārya) – aśuddhaśuddha-a.			
(C) tathāgata (= saṃbuddha) – suviśuddha-a.			
(Q)			40.16–41.5
(VIII) Sarvatraga			41.6–17
(Kārikā)	11	(= 49)	
(Commentary) ' All-pervadingness ' of ' cittaprakṛti ' (= dhātu), like ' ākāśa ' irrespective of (A)doṣa, (B)guṇa or (C) niṣṭhā (-guṇa)		50	
(Q)			41.15–17
(IX) Avikāra			41.18–54.15
' Unchangeability ' of the Germ throughout the 3 States			
Introduction			41.18–42.4
uddāna: doṣâgantukatāyogatva & guṇaprakṛtiyogatva		51	
(A) Unchangeability in the Impure State (aśuddhâvasthāyām avikāritva) – ' sattvadhātu '			42.5–46.4
(Kārikās) ' dhātu ' is like ākāśa being the basis of all phenomena but having no support on which it depends.	12–23	(= 52–63)	
origination of the worldly phenomena		(54)	
1. cittaprakṛti – ākāśa		(53)	
2. ayoniśomanasikāra – vāyu			
3. karmakleśa – vāri			
4. skandhadhātvāyatana – pṛthivī			
(Commentary)			

T	C	Q. & R.	BGŚ	DAŚ	AĀS
96 *a* 3–96 *b* 4	832 *a*–832 *b*		806 *a* (IV–7)	893 *a* (6) avasthāprabheda	469 *c*
	{ 814 *a* 832 *a*				
	832 *a*	AAN 467 *b*	806 *b* Q. AĀS	893 *a* Q. AAN	469 *c*
96 *b* 4–97 *a* 2	832 *b*		806 *b* (IV–8)		
	{ 814 *a* 832 *b*				
			806 *b* Q. AĀS		469 *c*
97 *a* 1–2	832 *b*	AAN 467 *b*			
97 *a* 2–103 *b* 6	832 *b*–835 *b*		806 *c* f. (IV–9)		
97 *a* 2–6	832 *b*				
	(all in verse)		as a Q from SNS		
97 *a* 6–99 *a* 5	832 *c*–833 *b*				
	{ 814 *a*–*b* 832 *c*			893 *a* (8) nitya	
				v. 12	
				v. 11	

	K	v	S
§ 1. Unoriginated Character of the Innate Mind (avikāra = anutpādânirodhatva of dhātu)			44.1–45.9
origination of the world does not originate 'cittaprakṛti', nor is 'cittaprakṛti' destroyed by the fire of 'mṛtyuvyādhijarā' (on KK 12–14)		64	
(Q) on 'cittaprakṛti'			
prakṛtiprabhāsvaraṃ cittaṃ āgantukair upakleśair upakliśyate			
§ 2. Indestructible Character of the Innate Mind			45.10–46.4
simile of 'agni' for 'mṛtyuvyādhijarā' as 'upasarga'		65	
yugântâgni – mṛtyu			
nārakâgni – vyādhi			
prākṛtâgni – jarā			
(Q) eternity of tathāgatagarbha			45.20–46.4
(B) Unchangeability in the Pure-and-Impure State (aśuddhaśuddhâvasthāyām avikāritva) – 'bodhisattva'			46.5–53.8
(Kārikā)	24	(= 66)	
§ 1. Pure Character and Impure Character of the Bodhisattva			46.10–47.7
1) 'pure' state: bodhisattva has no calamity (vyasana) as experienced among ordinary beings (on K 24 *a b*)		67	
2) 'impure' state: however, he pretends to have calamities because of his 'mahākaruṇā' (on K 24 *c d*)		68	
(References to the Scriptures) (§ 2–§ 6)			
§ 2. Defilements endowed with the Virtuous Root (kuśalamūlasaṃprayuktakleśa)			47.7–16
§ 3. Bodhisattva's Compassion – The Parable of a Householder			47.17–48.16
mīḍhakūpa → saṃsāra			
ekaputraka → sattvadhātu			
mātṛ, jñāti → śrāvakayānika, pratyekabuddhayānika			
gṛhapati(pitṛ) → bodhisattva			
§ 4. Bodhisattva's Perception of the Pure Mind			48.17–50.7
1) Perceiving that sarvadharmas are created illusionally, bodhisattva has neither disgust nor attachment to saṃsāra			
2) Parable of 'vaiḍūryamaṇi' on cittaprakṛti & āgantukakleśa			

T	C	Q. & R.	BGŚ	DAŚ	AĀS
97 *b* 6–98 *b* 5	832 *c*–833 *b*				
	adds 2 more verses				
		GagS 124 *c* AN } I.5.9–10 / IV.1–2 cf. Mahāvibhāṣā (*Taisho*, XXVII, 140 *b*)			469 *b*
98 *b* 5–99 *a* 5	833 *b*				
99 *a* 3–5	833 *b*	ŚMS 222 *b*		893 *b* (Q ŚMS)	
99 *a* 5–103 *a* 3	833 *b*–835 *a*				
	{ 814 *b* { 833 *b*				
99 *a* 6–99 *b* 3					
	(in prose)				
99 *b* 3–100 *a* 2	833 *c*	SagP 68 *b*			
100 *a* 2–100 *b* 4	834 *a*	SagP 68 *b*			470 *a*–*b*
100 *b* 4–101 *b* 1	om. the passage before the example of vaiḍūryamaṇi	SagP 68 *a* cf. MSbh (P) 259 *c*–260 *a* (Q AĀS)			469 *b*–*c*
	834 *b*				

	K	V	S
§ 5. Saṃsāra in the case of Bodhisattva			50.8–12
'saṃsāra' means 'traidhātukapratibimbako manomayakāyatrayaḥ' in anāsravadhātu – Impure state			
this is, at the same time, 'nirvāṇa' – Pure state			
(Q)			50.10–11
§ 6. Bodhisattva in his 6th Stage			50.13–51.9
1) Perfect Wisdom, but no experience of 'nirvāṇa' owing to his Compassion			
2) Parable of a castle (Q)			(missing in S.T.)
3) Readiness for 'āsravakṣaya' owing to 'jñāna' – śuddhâvasthā			
assuming of life in saṃsāra for the sake of others owing to 'karuṇā' – aśuddhâvasthā			
(Another Interpretation of K 24 (v. 66))	(a later interpolation)	69–78	51.10–53.8
§ 7. The Pure and Impure State of Bodhisattva in comparison with Ordinary Beings and the Buddha			
1) Comparison with sattva below Pramuditābhūmi			
(4 kinds of bodhisattva) (bhūmi)			
1. prathamacittôtpādika 1st (Pramuditā)			
2. caryāpratipanna 2nd (Vimalā) to 7th (Dūraṃgamā)			
3. avivartika 8th (Acalā)			
4. ekajātipratibaddha (9th &) 10th (Dharmameghā)			
2) Comparison of 'niṣṭhāgata-bodhisattva' with the Buddha (vv. 77–78)			
(C) Unchangeability in the Perfectly Pure State (suviśuddhâvasthāyām avikāritva) – 'Buddha'			53.9–54.15
(Kārikā)	25	(= 79)	
1) 4 Characters of 'avikāra' in 'buddhabhūmi'			
1. nitya – of no birth – with 'manomayakāya'		80–82	
2. dhruva – of no death – by 'acintyā pāriṇāmikī cyuti			
3. śiva – of no illness – by 'avidyāvāsabhūmi'			
4. śāśvata – of no decrepitude – by 'anāsravakarman'.			
2) Appliance of these 4 terms to K 25		83	54.8
1. nitya – ananyathâtmā – akṣayadharmayogataḥ			
2. dhruva – jagaccharaṇya – anaparântakotiṭaḥ			
3. śiva – sadā 'dvaya – avikalpatvataḥ			
4. śāśvata – avināśadharma – akṛtasvabhāvataḥ			
(Q)			54.12–15

T	C	Q. & R.	BGŚ	DAŚ	AĀS
101 *b* 1–4	834 *b–c*				
		ŚMS 221 *b*			
101 *b* 4–102 *a* 5	834 *c*–835 *a*				
	834 *c*	RCS 181 *a*			
102 *a* 5–103 *a* 3	om.				
103 *a* 3–103 *b* 6	835 *a–b*				
	814 *b* 835 *a*				
				892 *b* (1) phala	
103 *b* 2	835 *b*			892 *b*	
	835 *b*	AAN 467 *b*			

	K	V	S
(X) Asaṃbheda			55.1–59.8
Undifferentiation of the Germ from the Absolute			
(Kārikā)	26	(= 84)	
§ 1. Synonyms for the Essence of the Tathāgata (on K 26 *a b*)		85,86	55.7–56.6
1. 'dharmakāya' – buddhadharmâvinirbhāga (Q)			55.14–15
2. 'tathāgata' – gotrasya tathāgamaḥ (Q)			55.16–17
3. 'āryasatya' – amṛṣāmoṣadharmitva (Q)			55.18–19
4. 'parama-nirvāṇa – ādiprakṛtiśāntatā (Q)			55.20
Reference to 1) dharmakāya			56.2–3
2) tathāgata			56.3–4
3) āryasatya			56.4–5
4) nirvāṇa			56.5–6
§ 2. The Point: Buddhahood is Nirvāṇa (on K 26 *c d*)			56.7–57.5
1) buddhatva, as representing 'abhisaṃbuddha' is 'nirvāṇa being 'savāsanamala-uddhṛti'		87	
2) 4 characteristics of the Highest Nirvāṇa (caturākāraguṇaniṣpattyasaṃbhinnalakṣaṇanirvāṇa)			56.14–57.5
1. sarvākāra, 2. asaṃkhya, 3. acintya, 4. amala (Q)			56.14–15
(Q 1)			56.16–17
(Q 2)			56.18–57.2
§ 3. The Parable of Painters (on Tathāgata as 'sarvākāraguṇôpetaśūnyatā')			57.6–57.20
Without the accomplishment of all the 6 pāramitās, there is no Buddhahood		88–92	
§ 3′. The Relation of the 4 Characteristics to boddhisattvabhūmis			57.20–58.9
(stages) — (acquisition of)			
Acalā — 1. guṇa-sarvatā			
Sādhumati — 2. guṇa-aprameyatā			
Dharmameghā — 3. guṇa-acintyatā			
Buddhabhūmi — 4. guṇa-viśuddhiparamatā			
§ 4. Similarity of the Buddhahood to the Sun			58.10–59.8
1) 3 points of similarity – (viśeṣalakṣaṇa)		93	
1. prajñā (lokottara, nirvikalpa) – dīpti – prabhā			
2. jñāna (pṛṣṭhalabdha) – spharaṇa – raśmi			
3. vimukti of cittaprakṛti – viśuddhi – maṇḍala			
2) Individuality of properties with substance (sāmānyalakṣaṇa)		94	58.20 f.
(Q)			59.5–8

T	C	Q. & R.	BGŚ	DAŚ	AÅS
103 *b* 6–106 *a* 7	835 *b*–836 *c*		811 *c* ff. (IV-10) Asaṃbheda	893 *c*–894 *a* 12 ekatva	
	814 *b*			vv. 23 24	
	835 *b*				
103 *b* 7–104 *b* 2	835 *b*–*c*		811 *c*		
		ŚMS 221 *c*			
		ṢaḍS			
		cf. BBh 3, 2–4 unk.			469 *b*
		JÃA 341 *c*			
		AAN 467 *a*			
		ŚMS 220 *c*			
		ŚMS 222 *a*			
		ŚMS 220 *c*			
104 *b* 2–105 *a* 3	835 *c*–836 *a*				
			812 *c*		
		MSP (verse)			
		SMS 219 *c*			
		SMS 219 *c*			
105 *a* 3–105 *a* 7	836 *a* –836 *b*	cf. RCS 176			
	(C quotes the parallel passage				
105 *a* 7–105 *b* 5	836 *b*	cf. MSbh (P) 258 *b*	812 *c*		
105 *b* 5–106 *a* 7	836 *b*–*c*				
106 *a* 2 f.	836 *c*				
106 *a* 5–7	836 *c*	ŚMS 220 *b*		894 *a* (Q. ŚMS)	

	K	V	S
IX. THE 9 ILLUSTRATIONS OF THE GERM COVERED WITH DEFILEMENTS			59.9-73.8
§ 1. The 9 Illustrations according to the Tathāgatagarbhasūtra (Introduction & Summary) " aparyantakleśakośakoṭigūḍhas tathāgatagarbhaḥ " anādisāṃnidhyâsaṃbaddhasvabhāva-kleśakośatā } anādisāṃnidhya-saṃbaddhasvabhāva-śubhadharmatā }		95	59.9-67.2
(Kārikās) Summary of Illustrations	27-29	(= 96-98)	59.16-60.10
(Kārikās) The 9 Illustrations			
(I) ' kleśas ' are like an ugly ' padmakośa ' ' dhātu ' is like a ' buddha ' abiding inside a padma	30-32	(= 99-101)	60.11-61.2
(II) ' kleśas ' are like ' kṣaudra-prāṇaka ' (honey-bees) ' dhātu ' is like ' kṣaudra ' (honey)	33-35	(= 102-104)	61.3-61.15
(III) ' kleśas ' are like ' bahis-tuṣa ' (outer husk) ' dhātu ' is like ' sāra ' (inner kernel)	36-38	(= 105-107)	61.16-62.8
(IV) ' kleśas ' are like ' aśucisaṃkāradhāna ' (a dirty place filled with impurities) ' dhātu ' is like ' suvarṇa ' (gold)	39-42	(= 108-111)	62.9-63.6
(V) ' kleśas ' are like ' pṛthivītala ' (the bottom of the ground) ' dhātu ' is like ' ratnanidhi ' (treasure of jewels)	43-45	(= 112-114)	63.7-63.19
(VI) ' kleśas ' are like ' tvak-kośa ' (the bark-covering of a seed) ' dhātu ' is like ' bījâṅkura ' (the germ within a seed)	46-48	(= 115-117)	63.20-64.10
(VII) ' kleśas ' are like ' pūtivastra ' (tattered garment) ' dhātu ' is like ' ratnavigraha ' (a precious image)	49-51	(= 118-120)	64.11-65.2
(VIII) ' kleśas ' are like ' āpannasattvanārī ' (a pregnant woman) ' dhātu ' is like ' cakravartin ' (in the embryonal state)	52-54	(= 121-123)	65.3-65.16
(IX) ' kleśas ' are like ' mṛt-paṅka-lepa ' (an earthen mould) ' dhātu ' is like ' kanaka-bimba ' (a golden statue)	55-57	(= 124-126)	65.16-66.10
(Commentary)			
' udāharaṇa-piṇḍârtha ' cittasaṃkleśadharma-āgantukatva cittavyavadānadharma-sahajâvinirbhāgatā		127-129	66.11-67.2
(Q) " cittasaṃkleśāt sattvāḥ saṃkliśyante, cittavyavadānād viśuddhyánte "			67.1-2
§ 2. 9 Kinds of Defilements – the Impurities of the Mind (citta-saṃkleśa illustrated by ' padma ', etc.)			67.3-68.16

T	C	Q. & R.	BGŚ	DAŚ	AĀS
106 *a* 7–112 *a* 5	837 *a*–839 *b*		806 *c*–808 *c* (IV–9) avikāra		
106 *a* 7– 108 *b* 6	837 *a*				
		TGS 457 *c* cf. AAN 467 *b*	811 *b*		
106 *b* 2–106 *b* 5	814 *b*–*c* 837 *a*				
106 *b* 5–7	814 *c*	cf. TGS 457 *c*			
106 *b* 7–107 *a* 3	814 *c*–815 *a*	cf. TGS 457 *c*–458 *a*			
107 *a* 3–6	815 *a*	cf. TGS 458 *a*			
107 *a* 6–107 *b* 2	815 *a*–*b*	cf. TGS 458 *a*–*b*			
107 *b* 2–5	815 *b*	cf. TGS 458 *b* cf. MPS 407 *b*			
107 *b* 5–108 *a* 1	815 *b*–*c*	cf. TGS 458 *c*			
108 *a* 1–4	815 *c*	cf. TGS 458 *c*–459 *a*			
108 *a* 4–7	815 *c*–816 *a*	cf. TGS 459 *a*			
108 *a* 7–108 *b* 3	816 *a*	cf. TGS 459 *a*–*b*			
108 *b* 3–6	837 *b*				
		unk (cf. SN III, 151 Vim N. 563 *b*)			
108 *b* 6–109 *b* 7	837 *b*–*c*		806 *c*		

(kleśa)	(saṃtāna)	(jñāna by which kleśa is removed)	(phala)	K	v	S
1. rāgânuśayalakṣaṇa-kl.	laukikavītarāgasāṃtānika	lokottara-jñ.	rūpârūpyadhātu		130 131 132	
2. dveṣânuśayalakṣaṇa-kl.						
3. mohânuśayalakṣaṇa-kl.						
4. tīvra-rāgâdiparyavasthānalakṣaṇa-kl.	rāgâdicaritasattva-s.	aśubhâdibhāvanā-jñ.	kāmadhātu			
5. avidyāvāsabhūmisaṃgṛhīta-kl.	arhat-s.	tathāgatabodhi-jñ	manomayakāya			
6. darśanaprahātavya-kl.	pṛthagjanaśaikṣa-s.	prathamalokottaradharmadarśana-jñ.	(aśuddhabhūmi)			
7. bhāvanāprah.-kl.	āryapudgala-s.	yathādṛṣṭalokottaradharmabhāvanā-jñ.	(aśuddhabhūmi)			
8. aśuddhabhūmigata-kl.	aniṣṭhāgatabodhisattva-s.	aṣṭamyādibhūmitrayabhāvanā-jñ	(śuddhabhūmi)			
9. śuddhabhūmigata-kl.	niṣṭhāgatabodhisattva-s.	vajrôpamasamādhi-jñ.	(buddhabhūmi)			
4 kinds of 'sattvaṣ' with respect to their 'aśuddhatā'					133	68.11-16
1. pṛthagjana – kleśa 1.–4.						
2. arhat – kleśa 5.						
3. śaikṣa – kleśa 6. & 7.						
4. bodhisattva – kleśa 8. & 9.						
§ 3. Concordance between the 9 Illustrations and the 9 Kinds of Defilements						68.17-69.16
1. padma → rāgarati					134–143	
2. bhramarāḥ → dveṣa						
3. bahistuṣa → mohâṇḍakośa hiding sārârthadarśana						

T	C	Q. & R.	BGŚ	DAŚ	AĀS
(v. 132) 109 *b*–3	(v. 132 in prose)				
109 *b* 5 ff.	837 *c*	TGS 457 *c* (repetition)			
109 *b* 7–110 *a* 6	838 *a*		807 *c*–808 *a*		

	K	v	S
4. amedhya → paryutthāna			
5. vasudhā → avidyāvāsabhūmi hiding buddhatva			
6. bījatvak → darśanaheya-vyāvṛtti covering tattvadarśana			
7. pūtivastra → bhāvanājñānaheya			
8. garbhakośamala → saptabhūmigata-mala			
9. mṛtpaṅkalepa → tribhūmigata-mala			
§ 4. The 3-fold Nature of the Essence – the Purifying Element within the Mind and its concordance with the 9 Illustrations (trividhasvabhāva being 'cittavyavadānahetu')			69.17–73.8
Summary: 'trividha-svabhāva'			69.17–70.1
a) dharmakāya-svabhāva – Illustrations (I)–(III)		144	
b) tathatā-svabhāva – » (IV)			
c) gotra-svabhāva – » (V)–(IX)			
a) 'dharmakāya' (TG a)			70.1–71.4
1) dharmadhātu = pratyātmâdhigamadharma – buddha (1)		145	
2) tad-niṣyanda = deśanādharma			
i) bodhisattvapiṭaka → sūkṣma – paramārthasatya – (ekarasa) – madhu (2)		146	
ii) sūtra, geya, etc. → audārika – saṃvṛtisatya – (vicitrarasa) – sāra (3)		147	
Significance: "sattvadhātoḥ tathāgatadharmakāyena parispharaṇatā" (v. 28 a)			
'tathāgatagarbha' = "tathāgatasya ime garbhāḥ sarvasattvāḥ"			70, 18–19
(Q) simile of 'ākāśa'			71.1–4
b) 'tathatā' (TG b)			71.5–17
cittaprakṛti = tathatā (avikāra, kalyāṇa, viśudhi) – suvarṇa		148	
(4) 'tathāgata' = "prakṛteḥ viśuddhiṃ tathatām āgataḥ"			
Significance: "tathatâvyatibhedatā" (v. 28 b)			
'tathāgatagarbha' = "tathāgata tathatā eṣāṃ garbhaḥ sarvasattvānāṃ".			
(Q 1) avyatibhedatā between 'buddha' and 'sattva'			76.12–14
(Q 2) tathāgata = tathātā śuddhim āgatā			71.16–17
c) '(tathāgata-)gotra' (TG c)			71.18–73.8

T	C	Q. & R.	BGŚ	DAŚ	AĀS
110 *a* 6–112 *a* 5	838 *b*–839 *b*		808 *a*		
110 *a* 6–110 *b* 2	838 *b*				
110 *b* 2–111 *a* 3	833 *b*		808 *a*		
111 *a* 2–3	838 *b*	cf. MSbh (P) 252 *b* MSA IX, 15	808 *a* (Q)		
111 *a* 3–111 *b* 2	838 *b*		808 *b*		
111 *a* 7–111 *b* 1	838 *b*	JĀA 247 *a*			
111 *b* 1	838 *b*	MSA IX, 37			
111 *b* 2–112 *a* 5	838 *b*–*c*		808 *b*–*c*		

	K	v	S
(hetu) (phala) gotra prakṛtiṣṭha → svabhāvakāya (svābhāvika) samudānīta → { sambhogakāya (sāṃbhogika) nirmāṇakāya (nairmāṇika) } Analogy: hetu { prakṛtiṣṭhagotra – nidhāna (5) samudānītagotra – phalavṛkṣa (6) } phala { svābhāvika (akṛtaka, śubha) – ratnavigraha (7) sāṃbhogika (mahādharmâdhirāja) – cakravartin (8) nairmāṇika (pratibimba) – hemabimba (9) } gotra = dhātu = 'hetu' of buddhatva manifested in 3 kāyas Significance: trividhabuddhakāyôtpattigotrasvabhāvârtha cf. "bauddhe gotre tatphalasyôpacārāt" (v. 27) 'tathāgatagarbha' = tathāgatadhātur eṣāṃ garbhaḥ sarvasattvānām. (Q 1) "tathāgatadhātur utpanno garbhagataḥ saṃvidyate.." (Q 2) 'anādikāliko dhātuḥ' (from the Abhidharmamahāyānasūtra)		149–152	72.13–14
Commentary on (Q 2)			72.12–73.8
1) 'anādikāliko' (dhātu) "pūrvakoṭir na vidyate" (Q)			72.15–16
2) 'dhātu' tathāgatagarbha is 'lokottaragarbha' &c. (Q)			72.16–73.1
3) 'sarvadharmasamāśraya' āśraya = niśraya, ādhāra, pratiṣṭhā (Q)			73.2–73.5
4) 'tasmin sati gatiḥ sarvā' (Q)			73.6
5) 'nirvāṇâdhigamo 'pi ca' (Q)			73.7–8
X. The Essential Characteristics of the Matrix of the Tathāgata			73.9–77.8
§ 1. The Saying: 'All Living Beings are possessed of the Matrix of the Tathāgata', is the Highest Logical Truth (garbhāstitva is dharmatā being yukti, yoga, upāya)			73.9–16
1) 'dharmāṇāṃ dharmatā' – "utpādād vā tathāgatānām anutpādād vā ete sattvās tathāgatagarbhāḥ". (Q)			73.11–12
2) This 'dharmatā' is only accessible to 'śraddhā'			

T	C	Q. & R.	BGŚ	DAŚ	AĀS
		Cf. BBh 3 MSA III, 4			
			898 *c*		
	om.	unk. AbhidhS cf. Sthiramati on VMT p. 37.			
111 *b* 6–112 *a* 5	839 *a* –839 *b*	MSbh (P) 156 *c* 157 *a* cf. ŚMS 222 *b* SN II 178, 198, etc. MK XI 1 Candrakīrti thereon			
		ŚMS 222 *b* cf. MSbh (P) 264 *b*	796 *b* (5–garbha theory)		
		ŚMS 222 *b*			
		ŚMS 222 *b*			
		ŚMS 222 *b*			
112 *a* 5–114 *b* 5	839 *b*–840 *b*				
112 *a* 5–112 *b* 1	839 *b*				
		TGS 457 *c* cf. SN II, 25 Laṅk 142.	811 *c*		

	K	v	S
§ 2. The 4 Kinds of Individuals to Whom the Faith in this Essence is Necessary.			74.1–75.17
1) Emphasis of the faith in the Tathāgata		153	
2) 4 kinds of people 1. pṛthagjana, 2. śrāvaka, 3. pratyekabuddha, 4. navayānasaṃprasthita-bodhisattva			
3) 3 kinds of individuals referred in the Scripture (Q) a) satkāyadṛṣṭipatita, b) viparyāsâbhirata, c) śūnyatāvikṣiptacitta			74.5–6
a) 'satkāyadṛṣṭipatitāḥ' – 1. bālapṛthagjana, having 'ahaṃkāra, mamakāra' on sāsravadharmas, cannot understand 'anāsravadhātu characterized as satkāyanirodha'			74.7–10
b) 'viparyāsâbhiratāḥ – 2. śrāvaka & 3. pratyekabuddha are clinging to 'anitya, duḥkha, anātma, & aśubha-saṃjñā and cannot understand 'tathāgatagarbha as nitya-sukha-ātma-śubhapāramitā'			74.10–75.12
(Q) on 'viparyastasaṃjñā' (parable of water-sport)			74.22–75.11
c) 'śūnyatāvikṣiptacittāḥ' – 4. navayānasaṃprasthitā bodhisattvāḥ are 'tathāgatagarbhaśūnyatârthanaya-vipranaṣṭāḥ' and thinking: i) 'parinirvāṇa' means 'atyanta-vināśa of dharmas' ii) 'śūnyatā' is something substantial to be obtained			75.13–17
§ 3. The True Conception of the Matrix of the Tathāgata as representing Non-substantiality (tathāgatagarbha-śūnyatā'rthanaya) (continuation of c) śūnyatāvikṣiptacittāḥ)			75.17–77.8
1) 'śūnya' and 'aśūnya'		154	
There is nothing 'apaneya' nor 'upaneya', dhātu is 'śūnya' of 'āgantukamalas' but is 'aśūnya' of 'avinirbhāga-dharmas'		155	
(Q) true perception of śūnya and aśūnya. "yad yatra nāsti tat tena śūnyam; yat punar atrâvaśiṣṭaṃ bhavati tat sad ihâsti".			76.8–9
2) Definition of 'śūnyatāvikṣiptacitta' "yeṣām itaḥ śūnyatā 'rthanayād bahis cittaṃ vikṣipyate – te –". Without knowing 'paramaśūnyatārtha, dhātu is not understood.			
(Q) tathāgatagarbhajñāna = tathāgatānāṃ śūnyatājñāna.			
3) Inaccessibility of tathāgatagarbha tathāgatagarbha being:			76.15–16
1. dharmadhātugarbha – a) satkāyadṛṣṭipatitānām agocaraḥ 2. dharmakāya, lokottaradharmagarbha – b) viparyāsâbhiratānām agocaraḥ			76.16–77.8

T	C	Q. & R.	BGŚ	DAŚ	AĀS
112 *b* 1–113 *a* 6	839 *b*–840 *a*	cf. MSbh (P) 258 *b*–*c* cf. ŚMS 222 *a*	812 *a* f.		
112 *b* 3–4	839 *b*	ŚMS 222 *a*			
112 *b* 4–6	839 *b*				
112 *b* 6–113 *b*4	839 *c*–840 *a*				
113 *a* 4–113 *b* 3 113 *b* 4–6	839 *c*–840 *a* 840 *a*	MPS 377 *c*–378 *a*			
			812 *b*		
113 *b* 6–114 *b* 5	840 *a*–840 *b*		812 *b*		
		cf. AĀ v. V, 21 &c.	812 *b* (Q)	893 *b* (9) v. 14	
		ŚMS 221 *c* cf. MN III, 104			
114 *a* 6–114 *b* 5		ŚMS 221 *c* cf. ŚMS 222 *b* cf. MSbh (P) 156 *c* 264 *b*	796 *b* (5 kinds of garbha)		

	K	V	S
3. pṛakṛtipariśuddha-dharmagarbha – *c*) śūnyatāvikṣipta-cittānām agocaraḥ			
4. lokottaradharmakāya-prakṛtipariśuddhi – *d*) daśabhūmi-sthita-bodhisattvāḥ can perceive a little			77.2
(Q) " chidrâbhre nabhasīva – "			77. 5–8
XI. The purpose of Instruction (deśanāprayojana)			77.9–78.20
(Kārikās)			
question: Why is ' buddhadhātu-astitva ' maintained here ?	58	(= 156)	
answer: In order to prevent ' 5 doṣas '.	59	(= 157)	
(Commentary)			
1) Teaching in the previous sūtras (pūrvam uktam) is: ' śunyaṃ sarvam, meghâdivat '. In this ' uttara tantra ', dhātu-*astitva* is taught.		158–160	78.1–6
2) ' 5 doṣas ' to be prevented		161–165	78.7–16
1. līna-cutta – nīcacittānām ātmâvajñānadoṣa			
2. hīnasattvâvajñā – (having a pride of own ' bodhicitta ')			
3. abhūtagrāha – misconception of ' aśūnyatā, on ' abhūta-dharma			
4. bhūtadharmâpavāda – misconception of ' śūnyatā ' on ' bhūtadharma (i. e. dharmakāya, etc.)			
5. ātmasneho 'dhikaḥ – failure in taking ' sattvâtmasama-darśikā ' (maitrī)			
3) ' 5 guṇas ' to be obtained by this teaching		166–167	78.17–20
1. prôtsāha – niravajñā			
2. śāstṛgaurava – samaprekṣin			
3. prajñā – nirdoṣa (obtaining the śūnya conception of dharmas)			
4. jñāna – guṇavat (obtaining aśūnya conception on dhātu)			
5. mahāmaitrī – ātmasattvasamasneha (attainment of ' budd-hatā ')			
(Colophon) – End of Chapter I.			78.21–22
Chapter II – The Enlightenment. (bodhi)			79–90
(II. Nirmalā tathatā) (VP 5) (RG II) = bodhi, dharmakāya, āśrayaparivṛtti, buddhatva			
XII. General Characteristics of the Reality free from Pollutions (8 Categories of 'nirmalā tathatā ')			79.2–20

T	C	Q. & R.	BGŚ	DAŚ	AĀS
		cf. MPS 411 *a* (652 *c*, 887 *a*) unk. (in verse)			
114 *b* 5–115 *a* 6	840 *b–c*		787 *a–c* I nidāna 811 *b*		
	816 *a–b* 840 *b*				
		cf. PP &c	811 *b*		
			787 *b*		
			787 *c*		469–*b–c*
115 *a* 6–7					
115 *a* 7–119 *b* 5	841 *a*–843 *c*				Chap. III bodhi 470 *c*–473 *c*
115 *a* 7–116 *a* 1	841 *a*				

	K	v	S
(term in v. 1) (term in v. 2)	(C takes v. 1. as kārikā)	1, 2	
1. śuddhi svabhāva (I) (āśrayaparivṛtter svabhāva viśuddhiḥ)			
2. prāpti (means of attainment) hetu (II) a) avikalpa–lokottarajñāna b) tatpṛṣṭhalabdha–laukikajñāna			
3. visaṃyoga phala (III) a) kleśâvaraṇa-visaṃyoga b) jñeyâvaraṇa–visaṃyoga			
4. svaparârtha karman (IV) a) svârthasaṃpatti, b) parârthasaṃpatti			
5. tadāśrayaḥ yoga (V) (karmaṇor adhiṣṭhāna-samanvāgamaḥ)			
6. gāmbhīryâudāryamāhātmya) vṛtti (VI) (manifestation of āśrayaparivṛtti in the forms of trikāya)			
7. yāvatkālam (duration of manifestation) nitya (VII)			
8. yathā (mode of manifestation) acintya (VIII)			
(Q) on 'svabhāva'			79.11–12
XIII. 8 Points on the Undefiled Reality			80.1–90.13
(I) Svabhāva & (II) Hetu (buddhatva and its prāptyupāya).			80.1–80.15
(Kārikā)	1	(= 3)	
(Commentary)			80.6–80.15
1. 'buddhatva' is like the sun and the sky because of its 'jñāna' and 'prahāṇa' (on K 1 b)		4	
2. 'buddhatva' is endowed with numberless properties (prakṛtiprabhāsvara, amala, nitya, dhruva, śāśvata, etc.) (on K 1 a, c)		5	
3. 'kleśa– & jñeya–āvaraṇa' are like clouds being 'svabhāvāpariniṣpatti, vyāpi, āgantuka' (on K 1 b)		6	
4. The cause (hetu) of the acquisition of 'buddhatva' is the 'avikalpajñāna & tatpṛṣṭhalabha (on K 1 d)		7	
(III) Phala (vaimalyaśuddhi – visaṃyoga from āvaraṇa)			80.15–82.4
Two kinds of 'śuddhi'			80.15
a) prakṛtiviśuddhi – svabhāva – (common to samalā tathatā) (vimukti, but na visaṃyoga) b) vaimalyaviśuddhi – phala – (unique to nirmalā tathatā, (vimukti, and visaṃyoga)			

T	C	Q. & R.	BGŚ	DAŚ	AĀS
	816 *a* 841 *b*				470 *c*
		(cf. MSbh (P) 258 *b*			
			311 *a*		472 *b*
		ŚMS 221 *b*			
116 *a* 1–119 *b* 5	841 *b*–843 *c*				
116 *a* 1–116 *a* 7	841 *b*				
	816 *b* 841 *b*			893 *b* (v. 10)	
116 *a*–3					
116 *a* 5–116 *b* 6	841 *b*			893 *b*–*c* (11) artha-kriyā	
		cf. MSA XII 15			

	K	V	S
(Kārikās)	2,3	(= 8,9)	
(Commentary)			81.9–82.4
1. phala of 'avikalpajñāna' – kleśaviśuddhi (on K. 2 *a, b, c*)		10	
phala of 'tatpṛṣṭhalabdha-jñāna' – vimalaguṇopeta (on K. 2 *d*)		11	
2. 'visaṃyoga' and 'guṇopeta'			
a) removal of 'rāga' – 'dhyānavāryabhiṣyandana' – vimalâmbu on padma (on K. 2 *a*)		12	
b) release from 'Rāhu' of 'dveṣa' – jagatspharaṇa-karuṇā' – pūrṇacandra (on K. 2 *b*)		13	
c) release from 'moha' – 'tamovidhamanajñāna' – amalârka (on K. 2 *c*)		14	
3. similarity to 'buddha', etc. (9 illustrations taught in Chap. I) (on K. 3)			
1. atulyatulyadharmatva – buddha (1) 2. saddharmarasadānatā – honey (2) 3. phalguvyapagamatā – kernel (3)		15	
4. pavitratā (śuddhi) – gold (4) 5. dāridryavinivartanatā – treasure (5) 6. vimuktiphaladānatva – tree (6)		16	
7. dharmaratnâtmabhāva (dharmakāya) – precious image (7) 8. dvipadâgrâdhipati (sāṃbhogika) – king (8) 9. rūparatnâkṛti (nairmāṇika) – golden statue (9)		17	
(IV) Karman			82.5–84.2
a) svârthasaṃpatti – dharmakāyaprāpti (karman of avikalpa-jñ).			
b) parârthasaṃpatti – kāyadvayena pravṛttiḥ (karman of tatpṛṣṭhalabdha-jñ.).			
(Kārikās)	4–6	(= 18–20)	
(Commentary)			83.5–84.2

T	C	Q. & R.	BGŚ	DAŚ	AĀS
116 *a* 7–116 *b* 1	816 *b* 841 *b*				
116 *b* 2–116 *b* 6	841 *b–c*				
				(10) an-artha kriyā	
				893 *c* (v. 17)	
				893 *b* (v. 16)	
				893 *c* (v. 19)	
116 *b* 6–117 *b* 1	841 *c*–842 *a*				472 *c* (5) (karman)
117 *a* 2–4	816 *b* 842 *a*				
117 *a* 4–117 *b*1	842 *a*				

	K	V	S
1) Twofold function of 'dharmakāya' - svārthasampatti -(on K. *4ab*)		21	
1. vimuktikāyasya pūrṇam - (prakṛtiviśuddhi) dharmakāyasya śodhanam - (vaimalyaśuddhi)		21	
2. characteristics of dharmakāya - 1) anāsrava, 2) vyāpi 3) asaṃskṛtapada (avināśadharmi)		22	
3. 1) anāsravatva - kleśanirodha 2) vyāpitā - asaṅga, apratighāta 3) asaṃskṛtatva - avināśitva		23	
4. 'avināśitva'=dhruva, śiva, śāśvata, acyuta, being the counterpart of pūti, vikṛti, ucchitti, acintyā pāriṇāmikī cyuti, resp.		24 26 *a b* 25	
2) Basis of the objects of cognition (Function of rūpakāya) - parārthasampatti - (on KK 4 *c d*, 5, 6) tathāgata is 'pada' (= āspada. nimittabhūta) for: 1. vibhūtirūpārtha-*vidarśana* - (rūpa) 2. sukathāśuci*śrava* - (śabda) 3. śuciśīla*jighraṇa* - (gandha) 4. mahāryasaddharmarasāgra-*vindana* - (rasa)		26 *c d*–28	
5. samādhisaṃsparśa*sukhānubhūti* - (spṛśya) 6. svabhāvagāmbhīryanay*āvabodhana* - (dharma)		27	
3) Simile of ākāśa - nimittabhūtatva & animittatva		27 28	
(V) Yoga - Buddha is endowed with 'āveṇikadharmas' as paramārtha-lakṣana. "ākāśalakṣaṇo buddhaḥ" (Q) on the speciality of Buddha's character			84.3–85.6
(Kārikā)	7	(= 29)	
(Commentary)			84.11–85.6
1) Buddha is 'āśraya' of 'svaparārtha-karma'		30	
2) Buddha's 'āveṇikadharmas' *a*) (1) acintyatā, being			
1. saukṣmya - agocara to 'śrutamayajñāna' 2. paramārtha - agocara to 'cintā-m.-jñ.' 3. dharmatāgahvara - agocara to 'bhāvanā-m.-jñ.' (buddhatva is 'sarvajñajñānagocara)		31–33	

T	C	Q. & R.	BGŚ	DAŚ	AAS
					472 *c*
117 *b* 1–118 *a* 1	842 *a*–842 *c*				472 *c* (6) yoga
		cf. JĀA 243 *c* etc. Vaj C 752 *a* (skt. 42–43)			
117 *b* 3	816 *c* / 842 *b*				
117 *b* 3	842 *b*				

	K	V	S
b) (2) nitya – anutpādatā			
(3) dhruva – anirodhatā		34	
(4) śiva – advayatā			
(5) śāśvata – dharmasthititā			
c) (6) śānta – nirodhasatya		35	
(7) vyāpi – sarvâvabodhitā			
(8) avikalpa – apratiṣṭhānatā			
(9) asakta – kleśāvaraṇaprahāṇa		36	
(10) apratigha – jñeyâvaraṇaprahāṇa			
(11) paruṣasparśarahita – mṛdukarmaṇyabhāva			
(12) adṛśya – arūpitva		37	
(13) agrāhya – animittatā			
(14) śubha – prakṛtiśuddhatva			
(15) amala – malavigamatā			
(VI) Vṛtti			85.7–88.14
– manifestation of buddhatva in the form of 3 Bodies			
(Kārikās)	8–11	(= 38–41)	
(Commentary)			86.11–88.14
1) General survey of 'manifestation'			
1. *b*uddhatva is *a*) sarvajñatā, *b*) paramanirvāṇa, *c*) arhattva		42	
2. manifestation of buddhatva is in three ways: *a*) gāmbhīrya (svābhāvika), *b*) audārya (sāmbhogika), *c*) māhātmya (nairmāṇika)		43	
2)–*a*) the Body of the Absolute Essence (svābhāvika) – (on K 8, 9)			86.16–87.6
1. '5 lakṣaṇas' – (dharmadhātusvabhāva)		44	
(1) asaṃskṛta (anādimadhyânta)		46	
(2) abhinna (asaṃbhinna)			
(3) advaya (antadvayavivarjita)			
(4) trayâvaraṇaniḥsṛta (tridhāvimukta)			
(5) prabhāsvara & viśuddhi (vimalâvikalpa)			
2. '5 guṇas'			
(1) aprameya – (udāratva)		47	
(2) asaṃkhya – (agaṇyatva)		48	
(3) acintya – (tarkasya agocaratva)			
(4) asama – (kaivalyatva)			
(5) viśuddhipāramiprāpti – (vāsanôcchitteḥ)			

T	C	Q. & R.	BGŚ	DAŚ	AĀS
118 *a* 1–119 *a* 3	**842 *c*–843 *b***		**809 *a*–811 *a* (IV–9 avikāra)**		**473 *a* III–(7) vṛtti**
118 *a* 3–6	**816 *c* 842 *c***				
118 *a* 6	**842 *c*–843 *b***				
118 *a* 7–118 *b* 3	**843 *a***				
			809 *a*–810 *b*		**473 *a***
			810 *b*–*c*		**473 *a***

	K	v	S
b) the Body of Enjoyment (sāṃbhogika) (on K 10)			87.7–87.14
1. two kinds of 'saṃbhoga' **(1) vicitradharmasaṃbhoga – 'svasaṃbhoga'** **(2) sattvârthakriyā as karuṇāniṣyanda – 'parasaṃbhoga'**		49	
2. similarity to 'cintāmaṇi' (1) **anābhoga, avikalpa, yathā'bhiprāyapūritva**		50	
3. 5 ways of manifestation **(1) deśana, (2) darśana, (3) kṛtyâsraṃsana, (4) anabhisaṃskṛtakriyā, (5) atatsvabhāvâkhyā**		51	
4. manifestation is not of real nature – similarity to cintāmaṇi (2)		52	
c) the Apparitional Body (nairmāṇika) – (on K 11)			87.15–88.14
1. Buddha as 'lokavit' **14 affairs of the Buddha in 'apariśuddhakṣetra': 1) jātakāni, 2) tuṣiteṣv upapatti, 3) cyutis tuṣitebhyaḥ, 4) garvâvakramaṇa, 5) janman, 6) silpasthānāni kauśalam, 7) antaḥpraratikrīḍā, 8) naiṣkramya, 9) duḥkhacārikā, 10) bodhimaṇḍâvakrānti, 11) mārasainyapramadana, 12) saṃbodhi, 13) dharmacakra (–pravṛtti), 14) nirvāṇādhigamakriyā**		53–56	
2. Buddha as 'upāyavit' **1) śāntipathâvatāranidāna – (for Hīnayānists)** **aversion of saṃsāra – anitya, duḥkha, anātman** **leading to Nirvāṇa – śānti**		57	
2) prapâcanavyākaraṇe nidāna – (for Mahāyānists) **1. dharmatattvaprakāśana** **2. uttamayāne paripācana** **3. agrabodhaye vyākaraṇa**		58–59	
3) Characteristics of 'trikāya' **1. a) saukṣmya – gāmbhīrya – svābhāvika** **b) prabhāvasaṃpatti – audārya – sāṃbhogika** **c) bālasārthâtivāhana – māhātmya – nairmāṇika**		60	88.11
2. a) = dharmakāya: *b*) & *c*) = rūpakāya – (on K 11 *c d*) **'rūpakāya' is based on 'dharmakāya', as 'rūpa' on 'ākāśa'**		61	
(VII) Nitya			88.15–89.15
– Buddha's pravṛtti continues 'ā bhavagateḥ', therefore, it is eternal.			

T	C	Q. & R.	BGŚ	DAŚ	AĀS
118 *b* 3–118 *b* 5	843 *a*				
	om.				473 *a* (5 guṇas)
118 *b* 5–119 *a* 3	843 *a*–6				
			810 *c*		473 *a*
119 *a* 2	843 *b*				
119 *a* 3–119 *b* 1	843 *b*–*c*		811 *a*–*c*		473 *a* (III-8 nitya)

	K	v	S
(Kārikā)	12	(= 62)	
(Commentary) – 10 points on ' eternity '		63–67	89.3
1) ' hetvānantyatva ' – saddharmasaṃgraha			
2) ' sattvadhātvakṣayatva ' – ādipratijñā–uttaraṇa			
3) ' kāruṇya '–yogatva – karuṇā–pravṛtti			
4) ' ṛddhi '–yogatva – ṛddhipādaprakāśa			
5) ' jñāna '–yogatva – bhavanirvāṇadvayagrahavimukti			
6) ' saṃpatti '–yogatva – samādhānasukhasaṃpattiyogatva			
7) ' dharmaiśvarya ' – lokadharmair anupalepatva			
8) ' mṛtyumārâvabhaṅga ' – śamâmṛtapadaprāpti			
9) ' naiḥsvābhāvya ' – asaṃskṛta, ādipraśānta			
10) ' śāśvata–lokanātha ' – śaraṇâbhyupapatti			
1)–7) eternity of ' rūpakāya '		68	
8)–10) eternity of ' dharmakāya '			
(VIII) Acintya			89.16–90.13
– āśrayaparivṛttiprāptinaya is ' of inconceivable character '.			
(Kārikā)	13	(=69)	
(Commentary) – 6 points on ' acintya '		70–71	90.3
' acintya ' – 1) anabhilāpya (avākyavattva) – 2) paramârtha – 3) atarkya – 4) vyupameya – 5) anuttara – 6) anudgraha (in either saṃsāra or nirvāṇa)			
1)–5) inconceivability of ' dharmakāya '		72	
6) inconceivability of ' rūpakāya '			
Buddha's final stage is not accessible to Bodhisattvas of the highest rank (abhiṣekalabdhā bodhisattvāḥ)		73	
(Colophon) for Chapter II			90.14–15
Chapter III – The Properties of the Buddha			91–97
(III Buddha–Guṇāḥ)			
= guṇa, dharma, buddhadharma (VP 6) (RG III)			
XIV. General characteristics of the Buddha's properties			91.2–91.13
(Kārikā)	III. 1	(= 1)	

T	C	Q. & R.	BGŚ	DAŚ	AĀS
	816 *c* 843 *b*				
119 *a* 4					
119 *b* 1–119 *b* 5	843 *c*		810 *c*		473 *b* (III–10) acintya
	816 *c*–817 *a* 843 *c*				
	om.	probably a Quotation (unk.)			
119 *b* 5					
119 *b* 6–122 *a* 1	843 *c*–845 *c*	cf. RDS DRS			473 *c*–475 *c* (IV guṇa)
119 *b* 6–120 *a* 1	843 *c*–844 *a*				
	817 *a* 844 *a*				

	K	v	S
(Commentary)		2–3	
a) ādyam – dharmakāya / *b*) dvitīyam – rūpakāya 1. paramārthakāya (pāramarthika) / saṃvṛtikāya (sāṃketika) 2. svârthasaṃpattyadhiṣṭhāna / parârthasaṃpattyadhiṣṭhāna 3. visaṃyoga-phala / vipāka-phala 4. (endowed with) 10 balas, 4 vaiśāradhyas / 32 mahāpuruṣalakṣaṇas 18 āveṇikadharmas			
XV. 64. PROPERTIES OF THE BUDDHA			91.14–97.14
(Kārikās)			
Summary	2	(=4)	
(I) The 10 Powers	3–4	(=5–6)	91.19–92.7
buddha = balânvita			
jñānabala of 1. sthānâsthāna, 2. karmavipāka, 3. indriya, 4. dhātu, 5. adhimukti, 6. mārga sarvatragāminī, 7. dhyānâdi-kleśa-vaimalya, 8. nivāsânusmṛti, 9. divyācakṣus, 10. śānti (= āsravakṣaya).			
Simile of 'vajra'	5	(=7)	
'balas' do 'pierce the armour', 'break the fortress'. and 'cut down the tree' of ajñāna			
(II) The 4 Forms of Intrepidity buddha = caturvaiśāradyaprāpta			92.8–93.2
vaiśāradya (astaṃbhitatva) in	6–7	(=8–9)	
1. sarvadharmâbhisaṃbodhi – jñāna & jñāpana on jñeya 2. vibandhapratiṣedha – (hāni &) hānikāraṇakṛti on heya 3. mārgâkhyāna – (seva &) sevana on sevya 4. nirodhâpti – prāpta & prāpana on prāptavya			
Simile of 'siṃha'	8	(= 10)	
Among pariṣat, buddha is 'svastha, nirāsthạ, sthira, & vikramastha'.			
(III) The 18 Exclusive Properties buddha = aṣṭādaśâveṇikabuddhadharmasamanvāgata			93.3–94.7
1. nāsti skhalitam, 2. nāsti ravaḥ, 3. n. musitā smṛtiḥ, 4. n. asamāhitacittam, 5. n. nānātvasaṃjñitā, 6. n. upekṣā pratisaṃ-	9–13	(=11–15)	

T	C	Q. & R.	BGŚ	DAŚ	AĀS
120 *a* 2–122 *a* 1	844 *a*–845 *c*				
	817 *a* 844 *a*				
120 *a* 3–120 *a* 5	844 *a*	cf. RDS 34 *a*–*b* DRS 14 *c*–18 *a*			475 *b*
	817 *a* 844 *a*				
	817 *a* 845 *a*				
120 *a* 5–120 *b* 1	844 *b*	cf. RDS 34 *b* DRS 18 *a*–19 *a*			475 *b*
	817 *a*–*b* 844 *a*–*b*				
	817 *b* 845 *a*				
120 *b* 1–120 *b* 6	844 *b*	cf. RDS 34 *b* 35 *c* DRS 19 *a*–21 *b*			475 *b*
	817 *b* 844 *b*				

	K	v	S
khyāyām, 7. n. chandasya hāniḥ, 8. n. vīryataḥ h., 9. n. smṛteḥ h., 10. n. prajñāyā h., 11. n. vimukter h., 12. n. vimuktijñānadarśanāt h., 13–15. jñānapūrvaṃgamaṃ karmatrayam, 16–18, tryadhvajñānam anāvṛtam.			
Simile of 'ākāśa'	14	(=16)	
As 'space' has no nature in common with other materials, Buddha has 'exclusive nature' not in common with those worlds.			
(IV) The 32 Marks of the Superman			94.8–96.2
buddha = dvātriṃśanmahāpuruṣalakṣaṇarūpadhārin			
1. supratiṣṭhita-cakrâṅkavyāyata-utsaṅga-*pādatā* 2. dīrgā*ṅgulikatā* 3. jāla*pāṇipādâ*vanaddhatā 4. tvaṅmṛduśrī*taruṇatā* 5. saptôtsada-*śarīratā* 6. eṇeya*jaṅghatā* 7. nāgakośava*dvasti*guhyatā 8. siṃhapūrvârdha*kāyatva* 9. nirantaracit*âṃśatā* (antarāṃśa?) 10. saṃvṛtta*skandhatā* 11. vṛttaślakṣṇânunnāma*bāhutā* 12. pralambha*bāhutā* 13. śuddhaprabhāmaṇḍala*gātratā* 14. kambu*grīva*tvam. amalam 15. mṛgendra*hanutā* 16. samā catvāriṃśad*daśanatā* 17. svacchâvirara*dantatā* 18. viśuddha-sama-*dantatva* 19. śuklapravara*daṃṣṭratā* 20. prabhūta*jihvatā* 21. anantâcintya*rasa*rasâgratā 22. kalaviṅka*ruta* 23. brahma*svaratā* 24. nīlôtpalaśrī-vṛṣapakṣma-*netra* 25. sītâmala-ūrṇôdita-*cāruvaktra* 26. uṣṇīṣa*śīrṣa* 27. vyavadātasūkṣma-suvarṇavarṇa-*chavi* 28. ekaikaviśliṣṭa-mṛdu-ūrdhva-dehapradakṣiṇâvarta-susūkṣma-*roma* 29. mahêndranīlâmalaratna-*keśa* 30. nyagrodhapūrṇadrumamaṇḍal*âbhā* 31. nārāyaṇasthāmadṛḍh*âtmabhāva* 32. samantabhadra, apratima (*ātmabhāva*)?	15–23	(=17–25)	
Simile of 'dakacandra'	24	(=26)	
2 rūpakāyas are like the moon and its reflection in the pond.			
(Commentary)			96.3–97.14
1) 64 properties are taken from the Ratnadārikāsūtra		27	
2) Point of similarity (udāharaṇa-piṇḍârtha)			
General:		28	
(I) vajravat – nirvedhika; (II) siṃhavat – nirdainya			
(III) ākāśavat – kaivalya; (IV) dakacandravat – nirīha.			
(I) vajravat: bala is 'guru, sāra, dṛḍha & abhedya'		29–31	
1st–6th bala – jñeyāvaraṇaprahāṇa – piercing armour			
7th–9th bala – samāpattyāvaraṇa-p. – breaking wall			
10th bala – savāsanakleśâvaraṇa-p. – cutting down tree			
(II) siṃhavat: (because of)		32–34	
1. nirbhayatva — obtaining of 'sarvâbhijñā'			
2. nirāsthatva — no superiority–complex			

T	C	Q. & R.	BGŚ	DAŚ	AĀS
	817 *b–c* 845 *b*				
120 *b* 6–121 *a* 6	844 *b–c*	cf. RDS 36*a* – 40 *b*			475 *b*
	817 *c* 844 *b–c*	AA+AAĀ chap VIII etc.			
	817 *c*–818 *a* 845 *b*				
121 *a* 6–122 *a* 1	844 *c*–845 *c*				

	K	v	S
3. sthairyatva — obtaining ' cittasamādhāna '			
4. vikramasampad — ' avidyāvāsabhūmivyatikrānta '			
(III) ākāśavat:		35–37	
pṛthagjana, śrāvaka, pratyekabuddha, bodhisattva are like pṛthivī and the rest, but buddha is like ākāśa being of the subtlest Intellect.			
(I)–(III) – similes for ' dharmakāya '			
(IV) dakacandravat: simile for ' rūpakāya '		38–39	
saṃbhogakāya – in buddhamaṇḍala (bimba ?)			
nairmāṇika – in this world (pratibimba)			
(Colophon) for Chapter III			97.15–16
Chapter IV. – The acts of the Buddha			98.1–114
(IV. Jinakriyā) (VP 7) (RG IV)			
= karman, tathāgatakṛtyakriyā, buddhakarman			
XVI. General characteristics of the Acts of the Buddha			98.1–99.14
(Kārikās)	1,2	(=1–2)	
(Commentary)			98.12–99.14
a) ' anābhogatā ' of vinayakriyā (on K. 1)		3–4	
1. ' yasya ' – vineyadhātu ; 2. ' yena ' – vinayôpāya			
3. ' yāvat ' & 4. ' yadā ' – tad deśakālagamane			
b) ' apratipraśrabdhatā (or avikalpatā) ' of vinayakriyā (on K. 2)		5–12	

(6 points)	(subject)	(simile)	(point of simile)
1. niryāṇa (yāna)	daśabhūmi	mahôdadhi	jñānâmbu-guṇaratna
2. upastambha (hetu) of niryāṇa	saṃbhāradvaya (puṇya- & jñāna-)	ravi	sarvasattva-upajīvyatva
3. phala of saṃsāra	paramabodhi (buddhatva)	vyoman	vipulânanta-madhya
4. parigraha of bodhi	sarvasattva	nidhāna	samyaksaṃ-buddhadhar-matva
5. āvṛti on sattvadhātu	kleśāḥ(kleśa- & jñeyâvaraṇa)	ambuda	āgantuka, vyāpi, ani-ṣpatti
6. ucchitti-pra-tyaya of āvṛti	karuṇā	vāyu	āvṛtikṣipti-pratyupas-thāna

T	C	Q. & R.	BGŚ	DAŚ	AĀS
122 *a* 1					
122 *a* 1–127 *b* 4	845 *c*–846 *c*				chap. V Tathāgatakṛtyakriyāparivarta (but the content is different)
122 *a* 1–122 *b* 2	845 *c*–846 *a*				
122 *a* 2–122 *a* 4	818 *a* 845 *c* (C. 1.2*)				
122 *a* 4–122 *b* 2	845 *c*–846 *a*				

* Karikā number in C.

	K	V	S
XVII. THE 9 ILLUSTRATIONS OF THE BUDDHA'S ACTS			99.15-114.2
§ 1. Buddha's Magnanimity (māhātmya) - (General statement)			99.15-20
(Kārikā) tathāgata is like 'śakra', etc. in his acts	3	(=13)	
§ 2. 9 Illustrations taken from the Jñānâlokâlaṅkārasūtra (Kārikās)			
(I) śakrapratibhāsavat			100.3-102.4
1. Just as the appearance of Indra appears on the surface of pure Vaiḍūrya-stone, the Buddha's form appears on the pure mind of the living beings	4-16 17, 18	(=14-26) (=27-28)	
2. Appearance of image is due to the condition of 'svacitta'	19-20	(=29-30)	
(II) devadundubhivat			102.5-104.16
1. Just as 'devadundubhi' arises from 'svakarman' of gods, 'dharmadundubhi', the Buddha's voice, arises from 'svakarman' of 'sattva'	21-23 & 24	(=31-33) (=34)	
2. 'dharmadundubhi' alarms and encourages sattvas by the sound of 'anitya-duḥkha-anātma-śānta	25	(=35)	
3. On the superiority of the drum to other musical instruments		36-40	102.20-104.12
1) advantages of 'dharmadundubhi'			
1. aprādeśikatva, 2. hitatva, 3. sukhatva, 4. nairyāṇikatva			
2) '3 prātihāryas'			
(1. ṛddhi, 2. ādeśana, 3. anuśāsti)			
4. Buddha's voice is sometimes not audible because of the self-fault of sattvas (ātmâparādha of atatprahitas)	26	(=41)	104.12
(III) meghavat			104.17-106.19
1. Just as clouds discharge the rain and cause hervest, the Buddha discharges 'saddharma' on sattvas	27, 28 & 29, 30	(=42, 43) (=44, 45)	
2. Unequality of receptacles in measure (bhājana-vimātratā)	31	(=46)	105.11
3. The impartial attitude of the Buddha in discharging of the doctrine (nirapekṣapravṛtti)	32-34	(=47-49)	105.16
4. Functions of calming the fire of 'duḥkha' (duḥkhâgni - prâśamana)	35-37	(=50-52)	106.7
1) duḥkha - jñeya			
2) duḥkha-hetu - heya			
3) duḥkha-nirodha - sparśitavya			
4) mārga (towards duḥkhanirodha) - niṣevya			
(IV) mahābrahmavat			107.1-107.18
1. Just as Brahmā, without moving from his place, shows his form, similarly the Buddha, without moving from 'dharmakāya', shows his various 'nirmāṇakāya' before the people.	38-39 & 40-41	(=53,54) (=55,56)	
2. Invisibility of the Apparitional form to some people (anābhāsagamana).	42	(=57)	

T	C	Q. & R.	BGŚ	DAŚ	AĀS
122 *b* 3–127 *b* 4	846 *a*–846 *c*				
122 *b* 3–5	846 *a*				
	818 *a* 846 *a* (C 3)				
122 *b* 5–123 *b* 2		cf. JĀA 240 *b–c*			
	om. 818 *b* (C 6, 7)				
	818 *a–b* (C 4, 5)				
123 *b* 2–124 *b* 4		cf. JĀA 241 *a*			
	om. 818 *b* (C 12)				
	818 *c* (C 13)				
123 *b* 6–124 *b* 2	om.				
124 *b* 3	818 *c* (C 14)				
124 *b* 4–125 *a* 6		cf. JĀA 241 *b–c*			
	om. 818 *c* (C 16, 15)				
	818 *c* (C 17)				
	818 *c*–819 *a* (C 18–21)* C 19 is not in S & T				
	819 *a* (C 23 24.22)				
125 *a* 6–125 *b* 3		cf. JĀA 242 *a*			
	om. 819 *a* (C 26.25)				
	819 *a–b* (C 27)				

	K	v	S
(V) sūryavat			107.19–109.13
1. Just as the sun shines at once, causing blossoming of padma and closing of kumuda, the Buddha's shine makes to perish 'doṣa' and nourishes 'guṇa'	43	(=58)	
2. Two kinds of people compared to water-born flowers (vineya is svacchajalabhājanavat)		59-62	108.3-14
3. The order of sattvas on account of their receiving the Buddha's teaching (darśanādeśanāpravṛttikrama)	44, 45	(=63, 64)	
4. The superiority of the Buddha's light to that of the sun (prabhāmaṇḍala-viśeṣana)	46, 47	(=65, 66)	
(VI) cintāmaṇivat			109.14–110.7
1. Like cintāmaṇi, the Buddha fulfils the wishes of the people according to their merits, but he has neither 'vikalpa' nor 'ābhoga'	48, 50	(=67–69)	
2. 'durlabhatva' of the Buddha	51	(=70)	
(VII) pratiśrutkāśabdhavat			110.8–12
The Buddha's voice is, like echoes, 'parapratyayasaṃbhava'	52, 53	(=71, 72)	
(VIII) ākāśavat	54–55	(=73, 74)	110.13–110.17
Like space, the Buddha is invisible, immaterial			
(IX) pṛthivīvat			110.18–22
The Buddha is, like the earth, the ground of all the virtues.	56–57	(=75, 76)	
§ 3. Summary of the Illustrations given by the Commentator			111.1–17
1. the purpose of illustration – "sarvabuddhaviṣayâvatāra-jñānâlokâlaṅkāra"		77–79	
2. meaning of the 9 examples (point of similarity) (I) 'darśanā' – śakra (II) 'deśanā' – dundubhi (III) 'vyāpi' – megha (IV) 'vikṛti' – Brahmā (V) 'jñānaniḥsṛti' – sūrya (VI) 'mano–guhya' – cintāmaṇi (VII) 'vāg–guhya' – pratiśruti (VIII) 'kāya–guhya' – ākāśa (XI) 'prāpti' (buddhabhūmi) – pṛthivī		80–81	
3. Syllogism: pratijñā: – anābhogaśāntā buddhakriyāḥ hetu: – dhīnirvikalpatvāt dṛṣṭānta: – śakrâdivat (prakṛtârtha: – darśanâdi–navadho'rthaḥ)		82–84	
§ 4. Summary of Examples given in the Kārikās	58-61	(=85–88)	112.1–17
§ 5. Non-origination and Non-extinction of the Buddhahood (anutpādânirodhas tathāgatadharmakāyaḥ)		89–91	112.18–113.4

T	C	Q. & R.	BGŚ	DAŚ	AĀS
125 *b* 3–126 *a* 4		cf. JĀA 242 *b*			
	819 *b* (C 28)				
125 *b* 4–7	om.				
	819 *b* (C 29) (om. K 44)				
126 *a* 4–126 *a* 7	819 *b* (C 30–32) (C 30 is not in S & T)	cf. JĀA 242 *a*			
	819 *c* (C 33.34) om. K 50				
	om.				
126 *a* 7–126 *b* 1		cf. JĀA 243 *b*			
	819 *c* (C 35.36)				
126 *b* 1–2	819 *c* (C 37.38)	cf. JĀA 243 *c* (after *pṛthivīvat*)			
126 *b*		cf. JĀA 243 *c*			
	819 *c* (C 39.40)				
126 *b* 3–126 *b* 7	846 *b*				
127 *a* 1–127 *a* 4	819 *c* (C 41)				
	om. v. 85–87				
127 *a* 4–127 *a* 6	818 *b* (C 8–11) *C 8 is an addition				

	K	V	S
§ 6. The Point of Dissimilarity			113.5–114.2
(Dissimilarity of each example with the Buddha's act is removed by the succeeding one, respectively).		92-98	
(I) aghoṣavat (II) na sarvathā'rthakṛt (III) na sārthabījavat (IV) na atyantapācaka (V) na atyantatamo'paha (VI) na durlabhôdaya (VII) na pratyayasaṃbhava (VIII) na śuklâspada (IX) pṛthivī, being 'āspada', is the best example (?)			
(Colophon) for Chapter IV			114.3-4
Chapter V. – The Merits of Faith (adhimuktyanuśaṃsa)			115–119
XVIII. THE MERITS OF HAVING FAITH IN THE DOCTRINE OF THE ESSENCE OF BUDDHAHOOD			
§ 1. The Superiority of Faith to other Virtues in regard of their Merits			115.1–117.4
(Kārikās)	1-6	(=1-6	
(Commentary)			
1) acintyatā of buddhaviṣaya in its 4 aspects (on K 1) (I) buddhadhātu – āśraya (II) buddhabodhi – (āśrayasya) parāvṛttiḥ (III) buddhaguṇāḥ – (āśrayaparivṛtter) guṇāḥ (IV) buddhakṛtya – arthasādhana		7	
2) adhimukti of bodhisattva – the rise of 'bodhicitta' (on K 2) śraddhā-adhimukti on: 'astitva' (of dhātu) 'śaktatva' (of dhātu to attain bodhi) 'guṇavattva' (buddhadhrmâvinirbhāgatā of dhātu) resulting in puṇyapāramitā { 'pūri' – trimaṇḍalâvikalpa; 'pariśuddhi' – vipakṣaprahāṇa }		8-12	
3) puṇyapāramitā and prajñāpāramitā; the superiority of the latter (on K 3–6) (1) dāna – (K 3) (2) śīla – (K 4) dhyāna (bhāvanā) – (K 5) { (3) kṣānti, (5) dhyāna } { (1), (2), (3), (5) } (4) vīrya (common to all) – puṇyapāramitā		13-14	
(6) prajñā – (K 6) – the basis of puṇyapāramitā		15	
4) śruti → adhimukti → prajñā. therefore, śruti is the basis of all – (K 6)			

T	C	Q. & R.	BGŚ	DAŚ	AĀS
127 *a* 6–127 *b* 3	846 *b–c* C adds one verse more at the end				
127 *b* 3					
127 *b* 4–129 *a* 5	846 *c*–848 *a*				
127 *b* 4–128 *b* 1	846 *c*–847 *b*				
	819 *c*–820 *a* 846 *c*–847 *a*				
		cf. MSbh (P) 194 *b*, 200 *c*	799 *c* 812 *c*–813 *a*		

	K	v	S
§ 2. Authority, Motive, and Characteristics of this Text being the Correct Doctrine			117.5-118.2
(Kārikās)			
1) basis (yataḥ) – āptâgama & yukti			
2) motive (yannimittaṃ) – *a*) ātmaśuddhi, *b*) kuśalasaṃpat-sattvânugraha	7	(=16)	
3) how? (yathā) – by the light of muniprabhākara	8	(=17)	
4) characteristics (yad)	9	(=18)	
qualification of 'ārṣa-vacas' 1. arthavaddharmapadôpasaṃhita 2. tridhātusaṃkleśanibarhaṇa 3. śāntyanuśaṃsadarśaka			
5) means of explanation (yena) (yanniṣyanda-phala)	10	(=19)	
qualification of this treatise as being similar to 'ārṣa-vacas'			
§ 3. Means of Preserving Oneself within the Doctrine (ātmarakṣanôpāya) – purification of the mind	11-12	(=20-21)	118.3-118.10
§ 4. Causes and Results of the Loss of the Doctrine			118.11-119.4
a) dharmakṣati-hetu 1. dhī-māndya, 2. adhimuktaśukla-viraha, 3. mithyā'bhimānâśraya, 4. saddharmavyasanâvṛtâtmaka 5. neyârthatattvagraha, 6. lobhagredhatā, 7. (mithyā-)darśana, 8. dharmadviṣa-sevana, 9. dharmabhṛd-āra, 10. hīna(-yāna)-ruci	13	(=22)	
b) dharmakṣati-phala	14-15	(=23,24)	
'dharmakṣati' is the worst sin which leads one to Avīci. It is worse than '5 ānantaryāṇi'			
§ 5. Conclusion	16	(=25)	119.5-15
– dharmârthavādasya phala (āptapuṇya-pariṇamana) saṃsāramaṇḍala-kṣānti & bodhy-āpti 'puṇya-āpti' by teaching 'sapta-arthapada' (= 7 vajrapadas) 'pariṇamana' of puṇya – Let the people perceive the Lord Amitāyuṣ and get 'paramabodhi'			
(Commentary) Summary of topics discussed in § 2.-§ 5. (on KK 7-16)		26-28	
(Colophon) for Chapter V			119.16-17

T	C	Q. & R.	BGŚ	DAŚ	AĀS
128 *b* 1–128 *b* 4	847 *b*	cf. MSbh (P) 270 *a–b* (= vv. 16–25)			
	820 *a* 847 *b*				
	820 *a–b* 847 *b*				
	820 *b* 847 *b*				
	820 *b* 847 *b*				
128 *b* 4–128 *b* 6	847 *c* 820 *b*				
128 *b* 6–129 *a* 2	847 *c*				
	820 *b* 847 *c*				
	820 *b* 847 *c* C adds. one verse before v. 26				
129 *a* 2–129 *a* 5	848 *a* 820 *c*				
129 *a* 5, 6–7		cf. MSbh (P) 270 *b* (= vv. 26–28)			

TRANSLATION

TABLE OF CONTENTS

(for Translation & Notes thereon)

Chapter I. — THE MATRIX OF THE TATHĀGATA

Translation

Chapter II. — The Enlightenment

Chapter III. — The Properties of the Buddha

Chapter IV. — The Acts of the Buddha

Chapter V. — The Merits of Faith

ANALYSIS OF THE GERM OF THE JEWELS [1]

(A Treatise on the Ultimate Doctrine of the Great Vehicle) [2]

Chapter I.

THE MATRIX OF THE TATHĀGATA

(Salutation)

I bow to the Saint Vajrasattva [3].

I. INTRODUCTION – The 7 *Vajrapadas*

§ 1. The Meaning of the 7 *Vajrapadas*.

The Buddha, the Doctrine, and the Community [4],
The Essence [of the Buddha] [5], the Supreme Enlightenment [6],
The Virtuous Qualities [of the Buddha],
And, last of all, the Act of the Buddha; —
These are the 7 Adamantine Subjects, [which show]
Briefly, the body of the whole text. // 1 //

1) *Ratnagotravibhāga*. The word '*vibhāga*' is the correct Skt. form of Pāli '*vibhanga*' which means 'explanation', 'commentary'. In BHS, however, the form '*vibhaṅga*' is more often used as in cases of *Madhyântavibhaṅga*, *Dharmadharmatā–vibhaṅga* and so on. In these cases, '*vibhaṅga*' is taken in the sense of 'distinction between two'. But here, the meaning 'analysis' seems more suitable, because the word '*ratnagotra*' indicates '*dhātu*' or '*tathāgatagarbha*', and not '*ratna* & *gotra*'. Cf. *gotram ratnatrayasya* S. p. 21.6.

2) *Mahāyāna–uttaratantra–śāstra*. About the title, see my Introduction, Chap. I.

3) T. offers salutation to "the Buddhas and Bodhisattvas". C. om. the salutation, but has 18 verses instead before entering the main text. This salutation to Vajrasattva, who has an important rôle in the Tantric Buddhism, does not match with this text which has no connection with Tantrism in its doctrine, in spite of the use of the word '*tantra*' in the title. Probably this is a salutation made by the copyist of the present Skt. text under the influence of later Tantric Buddhism.

4) *gaṇa*, T. *tshogs*, C. 衆僧 (= *saṅgha*).

5) *dhātu*, T. *khams*, C. 性.

6) *bodhi*, T. *byaṅ-chub*, C. 道.

The word '*vajrapada*' (adamantine subject) [7] means the term (*pada*), i.e. the basis (*sthāna*), which expresses the meaning of the Enlightenment (*adhigama*) which is similar to a thunderbolt [or diamond] (*vajra*). Here, it being difficult to be penetrated [8] by the knowledge consisting in studying and thinking, the meaning [of the Enlightenment] which is not capable of being explained but is to be realized by oneself [9], should be understood as 'like a thunderbolt'. Those letters, which express that meaning by making manifest the way which is favourable for its acquisition, are called '*pada*', just because they are the basis of that meaning. Thus, by both meanings, i.e. being hard to be penetrated and being the basis, the character of '*vajrapada*', of the meaning as well as of the letters, is to be understood.

Now, what is '*artha*' (the meaning) and what is '*vyañjana*' (the letter)? '*Artha*' is the sevenfold meaning of the Enlightenment, viz. 1) the Buddha (*buddha*), 2) the Doctrine (*dharma*), 3) the Community (*saṃgha*), 4) the Essence of the Buddha (*dhātu*) [10], 5) the Supreme Enlightenment (*bodhi*), 6) the Virtuous Qualities of the Buddha (*guṇa*), and 7) the Acts of the Buddha (*karman*) [11]. These are called '*artha*' [12]. The letters, by which this sevenfold meaning of the Enlightenment is indicated or is manifested, are called '*vyañjana*' [13]. And this teaching of '*vajrapada*' should be understood in detail according to the Sūtras.

7) T. *rdo-rje gnas*, C. 金剛句.

8) *prativedha*, T. *phigs-pa* (to make a small hole, to penetrate).

9) *pratyātma-vedanīya*, T. *so-so-raṅ-bshin rig-par bya-ba*, C. 内身證法.

10) C. 衆生 (= *sattva*).

11) For these 7 subjects, T. & C. give the following terms: 1) *saṅs-rgyas*, 佛; 2) *chos*, 法; 3) *dge-ḥdun*, 僧; 4) *khams*, 性 (衆生); 5) *byaṅ-chub*, 菩提 (道); 6) *yon-tan*, 功德; 7) *phyin-las*, 業.

12) C. adds here the following scriptural passage: "又第一義諦者 (*paramârtha satya*) 所謂, 心緣尚不能知, 何况名字章句".

13) Instead of this sentence, C. puts the following one: "所言字者, 隨以何等名字, 章句 (phrase), 言語 (word), 風聲 (sound), 能表 (expression), 能說 (description), 能明 (explanation), 能示 (indication), 此七種義, 是名爲字".

And it adds the following scriptural passage: "又, 世諦 (*saṃvṛtisatya*) 者, 謂世間中所用之事, 名字, 章句, 言語, 所說".

These two passages are quoted from the *Akṣayamati-parivarta* (C. 大集經, 無盡意菩薩品, *Taisho*, XIII, p. 197 *b*).

§ 2. Authorities on the 7 Subjects.

1) '*Buddha*': "Verily, O Ānanda, invisible is the Tathāgata. He cannot be seen by eyes".

2) '*Dharma*': "Verily, O Ānanda, unutterable is the Doctrine. It cannot be heard by ears".

3) '*Saṃgha*': "Verily, O Ānanda, the Holy Community is of an immutable [14] character. It cannot be completely served, either by body or by mind".

These are the [first] 3 *vajrapadas*, which are to be understood according to the *Dṛḍhâdhyāśaya-parivarta* [15].

4) '*Dhātu*': "Verily, O Śāriputra, this meaning is a subject for the Tathāgata [and only belongs to] the sphere of the Tathāgata. This meaning, O Śāriputra, can neither be known [16] nor be seen, nor be examined correctly throngh the knowledge of the Śrāvakas and the Pratyekabuddhas. Needless to say, this applies to the case of ignorant and ordinary beings, except when they have faith [17] in the Tathāgata. O Śāriputra, the ultimate truth is really approachable only by faith [in the Tathāgata]. O Śāriputra, the ultimate Truth is a synonym of the mass of living beings (*sattva-dhātu*) [18]. The mass of living beings is, O Śāriputra, nothing but a synonym of the Matrix of the Tathāgata (*tathāgatagarbha*) [19]. The Matrix of the Tathāgata is, Śāriputra, nothing but a synonym of the Absolute Body (*dharmakāya*)".

14) *asaṃskṛta*, T. *ḥdus-ma-byas-pa*, C. 無爲, Lit. 'being not created by causes and conditions', or 'not caused by *saṃskāras* (the active forces)', i. e. 'not belonging to this Phenomenal World'.

15) T. *Lhag-paḥi bsam-pa bstan-paḥi leḥu*. Here, '*brtan-pa*' is preferable to '*bstan-pa*'. Cf. *Tohoku* No. 224 which gives the Skt title; *Sthirâdhyāśaya-parivarta*. This sūtra is lacking in Chinese Tripiṭaka.

16) According to T., '*jñātuṃ vā*' should be supplied after '*svaprajñayā*' (T. *śes-pa*).

17) *śraddhā-gamana*, T. *dad-pas rtogs-pa*. As for the importance of faith, see S. p. 74 l. 1 f. (v. I. 153).

18) T. *sems-can-gyi khams*, C. 衆生界, Here *dhātu* means 'a group' (*jāti* or *gotra*) and *sattvadhātu* is used as a collective noun for *sattvas*. At the same time, however, this word, being synonymous with *tathāgatagarbha*, may be interpreted as "the Essence of the sattva, being the 'cause' of the Buddhahood", according to the special use of the word '*dhātu*' in this text.

19) T. *de-bshin-gśegs-paḥi sñiṅ-po*, C. 如來藏. The meaning of *tathāgatagarbha* will be discussed under (VII) & (IX) - 4) (in Chap. I) (S. p. 26, 70 ff.).

Thus is the fourth '*vajrapada*' and is to be understood according to the *Anūnatvâpūrṇatvanirdeśa-parivarta* [20].

5) '*Bodhi*': "O Lord, the Supreme Perfect Enlightenment (*anuttarā samyaksambodhi*) is a synonym of the Sphere of the Nirvāṇa [21]. The Sphere of the Nirvāṇa is nothing but a synonym of the Absolute Body of the Tathāgata".

Thus is the fifth *Vajrapada* which is to be understood according to the *Ārya Śrīmālā-sūtra* [22].

6) '*Guṇa*': "O Śāriputra, that which is called the Absolute Body, preached by the Tathāgata, is of indivisible nature, of qualities inseparable from the Wisdom, that is to say, [indivisible from or endowed] with the properties of the Buddha which far surpass the particles of sands of the Gaṅgā in number" [23].

20) C. 不增不減經, *Taisho*, No. 668, XVI, 467 *a*. T. has no translation of this sūtra. Hereafter, AAN will be used as the abbreviation.

21) *nirvāṇadhātu*, T. *mya-ṅan-las-ḥdas-paḥi dbyiṅs*, C. 涅槃界. T. *dbyiṅs* (for *dhātu*) means 'a heavenly region'. '*bhagavan*' in the Text is, to be corrected into '*bhagavaṃs*'.

22) = *Śrīmālādevīsiṃhanāda-sūtra*. T. *Ḥphags-pa dpal-phreṅ-gi mdo* (*Dpal-phreṅ lha-mo seṅ-geḥi sgraḥi modo*) C. 聖者勝鬘經. There are two translations in C.: 1) 勝鬘師子吼一乘大方便方廣經 tr. by 求那跋陀羅 (Guṇabhadra), *Taisho*, No. 353. and 2) 勝鬘夫人會, vol. 48 of 大寶積經 (*Ratnakūṭa-sūtra*), *Taisho*, No. 310. Hereafter the first one will be used as the reference under the abbreviation of ŚMS. This passage, ŚMS, *Taisho*, XII, 220 *c*.

23) The whole quotation runs as follows:

(S.) *yo' yam, Śāriputra, tathagatanirdiṣṭo dharmakāyaḥ, so'yam avinirbhāgadharmā, avinirmuktajñānaguṇo, yaduta, gaṅgānadī-vālikā-vyatikrāntais tathāgatadharmaiḥ;*

(T.) *Śāri-bu, de-bshin-gśegs-pas bstan-paḥi chos-kyi sku gaṅ-yin-pa de-ni ḥdi-lta-ste, gaṅgāḥi kluṅ-gi bye-ma-sñed-las ḥdas-paḥi de-bshin-gśegs-paḥi chos-dag-daṅ / rnam-par dbyer-med-paḥi chos daṅ ldan-pa, ma-bral-baḥi ye-śes-kyi yon-tan-can yin-no.*

(C.) 舍利弗, 如來所說法身義者, 過於恒沙不離不脫不思議佛法如來智慧功德 (C. has a longer quotation, but its additional part is identical with the quotation in S. p. 39 from the same sūtra).

For '*avinirbhāgadharman*' ('*-dharman*', ifc. 'of the nature of'), T. *rnam-par dbyer-med-paḥi chos daṅ ldan-pa* (= ... *chos-can*), C. simply 不離 and om. '*dharman*' (usually, 不相捨離法).

For '*avinirmuktajñānaguṇa*', T. *ma-bral-baḥi ye-śes-kyi yon-tan-can*, which does not seem correct (it should be '*ye-śes-daṅ ma-bral-baḥi yon-tan can*'); C. 不

This is the sixth *Vajrapada* and is to be understood according to the *Anūnatvâpūrṇatvanirdeśa* [24].

7) '*Karman*': "O Mañjuśrī, the Tathāgata never imagines anything nor distinguishes falsely. That is to say, his acts of this kind flow forth without any effort, without any imagination or any thought construction".

This is the seventh *Vajrapada* which is to be understood according to the *Tathāgataguṇajñānâcintyaviṣayâvatāra-nirdeśa* [25].

In short, these are the 7 *Vajrapadas* which should be known as the body of this whole text, in the sense of being a collection of preliminary explanations [26].

脫.....智慧功德, but 智慧功德 is placed at the end, and probably the whole sentense could not be understood properly by C. translator. The term '*avinirmuktajñānaguṇa*', being appositional to '*dharmakāya*', is a Bahuvrīhi compound, in which the former part '*avinirmuktajñāna*' is relating to the latter part '*guṇa*' as an apposition. And hence, '*avinirmuktajñāna*', being an adjective to '*guṇa*' (which means '*buddhaguṇāḥ*' or '*tathāgatadharmāḥ*' i. e. the Qualities of the Buddha), forms again a kind of Bahuvrīhi compound. It should mean 'unreleased from *jñāna*'. Here, '*jñāna*' signifies '*buddhajñāna*', i. e. the Wisdom, by which the Buddha has realized '*bodhi*'. Therefore, this term '*avinirmuktajñāna*' is an attribute, exclusive to the Buddha's Qualities. (See S. p. 39, where a simile of lantern is used for clarifying this meaning and lantern is said to be of '*avinirmukta-guṇa*', omitting the word '*jñāna*').

In other passages, '*amuktajñāna*' or '*amuktajña*' is used as an attribute to '*guṇa*'. They are nothing but the abbreviated forms of '*avinirmuktajñāna*' and seem to have the same sense as the latter. See S. pp. 42,2–3; 55,14–15; 73,2–3; 76,9.

As for the term '*gaṅgānadīvālikā-vyatikrānta*' it is also an adjective, exclusive to the Buddha's Qualities and often used along with '*amuktajña*', '*avinirbhāga*' and '*acintya*'. (sometimes in the form of '*gaṅgānadīvālukāvyativṛtta*' (S. pp. 42,2; 55,14), '*gaṅgānadivālikā-vyativṛtta*' (p. 12,12), '*gaṅgātīrarajo 'tīta*' (p. 80,9) or '*gaṅgāsikatā 'tivṛtta*' (p. 85,16).

Instrumental case-ending of the word '*tathāgatadharma*' (which is translated into T. by '*daṅ*') shows the implied meaning of '*-upeta*', '*-yoga*', '*samanvāgama*', or otherwise is to be related to '*avinirbhāga*' as shown in the present translation. T. seems to show the latter interpretation. C. offers no help.

24) AAN 467 *a*.

25) Chinese Tripiṭaka retains 3 kinds of translations of this sūtra, namely: 1) 度諸佛境界智嚴經 (translator unknown), *Taisho*, No. 302, 2) 佛華嚴入如來德智不思議境界經 tr. by 闍那崛多 (Jñānagupta), *ibid.*, No. 303, 3) 大方廣入如來智德不思議經 tr. by Śikṣānanda, *ibid.*, No. 304. This passage is in *Taisho*, X, p. 915 *b* (No. 302).

26) *uddeśamukha*, T. *bstan-paḥi sgo*, C. not clear.

§ 3. The Essential Character of the 7 Subjects.

Of these [seven subjects],
Accompanied [27)] by their own characteristics,
One should know respectively the [first] three subjects
From the introductory chapter in the *Dhāraṇirāja-sūtra* [28)],
And the [latter] four from [the chapter on] the distinction
Between the qualities of the Bodhisattva
and those of the Buddha [29)]. // 2 //

[The meaning of this verse is as follows]: And of these seven *Vajrapadas*, accompanied [30)] by the explanation of their own characteristics, the three subjects should be known as being from [31)] the introductory chapter (*nidāna-parivarta*) of the Holy *Dhāraṇīśvararājasūtra*, and then the remaining four [are to be known] from the chapter on the distinction between the qualities of the Bodhisattva and those of the Buddha respectively [32)]. Therefore, it is said:

"The Lord has perfectly realized the equality of all things, has set the wheel of Doctrine going well and has kindly trained numberless disciples" [33)].

27) *anugata*, T. *rjes-ḥbrel-ba* (= *anubandha*), C. not clear.
Literally, '*anugata*' is related to '*trīṇi padāni*', as well as to '*catvāri [padāni]*'. For '*svalakṣaṇenânugatāni*', T. as if '*svalakṣaṇasyânngatāni*', and om. the case-ending of '*eṣām*' (*ḥdi-dag*).

28) = *Dhāraṇīśvararājasūtra*. See below.

29) *dhīmat* (= *bodhisattva*), and *jina* (= *buddha*). T. *blo-ldan* & *rgyal-ba*, respectively. For '*dharma*', C. 智 (*jñāna*).

30) For '*svalakṣaṇanirdeśena* ... *anugatāni*', T. *raṅ-gi mtshan-ñid bstan-pa daṅ / rjes-su ḥbrel-ba ni.* (*daṅ* is probably for Instrumental case-ending).

31) The reading '*nidānaparivartânugatāni*' is rather obscure. It should be '*nidānaparivartād anugatāni*'. So T. (ablative) Also v. 2 (*nidānataḥ*). But C. takes it as locative.

32) This sūtra is available in both Tibetan and Chinese Tripiṭakas. T. has the title '*Tathāgata-mahākaruṇā-nirdeśa-sūtra*', which is identical with the title of Chinese translation '大哀經' (*Taisho*, No. 398). Beside this independent sūtra, C. has another translation of the same sūtra as a part of the *Mahāvaipulya-mahāsaṃnipāta-sūtra* (大方等大集經) (*Taisho*, No. 397). In this *Mahāsaṃnipātasūtra*, the *Dhāraṇīrājasūtra* occupies the vols. 1–4, under the titles of Chap. I "*Alaṅkāra-parivarta*" and Chap. II "*Dhāraṇīśvararāja-bodhisattva-parivarta*". It seems that the "*Nidāna parivarta*" is equivalent to the *Alaṅkāra-parivarta*, and the "*Bodhisattva-tathāgata-dharmabheda-(parivarta)*", to the remaining part, i.e. Chap. II, denoting the contents of this chapter.

33) DRS 1 *a*. (=大哀經, *Taisho*, XIII, p. 409 *a*).

By these three fundamental sentences, respectively, one should know the arrangement of the three Jewels [in the aspect of] their successive origination and accomplishment [34]. The remaining four subjects are to be known as the statement of the accomplishment of the causes which correspond to the origin of the three Jewels [35]. Now, on the 8th Stage of Bodhisattva, as the power of controlling all elements of phenomena has been attained, so it is said:

> " He (= the Lord), sitting in the excellent Seat of the Englightenment [36], realized perfectly the equality of all things ".

On the 9th Stage of Bodhisattva, he is endowed with the power of expressing the Highest Doctrine [37], knows very easily the intentions of all living beings, brings all faculties [of living beings] [38] to the highest perfection and becomes an expert in the removal of the chain of Defiling forces [39] in all living beings. Therefore, it is said: "Having realized the perfect Enlightenment, he has well set the wheel of the Doctrine going ". On the 10th Stage of Bodhisattva, after attaining the anointment for the prince recognized as the next king in the highest religious empire of the Buddha, he is immediately calmed in the Buddha's effortless [40] acts uninterruptedly [41]. Therefore, it is said: "He who has well set the wheel of the Doctrine going has kindly trained number-

34) *anupūrva-samutpāda-samudāgama*, T. *rim-gyis skye-ba ḥgrub-pa*, C. 次第生起成就. Here the word '*samudāgama*' (also in the next line) means '*siddhi*'. (T. *ḥgrub-pa*, C. 成就).

35) *triratnôtpatty-anurūpahetu-samudāgama-nirdeśa*.

36) *bodhi-maṇḍa*. '*maṇḍa*' has originally meant 'the scum of cooked rice, or the essence of milk, i. e. cream'. In Pāli, it is used in the sense of 'essence' (*sāra*) 'excellent part'. T. translation '*sñiṅ-po*' shows the same meaning. Therefore '*bodhi-maṇḍa*' means literally 'the essence of the Enlightenment', 'the highest state of Enlightenment'. But in later scriptures, it denotes 'the excellent place of the Enlightenment' as C. translation '[坐於]道場勝妙之處', and is often accompanied by the word '*vara*' as in the text. Sometimes '*bodhi-maṇḍa*' is explained as denoting Bodhi-tree. Here I preferred C. translation.

37) *dharmabhāṇakatva*, T. *chos-smra-ba-ñid*, C. 法師 (teacher of the Doctrine, one who has the qualification for preaching the Doctrine).

38) *indriya*. There are 5 *indriyas*, namely *śraddhā-i.*, *vīrya-i.*, *smṛti-i.*, *samādhi-i.*, & *prajñā-i.* viz. Mvyut 41.

39) *vāsanā-anusaṃdhi*, T. *bag-chags-kyi mtshams-sbyor-ba*, C. 習氣 (om. *anusaṃdhi*).

40) *anābhoga*, T. *lhun-gyis grub*, C. 自然而行.

41) *apratipraśrabdha*, T. *rgyun mi-ḥchad-pa(r)*, C. 常不休息.

less disciples ". Furthermore, the same qualification of having trained numberless disciples is shown in the same text, immediately after this sentence. It runs as follows:

> " He was together with the assembly of a large number of monks [42], and with the assembly of numberless Bodhisattvas ".

As he has well trained those who are in the enlightenment of the Śrāvaka and up to that of the Buddha, step by step, it is said:

> " Thus being endowed with the virtuous qualities, . . ." &c.[43]

And then, immediately after the [passage of the] doctrine on the nature of qualities of Śrāvakas and Bodhisattvas, in the reference to the Buddha's inconceivable leadership [44] in regard to tranquillity, the establishment of the distinguishable qualities [45] of the Jewel of the Buddha is to be known through the accomplishment of a great palace adorned with circular ornament of jewels [46], through his bringing the people together [47] into the assembly of Tathāgatas, through the completion of various kinds of worship with divine things [48], and through the pouring of rain from the cloud of praises [49].

And next, through the splendid arrangement [50] of the seat of the Doctrine and its brightness, and through the glorification [51] of the name

[42] A – *yāvat* – B (beginning with A up to B), T. . . . *shes-bya-ba-nas* . . . *shes-bya-baḥi bar*, C. 乃至.

[43] DRS 1, *a–b*.

[44] *vṛṣabhitā* (BHS), T. *khyu-mchog* (' the best bull ' = *ṛṣabha*). The term is often used as an epithet of the Buddha. C. reads it as ' *viṣaya* '.

[45] For ' *guṇavibhāga* ', T. *yon-tan rnam-par dbye-ba*, C. 不思議事 (*acintya-vastu*). In the following cases, however, C. 功德差別 (*guṇaprabheda*).

[46] *vipula-ratna-vyūha-maṇḍala-vyūha-nivṛtti*. Of the two ' *vyūhas* ' in the text, the first one is translated into T. ' *bkod-pa* ', C. 莊嚴 (decoration), and the second one, into T. *khyams* (court-yard), C. 寶殿 (palace of jewel). C. ' 寶殿 ' seems to include the meaning of ' *maṇḍala* '. For ' *vipula* ', C. as ' *vimala* ', but T. as S.

[47] *samāvartana* < samāvartayati (BHS), ' gathers, collects ' (viz. BHS Dic. s.v.). For *pariṣat-samāvartana*, T. *bkhor-ḥdus-pa* (*ḥdus-pa* < *ḥdu-ba*, to come together). For *samāvartana*, C. 雲集, but seems to om. *pariṣad*.

[48] C. om. *dravya*, and has 種種供養 instead (*vividha-divyā-pūjā*?).

[49] These passages are extracted from the same sūtra. (DRS 1 *c*–3 *c*).

[50] *vyūha*, T. *bkod-ba*, C. 莊嚴.

[51] *parikīrtana*, T. *yoṅs-su bsgrags-pa*, C. 說 (示現).

and qualities of the variety of doctrines [52], there should be known the establishment of the distinguishable qualities of the Jewel of the Doctrine [53]. And next, in the light of the mutual [54] manifestation of the power of the acting sphere [55] of various tranquillities of the Bodhisattvas, and in the light of the description of their various forms of qualities, there should be known the establishment of the distinguishable qualities of the Jewel of the Community [56].

And again, immediately after this, in the reference to the Buddha's presentation [57] of the highest fearlessness and confidence [in speech] [58] on account of the prince of the supreme religious king [to the Bodhisattvas], through the sprinkling of the Buddha's light. And, through the explanation of the highest praise to the true virtues of the Tathāgata, through the description [59] in the form of discussion [60] of the highest Doctrine of the Great Vehicle, and, as the result of that knowledge, through the manifestation of the attainment of the highest sovereignty [61]; through these three, respectively, the highest establishment of the distinguishable qualities of three Jewels is to be understood [62]. And also therein the introductory chapter of this Sūtra is known to have come to the end [63].

Then, after the introductory chapter of this Sūtra, the Essence of the Buddha is explained by a description of the sixtyfold appliance as

52) *dharmaparyāya*, T. *chos-kyi rnam-grańs*, C. 法門.

53) Cf. DRS 3 *c*–4 *d*.

54) *anyonya*, T. *phan-tshun*, C. 迭共. As J. suggested, '*anyonya*' had better be connected with '*bodhisattva*' in a compound. C. seems to omit '*prabhā-saṃdarśana*'.

55) *gocara-viṣaya*, T. *spyod-yul*, C. 行境界.

56) DRS 4 *c*–5 *b*.

57) The reading '*upakaraṇatā*' is to be corrected into '*upaharaṇatā*', according to C., which translates it twice by 授 & 與 (to give, to offer), respectively, resolving the compound into '*anuttaradharmarāja-jyeṣṭhaputra-upaharaṇa*' and '*paramavaiśāradya-upaharaṇa*'. But this resolution of the compound is not good. Here the translation is according to T, except the term '*upaharaṇa*'. '... *jyeṣṭhiputra*' meaning Bodhisattva.

58) *pratibhāna* (from Pāli *paṭibhāna*, which has the special meaning of 'readiness in speech' or 'confidence of speech', besides the usual sense of intelligence or manifestation of mind), T. *spobs-pa* (courage, confidence), C. 不怯弱辯才 (cowardless talent of speech).

59) *upanyasana* (< upa-ni-√ as) T. *ne-bar bkod-pa*, C. 說.

60) *kathāvastu* (subject of story), T. *gtam-gyi dńos-po*, C. om.

61) C. om. *aiśvarya*. For '*tat-pratipatteḥ*', C. 如實修行彼大乘故 (because of the practice of that Mahāyāna by rule).

62) Cf. DRS 5 *b*–6 *c*.

63) *avasānagata*, T. *mthaḥ-ñid* (*avasānatva*) C. 已竟.

the purifying factors of that Essence [64]. Because the Essence of the Buddha deserves to be applied the purification, in so far as it has qualities of an object to be purified [65]. And because of the effect of this meaning, in the 10 Stages of Bodhisattva [66], there is illustrated again an analogy of the purifying process of gold. In this Sūtra (the *Dhāraṇirāja-sūtra*) too, after the description of the Acts of the Buddha, the allegory of unpurified Vaiḍūrya stone is illustrated. It runs as follows [67]:

> " O noble youth, take for instance a skilful jewel-maker who knows quite well how to purify precious stones. Having taken out an unpurified precious stone from the mine [68], and having washed [69] it with acid salt water [70], he then polishes it by rubbing [71] with black-

[64] *ṣaṣṭy-ākāra-tad* (=*dhātu*) *-viśuddhi-guṇa-parikarma-nirdeśena*. About '*viśuddhi-guṇa-parikarman*', see below.

[65] *viśodhye 'rthe guṇavati, tad -viśuddhi-parikarma-yogāt*.

In comparison with '*viśuddhi-guṇa-parikarman*' and '*buddhadhātoḥ ṣaṣṭyākāra-viśuddhi-parikarma-guṇāḥ*' in S. p. 6, l: 11, the meaning seems as follows '*viśuddhi-guṇa*' is '*viśuddhi-parikarman*' of '*dhātu*'. In other words, '*dhātu*' is '*viśodhya-guṇavad-artha*', and hence, '*viśuddhi-parikarman*' is inherent to '*dhātu*' in the form of '*ṣaṣṭyākāra-viśuddhiguṇa*'. For '*parikarman*', T. *yoṅs-su sbyoṅ-ba* (*pariśodhana*, cleaning), C. 法 (in the sense of 'method', or 'appliance') in the former two cases, and '業', in the third case (淨業功德, for *viśuddhi-parikarma-guṇa*). But in another case, i.e. for '*parikamma*' in the verse quoted in S. p. 6, C. translates it by '清淨', which has the same sense as T. '*yoṅs-su sbyoṅ-bȧ*'. After all, the most suitable translation for this term is 'process of purification or 'appliance for purification'.

[66] The significance of this '*daśaṣu bodhisattvabhūmiṣu*' is not clear, C. says instead 'in the Daśabhūmika-sūtra'. It sounds better in comparison with '*asminneva ca sūtre*' in the next sentence. (Cf. *Taisho*, 10, 186 *c*, 188 *c*, etc.).

[67] DRS p. 21 *c*.

[68] *maṇigotra*, T. *nor-bu rin-po-cheḥi rigs* (= *maṇiratnagotra*), C. [寶] 性山 [中]. Cf. Laṅk. p. 1,7 (*ratnagotra-puṣpapratimaṇḍite . . . samudra-malaya-śikhare*).

[69] *utkṣālya* in the text, but Ms. B reads '*unmilya*'. There seems to be no definite reason for changing '*unmilya*' into '*utkṣālya*' against Ms. reading. The meaning of this word is no doubt 'washing', but in the special sense of 'metaling', i.e. 'taking dust off in order to make jewel or metal manifest' (in causative sense). As this '*unmīlya*' is found twice in Ms., it seems rather difficult to consider it as a mistake. At the same time, however, we can not say '*unmīlya*' is absolutely correct, unless we find other examples of the same use.

[70] *tīkṣṇa khārôdakena*, T. *lan-tshvaḥi chu rnon-pos*, C. 以嚴灰 (sharp ash?) '*khāra*' is a Prakrit form of Skt '*kṣāra*'.

[71] *paryavadāpanena paryavadāpayati* (lit. 'makes perfectly clean by means of purifying instrument'), T. *yoṅs-su sbyoṅ-bas sbyoṅ-ba byed-do*. C. 以用措磨 seems to show the actual process of purification. So I adopted it in the translation.

hair cloth [72]. But with this much work, he never ceases to make efforts. After that, having washed the stone with meat juice [73] of bitter taste, he polishes it by rubbing with a woollen blanket [74]. Even with this much work, he never ceases to make efforts. After that, having washed it with great medical liquid [75], he polishes it with closely-woven cotton cloth [76]. After having been polished and having been separated from all impure metals mingled with it [77], it is called a precious [78] Vaiḍūrya stone. Similarly, O noble youth, the Tathāgata too, having known the unpurified element of living beings [79], creates disgust in the mind of those living beings who are attached to the world of transmigration through the teaching of being afraid of the non-eternity, suffering, impersonality and impurity [of this world] [80], and causes them to enter the discipline of the sacred Doctrine. With this much of act the Buddha never ceases to make efforts. After that, he makes them realize the guiding manner [81] of the Tathāgata by the teaching of [the threefold gate to the emancipation [82], viz.] 'non-substantiality' (*śūnyatā*), 'non-distinction' (*animitta*) and 'desirelessness' (*apraṇihita*). Even with this much of act, the Tathāgata never ceases to make efforts. After that, through the teaching of the irreversible wheel of the Doctrine [83] and through the teaching of the 'purification of three circles' [84], he causes those living beings who have

72) *kṛṣṇa-keśakambala*, T. *skraḥi re-ba* (om. *kṛṣṇa*), C. 黑頭髮衣.

73) *tīkṣa āmiṣa-rasa*, T. *zaṅs-kyi klu-pa rnon-po*, C. 辛味飲食汁.

74) *khaṇḍikā*, T. *lal-gyi la-ba*, C, 衣纏裹木 (a piece of wood covered with cloth).

75) *mahā-vaiṣajya-rasa.*

76) *sūkṣma-vastra*,

77) *apagatakāca* (Bahuvrīhi comp.), T. *dri-ma daṅ bral-ba(ni)*, C. 遠離銅鐵等鑛, 毗琉璃垢. According to C., '*kāca*' seems to be a general name for dust or piece of metal and glass mingled within jewels.

78) *abhijāta* ('well born', 'born in the noble family', 'noble'), T. *rigs-chen-po* (= *mahākula*), C. 大 (= *mahā*).

79) *sattvadhātu*, C. 衆生性. T. as usual.

80) These are called '*caturvidhâviparyāsa-saṃjñā*'. viz. S. p. 30.

81) *netrī*, T. *tshul* (= *naya*), but C. 法輪 (*dharmacakra*). Cf. BHS Dic. s. v.

82) (*trīṇi vimokṣa-mukhāni*).

83) *avivartya-dharmacakra.*

84) *trimaṇḍala-pariśuddhi*, T. *ḥkhor-gsum yoṅs-su dag-pa*, C. 不見三事 (against the usual translation, 三輪淸淨). It means usually the purity of three things in donation, i.e. the giver, the receiver, and the gift, and signifies 'non-substantiality' (*śūnyatā*).

different kinds of characteristics and origins, to enter the sphere of the Tathāgata. Having entered [the sphere of the Tathāgata], those same beings, when they have realized the true nature of the Tathāgata, are called unparalleled venerables " [85].

Having in view this Essence of the Tathāgata, which is of pure origin [86], it is said as follows:

" Just as gold, though it is invisible among stones and sands,
Comes to be seen by the process of purification,
Similarly, in this world of living beings
The Tathāgata [becomes visible by purification] ".

Now, which are the sixtyfold factors of purifying process [87] of the Essence of Buddhahood? They are, namely, (1) 4 kinds of ornament of Bodhisattvas, (2) 8 kinds of illumination of Bodhisattvas, (3) 16 kinds of Bodhisattva's great compassion, and (4) 32 kinds of Bodhisattva's deeds [88].

[85]) *dakṣiṇīya* (worthy to receive '*dakṣiṇā*', i.e. gift, donation), T. *yon-gnas* (place of gift), C. 福田 (*puṇya-kṣetra*).

[86]) *viśuddhigotra*, T. *yoṅs-su dag-paḥi rigs*, C. 自性清淨 (as if '*prakṛti-pariśuddhi*').

The source of this Prakrit verse is unknown. (It is apparently in Pāli, but is not found among the present Pāli Tripiṭaka.)

[87]) See above (Note 65).

[88]) According to DRS, these *guṇas* are as follows:

1) 4 '*alaṅkāras*' (瓔珞莊嚴): 1. 戒 (*śīla*), 2. 三昧 (*samādhi*), 3. 智慧 (*prajñā*) & 4. 陀羅尼 (*dhāraṇī*). (DRS 5 *b*–8 *b*).

2) 8 '*avabhāsas*' (光明): 1. 念 (*smṛti*), 2. 意 (*manas*), 3. 行 (*caryā* ?), 4. 法 (*dharma*), 5. 智 (*jñāna*), 6. 實 (*satya*), 7. 神通 (*abhijñā*), & 8. 無礙智 (*apratihatajñāna*). (DRS 9 *a*–10 *a*).

3) 16 '*karuṇās*', by which each of the following '*mithyās*' of the living beings is removed: 1. 邪見 (*mithyā-dṛṣṭi*), 2. 四顛倒 (*caturvidha-viparyāsa*), 3. 我我所見 (*ahaṃkāra, mamakāra*), 4. 五蓋 (*pañca-āvaraṇa*, i.e. *rāga-ā.*, *pratigha-ā.*, *styāna-middha-ā.*, *auddhatya-kaukṛtya-ā.*, & *vicikitsā-ā.*), 5. 執六入 (*ṣaḍāyatana-abhiniveśa*), 6. 七慢 (*sapta-māna*, i.e. *māna*, *adhimāna*, *mānâtimāna*, *asmimāna*, *abhimāna*, *ūnamāna* & *mithyāmāna*), 7. 世道 (*loka-mārga* ?), 8. 惡道 (*durgati*), 9. 惡業 (*daśa akuśalāni karmaṇi*), 10. 無明慳貪 (*avidyā-mātsarya-rāga* ?), 11. ignorance about the 12 *aṅga*'s of causality, 12. 十六邪見 (16 kinds of '*mi-*

Immediately after this statement, there is explained the Supreme Enlightenment of the Buddha by indicating the 16 kinds of Great Compassion [imparted by] the Supreme Enlightenment [89]. Next to this description, there is explained the Buddha's Virtuous Qualities by the indication of 10 Powers, 4 kinds of Intrepidity and 18 Exclusive Properties of the Buddha [90]. And next, the Acts of the Buddha are explained by the indication of 32 kinds of Supreme Acts of the Buddha [91]. Thus, these 7 *Vajrapadas* should be understood in detail through the indication of their own characters according to the Sūtra.

§ 4. The Inherent Connection between 7 Subjects.

And then, what is the inherent connection [92] between these subjects?

From the Buddha comes the Doctrine,
Owing to the Doctrine there is the Holy Community,
In the Community exists the Matrix, which is

thyādṛṣṭi '), 13. affliction to '*tribhava*', 14. 魔 (*māra*), 15. 快樂 (*kāma* ?), 16. ignorance about the gate to Nirvāṇa. (DRS 10 *a*–10 *c*).

4) 32 acts practised by Bodhisattvas, which are the counterpart of 32 bad behaviours of living beings. (DRS 10 *c*–11 *b*).

[89]) The Supreme Enlightenment is said to be accompanied by the following 16 qualities, namely: 1. 清淨寂靜 (*śuddhi–śānti*), 2. 自性清淨 (*prakṛtipariśuddhi*), 3. 不取, 不捨 (*anudgraha, anupekṣā* ?), 4. 無想無緣 (*asaṃjñā, anārambaṇa*), 5. 三世平等 (*tryadhva–samatā*), 6. 無身無爲 (*asaṃskṛta*), 7. 無分別句義 (*nirvikalpa–padârtha*), 8. 不可說 (*anabhilāpya*), 9. 無取無緣 (無住處) (*apratiṣṭhita*), 10. 空 (*śūnya*), 11. 虛空 (*ākāśavat*), 12. 眞實句 (*satya-pada*), 13. 非內非外 (無相無作) (*animitta–akṛtrima* ?), 14. 無漏無取 (無所受) (*anāsrava*, etc.), 15. 寂靜光明無諍 (*śānti, prabhā, araṇa*?), 16. (?) (DRS 11 *b*–14 *a*) (Chinese terms in brackets are taken from 大哀經, *Taisho*, 8, pp. 422 *a*–425 *a*).

Here the reason why these qualities are called '*mahākaruṇā*' is that they are inseparable from '*mahākaruṇā*' and Buddha's Enlightenment realizes itself in the form of the acts of '*mahākaruṇā*'. Cf. DRS 11 *b*, "無上菩提及大悲, 如是二法等而無分別". (The Supreme Enlightenment and the Great Compassion, these two are equal and undistinguishable from each other).

[90]) See Chap. IV (III).; DRS 14 *c*–21 *c* (there is no description of the 32 *Mahāpuruṣalakṣaṇa* in DRS).

[91]) DRS 26 *b*–27 *b*. Each of the 32 '*karman*'s is indistinct.

[92]) *anuśleṣa* (< *anu*–√ *śliṣ*), T. *ḥbrel–pa* (= *saṃbandha*), C. 次第 (*anu–krama*). The use of '*anuśleṣa*' seems to be quite rare. BHS Dic. records only the form of '*anu-*

The element of Wisdom, aiming at its acquisition [93];
Its acquisition of the Wisdom is the Supreme Enlightenment,
Which is endowed with the Qualities, 10 Powers and others,
And accompanied by altruistic Acts for all living beings. // 3 //

Finished [the explanation of] the relation between each subject in the text [94].

śliṣṭa ' (ppp.) found in *Mahāvastu*, iii-71-14. viz. BHS Dic., s. v. C. takes it merely to show the order of succession between each subject and uses, in each case, the ablative for the preceding one. But it is not agreeable. Therefore, the reading '*saṅghe*' in the text, though against T. & C. is quite correct.

[93] '*jñāna-dhātu-āptiniṣṭha*'. For '*niṣṭha*', T. *mthar.* ('*āpti-niṣṭha*' seems to mean 'having (*jñāna*-)*āpti* as the end'. In comparison with it, '*jñāna-dhātu*' seems to mean 'garbha', which is indicated by '*tad*' in the next line. C. reads as '*saṅghād apratihatadhātuḥ* (無礙性), *dhātor jñānam*' and om. '*jñānadhātvāptiniṣṭha*' & '*agrabodhi*'. (Supreme Enlightenment)

[94] *śāstrasaṃbandha*. For *saṃbandha*, T. *ḥbrel-pa*, C. 法義體相 (*dharmârtha-svalakṣaṇa* ?).

II. THE JEWEL OF THE BUDDHA

Hereafter we should explain the meaning of *Ślokas* (basic verses) [1]. Those living beings who were lead by the Tathāgata, while taking their refuge in the Tathāgata, also take refuge in the Doctrine and Community through the faith as the natural outflow of the Reality [2]. Therefore, first of all, there is one *śloka* with regard to the Jewel of The Buddha.

(Kārikā 1)

I bow to the one, who has realized [3] the Buddhahood [4]
Which has neither beginning, middle nor end, and is quiescent,
And who, having realized himself, taught the Path,
Fearless and eternal, in order to enlighten the ignorant [5],
And who, having in hand the excellent sword and thunderbolt
Of Wisdom and Mercy, cuts in pieces [6] all sprouts of Sufferings,
And breaks the wall of doubts [7] concealed
In the forest of various views [8]. // 4 //

1) The word *śloka* has a strict use in this text, especially in Chap. I. It is used mostly in case of certain verses which I picked up as the basic verses. In I. *Introduction*, it is clear, there is no *śloka*, though we have 3 'verses'. Śloka–or Kārikā– text starts with the following verse (v. 4). Hereafter I shall use the Sanskrit word *śloka* without translation when it indicates the basic verses. About a detailed discussion on the basic verses, see my Introduction.

2) *dharmatāniṣyandâbhiprasādena*, T. *chos–ñid–kyi rgyu–mthun–paḥi dvaṅ–ba*, C. 尊敬如來 (respecting the Tathāgata). For *abhiprasāda*, Pāli, *abhippasāda*, T. *dvaṅ–ba*, *dvaṅs–pa* (purity, faith, trust). Cf. ŚMS 221 *a*, where emphasis lies on the '*ekaśaraṇatā*' of the Buddha. See also V. *The three jewels as refuges.*

3) *vibuddha*, 'one who has enlightened'.

4) *buddhatva*, T. *saṅs–rgyas–ñid*, C. 佛身.

5) *abudha* (BHS), = Skt. *abuddha.*

6) *ekacchid*, both T. & C. omit *eka*.

7) *vimati*, T. *the–tshom* (doubt), C. 顚倒意 (*viparyasta–mati*, wrong view).

8) C. reads this passage as follows "and breaks the wrong view and all forests [of defilements] (稠林) concealed in the mountain of various views".

§ 1. The Eightfold Quality of the Buddhahood.

What is shown by this [*śloka*]?

Being immutable, free from efforts
And not being dependent upon the others,
[Also] Being endowed with Wisdom, Compassion and [supernatural] Power [imparted by both],
The Buddhahood has two kinds of benefit. // 5 //

By this verse there has been briefly explained the Buddhahood as being contracted by eight qualities. Which are the 8 qualities? Namely, 1) Immutability (*asaṃskṛtatva*), 2) being free from any effort (*anābhogatā*), 3) Enlightenment, not dependent on others (*aparapratyayâbhisaṃbodhi*) [9], 4) Wisdom (*jñāna*), 5) Compassion (*karuṇā*) [10], 6) [*supernatural*] power (*śakti*), 7) fulfilment of self-benefit (*svârthasaṃpad*), and 8) fulfilment of benefit for others (*parârthasaṃpad*) [11].

As having neither beginning, middle nor end by nature,
It is immutable;
Being the body of quiet character,
It is free from any effort, — thus remembered by tradition // 6 //
Being realized by oneself [12],
It is cognizable without any help of others;
Thus awakened in a threefold way, it is Wisdom,
Because of preaching the way, it is Compassion. // 7 //
It is Power because of destroying
Suffering and Defilements by Wisdom and Compassion;
By the first three qualities, benefit for oneself,
And by the latter three, benefit for others [is indicated]. // 8 //

1) *asaṃskṛta*: The word 'immutable' (*asaṃskṛta*) should be understood as being opposite to being conditioned or caused (*saṃskṛta*) [13]. Here

9) *aparapratyayôdita* in the verse.

10) *kāruṇya* in the verse.

11) Translations of these 8 qualities in T. & C. are as follows:

1) *ḥdus ma-byas-pa-ñid*, 無爲體; 2) *lhun-gyis-grub-pa*, 自然; 3) *gshan-gyi rkyen-gyis mṅon-par rtogs-pa ma yin-pa*, 不依他知; 4) *ye-śes*, 智; 5) *thugs-rje*, 悲; 6) *nus-pa*, 力; 7) *raṅ-gi don phun-sum tshogs-pa*, 自利益; 8) *gshan-gyi don phun-sum tshogs-pa*, 他利益.

12) *pratyātmam adhigamya*, C. 内身自證.

13) *saṃskṛta*, T. *ḥdus-byas-pa*, C. 有爲.

'being conditioned' (*saṃskṛta*) means the thing, of which origination, lasting, as well as destruction [14] are conceivable. Because of the absence of these characteristics, the Buddhahood should be seen as having neither beginning, middle nor end, and being represented as the immutable Absolute Body.

2) *anābhoga*: It is free from efforts because all dualistic views [15] and false discriminations [16] have ceased to exist.

3) *aparapratyayâbhisaṃbodhi:* It is 'enlightened without any help of others' (*aparapratyayôdaya*) because it is realized through one's innate knowledge. Here the word '*udaya*' means 'perfect enlightenment' (*abhisaṃbodha*), in which the sense 'origination' is implied [17]. Thus, as being Tathāgata, though it is immutable and of the characteristic of non-activity, the whole action of the Perfectly Enlightened One proceeds without any effort, ceaselessly and uninterruptedly as far as the world exists [18].

4) *Jñāna*, 5) *karuṇā*, & 6) *śakti:* Thus, not having heard the Buddhahood, which is a quite marvellous and unthinkable sphere, from somebody else, but having perfectly cognized its unutterable nature 'by oneself' (*svayam*), i.e. by means of self-born knowledge which needs no tea-

[14] *utpāda*, T. *skye-ba*, C. 生; *sthiti*, T. *gnas-pa*, C. 住; and *bhaṅga*, T. *ḥjig-pa*, C. 滅, respectively. Sometimes, inserting *anyathātva* (C. 異) between *sthiti* and *bhaṅga*, we count 4 characteristics of *saṃskṛta*. Cf. *Abhidharmakośa*. II. 45 and comm. Here, these 3 are implied the beginning, middle and end, as in the *śloka*.

[15] *prapañca* (Pāli *papañca*), T. *spros-pa*, C. 戯論. T. shows merely a literal translation of the term *prapanca* (*pra*-$\sqrt{}$*pac* or -$\sqrt{}$*pañc*, to spread out, to enlarge). But, in Buddhist thought, this term signifies 'pluralistic view'. i.e. a view, by which the one entity is regarded as plural, manifold (= *prapañca-vacana*) and not 'the phenomenal world' as in the Vedānta philosophy. C. means literally 'frivolous talk', which shows almost the exact sense of this Buddhist term. That is to say, from the Buddhist point of view, any pluralistic view is considered as a false view. In the Buddhist texts, the term is usually accompanied by *vikalpa*.

[16] *vikalpa*, T. *rnam-par rtog-pa*, C. 虚妄分別 (sometimes only 分別).

[17] T. reading "*odaya ni ḥdir mṅon-par-rtogs-pa-la ḥdod-kyi, skye-ba-la ni ma yin-no*" means "here the word '*udaya*' is to be understood in the sense of '*abhisambodha*' and not in the sense of '*utpāda*'", as O translated. Though it is not a literal translation of Skt, it catches the significance quite well. '*Kyi*' of '*ḥdod-kyi*' in the above sentence is a conjunction of two clauses, showing an opposite sense between them. (*udaya*, *utpāda* = *tathāgatôtpatti*, by which is meant originally the acquisition of Enlightenment by Śākyamuni. Cf. Pāli AN. I, 13. Ekapuggala-vaggo.)

[18] *ā saṃsārakoṭeḥ*, C. 無始世來 (from the beginningless past). Cf. S. p. 32, l. 4 (*ā saṃsārāt*), p. 79, l. 17 (*ā bhavagateḥ*), p. 88, l. 4 and p. 113, l. 4 (*ā bhavasthiteḥ*), p. 112, l. 9 (*ā bhavâgrataḥ*).

cher[19], and, with respect to his comprehension, in order to enlighten the others too, who are ignorant[20] and blind by birth, [the Buddha] has preached[21] the path to follow[22] that [Buddhahood]. Therefore, [the Buddha] should be understood as being endowed with the supreme Wisdom and Compassion. The fearlessness (*abhayatva*) of Path is due to its transcendency. The transcendency is due to its never again being turned back. With respect to their abolition of the roots of others' Suffering (*duḥkha*) and Defilement (*kleśa*), the power (*śakti*) of Wisdom and of Compassion of the Tathāgata, is explained by means of the examples of sword and thunderbolt, respectively. Of these, the root of Suffering is, in short, one kind of origination of Individuality[23] (*nāma-rūpa*) on the [three] existences[24]. The root of Defilement is anything which is based on the prejudice[25] to the individual existence[26], i.e. wrong view and doubt[27]. Here, the Suffering, as being contracted in the Individuality, should be regarded as having the state of sprout because of its character of origination. As having the character of cutting it, it should be known that the Buddha's power of both Wisdom and Compassion is illustrated by an example of sword. The Defilement, which is contracted in wrong view and doubt and is to be destroyed by the Path of true perception, is difficult to be understood and hardly to be overcome by means of mundane knowledge. Thence, it is akin to the wall concealed by a thick forest. As having the character of breaking, it should be known that Buddha's Power of both Wisdom and Compassion is illustrated by an example of thunderbolt.

19) *anācāryaka* (Pāli *anācaryaka*), T. *slob-dpon med-pa*, C. 不從師聞. Cf. Pāli MN vol. 1, p. 171 (Āryapariyesana-sutta).

20) *abudha* = S. *abuddha*.

21) *vyupadeśa* (BHS) (perhaps a wrong form for Skt. *vyapadeśa*), T. *ston-pa*, C. 說.

22) *anugāmin*, T. *rjes-su rtogs-pa* (= *anubodha*), C. reads instead '*anuttara*'.

23) *nāmarūpa*, T. *min dañ gzugs*, C. 名色. 'mental elements and material elements, by which the individuality is distinguished from each other', '*nāma*' means the 4 skandhas other than '*rūpa*', therefore, *nāmarūpa* is a synonym of *pañcaskandhāḥ*.

24) *bhavāḥ* T. *srid-rnams-pa*, C. 三有 (tribhava).

25) *abhiniveśa* (Pāli *abhinivesa*), false opinion, superstition, T. *mṅon-par źen-pa*, C. 見.

26) *satkāya* (P. *sakkāya*), T. *ḥjig-tshogs* (a collection perishable), C. 有身, physical body.

27) There are 4 kinds of '*kleśas*' which are caused by the wrong discrimination and are to perish by *darśana-mārga*. They are *mithyādṛṣṭi*, *dṛṣṭi-parāmarśa*, *śīlavrataparāmarśa* and *vicikitsā*. *satkāyadṛṣṭi* is, on the contrary, an innate defilement, and is to perish by *bhāvanā-mārga*.

§ 2. Reference to the *Jñānâlokâlaṅkāra-sūtra*.

Thus, the six qualities of the Tathāgata mentioned above should be understood by this very order [28] and with detailed and analytical explanation, according to the *Sarvabuddhaviṣayâvatārajñānâlokâlaṃkāra-sūtra* [29]. In that Sūtra, it is said as follows:

> " O Manjuśrī, he who is of no origination or destruction is (i.e. has the epithets) the Tathāgata, the Arhat, the Perfectly Enlightenend One " [30].

By this, first of all, it is explained that the Tathāgata is of immutable character. And immediately after this, by nine illustrations beginning with the illustration of a reflection of the Indra on the surface of an immaculate Vaiḍūrya stone [31], with reference to this very meaning of the Tathāgata's being neither originated nor destructed, it is said as follows [32]:

> " Thus, Mañjuśrī, the Tathāgata, the Arhat, the Perfectly Enlightened One neither moves nor produces any thought [33], neither explains in a dualistic way [34] nor imagines falsely nor discriminates. He is unimaginable, indiscriminative, devoid of thinking [35] and

[28]) *ānupūrvī* (*anupūrvī*?), Pāli, *anupubbī*. T. *go-rims*. Cf. S. p. 31, l. 7: *hetv-ānupurvyā* (Ms. B anu-). See BHS Dic. s.v.

[29]) We have 3 translations of this sūtra in the Chinese Tripiṭaka:

1) 如來莊嚴智慧光明入一切佛境界經 tr. by 曇摩流支 (Dharmaruci), (501 *A. D.*), *Taisho*, No. 357 (12, p. 239-250 *a*); 2) 度一切諸佛境界智莊嚴經 tr. by 僧伽婆羅 (Saṃghabhadra) & c. (511-520 *A. D.*), *Taisho* No. 358 (12, p. 250 *a*-253 *c*); 3) 佛說大乘入諸佛境界智光明莊嚴經 tr. by 法護 & c. (the 11th cent. *A. D.*), *Taisho*, No. 359 (12, p. 253 *c*-265 *b*). Of them, the simplest edition is 2), which seems to show the original type of this sūtra. However, the 9 illustrations on the Buddha's Acts utilized in the *Ratna.* are partly lacking in 2), hence hereafter the equivalency in C. will be shown according to 1) (abbr. JAĀ).

[30]) C. JAĀ, 240 *b*.

[31]) About the 9 illustrations, see Chap. IV (S. p. 99 ff.).

[32]) JAĀ, 240 *c*.

[33]) The term '*viṭhapati*' is to be corrected into '*viṭhapeti*', as a hybrid form of *viṭhapayati*, Caus. of Skt. *vi√sthā*. so, T. *sems-par byed-pa*, C. 不生[心]. Cf. S. p. 49, l. 1. *viṭhapyante*, l. 2. *viṭhapitā*, *viṭhapanā*.

[34]) *prapañcayati*. See Note II-15.

[35]) T. *bsam-du med-pa* (= *acintya*), C. 不思無思不思議 '*acintya*' should be inserted after '*acitta*'.

minding, of quiescent character, of neither origination nor destruction. He cannot be seen, or heard, or smelt, or tested, or touched and has no characteristic remark, has neither making known nor being made known." and so forth.

Such is the explanation of various kinds of aspects of quiescence[36]. By this it is indicated that, in his own acts, all dualistic views and false discriminations have ceased to exist; hence, the Tathāgata is free from efforts.

After this, i.e. after the explanation of [nine] illustrations, there is explained by the remaining texts the Tathāgata's perfect enlightenment realized without any help of others with respect to all the gates to the Perfect Enlightenment of the real nature of all elements[37].

And after this, with reference to the Tathāgata's 16 kinds of Enightenment[38], it is said as follows[39]:

> "There, O Mañjuśrī, as soon as the Tathāgata has enlightened all the elements of such a nature and has observed the essential nature of all living beings as 'impure' 'not removing stains' and 'blemished', the Creat Compassion named 'mastery' sets in forth on all living beings".

By this the Tathāgata's possession of Supreme Wisdom and Compassion is demonstrated. There, "all the elements of such a nature" means '[all the elements, having the nature] as has been said before', i.e. the character of non-existence[40]. Having enlightened" means 'having known truly by means of Buddha's non-discriminative Wisdom'. "Of [all] living beings" means 'of those [living beings] who are in the

36) *upaśamaprabheda-pradeśa*, T. *ñe-bar shi-baḥi tshig-gi rab-tu dbye-ba* (= *upaśamaśabda-prabheda* ?), C. 寂滅差別之相 (= *upaśama-prabheda-lakṣaṇa*). Here '*pradeśa*' seems to mean 'aspect' (*viṣaya* or *gocara*).

37) C. regards '*sarvatathatâbhisaṃbodhamukheṣu*' as a quotation, which is equivalent to JAĀ, 247 *b*.

38) Cf. Note 1–89.

39) JAĀ, 247 *b*. (如來如是覺一切法觀察一切衆生性卽生清淨無垢無點奮迅大慈悲心. ...observing the nature of all living beings, sets forth the Compassion which is 'pure', 'immaculate', 'not blemished' and 'mastery'), The former 3 epithets are translated in an opposite way, but it is probably a wrong translation.

40) '*abhāva-svabhāvāt*' in the text should be corrected to '*abhāvasvabhāvān*', by accepting T. reading '*dṅos-po med-paḥi ṅo-bo-ñid-du* (*Acc.*)*-ḥo*' as an apposition to '*nirdiṣṭān*'.

state of conformed [in right way] (*niyata*–), unconformed (*aniyata*–) and wrongly conformed (*mithyā–niyata*–) groups (*rāśi*) '. " Essential nature (*dharmadhātu*) " [41] means ' the Matrix of the Tathāgata, which is not different from his own quality by nature ' [42]. " Having observed " means ' having perceived all kinds (i.e. impure, etc.) through the Buddha's eye to which nothing is obscure ' [43]. " Impure (*aśuddha*) " means ' [impure nature] of the ignorant and common people ' because of obstruction caused by Moral Defilement (*klēśâvaraṇa*). " Not removing stains (*avimala*) " means ' [stainful nature] of the Śravākas and Pratyekabuddhas ' because of obstruction on account of knowable things (*jñeyâvaraṇa*). " Blemished (*sâṅgana*) " [44] means ' [blemished nature] of Bodhisattvas ', because of [their] retaining [the impression of] one of both [obstructions] [45]. [The Compassion is " named] mastery (*vikrīḍitā*) " [46] because it enters well into the gates of accomplished means of training in various ways (vividhā) [47]. " The great Compassion sets forth on all living beings ", because [the Buddha], having realized [48] the characteristics of all living beings through

[41]) T. *chos–kyi dbyiṅs*, C. 法性 in the quotation (instead of the usual '法界'). But here C. has '法界' 'along with' '法性, 法體' (*dharmatā, dharmasvabhāva* ?).

[42]) (*sattvānāṃ*) *dharmadhātu* = *svadharmatā–prakṛtinirviśiṣṭa–tathāgatagarbha.*

[43]) C. explains the words from '*sarvasattvānām*' to '*avalokya*' together.

[44]) T. *skyon–dań bcas–pa*, C. 有點 cf. BHS. Dic. *aṅgana*, *sāṅgana*, s.v.

[45]) Instead of '*tadubhayâniyatama–viśiṣṭayā*' in the text, the reading should be '*tadubhayânyatamâvaśiṣṭatayā*'. For '*avaśiṣṭatā*' (remained), T. *lhag–ma*, and C. '習氣' shows nearly the same meaning.

[46]) T. *rnam–par–brtse–ba*, instead of the usual *rnam–par rol–pa*, (*brtse–ba* = *sneha* [affection], hence the whole means 'taking compassion in various ways'?). On the contrary C. translates it by '奮迅', which is usually equivalent to '*vijṛmbhita*' (manifestation of the Buddha's power). The term *vikrīḍita* is often used in the sense of 'having perfect mastery' in BHS as E. mentioned (e. g. *trivimokṣamukha–vikrīḍito*, *Lalitavistara*). Here, being an epithet or an apposition to '*karuṇā*', the feminine form is used.

[47]) The reading of this passage is rather obvious. There is no exact concordance between S., T. & C. The prefix '*vi–*' is interpreted by '*vividhā*', in common with S., T. & C., but T. connects this '*vividhā*' to '*mukha*' and C. uses this word twice, once connecting to '*upāya*' and in the second case, to '*mukha*'. On the contrary, S. connects it to '*supraviṣṭa*'. For '*vinayôpāya*', both T. & C. read as '*vineyôpāya*'. But there seems to be not so much difference between both terms as to their sense. Cf. S. v. IV–1 '*vineyadhātau vinayâbhyupāye*'. C. translation of this passage runs as follows:

" It is '*vikrīḍitā*' because [the Buddha], having known (= *sampanna* ?) the various means by which living beings are to be converted, enters the various gates of that means ".

[48]) The reading '*abhisaṃbuddhabodheḥ*' in the text is doubtful. T. *mṅon–par rdsogs–*

equality [49], has the intention to lead [the living beings] to the acquisition of their own nature [50]. After this, i.e. having aroused the supreme Wisdom and Compassion, [the Buddha] has no relaxation of activity for effectuating the setting in motion of the Wheel of unparalleled Doctrine. This [activity] should be known as 'power' of both [Wisdom and Compassion] in regard of acting for the sake of others.

7) *Svârthasaṃpad* & 8) *parârthasaṃpad*: Here, of these six qualities of the Tathāgata, according to order [the quality] connected with the first three qualities, immutable, etc. is 'the fulfilment of self-benefit' (*svârthasampad*), and [the quality connected with] the remaining three, Wisdom, etc. is 'the fulfilment of benefit for others' (*parârthasaṃpad*). Besides [there is another meaning]. By the word 'Wisdom', the fulfilment of self-benefit is designated, in so far as the highest, eternal and quiescent place [51] has the character of being the basis of his own perfect enlightenment. By the words 'Compassion' and 'Power', the fulfilment of benefit for others is designated, because of their character of being the basis for setting forth the Wheel of the highest and greatest Doctrine.

par byaṅ-chub-pas na (*abhisaṃbodheḥ*), C. seems to have a double expression '證大菩提', but it is not certain whether it is the translation of this term or that of '*adhigamaprāpaṇa*' (leads to the acquisition), because there is another expression '成大菩提', after '*wahākaruṇā iti*', and '證大菩提' seems to be connected with '爲欲令 ...' (in order to, or having intention to) as an apposition to '如是覺知' (to enlighten the same as the Buddha, i.e. to enlighten the Highest Enlightnement). If so, '證大菩提' is merely an interpreting word by the Chinese translator. And even if we accept the double expression, still it is better to be '*abhisaṃbodhi-buddhyā*'.

49) *samatayā*, id., the equality, or the lack of difference (*nirviśiṣṭatā*) between the Buddha himself and all *sattvas*. See, Note II-42, VII - I. Cf. The *Tathāgatagarbhasūtra*, the *Tathāgatôpattisambhavanirdeśa* (Avat S).

50) C. reads the whole passage as follows:

"'*mahākaruṇā*' [signifies] that, having attained the Great Enlightenment, [the Buddha] obtains the Great Compassion equally for all living beings with intention to make living beings realize what the Buddha did, i.e. to make them enlighten the Great Enlightenment. Therefore, [it is called '*mahākaruṇā*']." It seems C. takes '*svadharmatā*' as 'Buddha's own nature', i.e. the Enlightenment.

51) *paramanityôpaśāntipada*, C. 第一寂靜法身. Usually, *upaśāntipada* signifies '*nirvāṇa*'.

III. THE JEWEL OF THE DOCTRINE

Now, from the Jewel of the Buddha, there arises the Jewel of the Doctrine. Therefore, immediately after [the explanation of] the former, we have one *śloka* concerning the latter.

(Kārikā 2).

I bow before the sun of the Doctrine,
Which is neither non-being nor being,
Nor both being and non-being together,
And neither different from being nor from non-being [1];
Which cannot be speculated upon and is beyond explanation,
But revealed [only] by introspection [2] and is quiescent;
And which, with rays of light of the immaculate Wisdom,
Destroys passion, hatred [3] and darkness [4]
with respect to all the basis of cognition [5]. // 9 //

[1] This alternative proposition is called '*catuṣkoṭikā*'. Cf. *Madhyamaka-kārikā* I, 7, *Mahāyānasūtrâlaṅkāra* VI, 1, *Laṅkāvatāra* p. 122, l. 4–8, etc.

[2] *pratyātmavedya* (= *pratyātmavedanīya* in comm.), T. *so-so-raṅ-gyis rig (-par-bya-ba)*, C. 內心知, 內證法.

[3] *doṣa* (BHS for Skt. *dveṣa*, Pāli *dosa*), T. *sdaṅ(-ba) (she-sdaṅ)*.

[4] *timira*, T., *rab-rib*. It means doctrinally the ignorance, *moha* or *avidyā*. So C. 癡 (*moha*). But, in comparison with the simile of the sun, what is to be destroyed is *timira* (the sun is often referred to by such terms as *timiracchid*, *timiranāśana*, *timiranud*, *timiraripu*, *timirâri*, etc., cf. M. W. Skt. Dictionary, s.v.) and C. 曀障 seems to show this sense.

[5] *ārambaṇa* (*āramvana* in the text is probably a misprint) (BHS fr. Pāli *ārammaṇa* = Skt. *ālambana*), T. *dmigs-pa*, C. 覺觀 or 曀障覺觀? C. translation is curious. '覺觀' means usually '*vitarka-vicāra*' and I could not trace the use of '覺觀' for '*ārambana*' in other texts. But, viz. Note VI–70 (for *cittârambaṇa*, C. 心所念觀) and XVII–187 (for '*nirālamba*', C. 無觀). The present transla-

§ 1. Eightfold Quality of the Doctrine [6].

What is shown by this *śloka*?

Because of its being unthinkable, non-dual,
and being non-discriminative,
And because of its pureness, manifestation and hostility;
The Doctrine, which is Deliverance and also
by which arises Deliverance
Has the characteristics of the two Truths. // 10 //

By this verse, in brief, the Jewel of the Doctrine is explained as being contracted by eight qualities. Which are the eight qualities? They are 1) unthinkability (*acintyatva*), 2) non-duality (*advayatā*), 3) non-discriminativeness (*nirvikalpatā*), 4) purity (*śuddhi*), 5) [being] manifest (*abhivyaktikaraṇa*), 6) hostility [against obstacles] (*pratipakṣatā*), 7) Deliverance [from passions] (*virāga*), and 8) cause of Deliverance (*virāgahetu*) [7].

tion is according to T. The C. translation for the whole line runs as follows:

"Destroys several kinds of darkness (瞪障), i.e. researching and investigation (覺觀) [by discriminative mind], passions, hatred and ignorance, and all [other] defilements".

In the light of the commentary, '瞪障' seems to be equivalent to *vibandha*', and '覺觀' to *vikalpa* or *ayoniśomanasikāra*, and C. translation is more understandable than S.

About the use of the term '*ārambaṇa*', see below (Note III-39). Cf. BHS Dic. s. v. (*ārambaṇa* & *ālambana*).

6) Cf. *Buddhagotraśāstra* (BGŚ) 801 *b* ff. (under Chap. IV, [V] *vṛtti*, where these 8 categories are explained as the qualities of the Buddha's '*āśrayaparivṛtti*').

7) Terms in v. 10 and translations of these 8 in T. & C., as well as in BGŚ are as follows:

1) *acintya, bsam-du med-pa-ñid,* 不可思議 (BGŚ 不可思量); 2) *advaya, gñis-su med-pa-ñid,* 不二 (BGŚ 無二); 3) *niṣkalpa, rnam-par rtog-pa med-pa-ñid,* 無分[別]; 4) *śuddhi, dag-pa,* 淨, (BGŚ 清淨); 5) *vyakti, mṅon-par gsal-bar (byed-pa),* 現, 顯現 (BGŚ 照了因); 6) *vipakṣa gñen-poḥi phyogs-ñid,* 對治, 對; 7) *yo virāgaḥ, ḥdod chags daṅ bral-ba,* 離果 (BGŚ 離欲), & 8) *yena virāgaḥ, ḥdod-chags daṅ bral-baḥi rgyu,* 離因 (BGŚ 離欲因). Cf. BGŚ 801 *b*.

§ 2. *Nirodha-satya* and *Mārga-satya*.

Deliverance [8] is summarized
In both truths, Extinction and Path,
Which [9] are each to be known
By three qualities according to order. // 11 //

Of these six qualities, by the first three qualities, i.e. unthinkability, non-duality and non-discriminativeness, the Truth of Extinction is explained. From this [explanation] it should be known that the Deliverance [itself] is contracted. And by the remaining three qualities, i.e. purity, manifestation and hostility, the Truth of Path is explained, and from this, it should be known that the cause of Deliverance is contracted. "That which is Deliverance" means [the Doctrine, as] the Truth of Extinction, and "by which arises the Deliverance" means 'by [the Doctrine as] the Truth of Path.' Having joined these two together [10], it is explained, 'being of the nature of Deliverance (*virāgadharma*) [11]' means 'having characteristic of the two purifying Truths [12].

§ 3. The Doctrine as the Truth of Extinction.

Because of its being beyond speculation and explanation,
And because of its being the knowledge of Saints [13],
Unthinkability [of the Doctrine should be known];

8) '*virāgitā*', the state of being *virāgin* (one who is passionless). T. '[*ḥdod*-]*chags* [*daṅ*] *bral*[-*ba*]-*ñid*' seems equivalent to '*virāgatā*'. C. '離' also shows nothing special. The meaning of this word is shown below by the term '*virāgadharma*', which is the common nature of both '*nirodhasatya*' & '*mārgasatya*'. Hence 'virāgatā' seems here a more natural form than '*virāgitā*'.

9) The reading '*ete*' in the text should be understood in the sense '*yābhyāṃ nirodha-mārgasatyābhyām* ... *te* (*ete*) *veditavye*'. C. translates '*nirodha-mārga-satyābhyām*' as the subject, and takes '*saṃgṛhīta*' as active voice. Consequently there is no difficulty in C. reading.

10) *abhisamasya* (gr. of *abhi-sam-√as*), T. *mṅon-par bsdus te*, C. 合 ....

11) C. 離法. This is an interpretation of the word '*virāgitā*' (or *virāgatā*) in v. 11. See above.

12) *vyavadāna-satyadvaya-lakṣaṇa*, T. *rnam-par byaṅ-baḥi bden-pa gñis-kyi mtshan-ñid*, C. 淨法二諦相 '*vyavadānasatyadvaya*' means 'the 2 *satyas* concerned with purification' i.e. *nirodhasatya* and *mārgasatya*, and is opposite to '*duḥkhasatya*' and '*samudayasatya*', which are, in their turn, to be termed '*saṃkleśasatyadvaya*'.

13) *ārya*, T. *ḥphags-pa*, C. 智者.

Because of quiescence it is non-dual and non-discriminative,
And three [qualities], purity etc., are akin to the sun. // 12 //

1) *acintyatva:* Unthinkability of the Truth of Extinction, in short, should be known by three causes. By which three? Because, 1) it is not a sphere of speculation even by four categories [of existence] [14], i.e non-being, being, being and non-being together, and neither being nor non-being; 2) it cannot be explained by any sound, voice, speech, way of speech, explanation, agreed term, designation, conversation [and so forth] [15]; and 3) it is to be revealed by the introspection of Saints.

2) *advayatā* & 3) *nirvikalpatā*. How should here be understood non-duality and non-discriminativeness of the Truth of Extinction? It is taught by the Lord as follows [16]:

" O Śāriputra, quiescent [17] is this Absolute Body [of the Buddha], having the nature [18] of being non-dual and non-discriminative ".

Here, 'dual' (*dvaya*) [19] means 'action' or 'active force' (*karman*), [as by deed, word and thought] ' [20] and 'Defilement (*kleśa*); 'discrimination (*vikalpa*) means 'Irrational Thought (*ayoniśomanasikāra*)' [21] which is the cause of origination of Action and Defilements. By knowing deeply that

14) So-called '*catuṣkoṭikā*'. See above.

15) *ruta*, T. *sgra* (= *śabda*), C. 聲 ; *ravita* (artificial sound), T. *skad* (= *bhāṣā*), C. 響 (echo ?); *ghoṣa*, T. *brjod-pa* (= *vacana*), C. 名 ; *vākpatha*, T. *ṅag-gi yul*, C. 字 ; *nirukti*, T. *ṅe-tshig*, C. 章 ; *saṃketa*, T. *brda*, C. 句 ; *vyavahāra*, T. *tha-sñad*, C. 相貌 ; *abhilāpa*, T. *mṅon-par brjod-pa*, C. 言語, respectively. Equivalency to each term in C. is not sure. About the etymology of '*vyavahāra*', see Note VIII-(IX) A-61.

16) AAN 467 *b*, (BGŚ also quotes this sentence).

17) *śiva*, C. 清涼. But T. *hgog-pa* (= *nirodha*), perhaps in the sense that '*śiva*' is an epithet of '*nirodha*'.

18) *dharman* (ifc). In another passage, the same sentence is quoted changing '*dharmā*' into '*dharmatayā*'. (S. p. 44, l. 14). It seems to be the original reading and is preferable here.

19) C· 何者是二而說不二 (what are two, of which is taught 'non-dual'?).

20) See below (S. p. 13, l. 7 ff.). Cf. PTS Dic ('*kamma*') Whenever '*karman*' and '*kleśa*' are mentioned side by side, the former signifies the actual deed by body, word and thought, of which the cause is '*kleśa*'. But in the relation to '*janman*', i.e. the next birth, '*karman*' is the cause of '*janman*' (or *bhava*). In this sense '*karman*' should be regarded as the 'active force', some kind of energy and has a sense similar to '*saṃskāra*'.

21) T. *tshul-bshin ma-yin-pa yid-la byed-pa*, C. 邪念 (不正思惟). As for its being a cause of Defilements and Actions, see S. p. 13 and p. 42, l. 10 ff.

this Irrational thought is extinct by nature, consequently, there is no origination of duality and discrimination; for this reason there is absolutely no origination of Suffering. This is called the Truth of Extinction of Suffering. It should never be explained that, because of extinction of something, it is [called] the Truth of Extinction of Suffering. It is said as follows [22]:

> "O Mañjuśrī, in case there is neither origination nor extinction, mental actions as mind, intellect and consciousness never take place [23]. Wherever no mental action takes place, there is no false imagination by which they would think irrationally. One who applies himself with rational thought never makes Ignorance arise. Non-arising of Ignorance means non-arising of the Twelve Parts of Existence (*dvādaśa-bhavâṅga*) [24]. It is called 'non-birth(*ajāti*) [25].'" and so forth.

Also said [in the scripture] [26].

> "O Lord, extinction of Suffering does not mean the disappearance of element. By the term, 'Extinction of Suffering', O Lord, there is designated the Absolute Body of the Tathāgata which is beginningless [27], immutable, of no birth, non-originated, of no destruction, free from destruction, eternal, constant, quiescent, everlasting [28], purified by nature, released from covering of

22) JAĀ 247 *a*. Cf. AĀS (beginning of Chap. II, p. 469 *b*) BGŚ quotes the first sentence from AĀS and regards the remaining as its own explanation. (BGŚ 801 *c*).

23) *citta-mano-vijñāna*, T. *sems dan yid dan rnam-par śes-pa*, C. 心意意識 (but AĀS & BGŚ, 心意識). These three are synonymous with each other and here seem to have no special meaning as in the Vijñānavāda. (in BGŚ, however, Paramārtha interprets that '*citta*' means the 'former' (i.e. the usual set of) 6 *vijñānas*, '*manas*' '*ādāna-vijñāna*', and '*vijñāna*', '*ālayavijñāna*'. It is quite against the Vijñānavādin's way of interpretation.)

24) i. e. the chain of causation (*pratītyasamutpāda*), starting with '*avidyā*'.

25) T. *mi-skye(-ba)*, C. 無生 (BGŚ 不生). '*ajāti*' = '*anutpādânirodha*'. The term '*ajāti*' reminds us of the idealistic philosophy of Gauḍapāda.

26) ŚMS 221 *c*. Cf. BGŚ 801 (quotation from ŚMS).

27) *anādikālika*, T. *thog-ma med-paḥi dus-can*, C. 無始 [無始世來]. This is usually an adjective to '*dhātu*'. See S. p. 72, l. 13.

28) These 4, *nitya*, *dhruva*, *śiva*, & *śāśvata*, (T. *rtag-pa*, *brtan-pa*, *shi-ba*, *mi-ḥjig-pa*; C. 常恒清涼不變) are often used in this treatise as the modifiers of '*dharmakāya*' or the Absolute Truth. See below (S. p. 20, l. 10; p. 53, vv. 81, 82, p. 54, l. 12 ff., etc.) Cf. AĀS (which has the passage after '*asaṃskṛta*' up to the end of this quotation), 常恒寂住, respectively (496 *b*) BGŚ 常住恒寂湛然 (801 *c*).

all moral defilements, and endowed with inseparable and unthinkable qualities of the Buddha, which are far more than the sands of the Gaṅgā in number[29]. And this very Absolute Body of the Tathāgata, O Lord, [when it is] unreleased from the covering of moral defilements, is called the Matrix of Tathāgata." [30]

Thus all the determination of the Truth of Extinction of Suffering should be understood wholly and in detail according to Sūtras.

§ 4. The Doctrine as the Truth of Path[31].

4) *śuddhi*, 5) *abhivyaktikaraṇa* & 6) *pratipakṣatā*: Now indeed, the way to attain the Absolute Body of Tathāgata named Extinction of Suffering is the Path of perception and practice[32] based upon the non-discriminative Wisdom (*avikalpa-jñāna*)[33]. And this [Path] is to be known as similar to the sun with threefold common characteristics[34]. [Namely] 1) through the common characteristic of purity of the disk, because of being apart from all the minor defilements and stains; 2) through the common characteristic of being the manifestor of forms, because of making manifest knowable things of all kinds; and 3) through the common

[29] ... *gaṅgāvālikāvyativṛttair avinirbhāgair acintyair buddhadharmaiḥ samanvāgatas* .... For this expression, see Note I-23. (quotation from AAN). The term '*amuktajñair*' had better be inserted after '*avinirbhāgair*', because, except the present Skt. text and T., all other editions i.e. C., ŚMS (both T. & C.), AĀS & BGŚ, have this term. (C. 不脱不異); ŚMS, T. *brol-bar śes-pa* (= *muktajña*), C. 具解脱智; AĀS; 不捨智 BGŚ 不捨離智 the last two seem to show the best translation.) The term '*samanvāgata*' makes the idea signified by '*gaṅgāvālikā* ... quite clear.

[30] *tathāgatakāyo* '*vinirmuktakleśakośas tathāgatagarbhaḥ* --. This is a famous definition of the term '*tathāgatagarbha*'. Chinese refer to this often by '在纏位法身'.

[31] Cf. BGŚ 802 *a* (離欲因).

[32] *darśana-mārga*, T. *mthoṅ-baḥi lam*, C. 見道; & *bhāvanā-mārga*, T. *sgom-paḥi lam*, C. 修道. '*darśana-mārga*' signifies the first Stage of the Bodhisattva, and '*bhāvanā-mārga*' those Stages after the second one.

[33] T. *rnam-par mi-rtog-paḥi ye-śes*, C. 無分別智.

[34] Similarity of '*jñāna*' to the sun is also referred to in S. p. 58, vv. 93 ff., p. 107 ff. (*sūryavad iti*, and forth), etc.

characteristic of hostility against darkness, because of being the enemy of all kinds of obstacles against the true perception [35].

And ' bondage ' (*vibandha*) [36] means the origination of Desire, Hatred and Ignorance [37] preceded by the thought [38] which takes its basis [of cognition] upon the characteristic of unreal things [39]. It is due to the union of the state of tendency (*anuśaya*) with manifested state (*paryutthāna*) [of defilement] [40]. Indeed, people regard the unreal, i.e., 'not of its nature (*atatsvabhāva*) ' thing as the [real] characteristic because of its desirable looks (*śubhâkāra*) [41] when Desire comes forth from its state of tendency; when Hatred comes forth [from its state of tendency], [they regard the unreal thing as the real characteristic] because of its detestable looks (*pratighâkāreṇa*); and when Ignorance comes forth, then it is the same because of its obscure looks (*avidyâkāreṇa*). And of those people who

35) T. *de-kho-na mthoṅ-ba* (= *tattva-darśana*). By reason of this T. translation as well as by the reading ' *sarvâkārasya tattvadarśanavibandhasya* ' in S. p. 13, l. 17, the uncertain passage in Ms. B. (see J. fn. 8 in S. p. 12) should be read ' *tattva* ' instead of ' *satya* ' inserted by J. C. has no equivalent term, but BGŚ, 真見.

36) T. *gegs*, C. 所治法 (the thing to be dispelled), BGŚ 暗障. This word seems to stand for ' *timira* ' in the kārikā.

37) *rāga*, T. *ḥdod-chags*, C. 貪; *dveṣa*, T. *she-sdaṅ*, C. 瞋 *moha*, T. *gti-mug*, C. 癡, respectively.

38) *manasikāra*, T. *yid-la byed-pa*, C. 虛妄分別念. As being based upon the unreal feature, it should be *ayoniśomanasikāra* ' in its implied sense. Or ' *ayoniśo manasikāra* ' = ' *abhūtavastu-nimitta-ārambaṇa-manasikāra* '. See below.

39) *abhūta-vastu-nimitta-ārambaṇa*, T. *yaṅ-dag-pa ma-yin-paḥi dṅos-po rgyu-mtshan-gyi yul*, C. 取不實事相. T. regards the term '*ārambaṇa*' as '*viṣaya*' (sense object) and connects it with '*abhūta-vastu-nimitta*' by the genitive case. As for the relation of this ' *ārambaṇa* ' to ' *manasikāra* ', T. seems to regard it as being appositional. On the contrary, C. understands '*ārambaṇa*' in the sense of 'taking hold of' or 'grasping'. This verbal sense seems better here than the nominal sense, because '*arāmbaṇa*' is a kind of act, determining the characteristic of ' *manasikāra* '. In other words, ' *manasikāra* ' here is determined as ' *abhūtavastunimitta-ārambaṇa* ', i.e. the act of taking hold of '*abhūtavastu-nimitta* ' [as real]. From the point of Skt. grammar, however, the compound ' *abhūta* ... *ārambaṇa* ', being appositional to ' *manasikāra* ', makes a Bahuvrīhi compound, and hence is to be understood in the sense '[*manasikāra*] whose *ārambaṇa* is *abhūtavastu-nimitta* ' and ' *ārambaṇa* ' can be translated into ' sense-object '. If we construe T. translation in the light of this Skt. way, ' *can* ' should be inserted after ' *yul* '.

40) *anuśaya*, T. *bag-la ñal-ba*, C. 結使煩惱 (but usually 隨眠) ' sleeping state ', ' potential state '; and for *paryutthāna*, T. *kun-nas ldan-pa*. C. om. (but usually 纏) = *paryavasthāna* (S. 67, l. 17). See note IX-77.

41) For ' *śubhâkāra* ', C. 念?

incorrectly take hold of characteristics of Desire, Hatred and Ignorance as the basis of cognition [42], the Irrational Thought occupies their mind. For those people whose mind is occupied with the Irrational Thought, there takes place the Defilement of any one of Desire, Hatred and Ignorance. Due to this [origination of Defilement], they make the actions born of Desire by means of body, speech and thought, and also [in the same way] they produce the action born of Hatred, the action born of Ignorance. Furthermore, from Action there results Rebirth. Thus these people, having tendencies [of Desire, Hatred and Ignorance], regarding the [unreal] characteristic [as real], and making it the basis of cognition, [affectionally] hanging on it [43], produce the Irrational Thought, from which consequently arises Defilement. Because of origination of Defilement, there arises Action; from the origination of Action, there arises Rebirth. And all kinds of impurity (*saṃkleśa*) [44] of these Defilements, Action Rebirth, etc. come forth because people do not know, nor perceive the one [real] essence [45] as it is [46].

42) *rāgadveṣamoha-nimittam ayathābhūtam ārambaṇam kurvatām.*

Here, for '*ārambaṇa*', T. *dmigs-pa*, C. as before (取). *ayathābhūtam* can be regarded as an adjective to *ārambaṇa*, but from the context, I rendered it into an adverbal sense.

43) Here ordinary beings (*bala*) are said to be '*anuśayavat*', '*nimitta-grāhin*' and '*ārambaṇa-carita*'. (C. om. the latter two). For '*nimitta-grāhin*', T. *mtshan-par ḥdsin-pa-can*, and for '*ārambaṇa-carita*' T. *dmigs-pa-la spyod-pa*. Here '*ārambaṇa* seems to show more clearly the sense of 'an action to hang on '. These three show successive activities of mind preceding to '*manasikāra*'. Cf. BGŚ 802 *a*: 真見暗障 (*tattvadarśana-vibandha*) 謂, 具足想, 煩惱難, 業難, 果報難. 具足想, 以隨眠煩惱 (*anuśaya*) 爲因, 五塵欲為緣, 不正思惟 (*ayoniṣomanasikāra*) 為俱起因, 具此三故, 名為具足想.

(The *tattvadarśanavibandha* means (1) a complexed action of mind, (2) *kleśa-saṃkleśa*, (3) *karma-saṃkleśa*, and (4) *janma-saṃkleśa*. [Of them], (1) a complexed action of mind is [a mental activity], of which the Defilements in dormant state are causes, affections towards the five sense-objects are conditions, and the Irrational Thought is the cause of associated origination. Because of the association of these three, it is called 'a complexed action of mind').

44) *saṃkleśa*, T. *kun-nas ñon-moṅs-pa*, C. 染 (雜染). A general term for *kleśa*, *karman* & *janman*, etc., i. e. all the phenomenal life.

45) *eka-dhātu*, C. 一實性界, (BGŚ 一界) T. *khams gcig*. It may be termed *dharmadhātu*, *dharmatā*, i. e. the Absolute. It is also identical with *cittaprakṛti*.

46) About the process of origination of the phenomenal life (*saṃkleśa*) see S. p. 42 f. (v. 58 f.). In this process, '*ayoniśomanasikāra*' occupies the important role, and this '*ayoniśomanasikāra*' is defined as '*vikalpa*' (S. p. 12, l. 2) or '*abhūtavastunimittārambaṇa-manasikāra*' (S. p. 13, l. 1) (see Note 38, 39). The function of '*ayoniśomanasikāra*' is to be compared to that of '*manas*' in the Vijñānavāda.

[On the other hand] these impurities should be seen in the same manner as by a perfect investigator[47] who does not perceive any [unreal] characteristic nor any basis of these impurities. [Because], when he perceives neither characteristic nor basis, then can he perceive the Reality[48]. Thus, these elements[49] are perfectly realized by the Tathāgata as equal through equality[50]. And thus, this realization of all natures by Wisdom, as being equal without any addition nor diminution because of these two facts, i.e. because we cannot see any characteristic nor basis of non-being[51], and we can see the real character of being as the absolute truth, this is to be known as the 'enemy' (*pratipakṣa*) of all kinds of obstacles against the true perception. And because of the origination of this enemy, there is absolutely no association nor harmony[52] of the obstacles. This is indeed the Path of perception and practice based upon the non-discriminative Wisdom, which is the cause of attaining the Absolute Body [of the Tathāgata] and which is to be understood in detail according to the Sūtra named *Prajñāpāramitā*[53].

47) *parigaveṣayat* (one who investigates) (< p. pres. of *parigaveṣayati*, caus. of *parigaveṣate*, seeks for, investigates. BHS Dic. s. v.), T. *yoṅs-su btsal-ba*, C. 觀察.

For '*nimittam ārambaṇam vā*', T. *rgyu-mtshan nam dmigs-pa*, C. 取相 (as if '*nimittârambaṇa*' as in the previous cases). Here the use of '*ārambaṇa*' is obviously objective.

48) *bhūta*, T. *yaṅ-dag-pa*, C. 實性.

49) *dharmāḥ* (pl.), C. 實性, but BGŚ 一切諸法 (*sarvadharmāḥ*).

50) By the term '*iti*', the content of realization is shown.

51) *asad nimittârambaṇa*, which had literally better be translated into 'unreal basis of characteristics'. (Skt. has the sg. g. case-ending) T. *med-pahi rgyu-mtshan-gyi dmigs-pa* and C. 虛妄法相 (unreal characteristics of things) and om. '*ārambaṇa*'.

52) *asaṃgati*, T. *bral-ba; asamavadhāna*, T. *med-pa;* C. 不復生起 for both together.

53) e. g. *Aṣṭasāhasrikā-Prajñāpāramitā* (Wogihara's Edition of AAA pp. 332, l. 9–12; 333, l. 4–7 & 11–15; 334, l. 2–5 & 15–16; 334, l. 22–335, l. 1; 353, l. 12– 14 & 17–18; 354, l. 5–9). Cf. AAA (GOS Edition, p. 230 ff. where a passage from ASP is quoted, for which the original reading is as follows:

"... *tatra bodhisattvayānikaḥ pudgalo yair vastubhiḥ anumodeta yair ārambaṇair yair ākārais tac cittam utpādayet api nu tāni vastūni tāni vā ārambaṇāni te vā ākārās tathôpalabhyeran yathā nimittīkaroti*". (*Wogihara*, p. 332, l. 9–12).

C. inserts a short quotation, running:

"須菩提,真如如來真如平等無差別". (e. g. *Taisho*, VIII, p. 335 *b*).

IV. THE JEWEL OF THE COMMUNITY

Now, from the Jewel of the Doctrine of the Great Vehicle, there arises the Jewel of the Community of Bodhisattvas who are abiding in the irreversible state [1]. Therefore, immediately after [the explanation of] the former, we have one *śloka* referring to the latter.

(Kārikā 3.)

I bow before those who, having understood [2] perfectly
The extremity of non-substantiality of all the worlds as quiescent,
Because of their perception of the unreality [3] of defilements
Through the brightness of the innate pure mind of all the world [4],
Perceive the Buddhahood [5] penetrating everywhere;
Those whose intellect is unobscured,
And whose eye of Wisdom has its objects
In the pureness and infinitude of the living beings. // 13 //

1) *avaivartika* (= *avinivartanīya*), T. *phyir mi-ldog-pa*, C. 不退轉. About the equivalence of this state to the Bodhisattva's '*bhūmi*' or '*vihāra*', there is a variety among the Mahāyāna texts. At the beginning of the development of the '*bhūmi*' theory, there seems to have been 4 divisions of states on account of the Bodhisattva's rank, namely: *prathamacittôtpādika*, *caryāpratipanna*, *avaivartika* & *ekajātipratibaddha* or *abhiṣeka* (of these 4, see S. p. 52, l. 16 ff.). Besides this division, the division of 10 stages also seems to have an old history and as a result of the combination of both, the former 4 have got their place among 10 stages, being ranked as the 1st, 3rd, 7th & 10th, respectively. Confusion occurred after the apperance of the *Avataṃsakasūtra* which established the 41 stages of Bodhisattva, ranking the old 10 stages at the beginning under the name of 10 '*vihāra*'s, and newly creating the 10 '*bhūmi*'s, Pramuditā & c. as the highest group of Bodhisattva's stages. As for '*avaivartika*', it is regarded on one hand as the name for the 7th '*vihāra*', but on another hand, as being equivalent sometimes to the 1st *bhūmi*, sometimes to the 7th *bhūmi*. Here the commentator seems to have used the term '*avaivartika*' as indicating the Bodhisattva on the 1st *bhūmi*. (Cf. S. p. 15, l. 13). See S. p. 16, l. 13; Notes IV-31.

2) *prati-vidh*, T. *rtogs(-pa)*, C. 覺 (or 知).

3) *asvabhāva*, T. *ṅo-bo-med[-pa]*, C. 無實.

4) '*tat*' of the 2nd line of v. 13 indicates '*sarvajagat*' in the 1st line, the '*jagat*' means 'people in the world'.

5) *saṃbuddhatā*, T. *rdsogs-paḥi saṅs-rgyas* (om. *-tā*), C. 佛法身境界 C. has some misunderstanding on the third line and due to this misunderstanding, C. changes the order of the commentary.

§ 1. Manner and Extent of the Perception of the Community.

What is shown by this *śloka*?

Because of its purity of perception by introspective knowledge,
So far as its manner and extent are concerned [6],
The Community of irreversible Bodhisattvas
[Is endowed] with the supreme qualities [7]. // 14 //

By this it is explained, in brief, that the Jewel of the Community of irreversible Bodhisattvas is endowed with supreme qualities, because of its purity of perception by supermundane knowledge, with respect to two aspects, [manner and extent] i.e. 'being as it is' (*yathāvad-bhāvikatā* and 'being as far as' (*yāvad-bhāvikatā*) [8].

[6] *yathāvad-yāvat*, T. *ji-bshin, ji-sñed*, C. 如實 and om. *yāvat*.

[7] C. refers only to '*yathāvat*' here, and consequently replaces the following prose commentary before v. 16.

[8] T. *ji-lta-ba-bshin-yod-pa & ji-sñed-yod-pa*, respectively: C. 如實修行 & 遍修行, resp. C. '修行' for '*bhāvikatā*' is probably a misreading, but see BGŚ 802 *b* where these two are said to be the cause of '*virāgadharma*' representing '*bhāvanā-mārga*' under the names of 如理修 & 如量修. This term '修' is however, replaced by '智' after the next occurrence (如理智 & 如量智). Cf. AĀS 如理, 如量 (470 *c*); *Yogācārabhūmi* (*Bodhisattvabhūmi*) 如所有性 & 盡所有性 (*Taisho*, XXX, 486 *b* etc., BBh, p. 39, ll. 1–2, 215, l. 2, 258, ll. 5–9); *Sandhinirmocanasūtra*, T. *ji-lta-ba bshin-du yod-pa-ñid & ji-sñed yod-pa-ñid* (Lamotte's edition, p. 98 & 99), C. 如所有性 & 盡所有性 (*Taisho*, XVI, 699 *c*). As for their meanings, *Sandhinirmocana* defines them, '*kun-nas ñon-moṅs-pa daṅ rnam-par byaṅ-baḥi chos rnams-la rnam-pa rab-tu dbye-ba thams-cad-kyi mthar thug-pa gaṅ-yin-pa de-ni ji-sñed-yod-pa yin ...*', & '*kun-nas ñon-moṅs-pa daṅ rnam-par byaṅ-baḥi chos de-dag ñid-kyi de-bshin-ñid gaṅ-yin-pa de-ni ji-lta-ba bshin-du yod-pa-ñid yin ...*', respectively. It means '*yāvadbhāvikatā*' signifies all phenomena, pure and impure, while '*yathāvadhbāvikatā*' signifies the essence or the Absolute (*tathatā*) inherent in all phenomena. While the *Bodhisattvabhūmi* says that *yathāvadbhāvikatā* of *dharmas* means their '*bhūtatā*', and *yāvadbhāvikatā* of *dharmas* means *sarvatā*, by both of which the two kinds of '*tattvârtha*' are represented. It seems to show the original sense of these terms. On the other hand. O translates the terms into 'Absolute and Empirical character', i.e. as if '*yathāvad-bh.*' signified *paramârtha-satya*', while '*yāvad-bh.*', '*saṃvṛti-satya*'. This is the traditional way of interpretation in Tibet. But as far as this text is concerned, both of these relate to '*lokottara-jñāna*' or '*lokottara-prajñā*' (S. p. 14, 1–19, p. 15, l. 11), i.e. '*avikalpa-jñāna*' and not to '*laukika-*' or '*tatpṛṣṭhalabdha-jñāna*'. This is rather close to the original interpretation, the only special feature being that the '*yāvad-bh.*' is said to relate to the perception of '*tathāgatagarbha-astitva*' in all living beings. Therefore, O's way seems an overinterpretation.

a) Right Manner of Perception (*yathāvad-bhāvikatā*).

Their manner [of perception] is 'as it is',
Because they have understood the quiescent nature [9] of the world,
And this [understanding] is caused by
The purity [of the innate mind] and
Their perception of the defilement as being destroyed from the outset [10]. // 15 //

Here, 'being as it is (*yathāvad-bhāvikatā*)' should be understood thus: because, [with respect to the manner], they (i.e. Bodhisattvas) have understood the extremity of non-substantiality (*nairātmyakoṭi*) of the whole world called Individualities and Separate Elements (*pudgala-dharma-ākhya*) as it is (*yathāvat*). And this understanding, relating to the non-annihilation [11] of Individualities and Separate Elements because of their nature of absolute quiescence from the outset, is produced, in short, by two causes. Namely, because of their perception of the innate brightness (*prakṛtiprabhāsvaratā*) [12] of the mind, and because of their perception of 'being destroyed from the outset' (*ādikṣaya*), i.e. the extinction of defilements on the mind. Here, these two, i.e. the innate brightness of the mind and the defilement on the mind, are quite difficult to be understood in relation to the fact that, in the immaculate sphere, there is no succession of a second mind because both minds, good and bad, act together as one and the same. Therefore, it is said [13]:

"O Lord, a good mind is momentary [14]; it cannot be afflicted by defilements. The bad mind is [also] momentary; even this [bad] mind cannot be afflicted by defilements. O Lord, defilements cannot

[9] *śānta-dharmatā*, T. *shi-baḥi chos-ñid*, C. 寂靜眞法身. This is a word for '*śivā nairātmyakoṭi*' in *k*. 3.

[10] *ādikṣaya*, T. *gdod-nas zad*, C. 本來無.

[11] *avināśa*, which shows the denial of the conception of destroying something. See S. p. 12, l. 4–5 (on '*nirodha-satya*'). T. *ḥjig-pa med-pa*. C. has a long interpretation: 如實知無始世來本來寂靜無我無法, 非滅煩惱證時始有 (Real perception means the perception of the non-existence and quiescence of individuality and separate element from the outset, and not such a perception as existing after the realization by dispelling the defilements.

Here, '*avināśa*' = *ādikṣaya*, *nirodha*, *niḥsvabhāva*.

[12] T. *raṅ-bshin-gyis ḥod-gsal-ba(-ñid)*, C. 自性清淨 (= *prakṛtipariśuddhi*).

[13] ŚMS 222 *b*.

[14] *kṣaṇika*, T. *skad-cig-ma*, C. 刹尼迦.

touch that mind. [And the mind cannot be touched by the Defilements][15]. O Lord, how is it possible that the mind, of untouchable character[16], can be afflicted by darkness? O Lord, still there is defilement and there is defiled mind. Moreover, O Lord, the meaning that the mind purified by nature is defiled[17] is difficult to be understood ".

Thus, with reference to [the manner of] 'being as it is', the explanation of the meaning 'difficult to be understood' should be understood in detail according to the Sūtra.

b) Unlimited Extent of Perception (*yāvad-bhāvikatā*).

Their extent [of perception] is 'as far as',
Because they perceive the existence
Of the nature of Omniscience[18] in all living beings,
By the intellect[19] reaching as far as
the limit of the knowable[20]. // 16 //

Here, 'being as far as (*yāvadbhāvikatā*)' should be understood thus: because [with respect to the extent], they perceive the existence of the Matrix of the *Tathāgata* in all living beings, up to those who are in the animal kingdom, by means of the supermundane intellect (*lokottara-prajñā*) which reaches as far as the limit of all knowable things[21]. And this perception of Bodhisattvas takes place in the first Stage of the Bodhisattva, because [verily in that Stage], the Absolute Essence is realized in the sense of all-pervading' (*sarvatraga*).

15) Acc. to T. & C., one sentence should be added here (as in brackets). T. *sems ñon-moṅs-pa yaṅ ma-lags na*, C. 心不觸煩惱 = *nâpi cittam saṃkliṣṭam bhavati.*

16) *asparśa-dharmin*, T. *reg-paḥi chos-can ma lags-pa*, C. 不觸法.

17) The reading '*upakleśârtho*' is preferably to be corrected into '*upakliṣṭârtho*'. Cf. S. p. 22, l. 2, *cittasyôpakliṣṭatā duṣprativedhyā.*

18) *sarvajña-dharmatā* = *tathāgatagarbha* (in the comm.)

19) *dhī* = *prajñā* (*lokottara prajñā*).

20) C. in prose: 遍修行 (*yāvadbhāvikatā*) 者，謂遍十地一切境界故 (*jñeya-paryantagatayā*), 見一切衆生有一切智故 (*sarvasattveṣu sarvajñâstitvadarśanāt*). ('*dhyā*' in the 1st line and '*dharmatā*' in the 2nd line are omitted).

21) Cf. S. p. 22, 10 ~ 24, 9 (Quotation from Avat S. *Tathâgatôtpattisaṃbhava-nirdeśa*).

§ 2. Introspective Character of Bodhisattva's Perception.

Thus, what is called 'understanding in such a way',
That is the perception by one's own wisdom.
It is pure in the Immaculate Sphere,
Because it is free from attachment
and has no hindrance [22]. // 17 //

'Thus, in such a way' (*ity evam*), by this way, i.e. through 'being as it is' and 'being as far as'; what is called 'understanding' (*avabodha*) of the supermundane path, is here intended to be the perception of the Saints by the supermundane wisdom of their own (*pratyātmam*), i.e. uncomon to others [23]. And this [perception] is called perfectly pure in comparison with [24] the superficial knowledge of everyday life [25] because, in brief, of two reasons. Which ones? Because it is 'free from any attachment' (*asaṅga*), and because it 'has no hindrance' (*apratihata*) [26]. Here, as its field is the innate purity of the essence of living beings through its being as it is, the perception [of the Saints] is free from any attachment; and through its being as far as, its field is the unlimited number of knowable objects, therefore, that perception has no hindrance [27].

§ 3. Superiority of Bodhisattva's Community.

Through the purity of their perception by wisdom [28],
It is superior as [being the same as] Buddha's Wisdom [29]

22) C. again in prose.

23) i. e. uncommon to Śrāvakas, Pratyekabuddhas and ordinary people. C. 不共二乘凡夫人等.

24) *upanidhāya*, T. -- la *ltos-nas.*

25) *itara-prādeśika-jñāna*, T., *cig-śes ñi-tshe-baḥi ye-śes.* C. takes it as showing the knowledge of Śrāvakas and Pratyekabuddhas. (聲聞辟支佛證智).

26) *asaṅga*, T. *chags-pa med-pa*, C. 無障; *apratihata* (*apratigha* in the verse), T. *thogs-pa med-pa*, C. 無閡 (=無礙); BGŚ 無著 & 無礙, respectively.

27) BGŚ adds some more sentences on '*yathāvad-bhāvikatā*' and '*yāvad-bhāvikatā*', saying that the former is '*hetu*', while the latter is '*phala*', or in comparison with the nature of '*viśuddhi-hetu* of the former, the latter is '*paripūrṇa-hetu*' (802 *b*).

28) The shortage of syllables after '...*śuddhyā*' can be made up by '*hi*' or '*eva*' (*śuddhyaiva*). T. has '*na*' after '*dag-pas*'.

29) For v. 18 *a b*, C. 如實知見道 見清淨佛智 (故) (Because of their perception of pure '*buddhajñāna*' through the Path of the true intuition).

C. has no word equivalent to '*anuttarā*' in the verse, but '勝' in the commentary shows it.

Therefore, the Saints abiding in the irreversible state [30]
Are [worthy of being] the refuge of all living beings. // 18 //

Thus, this 'purity of perception by wisdom' of Bodhisattvas who mounted to the Stage of being irreversible [31] is to be known as 'the supreme', because it approached [32] the highest purity of the perception of Buddha's Wisdom; or otherwise [33], because it is superior to the other qualities of Bodhisattva, donation, moral conduct, etc. [34]. On account of this purity, it is said that Bodhisattvas in the irreversible state are worthy of being the refuge of all living beings.

There is no mention of the Jewel of Community of the Śrāvakas, immediately after the Jewel of Community of the Bodhisattvas, because the former is not worthy of being worshipped [35]. Indeed, there is no wise man who, having known the distinction of qualities between Bodhisattvas and Śrāvakas, casting off the new-moon-like Bodhisattvas, who

30) The reading '*avaivartyād bhavanty āryāḥ*' should be corrected into '*avaivartyā bhavanty āryāḥ*' acc. to both T. & C.

31) *avinivartanīyabhūmi-samāruḍhānāṃ bodhisattvānām*, C. 初地菩薩摩訶薩見道不退地乘. It is clear that *avinirvartanīya-bhūmi* is here regarded as the 1st *bhūmi* of Bodhisattva on which stage he accomplishes '*darśana-mārga*'. In this sense, the term '*jñānadarśanasiddhi*' has the implied meaning of '*darśanamārga*' as in C. translation of v. 18.

32) *upaniṣadgata*, T. *ñe-bar gnas-par ḥgyur-ba.* Cf. AA III, 2. *samyag-āsannatôditaḥ* (produced by sitting perfectly near).

33) vā, T. (*r*)*am* (after *phyir*) It denotes another interpretation of '*anuttarā*'.

34) The first two of the 6 *pāramitās* are mentioned.

35) C. has one verse on the superiority of *bodhisattva-saṅga* from 10 points, and a prose commentary thereon. It seems the present Skt text is lacking one paragraph which was in the original text of C. translation. 10 points of superiority mentioned in C. are as follows:

1) 境界 '*viṣaya*', (觀勝), superiority in perception of objects; 2) 諸功德 *guṇāh*, (功德勝), sup. in qualities; 3) 證智 *adhigama*, (證智勝), sup. in acquisition; 4) 涅槃 *nirvāṇa*, (涅槃勝), sup. in Nirvāṇa as being obtained after salvation of all living beings; 5) 諸地 *bhūmayaḥ*, (諸地勝), sup. in their Stages; 6) 淨無垢 *śuddhi, amala*, (淸淨勝), sup. in purity; 7) 滿足大慈悲 *sampūrṇā,-mahākaruṇā*, (平等心勝), sup. in their compassionate mind regarding people equally; 8) 生於如來家 *jātis tathāgatakule*, (生勝), sup. in their birth, because their birth is *ajāti* (無生) in its ultimate sense; 9) 具足自在通 *vaśitâbhijñāsampad*, (神力勝), sup. in their supernatural powers, 10 *vaśitās*, 6 *abhijñās*, etc.; 10) 果勝最無上 *anuttara-phala*, (果勝) sup. in the accomplishment being the Supreme Enlightenment. (letters in parentheses show the terms in commentary).

have the lustre-disk of Wisdom and Compassion filling with great accumulation of merits and knowledge [36] for the Great Enlightenment, and are standing in the illumination over the group existence (*gaṇa-saṃtāna*) [37] of innumerable living beings and entering the way favourable for going toward the full-moon of the supreme Tathāgata, tries to bow before the Śrāvakas, who in their turn, although having attained certain limited superficial knowledge [38], are standing in the illumination for their own existence (*sva-saṃtāna*) like stars [39]. Indeed, even those Bodhisattvas who have resolved to attain the Enlightenment for the first time [40] by the quality based upon the purity of altruistic intention, can overcome the holy Śrāvakas who are pitiless [41], indifferent to the nourishment of others [42], although having attained perfect purity of immaculate moral conduct and discipline [43]. How much more is the case of the other qualities of Bodhisattvas, 10 Controlling Powers, [44] etc.? Really, it will be said [45]:

36) *puṇya-jñāna-sambhāra*, T. *bsod-nams daṅ ye-śes-kyi tshogs*, C. om. (usually, 福資糧 & 智資糧). Of the 6 *pāramitās*, *prajñā-pāramitā* is called '*jñānasaṃbhāra*', and the other 5 are called '*puṇya-s*'.

37) C. [衆生性] 行稠林 (*gahaṇa-saṃtāna?*), T. om. The meaning is clear as being compared with '*svasaṃtāna*' in case of Śrāvakas.

38) *prādeśika-jñāna*. See above (Note IV-25).

39) The whole passage illustrates the comparison between Buddhas, Bodhisattvas and Śrāvakas by an example of moon and stars, saying that the Buddha is like the full moon, Bodhisattvas are like the new moon; both of them have illumination for others, while the Śrāvakas, being like stars, have light only for their own illumination.

40) *prathamacittôtpādika ... bodhisattva*, T. *sems daṅ-po bskyed-paḥi byaṅ-chub-sems-dpaḥ*, C. 初始發起菩提之心諸菩薩等 (初發心菩薩).

41) *niranukrośa*, T. *rjes-su brtse-ba med-pa*, C. om.

42) *ananyapoṣigaṇya*, T. *gshan rgyas-par byed-pa mi-ldan-pa*, C. 不爲利益他衆生身. C. '衆生身' for '*poṣin*' is probably a misreading for '*poṣa*', which, in its turn, has the same sense as '*puruṣa*' in BHS. See BHS Dic. s. v.

43) *saṃvara*, T. *sdom-pa* (利). See BHS. D. *śilasaṃvara* (under *saṃvara* [1]).

44) 10 *vaśitās* are namely: 1) *āyur-vaśitā*, 2) *citta-v.*, 3) *pariṣkāra-v.* (wealth), 4) *karma-v.*, 5) *upapatti-v.*, 6) *adhimukti-v.*, 7) *dharma-v.*, 8) *praṇidhāna-v.*, 9) *ṛddhi-v.*, & 10) *jñāna-v.*, (Mvyut. 27).

45) '*vakṣyati hi*' in S. shows that the following verses belong to the same text, but not to a quotation from another scripture. Though both T. & C. regard only the following verse as a quotation (T. *gaṅ-gi phyir ...shes-gśad-do*, C. 經中偈言), it seems that the whole passage after '*na hi jātu paṇḍitā*' (Indeed, there is no wise man who ...) up to the end of the verse is a long quotation from some Sūtra (source unknown). The style of these passages seems near to the sūtra style. If it be so, the passage only available in C will be ascertained to be the original *śāstra* passage for which this long quotation is mentioned as the authority.

One who feeds [46] moral conduct for his own sake,
Apart from compassion on the living beings of bad conduct [47],
And who is endowed with pure wealth of moral conduct only for his own nourishment, [48]
Such a saint is never called a man of pure conduct.

One who, having aroused the highest Compassion toward others
And having accepted the moral conduct,
Renders services for others' livelihood like fire, wind, water and earth,
Such a one is a [real] moral man, and others are of sham [49] morality.

[46] *bibharti* (Pres. 3 sg. of *bhṛ*), T. *rnam-rgyas-śiṅ* (= *vivṛddhyā?*), C. 修行.

[47] *praśuddha*, T. *rab-dag-pa*, C. om.

[48] *ātmambhari*, (lit. nourishing oneself, one who nourishes himself) T. *bdag-ñid rgyas-byed*, C. 以爲自身故.

[49] *pratirūpaka* T. *gzugs-brñen*, C. 似非.

V. THE THREE JEWELS AS REFUGES

Now, for what purpose and for the sake [1] of whom did the Lord teach [2] the 3 Refuges (*śaraṇa-traya*)?

In order to show [the virtues of] [3]
The Teacher, the Teaching and Disciples,
With reference to those who belong to 3 Vehicles
And to those who devote themselves to religious observance [4]
Three Refuges were taught [2] [by the Lord]. // 19 // ⌊in 3 forms,

§ 1. 3 Refuges from the Empirical Standpoint.

The teaching: "the Buddha is a Refuge because he is the highest among human beings" [5]; it was established [2], in order to show the virtue of the Teacher (*śāstṛ*), for the sake of those people who approached the nature of Buddha [6] i.e. who belong to the Vehicle of Bodhisattva [7] and those [people who] devote themselves to the highest religious observance of the Buddha.

The teaching: "the Doctrine is a Refuge because it is the highest of what are devoid of passions"; it was established, in order to show the

1) '*adhikṛtya*' has a more concrete sense than usual here. T. '*dbaṅ-du byas-nas*' as usual, but C. 爲 (何 等 人) (for the sake of).

2) *prajñapta* (made known = taught), C. 說. But, T. *rnam-par gshag-pa* (*vyavasthita*) in the introductory sentence and in v. 19. In the commentary, however, there is used '*deśitaṃ prajñaptam*', for which T. *bstan-shiṅ rnam-par gshag-go*, C. 說 立. It seems that the term *prajñapta*' has both senses here.

3) *arthena* = .. *guṇa-udbhāvanârthena* (in the comm.).

4) *kāra* (BHS), C. 供 養. (= *pūjā*, 'homage, worship') (Cf. BHS Dic. s. v.). Usually this term is accompanied by '*kriyā*' and other forms delivered from *kṛ* as in the prose comm. T. translation '*byed*' or '*bya-ba byed*' shows nothing special.

5) *dvipada*. It is interpreted doctrinally that the Buddha is standing on the basis of '*jñāna*' and '*karuṇā*'. (T. *rkaṅ-gñis rnams*, C. 兩 足).

6) *buddhabhāva* (= *bodhi*), T. *saṅs-rgyas-kyi dṅos-po-ñid*, C. 佛 菩 提.

7) The reading is preferably '*bodhisattva-yānikān*' instead of '*bodhisattvān*' in comparison with the uses of '*pratyekabuddhayānikān*' and '*śrāvakayānikān*' in the following paragraphs. Also, T. *byaṅ-chub-seems-dpaḥi theg-pa-baḥi*.

virtue of the Teaching (*śāsana*) of the Teacher, for the sake of those people who approach the enlightenment of profound Doctrine of the dependent origination by [depending on] themselves[8], i.e. who belong to the Vehicle of the Pratyekabuddha and those who are devotees to the highest religious observance of the Doctrine.

The teaching: " the Community [of the disciples] is a Refuge because it is the highest of communities "[9]; it was established, in order to show the virtue of Disciples (*śiṣya*) well enrolled in the Teaching of the Teacher, for the sake of those people who approach in order to understand the voice heard from others, i.e. who belong to the Vehicle of Śrāvaka, and those who are devotees to the highest religious observance in the Community.

Thus, in short, for these three purposes, for the sake of six kinds of people, distinctively did the Lord establish the teaching of these three Refuges from the empirical standpoint [10], in order to make living beings enter the regular method [11].

§ 2. The Doctrine and Community are not the Ultimate Refuges.

As being abandoned, being of deceptive nature,
Being non-existence and being possessed of fear[12], [respectively],
The two kinds of Doctrine and the Community
Are ultimately not the highest Refuge. // 20 //

8) Ms.B reading '*svayaṃ gambhīra–pratītya–dharmânubodha*' is preferable. T. '*raṅ-ñid rten–ḥbrel–gyi chos zab–mo rje–su rtogs–pa . . .*', C. 自然知, 不依他知, 深因緣法. Here, '*pratītya*' (T. *rten–ḥbrel*, C. 因緣) seems to mean '*pratītya samutpāda*'. Pretyekabuddha is said to be a buddha who enlightened the doctrine of *pratītyasamutpāda*.

9) About these three formulae on '*ratna–traya*', see Mvyut. 267.

10) *saṃvṛti–pada–sthānena*. That is to say, from the empirical standpoint, there are 3 Refuges, but from the highest standpoint, only the Buddha is the Refuge. See below.

11) *anupūrvanaya*. T. equals '*yāna*' instead of '*naya*', but C. 次第. 'The regular method' means 'from the lower standard to the higher standard, i.e. from being *adhimukta* to *yānika*, from *saṅga–śaraṇa* to *buddha–śaraṇa*, from *śrāvakayāna* to *bodh.sattvayāna*, according to the faculties of living beings.

12) For these four reasons, the terms used in S. T. & C. are as follows:

1) *tyājya* (T. *spaṅ*, C. 可捨);
2) *moṣadharma* (T. *slu–baḥi chos–can*, C. 虛妄);
3) *abhāva* (T. *med*. C. 無物);
4) *sabhaya* (T. *ḥjigs–daṅ bcas–pa*, C. 怖畏).

T. (D.). reading, '*sdaṅ*' is to be corrected into '*spaṅ*' (fut. of '*spaṅ–ba*').

The Doctrine has two kinds, i.e. the Doctrine as Teaching (*deśanādharma*) and the Doctrine as Realization (*adhigamadharma*) [13]. Of them, the Doctrine as Teaching is [the Doctrine] of *sūtra* and other teachings and it consists of the collection [14] of name, word, and letter. And it is said that this Teaching is akin to the boat [15] because it ends [16] with the acquisition [17] of the Path. The Doctrine as Realization is [again] twofold by the division of cause and result. That is to say, the Truth of Path and the Truth of Extinction in the sense, 'by which realized' and 'that which in realized', [respectively] [18]. Of them, the Path is included in the artificial character. That which is included in the artificial character is of false, deceptive nature (*mṛṣāmoṣadharmin*) [19]. That which is of false, deceptive nature is untrue (*asatya*), that which is untrue is not eternal, and that which is non-eternal cannot be a refuge. And the Extinction realized by this Path also represents, according to the system (*naya*) of Śrāvaka [20], the mere absence of Defilement and Suffering, just like the extinction of a lamp. Also, a non-existence (*abhāva*) cannot be a refuge nor a non-refuge.

'The Community' is a term for the community [of the Saints] belonging to three Vehicles [21]. And they are always possessed of fear (*sabhaya*), because, as learned people, they have taken refuge in the Tathāgata and are seeking for deliverance [22]; [but still] they have [many]

13) On these two categories of '*dharma*', see S. p. 70 (v. 145 and comm.) T. *bstan-paḥi chos* & *rtogs-paḥi chos*, C. 所說法 & 所證法, resp.

14) *kāya*, T. *tshogs*, C. 身. As for these three *kāyas*. See Mvyut, § 104, 95–97.

15) *kola*, T. *gziṅs*, C. 船栰. For '*kolôpama*' Cf. Vaj. C. p. 23; MN, I, 134,135 (*kullūpamo dhammo*).

16) *paryavasāna*, T. *mthar-thug-pa* (*paryanta*). C. translation '證道時滅如捨船栰' catches the meaning well. (This term is for *tyājya* in v. 20).

17) *abhisamaya*, T. *mṅon-par rtogs-pa*, C. 證道.

18) See S. p. 11 (v. 10 and comm.).

19) ('*moṣadharma*' in v. 20). Pāli *musā–mosa–dhamma*. '*mosa*' in Pāli is the intensified form of '*musā*' (deceptive). C. 虛妄, T. *brdsun-pa slu-baḥi chos-can*. See BHS Dic., PTS Dic., s. v.

20) It is remarkable in this text that whenever the subject refers to the unworthiness of Dharma or Saṅgha, the author substitutes Śrāvaka for it and never refers to that of Bodhisattva.

21) For the following passage, see ŚMS 221 *a*. This passage is exactly an extract from that sūtra.

22) *niḥsaraṇa*, T. *ṅe-bar ḥbyuṅ-ba*, C. 離世間 (= *loka-niḥsaraṇa*). It is synonymous with '*mokṣa*'.

things to be done (*sakaraṇīya*) and are approaching (i.e. have not yet realized) [23] the Highest Perfect Enlightenment [24]. How are they possessed of fear? As the Arhats (the Saints of the Vehicle of Śrāvaka), though having extirpated rebirth [25], have not yet destroyed the Impression [of Defilements], there therefore exists always and constantly [26] a strong notion of fear in all physical life [27], as if standing in face of the executioner with raised sword [28]. So they have not attained the ultimate delightful Deliverance [22]. Indeed, [that which is] a refuge [by itself] never seeks for refuges [in others]. Just as living beings, having no refuge, are frightened by this or that fear, and consequently seek for the Deliverance, similarly even the Arhats have their fear, and, being frightened by fear they take refuge in the Tathāgata [29].

And thus one who seeks for a refuge because of his being possessed of fear, will inevitably seek for the deliverance from fear. And as being a seeker of deliverance, with reference to the destruction of the root of fear, a learned man [30] is 'one who has things to be done' (*sakaraṇīya*) [31]. As being a learned man, he is 'one who has undertaken' (*pratipannaka*) to attain the fearless, highest state [32], i.e. the Highest Perfect Enlightenment. For this reason, the Community, being a partial refuge, cannot be the

23) *pratipannaka* (Pāli *paṭipannaka* = *maggaṭṭhaka*, one who has entered upon the Path). It is used here in the sense of 'gone towards', 'entered the way', but not 'attained [the Enlightenment]', and the emphasis is on the approach. Hence C. '未究竟故猶進趣向阿耨多羅三藐三菩提' is quite correct. On the contrary, T. '*shugs-pa ma yin-no*' is probably due to a misunderstanding of this '*pratipannaka*' for the actual attainment of Enlightenment. (For the parallel passage in SMS, T. *shugs-pa lags-so*, where the negative '*ma*' is not used).

24) Cf. ŚMS 221 *a*.

25) *punarbhava*, T. *yaṅ-srid-pa*, C. 有漏 (= *sāsravadharma*).

26) *satata-samitaṃ* (BHS), T. *rtag-tu rgyun mi-ḥchad-par*, C. 常.

27) *saṃskāra*, T. *ḥdu-byed*, C. 有爲行相.

28) The text should have *Daṇḍa* between '*vadakapuruṣe*' and '*tasmāt*'. For *vadakapuruṣa*, T. *gśad-maḥi skye-bu*.

29) C. regards this passage (*arhatām api* ... *śaraṇam upagacchati*) as a quotation from ŚMS, and before the quotation has the same commentary passage as the Skt. text up to '*pratyupasthitā bhavanti*'. Cf. ŚMS 219 *b*.

30) *śaikṣa*, T. *slob-pa*, C. 黠慧人.

31) On the contrary, Buddha is said to be '*aśaikṣa*'. (Cf. *aśaikṣa-sāntānika*, S. p. 39, l. 3.)

32) *ārṣabha* (Lit. coming from a bull, *ṛṣabha*), descendant of Ṛṣabha (name of a former Buddha), Pāli '*āsabha*' means a hero or great man and is an epithet of the Buddha. T. *khyu-mchog* (the highest bull). C. om. '*ārṣabha*'. '*ārṣabha-sthāna*' = Pāli *āsabhaṭṭhāna*, the first place, leadership.

ultimate refuge. Thus these two Refuges, (i.e. the Doctrine and the Community), are called 'temporary refuges'[33].

§ 3. Only the Buddha is the Refuge from the Highest Standpoint.

From the ultimate standpoint[34],
Buddhahood is the sole Refuge of the world,
Because the Sage has the body of the Doctrine,
And because in that the Community sets the ultimate goal[35]. // 21 //

As has been said before, the Sage (*muni*), represented as neither becoming originated nor disappearing, is endowed with the body of the Doctrine, liberated from passions and [characterized[36]] as the Two Truths of purification (i.e. the Truth of Path and the Truth of Extinction), and in the purity of this Body of the Doctrine (= the Absolute Body, *dharmakāya*), the Community [of the Saints] belonging to the three Vehicles sets the ultimate goal of acquisition[37]. Therefore, from the ultimate standpoint, that which is the imperishable Refuge, eternal Refuge, and everlasting Refuge, which lasts as long as the utmost limit[38] in the unprotected and refugeless world, is [only one][39], that is to say, the Tathā-

[33] *paryantakāla-śaraṇa.* '*paryantakāla*' is a Bahuvrīhi comp. meaning 'having *kāla* which has *paryanta*, the end'. Both T. & C., putting a negative, interpret this term as '*nâtyantakāle śaraṇe*'. But it is wrong. (T. *mthar-thung-paḥi dus-na skyabs ma-yin-pa*, C. 非究竟歸依處). A correct translation is shown in ŚMS, where for '*paryantakāla*', T. *dus-kyi mthaḥ-mchis-paḥi*, C. 有限 (having limitation, limited). (ŚMS 221 *a*).

About '*sabhayatā*' of the Śrāvakas, see v. I, 32 and comm.

[34] *pāramārthikam.* In Skt., it is an adjective to '*buddhatva*'. But T. takes it in the adverbial sense, saying '*dam-paḥi don-tu*' (*paramârthataḥ*), which seems better to grasp the meaning in comparison with the Empirical standpoint in v. 19. Also, see the prose comm. on this verse. (C. 彼岸 being an adjective to *buddhatva* as S.).

[35] *niṣṭha* = *niṣṭhâdhigama-paryavasāna*, and *tanniṣṭhatva* = *dharmakāyaviśuddhiniṣṭha.* See below.

[36] T. inserts '*mtshan-ñid*' (*lakṣaṇa*) after '*vyavadana-satya-dvaya*'. It is helpful to make the meaning clear. See S. p. 11, l. 14 (*vyavadānasatyadvaya-lakṣaṇo virāgadharma iti*). C. reads probably '*śivâdvayavirāgadharma*).

[37] *niṣṭhâdhigama-paryavasāna*, T. *mthar-thug-pa thob-pas mthar phyin-par ḥgyur-ba*, C. 究竟清淨處 (om. *adhigama*).

[38] *aparântakoṭisama*, T. *phyi-maḥi mthaḥi mu-daṅ mñam-pa*, C. 無始本際畢竟 (as if '*pūrvântakoṭiniṣṭha*').

[39] '*ekam*' should be inserted after '*pāramārthikam*', being the explanation of the term '*ekatra*' in the verse. The same with T.

gata, the Arhat, the Perfectly Enlightened one[40]. And this teaching of the unique, eternal, ever-lasting, quiescent and unchangeable Refuge is to be understood in detail according to the *Āryaśrīmālā-sūtra*[41].

§ 4. The Meaning of the 3 'Jewels'.

[They are called] 'Jewels', because
Their appearance is difficult to obtain,
They are immaculate and powerful,
And because of their being the ornament of the world,
And being the highest and unchangeable. // 22 //

In short, by the sixfold common nature with Jewels, these three named Buddha, Doctrine and Community, are called 'Jewel'. That is to say, 1) through the common nature of their appearance being difficult to obtain[42]; because those people who have not ripened[43] the root of virtue cannot get any chance to meet them, even during a long succession of eaons[44]. 2) Through the common nature of being immaculate; because they are apart from all kinds of[45] dust. 3) Through the common nature of power[46]; because they are endowed with the quality of unthinkable power, the 6 Supernatural Powers (*abhijñā*)[47] and so forth. 4) Through the common nature of being the ornament of the world; because they are the cause of beauty[48] intended by the whole world. 5) Through the common nature of being superior to the artificial[49] jewel; because they are supermundane. And 6) through the common nature of being unchangeable by praise, blame etc.[50]; because of their non-artificial nature.

[40] pl. in the text.

[41] ŚMS 221 a. This '*ekayāna*'-theory is one of its main points of teaching.

[42] *durlabhôtpādabhāva*, T. *ḥbyuṅ-ba dkon-pa*, C. 世間難得 (in v. 22, 世希有). For this passage, cf. BGS 808 *a*.

[43] *anavāpta*, T. *ma bskrun-pa*, C. 不能得 (unable to obtain).

[44] *kalpa*, T. *bskal-pa*, C. 劫.

[45] I accepted T. reading '*sarvâkāra*' instead of '*sarvâcāra*'. C. translation is as '*sarva-sāsravadharma*'.

[46] *prabhā*, T. *mthu*, C. 威德.

[47] 1) *divyācakṣus*, 2) *divyāśrotra*, 3) *ceta-paryāya-jñāna*, 4) *pūrvanivāsânusmṛti-jñāna*, 5) *ṛddhividdhi-jñāna*, & 6) *āsravakṣaya-jñāna*. Cf. Mvyut. 14.

[48] *śobhā*, T. *dge-ba*, C. om.

[49] *prativarṇika*, T. *bsñan-pa*, C. om.

[50] These are called '*aṣṭa-lokadharmāḥ*, i.e. *lābha*, *alābha* (gain & loss); *yaśas*, *ayaśas* (praise and blame); *nindā* (blame), *praśaṃsā* (praise); *sukha*, *duḥkha*. Cf. Mvyut. 125. '*stuti*' is for *praśaṃsa*. So, instead of '*stuti-ninda*', C. 世間八法.

VI. THE GERM OF THREE JEWELS IN FOUR ASPECTS

Immediately after the explanation of the Three Jewels, there is one *śloka* with reference to the question, in what circumstances are there born the Three Jewels, what is the birth-place [1] of purity, mundane and supermundane.

(Kārikā 4)

The Reality mingled with pollution,
And [the Reality] apart from pollution,
The Immaculate Qualities of the Buddha, and his Acts;
[These are the four aspects of] the sphere
Of those who perceive the Highest Truth, [2]
From which arise the pure Three Jewels [3]. // 23 //

What is elucidated by this *śloka* ?

The Germ of these Three Jewels
Is the sphere of the Omniscience [2],

[1] *yoni*, T. *skye-bahi gnas*, C. om.

[2] *paramârthadarśin* = *sarvadarśin* (in v. 24) = *sarvajña* (in comm.) C. 諸佛, 諸佛, 如來, for the respective case. (T. has literal translations). Cf. *Saddharmapuṇḍarika*, I,. v. 97, etc. (*paramārthadarśin*).

[3] This is the stanza by which the basic subjects of this text are shown. Each one of these four is treated in each chapter (I–IV), and also these 4 stand for the latter 4 of the 7 *vajrapadas*.

There is a Sūtra named " *Anuttarâśrayasūtra* " (AÂS), of which now only the Chinese translation is available (C. 無上依經, *Taisho*, No. 669). This sūtra also mentions the same 4 subjects with which the main part of the *sūtra* is formed, namely: 界 (*dhātu*) of the Tathāgata in Chap. II, 菩提 (*bodhi*), in Chap. III, 功德 (*guṇa*), in Chap. IV, and 事 (*kriyā*) of the Tathāgata in Chap.V. It seems that this Sūtra, though it bears the name of ' *sūtra* ', has been composed after the *Ratna.*, probably in order to authorize this theory of the 4 subjects. Detailed discussion of this problem is given in my Introduction.

And it is inconceivable in fourfold
For four reasons, respectively. // 24 //

Here, 1) 'The Reality mingled with pollution (*samalā tathatā*)'[4] is a term for 'the Essence (*dhātu*), unreleased from the sheath of defilements', i.e. the Matrix of Tathāgata. 2) 'The Reality apart from pollution' (*nirmalā tathatā*)[5] is a term for the same Essence, when it is characterized as the Perfect Manifestation of Basis (*āśrayaparivṛtti*)[6] in the Stage of Buddha, i.e. the Absolute Body of the Tathāgata. 3) 'Immaculate Qualities of the Buddha' means Supermundane Qualities of the Buddha—10 Powers and so on—in this Absolute Body of the Tathāgata, characterized as the Perfect Manifestation of Basis. 4) 'The Buddha's Act' means the automatic[7], highest act of these Qualities of the Buddha, 10 Powers, etc., which continues to give prophecies[8] to Bodhisattvas, without end[9], without interruption, unceasingly. And also, these four subjects are inconceivable[10] for four reasons, respectively; therefore, they are called the Sphere of Omniscience[11].

Then, for which four reasons ?

[4] *samalā tathatā*, T. *dri(-ma-daṅ) bcas(-paḥi) de-bshin-ñid*, C. 真如有雜垢, 有垢真如, 有垢如.

[5] *nirmalā tathatā*, T. *dri-ma med-paḥi de-bshin-ñid*, C. 遠離諸垢, 無垢真如, 無垢如.

[6] T. *gnas yoṅs-su gyur-pa*, C. 轉身. The term '*āśraya-parivṛtti*' seems to have somehow a different sense than the '*āśrayaparāvṛtti*' often used among the Vijñānavādin. The difference is probably due to what is meant by '*āśraya*'. Here '*āśraya*' signifies '*dhātu*' or '*gotra*' in the sense of '*tathāgatagarbha*' (see v. V, 7), while in case of '*āśrayaparāvṛtti*', '*āśraya*' signifies also '*dhātu*' but in the sense of '*ālayavijñāna*' (see S. p. 73, comm. on the verse quoted from the *Mahāyānâbhidharmasūtra*). And here '*dhātu*', being '*cittaprakṛti*', is regarded as the same as '*dharmakāya*', i.e. the Reality. Only because of '*āgantukakleśa*' attached to it, it cannot manifest itself fully. By removing such '*kleśa*', this *dhātu* becomes manifested fully, as being the reality itself. This point is called '*parivṛtti*'. On the contrary, '*ālayavijñāna*' no longer remains the same when '*āśrayapārāvṛtti*' takes place, and this change of basis is called '*parāvṛtti*'. See my Introduction III, where the uses of these terms in the *Sūtrâlaṅkāra* are discussed.

[7] *pratisvam*, T. *so-so-raṅ-gi* (of its own), C. 自然 (natural).

[8] *vyākaraṇa-kathā*, T. *luṅ-bstan-paḥi gtam*, C. 授(菩提)記. The prophecy on the attainment of the Highest Enlightenment.

[9] *aniṣṭhita*, T. *med-par ma gyur-shiṅ*, C. 常 (?) '*niṣṭhita*' means 'being done, ready, fixed or completed, i.e. coming to an end. So, '*aniṣṭhita*' means 'always not coming to an end'.

[10] Cf. AĀS 469 *b* (beginning of Chap. II).

[11] See note VI-2.

§ 1. Inconceivability of the 4 Subjects.

Because, [the Germ is] pure but defiled [at one and the same time],
[The Absolute Body is] of no impurity, and yet purified,
[The Qualities are] of inseparable nature [12] [from the Absolute Body], and
[The Acts are] effortless and of no discrimination. // 25 //

Here, 1) ' the Reality mingled with pollution ' is always, at the same time, pure and defiled; this point is inconceivable [13]. [Here, ' inconceivable ' is] in the sense that even for the Pratyekabuddhas who believe in the way of profound Doctrine [14], this is not an understandable sphere [15]. Because it is said [16]:

" O Goddess [17], these two points are quite difficult to be cognized. It is difficult to be cognized that the mind is pure by nature. It is also difficult to be cognized that this very mind is defiled. O Goddess, those who can hear these two points [with understanding] are only either yourself or Bodhisattvas who are endowed with the great qualities. O Goddess, for the other Śrāvakas and Pratyekabuddhas, these two points are to be understood only through the faith in the Tathāgata " [18].

2) ' The Reality apart from pollution ', though it is originally not defiled by pollution, yet it is purified afterwards; this point is inconceivable. Because it is said [19]:

" The mind is clear by nature [20]. This is the real knowledge as it is [21]. Therefore it is said [22]: [the Tathāgata] perfectly enligh-

12) *avinirbhāgadharma*, T. *rnam-par dbye-ba-med chos*, C. 不相捨離法.

13) Cf. AĀS 470 *c*. (end of Chap. II). (= S. p. 21, ll. 17-18).

14) The doctrine of relativity (*pratītya-samutpāda*), so C. 深因緣法. C. mentions ' *śrāvaka* ' along with ' *pratyekabuddha* '. So does AĀS, too.

15) *agocara-viṣaya*, T. *spyod-yul-du ma gyur-paḥi yul*, C. 非境界.

16) ŚMS 220 *c*.

17) Indicating Śrīmālādevī, the heroine of the Sūtra.

18) Cf. AĀS 473 *c* (end of Chap. III). (= S. p. 22, l. 5).

19) DRS 20 *b*. (如來…知心性淨).

20) *prakṛti-prabhāsvaram cittam*, C. 心自性清淨.

21) *tat tathaiva jñānam*, T. *de-ni de-kho-na bshin śes-so* (*tat tattvavad jñānam*, C. 如彼心本體如來如是知.

22) C. 是故經言, but DRS itself has this sentence saying '是故唱言'. It seems the following saying is an old aphorism taken from some other source.

tened the Supreme[23] Perfect Enlightenment by the Intellect endowed with contemplation at one moment[24].

Next, 3) 'Immaculate Qualities of the Buddha' are always[25] found? even in the stage of those ordinary people who are absolutely[26] defiled, of no differentiation through the inseparable nature [from the Absolute Body]; this point is inconceivable[27]. Because it is said[28]:

"There is no one among the group of living beings in whose body the Wisdom of the Tathāgata does not penetrate at all[29]. Nevertheless, as taking [wrong] conceptions[30], he cannot cognize the Buddha's Wisdom [residing in himself]. By removing this taking of conceptions, the Wisdom of Omniscience, self-born Wisdom, makes its appearance again unobstructedly[31]. O Son of the Buddha, suppose there would be a big painting cloth[32], of the size equal to the Great 3-thousand thousands of Worlds. And indeed, on this big cloth, the whole Great 3-thousand thousands of Worlds would be described completely. The Great Earth would be described in

23) The text om: '*anuttarā*', but both T. & C. have it.

24) *ekakṣaṇa-samāyukta*; '*lakṣaṇa*' after '*ekakṣaṇa*' in the Text should be omitted. So do T. & C. T. *skad-cig-ma gcig dan ldan-pa*, C. 一念心相應 (*citta*, instead of *lakṣaṇa*) This is a modifier of '*prajñā*' by which the Buddha has attained '*anuttarā samyaksambodhi*', i.e. '*prajñā*' in which both *prajñā* and *dhyāna* are associated at one moment.

25) *paurvâparyena*, T. *sṅa-phyir*, C. 前際後際.

26) *ekânta*, T. *gcig-tu*, C. 一向.

27) Cf. AĀS 475 *c* (end of Chap. IV). (= S. p. 22, ll. 8-9).

28) The *Avataṃsakasūtra*, Chap. XXXII. *Tathāgatôtpattisaṃbhava-parivarta* (如來性起品), *Taisho*, IX, 623 *c*-624 *a* (No. 278). This Chap. XXXII is identical with another independent Sūtra named *Tathāgatôtpattisaṃbhavanirdeśa* (C. 如來興顯經, tr. by Dharmarakṣa, *Taisho*, No. 291).

29) '*tathāgatajñāna*' in this Sūtra is identical with '*dhātu*' and '*gotra*', and shows the origin of the *tathāgatagarbha* theory. See my Introduction IV. Cf. '*buddhajñānântargamāt*' (v. I, 27).

30) *saṃjñā-grāha*, T. *ḥdu-śes-kyi ḥdsin-pa*, C. 顛倒 (*viparyasta*).

31) *asaṅgataḥ*, T. *thogs-pa med-par*, C. 無礙. '*asaṅga*' is a modifier of [*Buddha*'s] *jñāna*, see S. p. 241, l. 2 (*asaṅgena tathāgatajñānena*). Cf. Laṅk. p. 157, l. 14, 16; *Gauḍapāda-Kārikā* IV, 96.

32) *mahāpusta* (big book), T. *dar-yug* (a narrow ribbonlike piece of silk stuff (Jäschke). '*dar*' & '*yug*' both mean silk. The use of such silk is for painting.), C. 經卷 (roll of scripture). T. mentions the material and C. shows the form of the 'big book', according to the manner peculiar to each country.

the exact size of the Great Earth. The 2-thousand Worlds [would be written] in their own full size. [In the same way] the thousands of Worlds, the Four Continents, the Great Ocean, the Southern Continent of Jambū, the Eastern Continent of Videha, the [Western] Continent of Godāvari, the Northern Continent of Kuru, the Mount Sumeru, the Palace of Gods living on the earth, that of Gods living in the Sphere of Desire, and of Gods living in the Sphere of Form[33]; all of these would be written in their own size. And [thus] this big cloth would have the same size as the expansion of the Great 3-thousand thousands of Worlds. Furthermore, this very big cloth would enter within one particle of an atom[34]. Just as this big cloth lies within one small particle of an atom, in the same way, in each of all the other[35] particles of atoms, too, there enters a big cloth of the same size. Suppose there

[33] This passage describes various worlds, from larger one to smaller one, according to the Buddhist cosmology. All the terms mentioned here are as follows:

1) *trisāhasra-mahāsāhasra-lokadhātu*, T. *stoṅ-gsum-gyi stoṅ-chen-poḥi ḥjig-rten-gyi khams*, C. 三千大千世界;

2) (*mahācakravāla*) (S. & C. om. but T. has it), T. *khor-yug chen-po*;

3) *mahāpṛthivī*, T. *sa chen-po*, C. om;

4) *dvisāhasra-lokadhatu*, T. *ston-gñis-paḥi*. . ., C. 二千世界;

5) *sāhasra-lokadhātu*, T. *stoṅ-gi ḥjig-rten-kyi khams*, C. 小千世界;

6) *cāturdvīpika*, T. *gliṅ bshiḥi ḥjig-rten-kyi khams*, C. 四天下;

7) *mahāsamudra*, T. *rgya-mtsho chen-po*, C. om;

8) *jambudvīpa*, T. *ḥdsam-buḥi gliṅ*, C. om. (but usually, 閻浮提州 or 南·瞻部州);

9) *pūrvavideha-dvīpa*, T. *śar-gyi lus ḥphags-kyi gliṅ*. C. om. (東勝身州);

10) *godāvarī-dvīpa*, T. *nub-kyi ba-laṅ spyod-kyi gliṅ* (= *avara godānīya-dvīpa*), C. om. (西午貨州); '*godānīya*' is preferable.

11) *uttarakuru-dvīpa*, T. *byaṅ-gi sgra-mi sñan-gyi gliṅ*, C. om. (北俱盧州);

12) *sumeru*, T. *ri-rab*, C. 須彌山(王);

13) *bhūmyavacara-devavimāna*, T. *sa-la spyod-paḥi lhaḥi gshal-yas-khaṅ*, C. 地天宮;

14) *kāmâvacara-d.*, T. *ḥdod-pa-na spyod-paḥi*. . ., C. 欲天宮;

15) (*rūpâvacara-d.*,) (T. *gzugs-*[illegible] *spyod-paḥi* . . ., C. 色天宮.

C. has 無色天宮 (*ārūpyâvacara-d.*) after '*rūpâvacara-d.*', but it is not the case here. Cf. Mvyut. 153-155.

[34] *paramâṇu*, T. *rdul-phra-rab*, C. 微塵.

[35] *anya*, but T. *ma-lus-pa* (*aśeṣa*) and om. *sarva*. C. om. *anya* but retains *sarva*. See below (S. I. 13: *tathāśeṣebhyaḥ paramâṇubhyas*. . .).

should appear one person, well learned, clever, intelligent, wise and possessed of the skill [36] to approach there (i.e. to the big cloth). And his divine eyes were perfectly pure and clear. With these divine eyes he would perceive [and say]: Why does this big cloth of such a great nature stay [37] here in such a limited small particle of an atom! It is of no use to anybody! So he would think: Now, I will break this particle of an atom by the force of great efforts [38] and let this great cloth become useful for the world. Then, producing the strength of great efforts, he would break this small particle of an atom with a subtle diamond [39] and would make that great cloth useful for the world as was his intention. Not only for one particle of an atom but also for [all] the remaining [40] atoms, he would act in the same way [41].

Similarly, O Son of the Buddha, the Wisdom of the Tathāgata, which is the immeasurable wisdom, the profitable wisdom for all living beings [42], thoroughly [43] penetrates within the mentality [44] of every living being. And every mental disposition of a living being has the same size as the Buddha's Wisdom [45]. Only the ignorant, however, being bound by misconceptions [46] does neither know nor cognize nor understand [47] nor realize the Wisdom of the Tathāgata [within himself]. Therefore, the Tathāgata, having observed the state [48] of all the living beings in all the universal re-

36) *mīmāṃsā*, T. *spyod-pa* (= *caryā*, 'habit'), C. om.

37) *anutiṣṭhate* (Ātmanepada).

38) C. 勤作方便 (*upāyena* or *upāya-saṃjanayitvā*). T. adds '*vajreṇa*', which appears in the next sentence in S.

39) C. om. '*sūkṣma-vajreṇa*'.

40) The reading is preferably '*tathā śeṣebhyaḥ*' instead of '*tathâśeṣethyaḥ*'. But T. reads '*lus-pa med-pa mthaḥ-dag-las*', as S.

41) C. om. the whole sentence.

42) C. instead has '無相智慧, 無閡智慧' (*animittajñānam asaṅgajñānam*).

43) *sakalaṃ*, T. *ma-tshaṅ-ba med-par* (*aśeṣeṇa*).

44) *citta-santāna*, T. *sems-kyi rgyud*, C. [衆生] 身. See BHS Dic. '*santāna*'. Often '*santāna*' alone is used in the same sense.

45) T. ...*ye-śes daṅ ḥdra-bar tshad med-do*. (*sattvasantāna*, being endowed with *tathāgatajñāna*, is also *apramāṇa*. C. om. this sentence.

46) *saṃjñāgrāha*, C. 顛倒意 (妄想顛倒, 虛妄顛倒).

47) *anu-*√*bhū*. C. 不生信心 (not producing faith in...). C. om. the last verb.

48) *bhavana*, T. *gnas* (= *sthāna*).

gion [49] by his unobstructed Wisdom, resolves to be a teacher [and says:] 'What a pity! These living beings cannot cognize properly the Wisdom of the Tathāgata, though it penetrates them. O! I shall try to withdraw all the obstacles made by wrong conceptions for the sake of these living beings through the teaching of [8-fold] Holy Path [50], in order that they would by themselves, by accepting the power of the Holy Path, cast off the big knot of conceptions and would recognize the Wisdom of the Tathāgata [within themselves], also that they would obtain equality with the Tathāgata'. [In accordance with this declaration], they remove all the obstacles made by wrong conceptions through the teaching of the [Holy] Path of the Tathāgata. And when all the obstacles created by wrong conceptions are withdrawn, then this immeasurable Wisdom of the Tathāgata becomes useful to all the world".

Now, 4) 'the Buddha's Acts' proceed forth at one time, everywhere, always, without efforts, without discrimination, according to the intention [of the living beings], according to [the faculty of] the living beings who are to be disciplined [51] without fault [52], in conformance with their merits [53]; this point is inconceivable [54]. Because it is said [55]:

"In order to enroll the living beings [in the Buddha's Doctrine] [56] the Acts of Tathāgata, though they are unlimited, are taught as if

[49] *sarvadharmadhātu-sattvabhavanāni*, T. *chos-kyi dbyiṅs sems-can-gyi gnas thams-cad-la*, T. regards '*sarva*' as relating to *bhavana*. But cf '*sarvadharmadhātuprasṛtaṃ tathāgatajñānam*' (*Rāṣṭrapālaparipṛcchā*, p. 4, l. 12) C. om. '*dharmadhātu*'.

[50] '*āryeṇa mārgôpadeśena*' in the text. But it should be corrected into '*ārya-mārgôpadeśena*', since '*ārya*' modifies '*mārga*' but not '*upadeśa*'). T. *ḥphags-paḥi lam*, C. 聖道. See below (S. p. 24, l. 5: *āryamārgabalâdhānena*.) (For this *mārga*, T. reads *jñāna*, probably by mistake).

[51] So in C. (隨順可化衆生根機), and it makes the meaning clear and supports the reading '*yathā*' in the text. Therefore, the reading is preferable '*-vaineyikeṣu* (*vaineyika* > *vineya* C. 可化, T. *gdul-bya*) instead of '*vainaikeṣu*'.

[52] *akṣūṇaṃ*, T. *mtshaṅ-ba med-ciṅ*, C. 不錯不謬. *kṣūṇa* = *doṣa* (see BHS Dic. '*akṣūṇa*').

[53] *anuguṇaṃ*. C. 隨順 (probably om. '*guṇa*'), T. *rjes-su mthun-par*.

[54] Cf. AĀS 476 *b* (end of Chap. V) where the following quotation from DRS is utilized. (= S. p. 24, l. 9; p. 25, l. 3).

[55] DRS 21 *c*.

[56] I accepted C. reading '令一切衆生入佛法中 (in *buddhadharma*)'.

they were somewhat limited[57], with summarized number[58]. However, o Noble Youth, that which is the true act of the Tathāgata is immeasurable, inconceivable, uncognizable by all the world, indescribable by letters, difficult to be acquired by others, established[59] in all Buddhas' lands, rendered in equality with all the Buddhas, far beyond all works of exertion[60], of no discrimination as being equal to the sky, of no differentiation[61] as being the act of the universal essence"[62] &c.

Then, after showing the example of pure, precious Vaiḍūlya stone[63], it is taught as follows[64].

"O noble youth, in this manner[65], this Buddha's inconceivable Act should be known as rendered in equality [with all the Buddhas], nowhere blamable[66], related to the three divisions of time[67], and not interrupting the lineage of the 3 Jewels[68]. Residing in this inconceivable Act of the Tathāgata, the Buddha never casts off the sky-like nature of his body[69] and he shows himself in all the Buddhas' lands; without casting off the indescribable nature of his

57) *pramāṇataḥ*, T. *tshad-daṅ ldan-par*, C. 有量.

58) *saṃkṣepamātrakena*. C. om.

59) *adhiṣṭhita*. T. *gnas-pa*. C. '不休息' shows a different reading (*apratipraśrabdha*).

60) *ābhogakriyā*, T. *ḥbad-rtsol daṅ bya-ba*, C. 心所作事.

61) *nirnānākāraṇam* (Ms B. reading corrected by T. Chowdhury in his introductory note to the Skt. text) is acceptable, but it is preferable to read '...*karaṇa*' instead of '...*kāraṇa*'. See BHS Dic. '*nānākaraṇa*'. T. *tha-dad-du dbyer-med-pa*, C. 無異無差別.

62) *dharmadhātu-kriyā*. So in T. C. 法性體 (*dharmadhātu-svabhāva*).

63) See S. p. 5, l. 9 ff.

64) DRS 21 *c*. Cf. AĀS. 476 *b*.

65) *anena paryāyeṇa*, T. *rnam-graṅs ḥdis*, C. 依此譬喩 (by this example).

66) *anavadya*, T. *kha-na-ma-tho-ba med-pa*, C. 不可呵 (AĀS 無失).

67) T. & C. agree to put one epithet more before '*triratnavaṃśa*...'. T. *dus gsum daṅ rjes-su ḥbrel-pa* (*tryadhvânubaddha*), C. 三世平等 (*tryadhvasamam*). Cf. AĀS 隨行三世處 (prob. as T.). T. reading is here accepted.

68) *triratna-vaṃśa*, T. *dkon-mchog-gsum-gyi gduṅ*, C. 三寶種 (AĀS 三寶性).

69) *ākāśasvabhāvatā*. C. 虛空法身. Hereafter the reference is to the 3 actions, by deed, word and mind. C. failed to catch this point, But AĀS is apparently correct.

speech, he teaches the Doctrine for the sake of living beings through the proper word-communication; and being apart from all objects of the mind [70], still he can understand the deeds and intentions of the minds [71] of all living beings.

§ 2. The Germ as Cause and Conditions of the 3 Jewels in its four Aspects.

The object to be enlightened, the Enlightenment,
The attributes of the enlightenment,
The act to instruct the enlightenment [72];
[Of these four], respectively,
One subject signifies the cause,
[The remaining] three are the conditions
For the purification of the former [73]. // 26 //

Indeed, of these four subjects, with reference to their inclusion of all knowable objects, the first subject should be known as 'the object to be enlightened' (*boddhavya*) [74]. The second subject, 'the Enlightenment' (*bodhi*) should be known in the sense that the object to be enlightened has been awakened, therefore it is the Enlightenment. Being the portions of enlightenment, they are called Buddha's attribute; in this sense the third subject, 'the attributes of the Enlightenment (*bodhyaṅga*)' is to be known. Only through the attributes of Enlightenment is there instruction for others; in this sense the fourth subject, 'the act to instruct the Enlightenment (*bodhana*)' is to be known [75]. Thus with reference to these

[70] *sarvacittârambaṇa*, C. 一切衆生心所念觀. Note C. translation of '*ārambaṇa*' by 觀 or 所念觀, and compare to S. p. 11, l. 2 (v. 9), where '*ārambaṇa*' is translated by '覺觀'. Also see S. p. 110 (v. IV, 73): *nirālambe* (C. 無觀). See Note III-5, 39. (Cf. AAS 境界).

[71] *cittacaritâśayāmś ca*. T. *sems-kyi spyod-pa dan bsam-pa yan*, C. 諸心行 (om. *āśaya*). Cf. AAS. 心根性志樂 (*citta-indriya-āśaya?*). Acc. to T., the reading is preferably corrected into '*cittacaritān āśayāṃs ca*', otherwise '*ca*' is to be removed as an excess.

[72] Four subjects from the standpoint of Enlightenment (*bodhi*).

[73] i.e. 'the object to be enlightened'. It correspond to '*gotra*' itself.

[74] '*bodhya*' in v. 26.

[75] Of these 4, C. has confusion in its interpretation, C. translation of the first line is as follows: '所覺 (*bodhya*) 菩提法 (*bodhi*), 依菩提分 (*bodhyaṅga*) 知, 菩提分教化 (*bodhana*, the reading *bodhanā* is to be corrected into *bodhana*),

four subjects, the arrangement of the Germ of the 3 Jewels in the state of cause and conditions is to be known.

Here, of these four subjects, the first one, as being the seed of the supermundane thing, should be understood as the cause (*hetu*) of origination of the 3 Jewels with reference to its (= of the Germ) purification based upon 'each own' correct thinking. Thus "one subject signifies the cause". How are there three conditions? The Tathāgata, having realized the Supreme Perfect Enlightenment, manifests the Act of Tathāgata of 32 features [76], being endowed with the Virtuous Qualities of the Buddha, 10 Powers, etc. This is to be understood as the condition (*pratyaya*) for the origination of the 3 Jewels with reference to the purification of Germ based upon the voice of others [77]. Thus "[the remaining] three are the condition".

Hereafter, of these four subjects, a detailed and analytical explanation will be made known in the remaining chapters.

衆生覺菩提'. The last pada '衆生覺菩提' should be taken as an explanatory adjective to '*bodhana*', and be read '*bodhana*, by which the people attain the enlightenment'. Nevertheless, C. applies each phrase for each subject in the prose commentary. It is obviously wrong.

76) Cf. S. p. 6, l. 16 (acc. to DRS).

77) *parataḥ*, which corresponds to '*pratyātma*' (each own) with reference to '*hetu*'. Of this correspondence, C. has no interpretation in the prose commentary, but in the verse C. adds 2 padas showing this. However, C. again failed to catch the sense and regards the former two subjects as relating to '*svârtha*', and the remaining two as '*parârtha*' (前二自利益, 後二利益他).

VII. THE SERMON: ALL LIVING BEINGS ARE POSSESSED OF THE MATRIX OF THE TATHĀGATA.

Now, with reference to 'the Reality mingled with pollution', it is said: All living beings are possessed of the Matrix of the Tathāgata [1]. By which meaning is it said thus [2] ?

[1] This formula shows a principle common to a group of Sūtras and Śāstras which express the *tathāgatagarbha* theory. The first appearance of this formula seems to be in the *Tathāgatagarbhasūtra* on which the *Ratna.* mainly depends. The Sūtra, of which the Skt. text is missing now, is retained in both T. & C.: T. Kg Mdo XXII, *Tohoku* No. 258, C. *Taisho*, No. 666 '大方等如來藏經' tr. by Buddhabhadra between 408–429 A.D. and No. 667 '大方廣如來藏經' tr. by Amoghavajra in the 8th cent. A.D. Hereafter C. No. 666 will be used for the reference with the abbreviation, TGS.

This formula runs in C. as follows:

一切衆生 雖在諸趣 煩惱身中 有如來藏 常無染汚 德相備足 如我無異 (TGS, 457 *c*).

Prior to this sentence, the Sūtra says:

我以佛眼，觀一切衆生，貪欲恚癡諸煩惱中，有如來智，如來眼，如來身，結加趺坐儼然不動，(*ibid.*).

(With Buddha's eyes, I observe that all living beings, though they are among the defilements of hatred, anger and ignorance, have the Buddha's Wisdom, Buddha's eye, Buddha's body sitting firmly in the meditating form).

This shows the reason for the statement mentioned above, i.e. "*sarvasattvās tathāgatagarbhāḥ*' and as this idea of the penetration of *buddhajñāna* is expressed in the *Avataṃsakasūtra* (*Tathāgatôtpattisaṃbhava-pariv*, see Note VI–28, 29, and my Introduction), it is clear that TGS borrowed this idea from that Sūtra and established the above formula.

After the first sentence, the Sūtra furthermore says:

諸佛法爾 若佛出世 若不出世 一切衆生 如來之藏 常住不變 (*ibid.*).

(*eṣā* -- *dharmāṇāṃ dharmatā, utpādād vā tathāgatānām anutpādād vā sadaîvaîte sattvās tathāgatagarbhāḥ*) (quoted in S. p. 73).

This third one shows that the formula is the eternal truth, and by combi-

Note 2 on foll. p.

(Kārikā 5)

The multidudes [3] of living beings are included
in the Buddha's Wisdom [4],
Their immaculateness is non-dual by nature,
Its result [5] manifests itself on the Germ of the Buddha [6];
Therefore, it is said: all living beings [7]
are possessed of the Matrix of the Buddha. // 27 //

[What is shown by this *śloka* ?] [8]

The Buddha's Body penetrates everywhere,
Reality is of undifferentiated nature,
And the Germ [of the Buddha] exists [in the living beings].
Therefore, all living beings are
always possessed of the Matrix of the Buddha. // 28 //

ning these three sentences together, we can get the main doctrine of the sūtra.

Here in the *Ratna.*, the main purpose of the teaching is to emphasize this point and, basing himself upon the TGS, the author analysed and systematized the *tathāgatagarbha* theory. First of all, the author picked up the fundamental characteristics of *tathāgatagarbha* in the 3 meanings, he next explained its features and functions summarized in 10 points, and lastly, the 9 illustrations in order to show how living beings are covered with defilements.

[2] The order of the text differs among S., T. & C. S. keeps quite a regular order starting with the Kārikā (v. 27), but omits the usual heading before the next commentary verse (v. 28). T. has clearly confusions in the prose commentary as J suggested. About C., on the contrary, starting with the commentary verse (v. 28) like T., it puts v. 27 after '*tathāgatagarbhasūtrânusāreṇa nirdeśo bhaviṣyati*' with the heading: as said in the Kārikā text (如偈本言). As regard this point, it looks all right and it is imaginable that the text used for C. translation had this order, i.e. v. 27 was put after the explanation. But from '*pūrvataraṃ tu*' up to '*uddānam*' is missing in C. and v. 28 is followed by v. 29 with no heading.

[3] *rāśi*, T. *tshogs*, C. 界.

[4] '*buddhajñānântargamāt sattvarāśeḥ*' means grammatically that *sattva-rāśi* goes into *buddhajñāna*. But T. as translation, C. 不離佛智 (being not separated from Buddha's Wisdom). This idea is shown in the *Avataṃsaka* quoted in S. p. 22. (see above, Note VII-1).

[5] The result of immaculateness i.e. *buddhatā*, *dharmakāya*, etc. or of *sattvarāśi*. Is C. '法性身' identified with it?

[6] *bauddhe gotre tatphalasyôpacārāt.* For *upacāra*, T. *ñer-brtags.* (In the sense of '*carati*', resides). C. translation of this line is as follows: 依一切諸佛. 平等法性身, (because of the body of real nature, equal to all the Buddhas). It is difficult to identify it with the present Skt. reading.

[7] *sarve dehinaḥ* = *sarvasattvāḥ* = [*sarva*] *śarīriṇaḥ* (in the following verse).

[8] Inserted according to the conformity. (*anena kiṃ darśitam* /).

In short, by three kinds of meaning, it is said by the Lord that all living beings are always possessed of the Matrix of Tathāgata. That is to say, by the following three meanings: 1) the Absolute Body (*dharmakāya*) of the Tathāgata penetrates all living beings; 2) the Tathāgata being the Reality (*tathātā*), is the undifferentiated whole; and 3) there exists the Germ of the Tathāgata (*tathāgatagotra*) [in every living being][9]. And of these three subjects[10], the [detailed] explanation will be made below[11] according to the *Tathāgatagarbha-sūtra*. Prior to it, however, there is [another] meaning by which this meaning in all its aspects is indicated in the Scripture[12] with no variance anywhere[13]. With reference to that as well, I shall now explain.

9) 1) (*sarvasattveṣu*) *tathāgata-dharmakāya-parispharaṇârtha*, T. *de-bshin-gśegs-paḥi chos-kyi skus ḥpho-baḥi don*;

2) *tathāgata-tathatā-'vyatirekârtha*, T. *de-bshin gśegs-paḥi de-bshin-ñid rnam-par dbyer med-paḥi don*;

3) *tathāgata-gotra-saṃbhavârtha*, T. *de-bshin-gśegs-paḥi rigs yod-paḥi don*.

C. has no equivalent word for each subject. The term '*saṃbhava*' would mean both 'being' and 'becoming'. T. '*yod-pa*' shows the first sense, but it seems to be not enough to express the idea contained here, in comparison with the phrase: '*gotre... upacārāt*' in v. 27. That is to say, the sense 'origination' or 'manifestation' is to be implied here. These three are the fundamental characteristics of *tathāgatagarbha*, as well as the ground of the statement: *sarvasattvās tathāgatagarbhāḥ*. Equality through *dharmakāya*, *tathatā* and *tathāgatagotra* is also a point of emphasis in the text. These are called '*trividha-svabhāva*' of *tathāgatadhātu* (S. p. 69, l. 17). Cf. BGŚ 808 *a*, 法身, 如如, 佛性, respectively. The threefold meaning of the term *tathāgatagarbha* mentioned below (S. p. 70, l. 16–18; p. 71, l. 10–12; p. 72, l. 7–9) as well as in BGŚ (795 *c*-ff.) is also an implication of this same idea.

Three terms in BGŚ are as follows:

1) 所攝藏: *tathāgata*, as *garbha* in which *sattvas* are 'enveloped';

2) 隱覆藏: *garbha* in which *tathāgata* is 'hidden';

3) 能攝藏: *sattvas* possessed of *garbha* of *tathāgata*, i.e. of *garbha* 'enveloping' *tathāgata*.

The first one shows the all-pervadingness of '*dharmakāya*' the 2nd should be applied to '*samalā tathatā*' in the sense '*sarvakleśakośópagūḍho dharmakāyaḥ*', and the 3rd shows the existence of '*gotra*' among *sattvas*. See Note X-139 140 150 151 169 170.

10) *arthapada*, T. *don-kyi gnas*, C. 句義.

11) See S. pp. 69–73.

12) *pravacana*. This sentence is missing in C. T. reads this word as the subject (*gsuṅ-rab*) See below.

13) *aviśeṣeṇa*. Significance of this sentence is as follows:

The 3 meanings mentioned above are applicable exclusively to *Tathāgatagarbha*; on the other hand, the following meanings, beginning with *svabhāva*, are applicable to any subject (*sarvatrâviśeṣena*) and are already used in the scripture. See Appendix III.

VIII. ANALYSIS OF THE GERM FROM 10 POINTS OF VIEW

Summary [1]:

The own nature and the cause,
The result, function, union and manifestation,
Various states and all-pervadingness,
The qualities always unchangeable and non-differentiation;
In these [points of view], there should be known
The implication [2] of the Absolute Essence [3]. // 29 //

In short, with reference to [4] these 10 meanings, there should be understood the various aspects [5] of the Essence of the Tathāgata, which is the sphere of the highest true knowledge [6]. What are the 10 meanings? They are namely: 1) the own nature (*svabhāva*) [of the Germ]; 2) the cause (*hetu*); 3) the result (*phala*) [of its purification]; 4) the function (*karman*) [towards the purification]; 5) the union (*yoga*) [of the Germ]; 6) the manifestation (*vṛtti*) [of the Germ]; 7) the various states (*avasthāprabheda*) [of its manifestation]; 8) all-pervadingness (*sarvatraga*) [7] [of the Germ]; 9) unchangeability (*avikāra*) [of the Germ through various states]; and 10) non-differentiation (*abheda*) [of the Germ with the Reality] [8].

1) *uddāna*, T. *sdom*, C. 偈言. This verse on the 10 meanings (v. 29) has a doubtful position as the original Kārikā, though it is mentioned in the Kārikā text of C. Because it follows immediately upon the word '*vakṣyāmi*' in the last sentence, it seems that this *uddāna* was composed by the commentator prior to explaining following Kārikās. Therefore, I ventured to omit this verse from the line of Kārikās.

2) *arthasaṃdhi*, T. *dgoṅs-don* (implied meaning), C. 妙義次第 (succeeding order of the excellent meanings).

3) *paramârtha-dhātu*, T. *don-dam-dbyiṅs*, C. 第一真法性 (*dhātu* in the sense of *tathāgatadhātu*, i.e. *gotra*).

4) *abhisaṃdhāya*, C. 依 ....

5) *vyavasthā*, T. *rnam-par gshag-pa*, C. 差別.

6) *paramatattva – jñānaviṣayas tathāgatadhātuḥ*. An explanation of the term *paramârthadhātu* in the verse. C. rendering of *tathāgatadhātu* here is '佛性'.

7) *sarvagatva* in the verse.

8) Corresponding terms for these 10 in T. & C. are as follows:

1) *ṅo-bo*, 體; 2) *rgyu*, 因; 3) *ḥbras[-bu]*, 果; 4) *las*, 業; 5) *ldan-pa*,

Chapter I (*Samalā Tathatā*)

(I) SVABHĀVA & (II) HETU [9]

Now, with reference to the meaning of 'own nature' and 'cause' there is one *śloka*.

(Kārikā 6)

[The Matrix of the Tathāgata] is always undefiled by nature [10],
Like the pure jewel, the sky and water;
It follows after [11] the faith in the Doctrine,
The highest Intellect, Meditation and Compassion [12]. // 30 //

§ 1. The Nature of the Essence of the Tathāgata.

Here, what is shown by the former half of this *śloka* ?

Because of its own nature of power,
Identity, and being moist; in these [three points]
[The Essence of the Tathāgata has] a resemblance [13]
To the quality of the wish-fulfilling jewel, the sky and water.
// 31 //

相應; 6) *hjug-pa*, 行; 7) *gnas-skabs-kyi rab-tu dbye-ba*, 時差別 (*kāla-prabheda*), 8) *kun-tu hgro-ba*, 遍一切處; 9) *mi-hgyur-ba*, 不變; *dbyer-med-pa*, 無差別.

Cf. BGŚ 796 *b*: 1) 自體相; 2) 因相; 3) 果相; 4) 事能相; 5) 總攝相; 6) 分別相; 7) 階位相; 8) 遍滿相; 9) 無變異相; 10) 無差別相, of these 10 categories, the first 6 are common to the 8 categories on '*nirmalā tathatā*' (Chap. II), and the application of the same 6, from *svabhāva* to *vṛtti*, is also observed in YBh. (*Taisho*, XXX, 36 *a*), MSA, IX, 56–59, comm., etc. Also the *Mahāyānadharmadhātvaviśeṣa-śāstra* (DAŚ) mentions 12 categories with respect to '*bodhicitta*' (DAŚ 892 *a*), namely: 1) 果; 2) 因; 3) 自性; 4) 異名; 5) 無差別; 6) 分位; 7) 無染; 8) 常恒; 9) 相應; 10) 不作義利; 11) 作義利; 12) 一性. See Appendix III.

9) Cf. BGŚ 796 *b* (I. *svabhāva* & II *hetu*), DAŚ 892 *a* (3. 自性, 2. 因).

10) *prakṛty-asaṃkliṣṭa*. For *prakṛti*, T. *raṅ-bshin*, C. 自性. The subject term for this and the following Kārikās is '*jinagarbha*' in v. 45.

11) *-anvaya*, T. ...*las byuṅ-ba* (come out from...), C. om.

12) *dharmâdhimukti*, *adhiprajñā*, *samādhi*, *karuṇā*, respectively, which show the cause of purification. See below.

13) *sādharmya*, T. *chos mthun-pa-ñid*, C. 相似相對法.

'In these' three [points], which are already mentioned above [14], the resemblance of the Essence of the Tathāgata to the purified quality of the wish-fulfilling jewel, the sky and water, respectively, should be known with reference to its particular and common characteristics. Now, first of all, a resemblance to the wish-fulfilling jewel is to be known of the Absolute Body of the Tathāgata, with reference to its particular characteristic, the own nature of powers (*prabhāva*), fulfillment [15] of desired objects [16] etc. A resemblance to the sky is to be known of the Reality, with reference to its own nature of identity [everywhere] (*ananyathābhāva*) as the particular characteristic. A resemblance to water is to be known [17] of the Germ of the Tathāgata, with reference to its moist nature (*snigdhabhāva*) of mercy towards living beings as the particular characteristic. And now, of all these, with reference to their being undefiled always, absolutely, by nature, i.e., the innate purity as the common characteristic, this very resemblance [of the Essence] to the purified qualities of wish-fulfilling jewel, the sky and water is to be understood.

§ 2. Obstructions and Causes of Purification [18].

Now, what is shown by the latter half of the *śloka* (v. 30)?

There are four kinds of Obstructions [19]:
Enmity [20] to the Doctrine and perception of the Self,

[14] vv. 27, 28 and its commentary. i.e. *trividhasvabhāva* of *tathāgatadhātu*.

[15] *samṛddhi*, T. *grub-pa* (= *siddhi*), C. 成就 (as T.).

[16] *cintitârtha*, T. *bsam-paḥi don*, C. 所思 (C. '所修' after '所思' is probably a misreading of *prabhā* for *bhāvanā*). C. has a lacuna after *samṛddhi* up to the end of the commentary on v. 31, but it puts '思者' (*cintā iti*)' before '*tathāgatadharmakāye*' and it seems to correspond to '思實體', in v. 31 of C., but not found in S.

[17] For these 3 terms showing the similarity in particular characteristics, T., C. & BGŚ (796 *b*) runs as follows:

1) T. *mthuḥi ṅo-bo-ñid*, C. 自在力, BGŚ 如意功德性;
2) T. *gshan-du ma-yin-pa-ñid-kyi raṅ-gi ṅo-bo*, C. 不變, BGŚ 無異性;
3) T. *brlan-paḥi raṅ-gi ṅo-bo*, C. 柔軟, BGŚ 潤滑性.

[18] Cf. BGŚ 797 *a*.

[19] *āvaraṇa*, T. *sgrib*, C. 障礙.

[20] *pratigha*, T. *khoṅ-khro* (hatred, wrath, enmity), C. 謗 (abuse).

Fear of Suffering in this world,
And indifference to the profit of living beings [21]; – // 32 //
[These are respectively] of the Icchantikas [22],
Of the Heretics [23], the Śrāvakas and the Pratyekabuddhas [24]; –
The virtues, the faith [in the Doctrine] etc., are
The four Causes of purification. // 33 //

In brief there are those three kinds of living beings among their multitudes [25]: 1) those who cling to the worldly life (*bhavâbhilāṣin*), 2) those who seek for deliverance from it (*vibhavâbhilāṣin*), 3) those who wish neither of both (*tadubhayânabhilāṣin*) [26]. Of them, 1) those who cling to the worldly life' should be known as twofold. *a*) The people whose intention is against the path to Emancipation and who never belong to the family of the perfect Nirvāṇa (*aparinirvāṇagotraka*) [27], Those are only seeking for Phenomenal Life and not for Nirvāṇa. And *b*) Those people who, although belonging to this Our Religion (*ihadhārmika*) [28], have definitely fallen into the former's way [29]. Some of these are hostile to the Doctrine of the Great Vehicle. With reference to them,

21) The reading should be '*sattvârtha-nirapekṣatā*' (or *-arthe nirape-*) instead of '*-arthaṃ nirapekṣatā*' in the text. T. *sems-can don-la ltos med-pa*.

22) *icchantika*, T. *ḥdod-chen*, C. 闡提 (一闡提) (of this literal meaning, BHS Dic. s. v.). As a Buddhist technical term, it means one who longs only for worldly pleasure (= *bhavâbhilāṣin*, see below), more strictly, one who abuses the Buddhist doctrine, esp. that of Mahāyāna. The capacity for Enlightenment of this Icchantika is usually denied as being '*aparinirvāṇagotraka*'. But from the viewpoint of the *tathāgatagarbha* theory, the Icchantika is said to be able to get Enlightenment as taught in this text (S. p. 37, l. 1 ff.).

23) *tīrthya*, T. *mu-stegs*, C. 外道 (= *anyatīrthika*) = *tīrthika*.

24) *svayaṃbhū* in the text (T. *raṅ-byuṅ*, C. 自覺). Cf. AA II, 6.

25) Cf. AĀS 471 *a*; BGŚ 797 *b* ff.

26) Of these 3, 1) T. *srid-pa ḥdod-pa*, C. 求有; 2) T. *srid-pa-daṅ bral-bar ḥdod-pa*, C. 遠離求有; 3) T. *de-gñis-ka mṅon-par mi-ḥdod-pa*, C. 不求彼二, respectively.

27) T. *yoṅs-su mya-ṅan-las mi-ḥdaḥ-baḥi rigs-can*, C. 無涅槃性. This sentence and the next show the definition of Icchantika.

28) T. *chos ḥdi-pa-ñid*, C. 於佛法中 (within the Buddhist fold). The word '*iha*' here means 'in this religion' but not 'in this world'. Cf. Pāli *idha*, which is used in this sense in Vibhaṅga 245 (PTS Dic. s. v.).

29) i.e. '*saṃsāram eva icchanti na nirvāṇam*', C. [於佛法中] 闡提同位 (as same as Icchantika in their position).

the Lord said as follows [30]:

> " I am not their teacher; they are not my pupils. O Śāriputra, I say of them that they are chiefly filled with darkness, as migrating from darkness to another darkness, from gloom to greater gloom [31].

Next, 2) 'those who seek for deliverance from this worldly life' are also twofold. *a*) Those who have fallen into a methodless way (*anupāyapatita*) and *b*) 'those who are in [the correct] method' (*upāyapatita*) [32]. Here, 'those who are of no method' are again divided into three [33]. *i*) Outsiders of this Religion (*itobāhya*) [34], i.e. various kinds of Heretics (*anyatīrthya*), i.e. the Carakas [35], the Parivrājakas [36], the Jains [37], etc. *ii*) & *iii*) Insiders of Our Religion, but whose conduct is in common with the Heretics [38]. They, though being faithful in [Buddhism], take hold of bad conceptions [39]. Then, what are they? They are namely, *ii*) those who have the perception of the substantial Ego (*pudgaladṛṣṭi*) [40] and have no faith in the Highest Truth. With reference to them, the Lord said [41]:

> " One who has no faith in Non-substantiality is not different from the Heretics ".

30) AAN 467 *c*. Cf. AĀS 471 *a*. C. (and AAN as well) 'I will call them *icchantikas*', instead of '*tamobhūyiṣṭhā*'.

31) *tamasas tamo 'ntaram andhakālān mahândhakālagāminaḥ*, C. 從闇入闇, 從冥入冥. But T. *mun-pa-las kyaṅ ches, mun-pa chen-por ḥgro-ba*.

32) Of these 2, 1) T. *thabs ma-yin-pa-la shugs-pa*, C. 無求道方便; 2) T. *thabs-la shugs-pa*, C. 有求道方便, respectively.

33) C. 'two', combining the latter two in S. & T. into one. So do AĀS. & BGŚ. as well. This seems to be the original reading.

34) In contrast with '*ihadhārmika*'. The word '*itobāhya*' is literally an adjective to '*tīrthya*'. T. *ḥdi-las phyi-rol-tu gyur-pa*, C. om.

35) *caraka* (lit. wanderer), T. *tsa-ra-ka*, C. regards them as the Sāṃkhya (僧佉).

36) (lit. religious wanderer), T. *kun-tu rgyu* (one who goes everywhere), C. regards them as the Vaiśeṣika (衛世師).

37) *nirgranthi-putra*, T. *gcer-bu-ba* (naked people), C. 尼健陀若提子.

38) C. 於佛法中同外道行.

39) *durgṛhītagrāhin*, T. *dkaḥ-baḥi lta-ba ḥdsin-pa* (*durdṛṣṭigrāhin*), C. 顚倒取 (*viparyāsagrāhin*). T. reading is accepted in this translation.

40) C. mentions Vātsīputrīyas (犢子部) as an example.

41) The source is unknown.

iii) Those who have the conception of the Non-substantiality and are proud of it are doubtless at the door of Emancipation through the Non-substantiality [42] in this religion [43]. But as they are intoxicated with this Non-substantiality, it follows for them that Non-substantiality itself becomes a [wrong] conception [44]. With reference to these, he (= the Lord) said [in the Scripture] [45]:

> "O Kāśyapa, really even such a conception which maintains substantial Ego as much as Mt. Sumeru is better than the conception of Non-substantiality on the part of those who are proud of it".

Here, *b*) 'those who are in [the correct] method' are again twofold. *i*) Those who belong to the Vehicle of the Śrāvaka and *ii*) those who belong to the Vehicle of the Pratyekabuddha. [Both of them] have proceeded on the fixed way of rightfulness [46].

And next, 3) 'those who wish neither of both the worldly life and deliverance from it' are the people who are standing firmly amidst the Great Vehicle and are of the highest, talented faculty. They are not seeking for the Phenomenal Life as the Icchantikas do, nor are they those who are in no method like Heretics, nor those who are in the correct method [for deliverance] like Śrāvakas and Pratyekabuddhas, but, having entered [47] the Path to obtain [48] [the intuition of] the equality of this Phenomenal Life with Nirvāṇa, they intend not to stay fixedly in the Nirvāṇa (*apratiṣṭhitanirvāṇa*) [49]; their activities [50] are based upon Phenomenal Life [51] but without being defiled by it, and their root is perfectly

[42] *tad-vimokṣamukhe*. C. 空解脫門.

[43] *iha*. The same use as in '*ihadhārmika*'.

[44] C. 計唯空無實.

[45] C. 寶積經中 (*Ratnakūtasūtre*). This is a passage in *Kāśyapa-parivarta* of the *Ratnakūṭasūtra*. (*Taisho*, XI, p. 634 *a*). Cf. AĀS 471 *b*; BGŚ 797 *b* (quotation from AĀS); Laṅk. p. 146, 11-13.

[46] *samyaktva-niyāma*, T. *yaṅ-dag-par ṅes-pa-ñid*. C. om. the whole compound.

[47] *pratipanna*, T. *shugs-pa* (to enter), see Note V-23.

[48] *āpatti* in the text, but T. *thob-pa*, (C. offers no help). As by J.'s suggestion, *āpti* had better be accepted. (Cf. S. p. 29 l. 4 *samatâpti-mārga-pratipannāḥ*).

[49] T. *mi-gnas-paḥi mya-ṅan-las-ḥdas-pa*. (T. adds *brten-pa* (*āśrita*) after *nirvāṇa*), C. 不住涅槃 (無住處涅槃). This is the highest and ideal feature of *nirvāṇa* in the Mahāyāna doctrine. See S. p. 35, l. 2 ff.

[50] *prayoga*, T. *sbyor-ba-can*, C. 修行.

[51] *saṃsāragata*, C. 世間行. For '*-gata*', T. *brten-pa*(= *āśrita*).

pure as being grounded in the firm Compassion and Superior Intention [52].

And here [53], 1) those people who cling to this wordly life, i.e. the Icchantikas and [54] those who, though belonging to this Our Religion, have definitely fallen into the former's way are called (A) the group of people who conform in the wrong way (*mithyātvaniyataḥ sattvarāśiḥ*). 2–*a*) 'Those people who seek for deliverance from the worldly life but have no method' are called (B) the group of people unconformed (*aniyataḥ s.*). 2–*b*) 'Those people who seek for deliverance with the correct method' and 3) 'those who wish neither of both and have entered the path through which [the intuition of] the equality [of the Phenomenal Life with the Nirvāṇa] is attained are called (C) the group of people who conform in the right way (*samyaktvaniyataḥ s.*).

Of [55] these [groups of living beings], keeping aside those people who stand firmly in the Great Vehicle and follow the unobstructed way [56], other people are [fourfold] [57], i.e. the Icchantikas, the Heretics, the Śrāvakas and the Pratyekabuddhas. Of these [four groups], there are four kinds of Obstructions on account of which they cannot understand or realize the Essence of the Tathāgata. What are then the four Obstructions? That is to say, 1) the enmity [58] to the Doctrine of the Great Vehicle (*mahāyānadharmapratigha*). This is the Obstruction of the Icchantikas, and its Antidote [59] is the practice of the faith in the Doctrine of the Great Vehicle (*mahāyānadharmâdhimukti–bhāvanā*) by the Bodhisattvas. 2) The conception of the Self (*ātmadarśana*) on the separate elements (*dharmeṣu*). This is the Obstruction of the Heretics, and its Antidote is the practice of Supremacy in the transcendental Intellect (*prajñāpāramitā-bh.*) by the Bodhisattvas. 3) The notion of Suffering (*duḥkha–saṃjñā*) [or rather] the fear of Suffering (*duḥkha–bhīrutva*) in Phenomenal Life.

52) *adhyāśaya*, T. *lhag–paḥi bsam–pa*, C. 涅槃心 (the intention to attain *Nirvāṇa*).

53) Hereafter, reference is made to the relation between the 3 kinds of people above mentioned and the 3 groups of people.

54) '*ca*' should be inserted before '*ihadhārmikā*', though it is missing in S. & T. C. has it.

55) Hereafter, reference is made to the 4 kinds of people and their impediments.

56) *anāvaraṇa–gāmin* (one who goes without any obstacle). But T. *sgrib-pa med-pa rtogs-pa* (one who knows the unobstructed thing) and C. 求於無障礙道 (one who seeks for the unobstructed way). Here '*anāvaraṇa*' indicates strictly Nirvāṇa. I preferred C. translation.

57) S. om. '*caturvidha*', but both T. & C. have it.

58) T. *sṅaṅ–ba*, C. 謗. Cf. BGŚ 憎背.

59) *pratipakṣa*, T. *gñen–po*, C. 對治.

This is the Obstruction of those who belong to the Vehicle of the Śrāvaka and its Antidote is the practice of Meditations (*samādhi-bh.*), *Gaganagañjā* [60] etc., by the Bodhisattvas. 4) Aversion to the profit of living beings (*sattvārtha-vimukhatā*) or Indifference to the profit of living beings (*sattva-artha-nirapekṣatā*). This is the Obstruction of those who belong to the Vehicle of the Pratyekabuddha and its Antidote is the practice of Great Compassion (*mahākaruṇā-bh.*) by the Boddhisattvas [61].

These are the four kinds of Obstructions of the four kinds of living beings. And having practised the four kinds of Antidotes to these Obstructions, i.e. the faith [in the Doctrine of the Great Vehicle] etc., the Bodhisattvas attain the highest purity, the highest truth, i.e. the Absolute Body. And, accompanied by these four causes of origination of purity, they become the sons of the Religious King in the Buddha's family. How are they? It is said [62]:

[60] T. *nam-mkhaḥ-mdsod*, C. 虛空藏 (*ākāśagarbha*). C. adds '*śūraṅgama*' (首楞嚴) as a name of *samādhi*.

[61] The terms for the 4 obstructions in T. & C. are as follows:

1) [*thegs-pa chen-poḥi*] *chos-la sṅaṅ-ba*, 謗法;

2) *bdag-tu lta-ba*, 著我;

3) *ḥkhor-ba-la sdug-bsṅal hjigs-pa*, 怖畏世間苦;

4) *sems-can-gyi don-la mi-ltos-pa*, 捨離著衆生.

And the terms for the 4 causes of purification.

1) [*thegs-pa chen-poḥi*] *chos-la mos-pa*. 信法;

2) *śes-rab* [*-kyi pha-rol-tu phyin-pa*], 般若;

3) *tiṅ-ṅe-ḥdsin*, 三昧;

4) *sñiṅ-rje chen-po*, 大悲.

[62] The following verse is probably a quotation from some canonical work. At least, the idea must be borrowed from an old source. The same idea is expressed with slight difference in the following Śāstras; each of them, however, regards it as its own.

1) MSA IV, 11:

dharmâdhimuktibījāt pāramitāśreṣṭhamātṛto jātaḥ
dhyānamaye sukhagarbhe karuṇā saṃvardhikā dhātrī

C. has no corresponding verse, but in the commentary there is a passage saying: 一種子勝, 信大乘法爲種子故. 二生母勝, 般若波羅蜜爲生母故. 三胎藏勝, 大禪定業爲胎藏故. 四乳母勝, 大悲長養爲乳母故 (*Taisho*, XXXI, p. 596 *b*).

Those whose seed is the faith in the highest Vehicle,
Whose mother is the transcendental Intellect [63],
On account of the origination of Buddha's Doctrine;
Whose abiding womb is the blissful meditation
And whose nurse is called Mercy;
They are the sons, the after-comers [64] of the Buddhas. // 34 //

(III) PHALA & (IV) KARMAN

Now, with reference to the meaning of 'result' and 'function', there is one *śloka*.

(Kārikā 7)

The Supreme Virtues [65] of Purity, Unity [66], Bliss and Eternity; –
[These] are its results [of the purification] [67];
[Towards this purification] it has the functions,
Aversion to Suffering, longing for and praying for
the acquisition of Quiescence [68]. // 35 //

2) BGŚ 798 *a*: 一因如父身分, 一緣如母, 三依止如胞胎, 四成就如乳母 (*hetu* is like *pitṛ*, *pratyaya* like *mātṛ*, *āśraya* like *garbha*, and *siddhi* like *dhātrī*).

3) DAŚ v. 3: 信爲具種子 般若爲其母 三昧爲胎藏 大悲乳養人. Cf. C. translation of the *Ratna*.: 大乘信爲子 般若以爲母 禪胎大悲乳 諸佛如實子.

[63] *prajñāpāramitā* is often called '*buddhamātṛka*' in the *Prajñāpāramitāsūtra*.

[64] *anujāta*, T. *rjes[-su] skyes*, C. 如實子 (together with '*putra*').

[65] *guṇa-pāramitā*, T. *yon-tan pha-rol[-tu] phyin-pa*, C. 彼岸功德.

[66] *ātman*, T. *bdag*, C. 我 = *paramâtman*. Here '*ātman*' should be understood in the sense of '*dharmakāya*' or '*dharmadhātu*' as the universal essence or truth itself, which represents, in its turn, the Non-substantiality (*nairātmya*) of separate elements and individuals.

[67] As being in the series of Kārikās, v. 35 *a b* had better be read as '... *guṇa-pāramitā-phalaḥ*' (Bahuvrīhi comp.), whose subject or *viśiṣya* is '*jinagarbha*' in v. 45.

[68] *śama-prāpti*, T. *shi thob-pa*, C. 涅槃 (= *nirvāṇa*) and om. *prāpti*.

§ 1. The Four Supreme Virtues as the Result of Purification [69].

Here, what is shown by the former half of this *śloka*?

Because of the change of value [70] in the Absolute Body,
The results of these [4 causes] are, in short,
[The Purity, etc.] represented as the Antidote [71]
To the four kinds of delusion [72]. // 36 //

Those terms, 'the faith' etc., have been taught [73] as the causes of purification of the Essence of the Tathāgata. 'Of these [four causes]', in brief, the four kinds of Supreme Virtues (*guṇapāramitā*) of the Absolute Body of the Tathāgata are to be understood as 'the results' on account of their being Antidotes to the opposites of four kinds of delusion, respectively. Now, there is a notion of being eternal (*nitya*), blissful (*sukha*), of substantial Ego (*ātman*), of being pure (*śubha*) regarding the separate things consisting of form and others [74] which are really non-eternal, full of sufferings, of no substantial Ego and impure, respectively. Such a notion is called 'the fourfold delusion' (*viparyāsa*). Being opposite to this notion, there should be known 'the fourfold non-delusion (*aviparyāsa*) [75]. Which four? That is to say, the notion of being non-eternal, full of sufferings, of no substantial Ego, and impure regarding just those separate

[69] Cf. BGŚ 798 *a*, AĀS 471 *c*.

[70] *viparyaya*, T. *bzlog-pa*, C. 倒 (lit. reversed). This word does not include the sense of 'wrong' or 'mistake'. On the other hand, '*viparyasta*' or '*viparyāsa*' is always used in a bad sense. See below.

[71] *pratipakṣa*, T. *gñen-po* (antidote to poison), C. [修行] 對治法.

[72] *viparyāsa*, T. *phyin-ci-log* (anything wrong, deceptive), C. 顚倒 [法]. The context of this verse is not so clear. According to the prose commentary, these 4 *pāramitās* should be the antidotes to '*viparyāsa-viparyaya*', i.e. *aviparyāsa*. In this sense, by the reading '*caturvidha-aviparyāsa*', instead of '*caturvidha-viparyāsa*', it will be easier to catch the meaning, though it has no support in T. & C. Or otherwise, this '*caturvidha-viparyāsa*' should be taken as including two kinds of '4-fold delusion'. T. translation shows the following meaning: "These results are, in short, shown as *pratipakṣa* of *viparyaya* of the 4-fold *viparyāsa* in *dharmakāya*."

C. picks up three phrases, viz. *caturvidha-viparyāsa*, *dharmakāye viparyayaḥ* (instead of *viparyayāt*), and *pratipakṣaprabhāvita*, as being correspondent to '*viparyāsa*', '*viparyāsa-viparyaya*' and '*guṇapāramitā*', respectively.

[73] The insertion of '*uktāḥ*' after *viśuddhihetu*, indicated by T. Chowdhury, is supported by T. as well as C. (T. *bśad-pahi*, C. 向說).

[74] *rūpâdike vastuni*. C. 於色等無常事中. T. as C. (= *rūpâdi-vastuni anitye*).

[75] T. *phyin-ci ma log-pa*, C. 非顚倒法.

things of form, etc. Such a notion is called the fourfold Opposite of delusion (*viparyāsaviparyaya*) [76]. And again, this very [notion of non-delusion] is implied as 'delusion' with reference to the Absolute Body of the Tathāgata whose characteristics are eternal, etc. Being the Antidote of this notion, there is established the fourfold Supreme Virtue of the Absolute Body of the Tathāgata. That is to say, the Supreme Eternity (*nitya-pāramitā*), the Supreme Bliss (*sukha-pāramitā*), the Supreme Unity (*ātma-p.*), and the Supreme Purity (*śubha-p.*) [77].

And this subject [78] is to be known in detail according to the Scripture [79]. [It runs as follows]:

> "O Lord, the people have a miscomprehension regarding the phenomenal things consisting of five personality aggregates which cling to existence [80]. They have a notion of eternity on the non-eternal things, a notion of bliss regarding painful things, of substantial Ego regarding non-substantial things, and have a notion of purity regarding impure things. Even all the Śrāvakas and Pratyekabuddhas, O Lord, also have a miscomprehension in regard to the Absolute Body of the Tathāgata which is the sphere of the Wisdom of Omniscience and has never been seen before [81] just because of their knowledge of Non-substantiality [82]. O Lord, if there would be the people who have the notion of Eternity, Unity, Bliss, and Purity [regarding the Absolute Body], they would be the legal [83]

[76] C. 顛倒對治 (the reading '不' before '顛倒' in the *Taisho* edition, should be removed).

[77] These 4 *pāramitās* are taught in ŚMS, MPS, etc. and are peculiar to the *garbha* theory. The first appearance of this theory is probably in ŚMS.

[78] *grantha*, T. *bshuṅ*, C. om.

[79] ŚMS 222 *a*.

[80] *upātteṣu pañcasûpādāna-skandheṣu*. For *upātta* (Pāli *upāta*), T. *zin-pa* (finished, raised). O gives the translation: as far as manifesting themselves in an individual. The meaning is '*skandha* in the form of individual or phenomenal things and not in the form of each separate element'. Usually when '*pañca-upādānaskandha*' is spoken of, this sense is implied. So C. merely '五陰法'.

[81] *adṛṣṭa-pūrva*, T. *sṅar ma mthoṅ-ba*, C. 本所不見.

[82] *śūnyatā-jñāna*, T. *stoṅ-pa-ñid-kyi ye-śes*, C. 空智. About this *śūnyatā-jñāna*, see S. p. 76 (a quotation from the same Sūtra).

[83] *aurasa* (< *uras*) (produced from the heart), T. *thugs-las skyes-pa*, but C. instead has '信佛語故' (because of their believing in the Buddha's word). AĀS as C. But in the last sentence of this quotation, C. 真子 and adds '從佛口生 (produced from the Buddha's mouth), 從正法生從法化生得法餘財, being as the explanation of the word '*aurasa putra*'. Cf. Manu Smṛti IX, 166.

sons of the Buddhas and be of no miscomprehension. O Lord, [verily] they would be of perfect perception. For what reason? [Because], O Lord, the Absolute Body of the Tathāgata is verily the Supreme Eternity, the Supreme Bliss, the Supreme Unity and the Supreme Purity. O Lord, those people [84] who perceive the Absolute Body of the Tathāgata in this way, perceive perfectly. Those who perceive perfectly are, O Lord, the legal sons of the Buddhas" &c. [85].

§ 2. Concordance between 4 Supreme Virtues and 4 Causes of Purification [86].

And again, of these four Supreme Virtues of the Absolute Body of the Tathāgata, one should know the reversed arrangement [87] according to the order of causes. Here, 1) being opposite to the taking of delight in [88] the 'impure' Phenomenal Life by the Icchantikas who have hatred against the Doctrine of Great Vehicle, it should be understood that the acquisition of the Supreme Purity is the result of 'Practice of the Faith in the Doctrine of Great Vehicle' by the Bodhisattvas.

2) Being opposite to the taking of delight in the perception [89] of unreal Ego by the Heretics who perceive an Ego in the individual things consisting of five personality aggregates, it should be understood that the acquisition of the Supreme Unity is the result of 'practice of supremacy in the transcendental Intellect'. Indeed, all the other Heretics consider the things consisting of form, etc. as the Ego though they are of the unreal nature. And this very thing as has been perceived by the Heretics does not correspond with [90] the [real] characteristic of Ego, hence it is always non-Ego. On the contrary, the Tathāgata has attained the highest supremacy, [91] [knowing [92]] non-substantiality of all the phenomena by means

84) T. adds '*sarve*' after '*te*'.

85) Cf. AĀS 471 *c* f. (for the whole quotation).

86) Cf. BGŚ 798 *b* f.; AĀS 472 *a* f.

87) *pratiroma-krama*, T. *bzlog ste*, C. mentions the actual order (浄我樂常).

88) *abhirati*, T. *mṅon-par dgaḥ-ba*, C. [心] 樂, and adds '諸取' (*graha*).

89) *graha*, T. *ḥdsin-pa*, C. 諸取. For '*ātman*' of the Heretics, C. uses the term '神我'.

90) *visaṃvāditva*, T. *slu-ba-daṅ ldan-pa* (*slu-ba*, falsehood), C. 虛妄顛倒.

91) *para-pārami-prāpta*, T. *dam-paḥi pha-rol-tu phyin-pa brñes*, C. 到第一彼岸. '*para*' in the sense of '*parama*'.

92) So C. (知...). T. regards '*para*' as an attribute to '*nairātmya*'.

of his Wisdom perceiving the truth [93]. And this very non-substantiality as has been perceived by the Tathāgata is quite consistent with [94] the characteristic of non-ego, hence there is always the implication of Ego (ātman) [95], by taking non-Egoity (*nairātmya*) in the meaning of Ego, as has been said:

"He stands by application of no standing place" [96].

[93] *yathābhūta-jñāna*, T. *yaṅ-dag-pa ji-lta-ba-bshin-kyi ye-śes*, C. 如實智 (om. instrumental case-ending).

[94] *avisaṃvāditva*, C. 不虛妄, 非顚倒.

[95] *ātmâbhipreta*. C. 卽無我名爲有我 and seems to omit '*nairātmyam eva ātmani kṛtvā*'.

[96] C. om. this quotation whose source is unknown, and adds the explanation of '*nairātmyam eva*' (卽無我) and '*ātmâbhipreta*' (名爲有我), saying that the former is in the sense of the absence of the Heretical *ātman*, while the latter is the Buddha that has attained the 'mighty Ego'. And furthermore, with reference to this 'supreme Ego', C. adds a verse with commentary thereon. It runs as follows:

"如清淨真空 得第一無我 諸佛得淨體 是名得大身

Having attained the highest Non-substantiality.
As the pure and real emptiness,
The Buddhas obtained the pure body.
Therefore, it is said that they attained the great body.

Here 'attained the great body' (得大身) means that the Tathāgata has attained the highest pure Reality, the Absolute Body (第一清淨真如法身), which is the real nature (實我) of all the Buddhas. Having attained the self-controlling body (自在體), he got the pure body (清淨身). Therefore the Buddhas are said to have attained the pure controlling[power] (得清淨自在). In this sense the Buddhas could be the highest powerful Ego (第一最自在我) in the Immaculate Sphere.

And again, with reference to this meaning, the Absolute Body of the Tathāgata is not called the being (有). Because [all phenomena are] of non-substantial nature (無我相), of the nature of non-being (無法相). Hence he cannot be called 'the being'. Because, as his nature, he himself is absent (如彼相如是無故). At the same time, with reference to the same meaning, the Absolute Body of the Tathāgata is not called 'non-being' (無). Only because his body is the Reality itself (以唯有彼真如我體). Hence, we cannot say there is no Absolute Body. Because, as his feature, he does exist. For this reason, when Heretics asked the Buddha whether the Tathāgata would have body (有身耶) after death or not (無身耶), etc., he did neither explain (不記) nor reply (不答)".

The verse mentioned at the top has a similarity to the verse IX-23 of the

3) Being opposite to the taking of delight in the cessation [97] of Sufferings of the Phenomenal Life alone by those who belong to the Vehicle of Śrāvaka and who have fear of the sufferings of Phenomenal Life, it should be understood that the result of the practice of various kinds of meditation, named Gaganagañjā, etc. is the acquisition of the Supreme Bliss [98] concerned with all matters, mundane and supermundane.

4) Being opposite to the taking of delight in the isolated [99] abode by those who belong to the Vehicle of Pratyekabuddha and who are indifferent to the benefits of living beings, it should be understood that the Bodhisattvas' practice of Great Compassion has the acquisition of the Supreme Eternity as its result, because practising [for the sake of others]

Sūtrâlaṅkāra, which runs as follows:

> " *śūnyatāyāṃ viśuddhāyāṃ nairātmyān mārgalābhataḥ /*
> *buddhāḥ śuddhâtmalābhitvād gatā âtmamahātmatām //* ".

Also, we can find a similar passage of the prose commentary mentioned above in the following passage of the *Sūtrâlaṅkāra* along with the next verse (IX-24) and the commentary thereon. It runs as follows:

> " *tatra cânāsrave dhātau buddhānāṃ paramâtmā nirdiśyate / kiṃ kāraṇam ? / agranairātmyâtmakatvāt / agraṃ nairātmyaṃ viśuddhā tathatā sā ca buddhānām ātmā svabhāvârthena tasyām viśuddhāyām agraṃ nairātmyam ātmānam buddhā lābhante śuddham / ataḥ śuddha-ātmalābhitvād buddhā ātmamahātmyaṃ prāptā iti paramâtmā vyavasthāpyate //*
> *na bhāvo nâpi câbhāvo buddhatvaṃ tena kathyate /*
> *tasmād buddha tathāpraśne avyākṛtanayo mataḥ //*
> *tenaîva kāraṇena buddhatvaṃ na bhāva ucyate / pudgaladharmâbhāvalakṣaṇatvāt tādātmakatvāc ca buddhatvasya / nâbhāva ucyate tathatālakṣaṇaṃ bhāvāt / ato buddhatvasya bhāvâbhāvapraśne bhavati tathāgataḥ paraṃ maraṇān, na bhavatîty evam ādir avyākṛtanayo mataḥ //* (MSA p. 37-38).

Most probably the verse kept in C. is a quotation from the MSA by the commentator from the same source he quoted in other passages (e.g. S. p. 71) and the present Skt. text has a lacuna of this passage. One strong reason for this supposition is that BGŚ, which has parallel passages with the *Ratna.* throughout the text, also mentions this verse in the equivalent passage, but without commentary and regarding it as a 'sūtragāthā' (如經偈說), saying: 二空已清淨 . 得無我勝我 佛得淨性故 無我轉成我 (798 *a*).

As for the prose commentary, however, it was probably not in the original text, but we have no definite proof for saying this.

97) *upaśama*, T. *ñe-bar shi-ba.* C. om. it along with '*abhirati*' and instead has 'bhīru' (fear).

98) T. and C. add *parama.* (*paramasukhapāramitā*).

99) *asaṃsarga*, T. *ḥdu-ḥdsi med-pa* (*saṃsarga* means 'company'), C. 寂靜 (樂住寂靜 for *asaṃsargavihārâbhirati*).

as long as the world exists, without interruption, their attachment [100] to the benefits for living beings is perfectly pure.

Thus, 4 kinds of Supreme Virtues named Purity, Unity, Bliss and Eternity are brought about on the Absolute Body of the Tathāgata as the result of Bodhisattvas' 4 kinds of practices, namely, those of Faith [in the Doctrine of Great Vehicle], the Supremacy in the transcendental Intellect, the Meditations and the Great Compassion, respectively.

And [101] because of these four [Supreme Virtues in the Absolute Body] it is said, the Tathāgata is the highest Absolute Essence, he reaches up to the limit of the space and he lasts as long as the utmost limit [of the world] [102]. Indeed, the Tathāgata, through the practice of faith in the highest Doctrine of the Great Vehicle, has attained the highest state of the Absolute Essence which is the ultimate purity, hence he has become the highest Absolute Essence. Through the practice of the supremacy in the transcendental Intellect, [the Tathāgata] has realized perfectly [103] the non-substantiality of living beings and of the material world, just as the sky [reaches up to the limit of the world] [104] and, through the practice of

100) *phaligodha* in the text. T. *yoṅs-su sbyoṅ-ba* (D) (*pariśodha*, same as Ms. B.) T. shows a sense similar to '*pariśuddha*', but from the context, the meaning 'attachment' or 'clinging to' seems better. For this meaning we have a word '*paligodha*' (BHS Dic. s. v.) and if we change a letter '*ṅ*' into '*r*' in T. *sbyoṅ*, we get this meaning, hence '*yoṅs-su sbyor-ba*' might be the translation of '*paligodha*'. As for the form '*phaligodha*' instead of *paligodha*, we should record this form as a *varia lectio*, but most probably it is a wrong reading. ('*pali*' is a rather common transformation of the prefix '*pari*' in Middle Indic. Cf. Pāli *paligedha*).

101) C. 又復有義. On this passage, cf. AĀS 472 *a*; BGŚ 798 *c*.

102) Cf. *Daśabhūmikasūtra* (ed. by J. Rahder, p. 14).

"*dharmadhātu-vipulam ākāśadhātu-paryavasānam aparântakoṭiniṣṭham*"

(C. 廣大如法界 究竟如虛空 盡未來際. Avat S. 545 *b*, etc.).
These are used there as modifiers of '*praṇidhāna*' of Bodhisattvas. Cf. AĀS 472 *a*: 阿難, 因此四德 一切如來 實稱法界 不著有無 如大虛空 修空界最究竟 過三界永安住. BGŚ 798 *c*: 是故佛說 (therefore it is taught by the Buddha), 由此四德 一切如來 唯爲法界勝 由如虛空 取虛空爲邊際 極後際.

103) *niṣṭhâgamana* (lit. reaching up to the limit), T. *mthar-thug-pa-ñid-tu rtogs-pa*

104) *ākāśôpama* (T. *nam-mkhaḥ ltar*) is relating to *niṣṭhāgamana*. C. renders this passage as follows: The Tathāgata completes the sky-like *dharmakāya* through [the realization of] the absolute (究竟 *niṣṭha*) non-Substantiality of *bhājana-loka* (om. *sattva*).

The reading '*sarvatra parama-*' is to be corrected into '*sarvatra-parama-*' (in one compound).

various kinds of meditations named Gaganagañjā, etc. he has perfectly perceived the omnipresence [105] of the power of the highest truth everywhere. Because of these two acquisitions, he reaches up to the limit of space. [And lastly], through the practice of the Great Compassion, [he has] mercy towards all living beings beyond the limitation of time. Therefore, with reference to [106] this point, it is said he lasts as long as the utmost limit [of the world].

§ 3. 4 Impediments to the Attainment of the Supreme Virtues [107].

And now, for the acquisition of these four kinds of Supreme Virtues of the Absolute Body of the Tathāgata, there are four Impediments (*paripantha*) [108] even in case of the Arhats, Pratyekabuddhas and those Bodhisattvas who have obtained [10] Controlling Powers [109], though they are abiding in the Immaculate Sphere [110]. That is to say, 1) 'phenomenon of condition' (*pratyaya-lakṣaṇa*); 2) 'phenomenon of cause' (*hetu-lakṣaṇa*); 3) 'phenomenon of origination (*saṃbhava-lakṣaṇa*); and 4) 'phenomenon of destruction' (*vibhava-lakṣaṇa*) [111]. Here, 1) 'Phenomenon of condition' means the Dwelling-place of Ignorance (*avidyāvāsabhūmi*) [112].

[105] *parama-dharmaiśvarya, chos-kyi dbaṅ-phyug dam-pa.* C. rendering of this passage is as '*sarvatra sarvadharmeṣu aiśvarya-prāptatvāt*'.

[106] *upādāya.* T. & C. show it by ablative case-ending only.

[107] Cf. AĀS 472 *b*; BGŚ 799 *a*.

[108] T. *gegs*, C. 障. In BHS, it is mostly concerning the obstacles or impediments in Bodhisattvas for attaining *bodhi*. Cf. the *Rāṣṭrapālaparipṛcchā*, p. 18, l. 1 ff.

[109] *vaśitāprāpta-bodhisattva*, T. *dbaṅ-thob-paḥi byaṅ-chub-sems-dpaḥ*, C. 大力菩薩. It is not necessary to limit this qualification to those Bodhisattvas who abide on the 10th *bhūmi* as mentioned in the Tibetan commentary. We can regard this '*vaśitā-prāpta*' as an epithet for Bodhisattwas in general. (Cf. *Laṅkāvatāra*, p. 274, l. 21: *sarva-bodhisattvabhūmiṣu vaśitāprāptaḥ*).

[110] *anāsravadhātu.* It is equivalent to '*lokottara*' and its counterpart is '*sāsrava*' equivalent to '*laukika*'. The contrast between *anāsrava* and *sāsrava* will be seen in the following passage.

[111] Of these 4 terms, T. & C. are as follows:

1) *rkyen-gyi mtshan-ñid*, 緣相; 2) *rgyuḥi mtshan-ñid*, 因相; 3) *ḥbyuṅ-baḥi mtshan-ñid*, 生相; 4) *ḥjig-paḥi mtshan-ñid*, 壞相.

Cf. BGŚ: 1) 方便生死; 2) 因緣生死; 3) 有有生死: 4) 無有生死 (四種怨障). AĀS: 1) 生緣惑; 2) 生因惑; 3) 有有; 4) 無有.

[112] C. 無明住地 but T. *ma-rig-paḥi bag-chags-kyi sa* (*avidyā-vāsanā-*

[It is the condition of birth of the Body made of mind for the Saints] just as Ignorance (*avidyā*) is [the condition] of Predispositions (*saṃskārāḥ*) [for ordinary people]. 2) 'Phenomenon of cause' means the Immaculate Action (*anāsravaṃ karma*)[113] conditioned by the Dwelling-place of Ignorance [as the cause of the Body made of mind], [and it is to be] compared with the Predispositions [of ordinary people][114]. 3) 'Phenomenon of origination' means the origination of the 3-fold Body made of mind (*manomayâtmabhāva.*)[115], conditioned by the Dwelling-place of Ignorance and caused by the Immaculate Action, just as the origination[116] of the Three-Worlds (*tribhava*)[117] is conditioned by 4 kinds of Graspings (*upādāna*)[118] and caused by the Passioned Actions

bhūmi). which agrees with Ms. B reading. See S. p. 33, n. 6. Acc. to ŚMS (220 *a*), there are said to be five *vāsa-bhūmis*, of which *avidyā-vāsabhūmi* is the basic and the strongest. The other four are 1) C. 見一切處住地, T. *lta-ba gcig-la gnas-paḥi gnas-kyi sa* (**ekadṛṣṭisthita-vāsabhūmi*); 2) C. 欲愛住地, T. *ḥdod-paḥi ḥdod-chag-la gnas-paḥi . . .* (**kāmarāgasthita-v.*); 3) C. 色愛住地, T. *gzugs-kyi ḥdod-chag-la gnas-paḥi . . .* (**rūparāgasthita-v.*), and 4) C. 有愛住地, T. *srid-paḥi ḥdod-chags-la gnas-paḥi . . .* (**bhavarāgasthita-v.*), and are said to be the basic *kleśas* from which all the defilements in the form of intense outburst (*paryavasthāna-* or *paryutthāna-kleśa*) come out. Furthermore, it is said, these four are '*kṣaṇika*', while '*avidyāvāsabhūmi*' (T. *ma-rig-paḥi gnas-kyi sa*) is '*anādikālikā*' and cannot be destroyed except by '*bodhijñāna*' of the Tathāgata; therefore, it is the strongest. In this sense *avidyāvāsabhūmi* is here related to the defilement existing in Bodhisattvas (in another passage in the *Ratna.*, this *kleśa* is said to be that of Arhats. see S. p. 67, l. 17–19). As for the meaning of '*vāsabūmi*', there are traditionally two ways of interpretation: one is shown in C. and T. translation of ŚMS, the other is shown in T. translation of the *Ratna.* It relates more or less to the etymology of the term *vāsanā* (from √ *vas*, to dwell, or from *vas*, to perfume). The second interpretation is also shown in this *Ratna.*, v. I, 130 where the term '*vāsanā*' is used for indicating '*avidyāvāsabhūmi*'.

113) T. *zag-pa med-paḥi las*, C. 無漏業. Here *anāsravakarman*, of which the exact counterpart is *sāsravakarman*, is compared to *saṃskāras* in the sense that *karman* is the cause of the next birth.

114) C. has confusion in interpreting this passage. C. says '*hetulakṣaṇa*' means '*avidyāvāsabhūmi-pratyayā saṃskārāḥ*', and from this *saṃskāra*, there is conditioned '*anāsravakarman*', just as '*vijñāna*' is produced from '*saṃskāra*'. C. seems to regard '*saṃskāra*' of *avidyā-vāsabhūmi* as something different from '*anāsravakarman*'. But it may not be the case here.

115) (= *manomaya-kāya*), T. *yid-kyi raṅ-bshin-kyi lus*, C. 意生身. The body of the saints is said to be consisting merely of '*mano-skandha*', instead of 5 *upādāna-skandhas* as in the case of ordinary beings.

116) *abhinirvṛtti*, T. *mṅon-par grub-pa*, C. 生.

117) T. *srid-pa gsum*, C. 三界 (= *tridhātu*).

118) T. *ñe-bar len-pa bshi*, C. 四種取. Here '*upādāna*' is synonymous with *kleśa*. The four *upādānas* are usually; 1) *kāma*; 2) *dṛṣṭi*; 3) *śīlavrata* and 4) *ātmavāda*.

(*sāsravakarman*)[119]. 4) ' Phenomenon of destruction ' means Death as the inconceivable Transformation (*acintyā pāriṇāmikī cyuti*)[120] conditioned by the origination of the 3-fold Body made of mind. It corresponds to the Decrepitude and Death (*jarāmaraṇa*) conditioned by the Birth (*jāti*) [in the Three-Worlds].

Now, the Arhats, Pratyekabuddhas and those Bodhisattvas who have attained (10) Controlling Powers, have not extirpated the Dwelling-place of Ignorance which is the ground of all the subsequent Defilements[121], hence they cannot attain the Supreme Purity as the end of removal[122] of all the dusts of defilements with their bad-smelling impressions[123]. And, on account of that Dwelling-place of Ignorance, and because of their being accompanied with[124] the arising of the subtle-featured dualistic view[125], they cannot attain ultimately[126] the Supreme Unity which is characterized as no accumulation of Active Force[127]. And, on account of that Dwelling-place of Ignorance and Immaculate Action caused by the arising of the subtle-featured dualistic view conditioned by the Dwelling-place of Ignorance, there is [still] the arising of the Mind-made aggregate

119) T. *zag-pa daṅ bcas-pāḥi las*, C. 有漏業. See above (Note VIII-113).

120) T. *mi-khyab-par yoṅs-su bsgyur-paḥi ḥchi-ḥpho-ba*, C. 不可思議變易死 (*cyuti* means literally ' fall '). The counterpart of this death in the case of ordinary beings is called C. 分段死, T. *rgyun-chad-paḥi ḥchi-ḥpho* (death as the interruption of flowing). Cf. ŚMS 219 *c* (this term seems peculiar to ŚMS).

121) *upakleśa*, T. *ñe-baḥi ñon-moṅs-pa*, C. 煩惱 (om. *upa*). About *avidyā-vāsa-bhūmi* being the ground of all *upakleśas*, see ŚMS 220 *a*: 如是無明住地力... 恒沙等數上煩惱依 (*ñe-baḥi ñon-moṅs-pa gaṅ-gāḥi kluṅ-gi bye-ma-las ḥdas-pa sñed-kyi rten-du gyur-pa*).

122) ... *apakarṣa-paryanta* (lit. ending with the removal of . . .). But the reading is not clear. Both T. & C. take ' *paryanta* ' as ' *atyanta* ' and attach it to *śubhapāramitā* as an attribute. About *apakarṣa*, T. reads instead ' *bag-chags . . . daṅ ldan-paḥi phyir* ', and C. 未得遠離... (*apakarṣāparyantatvāt*).

123) *daurgandhya-vāsanā*. T. *drir-baḥi bag-chags*, but connects *drir-ba* with *mala*. C. gives no translation of *daurgandhya* and has instead ' *avidyāvāsabhūmigata-mala* '.

124) C. reads as ' . . . *apakarṣāparyantatvāt* ' (未得永滅) instead of ' *yogāt* '.

125) *sūkṣmanimitta-prapañca*, C. 細相戲論.

126) C. as an attribute to *ātmapāramitā*. T. takes it probably as an attribute to *anabhisaṃskāra*.

127) *anabhisaṃskāra*, T. *ḥdus ma-byas-pa*, C. 無爲. C. takes this as an attribute to all the 4 *pāramitās* along with *atyanta*.

The reading *anabhisaṃskāram* is, at J's suggestion, to be corrected into *anabhisaṃskārām*.

(*manomaya-skandha*)[128]. Therefore, they cannot attain the ultimate Supreme Bliss as the extinction of this Spiritual Aggregate. And [lastly], unless they realize the Essence[129] of the Tathāgata as being arisen from the entire extinction of all impurities in forms of Defilements, Actions and Originations, they cannot remove Death as the Inconceivable Transformation. Consequently, they cannot attain the absolutely unchangeable[130] Supreme Eternity.

Here, the Dwelling-place of Ignorance is to be compared with the Impurity of Defilements [in the case of ordinary people]. The performance[131] of Immaculate Action corresponds to the Impurity of Actions. [And] the 3-fold origination of the Body made of mind and Death as the Inconceivable Transformation corresponds to the Impurity of Origination[132].

And this passage is to be understood in detail according to the Scripture[133]. [It runs as follows]:

> " O Lord, just as, being conditioned by [4] graspings and caused by passionate actions, there are produced the three spheres of existence; likewise, O Lord, being conditioned by the dwelling-place of ignorance and caused by the immaculate actions, there are born the 3 kinds of body made of mind of the Arhats, Pratyekabuddhas and those Bodhisattvas who have attained the [10] Controlling Powers. [Thus] O Lord, for the birth of the 3-fold Body made of mind in these 3 lands[134] and for the origination of the immaculate actions the dwelling-place of Ignorance is the [inevitable] condition, & c.".

Thus, in these 3 Bodies made of mind of the Arhats, Pratyekabuddhas and Bodhisattvas, there are no Supreme Virtues of Purity, Unity, Bliss

128) T. *yid-kyi raṅ-bshin-gyi phuṅ-po*, C. 意陰. See above (Note VIII-115).

129) C. has instead '*dharmakāya*'.

130) *atyantânanyathābhāva*, T. *gshan-du gyur-pa med-pa*, (om. *atyanta*), C. 不變異體. C. connects *atyanta* to *nityapāramitā*.

131) *abhisaṃskāra*, T. regards it as an apposition to *anāsravakarman*. C. 行.

132) *saṃkleśa* (T. *kun-nas ñon-moṅs-pa*, C. 染) is a general term for all the process of *saṃsāra* in which *kleśa*, *karman* and *janman* are included. Sometimes, for *janman*, *duḥkha* is mentioned (C. 惑, 業, 苦, for the three); also, it is replaced by '*vipāka*' or '*skandha-dhātv-āyatana*'. In all cases what is meant by them is the same Phenomenal Life.

133) ŚMS 220 *a*.

134) *tisṛṣu bhūmiṣu*, T. om., but C. [此] 三乘地 (the lands of the 3 vehicles).

and Eternity. Therefore, it is said[135]:

> "Only the Absolute Body of the Tathāgata is the Supreme Eternity, the Supreme Bliss, the Supreme Unity and the Supreme Purity".

§ 4. The Motives of the 4 Supreme Virtues[136].

Verily[137], the Absolute Body of the Tathāgata is pure
Because of his innate purity and removal of Impressions;
He is the highest Unity because he is quiescent,
Having destroyed[138] the dualistic view of Ego and non-Ego. // 37 //
He is blissful because the Mind-made Aggregate
And its causes have been removed [completely];
He is eternal because he has realized[139]
The equality of the Phenomenal Life and Nirvāṇa. // 38 //

In short, by two reasons there should be known the Supreme Purity in the Absolute Body of the Tathāgata. That is to say, 1) through his being perfectly pure by nature, as the common feature; and 2) through his being perfectly pure by the removal of pollution, as the special feature [to the Buddha][140]. The Supreme Unity, too, should be understood by two reasons: 1) because of the removal of false imagination of Ego by rejecting the extremity peculiar to the Heretics, and 2) because of the removal of false imagination concerning non-substantiality by rejecting

[135] ŚMS 222 *a* (C. 是故聖者勝鬘經言).

[136] Cf. BGŚ 799 *b*; AĀS 472 *b*. Both of them have one passage preceding to it, on the 4 troubles (難) corresponding to the respective impediments, namely: 1) 煩惱難; 2) 業難; 3) 生執難; 4) 過失難 (trouble by fault or death).

[137] C. treats these two verses in prose and regards them as the commentary on the quotation above mentioned.

[138] *kṣaya*, T. om., C. 離 (having removed). C. om. *ātma-*.

[139] *prativedha*, T. *rtogs(-pa)*, C. 證.

[140] *sāmānyalakṣaṇa* & *viśeṣalakṣaṇa*, C. 因相 & 勝相, respectively. T. as usual. Here '*sāmānya*' means common to all living beings; therefore, it is the cause (因) for the attainment of the highest purity. On the other hand, removal of pollution is not innate to living beings, and the Buddha got his appellation because of his attainment of this purity. Therefore, it is peculiar to the Buddha and shows the superiority (勝) of the Buddha.

the extremity peculiar to the Śrāvakas. The Supreme Bliss is to be known likewise by two reasons: 1) because of the abandonment of the origination of all sufferings as well as the extirpation of succeeding origination [141] of Impressions; and 2) because of the realization of all sufferings as well as the realization of extinction of the Mind-made Aggregates [142]. [And finally] by two reasons the Supreme Eternity is to be known: 1) Because he does not fall into the Nihilistic Extremity through his not diminishing [143], neglecting the non-eternal Phenomenal Life; 2) nor does he fall into the Eternalistic Extremity through his not intensifying [144] the eternal Nirvāṇa. It is said as follows [145]:

> " If someone would perceive that all the Phenomenal Worlds are non-eternal, O Lord, this view would be a Nihilistic Perception [146]. It would never be the true perception at all. If someone would perceive that the Nirvāṇa is eternal, O Lord, this view would be an Eternalistic Perception [147]. And it would never be the True Perception at all ".

§ 4′ (The Unstable Nirvāṇa).

Therefore, by this introduction to the theory [148] of the Absolute Essence, it is said from the highest view-point that the Phenomenal Life itself is Nirvāṇa, because [the Bodhisattvas] realize the Unstable Nirvāṇa (*apratiṣṭhitanirvāṇa*), being indiscriminative of both [the Phenomenal Life and

141) *anusandhi*, T. *mtshams-sbyor-ba*, C. om. This '*vāsanā-anusandhi*' corresponds to *manomayakāya* of the Saints, and similarly '*duḥkha*' signifies that of ordinary people.

142) Both T. & C. have *kāya* instead of *skandha*. (But the meaning is the same) Of these two columns, 1) shows an actual 'annihilation' and 2), its cause. In other words, to annihilate *duḥkha* means to realize that *duḥkha* is extinguished by nature, i.e. there is no *duḥkha* in the ultimate sense. Logically, therefore, it would be better to consider the annihilation of *duḥkha* and that of *vāsanā* as 'two reasons'. C. shows this way of interpretation, though it has some confusion on the way.

143) & 144) *anapakarṣaṇa* & *asamāropaṇa*, (a negative particle is required before *samāropa*. Hence the reading should be *nirvāṇâsamāropaṇa*–). C. 不滅 & 不取, respectively. BGŚ 不損減 & 無増益, resp. For *apakarṣaṇa*, T. has *ḥbrid-pa*, which means 'to impose' and is close to *samāropa* (T. *snon-pa*) in its sense. From the context, the reading in C. seems better.

145) ŚMS 220 *a*.

146) & 147) *ucchedadṛṣṭi* & *śāśvatadṛṣṭi*, respectively.

148) *nayamukha*, T. *tshul-gyi sgo*, C. 法門. For this passage, cf. BGŚ 799 *c*.

Nirvāṇa] [149]. Moreover, they are neither entirely involved among all living beings nor remote from them [150], for two reasons. Here, therefore, the explanation will be made merely about how to attain this Unstable stability [151]. Then, for which two reasons? Here, in this world, the Bodhisattva is not entirely involved among all living beings because he has completely rejected all tendencies of desires by means of the Transcendental Intellect. [At the same time], he is not remote from them since he never abandons them owing to his Great Compassion. This is the means for the acquisition of the Supreme Enlightenment of which the Unstability is the essential nature. By means of the Intellect, indeed, the Bodhisattva has exterminated without remainder the tendency of desire, hence, being deeply intent towards the Nirvāṇa for his own sake, he does not stay in the Phenomenal Life as the lineage of no Nirvāṇa (*aparinirvāṇagotra*). [At the same time], owing to his Great Compassion, he never abandons those suffering people, hence, having activity [152] in this Phenomenal Life, for the sake of others, he does not abide in the Nirvāṇa, as do those who seek only for Quiescence (*śamaikayānagotra*) [153].

Thus these two qualities (i.e. the Intellect and Great Compassion) are the root, i.e. the foundation of the Highest Enlightenment. [So it is said] [154]:

[Though] Having destroyed affection for himself
By means of the Intellect, completely,

[149] *ubhayathā'vikalpana*, C. 以此二法不分別故. Of this point, S. & T. have no further explanation. But C. puts one verse which explains this point:
無分別之人 不分別世間 不分別涅槃 涅槃有平等
(One who has non-discriminative [Wisdom] distinguishes neither Phenomenal Life nor Nirvāṇa, and perceives the equality of both Nirvāṇa and Phenomenal Life).

This verse has a similarity to some extent with v. 39 in its contents, but it is difficult to identify both verses. C. om. the following sentences along with v. 39. These facts seem to show that the original text was as C. (but the verse is a quotation) and that later on that verse was replaced by the following passage along with v. 39.

[150] *āsanna-dūrī-bhāva*. Lit. near and remote state.

[151] *apratiṣṭhita-pada*, T. *mi-gnas-paḥi gnas*. The term *pada* signifies actually *nirvāṇa*.

[152] *prayoga*, T. *sbyor-ba*.

[153] T. *shi-ba bgrod-pa gcig-paḥi rigs*. It signifies *śrāvakayānika* & *pratyekabuddhayānika*, in whom the mind of Compassion towards living beings is lacking. Being opposed to either of them, *aparinirvāṇagotra* and *śamaikayānagotra*, Bodhisattvas may be termed as '*parinirvāṇagotraka*', and *parinirvāṇa* is, in the ultimate point, this *apratiṣṭhitanirvāṇa*.

[154] This verse seems to be a quotation even if the preceding prose commentary is genuine.

The Saint, being full of Mercy, does not approach
Quiescence because of his affection for the people;
Thus standing on [155] both the Intellect and Mercy,
These two means of Enlightenment,
The Saint approaches neither this world nor Nirvāṇa [156]. // 39 //

§ 5. The Functions of the Germ for its Purification (IV) [157].

Now, with reference to the subject of 'function' which is previously maintained (in verse 35), what is shown by the latter half of that *śloka?*

If [158] there is no Essence of the Buddha,
There will be no aversion to Suffering,
Nor will there be desire nor earnest wish,
Nor prayer for Nirvāṇa. // 40 //

So it is said [159]:

"O Lord, if there were no Matrix of the Tathāgata, then there would arise neither aversion to Suffering nor desire for Nirvāṇa, nor earnest wish for it or prayer for it".

Here, in brief, the Essence of the Buddha, the perfectly pure Germ [160], even of those people who are fixed in the wrong way [161] has the two kinds of foundation [162] of its actions. That is to say, it produces disgust

[155] *niḥśritya*, T. *brten-nas.* The form *niḥ-śri* is etymologically a wrong reading for *ni-śri* and probably caused by actual pronunciation, i.e. insertion of Visarga after *ni-* before double consonant bearing a sibilant at the head. (e.g. *niḥṣyanda* for *niṣyanda*).

[156] *saṃvṛti* (covered) and *nirvṛti* (dis-covered) in the text. T. as *saṃsāra* and *nirvāṇa.*

[157] Cf. BGŚ 799 *c*–800 *c* (4. *karman*).

[158] *sacet* (BHS). Pāli *sace.*

[159] ŚMS 222 *b.*

[160] *viśuddhigotra*, T. *rnam-par dag-paḥi rigs*, C. 清淨正因 (*viśuddhi-hetu*). (Cf., BGŚ, 清淨性). This is an apposition to *buddhadhātu.* See S. p. 6, l. 9.

[161] For *mithyātvaniyata-*, C. 不定聚, (*aniyata-sattvarāśi*) and BGŚ agree with C. (T. as S.) '*aniyata-*' seems to be the original reading, since by the term '*mithyātvaniyata- s.*' the Icchantikas are implied and this passage does not refer to the Icchantikas.

[162] *pratyupasthāna*, T. *ñe-bar gnas-par byed-de* (*upasthita*), C. 能作... (to cause to work). See Note VIII-211.

witn Phenomenal Life basing itself upon [163] the perception of the fault of Suffering, and it calls forth longing, desire, earnest wish and prayer for the Nirvāṇa, basing itself upon the perception that happiness is the merit [164]. Here, 'longing' (*chanda*) means 'expectation' (*abhilāṣa*) [165]. 'Desire' (*icchā*) means 'uncowardliness' (*asaṃkoca*) [166] for the attainment of the intended object. 'Earnest Wish' (*prârthanā*) means 'searching for' (*parimārgaṇā*) [167] the means to attain the intended object. 'Prayer' (*praṇidhi*) means 'will' (*cetanā*) or 'manifestation (*abhisaṃskāra*) of the mind' [168].

The perception of Phenomenal Life and Nirvāṇa, —
The former is full of Suffering, hence it is the fault,
The latter is of bliss, therefore it is the merit;
It exists only in case the Germ of the Buddha exists,
And does not exist with people of no Germ. // 41 //

The perception that Phenomenal Life is full of suffering, hence is the fault, and that Nirvāṇa is blissful, hence it is the merit, – this perception belongs to those people who are possessed of good virtues [169] and exists only in case the Germ [of the Tathāgata] exists. Thus this perception does not take place without causes or without conditions. Indeed, if it were without Germ [170], without causes and conditions and were not brought about through the extirpation of sin [171], it would exist even with

163) *niḥśrayena*, C. 依.

164) *anuśaṃsa*, T. *phan-yon*, C. 寂樂 for *sukhânuśaṃsa*. Here *anuśaṃsa* stands for *guṇa* in the following verse and corresponds to *doṣa* in case of *saṃsāra*.

165) This sentence is lacking in S. But T. *de-la ḥdun-pa ni mṅon-par ḥhod-paḥo*; C. has a similar sentence. The context shows its necessity. The rendering from T. is as follows:

tatra cchando 'bhilāṣaḥ

166) T. *phyogs-pa* (*abhimukha*, going ahead), C. 不怯弱.

167) T. *tshol-ba*, C. 追求 & 諮問. *parimārgaṇā* is a unique form in BHS for Skt. *parimārgaṇa*. For *prârthanā*, T. *don-du gñer-ba* (to provide for, to strive to procure), C. 欲得.

168) *cetanā cittâbhisaṃskāra*, C. 心心相行, but T. om. *cetanā*.

169) *śuklâṃśa*, T. *dkar-po [ḥi] cha* / (so J's fn., but D. *dkar-poḥi chos*... (*śukladharma*), C. 善根 (= *kuśalamūla*). Cf. BGŚ, 淨分 (as S.), together with an explanation of this term (3 aṃśas- 福德分 (*puṇya*), 解脫分 (*mukti*), 通達分 (*adhigama*)). Cf. Pāli *sukkâṃsa*, bright lot, fortune.

170) *gotram antareṇa*. T. & C. om. it.

171) The reading should be corrected into '*pāpâsamuccheddayogena*' from *pāpasamucchedayogena* (acc. to T.).

the Icchantikas who are of the lineage of no Nirvāṇa. Really, it cannot take place unless they bring about the Germ which is purified from accidental pollutions and the faith in any one of three Vehicles [172] through being endowed with [173] the 4 kinds of good actions [174], beginning with having contact with a personage of high virtue [175].

(The saying: the Icchantikas are of no Nirvāṇa, is only conventional) [176]

It is however said [in the Scripture] [177]:

" After this [178] the rays of the disk of the sun-like Tathāgata [179]

[172] *dharma* is here used for *yāna*. T. *chos*, but C. 乘 (C. '一乘' stands for *anyatamadharma*).

[173] *samavadhāna*, T. *yaṅ-dag-par ḥbyor-ba*, C. 修習 (to practise).

[174] *catuḥśukla*. T. *ḥkhor-lo bshi* (*catuścakra*), which are, according to O, 1) the reliance upon a saintly personage; 2) the accumulation of virtue; 3) a favourable dwelling-place; and 4) sublime vows and correct appreciation. They are the 4 wheels of the great vehicle. There is, however, another fourfold group in Tibetan under the name of '*catuḥśukladharma* (*dkar-poḥi chos bshi*)' or '*caturākaraśukla* (*dkar-po rnam bshi*)' (they are namely: 1) *dge-baḥi chos ma skyes-pa bskyed-pa*, to produce good quality which has not been produced; 2) *skyes-pa mi-ñams-pa*, to retain what is produced; 3) *mi-dge-baḥi chos skyes-pa spoṅ-ba*, to avoid the bad quality already produced; and 4) *mi-dge-baḥi chos ma-skyes-pa rnams mi-bskyed-pa*, to prevent the generation of bad quality which has not yet appeared). The latter fourfold group seems not relevant to this passage.

The third and perhaps the most suitable one is found in the *Mahāparinirvāṇasūtra* of Mahāyāna. According to C. translation, it is called '四善法' (*catuṣkuśaladharma*, but most probably for *catuḥśukladharma*), and its four items are 1) to approach the personage of high virtue; 2) to attend and accept the teaching; 3) to contemplate the meaning of the doctrine; and 4) to practise according to the teaching.

Cf. BGŚ 四種聖輪 (*catur[ārya]cakra* as T.), which are 1) 如法住國土; 2) 信善知識; 3) 自調伏身; 4) 宿植善根. It has an explanation of the term '*cakra*'.

[175] *satpuruṣa*, T. *skyes-bu dam-pa*, C. 善知識, which includes monks as well as laymen.

[176] Cf. BGŚ 787 *c*–788 *c* (破執分第二中 破小乘執品第一), where discussion is held around the existence of '*buddhagotra*' among various schools of Buddhism.

[177] Avat S. 616 *b* (in Chap. 32: *Tathāgatôtpattisaṃbhava-parivarta*), according to C. But a sentence closer to this quotation is found in JAĀ, 242 *c*. (as O's note).

[178] The reading '*yatra hy āha / tatra paścād*' is somewhat doubtful. T. *gaṅ-gi phyir, de-ḥi ḥog-tu ... shes gsuṅs-sc*' (*yata āha / tataḥ paścād ...*), and C. 是故華嚴性起中言 (*tasmād uktam Avataṃsaka-gotrôtpattau / tataḥ paścād ...*).

[179] T. adds *jñāna* after *tathāgata*.

fall upon the bodies of even those people who are fixed in the wrong way and make benefits for them [180]. And furthermore producing the cause of future [bliss] [in them], they cause them to thrive with virtuous qualities [181].

And also the saying : " the Icchantikas are by all means of the nature of no Perfect Nirvāṇa " [182] is taught in order to remove the hatred against the Doctrine of the Great Vehicle, this being the cause of their being Icchantikas and refers to a certain period of time [183]. Indeed, as there exists the Germ which is pure by nature, none could be of the absolutely impure nature [184]. Therefore, with reference to the fact that all living beings, with no difference, have the possibility [185] of being purified, the Lord has said again [186] :

" Though being beginningless, indeed,
[The Phenomenal Life] has its end [187] ;
Being pure by nature,
It is endowed with Eternity [188] ;
Being covered from outside
By the beginningless sheath [of defilements],
[This nature] is however invisible,
Just as the gold [189] concealed [190] [in sand and dust] ".

180) Acc. to T. & C., one phrase of '*tān upakurvanti*' should be inserted. (T. *de-dag-la phan ḥdogs-par ḥgyur shiṅ*, C. 作彼衆生利益.

181) *kuśalair dharmaiḥ*, C. 白法 (*śukladhamra*).

182) In the *Mahāparinirvāṇasūtra*, &c.

183) According to O's interpretation. T. *dus-gshan-la dgoṅs-nas*, C. 依無量時. The meaning is that the Icchantikas remain as *aparinirvāṇagotraka* only for the certain period of time when they have hatred against the doctrine of Mahāyāna, but not forever. Cf. BGŚ 786 *c*: 於長時中.

184) *-dharman* (ifc.), T. om., C. 性.

185) *bhavyatā*, T. *ruṅ-pa-ñid*. This sentence and the following verse are missing in C.

186) The source unknown.

187) *avasānika*, T. *tha-ma daṅ ldan-pa*. About this beginningless nature of *saṃsāra*, see S. p. 72 ll. 13-16. It should be noted that *saṃsāra* is not endless. See Note VIII-242.

188) *dhruvadharma*.

189) *suvarṇabimba* Lit. 'the shape of gold', T. *gser-gyi gzugs*.

190) *paricchādita*, T. *bsgribs* (= *vṛta*).

(V) YOGA [191]

Now, with reference to the meaning of 'Union' (*yoga*), there is one *śloka*.

(Kārikā 8)

Being the inexhaustible storage [192] of jewels of immeasurable virtues,
[The Germ of the Buddha is] like the Ocean;
It is akin to the lantern, because of its nature of
Being endowed with properties indivisible [from it] [193]. // 42 //

§ 1. The Union of the Germ with the Factors of its Purification.

Here, what is shown by the former half of this *śloka?*

Because it consists of the sources [194] of the Absolute Body,
Of the Buddha's Wisdom and Compassion [195],
There is shown the similarity of the Germ with the ocean,
Through being receptacle, jewels and water. // 43 //

On account of three points, the Essence of the Tathāgata has a resemblance to the great ocean in three ways, respectively, and through this

[191] Under this subject of '*yoga*', two kinds of 'union' are discussed. One is the union of *dhātu*, in the sense of *hetu*, with *dharmakāya*. The other is the relation of *dhātu*, in the sense of *dharmadhātu*, i. e. *phala*, with its properties. And this union is an unseparable accompaniment (*samanvāgama, avyatireka, saṃbaddha, avinirbhāga*). That is to say, being possessed of *hetu* of *dharmakāya*, consisting of *prajñā* and *karuṇā*, a *sattva* is called *dhātu*: and just because he is *dhātu*, consequently he is endowed with *abhijñā*, *jñāna* and *āsravakṣaya*.

Cf. BGŚ 801 *a* (5. yoga), where '*āśrayaparivṛtti*' and '*nirvāṇa*' are discussed along with this subject.

[192] *ākara*, T. *gnas*, C. 器.

[193] Cf. DAŚ 893 *b*: 如光明熱色,與燈無異相.

[194] *dhātu*, T. *khams*, C. 衆生性 *sattvas* are '*dhātu*' because of their being '*dharmadhātu-saṃgraha*' of *dharmakāya*. *dhātu*, here in the sense of '*hetu*'. See commentary.

[195] C. inserts '*samādhi*' (定) between *jñāna* and *karuṇā*.

similarity, the subject ' Union ' should be understood in the sense that the Essence of the Tathāgata is provided with causes [of its purification] (*hetu-samanvāgama*)[196]. Then, which are the three points ? They are namely: [its being provided with] 1) the cause of purification of the Absolute Body (*dharmakāyaviśuddhihetu*)[197]; 2) the cause of the attainment of Buddha's Wisdom (*buddhajñānasamudāgamahetu*); and 3) the cause of the manifestation of Buddha's Great Compassion (*tathāgatamahākaruṇāvṛttihetu*)[198]. Here, 1) ' the cause of purification of the Absolute Body ' is to be known as the practice of faith in [the Doctrine of] the Great Vehicle; 2) 'the cause of the attainment of Buddha's Wisdom', the practice of the introduction to the highest Intellect and Meditation; and 3) 'the cause of the manifestation[199] of Buddha's Great Compassion', the practice of Bodhisattva's Great Compassion[200].

Here, the practice of faith in [the Doctrine][201] of the Great Vehicle has a similarity to the ' receptacle ' because, in this [receptacle], there is an accumulation[202] of the jewel of Intellect and Meditation as well as the water of Compassion which are immeasurable and inexhaustible. The practice of the introduction to the highest Intellect and Meditation has a similarity to ' jewel ' because of its being indiscriminative and being endowed with inconceivable and powerful virtues. The practice of Bodhisattva's Compassion has a similarity to ' water ' because, in all the world, it manifests the highest moisture with the feature of one and the same taste[203]. This coherence (*saṃbaddha*)[204] i.e. the accompaniment

196) T. *rgyu daṅ ldan-pa*, C. 依因畢竟成就 '*dhātu-saṃgraha*' in the verse is here explained by this '*hetu-samanvāgama*'.

197) Against J's note, T. (D) has '*kāya*'.

198) C. has '得' (*prāpti*) instead of '*vṛtti*'. But T. *ḥjug-pa*.

199) Against J's note, T. (D) has '*tathāgatamahākaruṇā* (*de-bshin-gśegs-paḥi thugs-rje chen-po*). About '*pravṛtti*', T. always translates it into '*ḥjugs*' without prefix.

200) T. distinguishes the *karuṇā* of the Buddha from that of the Bodhisattva by using '*thugs-rje*' for the former and '*sñiṅ-rje*' for the latter.

201) T. has '*dharma*' after '*mahāyāna*'.

202) *samavasaraṇa*, T. *ḥdu-ba* (mixing up). C. simply '*tasyām aparimeya-akṣayatvāt*' and om. '*prajñāsamādhiratnakaruṇāvāri-samavasaraṇa*'. But, BGŚ says '此中有無量定慧大寶遍滿故, 故說界相似', which is apparently equal to S.

203) T. reads 'its nature of the highest moisture in all the world is endowed with one taste' and om. *lakṣaṇa*, which C. has. For *prayoga*, T. *-daṅ ldan-pa*, but C. 行 (= *pravṛtti*). Here *prayoga* has the sense of ' presentation or manifestation ' in connection with the term *lakṣaṇa* (*lakṣaṇa-prayoga*, C. 相行).

(*samanvāgama*) [205] of these three things (the Absolute Body and others), with these three causes, the practice of faith, etc., is here called 'Union'.

§ 2. The Union of the Germ with the Result of Purification.

Now, what is shown by the latter half of the *śloka* ?

> In the immaculate basis [206], the supernatural faculties,
> The Wisdom and Immaculateness [207] are inseparable from Reality;
> Therefore, they have a resemblance to a lantern,
> On account of its light, heat and colour [208]. // 44 //

The subject, 'Union' is here to be understood in the sense that the Essence of the Tathāgata is accompanied by the results [of its purification] (*phala-samanvāgama*), through its similarity to a lantern in three ways on account of three points, respectively. Then, which are the three points ? Namely, [the Essence of the Buddha is endowed with] 1) the Supernatural Faculties (*abhijñā*); 2) the Wisdom by which the evil influence is destroyed, (*āsravakṣayajñāna*); and 3) the Extinction of Evil Influence (*āsravakṣaya*) [209]. Here, the 5 Supernatural faculties [210] have a resemblance to 'light of flame' because they have a characteristic of engaging in [211] the extinction of darkness which is opposite to the know-

204) T. [-daṅ] *ḥbral-pa*, C. 和合.

205) T. *-daṅ ldan-pa*, C. 畢竟不捨離 (absolutely inseparable).

206) *vimalâśraya*, T. *dri-med-gnas*, C. 無垢界 (*vimala-dhātu*). Here *āśraya* is used for *dhātu*, and hence, *vimalâśraya* is synonymous with *dharmakāya*.

207) C. 通, 智, 無垢, for respective term,

208) Cf. DAŚ 893 *b* (v. 13): 如光明熱色 與燈無異相 如是諸佛法 於法性亦然.

209) T. & C. for these 3 terms are respectively:

1) *mṅon-par śes-pa*, 通 (= 神通); 2) *zag-pa zad-paḥi ye-śes*, 知漏盡智 (*jñāna* in the verse, T. *ye-śes*, C. 智); 3) *zag-pa zad-pa*, 漏盡 (*vaimalya* in the verse, T. *dri-med*, C. 無垢).

210) 1) *ṛddhi-viṣaya-jñāna-sākṣātkriyā-abhijñā*; 2) *divyacakṣuḥ -j.-s.-a*; 3) *divyaśrotra-j.-s.-a.*; 4) *paracetaḥ-paryāya-j.-s.-a.*; & 5) *pūrvanivāsânusmṛti-j.-s.-a*. Cf. Mvyut. 14.

211) *pratyupasthāna*, T. *ñe-bar gnas-pa* (originally from Pāli *paccaṭṭhāna*). In C. '能' of '能治, 能燒' stands for this term and shows the meaning of 'being capable of'.

ledge which perceives an object [212]. The Wisdom by which the Evil Influence is destroyed is similar to 'heat' because of its characteristic of engaging in consuming the fuel [213] of the Active force and Defilements, leaving no residue.

The Extinction of Evil Influence as the [result of] the Perfect Manifestation of the Basis has resemblance to 'colour' because of its characteristic of being perfectly stainless (*vimala*), pure (*viśuddha*) and radiant (*prabhāsvara*). Here, it is 'stainless' because it has destroyed the Obstruction caused by moral Defilements. It is 'pure' because it has destroyed the Obstruction on account of knowable things. It is 'radiant' [by nature] because these two [Obstructions] are merely of an occasional nature [214]. Thus, in brief, the properties of those people who have nothing further to learn [215] summarized in these seven, i.e. the 5 Supernatural Faculties, the Wisdom destroying the Evil Influence and the Destruction [of Evil Influence] [216], are in the Immaculate Sphere, inseparable from each other, not different [from each other] and coherent with [217] the Absolute. This point is here called 'Union'.

And with reference to this subject of 'Union', the example of a lantern is to be understood in detail according to the Sūtra [218].

> "O Śāriputra, just as a lantern is of indivisible nature and its qualities are inseparable from it [219]. That is to say, [it is] indivisible [inseparable], from light, heat and colour. The precious stone is also [indivisible, inseparable], from its light, colour and shape. In the same way, O Śāriputra, the Absolute Body, taught by the

212) *arthânubhava*, T. *don ñams-su myoṅ-ba*, C. 受用事. T. om. *jñāna*.

213) C. om. *indhana* (T. *bud-śiṅ*).

214) T. reads as '*tad-ubhaya-āgantukatā-aprakṛtitaḥ*' (*glo-bur-pa-ñid-kyi raṅ-bshin ma yin-paḥi phyir-ro*, being *āgantukatā*, they are not the innate character). C. reads '如自性清淨體 彼二是客塵煩惱' (its being the body of innate purity, these two are occasional defilements), taking *prakṛti* as *cittaprakṛti*.

215) *aśaikṣa-sāntānika*, T. *mi-slob-paḥi rgyud*, C. 無學身.

216) *prahāṇa*, T. *spaṅs-pa*, C. 離煩惱. It stands for *āśrayakṣaya*. Instead of '*sapta*', C. counts 6 *anāsravajñānas* and *prahāṇa* separately. T. adds *anāsrava* before *abhijñā*.

217) For *samanvāgama*, C. has a peculiar translation, '平等畢竟' (*samânvāgama?*).

218) AAN 467 *a*. C. om. the whole paragraph after '*eṣa ca yogârthaṃ*...'. Cf. DAŚ 893 *b*, which quote the same passage.

219) *avinirmukta-guṇa*. Here the word *jñāna*, which appears in the case of *dharmakāya* (*avinirmuktajñānaguṇa*), is omitted.

Tathāgata is of indivisible nature, of the qualities inseparable from Wisdom (i.e. Enlightenment). That is to say, [indivisible, inseparable], from the Properties of the Tathāgata which are far beyond the sand of the Gaṅgā in number".

(VI) VṚTTI[220]

Now, with reference to the meaning of 'manifestation' (*vṛtti*), there is one *śloka*.

(Kārikā 10)

The Ordinary People, the Saints, and the Buddhas, —
They are indivisible from Reality[221],
Therefore, the Matrix of the Buddha[222] exists among [all] living beings; —
Thus it is taught by the perceivers of the Reality. // 45 //

What is shown by this *śloka* ?

The Ordinary People are of erroneous conception,
Being opposite to them, [the Saints are] the perceivers of the truth,[223]
And being of the perfectly[224] right conception,
The Buddhas are apart from the dualistic view. // 46 //

In connection with the introductory teaching[225] of the Non-discriminative Wisdom, it has been taught, in the *Prajñāpāramitā*, etc., for the Bodhisattvas that the Essence of the Tathāgata[226] has the general charac-

220) Cf. BGŚ 805 *c* f. (6. *vṛtti*).

221) T. reads as '*tathatā-vyatirekataḥ*' and inserts *vṛtti* (manifests the *tathatā* in different way), but C. as usual.

222) *jinagarbha* = *tathāgatagarbha*.

223) *dṛṣṭasatya* = *tattvadarśin* (C. 見實者), T. *bden-pa mthoṇ-ba*.

224) *yathāvat* = *samyak*.

225) *mukhâvadāna*, T. *sgo-la gdams-pa*, C. [智] 法門 (in the sense of *dharmamukhâvadāna*).

226) T. as locative, in the sense 'with reference to *tathāgatadhātu*'. C. also as locative, but regards *dhātu* as *dharmadhātu* (如來法界中). Consequently, it shows a slight difference in the meaning.

teristic of being Reality, the perfect purity, i.e. the Suchness[227] of all the elements. On the basis of this general characteristic, it should be known in brief, there are threefold different manifestations (*pravṛtti*)[228] of three kinds of people:... of the Ordinary People who do not perceive the Truth, of the Saints who perceive the Truth and of the Tathāgata[229] who has attained the ultimate purity. In other words, they are 'of the erroneous conception' (*viparyasta*), 'of the right conception' (*aviparyasta*), and 'of the perfectly right conception[230] and of no dualistic view', respectively. Here, 'of the erroneous conception' is because Ordinary People have delusion on account of their conception, mind and perception[231]. 'Of the right conception' is because the Saints, being opposite to them, have destroyed the delusion. [And lastly], 'of the perfectly right conception and of no dualistic view' is because the Perfectly Enlightened Ones have dispelled the Obstructions of moral defilement and of knowable things along with their Impressions.

(VII) AVASTHĀPRABHEDA[232]

Hereafter, with reference to this subject of 'manifestation', other four subjects should be understood through the detailed explanation [on each subject]. Here, [first of all], with reference to the subject, 'different states (*avasthāprabheda*)' among these three kinds of people, there is one *śloka*.

(Kārikā 10)

Impure, [partly] pure and [partly] impure,
And perfectly pure — these are said of

[227] *tathatā*. In this translation, I repeated the word *tathatā* twice in order to make the meaning clear.

[228] = *vṛtti*. T. & C. has the same translation as in the case of *vṛtti*.

[229] C. adds *dharmakāya* after *tathāgata*.

[230] C. om. here *samyag-aviparyasta*.

[231] *saṃjñā*, T. *ḥdu-śes*, C. 想; *citta*, T. *sems*, C. 心; *dṛṣti*, T. *lta-ba*, C. 見, respectively. Cf. *Yogācārabhūmiśāstra* vol. 8 (*Taisho*, XXX, p. 314 *b*): 1) *saṃjñāviparyasta* means '*anitye vastuni nitya-parikalpa-pravṛttiḥ*; 2) *dṛṣti-v.* means '*tatparikalpite chandaḥ, abhilāṣaḥ*; and 3) *citta-v.* means '*abhilaṣitakleśasya kriyā*'. Also cf. BGŚ 806 *a*.

[232] Cf. BGŚ 806 *a*; AĀS 469 *c*.

The Ordinary beings, the Bodhisattvas [233],
And the Tathāgata, respectively [234]. // 47 //

What is shown by this *śloka* ?

The Essence [of the Buddha] [235], [hitherto briefly explained]
By these six subjects, beginning with 'own nature',
Is, in accordance with its 3 states,
Designated by 3 different names. // 48 //

Any teaching referring to the immaculate Essence [of the Buddha] [236], taught by the Lord in detail through various divisions of Scripture [237] is hitherto briefly summarized by six subjects, namely, 'own nature', 'cause' [of purification], 'result' [of purification], 'function' [towards purification], 'union' [with the cause and result], and 'manifestation' [238]. This very Essence of the Buddha is here to be known as being taught through the teaching of 3 different names in accordance with its 3 states, respectively. That is to say, 1) in the 'impure' (*aśuddha*) state [the Essence of the Buddha is named) 'the Ordinary Beings' (*sattvadhātu*) [239]; 2) in the '[partly] pure and [partly] impure' (*aśuddhasuddha*) state, the Bodhisattva; and 3) in the 'perfectly pure' (*suviśuddha*), the Tathāgata.

It has been said by the Lord [240].

"O Śāriputra, this Absolute Body, when it is covered with the limitless [241] sheath of defilements, being carried by the stream of

[233] For *ārya* in the previous Kārikā. Here it is specified that *ārya* is *par excellence* the Bodhisattvas.

[234] Cf. DAŚ 893 *a*: 不淨衆生界 染中淨菩薩 最極清淨者是說爲如來.

[235] For *dhātu*, C. 法性體.

[236] *anāsravadhātu*. For *dhātu*, T. *khams*, C. 法性.

[237] *nānādharmaparyāyamukheṣu*. C. 種種法門 (*mukheṣu* = *dvāreṇa*).

[238] It shows us that the 6 subjects mentioned above are the fundamental categories by which any kind of teaching can be summarized, whereas the remaining four subjects are peculiar to the *tathāgatadhātu*, as forming sub-divisions of the sixth category, *vṛtti* See note VIII-8. As for the six *padârthas*, see *Appendix*, III.

[239] C. 衆生. Here *sattvadhātu* stands for *pṛthagjana*.

[240] AAN 467 *b*. Cf. AĀS 469 *c*.

[241] *aparyanta... koṭi* (-*gūḍha*), T. *bye-ba mthaḥ-yas-pas* (*gtums-pa*), (*koṭi* is regarded as a unit of number), C. 過於恒沙無量... [所纏].

the Phenomenal Life and moving to and fro between death and birth in the course of the beginningless [242] Phenomenal Life, is called 'the [ordinary] living beings'. This same Absolute Body, O Śāriputra, when it has become averse to the Suffering in the stream of Phenomenal Life and become free from all the objects of desire, doing the practice towards Enlightenment by means of the 10 Supreme Virtues [243] as including and representing [244] all of the 84 thousands groups of Doctrines [245], it is called 'the Bodhisattva'. Furthermore, O Śāriputra, this very Absolute Body, when, having been perfectly released from all the sheaths of defilements, having surpassed all the Sufferings, having rejected all stains of subsequent defilements, it has become pure, perfectly pure, and, abiding in the Absolute Essence which is the highest point of purity [246], ascending to the stage to be looked upon [247] by all living beings, has attained the unexcelled, manly strength [248] among all

242) *anavarâgra*, T. *thog-ma daṅ tha-ma med-pa* (of neither bottom nor top, without beginning nor end), C. 從無始來 (of beginningless time). As an epithet to *saṃsāra*, it has its origin in Pāli *anamatagga*, which seems to mean 'whose beginning is unknown', (*an'-amata-agga*, *an'* = *anu*, a prefix of intensitive sense). (viz. V. P. Bapat, *Review of Buddhist Hybrid Sanskrit Dictionary*, *ABORI*, vol. XXXV, p. 234-5). By Sanskritization, *anamata* was changed into *anavara* (reason unknown) and regarded as the compound of '*an-avara-agra*'. T. translation shows this sense. On the contrary, C. has retained the original sense of this term. In Sanskrit sources, however, this term was interpreted in two ways. We have a good example in Candrakīrti's *Prasannapadā*.

pūrvā prajñāyate koṭir nety vāca mahāmuniḥ /
saṃsāro'navarâgro hi nâsyâdir nâpi paścimam // (MK XI, 1)

uktaṃ hi Bhagavatā / Anavarâgro hi, bhikṣavo, jātijarāmaraṇasaṃsāra iti / avidyā-nivaraṇānāṃ . . . sattvānāṃ . . . saṃsaratāṃ . . . pūrvakoṭir na prajñāyata iti // (*Prasannapadā*, Poussin, p. 218) (Cf. SN II, 178, 193: III, 144, 151, etc.).

Here I suppose that the term *anamatágga* had originally the sense '*pūrvā koṭir na prajñāyate*', but from the literal meaning of its Sanskritized form '*anavarâgra*', a new interpretation of '*nâdir nâpi paścimam*' was added to its meaning.

243) *daśapāramitāḥ*. Besides the 6 *pāramitās* taught in the *Prajñāpāramitā*, '*upāya*', '*praṇidhi*', '*bala*', and '*jñāna*' are counted under this.

244) *antargata*, lit. represented by or summarized in [the 10 pāramitās].

245) *dharmaskandha*, T. *chos-kyi phuṅ-po*, C. 法門 (=法聚, 法蘊). The number of group is usually counted as 84 thousand. It is used in nearly the same sense as *dharmaparyāya* or *dharmapiṭaka*.

246) *paramaviśuddhadharmatā*, C. 彼岸淸淨法.

247) *ālokanīya*, T. *blta-bar bya-ba*, C. 所觀.

248) *advitīyaṃ pauruṣaṃ sthāma*, T. *gñis-su med-paḥi skyes-buḥi mthu*, C. 更無勝者 (there is nobody superior to him).

knowable spheres, and has attained the Controlling Power on all separate elements, which is of no obstruction[249] and of no hindrance, then it is called the Tathāgata, the Arhat, the Perfectly Enlightened One ".

(VIII) SARVATRAGA [250]

The Essence of the Tathāgata is ' all-pervading (*sarvatraga*) ' in these three states. With reference to this meaning, there is one *śloka*.

(Kārikā 11)

Just as being of indiscriminative nature,
Space pervades everywhere,
Similarly all-pervading is the Essence,
The immaculate nature of the mind [251]. // 49 //

What is shown by this Śloka ?

It pervades with common feature
The defective, the virtuous and the ultimate [252],
Just as space occupies all the visible forms [253],
Either inferior, middle, or superior. // 50 //

That which is the indiscriminative Innate Mind (*cittaprakṛti*)[254] of the ordinary people, of the Saints and of the Buddhas has a common feature in these three states, irrespective of their being defective, virtuous or the ultimate point of pure virtue. Therefore, just as space penetrates all the receptacles regardless of material, whether clay, silver or gold, it is all-per-

249) *anāvaraṇa-dharma*, T. *sgrib-pa med-paḥi chos-can*, C. 離一切障.

250) Cf. BGŚ 806 *b* (8. *sarvatraga*); AĀS 469 *c*–470 *a*.

251) *cittaprakṛti-vaimalyadhātu*, T. *sems-kyi raṅ-bshin dri-med dbyiṅs*, C. 自性無垢心 (*prakṛti-vaimalya-citta*).

252) *doṣa*, T. *gñes-pa*, C. 過; *guṇa*, T. *yon-tan*, C. 功德; *niṣṭhā*, T. *mthar-thug*, C. 畢竟, respectively. *niṣṭhā* is replaced by '*guṇaviśuddhiniṣṭhā*' in the commentary. Of these three, see next (IX) Avikāra.

253) *rūpagata* (= *rūpa*). T. *gzugs*–, C. 色. viz. BHS Dic. s. v.

254) C. 自性淸淨心. T. as in the Kārikā.

vading, all-embracing, equal, of no difference and is present always[255].

For this reason, it has been said in the same scripture[256], immediately after the explanation of different states:

> " Therefore, O Śāriputra, the [ordinary] living beings and the Absolute Body are not different from each other. The living beings are nothing but the Absolute Body, and the Absolute Body is nothing but the living beings. These two are non-dual by meaning, and different merely by letters ".

(IX) AVIKĀRA[257]

Now, the Essence of the Tathāgata, being all-pervading in these three states, is, moreover, unchangeable (*avikāra*) either by Impurity or through purification[258]. With reference to this subject, there are 14 *ślokas*. [Prior to the explanation of these *ślokas*], the summarized meaning[259] of these *ślokas* is to be known by the following verse:

> Being possessed of faults by occasion,
> It is, however, endowed with virtues by nature;
> Therefore it is of unchangeable character
> In the beginning as well as afterwards[260]. // 51 //

In the impure state as well as in the pure and impure state, which are shown by the [first] 12 *ślokas* and by the [next] one *śloka*, respective-

255) *prāptā sarvakālam*, C. 一切時有. T., connecting *nirviśiṣṭā* with this phrase, has '*dus tham-cad-du khyad-par med-par gyur-pa*'.

A quite equivalent passage is found in AĀS (469 *c*), which is quoted in BGŚ (806 *b*) with a heading '如無上依經言' (as has been said in the *Anuttarâśrayasūtra*).

256) AAN 467 *b*.

257) Cf. BGŚ 806 *c* (9. Avikāra) Under this subject, it treats '*avikāritva*' from 6 points, viz. *pūrva-paryanta*, *saṃkleśa-vyavadāna*, *jāti*, *pravṛtti*, *sthiti*, and *bhaṅga*. Furthermore it adds the 9 illustrations on *kleśa* there.

258) *saṃkleśa-vyavadāna*, C. 染浄 (impurity and purity).

259) *piṇḍârtha*, T. *bsdus-has-paḥi don*, C. 略說, 要義.

260) The same verse appears in BGŚ 806 *c*: 客塵相應故 有自性德故如前後亦爾 是無變異相. It is regarded in BGŚ as a verse from the *Sandhinirmocanasūtra* (如佛爲海智菩薩說 解節經偈言). We cannot, however, find out any similar verse in the present texts of the *Sandhinirmocana*. For *dharmatā*, C. 真法體, BGŚ 相.

ly, [the Essence of the Tathāgata] is possessed of faults caused by fundamental and subsequent defilements 'by occasion'. [On the contrary], in the perfectly pure state, shown by the 14th *śloka*, it is 'essentially' endowed with the Buddha's virtues [261] which are indivisible [from the Absolute Body], inseparable from Wisdom [262], inconceiva le and far greater in number than the sands of Gaṅgā. Therefore it is explained that the Essence of the Tathāgata [263], like space, is of absolutely unchangeable character throughout different states [264].

(A) Unchangeability in the Impure State

First of all, with reference to the subject of 'unchangeability' [of the Essence of the Tathāgata] in the Impure State, what is said in 12 *ślokas* ?

(Kārikās 12–23)

Just as space, being all-pervading,
Cannot be polluted because of its subtle nature;
Similarly, abiding everywhere among living beings [265],
This [Essence [265]] remains unpolluted [by defilements]. // 52 //

261) *dharma* = *guṇa*.

262) *amuktajña* (BHS, adj.). This is an abbreviated form of '*avinirmuktajñāna*' which occurred in a quotation from AAN (S. pp. 3 & 39) and its first use is probably in ŚMS (see quotations from ŚMS in S. pp. 55 & 76). This is a special adjective to *buddha-dharma* or *-guṇa*, showing inseparability of *guṇa* from *buddhajñāna*, i.e. *bodhi*. Therefore, T. *bral mi-śes* or C. '不脫' (unreleased) does not exactly convey its meaning. It should be '*ye-śes daṅ ma bral-ba*'. See Note I-23.

263) For *dhātu*, C. 真如性.

264) C. treats this passage in verse.

265) A doubt about the reading '*sattve*' in the text (for *satvo* in Ms. B) is raised by Prof. V. V. Gokhale, who, indicating the identification of this verse with v. XIII, 32 in the *Bhagavadgītā*, suggested the reading '*sattvas*' instead of *sattve*, being the subject noun for '*ayam*'. (*A Note on Ratnagotravibhāga I*, 52 = *Bhagavadgītā XIII* 32. Studies in Indology and Buddhology, Presented in Honour of Prof. S. Yamaguchi, Kyoto, 1955, pp. 90–91). However, as far as the independent use of '*ayam*' is concerned, there seems to be no problem, since this verse is in a series of Kārikās and *ayam* denotes '*cittaprakṛtivaimalyadhātu*' in v. 49. (So C. translates *ayam* into '佛性', *buddhadhātu*). A similar case is found in v. 54, where *enam* is also used independently, denoting the same subject of *cittaprakṛtivaimalyadhātu* (C. also '佛性'). T. & C. seem to support the reading in loc., but T. reads the second line as '*sarvasattveṣv avasthitas tathā'yaṃ nôpalipyate* / Here '*sattva*' seems to be used in a collective sense, the same as *sattvadhātu*.

Just as the worlds have everywhere
Their origination and destruction in space;
Similarly, on the basis of the Innate Essence [266],
The sense-organs appear and disappear [267]. // 53 //
Just as space has never been burnt [268],
By the fire [at the end of the world];
Likewise the fires of death, of illness and decrepitude [269]
Cannot consume [270] this [Essence of the Buddha] [271]. // 54 //
The earth is supported by water,
Water by air, and air by space;
Space has, however, no support
Neither in air, nor in water, nor in the earth. // 55 //
Similarly all the component elements [of Phenomenal Life] [272]
Have their foundation in the Active Force and Defilements,
And the Active Force and Defilements exist always
On the basis of the Irrational Thought [273]. // 56 //
The Irrational Thought is founded
In the [innate] mind which is pure [274],
The innate mind has, however, no support
In any [of the worldly] phenomena. // 57 //
All the component elements of Phenomenal Life

266) *asaṃskṛta-dhātu*, T. *ḥdus ma-byas dbyiṅs*, C. 無漏界 (= *anāsravadhātu*). It seems to indicate *cittaprakṛti* (see v. 57).

267) Cf. DAŚ 893 *a* (v. 12): 如一切世間 依虛空起盡 諸根亦如是 依無爲生滅.

268) *dagdha-pūrva*.

269) *mṛtyu, vyādhi, jarā*: T. *ḥchi-ba, na-ba, rga-ba*; C. 死, 病, 老, resp.

270) Grammatically the form should be '*pradahanti*' instead of '*pradahati*'.

271) Cf. DAŚ 893 *a* (v. 11): 譬如劫盡火 不能燒虛空 如是老病死 不能燒世界.

272) *skandha-dhātv-indriya* = *skandhâyatanadhātavaḥ* (vv. 58, 61), T. *phuṅ-po [daṅ] kham [daṅ] dbaṅ [-po]* (= *skye-mched*), C. 陰界根 (陰界入). By these, all the Phenomenal world is indicated.

273) *ayonimanaskāra* = *ayoniśomanaskāra*, *ayoniśomanasikāra*. T. *tshul-bshin ma-yin yid[-la] byed[-pa]*: C. 不善思惟, 不正思惟, 不正念, 邪念.

274) *cittaviśuddhi* = *cittaprakṛti*, *cittasya prakṛti*, *prakṛti*. C. 淨心, 清淨心, 自性清淨心, 性, resp.

Are known as akin to the earth,
And the Active Force and Defilements of living beings
Are known as akin to water. // 58 //
The Irrational Thought is known
As having resemblance to air;
Being of no root and of no support [275],
The Innate Mind is like space. // 59 //
Abiding in [276] the Innate Mind,
There occurs the irrational action of mind [277].
By the Irrational Action of mind,
The Active Force and Defilements are produced. // 60 //
All the component elements of Phenomenal Life,
Originated from the water-like Active Force and Defilements,
Show their appearance and disappearance [repeatedly],
Just as [the world repeats its] evolution and devolution [278]. // 61 //

The Innate Mind is like space,
Being of no cause or condition,
Or complex [of producing factors] [279],
It has neither origination nor destruction,
Nor even stability [between two points]. // 62 //
The innate nature of the mind is brilliant
And, like space, has no transformation at all;
It bears, however, the impurity [280] by stains of desires, etc.
Which are of accident and produced by wrong conception [281]. // 63 //

275) For '*tad*', T. has '*de-bshin*' (*tadvat*).

276) *ālīna* (*ā lī*) (c. acc.), T. *gnas*, C. 依 ... This word reminds us of *ālayavijñāna*.

277) *ayoniśo manasaḥ kṛtiḥ* = *ayoniśomanasikāra*.

278) *tat-saṃvarta-vivartavat* (lit. devolution and evolution). For *saṃvarta*, T. *ḥjig-pa*, C. 壞, and for *vivarta* (= *vividhaṃ vartate*), T. *ḥchags-pa*, C. 成. These are two of four periods within one Kalpa, a circle of world process. The 4 are namely: *vivarta* (成), *vivartasthāyin* (住), *saṃvarta* (壞), and *saṃvartasthāyin* (空, empty).

279) *sāmagrī*, T. *tshogs-pa*, C. 和合.

280) T. shows negative sense: '*ñon-moṅs mi-ḥgyur*'. But C. as S. (客塵煩惱染).

Negative interpretation of T. with respect to pollution by *āgantukakleśa* seems to be the usual way in Tibetan tradition. See Note VIII-305.

281) *abhūtakalpa*, T. *yaṅ-dag min rtogs*, C. 虛妄分別. It stands for *ayoniśomanasikāra*. See S. p. 12, l. 3 (*vikalpa* = *ayoniśomanasikāra*).

§ 1. Unoriginated Character of the Innate Mind.

By this analogy of space, how is the unchangeable character of the Essence[282] of the Tathāgata in the impure state explained? It is said as follows[283]:

> The accumulation of water-like Active Force and Defilements
> Cannot produce[284] this space-like [Innate Mind],
> And even the growing fires of death, of illness and old age
> Cannot consume [this Innate Mind]. // 64 //

The origination of the world classified into [5] elementary groups, [18] component elements or [12] bases of cognition is conditioned by the accumulation of water-like Active Force and Defilements, which is, in its turn, based upon wind-circle[285] of Irrational Thought. But this origination of the world never causes the evolution[286] of the Innate Mind which has a resemblance to space. In the same way, a group[287] of fires of death, of illness and decrepitude arises in order to destroy[288] the world classified into five elementary groups, 18 component elements or 12 bases of cognition which is founded on the accumulation of air-like Irrational Thought and water-like Active Force and Defilements[289]. But even by this ari-

[282] For *dhātu*, T. *sñiṅ-po*, C. 如來性.

[283] C. has other two verses before v. 64. From the context in the following commentary, both S. & T. seem to have a lacuna of two verses here.

Two verses in C. run as follows:

1) 不正思惟風 諸業煩惱水 自性心虛空 不爲彼一生;
2) 自性清淨心 其相如虛空 邪念思惟風 所不能散壞.

C. regards the first sentence in the commentary as the explanation of the first verse, and the next sentence as that of the next two. And, as J suggested, the term *ayoniśomanasikāra* is required by the prose commentary and also there might be terms such as *loka* or *skandhāyatanadhātavaḥ* in verses. C. seems, however, to have failed to catch the contrast between *vivarta* and *saṃvarta* by treating *ayoniśomanasikāra* and *kleśakarma* as something of destructive force.

J's further suggestion of v. 64 as a quotation is not reasonable, since this text puts always a certain number of commentary verses after original Kārikā or Kārikās.

[284] *abhinivartayati*. C. '湼爛' is probably a misunderstanding.

[285] *vāta-maṇḍala*, T. *rluṅ-gi dkyir-ḥkhor*, C. 風輪.

[286] *vivarta* = *abhinirvarta*. For '*vivarto na bhavati*', C. 不生不起.

[287] *skandha*, T. *tshogs*, (= *saṃcaya*, *rāśi*, accumulation). C. om.

[288] *astaṃgama*, T. *ḥjig-par byed-pa*, C. 壞 (= *nirodha*).

[289] C. inserts '行' (*saṃskāra*) after *karma*- (業行煩惱水).

sing of the fires of death, etc., it should be known that the Innate Mind cannot be destroyed. Thus, in the impure state, though all the Impurity of Defilements, of Active Force and Birth show their appearance and disappearance like the material world[290], the Innate Essence of the Tathāgata is, like space, of no origination and destruction. Therefore, it is explained as being absolutely of unchangeable character.

And this example of space which refers to the introduction to the light of doctrine[291] on the Innate Purity [of the mind] is to be understood in detail according to the Scripture[292]:

> "O Honourable[293] Men, Defilements are the darkness[294], the Pure [Mind][295] is the light. Defilements are of weak power but the correct intuition[296] is powerful. Defilements are merely accidental, but the Innate Mind is of a pure root[297]. Defilements are of wrong discrimination, but the Innate Mind is indiscriminative. For example, O Honourable Men, this great earth has its foundation in water. Water is supported by air, and air is founded on space. But space, in its turn, has no foundation. Thus, among these four gross elements, space is more powerful[298] than any of the other three elements, earth, water or air. It is also firm, immovable, neither increasing nor diminishing[299], neither originated nor dest-

290) *bhājanaloka*, T. *snod-kyi ḥjig-rten*, C. 器世間 (opp. to *sattvaloka*).

291) *dharmâlokamukha*, T. *chos snaṅ-baḥi sgo*, C. 法門. '*dharmâloka*' would mean '*dharma* as *āloka*', and hence *dharmâlokamukha* means *dharmamukha* as C. translated.

292) Against C. attribution, this quotation is from the *Gaganagañjā-paripṛcchā* as O found. Cf. 大集經虛空藏菩薩品第八 (*Taisho*, XIII, p. 124 *c*). 大集大虛空藏菩薩所問經, vol. 8 (*Taisho*, XIII, 643 *b–c*).

293) *mārṣa*, T. *draṅ-sroṅ-chen*, = *maharṣi* C. 佛子 (善男子).

294) *kavi* (probably *chavi* is the better reading), T. *mun-pa* (= *tamas*), C. 無體 (= 虛妄, *mṛṣa* ?). In contrast with '*āloka*', T. translation is better, and '*chavi*' here seems to mean 'coloured' or 'dark-coloured' (= *kṛṣnacchavi* or black-cloud ?).

295) *prakṛti*, C. 眞如性.

296) *vipaśyanā*, T. *lhag-mthoṅ*, C. 毗婆舍那 (usually, 觀).

297) *mūlaviśuddhā prakṛtiḥ*, T. *raṅ-bshin-gyis rnam-par dag-pa ni rtsa-baḥo.* (= *prakṛtiviśuddhaṃ mūlam*). But, '*prakṛti*' here stands for *cittaprakṛti*. C. om. from '*mūla*' to '*parikalpāḥ kleśāḥ*'.

298) The reading '*balī yo*' in the text should be corrected into '*balīyo*' (comparative degree).

299) *anupacayo* '*napacayo*. C. 不散...不作 (neither composing nor scattering himself). T. om. '*anupacaya*' (for *anapacaya*, *ḥgrib-pa med-pa*).

royed and is stable with its own essence [300]. [On the contrary], these three gross elements [other than space] are possessed of origination and destruction, unstable [301] and of no long duration [302]. It will be perceived that these three gross elements are changeable, but space is by no means changeable [303]. "In a similar manner [304], all the component elements [of the Phenomenal Life classified into] 5 elementary groups, 18 component elements, or 12 bases of cognition have their support in the Active Force and Defilements. The Active Force and Defilements are founded on the Irrational Thought and the latter has its support in the Innate Pure Mind. Therefore, it is said: the Mind is radiant by nature, [but it]is polluted by the occasional defilements [305] ".

After this passage, it is continued as follows [306]:

"Now, all these phenomena, the Irrational Thought, the Active

300) *svarasa-yogena*, T. *raṅ-gi ṅaṅ-gis*, C. 自然. (*rasa* = *dharmatā*, nature).

301) *anavasthita*, T. *mi-gnas-pa*, C. 無實體性 (= *abhūtadharmā* ?).

302) *acirasthāyin*, T. *yun riṅ-du mi-gnas-pa*, C. 剎那不住.

303) C. adds *anitya* and *nitya* after *vikāra* and *avikāra*, respectively. (Most probably for arranging the style of the Chinese sentence).

304) Hereafter, the Skt. text has no vocative case (*mārṣāḥ*), and the style looks as the commentator's own explanation. But, from the context and C. which mentions '*mārṣāḥ*' or '*kulaputrā*' between sentences, the quotation seems still to be continuing.

305) T. '*na kliṣyate*' (*ñon ma moṅs-paḥo*).

This sermon has its origin in Pāli canon (e.g. AN I, 5, 9–10; IV, 1–2). But it seems that not all the Buddhist schools accepted it. The *Mahāvibhāṣāśāstra* of Sarvāstivādin, who did not accept this *cittaprakṛti* theory, mentions it as an opinion of the Vibhajyavādin (分別說部), saying: 謂, 或有執心性清淨, 如分別論者, 彼說心本性清淨, 客塵煩惱所染汚故, 相不清淨. (Someone, like the Vibhajyavādin, has the opinion of *viśuddhi cittaprakṛti*. They say that the mind is pure by nature, but, being polluted by accidental defilements, its feature is impure) (*Taisho*, XVIIX, p. 140 *b*). See also 舍利弗阿毗曇論 (*Śāriputrâbhidharmaśāstra* ?) (*Taisho*, XXVIII, p. 697 *b*), where this theory is attributed to the Vātsīputrīya.

It is clear that T. interpretation has no foundation in the sūtras as far as its literal sense is concerned, but we have an example of the same interpretation as T. in the *Mahāprajñāpāramitāśāstra* (大智度論) attributed to Nāgārjuna, saying: 以是心清淨故 不爲客塵煩惱所染 (*Taisho*, XXV, p. 204 *a*). So there seem to be two ways of interpretation with respect to 'pollution', namely whether or not *cittaprakṛti* can be polluted.

306 The reading '*tatra paścād*' is somewhat doubtful. T. has simply *de-la* (*tatra*). C. om. the whole.

Force and Defilements, and all of the component elements of the Phenomenal Life are originated by the complex of their causes and conditions. When these causes and conditions lose their complexity [307] they are immediately extinguished. On the contrary, the Innate Mind is of no cause nor condition. Consequently, it has no complex [of cause and condition] and hence there is neither origination nor destruction of it. Here, the Innate Mind is like space, the Irrational Thought is like air, the Active Force and Defilements are like water and all of the component elements of the Phenomenal Life are akin to earth. Therefore, it is said:—, all phenomena are completely devoid of any root [308] and based upon an unreal and unstable foundation, [because they are of unreal nature, but at the same time] they are founded on a pure [essence] which is, in its turn, of no root ".

§ 2. Indestructible Character of the Innate Mind.

We have already explained that in the impure state the Innate Mind has a resemblance to space on account of its 'unchangeable' (*avikāra*) characteristic; the Irrational Thought and the Active Force and Defilements, being founded on the Innate Mind, have a resemblance to air and water, respectively, on account of their characteristic of 'cause' (*hetu*), and [lastly] all of the Component Elements of Phenomenal Life, being produced from the former two, have a resemblance to the earth on account of their characteristic of 'fruit' (*vipāka*). We have not, however, discussed the similarity of the fires of death, illness and decrepitude to the gross element of fire as being the cause of the annihilation of Life [309] and on account of their characteristic of being 'infection' [310]. So, on this point it is said as follows:

The three fires, the fire at the end of the world,

307) *visāmagrī* (losing complexity), T. [*dan*] *bral*, C. 壞.

308) *mūlaparicchinna* (which is to be inserted acc. to Ms. B., as well as T.), T. *rtsa-ba yoṅs-su chad-pa*, C. 皆無根本. The whole saying is as follows: *sarvadharmā mūlaparicchinnā asāramūlā apratiṣṭhānamūlāḥ śuddhamūlā amūlamūlā iti* Cf. AAS 496 *b*.

309) *vibhava*, T. *ḥjig-pa*, C. 焚燒 (an analogical translation).

310) *upasarga*, T. *mgoḥi nad*, C. 過患 (calamity). Three aspects of '*vikāra*' in the Phenomenal World are named here '*hetu*', '*vipāka*' and '*upasarga*', and all of these stand for the counterpart of '*avikāritva*' of *cittaprakṛti* or *tathāgatadhātu*.

The fire of hell and the ordinary[311] fire,
These are to be known respectively as the analogy
For three fires, that of death, of sickness and old age. // 65 //

The similarity of death, illness and old age to fire should be known for three reasons, respectively. [Which are the three reasons? They are namely]: 1) because [death] leads the 6 [internal] bases of cognition to destruction[312]; 2) [illness] makes sufferings of various kinds of torments[313]; and 3) [old age] leads the Active Forces to their ripening[314]. Even by these fires, the Essence of the Tathāgata in its impure state cannot be changed at all. With reference to this point, it is said [in the Scripture][315]:

"O Lord, something is dead, something is born, such sayings are merely a worldly usage[316]. The saying 'something is dead', O Lord, this means the destruction[317] of sense organs. Something is born means, O Lord, origination[318] of new sense organs. However, O Lord, the Matrix of the Tathāgata is never born, never decays,

[311] *prākṛta*, T. *tha-mal-ba*, C. 人 [火] (fire made by human being).

[312] *nirmamī-karaṇa* (*cause to destroy something conceived as* '*mine*'), T. *bdag-gi-ba med-par byed-pa* (*bdag-gi-ba* stands for *mamatva*). C. om. this phrase and regards the other two as part of a verse.

[313] *vicitra-kāraṇânubhavana*, T. *sdug-bsṅal sna-tshogs myoṅ-bar byed-pa*, C. 能作種種苦. For *kāraṇā*, T. & C. have '*duḥkha*'. The word *kāraṇā* (f.), being delivered from Pāli *kāraṇa*, has a sense of 'torture' or 'torment', 'punishment', and is often used along with *kṛ*, in the sense to make punishment, to make pain on somebody by torment'. Cf. BHS Dic. p. 178, '*kāraṇa*'; PTS Dic. II, 38 '*kāraṇā*' 1. (M. W. gives the meaning 'pain', which is picked up from *Daśakumālacarita*). Here in connection with *anu-bhū*, we can easily find out the sense, 'to feel pain as a result of experiencing torment.

[314] *saṃskāra-paripāka*, which means the readiness for the next birth, repetition of life in *saṃsāra*.

[315] ŚMS 222 *b*.

[316] *lokavyavahāra*, T. *ḥjig-rten-gyi tha-sñad*, C. [依] 世諦 [故說]. *vyavahāra*, as the sanskritized form of Pāli *vohāra*, has two senses, *vyāhāra* (speech) and *vyavahāra* (behaviour), and mixing both, the sense 'usage' is attached to the term *vyavahāra*. This *vyavahāra* is also used as a synonym of '*saṃvṛti*' in connection with '*satya*'. C. translation shows this meaning. Cf. Prof. P. V. Bapat, *A Review of Buddhist Hybrid Sanskrit Dictionary*, *ABORI*, XXXV, p. 235.

[317] *uparodha*, T. *ḥgags-pa* (= *nirodha*), C. 壞.

[318] *prādurbhāva*, T. *thob-pa* (= *prāpti*), C. 生.

never deceases, never passes away [319] or arises [again]. For what reasons ? Because, O Lord, the Matrix of the Tathāgata, being beyond the sphere characterized as being caused and conditioned, is eternal, constant, quiescent and everlasting ".

(B) Unchangeability in the Pure and Impure State

Now there comes one *śloka* referring to the meaning of 'unchangeability' in the pure and impure state [of Bodhisattvas].

(Kārikā 24)

Having truly [320] realized the Innate Mind
As being released [321] from birth and death
As well as from illness and decrepitude,
The Bodhisattvas have no calamity [322] of birth and so forth;
Still, because of the rising of Compassions towards the world,
They assume the cause of calamities [323]. // 66 //

§ 1. The Pure Character and Impure Character of the Bodhisattva.

What is shown by this *śloka* ?

The sufferings of death, illness and decrepitude

[319] *cyavate* (< *cyu*), T. *ḥpho-ba*, C. 變 (to change, to move from one place (life) to another place (life).

[320] *ananyathā*, T. *ji-bshin-ñid*, C. 如實. *ananyathā'vagamya* = *yathābhūtasya darśanāt* (v. 68).

[321] The reading '*-vimuktām*', instead of '*vimuktā*', should be adopted. So C. T. reading is not clear. Cf. S. v. I. 54 (*na pradahanty enaṃ mṛtyuvyādijarāgnayaḥ*, *enam* = *cittaprakṛtiṃ*).

[322] *vyasana*, T. *phoṅs*[*-pa*]. C. has '生死' for *janmâdivyasana*.

[323] *tan-nidānaṃ . . . bhajante*. C. 示現有生滅 (assume the existence of origination and destruction), T. *de-yi rgyus for tan-nidānam*, regarding this term as an adverbial use. See BHS Dic. p. 295 (under '*nidāna*'): *tan-nidānam*, for that reason. Acc. to C., however, *nidāna* seems to mean the existence (*bhava*) on which *janman*, etc. take place.

Are destroyed by the Saints to the root;
There is a birth by the power of Active Force and Defilements;
As there is no birth [of such a kind]
The saints have no root [of defilements]. // 67 //

Now, in the impure state, the ***causa materialis*** [324] of the fires of sufferings [325] like death, illness and decrepitude is the Birth based upon the Irrational Thought, the Active Force and Defilements, just as the fuel [is the *causa materialis* of ordinary fires]. In the pure and impure state, however, there is no appearance [326] whatever of such a cause that we can know of; there is also no flame of fires of suffering at all in the Bodhisattvas who have attained the Body made of mind.

They, being full of mercy, make appearance
Of birth, death, decrepitude and illness,
Though they have got rid of [327] birth, etc.
Because of their perception of the truth. // 68 //

Indeed, because of their contact [328] with the virtuous root [329], Bodhisattvas attach themselves [330] to the Phenomenal World consisting of three spheres, basing themselves upon [331] the power of origination by their will [332]. Also they make appearance of birth, of old age, of illness and of death. Still, there are in reality no such phenomena of birth, etc. among them. Because [333], of course, they have truly perceived that the Essence [of the Buddha] [334] is of no birth and of no origination [335].

(References to the Scriptures)

[324] *upādāna*, T. *ñe-bar len-pa*, C. 依 ... 本 (= *pūrvika*).

[325] T. om. *duḥkha*.

[326] *anābhāsa-gamana*, T. *snaṅ-bar med-par gyur-pa*, C. 永滅盡.

[327] *vinivṛtta* T. *ḥdas gyur*, C. 遠離.

[328] *saṃyojana* (= *saṃprayukta*), T. *kun-tu sbyor-ba*, C. 結使. T. adds *srid-pa* (*bhava*) before *saṃyojana*.

[329] *kuśala-mūla*, T. *dge-baḥi rtsa-ba*, C. 善根.

[330] *saṃ√śliṣ* T. *yaṅ-dag-par sbyor*[*-ba*], C. 現 (to make appearance).

[331] The form *saṃniḥśraya* for *saṃniśraya* is notable.

[332] *saṃcintya* (ind.), T. *bsams-bshin-du*, C. 依心.

[333] *yathāpi* is omitted in T.

[334] *dhātu*, T. *khams*, C. 真如佛性.

[335] Instead of *ajāty-anutpatti*, C. has *anutpatty-anirodha*.

§ 2. Defilements endowed with Virtuous Root.

And this state of Bodhisattvas is to be understood in detail according to the Scripture. It is said[336]:

"Which are the Defilements endowed with virtuous root[337] that cause [Bodhisattvas] to reside in the Phenomenal World? They are namely: Non-satisfaction[338] in searching for the accumulation of merits[339]; Acceptance[340] of existence through origination by their own will; The earnest wish to meet with[341] the Buddhas; Unweariness towards the perfect maturity[342] of living beings. Efforts for the perfect apprehension[343] of the sublime Doctrine[344]; Endeavour[345] after works to be done[346] for the living beings; Non-abandonment of propensity[347] of desire for phenomena; Non-reluctance from fetters[348] of the Highest Virtues. O Sāgaramati, thus are the Defilements endowed with the virtuous roots by which the Bodhisattvas attach themselves [to this world], but they are never affected by the fault of Defilements. ... Then [Sāgaramati] asked: Why then, O Lord, are the virtuous roots called 'Defilements'? ... [The Lord] answered: Because, O Sāgaramati, by these Defilements of such kinds Bodhisattvas attach themselves to the Phenomenal World. And this Phenomenal World is of origination

[336] The *Sāgaramati-paripṛcchā*. C. 大集經海慧菩薩品第五 (*Taisho*, XIII, p. 46–74); 海慧菩薩所問淨印法門經 (tr. by 惟淨 of Suang. *Taisho*, No. 400). This passage is in *Taisho*, XIII, p. 68 *a*, *b*, but quite simplified.

[337] *kuśalamūla-saṃprayuktā kleśāḥ*, C. 善根相應煩惱.

[338] *atṛptatā*, T. *mi-ṅoms-pa*, C. 無有厭足.

[339] *puṇya-saṃbhāra*, T. *bsod-nams-kyi tshogs*, C. 諸善根 (*kuśalamūlāni*).

[340] *parigraha*, T. *yoṅs-su hdsin-pa*, C. 攝取.

[341] *samavadhāna*, T. *phrad-pa*, C. 見. See S. p. 13, l. 18.

[342] *paripāka*, T. *yoṅs-su smin-pa*, C. 教化.

[343] *parigraha*. T. & C., the same as above (Note 340).

[344] *saddharma*, T. *dam-paḥi, chos*, C. [一切諸佛] 妙法.

[345] *kiṃkaraṇīya*, T. *bya-ba ci-yod-pa*. C. '利益' is implying the sense, 'for the living beings'.

[346] *utsukatā*, T. *ḥgrus-pa*, C. 常作...

[347] *anuśaya*, T. *bsam-pa* (intention), C. 結使.

[348] *saṃyojana*.

from Defilements. There, to this very Phenomenal World, Bodhisattvas attach themselves at their own wishes by their skill of means [349] and through producing [350] the power of virtuous roots. Therefore, it is called 'Defilements endowed with the roots of virtuous qualities. [It is called so] inasmuch as they attach themselves to the Phenomenal World, but not because of [actual] defilements on the mind".

§ 3. Bodhisattvas' Compassion. The parable of a Householder.

"For example [351], O Sāgaramati, suppose there were an only son of some distinguished person or [352] householder. Suppose he were beloved, handsome, affectionate [353] quite agreeable in his appearance [354]. Now suppose this boy, being a child, would fall into a pit of night-soil while playing. Thereupon the mother and relatives [355] of this boy would see him fall into the impure pit. Upon seeing this they would deeply sigh, lament and would cry out. They could not, however, take the boy out [356] by entering into the pit. After that the boy's father would come to that place, and would see his only son fallen in the pit of night-soil. Upon seeing that sight, he being affected by the intention to pull out his only son [357],

349) *upāya-kauśalya*, T. *thabs-la mkhas-pa*, C. 方便智力.

350) *anvādhāna*, T. *skyed-pa*, C. om.

351) Continuation from § 2 (quotation from the same Sūtra). This parable is also found in AĀS (470 *a-b*).

352) Both T. & C. insert a word for '*vā*'. So '*śreṣṭiṇo vā gṛhapater vā*' would be a better reading.

353) *manāpa* (BHS), T. *yid-du hoṅ-ba*, C. [甚] 念. (For the previous three, C. simply 甚愛).

354) *apratikūlo darśanena* (lit. not disagreeable), T. *mthoṅ-na mi-sdug-pa med-pa*, C. 見者歡喜. After *darśanena*, there should be a Danda.

355) C. inserts '*pitā*', but it is not the case.

356) *adhyālaṃbati* (BHS), T. *ḥdon-pa* (pulls out), C. 出.

357) The reading '*ekaputrakâdhyāśaya-premânunīta*' is doubtful as J said. This translation is according to T., which reads '*bu gcig-po ḥdon-par ḥdod-paḥi sred-pas byas*'. The word '*ḥdon-pa*' is used in the preceding sentence for '*adhyālaṃba*', and for '*abhyutkṣepa*' in S. p. 48, l. 8, in the sense of 'taking out, pulling out'. But C. seems to omit this word and reads: 生一子想 生愛念心 (having *ekaputraka*-

would hurry to enter the pit with full speed without any feeling of disgust, and would take out[358] his only son. O Sāgaramati, this example was made in order to make known a special meaning. Which relation[359] should be known [between illustrations and illustrated meaning]? O Sāgamarati, 'a pit of night-soil' is a name for the Phenomenal Life. 'An only son' is a name for the living beings, because Bodhisattvas have a notion of the only son towards all living beings. 'Mother and relatives' is a name for those people who belong to the Vehicles of Śrāvaka and Pratyekabuddha, since they, having seen the living beings fallen into the world of transmigration, are distressed and lament, but have no capacity to rescue [the living beings]. 'The distinguished person or[360] the householder' is a name for the Bodhisattva who is pure, unpolluted, of unpolluted mind, has attained the direct perception of the immutable Absolute[361], but still, in order to bring living beings to the maturity, connects himself[362] to the Phenomenal World by his own will. O Sāgaramati, such is the Great Compassion of the Bodhisattva that, being perfectly free from all bondages, he again assumes[363] the origination into Existence. Being possessed of the skill of means and the Transcendental Intellect, he is never affected by impurities; and, in order to extirpate all the bondage of Defilements from the living beings, he preaches the Doctrine".

By this explanation of words in the Scripture[364], there is explained the pure and impure state of Bodhisattvas who have the Controlling Power through two points: [namely] the Bodhisattva attaches himself at his will to the origination in the world, for the sake of others, by the powers of virtuous roots and Compassion, but, at the same time, he is not polluted by the world owing to the powers of means and the Intellect.

saṃjñā and *premâdhyāśaya*). Cf. AĀS 念子心重. (Instead of '*anunīta*', '*adhyālambanataḥ*' would be preferable to accept).

358) *abhy-ut√kṣip*, T. *phyuṅ-ba*, C. 出.

359) *prabandha*, T. don, C. 義 (*artha*).

360) S. om. *vā*, but T. & C. have it.

361) *asaṃskṛta-dharma*. T. as S., but C. 無爲眞如法界 (*dharmadhātu*).

362) *pratisaṃ √dhā*, T. *mtshams sbyor-ba*, C. 現.

363) *upa√dā*, T. *len-pa*, C. 廻生.

364) C. regards this passage as a quotation from the same Sūtra (SāgP.). T. om. *nirdeśa*. For *pada*, T. *dum-bu*.

§ 4. Bodhisattva's Perception on the Pure Mind.

Now, when a Bodhisattva has attained the correct perception of the Essence of the Tathāgata as being of no birth, no origination, then he can obtain this essential quality [365] as a Bodhisattva. This point should be understood in detail [366] according to the [same] Scripture. It is said:

" O Sāgaramati, perceive that separate elements are of no real essence, of no creator, of no substance, non-existence, lifeless, of no personality and of no owner [367] ! Indeed, these elements are illusorily created [368] according to desire. As being [369] illusorily created, they cannot cause [one] to think or to imagine [370]. Believing in the fact that separate elements are created illusorily [371], O Sāgaramati, the Bodhisattva does never produce the feeling of disgust for any phenomenon. He will be possessed of the pure and immaculate perception based upon the Wisdom that there is nothing which causes benefit or harm [372]. Thus, he knows correctly the essential nature [373] of separate elements. And thus he does never cast off the armour [374] of the Great Compassion [375]. For example, O Sāgaramati, suppose there were an invaluable [376] Vaiḍūrya stone, well polished, well purified, well cleaned. Suppose it might be thrown into mud and would remain there for a thousand years [377].

[365] *dharmatā*, T. *chos-ñid*, C. 功德法體.

[366] T. om. *vistareṇa*. C. 此修多羅句向前已說 (this word of the Sūtra has already been taught), and starts the next quotation with the parable of the Vaiḍūrya stone. The quotation is from SāgP. 68 *a*. Cf. AĀS 469 *b–c*.

[367] *asvāmikatā*, T. *bdag med-pa-ñid*. For *nirātmatā*, T. *bdag-po med-pa-ñid*.

[368] *viṭhapyante* (pass. 3. p. of caus. of *vi* √ *sthā*, a hybrid form. Cf. BHS Dic. s.v.). T. om. '*tathā viṭhapyante viṭhapitāś ca samānā*'.

[369] *samāna* (= *sat*, after adjective) (Pāli, the same). Cf. BHS Dic. s. v.

[370] *prakalpayati*, T. *rab-tu rtogs-par . . . byed*.

[371] *dharma-viṭhapanā*. T. *gshan-du mi-ḥgyur-baḥi chos* (*ananyathābhāvadharma*) is probably caused by a misunderstanding of the term *dharma*. After all, T. offers no help to fix the meaning of '*viṭhapyate*'.

[372] *upakāro vā 'pakāro vā*, T. *pham-ḥdogs-paḥam gnod-par byed-pa*.

[373] *dharmatā*.

[374] *saṃnāha*, T. *go-cha*.

[375] C. om. up to here.

[376] *anargha*, T. *rin than-pa* (*mahārgha*), C. 無價.

[377] Cf. SāgP.: 'hundred years'. (But the second Chinese translation of the SāgP. has 'thousand years').

After the passing of a thousand years [in mud], this stone would be drawn out from mud and would be washed [378] and cleaned. As being washed well, perfectly cleaned and polished, it would never abandon its nature of jewel, pure and immaculate. In the same way, O Sāgaramati, the Bodhisattva knows the innate radiant nature of the mind of living beings. He perceives also that the same mind is defiled by the accidental defilements. Then the Bodhisattva thinks as follows: ... These defilements would never penetrate into the radiant Innate Mind of the living beings. Being accidental, these defilements are the production of unreal, wrong discrimination. I can teach the Doctrine for the sake of these living beings in order to remove their accidental [379] defilements. Thus, he never has his mind demoralized [380] and, with great intensity, he gives rise to the intention towards liberation [381] in the case of [382] living beings. Again he thinks as follows: These defilements have no power and ability. They are powerless, of weak power. They have no real foundation at all. These defilements are [produced] by incorrect discrimination. These defilements, when they are inspected by the real and correct perception [383], cannot be excited [384] by any means. They should be investigated by us so that they might not contaminate again. Indeed, it is a good thing not to be contaminated by defilements, not a good thing to be contaminated [385]. If I were contaminated by

378) *loḍyeta* (caus. opt. of √ *luḍ*), T. *sbyaṅ-ba*, C. [水]洗.

379) T. om. *āgantuka* and instead has *upakleśa*.

This passage (S. p. 49, l. 9—p. 50, l. 7) is quoted in Paramārtha's translation of the *Mahāyānasaṃgraha-bhāṣya* as from AĀS. (MSbh (P) 259 *c*–260 *a*). It is notable that Paramārtha's translation is, though abbreviated, rather closer to the *Ratna.* passage than to AĀS, which has, in turn, insertions equivalent to other passages of the *Ratna.* (S. p. 78, ll. 17–20; p. 45, ll. 3–9).

380) *avalīyanā*, T. *shum-pa*, C. 怯弱 (timid). Probably from Pāli *oliyanā* (Skt. *avalīyana* ?) Cf. BHS Dic. s. v. *avalīyate*, *anavalīyanatā*, etc.

381) *pramokṣa-citta*, T. *rab-tu ḥbro-ba* (but it should be *-ḥgrol-ba*), C. 解脫.

382) *-antike*, T. *thad-tu*, C. 轉於.

383) *yathābhūta-yoniśomanasikāra*, T. *ji-lta-ba-bshin-du tshul-bshin-du yid-la byed-pa*, C. 正見.

384) *na kupyanti*, C. 不能得起 (cannot rise).

385) C. om. '*na punaḥ śleṣaḥ*', and for the former part, has '以不生煩惱故生諸善法'.

defilements, how could I teach the Doctrine for the sake of the living beings who are bound by the bondages of defilements, in order to remove these bondages of defilements? Oh! really, we are not attached to defilements; therefore, we shall teach the Doctrine to the living beings in order to remove the bondage of defilements. And moreover, in order to bring the living beings to their maturity, we should be attached to the defilements [386], by which we are bound to the world of transmigration, which are at the same time endowed with the roots of virtues ".

§ 5. '*Saṃsāra*' in the Case of Bodhisattva.

And here, the expression 'World of transmigration' (*saṃsāra*) implies the three kinds of Body made of mind in the Immaculate Sphere, being an image similar to that [387] in the Phenomenal World. Indeed, it is the World of Transmigration because it is manifested [388] under the influence of immaculate roots of virtue. At the same time, it is the Nirvāṇa because it is not manifested under the influence of the passionate Active Force and Defilements. With regard to this point, it is said [389]:

"Therefore, O Lord, there is the Phenomenal World, conditioned as well as unconditioned. There is the Nirvāṇa, conditioned as well as unconditioned ".

Here, being endowed with the manifestation of mind and mental states [390] mixing [391] both, the conditioned and the unconditioned, this is called 'the pure and impure state'.

§ 6. Bodhisattva in His 6th Stage.

And this state is predominantly established in the 6th Stage of Bodhisattva called Abhimukhī (ready for the Enlightenment) [392]. Because,

386) C. inserts '修行諸波羅蜜' (to practise *pāramitās*).

387) *–pratibimbaka*, T. *gzugs–brñan–yid*, C. 相似鏡像法.

388) *abhisaṃskṛta*, C. 所作. T. as usual.

389) ŚMS 221 *b*.

390) *citta–caitasika*, C. 心心數法. T. om. *citta*.

391) *saṃśliṣṭa*, T. *ḥdres–pa*, C. om.

392) T. *mṅon–du gyur–pa*, C. 第六…現前[地].

[in this Stage], the Bodhisattva, facing the acquisition [393] of the Extinction of Evil Influences [394] through his practices of unobstructed Highest Intellect and the Great Compassion [395], still does never realize that acquisition in order to protect all living beings [396].

With reference to this Wisdom for the Extinction of Evil Influences, there is an illustration of a castle [397] in the Scripture.

It runs as follows: (... omission) [398].

[393] *-abhimukhī*, T. *mṅon-du phyogs-pa*, C. [解脫]現前.

[394] The word *abhijñā* in both S. & T. is better omitted. C. om. it and instead has *mokṣa*.

[395] C. regards *mahākaruṇā-bhāvanayā* as being connected with *asākṣātkaraṇa*.

[396] *sattvadhātu*, T. as usual, C. 衆生.

[397] T. (D) has *mi*(= *nara*) instead of *nagara*. But it is not the case.

[398] The *Ratnacūḍa-paripṛcchā* (C. 寶髮經 is a mistake for 寶髻經). Chinese Tripiṭaka retains two versions of this Sūtra, namely 1) 大方等大集經, 寶髻菩薩品第十一 (*Mahāsaṃnipātasūtra*, Chap. 11. *Ratnacūḍabodhisattva-parivarta*), *Taishò*, XIII, p. 173–184; 2) 大寶積經第四十七會寶髻菩薩會 (*Mahāratnakūṭasūtra*, 47th Pariṣat) (originally called 寶髻菩薩所問經, *Ratnacūḍabodhisattva-paripṛcchā*), *Taisho*, XI, No. 310 (47). The illustration of a castle is available only in C., but probably S. & T. have a lacuna here. According to C., the illustration is as follows:

"Suppose, O noble youth, there were a castle of one square *yojana*, which has many gates, but the path towards its gates were steep and dark, and full of dangers. However, the people who could enter this castle were enjoying a lot of pleasure. Suppose again there were one person who had an only son and loved him. Having heard of the pleasure within the castle, he wanted to enter that castle leaving his son behind. By skilful means, he could pass over the steep path and reach a gate of the castle. But when he stepped inside with one leg, the other leg remaining outside, he would remember his son and think: Why hadn't I accompanied my only son! Who could nourish him and let him get rid of suffering? And rejecting the pleasure in the castle, he would go back to his only son. O noble youth, the Bodhisattva is also like him. For the sake of the people, he accumulated the 5 *abhijñās*. Having accumulated them and being ready for the acquiring of *āsravakṣaya*, he does never realize the Enlightenment. Why? Because, due to his compassion towards living beings, he, without making use of his *abhijñā* for *āsravakṣaya*, does act among the world of ordinary beings. Here, O noble youth, 'a castle' is the parable for *mahāparinirvāṇa*; 'many gates' are for the gates of *samādhi*, 80 thousand in number; 'the steep path' is for the various actions of demons; 'to reach the gate of the castle' is for [the attainment of] 5 *abhijñās*; 'stepped inside with one leg' is for [the attainment of] the Wisdom; 'the other leg remained outside' is for the Bodhisattva's non-realization of *mokṣa*; 'the only son' is for all living beings wandering in 5 paths (*gati*): 'to remember his son' is for the Great Compassion; and 'to go back to his son' is the parable for [the Bodhisattva's] leading of living beings. 'Though having the capacity of attaining the Liberation, he does never realize it'... this is due to [the Bodhisattva's]

Thus, through the origination of the Great Intention [towards the Nirvāṇa] [399] by great efforts and exertion, the Bodhisattva gives rise to the 5 Supernatural Faculties. Having the mind purified [400] by the contemplation and Supernatural faculties, he becomes ready for the Extinction of Evil Influences. Having cultivated [401] the Wisdom for the Extinction of Evil Influences in order to rescue all living beings through the origination of the mind of Compassion, he, with perfectly purified mind [402], produces the unobstructed Intellect in the 6th Stage and again becomes ready for the Extinction of Evil Influences. In this way is explained the 'pure' state of the Bodhisattva who has obtained the power for realization of the Extinction of Evil Influences in the [6th] Stage of the Bodhisattva named *Abhimukhī*. [On the other hand], he, though having practised [403] correctly for his own sake, still wishes to save the living beings who are on the wrong way [404], owing to the Great Compassion, saying: I will lead the others also to this true practice [405]. While cultivating the means for the bliss of the Quiescence, but not in order to taste it [by himself] [406] he turns his face [407] away from Nirvāṇa, for the sake of the living beings who are facing the world of transmigration. Though abiding [in the desireless World of Form] with [4 kinds of] contemplations [408] in order to accomplish the factors for the acquisition of Enlightenment [409],

skilful means (*upāya*). Thus, O noble youth, the Great Mercy and Compassion of the Bodhisattva is inconceivable". (Cf. RCP, *Taisho*, XIII, p. 181 *a*).

The following passage is actually not a quotation, and the word '*kulaputra*' (S., T. & C.) is probably an excess. I ventured to omit this vocative word in this translation and treated the whole passage as an explanation by the commentator.

399) *dṛdhâdhyāśaya*, T. *lhag-paḥi bsam-pa brtan-pa*, C. 堅固心. T. reads as '*dṛdhâdhyāśaya-pratipattyā*', which seems better.

400) *parikarma-kṛta*, T. *yoṅs-su sbyoṅ-ba byas-pa* (*pariśuddha-kṛta*), C. om.

401) *parijayaṃ kṛtvā*. For *parijaya*, T. *yoṅs-su sbyoṅ-ba*, C. unclear.

402) *suparikarmakṛtacetāḥ*. C. 善熟心行. C. inserts an explanation on the attainment of the 4th and 5th Stages (*bhūmi*) here.

403) [*samyak-*]*pratipanna*, T. [*yaṅ-dag-par*] *shugs-pa* (to enter), C. [正] 修行.

404) *vipratipanna*, T. *log-par shugs-pa*, C. 顛倒.

405) *samyakpratipatti*, T. *yaṅ-dag-par rtogs-pa*, C. not clear.

406) *anāsvādana*, T. *ro mi-myaṅ-ba*, C. 不著.

407) *vimukha*. But both T. & C. read as *abhimukhasya*.

408) (*catur*)*dhyāna*, T. *bsam-gtan dag* (pl.), C. 四禪. It is said that by the practice of these four *dhyānas*, one can be born in the World of Form (*rūpa-dhātu*).

409) *bodhyaṅga*, T. *byaṅ-chub-kyi yan-lag*, C. 菩提分. They are said to be 7 in number.

he voluntarily assumes[410] again the existence in the World of Desire and wishes to work for the sake of living beings as quickly as possible[411]. [Thus] he has obtained the power for manifesting the body of ordinary beings by assuming various births [even] in the form of animals. From these points mentioned above his state is explained as 'not perfectly pure'.

§ 7. The Pure and Impure State of the Bodhisattva in comparison with the Ordinary Being and the Buddha.

(Another interpretation of the verse 66)[412].
There is another meaning of the *śloka* (Kārikā 24, v. 66).

The son of the Buddha, though having understood[413] that
This Absolute Essence is unchangeable,
Is still perceived by the ignorant
In the appearances of birth, etc.:-
This is really wonderful! // 69 //
Having attained the position of the Saints[414],
He is nevertheless seen among ordinary beings;
Therefore, he is, for the friends of all the world,
The Highest Means and Compassion. // 70 //
Being superior to all kinds of worlds,
He is nevertheless not apart from the world,
He acts in the world for the sake of the world
Without being affected by the worldly pollution. // 71 //
Just as a lotus flower growing in the water
Is not polluted by the latter,
Similarly, though having been born in the world
He is never polluted by worldly matters. // 72 //
His intelligence is always burning like fire
For bringing about the welfare[415] [to the world];

410) *parigrahaṇa*, T. *yoṅs-su ḥdsin-pa*, C. 迴生.

411) C. om. '*yāvad āśu*'.

412) C. om. the whole of the following paragraph, which is therefore probably a later insertion. The heading '*aparaḥ ślokârthaḥ*' also supports this suggestion.

413) The reading *pratividhya* (Ms. B, as Chawdhuri noted) would be better than *prativicya* in the text. See S. p. 52, l. 19: *dharmatā-pratived hāt*. Cf. BHS Dic.: '*pratividhyati*' (Pāli *paṭivijjhati*). T. *rtogs-nas* (having understood).

414) *ārya-gocaia*. (*gocara* = *caryāviṣaya*).

415) *kṛtya-sampādana*, T. *bya-ba sgrub*.

At the same time, he is always practising [416]
Meditation and concentration on the Quiescence [417]; // 73 //
Owing to the continuing force [418] of the previous life,
And because of being free from all discriminations,
He does not use any exertion at all
For bringing the living beings to their maturity. // 74 //
The Bodhisattva, knowing who is to be trained
In what manner and by what means
[Performs it] in the proper manner:
By means of teaching, of two apparitional forms [419],
By conduct [of ordinary life] or by religious observances [420]. //75//
In such a way, he does always,
With no effort and with unobstructed Wisdom,
Bring benefits for the living beings
Among the world, limitless [421] like the sky. // 76 //
Having obtained this position [422],
The Bodhisattva becomes equal to the Tathāgata
On account of his act of conveying [423] the living beings
In various worlds, to the other shore. // 77 //
There is however a great difference
Between Bodhisattvas and the Buddha,
Such difference as lies between the atom and the earth,
Or in [the water] in a foot-print of a bull [424] and in the ocean. //78//

Of these ten verses taken respectively, [the first] 9 verses refer to the comparison [of the state of Bodhisattva] with the absolute impurity of those who rank below the 1st Stage of Bodhisattva named *Pramuditā*

[416] *pratipanna*, T. *sñoms-par shugs-pa.*

[417] This and the following 5 verses (vv. 74-78) were quoted in Amṛtākara's Ṭīka on the *Catuḥśubha* of Nāgārjuna, of which a Sanskrit Ms. was found by Prof. G. Tucci, and is edited along with the Tibetan version by him. (*Minor Buddhist Works*, II pp. 236-246, IsMEO, Rome, 1958).

[418] *āvedha*, T. *ḥphen-pa* (= *ākṣipta*). '*pūrvâvedhavaśāt*' or '*pūrvâvedhāt*' is the usual form. See BHS Dic. p. 109, *āvedha* (2).

[419] For *deśanyā rūpakāyābhyāṃ*, Amṛtākara's quotation reads *deśanā-rūpakāyābhyāṃ*. But T. *bstan daṅ gzugs-sku dag daṅ ni*, which suggests two *rūpakāyas* (i.e. *saṃbhoga-k*, & *nirmāṇa-k*). *deśanī* is a rare form.

[420] *īryā-patha*, T. *sbyod-lam.*

[421] *-paryanta*, T. *mthaḥ klas* (*ananta*).

[422] For *gati*, T. *tshul* (= *naya*).

[423] *saṃtāraṇa*, T. *yaṅ-dag sgrol-ba.*

[424] *gospada* (BHS. *goṣpada* in Skt.).

(Joy)[425], and the 10th verse refers to the comparison with the supreme purity of the Stage above the [10th] Stage of Bodhisattva named *Dharmameghā* (Cloud of Doctrine)[426] (i.e. the Stage of the Buddha). [In comparison with the states, both below and above], there is explained in brief the purity and impurity of the four kinds of Bodhisattvas in the 10 Stages of Bodhisattva. The four kinds of Bodhisattvas are as follows: 1) He who has resolved upon the acquisition for the first time (*prathamacittôtpādika*); 2) He who is practising the way towards the acquisition (*caryāpratipanna*); 3) He who has ascended the irreversible stage (*avaivartika*), and; 4) He who is expected to be the Buddha in the next birth (*ekajātipratibaddha*)[427].

Here, by the first and second verses, there are explained the pure characteristics of qualities[428] of the Bodhisattva who is abiding on the Stage of *Pramuditā* resolving upon the acquisition for the first time, because [in this stage] he has understood[429] the highest supermundane Essence which had never been seen before since beginningless time. By the third and the fourth verses, there are explained the pure characteristics of qualities of the Bodhisattva who is practising the way to the acquisition in the Stages beginning with [the 2nd named] *Vimalā*[430] up to [the 7th named] *Dūraṃgamā* (Far-Going)[431], because [in these stages] he practises the unpolluted practices. By the 5th verse, there are explained the pure characteristics of qualities of the Bodhisattva who has got the irreversible

425) T. *rab-tu dgaḥ-ba* (C. 歡喜地).

426) T. *chos-kyi sprin* (C. 法雲地).

427) T. 1) *sems daṅ-po bskyed-pa* (C. 初發心); 2) *spyod-pa-la shugs-pa* (C. 行道); 3) *phyir mi-ldog-pa*; (C. 不退轉); 4) *skye-ba gcig-gis thogs-pa* (C. 一生補處). Of these four, the first one is said to be equivalent to *darśanamārga* and the second to *bhāvanāmārga*. From the point of wiew of the development of the *bhūmi* theory, these four stages are regarded as older than the 10-*bhūmis* theory of the *Daśa bhūmikā*. The combination of these 4 groups with the 10-*bhūmis* seems to be the latest development, but how to combine both sets is not determined. Often these four are identified with the first, the 3rd, the 7th and the 10th of the 10 *vihāras* (C. 十住), respectively.

428) The reading '*gaṇa*' in the text is corrected into '*guṇa*', in comparison with the following three examples. T. also has '*yon-tan*'. For *viśuddhi*, T. *yoṅs-su dag-pa* (*pariśuddhi*).

429) *prativedha* (BHS for Skt. *prati* √ *vyadh*), T. *mthoṅ-baḥi phyir* (*darśanāt* for *prativedhāt*).

430) T. *dri-ma med-pa* (C. 離垢地).

431) T. instead has *mi-gyo-ba* (*acalā*, the 8th Stage). This is probably a mistake.

state in the [8th] Stage named *Acalā* (Immovable), because [in this stage] he has firmly stood in the meditation as the practice immediately connected with the acquisition of the Great Enlightenment. By the 6th, 7th and 8th verses, there are explained the pure characteristics of qualities of the Bodhisattva who is abiding on the 10th Stage named *Dharmameghā*, being expected to be the Buddha in the next birth, because [in this last stage] he, having attained the ultimate point of means for fulfilling all the benefits for his own as well as for others, is connected with the Stage of the Buddha by one and the last birth [432] on account of the acquisition of the Supreme Perfect Enlightenment. By the 9th and 10th verses, there are explained the equality and difference between the purity of qualities of the Bodhisattva who has reached the ultimate point with regard to the aim of others and of his own, and that of the Buddha's qualities.

(C) Unchangeability in the Perfectly Pure State.

Now, we have one *śloka* with reference to the meaning of 'unchangeability' in the perfectly pure state [of the Buddha].

(Kārikā 25)

This [Essence of the Buddha] is of unalterable nature [433]
Because it is endowed with inexhaustible properties,
It is the refuge of the world
Because it has no limit in the future [434];
It is always non-dual
Because it is indiscriminative,
Also it is of undestructible nature
Because its own nature is not created [by conditions] [435]. // 79 //

What is shown by this *śloka* ?

It is not born, nor does it die;
It does not suffer [from illness], nor is it decrepit.
Because it is eternal,

432) ***buddhabhūmy-ekacarama-janma-pratibaddha.***

433) ***ananyathâtmā*, T. *gshan-ḥgyur-min-bdag*, C. 不變異. See v. 66.**

434) ***anaparântakoṭi*, T. *phyi-maḥi mthaḥ-med myur-thug*, C. 無邊際.**

435) **For v. 79 *d*. C. 恒不執, 不作清淨心力故, which is difficult to be identified with S.**

Everlasting, quiescent and costant [436]. // 80 //
Being eternal, it is not born
Even with [the form of] the Body made of mind [437],
Being everlasting, it does not die
Even with the Inconceivable Transformation. // 81 //
Being quiescent, it has no suffering
From the illness of subtle defiling forces,
And, being constant, it does not become decrepit
By the accumulation of the Passionless Active Force [438]. // 82 //

Indeed, this Essence of the Tathāgata, in case it is abiding on the Stage of the Buddha which is absolutely immaculate, pure and radiant by its own nature, is 'eternal' in regard to its beginning. Therefore, it is never born even in the form of Body made of mind. Being 'everlasting' in regard to its end, it does not die in the manner of the inconceivable Transformation. Being 'quiescent' in regard to both, beginning and end, it never suffers from illness depending on [439] the Dwelling Place of Ignorance. Thus, not falling into misery [440], it is 'constant', and consequently never becomes decrepit through the transformation brought about by the Passionless Active Force.

Here, the meaning of Eternity, etc.
In regard to the immutable Sphere [441]
Is to be known, respectively,
By each couple of terms. // 83 //

436) These 4 terms are as follows: 1) *nitya*, T. *rtag-pa*, C. 常; 2) *dhruva*, T. *brten-pa*, C. 恒; 3) *śiva*, T. *shi-ba*, C. 清凉; 4) *śāśvata*, T. *gyuṅ-druṅ*, C. 不變.

437) *manomayakāya*, etc. are of Bodhisattvas and don't belong to the Buddha. Because of the birth in the form of *manomayakāya* and others, Bodhisattvas are regarded as 'partly impure'.

438) Cf. DAŚ 892 *b*: (under the item 1. *phala* of *bodhicitta*) 唯佛如來 能求滅盡一切微細煩惱執故 於中無生永復不生意生諸蘊故,無老,此功德增上殊勝 圓滿究竟無變異故,無死永捨離 不思議變易死故,無病一切煩惱所知障病及與習氣皆永斷故.

439) *parigraha*, T. *yoṅs-su hdsin-pa*, C. 所攝 (*parigṛhīta*).

440) *anartha*, T. *don-med-pa*, C. 三世 (= the world of transmigration). *anarthāpatita* is to be resolved into *anartha-apatita*. For *apatita*, T. *ma thog-pa*, C. 不墮.

441) *asaṃskṛta-pada*, T. *ḥdus-ma-byas-kyi dbyiṅs*, C. 無漏境界 (*anāsrava-*). (*asaṃskṛtadhātu* in the prose comm.).

Of these four terms, namely 'eternal', 'everlasting', 'quiescent' and 'constant', the distinction of the meaning of each term in regard of the Immutable Sphere is to be understood by each couple of terms showing 'statement' and 'explanation'[442], respectively, according to the Scripture[443]. It is said as follows:

> " This Absolute Body, O Śāriputra, is Eternal since it is of unalterable nature through its inexhaustible properties. This Absolute Body, O Śāriputra, is Everlasting, the everlasting refuge, because it exists as far as the farthest limit. Being of indiscriminative nature, O Śāriputra, this Absolute Body is Quiescent, of non-dualistic nature. Being of uncreated nature[444], O Śāriputra, this Absolute Body is Constant, of undestructible character ".

(X) ASAṂBHEDA[445]

The Essence[446] of the Tathāgata characterized as having reached the ultimate point of perfect purification in this pure state is of undifferentiated (*asaṃbheda*) nature. With reference to this meaning of 'undifferentiation' we have one *śloka*.

(Kārikā 26)

It is the Absolute Body, it is the Tathāgata,
Also it is the Holy Truth, the Highest[447] Nirvāṇa;
Therefore, being indivisible from qualities like the sun with its rays,
There is no Nirvāṇa, apart from the Buddhahood. // 84 //

442) *uddeśa* & *nirdeśa*, T. *bstan-pa* & *bśad- pa*, C. 本, 釋, respectively.

443) AAN 467 *b*. T. (as well as Ms. B.) adds two verses here, which are no doubt interpolations.

444) *akṛtrima-dharma*, C. 非作法.

445) Cf. BGŚ 811 *c* ff. (10. Asaṃbheda).

446) The reading '*tathāgatadhātor*' in Ms. B. does not have to be corrected with '*-garbhasya*', because it was the usual case to use the term *dhātu* in such headings in this text, and there is no essential difference between both terms.

447) The combination of *paramârtha* with *nirvāṇa* (*nirvṛti* in the text) is peculiar. T. rendering is helpless to fix the meaning and C. om. *paramârtha*. Does it mean *Nirvāṇa* of the Buddha and not that of Śrāvaka and Pratyekabuddha?

Cf. DAŚ 893 *c* (on Ekatva): 此即是法身 亦即是如來 如是亦即是 聖諦第一義 涅槃不異佛 猶如冷即水 功德不相離 故無異涅槃.

§ 1. Synonyms of the Essence of the Tathāgata.

Here, what is shown by the former half of the *śloka?*

It should be known, in brief,
There are 4 synonyms, the Absolute Body and others
Since [the Germ] in the Immaculate Sphere
Has four meanings from different aspects. // 85 //

In short, there are four meanings in regard to the Matrix of the Tathāgata as the Immaculate Sphere (or Essence). In accordance with these 4 meanings, there should be known 4 synonyms [448]. Then which are the 4 meanings?

It is indivisible from the Buddha's Properties,
Its Germ has been perfected as it is [449],
It is not of false, deceptive nature [450],
And it is quiescent from the very outset [451]. // 86 //

1) The first meaning: [the Essence of the Buddha] is indivisible from the Buddha's properties. With reference to this meaning, it is said as follows [452]:

"O Lord, the Matrix of the Tathāgata is not empty [453] [because it is endowed] with the Buddha's Properties which are inconceivable, indivisible, inseparable [from Wisdom] [454] and are greater in number than the sands of the Gaṅgā".

448) *nāmaparyāya*, T. *miṅ-gi rnam-graṅs*, C. 名 (異名).

449) *tathāgama*, T. *de-bshin thob-pa*, C. 真如 (彼真如性 for *tadgotrasya tathāgamaḥ*). An explanation of the meaning of '*tathāgata*'.

450) *amṛṣāmoṣadharmitva*, C. 法體不虛妄.

451) *ādiprakṛtiśāntatā*, C. 自性本來淨 ('淨' should be '寂' according to the meaning). Cf. BGŚ *ibid.*: 四義者 1) 一切佛法前後不相離; 2) 一切處皆如; 3) 非妄想顛倒法; 4) 本來寂靜.

452) ŚMS 221 *c*.

453) *aśūnya*, T. *mi-stoṅ-pa*, C. 不空. On this conception, further explanation will be given in S. p. 76, vv. 154-5 and commentary thereon. Lit. *tathāgatagarbha* is not empty of *buddhadharmāḥ* (*buddhadharmair aśūnyam*).

454) *amuktajña*, T. *bral mi-śes-pa*, C. 不脫 (lit. unreleased from the wisdom).

2) The second meaning: Its Germ, i.e. the Innate Nature has been perfected[455] in an inconceivable manner[456]. With reference to this point, it is said as follows[457]:

"[This Germ], having attained the Absolute Essence, has come down since beginningless time from one existence to another existence[458] assuming[459] various forms consisting of six organs of cognitions, (i.e. in the form of various living beings)".

3) The third meaning: It is not of false, deceptive nature. With reference to this point, it is said as follows[460]:

"Here, that which is the Highest Truth is Nirvāṇa, whose nature is undeceptive. For what reason? Because the Germ is eternal by its being quiescent"[461].

4) The fourth meaning: It is of the nature of absolute quiescence. With reference to this point, it is said as follows[462]:

"Being in Nirvāṇa from the very outset, the Tathāgata, the Arhat, the Perfectly enlightened One is of neither origination nor destruction".

455) *samudāgama*, T. *thob-pa*. = *āgama* (in the verse). C. has no literal translation.

456) *acintya-prakāra*, T. *bsam-gyis mi-khyab-paḥi rnam-pa*. It stands for *tathā* in the verse.

457) C. mentions the name of the source, *Ṣaḍāyatanasūtra* (or *Ṣaḍindriyarāśi-sūtra*) (六根聚經), which is missing now. The following quotation shows a quite unique interpretation of the word *tathāgata*. AĀS 469*b* 一切衆生有陰界入勝相種類內外所顯,無始時節相續流法爾所得,至明妙善. BGŚ quotes the sentence as from AĀS (812 *a*) (法然 for 法爾). Cf. BBh. 3. ll. 2–4 (on *prakṛtistha-gotra*).

458) *paraṃpara*, T. *brgyud-nas* (from ancestors).

459) *tādṛśaḥ*, T. *de-ḥdra-ba* (connecting with *ṣaḍāyatanaviśeṣaḥ*), C. [六根] 如是.

460) The source is uncertain. (Cf. AkṣP. 197 *b*). O attributes it to ŚMS, but C. does not mention the name of the source, and I could not find the exact passage in ŚMS. I suppose this quotation is also from the Ṣaḍāyatanasūtra, because, according to C., a vocative '*bhagavan*' is also inserted in the previous quotation and the Ṣaḍāyatanasūtra seems to have had a structure similar to the ŚMS, i.e. someone is expressing his understanding in front of the Buddha and the Buddha acknowledges it.

461) T. reading *shi-ba*(*śama*) is preferable from the context. C. 法體不變故 (*śāśvatadharmatayā*).

462) JĀA 241 *c*.

For these four meanings, there are four synonyms, namely, 1) the Absolute Body; 2) the Tathāgata; 3) the Highest Truth, and 4) the Nirvāṇa, respectively. It is said as follows [463]:

> "The Matrix of the Tathāgata, O Śāriputra, is the name for the Absolute Body.
>
> "O Lord, the Tathāgata and the Absolute Body, these both are not different from each other [464]. The Absolute Body is, O Lord, nothing but the Tathāgata".
>
> "Under the name of the Extinction of the Suffering, O Lord, there is indicated the Absolute Body of the Tathāgata, being endowed with such properties".
>
> "The Sphere of the Nirvāṇa, O Lord, is the name for the Absolute Body of the Tathāgata".

§ 2. The Point: Buddhahood is Nirvāṇa.

Now, what is shown by the latter half of the *śloka?*

Being the Perfect Enlightenment in all aspects,
And being the removal of pollutions along their root [465],
Buddhahood and Nirvāṇa
Are one and the same in the highest viewpoint [466]. // 87 //

These four synonyms of the Immaculate Essence converge into the undifferentiated [467] meaning of the Essence of the Tathāgata. Therefore, these four are one in their sense, and hence, by means of [468] the Doctrine of non-duality, the following fact is to be known. Namely, that which is called 'Buddhahood' because of its Perfect Enlightenment regarding all kinds of phenomena, and that which is called 'Nirvāṇa' because of its removal of pollutions along with their remaining forces which takes

463) AAN 467 *a*; ŚMS 220*c*, 222 *a*, 220 *c*, respectively.

464) A negative particle '*na*' is to be inserted before '*anyo dharmakāyaḥ*' (-*gato nānyo dharmakāyaḥ*).

465) The first one is for *buddhatva* and the next one is for *nirvāṇa*. See commentary.

466) C. reads 'inseparable from the highest truth' (不離第一義).

467) T. om. *abbhinna*, for which C. 一味 (*ekarasa*).

468) *nayamukhena*, T. *tshul-gyi sgo-nas*, C. [法] 門 ('不離一法門不離一法體' for *advayadharmanayamukhena*).

place simultaneously with[469] the Perfect Enlightenment, these two are non-dual, indivisible and inseparable [470] in the Immaculate Sphere.

[So it is said][471]:

" Liberation is of the characteristic
Indivisible from the properties, which are
Of all kinds, innumerable, unthinkable and immaculate[472];
This Liberation, that is the Tathāgata ".

Also, it is said in the Scripture[473] with reference to the Nirvāṇa of the Arhat and Pratyekabuddha:

" [Here], O Lord, the Nirvāṇa is merely a means used by the Tathāgata ".

By this passage it is explained that this [Nirvāṇa of the Arhats and the Pratyekabuddhas] is a means made by the Perfectly Enlightened Ones who have the highest Controlling Power on [all] phenomena[474] in order to protect them (i.e. Arhats and Pratyekabuddhas) against retreat; it is just like the illusory city in the forest[475] made for the travellers who are tired[476] after their long way [in order to encourage them].

[On the other hand] it is said:[477]:

" By reason of having attained Nirvāṇa, O Lord, the Tathāgatas, the Arhats, the Perfectly Enlightened Ones are endowed with properties showing the ultimate point of the entireness, immeasurebility, inconceivability and purity ".

By this passage it is explained that, having realized the Nirvāṇa which is characterized as being inseparable from the accomplishment[478]

[469] *mahâbhisaṃbodhāt.* C. as S. But T. adds *lhan-cig* (together), which makes the meaning clear. C. om. *buddhatva* & *nirvāṇa*.

[470] C. adds one epithet more: 不相離 (*avinirbhāga*).

[471] Both S. & T. are lacking the heading. But C. 以是義故大涅槃經中偈言 (*yata āha Mahāparinirvāṇasūtre*). The place in MPS remained untraced.

[472] *sarvākāra, asaṃkhyeya, acintya, amala*, respectively. These 4 are called '*caturākāraguṇaniṣpatti*' in the commentary.

[473] ŚMS 219 *c*.

[474] *dharma-paramêśvara.* An epithet of the Buddha.

[475] *aṭavī*, T. *ḥbrog-dgon*, C. 曠野.

[476] *pariśrānta*, T. *dub-pa*, C. 疲惓.

[477] ŚMS 219 c.

[478] *niṣpatti* (the reading '*niṣpatsv-*' in the text should be corrected. See S. p. 58, l. 9 & 12), T. *grub-pa*, C. 畢竟. *niṣṭhāgata* (in the quotation).

of properties of four kinds [479], the Perfectly Enlightened Ones identify themselves with Nirvāṇa [480]; therefore, as both of these, Buddhahood and Nirvāṇa, are endowed with inseparable properties, no one [481] can realize Nirvāṇa apart from Buddhahood.

§ 3. The Parable of the Painters.

Now, in the Immaculate Sphere, the Buddhas are possessed of all kinds of properties since they have accomplished [482] the Non-substantiality endowed with all sorts of excellency [483]. This is here to be known through the illustration of the painters [484].

Suppose there were some painters [485],
[Each of them] expert in a different sphere,
So that whatever skill possessed by one of them,
The others could not understand [486]. // 88 //
Then a mighty king would give them
A painting cloth [487] with the following commandment:
On this [cloth] ye all should draw my portrait [488]. // 89 //
Then the painters, having promised [489] [to the king],
Would start their work of painting.
Of these [painters] engaged in this work,

479) See Note 471. Here (in ŚMS), the four terms are as follows: 1) *sarva*; 2) *aprameya*; 3) *acintya*; 4) *viśuddhi*. Cf. BGŚ 812 *c*: 復次, 四種功德者, 一者一切功德, 二者無量功德, 三者不可思惟功德, 四者究竟清淨功德.

480) *tadātmakaṃ bhavati*.

481) T. *ḥgaḥ yaṅ* (= *kaścid*), C. 更無餘人 (*kasyacid . . . na*).

482) *abhinirhāra*, T. *mṅon-par bsgrubs-pa*, C. 示現.

483) *vara*, T. *mchog* (= *śreṣṭha*), C. om.

484) This illustration of the painters is originally taken from the *Ratnacūḍasūtra*. C. quotes the original account after the verses. Cf. RCS 176 *a*.

485) *citra-lekhaka*, T. *ri-mo ḥdri-byed-pa* (for *ḥdri*, *ḥbri*, to draw, would be better in sense, though the former is often used).

486) *avadhārayati* (to understand), T. *zin-pa* (to apprehend), C. 知.

487) *dūṣya*, T. *ras*, C. 摽(採)畫處.

488) *pratikṛti*, T. *gzugs*, C. (像).

489) *pratiśrutya*, T. *thos-gyur te* (having heard of it), C. 受勅已 (having accepted the commandment of the king).

One would have gone abroad [490]. // 90 //
Because of his absence during his being abroad
This picture would remain
Without the completion of all parts;
Thus the parable is made. // 91 //
The painters who are meant here are
Charity, Morals, Patience and other dispositions [491]
Being endowed with all kinds of these excellencies,
The Non-substantiality is called the picture [492]. // 92 //

Here, of these [excellent virtues], charity and the rest, each one is differentiated into limitless varieties in accordance with the Buddha's Sphere [of activity]. Therefore, it should be known as 'immeasurable' [493]. On account of its number and power, it should be known as being 'inconceivable' and, having exterminated the remaining force of pollutions [494] by its enemies, in the form of 'envy', etc. [495], [each virtue] is to be known as being 'pure'.

Now [496], through practice by means of Meditation on the Non-substantiality endowed with all sorts of excellencies, the Non-origination of [all] the elements [497] is realized. Because of this realization, [Bodhisattvas can] ascend to their 8th Stage called *Acalā* (Immovable), where they can get the knowledge of the Path which is indiscriminative, faultless [498], without any break and bearing its own taste [499]. On the basis

[490] *viyoga*, T. *ma tshaṅ* (incomplete), C. 無.

[491] T. om. *ākāra*, for which C. 行. These are the so-called *ṣaṭ-pāramitāḥ*.

[492] C. adds one verse saying: 'One painter is absent' means the lack of one *ākāra*, 'non-completion of the king's portrait' means the non-endurance of the knowledge of non-substantiality. T. (D) inserts unnecessarily one Pada between *c* and *d* of v. 92, saying: *de-la mṅon-par sbyin rnams-kyi*.

[493] *aparimita*, T. *tshad med-pa*, C. 無邊. This is for *aprameya*, the 2nd of the 4 characteristics.

[494] T. om. *mala*, but C. has it.

[495] 1) *mātsarya* (C. 慳); 2) *kaukṛtya* (C. 惡作); 3) *dveṣa* (C. 瞋); 4) *kausīdya* (C. 懈怠); 5) *vikṣepa* (C. 散亂); and 6) *moha* (C. 癡); are *vipakṣas* of *dāna*, *śīla*, *kṣānti*, *vīrya*, *dhyāna*, and *prajñā*, respectively.

[496] Hereafter, on the relation of the 4 characteristics to the Stages of Bodhisattva. Cf. BGŚ 813 *a*, MSbh (P), 258 *b*.

[497] *anutpattika-dharma*, T. *mi-skye-baḥi chos-ñid*, C. 無生法忍 (= *anutpattika-dharma-kṣānti*).

[498] *niśchidra*, T. *skyon med-pa* (without defect), C. 無間 (without interruption).

[499] *svarasavāhin*, *raṅ-gi ṅaṅ-gis ḥjug-pa*. C. 自然 (natural).

of this knowledge, the entireness of Buddhas' properties in the Immaculate Sphere is completed. On the Stage of Bodhisattva called *Sādhumati* (Perfect Knowledge), by means of immeasurable forms of Meditation and magic formulas like the ocean [500], they can obtain the knowledge [501] for assuming the immeasurable properties of the Buddha. On the basis of this knowledge, the 'immeasurability' of [Buddhas'] properties is completed. On the Bodhisattva's [last] Stage called *Dharmameghā*, basing himself upon the knowledge revealing [502] the secret [503] state of all the Buddhas, the 'inconceivability' of Buddhas' properties is completed. Immediately after this stage, on the basis of knowledge which leads to the liberation from all impediments on account of Defilements and Knowables along with their remaining forces, aiming at the acquisition of the Stage of Buddha, the highest 'purity' of Buddhas' properties is completed. As the Arhats and the Pratyekabuddhas cannot perceive [504] these four knowledges, the foundations of these Stages [above *Acalā*], they are said to be far from the Sphere of the Nirvāṇa [505] characterized as being indivisible from the accomplishment of the properties of the [above mentioned] four kinds.

§ 4. Similarity of the Buddhahood to the Sun.

The Intellect, the Wisdom and the Liberation
Are [respectively] bright, radiant, and clear,
And they are inseparable [506] from [the Absolute Essence];
Therefore, they are similar to the light,
The rays, and the disk of the sun. // 93 //

That which is indicated as the Sphere of the Nirvāṇa characterized as being inseparable from he accomplishment of four kinds of properties through the Intellect, the Wisdom and the Liberation, is explained to

500) For *samudra*, T. reads *brgya-stoṅ* (= *śatasahasra*), but C. 海.

501) C. calls this *jñāna* '*śūnya(tā)-jñāna*' (空智).

502) *aviparokṣa*, T. *lkog-tu ma gyur-pa*, C. 現前.

503) *guhya*, T. *gsaṅ-ba*, C. 密.

504) *saṃdṛśyate*, T. *mthoṅ-ba*, (as Parasmaipada), C. 'to be'.

505) Cf. ŚMS 219 *c* (after the explanation of '*caturākāraguṇa*' of the Tathāgata): 是故阿羅漢辟支佛 去涅槃界遠.

506) *abheda*, T. *tha-dad-med*, C.

have similarity to the sun in four aspects, namely, by three aspects [507] on account of the Intellect, etc., respectively, and by one [in general]. Here in the Buddha's body [508], 1) The transcendental Intellect which is supermundane and indiscriminative is, through its engaging in the destruction of darkness [that hides] the highest true essence of everything cognizable, akin to the light [of the sun]; 2) The Wisdom of Omniscience [509] which is attained subsequently [510] is, through its penetrating everything knowable of all kinds, without exception, akin to the radiance of the net [511] of rays; 3) The Liberation of the Innate Mind, the basis of the above two (Intellect and Wisdom), has a resemblance to the purity of the disk of the sun through its being perfectly free from pollution and its being radiant; and 4) As these three are undifferentiated from the Absolute Essence, there is a similarity to the light and others through their indivisibility [from the sun].

Therefore, without the acquisition of Buddhahood,
There is no attainment of Nirvāṇa,
Just as it is impossible to see the sun,
Avoiding [512] its light and rays. // 94 //

Thus, within the Essence [of the Buddha] which is endowed with [513] the virtuous qualities as its own nature constantly associated [514] since beginningless time, there exists the essential nature [515] of the indivisible properties of Tathāgatas. Therefore, unless the Buddhahood [516], i.e. the true introspection [517] by the Intellect [518] free from attachment and of no

[507] *kāraṇa* in the text. It is preferably corrected into *ākāra*. (T. *rnam-pa*). C. om. '*tribhir ekena ca kāraṇena*'.

[508] *buddhasāntānika*, T. *saṅs-rgyas-kyi rgyud-la mṅaḥ-ba*, C. 佛法身.

[509] *sarvajña-jñāna*, T. *śes-bya thams-cad-kyi ye-śes* (*sarvajñeyajñāna*), C. 一切智智.

[510] *pṛṣṭhalabdha*, T. *rjes-la thob-pa*. C. simply 智 (in comparison with *prajñā* 慧).

[511] *jāla*, T. *dra-ba*, C. 羅網.

[512] *nirvṛjya* (fr. *nir* √ *vṛj*, Pali *nibbajjeti*), T. *spaṅs-nas*, C. 棄捨.

[513] *upahita*, T. *-daṅ ldan-pa*.

[514] *sāṃnidhya*, T. *ñe-bar gnas-pa* (= *upasthita*). C. om. from *sāṃnidhya* up to *upahite*, and instead has *anāsrava*.

[515] *avinirbhāga-guṇadharmatva*, T. *yon-tan rnam-par dbyer-med-paḥi chos-ñid yin-pa*. For *dharmatva*, C. 法身 (= *dharmakāya*).

[516] *tathāgatatva* = *buddhatva*. T. om. *-tva*.

[517] *jñāna-darśana*, T. *ye-śes-kyi gzigs-pa*, C. om. *darśana*.

[518] T. om. *prajñā*, for which C. has '智慧'.

hindrance, is understood, the acquisition will not take place, i.e. the realization of the Sphere of Nirvāṇa characterized as the liberation from all the impediments, just as we cannot see the disk of the sun without perceiving its light and rays. Therefore, it is said [519]:

> " O Lord, there is no acquisition of the Nirvāṇa for [those who maintain] the inferiority or superiority of [all] the elements [520]. The acquisition of the Nirvāṇa is, O Lord, available [only] to [those who know] the equality of all the elements. [In other words], O Lord, it is for those who have the Wisdom of equality, those who have the liberation of equality [521], or those who have attained the true introspection through the liberation of equality. Therefore, O Lord, it is said the Sphere [522] of the Nirvāṇa is of unique taste, of equal taste. That is to say, [it is of one and the same] taste with Wisdom [523] and Liberation ".

[519] ŚMS 220 *b*. (Lit. therefore she (= *Śrīmālādevī*) said).

[520] *hīna-praṇīta-dharmāṇām* (Bahuvrīhi comp.).

DAŚ also quotes the same passage and, prior to the quotation has an interpretation of this subject. It runs as follows:

" It should be known, furthermore, that there is only one way of the One Vehicle. If otherwise, there should be another *nirvāṇa* than this. How may it be possible for the superior *nirvāṇa* and the inferior *nirvāṇa* to exist within one *dharmadhātu*? Also, we cannot say we get one result on the basis of higher or lower causes. If there were a difference among the causes, there would also be a difference among the results ". (DAŚ 894 *a*).

[521] *sama-vimukti*.

[522] T. om. *dhātu*, but C. has it.

[523] *vidyā*, T. *rig-pa*, C. 明.

IX. THE 9 ILLUSTRATIONS ON THE GERM COVERED WITH DEFILEMENTS [1]

§ 1. The 9 Illustrations according to the *Tathāgatagarbhasūtra*.

Thus have been explained the characteristics
Of the Matrix of the Buddha from 10 aspects;
Now, this Matrix, as concealed by the covering of defilements
Is to be known by the following illustrations. // 95 //

Thus, with reference to the existence [2] of the Essential Nature [3], as eternal as the ultimate limit [of the world] [4], we have hitherto explained the characteristics of the Matrix of the Tathāgata from 10 points of view. And hereafter, with reference to the fact that the covering of defilements is essentially unconnected [5] [with the Innate Mind] although associating with [6] it since the beginningless time [7], and the pure Essential Nature, likewise associating since the beginningless time, is essentially connected with it [as being its own nature], it should be understood, by 9 illustrations based upon the Scripture [8], that the Matrix of the Tathāgata is concealed by the limitless [9] coverings of defilements. Which are the 9 illustrations?

(Kārikās 27–57)

Like the Buddha in an ugly lotus flower,
Like honey surrounded by bees,

[1] C. 無量煩惱所纏品第六. Cf. BGŚ 806 *c*–808 *c*.

[2] *saṃvidyamānatā*, T. *rig-par bya-ba-ñid*, C. not clear.

[3] *dharmatā*, T. *chos-ñid*, C. 法體.

[4] *aparântakoṭi-sama*, T. *phyi-maḥi mthaḥi mu daṅ mtshuṅs-pa*. This formula (*aparântakoṭisama-dhruvadharmatā-saṃvidyamānatā*) is, together with the next two formulae (on *kleśakośatā* and *śubhadharmatā*), originally taken from AAN. 467 *b*. See my Introduction, n. 66.

[5] *asaṃbaddha*, T. *ma ḥbrel-ba*, C. om.

[6] *sāṃnidhya*, T. *ñe-bar gnas-pa* (*upasthita*), C. 'covered' in the meaning.

[7] So T. (*thog-ma med-paḥi dus-nas*) and C. (無始世界來). But S. *anādi*–.

[8] TGS 457 *a*–460 *b*.

[9] For *aparyanta* ... *koṭi*, C. 過於恒沙.

Like kernels of[10] grains covered by the husk,
Like gold fallen into impurities,
Like a treasure under the ground,
Like a sprout, etc. grown from a small fruit[11],
Like an image of the Buddha wrapped in a tattered[12] garment,
// 96 //

Like the kinghood[13] in the womb[14] of a poor[15] woman,
And like a precious statue in the earthen mould;
In such a way, there abides this Essence
In the living beings obscured by occasional stains of defilements.
// 97 //

[In these illustrations], pollutions are like
A lotus flower, bees, husk, impurities and the ground,
Like the bark of a fruit, like a tattered garment,
Like a woman of misery, and like earth tormented by the fire of pains;
And the Buddha, honey, cleaned kernels[16], gold, treasure,
A Nyagrodha tree, a precious image, the Highest Lord of the world,
And a purified precious statue,
The excellent Essence has a resemblance to them. // 98 //

(I) The Defilements are like the ugly sheath of lotus flowers, and the Essence of the Tathāgata is akin to the Buddha[17].

Suppose the Buddha, shining with a thousand marks [of virtue],
Were abiding in the inside[18] a faded lotus flower,

[10] *sāra*, T. *sñiṅ-po*, C. 實. The edible part of grains.

[11] *alpa-phala*, T. *ḥbras-chuṅs*, C. 果 (om. *alpa*).

[12] *praklinna* = *pūti* (v. 98), T. *hrul*, C. 朽故弊壞 (故弊).

[13] *nṛpatva*, = *dvīpâgrâdhipa* (*v. 98*) T. *mi-bdag*, C. 轉輪聖王 (*cakravartin*).

[14] *jaṭhala*, T. *lto*[*-ba*] (belly).

[15] *jaghanya*, T. *ṅan* (ugly), C. 貧賤醜陋 (poor and ugly).

[16] *susāra*.

[17] Cf. TGS 457 c. The story given in the Sūtra is as follows: Once the Lord, sitting in the assembly of Bodhisattvas, showed a miracle. There appeared thousands of lotus flowers having the apparitional Buddha within and shining with splendour fragrant. They came to blossom at the same time, but all at once they became faded and began to give a bad smell. But still there was the Buddha sitting within each flower. Bodhisattvas were surprised at this sight and asked the Lord for the explanation of this miracle. Then the Lord started his pronouncement on the Essence of the Tathāgata abiding within each living being.

This idea of the origination of the Tathāgata is probably borrowed from the *Tathāgatôtpattisaṃbhavanirdeśa* of the *Avataṃsaka*.

[18] *garbha-veṣṭita*, T. ... *ḥi khoṅ gnas-pa*, C. 住...中.

And a man of immaculate divine sight would perceive him
And release him from the sheath of petals[19] of lotus; — // 99 //
Similarly, the Lord, with his Buddha's eyes,
Perceives his own nature even in those who are in the lowest world,
And, being immaculate, standing at the utmost limit[20] and being full of Compassion,
He releases them from the obscurations. // 100 //
Just as a person of divine sight perceives
A faded[21] and ugly lotus flower and the Buddha within it,
And rends asunder the petals [in order to draw him out]; —
In the same way, the Lord perceives the world,
The Matrix of the Buddha, covered with the sheath of stains, Desire, Hatred[22], etc.,
And kills[23] its Obscurations[24] because of Compassion. // 101 //

(II) The Defilements are like honey-bees, and the Essence of the Tathāgata is akin to the honey[25].

Suppose a clever person, having seen
Honey surrounded by[26] cloudy bees,
And wishing to get it, with skillful means,
Would deprive the bees completely of it; — // 102 //
Similarly, the Great Sage, possessed of the eyes of the Omniscience,
Perceiving this Essence known as akin to honey,
Accomplishes the non-connection[27] of the Essence
With the bees-like obscurations, completely. // 103 //
Just as a man who is desirous of getting honey
Hidden by thousands, millions[28] of bees,

19) *pattra*, T. reads *padma* instead of *pattra*. Here *pattra* stands for *kośa*.

20) = being eternal (C. 處常住際).

21) *sammiñjita*, T. *thum*[*-pa*] (something packed or wrapped up), C. 朽枯，萎. T. reads *jalaruha* as locative, instead of accusative in S.

22) C. '*kleśa*'. T. as S.

23) *nir* √ *han*, T. *ḥjoms-pa*, C. 除 (to remove).

24) *nivaraṇa*, T. *sgrib-pa* (= *āvaraṇa*). C. reads analogically '花葉' (petals).

25) Cf. TGS 457 *c*–458 *a*.

26) *upagūḍha* (concealed), T. *bskor* (surrounded), C. 圍遶 (as T.).

27) *aśleṣa*, T. *rab-tu spoṅ-ba* (= *prahāṇa*), C. similar to T.

28) *sahasra-koṭi-niyuta*, T. *bya-ba khrab-khrig ston* (*niyuta-koṭi-sahasra*), C. 百千億那由他. (那由他 = *nayuta*, for *niyuta*).

Drives the bees away[29] and makes use of the honey[30] as he wishes;
In the same way, the immaculate Wisdom in the living beings
Is like honey, and the Defilements are like bees;
The Buddha, like that man, knows how to remove the stains. //104//

(III) The Defilements are like the outer husk, and the Essence of the Tathāgata is akin to the inner kernel[31].

The kernel of grains covered with the husk
Cannot be eaten by any person;
Those who wish to utilize it as food and the like[32]
Take it out from the husk; — // 105 //
Similarly, the Buddhahood in the living beings
Is polluted with the stains of Defilements,
And unless it is freed from the association of stains of Defilements,
It cannot perform the Acts of Buddha in the 3 Spheres. //106//
Just as the kernel of grains like rice, wheat, barley, etc.[33],
As long as it is unreleased from the husk and not cleaned well[34],
Cannot be the sweet edible for the people;
Similarly, the religious king[35] residing in the living beings,
Having his feature unreleased from the husk of Defilements,
Does not become one who can grant the pleasurable taste of the Doctrine,
To the people who are afflicted by the hunger of Defilements. //107//

[29] *vinihatya* (fr. *vi-ni*√*han*), C. 殺害 (killing). But T. *bsal te* (fr. *sel-ba*, to remove), which gives a better sense.

[30] The form *madhvā* as inst. sg. of *madhu* (neut.) is peculiar. (Is it a special form in some Prakrit or merely a wrong reading of *madhunā*?).

[31] Cf. TGS 458 *a*.

[32] *annâdibhir* (inst.) is grammatically peculiar (usually in loc.).

[33] *kaṅguka-śāli-kodrava-yava-vrīhi.* All these are varieties of grains, their equivalents are not so clear. The last one, *vrīhi* seems to stand for corn or grain in general, for which T. & C. are *ḥbru*, 穀, respectively. T. *sālu*, *bra-bo*, *nas*, *ḥbru* (the second one is a kind of wheat), C. 稻, 穀, 麥等.

[34] *khāḍy-asusaṃskṛta*, T. *gra-ma-can legs-par ma bgrus* (having hairs and not yet cleaned) (*bgrus* means 'to step on the bag filled with corns in order to remove the husk). C. 未浄治. See J's note 1 on S. p. 62.

[35] *dharmêśvara*, C. 佛自在法王.

(IV) The Defilements are like a dirty place [36] filled with impurities, and the Essence of the Tathāgata is akin to gold [37].

Suppose a traveller would happen to drop
A piece of gold in a place filled with impurities [38],
And the gold would stay there for many hundreds of years
As it were, without changing its quality; — // 108 //
Then a god possessed of immaculate divine eyes
Would see it there and tell a man: —
Here is a piece of gold, fresh [39] and the highest of precious things.
You should purify it and make use of it as a treasure; — // 109 //
Similarly, the Buddha perceives the quality of living beings
Drowned in the Defilements which are like impurities,
And pours the rain of the Doctrine over the living beings
In order to wash off that dirt of defilements. // 110 //
Just as a god, perceiving a piece of gold, the most beautiful one,
Fallen into a dirty place filled with impurities,
Would show it to the people in order to purify [40] it from dirt [41];
In the same way, the Buddha, perceiving the treasure of the Buddha in the living beings
Which is fallen into a big pit of impurities of defilements,
Teaches the Doctrine to the living beings in order to purify the treasure. // 111 //

(V) The Defilements are like the underground [42], and the Essence of the Tathāgata is akin to a treasure of jewels [43].

Suppose there were an inexhaustible treasure
Under the ground within the house of a poor man;
However this man might not know about that treasure,

[36] *saṃkāra-dhāna*, T. *ljan-ljin-kyi gnas*, C. simply 'impurities'. *dhāna* stands here for *ādhāna*. *saṃkāra* is replaced in verses by *saṃkara*.

[37] Cf. TGS 458 *a-b*.

[38] *saṃkara-pūti-dhāna*, T. *ljan-ljin rul-baḥi gnas*.

[39] *nava*. T. & C. om. it.

[40] T. reads '*kun-tu dgaḥ-bar bya phyir*' (in order to gladden them, O.), which is probably a misreading for '*kun-tu dag-par bya phyir*'.

[41] T. reads '*bālāt*' (nan-gyis) instead of *malāt*. But C. as S.

[42] *tala*, T. *mthil* (depth), C. om.

[43] Cf. TGS 458 *b*. Also cf. MPS (*Taisho*, XII, p. 407 *b*).

And the latter could not say to him 'I am here'; — // 112 //
Similarly, though there is a treasure of immaculate jewel,
The inconceivable, inexhaustible[44] properties in the mind,
The living beings of the world, without knowing it,
Constantly[45] experience the suffering of poverty in various ways. // 113 //

Just as a treasure of jewels in the house of a poor man
Would not say to him 'I am here',
Nor the man could know 'here is a treasure of jewels';
Likewise is the treasure of properties dwelling in the house of the mind[46],
And the living beings are like a poor man;
To enable those people to obtain this treasure,
The Sage makes his appearance in the world. // 114 //

(VI) The Defilements are like the bark-covering [of a seed], and the Essence of the Tathāgata is akin to the germ within a seed[47].

Just as the germ of a seed inside the fruit of trees
Of Mango, Tāla[48], etc. is of an imperishable nature,
And, being sowed in the ground, by contact with water, etc.,
Gradually attains the nature of the king of trees; — // 115 //
In the same way, the pure Absolute Essence, abiding in the living beings,
Covered by the sheath within the bark of the fruit of ignorance and the like,
[Grows] gradually by the help of this and that virtue
And obtains [finally] the state of the king of Sages. // 116 //
Conditioned by water, by the light of the sun,
By air, soil, time and space,
From within the husk of the fruit of the Tāla or mango
There comes out a tree;
Similarly, the germ of the seed of the Buddha,
Residing within the bark of the fruit, the defilements of living beings,

[44] *akṣayya* (= *akṣaya*).
[45] *ajasraṃ*, T. *rgyun-tu*, C. om.
[46] Remind of a similarity with the *ālayavijñāna* theory.
[47] Cf. TGS 458 *c*.
[48] T. om. *tāla*, C. simply 'various kinds of tree'.

Thrives by the help of this and that virtue,
Resulting in the tree [49] of the Highest Truth. // 117 //

(VII) The Defilements are like a tattered garment, and the Essence of the Tathāgata is akin to a precious image [50].

Suppose an image of the Buddha made of precious jewels
Wrapped in the tattered garment of bad smell
Were cast off [51] on the road, and
A god, perceiving it, would speak to travellers
About this matter [52], in order to retrieve it; — // 118 //
Similarly, the One who has eyes [53] of no obstacle
Perceives, even among those in the world of animals [54],
The nature [55] of the Buddha concealed by the stains [56] of various kinds of Defilements,
And, for the sake of its liberation [from Defilements],
Provides the means [57] [of deliverance]. // 119 //
Just as a god with divine eyes, seeing the Buddha's image
Wrapped in a bad-smelling garment, and rejected [58] on the road,
Would show it to the people in order to retrieve it;
In the same way the Lord, perceiving even among animals,
The Essence [of the Buddha] thrown on the road of transmigration,

49) *viṭapa* (small plant), T. *ḥthon* (coming out), C. 佛大法王 for *dharma-viṭapa*.

50) Cf. TGS 458 *c*–459 *a*. The story given in the Sūtra is as follows: There was a person who kept one golden image of the Buddha. He was on the way to another country along a dangerous path. For fear of robbers, he wrapped that image in tattered garment so that nobody could notice of it. As this person passed all of a sudden on the way, the image was abandoned in a field and left unknown to travellers who thought it merely a dirty cloth of no value. There happened to come a man of divine eyes, who, recognizing the image within the tattered garment, picked it up out of the garment and saluted it.

51) For *ujjhita*, T. *gnas* (placed), C. 在 or 墮在 (fallen) in v. 120.

52) *etam artham* (this thing).

53) T. om. *cakṣuḥ*, which C. has.

54) C. 'in the lowest world (*avīci*)'.

55) *ātmabhāva*, T. *dṅos-po* (nature), C. [如 來] 身 (= *kāya*).

56) T. om. *mala*, which C. has.

57) *abhyupāya*, T. *thabs*, C. 方便. For *vidadhāti*, T. *ston-mdsad*, C. 說 (妙法) (preaches the highest doctrine).

58) *ujjñita* in the text should be corrected into *ujjhita*.

With the covering of the tattered garment of Defilements,
Taught the Doctrine for the sake of its deliverance. // 120 //

(VIII) The Defilements are like a pregnant woman[59] and the Essence of the Tathāgata is akin to an Emperor contained in the Embryonal elements[60].

Suppose an ugly woman without a protector[61]
Were abiding in an orphanage[62],
And, bearing the glory of royalty as an embryo[63],
Might not know the king in her own womb[64]. // 121 //
The generation of worldly existence is like an orphanage,
Like a pregnant[65] woman are the impure living beings,
And the immaculate Essence in them is like that embryo[66],
Owing to the existence of which, they become possessed of protection. // 122 //
Just as a woman, whose body is covered with a dirty garment
And having ugly features, experiences in an orphanage,
The greatest pain when the king is in her womb;
Similarly the living beings abiding in the house of misery,
And whose mind is not quiet by the power of Defilements,
Imagine themselves without a protector
Though the good protectors[67] are residing in their own bodies. // 123 //

[59] *āpanna-sattva-nārī*, T. *sems-can shugs-paḥi mi-mo* (a woman who is bearing an embryo). *sattva* here means an embryo.

[60] *kalala-mahābhūtagata*. For *kalala*, T. *mer-mer-po*, C. 歌羅 [邏]. *kalala* is the first stage of embryo. Of this example, cf. TGS 459 *a*.

[61] *anātha* (Lit. without a protector) T. *mgon-med*, C. 孤獨. (It means 'abandoned by her husband', or 'widow').

[62] *anātha-āvasatha*, T. *mgon-med ḥbug-gnas*, = *anātha-śāla* (T. . . . *khyim*), *anātha-veśman* (T. . . . *khaṅ-pa*), C. 貧窮舍.

[63] *garbha*, T. *mṅal*. *mṅal* means 'womb' and not 'embryo', but here *garbha* seems to mean embryo. See below.

[64] *kukṣu*, T. *lte* (centre), C. 'inside of body'.

[65] *antarvat*, T. *mṅal-ldan* (*garbhavat*), C. 懷胎 (possessed of embryo).

[66] *tad-garbhavat*. For *garbha*, T. *mṅal-gnas* (= *garbha-sthita*, that which is within the womb), C. 藏中胎 (embryo within the womb).

[67] *sannātha*, T. *mgon-bcas*, C. 有歸依處. Both takes it as *sanātha*.

(IX) The Defilements are like an earthen mould [68] and the Essence of the Tathāgata is akin to a golden statue [69].

Suppose a man who knows [how to make a statue],
Seeing that the statue, filled with melted gold inside
And covered with clay outside, had become cool,
Would, for purifying the inner gold, remove the outer covering; —
// 124 //
Similarly, the One who has got the highest Enlightenment,
Perceiving always [70] the radiance of the Innate Mind
And the occasionality of the stains,
Purifies the world, which is like a mine of jewels, from obstructions.
// 125 //
Just as a statue made of pure, shining gold
Would become cool within the earthen covering,
And, knowing this, a skillful jewel-maker would remove the clay;
In the same way the Omniscient perceives that
The Mind [71], which is like pure gold, is quiescent [72],
And, by means of a stroke [73] [called] the method of teaching the Doctrine [74],
He removes the obscurations. // 126 //

The summarized meaning of the illustrations is as follows:

Inside a lotus flower, amidst bees,
Inside the husk, impurities, and the ground,
Within the bark of a fruit, within a tattered garment,
In the womb of a woman, and inside clay, respectively, // 127 //
Like the Buddha, like honey, like the kernel of grains,
Like gold, like a treasure, and like a tree,
Like a precious image, like the Emperor,
And like a golden statue, // 128 //
The Innate Mind of the living beings
Which is pure from beginningless time,

68) *mṛt-paṅka-lepa*, T. *sahi ḥdam gos-pa*, C. 泥模.
69) Cf. TGS 459 *a–b*.
70) T. om. *sadā*, which C. has.
71) *manas*, T. *yid*, C. 衆王佛性. *manas* here stands for *cittaprakṛti*.
72) For *śiva*, C. 儼然 (firmly).
73) *prahāra*, T. *brdeg-spyad*, C. 椎 (hammer).
74) *dharmâkhyāna-naya*, T. *chos-ḥchad-tshul*, C. 說法.

And is not bound by the covering of Defilements,
Though being within them from the outset is thus illustrated [75].
// 129 //

In brief, by this explanation of the illustrations given in the *Tathāgatagarbha-sūtra*, there is shown the fact that, for all living beings, the defiling elements [which cover] over their mind from the beginningless time are [merely] of an accidental nature, whereas the purifying elements existing in the mind since beginningless time were born together [with the mind], and hence, they are of an indivisible nature [76]. Therefore, it is said [77]:

"Owing to the impurities on the Mind, the living beings are defiled; owing to the Mind [itself], pure [by nature], they are purified".

§ 2. 9 Kinds of Defilements — the Impurities on the Mind [78].

Here, which are the impurities on the Mind, with reference to which the 9 illustrations, a sheath of lotus flower, &c., have been explained?

Desire, Hatred and Ignorance [79], and their intense outburst,
[Ignorance in] the form of Impression [80]

[75] C. abbreviates these 3 verses into two by avoiding repetition of the 9 examples. C. distinguishes the situation of *kleśas* and *cittaprakṛti* by using '有' for the former and '具足' (endowed with) for the latter.

[76] Here is given the contrast between *citta-saṃkleśa-dharma* and *citta-vyavadāna-dharma*, namely the former is merely *āgantuka*, while the latter is *sahaja* and *avinirbhāga*, although both are *anādisāṃnidhya* (S. p. 59, l. 12 ff.) with *sattvas*. This contrast is explained in a previous passage by the terms *asaṃbaddha* and *saṃbaddha*.

[77] The source of this quotation is unknown, but we have a similar expression in the *Vimalakīrti-nirdeśa* (*Taisho*, XV, 563 *b*). This idea seems to be quite old and perhaps we can trace back its origin as far as the Pāli Nikāyas (e.g. SN III, 151).

[78] Cf. BGŚ 806 *c*.

[79] C. adds a word '相續', of which the equivalent in Skt. is not clear. Probably it stands for *anuśaya* or *bandhana* (literally '相續' is near to *bandhana*, but in the commentary, these three *kleśas* are said to be in the state of *anuśaya*, and furthermore, *bandhana* is usually rendered in Chinese by '結使', while in this text, the same '結使' (or 使) is often used for *anuśaya*. If so, even more curious is the use of this '結使' for *tīvra-paryavasthāna* in this verse. It seems quite wrong.

For *paryavasthāna*, T. has *kun-ldaṅ* (= *kun-nas ldaṅ-ba*) (= *paryutthāna*). See v. 137.

[80] Here *vāsanā* stands for *avidyāvāsabhūmi*. See prose commentary on this verse. This use of *vāsanā* seems to support the Tibetan interpretation of the term *avidyāvāsabhūmi*. See Note VIII-112.

The pollutions [which are to be removed by [81]]
The Path of Perception and that of Practice [82],
And those remaining in the impure and the pure Stages [of Bodhisattva, respectively], // 130 //
These 9 kinds of [defilements] are illustrated
By the example of the sheath of a lotus flower and others;
In their variety, however, the coverings of Defilements [83]
Extend beyond the limit of extremity in number. // 131 //

In brief, these 9 kinds of Defilements make always their appearance [on the Essence of the Tathāgata] as the incidental [attachment] [84], although the latter is perfectly pure by nature, just like the sheath of a lotus flower [covering] over the Buddha's image, and other examples. What are the 9 Defilements? They are, namely: 1) the Defilement characterized as the dormant state [85] of Desire (*rāgânuśayalakṣaṇa-kleśa*); 2) the Defilement characterized as the dormant state of Hatred (*dveṣânuśayalakṣaṇa-k.*); 3) the Defilement characterized as the dormant state of Ignorance (*mohânuśayalakṣaṇa-k.*); 4) the Defilement characterized as the intense outburst of Desire, Hatred and Ignorance (*tīvrarāgadveṣamohaparyavasthānalaṣaṇa-k.*); 5) the Defilement contained in the Dwelling Place of Ignorance (*avidyāvāsabhūmisaṃgṛhīta-k.*); 6) the Defilement to be extirpated by means of Perception (*darśanaprahātavya-k.*); 7) the Defilement to be extirpated by means of Practice (*bhāvanāprahātavya-k.*); 8) the Defilement remaining in the impure Stage [of Bodhisattva] (*aśuddhabhūmigata-k.*); & 9) the Defilement remaining in the pure Stage [of Bodhisattva] (*śuddhabhūmigata-k.*) [86].

[81] T. inserts *spoṅs* (= *heya, prahātavya*) after *mārga*. It is better for understanding.

[82] *dṛn-mārga-bhāvanā*. But T. & C., in usual order of *darśana-bhāvanā-mārga*.

[83] *upasaṃkleśa*, T. *ñe-baḥi ñon-moṅs*, C. 煩惱.

[84] C. 外客相.

[85] *anuśaya*, T. *bag-la ñal*, C. 使 (BGŚ 隨眠).

[86] For these 9, T., C. & BGŚ have as follows (BGŚ in parentheses):

1) *ḥdod-chags bag-la ñal-gyi mtshan-ñid-kyi ñon-moṅs-pa*, 貪使煩惱, (隨眠貪欲煩惱);

2) *she-sdaṅ*, 瞋使煩惱, (隨眠瞋煩惱);

3) *gti-mug*, 癡使煩惱, (隨眠癡煩惱);

4) *ḥdod-chags daṅ she-sdaṅ daṅ gti-mug drag-pos kun-nas ldaṅ-baḥi mtshan-ñid*, 增上貪瞋癡結使煩惱, (貪瞋癡等極重上心惑);

Now first of all, 1)–3), there are those Defilements which are in the bodies [87] of those worldly people who are freed from [88] Desire, and, being the causes of Forces which accumulate the motionless State [89], give rise to the Material and the Immaterial Sphere, and which are to be killed [90] by means of the Supermundane Wisdom. These are here termed the Defilements characterized as the dormant state of Desire, Hatred and Ignorance. 4) Next, we have those Defilements which exist in the bodies of those living beings who indulge in Desire and the rest, and which, being the cause of Forces that accumulate merit and demerit, give rise only to the Sphere of Desire, and are to be killed by means of the Wisdom, [obtained] through the Contemplation of Impurity [91], etc. They are called the Defilements characterized as the intense outburst of Desire, Hatred and Ignorance. Then, 5) there are those Defilements which are in the bodies of the Arhats, and, being the cause that produces the Immaculate Actions, result in the birth of the pure Body made of mind, and are to be killed by the Tathāgata's Wisdom of Enlightenment. These are called the Defilements contained in the Dwelling Place of Ignorance [92].

There are two kinds of individuals who undergo training [on the

5) *ma-rig-paḥi bag-chags-kyi sas bsdus-pa*, 無明住地所攝煩惱. (無明住地);

6) *mthoṅ-bas spaṅ-bar bya-ba*, 見道所攝煩惱, (見諦所滅);

7) *bsgom-pas spaṅ-bar bya-ba*, 修道所攝煩惱, (修習所滅);

8) *ma-dag-paḥi sa-la brten-pa*, 不淨地煩惱, (不淨地惑);

9) *dag-paḥi sa-la brten-pa*, 淨地煩惱, (淨地惑).

87) *sāntānika*, (of *santāna*, lit. flux, stream), T. *rgyud-la yod-pa*, C. 衆生身中所攝.

88) *vīta*, T. *-daṅ bral-ba*. C. failed to catch the sense, but BGŚ 離欲.

89) *āniñjya-saṃskārôpacaya* T. *mi-gyo-baḥi ḥdu-byed-la sogs-pa*, C. 不動地業所緣. About *āniñjya* (= *anijya*, *aniñjya*, Pāli *ānejja*), see BHS Dic. s. v. Along with *puṇya* and *apuṇya*, this *āninjya* forms *saṃskāra* which accumulates the Phenomenal Existence (*bhava*). See below.

90) *vadhya*, T. *gshom-par bya-ba*, C. 斷.

91) *aśuddhabhāvanā* (text reading *bhāva* should be corrected), T. *mi sdug-paḥi sgom-pa*, C. 不淨觀. See BHS Dic. s. v., Mvyut. 52.

92) About *avidyāvāsabhūmi*, *anāsravakarman* and *manomayakāya*, see Note VIII-112, 115. (where Bodhisattva is also included in this group).

Path] [93]: *a*) the ordinary beings and *b*) the Saints. Now, 6) the Defilements which exist in the body of ordinary beings training on the Path and which are to be killed by the Wisdom [obtained through] the first [94] Perception of the Transcendental Truth are termed the Defilements to be extirpated by means of Perception. And, 7) the Defilements which exist in the body of the Saints training on the Path and which are to be killed by the Wisdom [obtained through] the Transcendental Practice of the Truth according to their [Transcendental] Perception [95] are called the Defilements to be extirpated by Practice.

[Lastly there are two kinds of Defilements associating with Bodhisattwas]. 8) Those which are in the body of Bodhisattvas who have not reached the ultimate perfection, and which are the enemy to the Wisdom [attained] on the [first] 7 Stages [96] and are to be killed by means of the Wisdom [obtained through] the Practice of the 3 Stages beginning with the 8th, these are called the Defilements remaining in the impure Stage [of Bodhisattva]. 9) The Defilements which exist in the body of Bodhisattvas who have reached the ultimate perfection, and which are the enemy to the Wisdom [attained through] the Practice on the (last) 3 Stages beginning with 8th and are to be killed by means of the Wisdom [of the Buddha, obtained through] the Meditation called 'the Diamond-like' [97], these are called the Defilements remaining in the pure Stage [of Bodhisattva].

These [98]

93) *śaikṣa*, T. *slob-pa*, C. 學人. They may be called '*bodhisattvayānika*', i.e. Mahāyānist. '*ārya*', here, seems to denote those Bodhisattvas who are below the 1st Stage, in comparison with no. 8. But usually the attainment of *darśanamārga* is said to take place on the 1st Stage of Bodhisattva.

94) T. regards *prathama* as *prathamabhūmi*. C. repeats *lokottara* and seems to render this *prathama* by *prathamalokottaracitta* (初出世間心). But BGŚ inserts '無始已來未曾見理' (*anādikālâdṛṣṭapūrva*) before *prathama*. It seems to be a good interpretation of this *prathama*. That is to say, in comparison with '*yathādṛṣṭa*' in the next, '*prathama*' means that this *darśana* has never been observed by the Hīnayānists and is to be attained 'for the first time' by the Mahāyānist. Paramārtha gives a detailed explanation on this subject in his commentary on BGŚ (BGŚ 807 *b*).

95) *yathādṛṣṭa*. See above. C. 如先見 (*yathā-pūrvadṛṣṭa*).

96) i.e. those which are not exterminated by the Wisdom attained in the first 7 Stages.

97) *vajropama-samādhi*. It is said to be the meditation in the highest stage of practice. (Mvyut. 21 & 55).

98) The following verse is, as J suggested, not a verse at all. This passage is merely

Nine Defilements, beginning with Desire,
Being taken in short, respectively,
Are illustrated by 9 examples,
That of the sheath of a lotus flower and others. // 132 //

And, if taken in detail, [these Defilements] which are differentiated into 84,000 groups, are as infinite as the Wisdom of the Tathāgata. On this point, therefore, it is said that the Matrix of the Tathāgata is concealed by the coverings of Defilements which extend beyond the limit of extremity in number [99].

(Variety of Living Beings according to their Defilements).

The impurity [retained] in the ordinary beings,
The Arhats, the individuals in training [on the Path],
And the Bodhisattvas is [explained], respectively,
By these four, one, two and two kinds of pollution. // 133 //

It has been said by the Lord that all living beings are possessed of the Matrix of the Tathāgata [100]. Here, 'all living beings' are said to be, in short, fourfold: namely, 1) the ordinary beings; 2) the Arhats; 3) the individuals in training [on the Path]; and 4) the Bodhisattvas. Their impurity, on account of [which they cannot identify themselves with] the Immaculate Sphere, is here explained by [the first] four, [the next] one (the 5th) and two (the 6th & 7th) and again by two (the 8th & 9th) kinds of Pollution, [101] respectively.

§ 3. Concordance between the 9 Illustrations and the 9 Defilements [102].

Now, how should the resemblance of 9 Defilements be known, Desire and the rest, to the sheath of a lotus flower and others, respectively, and how should the similarity be understood between the Essence of the Tathāgata and [the examples], the Buddha's image and the rest?

an explanation of v. 131 *a b* and the following sentences are those of v. 131 *c d*. Perhaps C. keeps the original form.

99) Cf. TGS (The second formula on *tathāgatagarbha*).

100) Cf. TGS (The first formula on *tathāgatagarbha*). (The reading *garbha iti* is to be corrected into *garbhā iti*).

101) *kleśa-mala*. T. om. *mala*.

102) Cf. BGŚ 807 *c*–808 *a*.

Just as the lotus flower born from the mud
Is delightful[103] in its first appearance,
But later on [when it withers], it is no more attractive;
Similar to it is the delight of Desire. // 137 //
Just as the honey-bees[104], being excited,
Sting sharply [and cause pain][105];
In the same way, Hatred, being aroused,
Produces suffering in the heart. // 135 //
Just as the kernel of rice[106] and others
Are concealed[107] by the outside husk,
Similarly, the perception of the Essential Truth[108]
Is hindered by the covering[109] of ignorance. // 136 //
Just as the impurities are somewhat disagreeable;
Likewise those who have got rid of desire[110]
[Regard] Passion as something disagreeable,
Being characterized as devoted to [such] Passion,
The outburst of Passions is repulsive like impurities. // 137 //
Just as the people[111], because of their ignorance,
Cannot obtain the treasure hidden under the ground[112],
In a similar way, they cannot obtain the Buddhahood
Hindered by the Dwelling Place of Ignorance[113]. // 138 //
Just as a sprout and the like, growing gradually,

[103] *mano-rama*, T. *yid-dgaḥ*, C. 愛. The analogies in the following verses seem quite artificial.

[104] *bhramarāḥ prāṇinaḥ* (pl.), T. *srog-chags sbraṅ-ma*, C. 群蜂.

[105] C. interprets: 'when they are making honey, they bite the flowers'.

[106] For *śāli*, T. *ḥbras* (= *vrihi*, corn).

[107] *avacchanna* = *saṃcanna*, T. *bsgribs-pa*.

[108] *sārârtha*, C. 内堅實.

[109] *aṇḍakośa* (lit. egg-shell).

[110] For '*kāmā virāgiṇām*', T. reads '*chags daṅ bcas rnams-kyi*' (*kāma-avirāgiṇām*, as J suggested). But C. reading '智觀貪亦爾' (similar is the case with the wise man's observation of *rāga*), though being far from the literal translation, is still close to S. And BGŚ has '離欲之人' (*virāgin*) in the parallel passage, which supports the text reading.

[111] T. reads as *jane* (*skye-la*). But *janāḥ* is the subject word of *āpunyur* and is used for both illustrating and being illustrated. C. shows this reading by repeating *janāḥ*.

[112] *vasudhā-antarita*, C. 地中. T. '*nor ni bsgribs-pas na*' for this and '*mi-śes gter*' for *ajñānād nidhi* is a misreading caused by the reading of *jane* for *janāḥ*.

[113] The reading '*avidyāvāsabhūmy-āvṛtā* had preferably be corrected into *-āvṛtaṃ*, being an adjective for *svayaṃbhūtvaṃ*, in comparison with the illustration above. So have T. & C.

Break out the husk of the seed,
Similarly, by the Intuition of the Truth,
Those Defilements are removed which are to be extirpated by Perception[114]. // 139 //
Those who have destroyed the ground of conception of personality[115]
Are following[116] in the [Practice of the] Saintly Path;
Therefore, their Defilements which are to be rejected
By the Wisdom of Practice are said to be like a tattered garment. // 140 //
The stains remaining in the [first] 7 Stages
Are like[117] the impurities of the receptacle of an embryo[118],
And the non-discriminative Wisdom has a resemblance
To the matured form of an embryo delivered from its covering. // 141 //
The stains connected with[119] the [last] 3 Stages
Are known as being like the earthen mould,
And are to be destroyed by the Wisdom of the Buddhas[120]
[Obtained through] Meditation called 'the Diamondlike'. // 142 //
Thus the 9 pollutions, Desire and the rest,
Have a resemblance to a lotus flower and others,
And the Essence [of the Buddha], consisting of 3-fold nature,
Bears a similarity to the Buddha and the rest. // 143 //

§ 4. The 3-fold Nature of the Essence, the Purifying Element within the Mind, and its Concordance with the 9 Illustrations[121].

The resemblance of the Matrix of the Tathāgata, being the cause for purifying the Mind[122], in 9-fold, i. e. to the image of the Buddha and so

[114] The analogy is not clear. C. says: '*darśanamārga* removes the defilements and makes the Stages grow up gradually'.

[115] *hata-satkāya-sārāṇām.* T. *ḥjig-tshogs sniṅ-po bcom rnams-kyi.* C. om. *sāra.*

[116] *anuṣaṅga*, T. ... *daṅ ḥbrel-pa* (= *sambandha*). C. 攝受.

[117] *prakhyā*, T. ... *daṅ mtshuṅs*, C. 猶如.

[118] *garbha-kośa-mala*, T. *mṅal-sbubs dri-ma*, C. 胎所纏. *garbhakośa* means *uterus.*

[119] *anugata*, T. *rjes-ḥbrel* (= *anubaddha*), C. 知 (known).

[120] *mahâtman*, T. *bdag-ñid chen-po*, C. 大智諸菩薩, which is not correct.

[121] Cf. BGŚ 808 *a* (如來三種自性).

[122] C. reads '法身, 自性清淨心, 如來藏' and connects them with each of *trividha svabhāva*, respectively.

forth, is to be understood in the reference to the 3-fold Nature (*tri-vidhaḥ svabhāvaḥ*) of the Matrix of the Tathāgata [123]. What is the 3-fold Nature?

The Nature of this [Essence] is the Absolute Body,
The Reality, as well as the Germ,
Which is known by the examples,
Three, one and five, [respectively]. // 144 //

By the 3 examples, i.e. those of the image of the Buddha, honey and the kernel [of grains], this Essence is to be understood as being of the nature of the Absolute Body (*dharmakāya-svabhāva*). By one example, i.e. that of gold, its being of the nature of Reality (*tathathā-svabhāva*), and by [the remaining] 5 examples, i.e. those of the treasure, the tree, the precious image, the highest Lord of Universe, and the golden statue, its being of the nature of the Germ (*gotra-svabhāva*) from which the 3 kinds of Buddha's Body are originated [124] [is to be understood].

a) *Dharmakāya.*

Here, how is the Absolute Body?

The Absolute Body is to be known in 2 aspects,
[One] is the Absolute Entity which is perfectly immaculate,
[The other] is its natural outflow [125], the teaching
Of the profound [truth] and of the diverse guidance. // 145 //

The Absolute Body of the Buddha is to be understood in 2 aspects. [Namely], 1) the perfectly pure Absolute Entity itself (*dharmadhātu*) [126],

[123] C. 三種實體. The following passage is a detailed explanation of v. 27 and v. 28 (S. p. 26). It is also to be compared with (I) *svabhāva* (the first of the 10 meanings of *tathāgatadhātu*, S. p. 27).

[124] Cf. v. 23 (K. 4) & v. 24, where *gotra* is explained as the germ of *ratnatraya*. From the viewpoint of *ekayāna*, *ratnatraya* is ultimately resolved into one '*buddha-ratna*'. In this sense, these two different explanations of *gotra* are identical.

[125] *niṣyanda*, T. *rgyu-mthun*, C. 習氣 (which is a peculiar translation. Usually, '等流'). This is interpreted in the commentary by '*tat-prāpti-hetu*'.

[126] The reading '*dharmadhātor avi-*' is to be corrected into '*dharmadhātur avi-*'. Both T. & C. read it as nominative.

which is the acting sphere of Non-discriminative Wisdom; and this is to be known in the reference to the Truth realized by the Tathāgata through introspection (*pratyātmâdhigama-dharma*). And, 2) the natural outflow of the perfectly pure Absolute Entity (*dharmadhātu-niṣyanda*) as the cause for its attainment [127], which produces [128] the communication [129] among other living beings according to their faculties in discipline [130]. And this is to be known in the reference to the Truth as the doctrine to be taught (*deśanā-dharma*) [131].

This teaching is again divided into two, owing to the difference of means for exposition [132] of the Doctrine, whether subtle or extensive [133]. Namely, 2)-1) the Code of Bodhisattva [134], the teaching by the profound means for exposition [135] of the Doctrine referring to the Highest Truth (*paramārtha-satya*), and 2)-2) the Aphorism, the Scripture in prose and verse, the Prophecy, the Verse, the Solemn Utterance, the Statement of subject matter, &c. [136] which are the teaching by various kinds of means for exposition of the Doctrine and are related to the Empirical Truth (*saṃvṛti-satya*) [137].

Being supermundane, nothing can be given
As an example for the Essence, in this world;
Therefore, it is shown in its similarity

[127] In the sense that, by means of *deśanā-dharma*, *sattvas* are led to *bodhi*.

[128] *prabhava*, T. *ḥbyuṅ*, C. 依…有.

[129] *vijñapti*, T. *rnam-par rig-pa*, C. 說 (?).

[130] *yathāvainayika* is to be corrected into *yathāvaineyika*. T. *gdul-bya ji-lta-bar*. C. 可化. So has BGŚ (所化).

[131] See back, the passage on *dharmaratna* (S. p. 10 ff.) and on *śaraṇatraya* (S. p. 18, l. 14 ff.). Of these two divisions of *dharma*, BGŚ: 正得法身 & 正說法身, respectively. Also cf. the *Mahāyānasaṃgraha-bhāṣya* (tr. by Paramārtha), *Taisho*, XXXI, p. 268 *c*: 真如法 & 正說法.

[132] *vyavasthāna*, T. *rnam-par ḥjog-pa*. C. om. *dharmavyavasthānanayabhedāt*.

[133] *sūkṣma*, T. *phra-ba*, C. 細, & *audārika*, T. *rgya-chen*, C. 麤, resp.

[134] *bodhisattva-piṭaka*, T. *byaṅ-chub-sems-dpaḥi sde-snod*, C. 菩薩法藏.

[135] T. om. *vyavasthāna*. C. 爲…演說 for *vyavasthāna-naya-deśanā*.

[136] *sūtra*, *geya*, *vyākaraṇa*, *gāthā*, *udāna*, *nidāna*, respectively. These are the first 6 of *dvādaśâṅga-dharmapravacana* (see Mvyut. 62). They are here regarded as the doctrine for Śrāvaka- and Pratyekabuddhayānika. Cf. BGŚ: 爲二乘人說此道理.

[137] These two divisions of *deśanā-dharma* correspond to *nītârtha* and *neyârtha*, respectively. (Cf. *Abhidharmakośa-vyākhyā*, Wogihara's Edition, p. 174). Also cf. Laṅk, p. 147, 171: *siddhānta-naya* & *deśanānaya*.

To the [apparitional form of the] Buddha himself. // 146 //
[The Doctrine] taught by subtle, profound means
Is to be known as being akin to honey of one taste,
And taught by various kinds of means,
As being similar to the kernel of various grains [138]. // 147 //

Thus, by 3 examples, those of the image of the Buddha, the honey and the kernel, in reference to the meaning that all living beings, with no exception, are penetrated by the Absolute Body of the Tathāgata [139], it is explained that 'these, all living beings, are the Matrix (interior) of the Tathāgata [140], (i.e. the Matrix in which the Tathāgata penetrates). Indeed, there is no one among the living beings [141] who stands outside the Absolute Body of the Tathāgata [142], just as no kind of physical form can exist outside of space. Because it is said [143]:

" Just as space is considered to be all-pervading always,
Similarly, it [144] is held to be always all-pervading;
Just as space pervades all visible forms,
Similarly, it pervades all the multitudes of living beings ".

138) *aṇḍa-sāra*, T. *sbubs-sñiṅ* (= *kośa-sāra*), C. (種種) 異味 (of different taste). The meaning of *aṇḍa* here is not clear.

139) Cf. S. p. 26, v. 27 *a*: *buddhajñānântargamāt sattvarāśeḥ*; v, 28 *a*: *saṃbuddhakāya-spharaṇāt*; & l. 8: *sarvasattveṣu tathāgata-dharmakāya-parispharaṇârthena.*

140) *tathāgatasya ime garbhāḥ sarvasattvāḥ.* This is the first way of interpreting the term *tathāgatagarbha*, regarding this Bahuvrīhi compound as consisting of two words whose interrelation is the dependent determinative (Tatpuruṣa). Here, '*garbha*' means 'interior', and hence the compound has the sense of 'one who is within the Tathāgata'. This meaning comes from the idea of '*antargama* of *buddhajnāna*', i.e. the penetration of the Absolute into everything from inside and this signifies the all-pervadingness of the Absolute. In this sense, BGŚ calls this 1st meaning '所攝藏' (*garbha* in the sense of *saṃgṛhīta*). By the way, T. translates the above sentence into '*de-bshin-gśegs-paḥi sñiṅ-po-can* (being possessed of the essence of the Tathāgata). C. shows no difference between this and the subsequent other two interpretations (有如來藏).

141) *sattvadhātu*, as a collective noun, the aggregate of living beings. T. & C. as usual (for *dhātu*, T. *khams*, C. 界).

142) C. inserts '*tathāgatajñānād bahir*' after '*dharmakāyād bahir*'. BGŚ regards this passage as a quotation from some scripture (808 *a*). Also, see MSbh (P), 252 *b*.

143) MSA IX, 15 (which has *rūpagaṇa* instead of *rūpagata*).

144) "*tat*" stands for *buddhatva*, acc. to the commentary on MSA. For the 2nd and 4th Pada, C. has a rather free rendering, saying:

'similarly, *sattvakāya* is indivisible from *buddhajñāna*', & 'therefore, it is said that *sarvasattvās tathāgatagarbhāḥ*', respectively.

b) *Tathatā.*

Being unchangeable, by nature,
Sublime [145], and perfectly pure,
Reality is illustrated
By the analogy with a piece of [146] gold. // 148 //

That which is the Mind, though it is associated with [147] the phenomena [148] of Suffering [caused by] innumerable forms of Defilement, is unable to be shown as being alterable because of its being radiant by nature. Therefore, it is called 'Reality' in the sense of being unchangeable like excellent gold. This very Mind gets also the appellation of 'the Tathāgata', whenever it perfects the purification [149] from all accidental pollutions even in the case of those living beings who are ranked among the groups in the definitely wrong way, since all of them are not different by nature. Thus, with reference to the sense that Reality is the undifferentiated whole [150], it is explained by the one example of gold, that 'the Tathāgata, being Reality, is [identical with] the Matrix (i.e. the inner essence) of these living beings [151]. Having in view [this] Innate Mind, the pure and non-dual Essential Nature [152], it is said by the Lord [153]:

145) C. om. *kalyāṇa*. For these three qualities, BGŚ: 1) 性無變異; 2) 功德無窮; 3) 淸淨無二 (808 *b*).

146) *maṇḍalaka*, T. *gzugs* (= *rūpa*), C. om.

147) *anugata*, T. *rjes-su ḥbrel*. C. om. the whole sentence.

148) T. om. *dharma*.

149) *viśuddhim āgatas*. An etymology of the term *tathāgata*. See the quotation below.

150) Cf. S. p. 26, v. 27: *tam-nairmalyasyâdvayatvāt*, v. 28: *tathatā'vyatibhedataḥ*, and l. 8: *tathāgata-tathatā'vyatibhedârthena*.

151) *tathāgatas tathatā eṣāṃ garbhaḥ sarvasattvānām*. This is the second interpretation of the term *tathāgatagarbha*, in which the two words *tathāgata* and *garbha* are related appositionally to each other, i.e. *garbha* being *tathāgata*. Here the word *garbha* means 'essence', i.e. *tathatā* which is represented by *tathāgata*. Because of this identification with *tathatā*, *tathāgatagarbha* is called '*samalā tathatā*'. The difference, if there is any, between *tathāgata* and *tathāgatagarbha* is merely in their appearance, the former being '*śuddhim āgatā tathatā*', i.e. '*nirmalā tathatā*' and the latter being '*samalā tathatā*'. From this point, *tathāgatagarbha* is a special name for *tathatā* when it is hidden by (or covered with) *kleśas*. In this sense, BGŚ calls this second interpretation '隱覆藏' (*garbha* in the form of *upagūḍha*).

152) C. reads this passage curiously as that '*cittaprakṛti*, though it is *śuddhi*, still is *advayadharma* by nature; therefore...

153) JĀA 247 *a*.

"Here, O Mañjusrī, the Tathāgata is one who has the full knowledge about the root of his own substratum [154]. Through his self-purification, he has understood [155] the purity of living beings. That which is the purity of his own and that which is the purity of the living beings, these two are one and the same, they cannot be divided into two [156].

[Also] it is said [157]:

"Though being undifferentiated among all,
Reality, in case the purification is perfected,
Is [called] Buddhahood; therefore,
All living beings are possessed of the Matrix of Buddhahood".

c) *Tathāgatagotra.*

The Germ [of the Buddha] is known to be twofold,
Being like a treasure and like a tree [grown] from a seed;
The Innate [158] [Germ] existing since the beginningless time
And that which has acquired the highest development [159]. // 149 //
From this twofold Germ, it is considered [160],
The 3 Bodies of the Buddha are obtained;
From the first one, the first Body,
And, from the second, the latter two [161]. // 150 //

154) *ātmôpādānamūla*, T. *bdag-gi ñe-bar len-paḥi gshi-rtsa*, C. 自身根本(清淨智) BGŚ 我取根本. For *parijñātāvin*, T. as 'protected by *parijñā*', BGŚ 已出離. It seems that to know *ātma-upādāna* means to purify his mind'.

155) *anugata*, T. *rtogs-pa* (= *āgata*), C. 知.

156) '*kāro ti*' should gramatically be '*kāreti*'.

157) MSA IX, 37.

158) *prakṛtistha (-gotra)*, T. *raṅ-bshin gnas-pa*, C. 自性清淨心. Cf. BGŚ 住自性性. BGŚ gives 6 points of similarity of *prakṛtistha-gotra* to a treasure, but they are exactly identical with those in *Ratna*. v. I, 22 (S. p. 20) where *ratnatraya* is referred to.

159) *samudānita (-gotra)*, T. *yaṅ-dag blaṅ-ba*, C. 修行[無上]道. Cf. BGŚ 引出性. As for these two kinds of '*gotra*', see BBh p. 3. MSA III, 4. comm. (*prakṛtistha*, *paripuṣṭa* or *samudānita*).

160) The reading '*matā*' is acceptable in the light of T. & C. T. *thob-par ḥdod-pa yin (prāptir matā)*, C. 知.

161) From this statement, *dharmakāya* seems to be divided into two: one is *dhar-*

The Body of the Absolute Essence[162] is pure
And is known to be like the precious image,
Since, by nature, it is non-artificial[163]
And is the substratum[164] of precious properties. // 151 //
The [Body of] Enjoyment[165] is like the Universal Lord
Since it is the great Emperor of Religion[166];
The Apparitional Body[167] is like a golden statue
Since is has the nature of being an image[168]. // 152 //

Thus, by these 5 examples, namely, those of a treasure, a tree, a precious image, a Lord of the Universe, and a golden statue, in the refer-

madhātu or *tathatā* which is called here the first body, and the other, *dharmakāya* as *bodhi*, i.e. the result of purification of *dhātu*, which is included in the second *kāya* being (*sva-*) *saṃbhogakāya*. In other words, it signifies the separation of *jñāna* from *dharmakāya* remaining the latter as pure reality or truth. This point is, however, not clear in this text, and in a later passage *dharmakāya* is spoken of as being the truth inseparable from wisdom (Chaps. II, III). It was BGŚ which, basing itself on this passage, made this point clear and regarded *saṃbhogakāya* as a part of *dharmakāya* being *svasaṃbhoga*.

162) *svābhāvika-kāya*, T. *ṅo-bo-ñid-sku*, C. 真佛法身 (BGŚ 法身).

163) *akṛtrima*, T. *byas-min*, C. 不改變 (unchangeable).

164) *āśraya*, T. *gter* (= *nidhi*), C. 實體 (攝功德實體). Cf. BGŚ 所依處. BGŚ mentions 4 kinds of similarity of *dharmakāya* to gold. Of them, the first three are the same as those mentioned here, the last one is called '平等所得' (*sama-prāpta*), which means that anybody can obtain *dharmakāya*, just as gold does not belong to any particular person (如金無的主, 衆人共有) (808 *c*).

165) *sāṃbhoga*, T. *rdsogs-loṅs*, C. om., BGŚ 應身.

166) For '*mahādharmâdhirājatvād*', T. reads '*chos chen rgyal-srid-du ldan phyir*' (*mahādharmâdhirājyatvād*'). Probably it is a better reading. C. 證大法王位 (attaining the position of a great religious king). BGŚ gives 4 qualities to this *kāya*, viz. 1) 依止 (based upon the former merit); 2) 正生 (= 應得, *prāptavya*); 3) 正住 (= 正得, *prāpta*); and 4) 正受用 (*saṃbhoga*) and regards each of these qualities as being correspondent to that of *cakravartin*.

167) *nirmāṇa*, T. *sprul-ba*, C. 化佛, BGŚ 化身. The same terminology on *trikāya* is used in MSA (IX, 59): *svabhāva-dharmasaṃbhoga-nirmāṇair*, *ibid.*, 60: *svābhāviko 'tha sāṃbhogaḥ kāyo nairmāṇiko.*

168) *pratibimba*, T. *gzugs-brñan*, C. 鏡像. BGŚ maintains 3 characteristics of *nirmāṇa*, through which the similarity to *pratibimba* is observed: 1) 有相 (having apparitional form); 2) 由功力 (produced by '*praṇidhāna*' (therefore, artificial); 3) 有始有終 (having beginning and end, therefore, not eternal) (808 *c*).

ence to the nature as the Germ from which the 3 Bodies of the Buddha are originated [169], it is said that 'the Matrix (i.e. the inner essence) of these living beings is the Essence (i.e. the cause) of the Tathāgata' [170]. Indeed, the Buddhahood is usually manifested [171] in the 3 Bodies of the Buddha. Hence, it is said that the Essence of the Tathāgata is the cause for the acquisition of these [3 Bodies]. Here, the word '*dhātu*' (essence) is especially used in the sense of '*hetu*' (a cause) [172]. So it is said [173]:

> "And now, in every living being, there exists the Essence of the Tathāgata arisen, in the form of embryo [174]. But these living beings do not know about it".

(Reference to the *Abhidharma-sūtra* on the 'Essence') [175].

169) Cf. S. p. 26, v. 27: *bauddhe gotre tatphalasyôpacārāt*, v. 28: *gotrataḥ*, and l. 8–9: *tathāgatagotrasaṃbhavārthena*.

170) *tathāgatadhātur eṣāṃ garbhaḥ sarvasattvānām*. This is the third interpretation of the term *tathāgatagarbha*, '*garbha*' here means inner essence (*dhātu*), being the cause (*hetu*) from which the Tathāgata is arisen. This stands for the original sense of the term *tathāgatagarbha*. BGŚ gives a name of '能攝藏' (*garbha* in the sense of *saṃgrahaka*, i.e. that which contains the Tathāgata).

171) *prabhāvita*, T. *rab-tu phye-ba*, C. 得名義 (has got the appellation).

172) Throughout this text, those terms, *garbha*, *gotra*, and *dhātu*, are used synonymously, being possessed of the meaning of '*hetu*'. And this *hetu* means '*āśraya*' as will be explained.

173) The source of this quotation is not yet identified. C. om. this quotation. The idea is close to the *Avataṃsakasūtra*.

174) *garbhagata*, T. *sñiṅ-por gyur-pa*.

175) A quotation from the *Mahāyāna-abhidharmasūtra*, of which no S., T. or C. version is available now. This Sūtra is regarded as one of the important sources of the Vijñānavāda and often quoted in the works of that theory. As for this verse, it is quoted in the *Mahāyānasaṃgraha-bhāṣya* of Vasubandhu (MS bh (P), p. 157 *a*) and also in Sthiramati's commentary on the *Triṃṣikā* of Vasubandhu (Skt., ed. par Sylvain Lévi, p. 37). In these two cases, the word *dhātu* is applied to *ālāyavijñāna*. One interesting point to be noted is that, in the case of *Triṃśikābhāṣya*, *dhātu* is translated by '*dbyiṅs*' in T. and by '界' in C., instead of by '*khams*' and '性' as in this text. The different way of translation seems to show the difference of meaning implied by these different theories. But as a matter of meaning in each language, the distinction is not so clear. In the case of C., '界' means originally 'boundary' 'sphere of certain limited extent', and derivatively, 'region', 'universe' and is usually used for the '*dhātu*' of *dharmadhātu*, *nirvāṇadhātu*, *lokadhātu*, *traidhātuka*, or *sattvadhātu*. At the same time, '界' is used for *dhātu* of *skandha-dhātv-āyatana*, *pṛthividhātu*, *ākāśadhātu*, etc. showing the sense of 'element'. This last sense cannot be derived from the Chinese word '界', but is merely a translation of the Skt. word *dhātu*. On the other hand, the Chinese word '性' has a sense of 'nature', 'character', 'essence' or sex. It is usually used for the tran-

Indeed, it is said [in the Scripture] as follows:

"The Essence that exists since beginningless time
Is the foundation of all the elements,
Owing to its existence, all Phenomenal Life [176],
As well as the acquisition of Nirvāṇa exists".

Here, how is it that 'it exists since beginningless time'? With reference to this very Matrix of the Tathāgata, it has been taught and ascertained by the Lord: "An initial limit is not to be perceived" [177].

About the 'Essence', it is said as follows [178]:

"O Lord, this Matrix of the Tathāgata is the transcendental Matrix; the Matrix, perfectly pure by nature".

slation of such Skt. words as '*svabhāva*', '*prakṛti*' and '*-tā*', '*-tva*', affixes showing an abstract sense. To translate *dhātu* into '性' as in this text is a rather peculiar case. But it is quite suitable here ('性' is also used for '*gotra*' here, which is usually replaced by '姓'). In short, of '界' and '性' as translations of Skt. *dhātu*, the former shows the meaning of something spatial, while the latter, of something internal or essential. In the case of Tibetan, the distinction between '*dbyiṅs*' and '*khams*' is not so clear as between the two C. translations. Both Tibetan words have a similar sense of 'place' or 'region', but as the translation of Skt. *dhātu*, the former is used in the cases of *dharmadhātu*, *nirvāṇadhātu*, and *ākāśadhātu*, while the latter, in the cases of *lokadhātu*, the 4 elements other than *ākāśadhātu*, 18 component elements, *sattvadhātu*, and in this text, the *tathāgatadhātu* of which we are now speaking. Originally '*khams*' seems to relate to the human body in the sense 'physical state of body' or sometimes 'body' itself, and derivatively to things smaller than the human body, like each of 18 elements, and also to worldly things in general. On the contrary, '*dbyiṅs*' always relates to something transcendental or heavenly. But this distinction is not absolutely fixed. As far as this text is concerned, C. shows a better and clearer distinction between the two senses of the word *dhātu*.

176) *gati*, T. *ḥgro*, C. 道.

177) C. regards this whole sentence as a quotation from ŚMS (cf. ŚMS 222 *b*: '世尊, 生死者依如來藏, 以如來藏故說本際不可知'). Originally this formula is an explanation of *saṃsāra* (cf. SN, II, 178, 193, etc. See Note VIII-(VII)-242, on *anavarâgra*). It is ŚMS which has inserted '*tathāgatagarbham adhikṛtya*' to this famous formula for the first time in order to show that the *tathāgatagarbha* is the basis of *saṃsāra*. Cf. MSbh (P), p. 157 *a*. (Quotation is apparently from SN).

178) ŚMS 222 *b*, where two other epithets are given of the *tathāgatagarbha* which are mentioned in C. (世尊, 如來藏者, 是法界藏, 法身藏, 出世間上上藏, 自性清淨藏. These four, viz. *dharmadhātu-garbha*, *dharmakāya-g.*, *lokottara*[*-dharma*]*-g.*, and *prakṛtipariśuddha*[*-dharma*]*-g.* are used in a later passage (S. p. 76, l. 16 ff.) as corresponding to 4 kinds of people. BGŚ mentions them

The statement 'The foundation of all the elements' means as follows [179]:

> "Therefore, O Lord, the Matrix of the Tathāgata is the foundation, the support, and the substratum [180] of the immutable elements (properties) [181] which are essentially connected with, indivisible from [the Absolute Entity], and unreleased from Wisdom [182]. [At the same time], this very Matrix of the Tathāgata is also, O Lord, the foundation, the support, and the substratum of the [worldly] elements that are produced by causes and conditions, which are by all means disconnected, differentiated [from the Absolute Essence], and separated from Wisdom [183].

The statement 'Owing to its existence, there is all the Phenomenal Life' means as follows [184]:

> "Owing to the existence of the Matrix of the Tathāgata, there is Phenomenal Life, this, O Lord, is the proper saying on account of the Phenomenal Life [185].

along with *tathāgatagarbha* as the 5 meanings of *garbha* (五藏義, 796 *b*).

Paramārtha makes use of this 5-fold meaning of *garbha* established in BGŚ twice in his translation of MS-bhāṣya: once explaining '*dhātu*', i.e. in the passage equivalent to this *Ratna.* passage (MSbh (P), 157 *a*), and another, explaining '*dharmadhātu*' (ibid. 264 *b*). Also, we have another modified application of this set of meanings to the explanation of '*svabhāva*' of *trisvabhāva* (*parikalpita* and others) in the Hsien-shih-lun (顯識論) translated by him. This theory is unique to those works translated by Paramārtha, and its originality seems to be due to Paramārtha himself.

179) ŚMS 222 *b*. Cf. MSbh (P) 157 *a* (Q. from ŚMS).

180) *niśraya*, T. *gnas*, C. 依; *ādhāra*, T. *gshi*, C. 持; *pratiṣṭhā*, T. *rten*, C. 建立, respectively. C. has one more word '住持' after '持', but C. tr., of ŚMS does not have it.

181) For *dharma*, C. 佛法 (Buddha's Properties). C. adds *acintya* and some more adjectives.

182) *amuktajñāna*, T. *bral mi-śes-pa*, C. 不離智 (not separated from jñāna).

183) *asaṃbaddha*, *vinirbhāgadharma*, *muktajñāna*, resp. These terms are used as adjectives to *saṃskṛta-dharmas* in contrast with *saṃbaddha*, *avinirbhāgadharma*, *amuktajñāna* in case of *asaṃskṛda-dharmas*, i.e. *buddhadharmas*.

184) ŚMS 222 *b*. Cf. MSbh (P) 157 *a* (Q. from ŚMS).

185) The reading '*iti parikalpam asya vacanāyēti*' is doubtful. C. reads '是名善說' (this is called a good saying), which agrees with C. tr. of ŚMS. T. reads for the whole sentence '*de-bshin-gśegs-paḥi sñiṅ-po mchis-na* (*tathāgatagarbhe sati*), *de-la ḥkhor-ba shes tshig-gis gdags-pa lags-so* (*saṃsāra iti vacanena asya prajñaptam*)'. On the other hand, T. tr. of ŚMS says: '... *mchis-na*, *ḥkhor-ba shes mchi-na ni*, *tshig de rigs-pa*

The statement 'There is also the acquisition of the Nirvāṇa' is said in the following sense [186]:

> "O Lord, if there were no Matrix of the Tathāgata, there would not take place aversion to Suffering, or arise desire, earnest wish, or prayer for Nirvāṇa". &c.

lags-so (... *saṃsāra iti yuktam etad vacanam*). At least the Skt. reading should be corrected into '*iti parikalpitam*...', but *parikalpitam* probably means here '*prajñaptam*' as given by T. But ŚMS shows better sense, so I read it according to ŚMS.

186) ŚMS 222 *b*. Cf. MSbh(P) 157 *a* (Q. from ŚMS).

X. THE ESSENTIAL CHARACTERISTICS OF THE MATRIX OF THE TATHĀGATA

§ 1. The Saying: All Living Beings are Possessed of the Matrix of the Tathāgata — is the Highest Logical Truth.

Now, this Matrix of the Tathāgata, being united with [1] the Absolute Body, having the characteristics inseparable from Reality, and being of the nature of the germ properly fixed [towards the attainment of the Buddhahood] [2], exists everywhere, at whatever time and without exception [3] among the living beings, this is indeed to be perceived in the light of the Absolute Essence as the [highest] logical ground [4]. It is said [5]:

> "O noble youth, such is the essential nature of the elements [6]. Whether the Tathāgatas appear in this world, or whether they do

[1] *avipralambha*. The reading is not clear. In comparison with two other epithets, i.e. those relating to *tathatā* and *gotra* which stand for *trividhasvabhāva* along with *dharmakāya*, this word has to express an idea similar to '*parispharaṇa*'. T. reads this passage as '*dharmakāya(-vat) vipulaḥ*' and C., '究竟如來法身' (probably '不差別' is connected with *tathatā* and is a translation of *asaṃbhinna*). We can get some idea from T. reading, though it is probably caused by a misreading. C. '究竟' (*atyanta*) is also not the proper translation at all. On the other hand, M. W. records a sense of 'disunion' for *vipralambha* as taken from Wilson's vocabulary. If the reading is correct the only meaning which can construe the sentence would be 'not disunited', i.e. 'united with'. (In this case, *avipralabdha* would be better than *avipralambha*).

[2] *niyatagotra-svabhāva*, T. *ṅes-paḥi rigs-kyi raṅ-bshin*, C. 畢竟定佛性體.

[3] *niravaśeṣa-yogena*, T. *khyad-par med-paḥi tshul-du*, C. 無餘盡. ('*khyad-par med-pa*' *nirviśeṣa*.)

[4] *dharmatāṃ pramāṇīkṛtya*, T. *chos-ñid tshas-mar byas-nas*, C. 依法相. It means '*dharmatā* is *pramāṇa*, i.e. only the truth is the authority for knowledge'.

[5] TGS 547 c.

[6] *dharmāṇāṃ dharmatā*, C. 此法性法體性自性常住, TGS 諸佛法爾.

not[7], these living beings are always possessed of the Matrix of the Tathāgata".

That which is meant by this 'essential nature' (*dharmatā*) is here synonymous for[8] the 'argument' (*yukti*), the mode of proof (*yoga*) and the means [of cognition] (*upāya*)[9], in the sense: — such is the real state of things and not otherwise[10]. In any case only the Absolute Essence is the resort[11] for the contemplation of the mind[12], only the Absolute Essence is the argument for the proper understanding[13] of

[7] *utpādād vā tathāgatānām anutpādād vā.* This expression is quite popular since the Pāli Canon. For instance, SN vol. 2, p. 25:

" *jāti paccayā, bhikkhave, jarāmaraṇam, uppādā vā tathāgatānam anuppādā vā tathāgatānaṃ, ṭhitā va sā dhātu dhamma-ṭṭhitatā dhamma-niyāmatā idappaccayatā* ".

In this example, the emphasis is on *idappaccayatā* (Skt. *idaṃpratyayatā* = *pratītya-samutpāda*) as the eternal truth (*dhātu*, fem. in Pāli). In a similar manner, this expression is here used for emphasizing the *garbha* theory as the eternal truth. BGŚ has a similar quotation regarding it as from the *Sandhinirmocanasūtra*, saying:

如解節經說 佛告無盡意菩薩 善男子 如來性者是眞實諦 若如來出世及不出世 性相常然 非虛妄法 (812 *a*).

Actually, however, we have no equivalent passage in the present text of the *Sandhinirmocana*, except for a reference to '*dharmadhātu-sthititā*' being '*dharmatā-naya*' (法爾道理), *where* the phrase '*utpādād vā tathāgatānām anuntpādād vā*' is used. (*de-la de-bshin-gśegs-pa rnams byuṅ yaṅ ruṅ/ma byuṅ yaṅ ruṅ ste/chos gnas-par bya-baḥi phyir, chos-ñid dbyiṅs gnas-pa-ñid gaṅ-yin-pa de-ni chos-ñid-kyi rigs-pa yin-no*) (E. Lamotte's Ed. p. 258) (法爾道理，謂如來若出世若不出世，法性安住，法住法界).

Also see Laṅk. p. 143, where the eternity of truth is called '*dharmadhātu-sthititā*'.

[8] *paryāya.* Both T. & C. have no translation of this word. So I take it as a predicate.

[9] T. *rigs-pa, sbyor-ba* & *thabs*; C. 法相應法方便 and om. *yukti*. ('法體' seems to be a repeated translation of *dharmatā*).

[10] *evam eva tat syāt/ anyathā naîva tat syāt.* C. adds: 'it is therefore *acintya*.

[11] *pratiśaraṇa*, T. *rtogs-pa* (= *adhigama*), C. 依 (or 信). C. reads for '*dharmataîva pratiśaraṇaṃ, dharmataîva yuktis*', '依法，依法量，依法信'.

[12] *citta-nidhyāpana* (*nidhyāpana* fr. *ni* √ *dhyai*, to observe, meditate), T. *sems ñe-bar rtogs-pa*, C. 心定. This corresponds to *pratiśaraṇa*.

[13] *citta-saṃjñāpana*, T. *sems yaṅ-dag-par śes-pa* (T. takes *saṃ-* in the sense of *samyak-*), C. 心淨 (*citta-pariśuddha*). T. gives the best sense. This corresponds to *yukti*.

the mind. This essence itself is not accessible to imagination nor to discrimination. It is accessible only to faith [14].

§ 2. The 4 Kinds of Individuals to Whom the Faith in this Essence is Necessary [15].

> The Highest Truth of the Buddhas [16]
> Can be understood only by faith,
> Indeed, the eyeless one cannot see
> The blazing disk of the sun [17]. // 153 //

In brief, there are four kinds of individuals who are defined as being blind [18] with regard to the perception of the Matrix of the Tathāgata. Who are these four? They are namely: 1) the ordinary beings; 2) the Śrāvakas; 3) the Pratyekabuddhas; and 4) the Bodhisattvas who have recently entered the Vehicle [19]. It is said [20]:

> " O Lord, the Matrix of the Tathāgata is not the accessible sphere for those who have fallen into the erroneous conception maintaining the existence of individuality [21], for those who are attached to delusion [22], and for those whose mind has deviated from the conception of Non-substantiality " [23].

14) Acc. to T. & C., the reading of this sentence is preferably corrected into the following:

... *na vikalpayitavyā* [*kevalaṃ tv*] *adhimoktavyêti* /.

(T. *ḥbaḥ-shig-tu*, C. 唯). C. om. *cintayitavyā*.

15) Cf. BGŚ 812 *a* ff., where the 4 kinds of people are connected with the 4 synonyms for *dharmakāya*, viz. *dharmakāya*, *tathāgata*, *paramârthasatya* and *nirvāṇa*, respectively. See VIII-(X). Cf. MSbh (P) 258 *b–c*. (Commenting of MSA verse quoted.)

16) *svayambhū*. T. reads *paramârtha* as the subject (*śraddhyaivânugantavyaḥ paramârthaḥ svayambhuvām* /). C. reading is uncertain but reads *paramârtha* as a locative and connects it with *śraddhā* (*paramârthe śraddhā*...), and om. *anugantavya*. Here the translation is acc. to T.

17) Cf. ŚMS 222 *a*: 譬如生盲不見衆色 七日嬰兒不見日輪.

18) *acakṣumat*, C. 生盲人 (*jātândha*).

19) *navayāna-saṃprasthita*, T. *theg-pa-la gsar-du shugs-pa*, C. 初菩提心 (*nava-bodhicitta*).

20) ŚMS 222 *a*.

21) *satkāyadṛṣṭi-patita*, T. *ḥjig-tshogs-la lta-bar lhuṅ-ba*, C. 身見 [衆生].

22) *viparyāsâbhirata*, T. *phyin-ci-log-la mṅon-par ḥdod-pa*, C. 取四顛倒 [衆生].

23) *śūnyatā-vikṣipta-citta*, T. *stoṅ-pa-ñid-las sems rnam-par gyeṅs-pa*, C. 散亂心失空衆生.

Here, 'those who have fallen into the erroneous conception maintaining the existence of individuality' are the ordinary beings. Indeed, having fully[24] admitted[25] those elements classified into [5] groups and others, which are possessed of Evil Influences[26], as being the real Ego and its belongings, they are clinging to the conception of 'Ego' and 'Mine'[27], and, due to this conception, they cannot believe even in the Immaculate Essence which represents the annihilation of the [conception of the] existence of real individuality[28]. Being so, how is it possible for them to cognize the Matrix of the Tathāgata which is the object accessible only to the Omniscient? There is [absolutely] no room for it.

Now, 'those who are attached to delusion' represent 2) the Śrāvakas and 3) the Pratyekabuddhas. Why? Because, although the Matrix of the Tathāgata is to be considered as 'eternal' in its transcendental sense[29], they indulge in the contemplation of the 'evanescence' [of the phenomena[30]] instead of meditating upon the 'eternity' of the former. Likewise, although the Matrix of the Tathāgata is to be considered as 'blissful' in its transcendental sense, still they indulge in the contemplation of the 'suffering' [of the phenomena] instead of meditating upon the 'bliss' of the former. Although the Matrix of the Tathāgata is to be regarded as 'the [highest] Unity', they nevertheless cling to the practice of meditation on the idea of 'non-Ego' [of the separate elements] instead of concentrating their mind on the notion of the Unity of the former. And, though the Matrix of the Tathāgata is to be considered as 'pure' in the transcendental sense, they devote themselves to the practice of meditation on the notion of the 'impurity' [of the Phenomenal World] without doing meditation on 'Purity' of the former. Thus,

24) The reading should be *atyantam* (adv.), instead of *atyanta-* in the text.

25) *upagamya*, T. *khas-blaṅs-nas*, C. 取.

26) C. om. *sāsrava*. C. seems to read '*atyantâbhūta-rūpâdi-skandhān dharmān*' (實無色等五陰諸法).

27) *ahaṃkāra & mamakāra*, T. *ṅar-ḥdsin-pa & ṅa-yir ḥdsin-pa*, C. 我我所慢.

28) *satkāya-nirodha* (as an adjective to *anāsravadhātu*), T. *ḥjig-tshogs ḥgag-pa*, C. 離身見等滅諦 (*nirodhasatya* represented by the removal of *satkāyadṛṣṭi*, etc.). For *anāsravadhātu*, C. 無漏性, and adds '甘露之法' (*amṛta-dharma*).

29) *uttari bhāvayitavya*, T. *bsgom-par bya-ba*, C. 應修行 (T. & C. om. *uttari*), '*uttari*' as a preceding part of a compound has a sense of 'further, beyond', etc. (BHS Dic. s. v.). So it seems not to have so important sense in this compound.

30) C. inserts *sarvadharmeṣu*. The sense is that those people know only about *anityatā* of *sarvadharma*, but cannot notice *nityatva* of *tathāgata* behind the phenomena.

in such a way, all the Śrāvakas and Pratyekabuddhas are attached to the Path which is quite opposite[31] to the realization of the Absolute Body, and hence the Essence [of the Tathāgata] which is characterized as the Supreme Eternity, the Supreme Bliss, the Supreme Unity, and the Supreme Purity, is said not to be accessible to them, too.

About[32] this inaccessibility of the Essence to those who are attached to delusion, i.e. who have the notion of Evenescence, Suffering, Impersonality and Impurity [as the almighty maximum], the Lord has made it clear[33] in detail in the *Mahāparinirvāṇa-sūtra* with the example of a jewel in the water of a pond. It runs as follows[34]:

> "Suppose, for instance, O monks, that in the hot season, the people, putting on the bathing underwear[35], were playing in the water with various ornaments and equipments for their individual pastime[36]. Suppose then, someone would cast[37] into the water the genuine[38] Vaiḍūrya stone. Thus, in order to get this Vaiḍūrya stone, all the people, leaving aside their ornaments, would dive into the water. They would mistake pebbles and gravels in the pond for the real jewel, seize them and draw them out, thinking: I have got a jewel. After having stood[39] on the bank of the pond, they would notice: It is not the real jewel at all! At that moment, the water of that pond would, owing to the power of that jewel, shine as if water itself were shining, and seeing that water sparkling, they would say: O the jewel is still there [in the water], and would notice how that jewel had great quality[40]. Thereafter, one who is experienced and clever would really get the jewel out. In the same way, O brethren, ye who are ignorant of the real

31) *vidhura*, T. ... *dań ḥgal-ba*. C. has no literal translation.

32) Better to change the paragraph after '*yathā ca sa viparyāsa* ... (S. p. 74, l. 19).

33) *prasādhita*, T. *rab-tu bsgrubs*, C. 明.

34) MPS 377 *c*–378 *a*.

35) *salila-bandhana*, T. *khrus-ras* (bath-cloth), C. om. This compound word seems to have not been recorded anywhere else.

36) *svaiḥ svaiḥ maṇḍanakôpabhogair*. T. *rań-rań-gi rgyan dań ñe-bar spyod-pa dag-gis*, C. 浴乘船遊戲 (playing bathing and boating). The concrete idea is uncertain. T. reads '*maṇḍanaka* (= *alaṅkāra*) and *upabhoga* (any equipment for pastime)'. Here I followed T. reading.

37) *sthāpayati*, T. *gshag-pa*. But C. 失 (has lost by mistake).

38) *jātya*, T. *rigs dań ldan-pa*, C. (真).

39) T. reads as '*dṛṣṭvā*' instead of *sthitvā*. But S. shows a clearer sense.

40) C. om. '*aho maṇir iti guṇa-saṃjñā pravartate*' and instead has 'just as one sees the moon in the sky'.

essence of things [41], maintaining the general conception that all things are evanescent, that there is only suffering, and that everything is impersonal and impure, practise the meditation [on that conception] repeatedly, and increasingly. But all that was attempted [42] by you, [ye should keep in mind], is [in reality] of no use. Therefore, O monks, ye should become skilful in order not to be determined by this [false conception] like the pebbles and gravels in the pond. O monks, with those elements which ye maintain to be in every case evanescent, suffering, impersonal, and impure, and on which ye practise the meditation [on that notion] repeatedly and increasingly [43], there exists [an essence which represents] the Eternity, the Bliss, the Purity [44], and the Highest Unity".

Thus should be understood in detail, according to the Scripture, the teaching of the incorrectness with regard to the feature of the highest true nature of the elements.

Lastly, 'those whose mind has deviated from the conception of Non-substantiality' denotes 4) the Bodhisattvas who have recently entered the Vehicle, [since] they are deprived of [45] [the cognition of] the Matrix of the Tathāgata in regard to the true meaning of Non-substantiality [46]. They are the people who look toward Non-substantiality as the medium of Liberation [47] in order to destroy the substance [48], thinking that the perfect Nirvāṇa means the Extinction, i.e. the destruction of the elements [for the Phenomenal Existence] in future [49]. There are also some people

41) *dharma-tattva*. T., as if '*dharmârtha-tattva*', C. 眞實 (apparently om. *dharma*).

42) *ghaṭita*, T. *ñe-bar gshags-pa* (= *upasthita*), C. 所修集 (being accumulated by practice).

43) C. om. this repetition.

44) '*śobha*' in the text is a misprint for '*śubha*'.

45) *vipranaṣṭa*, T. *ñams-pa* (disappeared), C. 離.

46) *tathāgatagarbha-śūnyatârthanaya*, T. *stoṅ-pa-ñid-kyi tshul-du* (*śunyatā-nayena*, om. *artha*) as adverbial use and reads '*tathāgatagarbhataḥ vipranaṣṭāḥ*', C. 空如來藏義 (*śūnyatā-tathāgatagarbhârtha*, the meaning that *tathāgatagarbha* is *śūnyatā*). What is meant here is that the *garbha* theory represents the real meaning of *śūnyatā*.

47) *vimokṣa-mukha*, C. 解脫門. Cognition of Non-substantiality is one of the 3 *vimokṣa-mukhas*.

48) *bhāva-vināśāya*, C. 以失變異物. '變異物' (things changeable) is for *bhāva*.

49) *uttarakālam*, T. *dus phyis*. C. reads 'after destroying existence, one can get *nirvāṇa*'. This conception amounts to the nihilistic view. Cf. BGŚ 執無.

among them who think that there is something substantial called 'the Non-substantiality' which is quite different from 'form' and other [elements], and that is the one which we should understand, upon which we should meditate, and, fancying[50] Non-substantiality in this way, they are persuaded of[51] Non-substantiality.

§ 3. The True Conception of the Matrix of the Tathāgata as Representing Non-substantiality[52].

Then how is what is called here '[the cognition of] the Matrix of the Tathāgata in regard to the true meaning of Non-substantiality'?

Here there is nothing to be removed
And absolutely nothing to be added;
The Truth should be perceived as it is,
And he who sees the Truth becomes liberated[53]. // 154 //

50) *upalambha*, T. *dmigs-pa*, C. 得.

51) *pratisarati*, T. *brten-pa*, C. om. Cf. BHS Dic., s. v. This conception represents the eternalistc view. Cf. BGŚ 執有.

52) The following is actually a part of the explanation on '*śūnyatāvikaṣiptacitta*'. Cf. BGŚ 812 *b*.

53) This is one of the most famous verses in Mahāyanistic literature. Besides this occurrence in the *Ratna.*, there are 9 occurrences of this verse recorded in *Mélanges chinois et bouddhiques*, l. 394. They are:

1) Tibetan version of *Pratītyasamutpāda-hṛdaya-kārikā*, v. 7, by Nāgārjuna (Acc. to Prof. V. V. Gokhale's report, however, the original Skt text. has merely 5 kārikās, and hence the authorship of Nāgārjuna for this verse is doubtful. See V. V. Gokhale, *Der Sanskrit-Text von Nāgārjuna's Pratītyasamutpādahṛdayakārikā*, *Studia Indologica*, Festschrift für Willibald Kirfel, Bonn, 1955, S. 101 ff.);

2) *Nāma-saṃgīti* (Tib.) 6-5, attributed to Nāgārjuna;

3) *Sumaṅgala-visāraṇī* of Buddhaghosa (in Pāli), part I, 12. (a similar idea attributed to the Buddha;

4) *Saundaranandakāvya* of Aśvaghoṣa, XIII, 44;

5) *Abhisamayâlaṅkāra*, V, 21, which has a little difference in *b*. (*prakṣeptavyaṃ na kiṃcana*);

6) *Śuklavidarśanā* (Bendall Mss.);

7) *Bodhisattva-bhūmi*, Wogihara's ed. p. 48. (not in verse);

8) *Madhyântavibhāga-vyākhyā* by Sthiramati (as a quotation, it is identical with that in the *Abhisamayâlaṅkāra*);

9) *Mahāyāna-śraddhôtpāda*, Suzuki's tr., p. 57 (not in verse).

We now can add one example to this list. BGŚ mentions this verse along with v. 155 as a quotation (812 *b*), saying:

無一法可損 無一法可增 應見實如實 見實得解脱
由客塵故空 與法界相離 無上法不空 與法界相隨

The Essence [of the Buddha] is [by nature] devoid [54)]
Of the accidental [pollutions] which differ from it;
But it is by no means devoid of the highest properties
Which are, essentially, indivisible from it. // 155 //

What is explained by this ? There is no defiling element [55)] which is to be removed from this Essence of the Tathāgata, perfectly purified by nature, since it is by nature devoid of accidental pollutions. Also, there is no purifying element which is to be added to it, since it is by nature indivisible from the pure properties [of the Buddha] [56)]. On account of this point, it is said [in the Scripture] [57)]:

"The Matrix of the Tathāgata is devoid of all the sheath of Defilements which are differentiated and separated [from the Absolute Essence]. The Matrix of the Tathāgata is by no means devoid of the Buddha's Properties which are indivisible, inseparable [from the Absolute Essence], inconceivable and far beyond the sands of the Gaṅgā in number".

Thus, wherever something is lacking, this is observed [58)] as 'void' (*śūnya*) in that place (*tena*), whatever remains there, one knows that this being must exist here [59)]: This is really the true [conception of Non-substanti-

This is no doubt a quotation from the *Ratna.* and shows a closer translation of the original than C. tr. of the same in the *Ratna.*

In the case of such a verse of widely applicable idea, there was probably a custom in those days to borrow the same expression without permission or mention of the source in order to express one's own idea freely, and hence it is not necessary to regard this v. 154 as a quotation from any particular source. The originality of the *Ratna.* on account of this verse lies in its application to the explanation of '*garbha-śūnyatā-arthanaya*' shown in the second verse (v. 155). As for the second verse, cf. DAŚ 813 *b* (v. 14).

54) *śūnya*, T. *stoṅ*, C. 空. This is an original sense of the term *śūnya*. See below.

55) *saṃkleśa-nimitta*, T. *kun-nas ñon-moṅs-paḥi rgyu-mtshan*, C. simply '*kleśa*'.

56) T. inserts *dharmatā* after *śuddhadharma*.

57) ŚMS 221 *c*.

58) *sam-anupaśyati*, T. *yaṅ-dag-par rjes-su mthoṅ(-ba)*, C. 如實見知. *sam-* = *samyak*.

59) *yad yatra nâsti tat tena śūnyam iti samanupaśyati / yat punar atrâvaśiṣṭaṃ bhavati tat sad ihâstîti yathābhūtam prajānāti /*. T. *gaṅ-shig gaṅ-na med-pa de-ni des stoṅ-ṅo . . . gaṅ-shig lhag-par gyur-pa de-ni de-la rtag-par yod-do.* (For *sad*, T. reads '*sadā*'). C. 如是以何等煩惱, 以何等處無, 如是, 如實見知名為空智, 又何等諸佛法, 何處具足有, 如是如實見知名不空智. Cf. Pāli MN. III, 104-5, etc. (*Suññata-vagga*, *Cū-*

ality] [60]. **[Thus], by removing the extremities of affirmation and negation** [61]**, the real** [62] **characteristic of Non-substantiality is explained by these two verses.**

Now, those individuals whose mind has deviated from this principle of Non-substantiality, and, turning in various directions [63]**, neither meditates nor concentrates upon** [64] **it, we call them by this very reason 'those whose mind has deviated from [the true conception of] Non-substantiality. Indeed, without the introduction** [65] **to the knowledge of the highest truth of Non-substantiality, nobody can attain or realize** [66] **the non-discriminative Sphere** [67] **[of the Tathāgata]. Implying this point, it has been said** [68]**:**

> **"The Wisdom cognizing the Matrix of the Tathāgata is nothing but the Wisdom about Non-substantiality of the Buddhas. And**

lasuññata-sutta)

> *yaṃ hi kho tattha na hoti, tena taṃ suññaṃ samanupassati;*
> *yaṃ pana tattha avasiṭṭhaṃ hoti, taṃ santam idam atthêti pajānāti.*

There are two kinds of usages of the term '*śūnya*': 1) 'A is *śūnya* of B' (B with instrumental case-ending), as in the case of '*śūnyo dhātuḥ*'; 2) 'B is *śūnya* (in A)' (A with locative case-ending, sometimes in BHS with instrumental), as used in the aphorism mentioned above. The first usage is also observed in the same Pāli canon (*migāramātu pāsādo suñño hatthi-gavâssa-valavena* ..., in the preceding illustration), where the term '*śūnya*' (*suñña*) is to be translated into 'empty of', 'void of', or 'devoid of'. In the second usage, '*śūnya*' is synonymous with '*na asti*' (*na hoti*), absent, and this usage relates to the meaning of '*śūnya*' in Buddhist doctrine as appearing in the statement: *śūnyaṃ sarvam*'. See Note XI-14. Cf. BBh, p. 48.

60) In the translation, '*true*' represents both, '*sam-*' of *samanupaśyati* and '*yathābhūtam*'.

61) *samāropa* & *apavāda*, T. *sgro-ḥgod-pa* & *skur-pa ḥdebs-pa*, C. 有 無, respectively.

62) The reading '*aparyantam*' is to be corrected into '*aviparyastaṃ*' according to T. (*phyin-ci ma-log-pa*) and C. (如 實, = *yathābhūtaṃ*).

63) *visarati*, T. *rnam-par ḥphrol* (*ḥphrol* fr. *bral-ba*, to separate). C., instead of '*cittam vikṣipyate visarati*', simply '不 相 應' (*ayogyaṃ*), and for *śūnyatârthanayād*, '佛 境 界' (*buddhagocaraviṣayād*).

64) *ekâgrī bhavati*, T. *rtse-gcig-tu* ... *ḥgyur-ba*, C. 一 心. It signifies *cittaikâgratā* (心 一 境 性).

65) T. om. *mukha*.

66) *sākṣāt* √ *kṛ*, T. *mṅon-par ḥdu-bya-ba* (= *abhisamayati, abhisameti*), C. 見.

67) *avikalpa-dhātu*, C. 無 分 別 境 界. T. inserts *śuddha* between two and for *dhātu*, *dbyiṅs*.

68) ŚMS 221 c.

this Matrix of the Tathāgata has never been seen, has never been realized by the Śrāvakas and the Pratyekabuddhas[69]" &c.

Now, this Matrix of the Tathāgata, inasmuch as it represents the Matrix of the Absolute Essence, is said to be a sphere not accessible to 'those who have fallen into the erroneous conception maintaining the existence of individuality', because the Absolute Essence is an antidote against such erroneous conception[70]. Inasmuch as it represents the Matrix of the Absolute Body, or the Matrix of the Transcendental Element, it is said not to be accessible to 'those who are attached to delusion', since the Transcendental Element is spoken of as being an antidote against the mundane elements of such nature as evanescence, etc. [Furthermore], inasmuch as it represents the Matrix of the properties, perfectly pure by nature, [the Matrix of the Tathāgata] is said not to be accessible to 'those whose mind has deviated from Non-substantiality', since the [Buddha's] pure virtuous Properties[71], being represented by the Transcendental Absolute Body which is indivisible from them, are by nature devoid of accidental pollutions.

Here, to perceive that the Transcendental Absolute Body is perfectly pure by nature, by means of the cognition of the unique[72] introduction to the Wisdom which is essentially connected with the Absolute Essence, implies here the True Intuition[73]. On account of this perception, it is said that [even] those Bodhisattvas who are abiding in their 10 Stages

69) C. adds a few sentences more which are not available in the present ŚMS except for the passage 'only the Buddha can obtain it' and are probably an insertion by the translator.

70) Hereafter, the commentator tries to combine the 4 meanings of *tathāgatagarbha* mentioned in ŚMS (see Note IX-178) with the 4 kinds of people to whom the former 4 have the power of being *pratipakṣa*, respectively:

1) *dharmadhātugarbha* is not accessible to *satkāyadṛṣṭipatitāḥ*;
2) *dharmakāya*-[garbha], and
3) *lokottaradharmagarbha* are not accessible to *viparyāsâbhiratāḥ*;
4) *prakṛtipariśuddhadharmagarbha* is not accessible to *śūnyatāvikṣiptacittāḥ*.

For 1) *dharmadhātu*, T. as '*dharmakāya*'; in 3) T. & C. om. *dharma*; in 4), instead of *prakṛti*, T. as *dharmakāya*, and C. adds *śūnya*, *tathāgata*, *dharmadhātu* in place of *dharma*. But S. is identical with those mentioned in ŚMS. See note IX-178

71) *guṇa-dharmāḥ*, T. *yon-tan-gyi chos*, C. 功德法.

72) *ekanaya*, T. *tshul gcig-po*, C. 一味等味 (*ekarasa samarasa*).

73) *yathābhūta-darśana*. T. adds '*samyak*' before it. T. resolves '*jñānadarśana*' into '*jñānena saṃdarśanam*'. C. 如實知見 and adds '真如' (*tathatā*) as the object of *darśana*.

can [but] slightly understand the Matrix of the Tathāgata[74]. Indeed, thus it is said[75]:

[O Lord], thou art unable to be seen fully,
Just as here the sun, in the sky with torn clouds[76],
Even by the Saints, of pure intellectual vision,
Since their intellect is still partial;
O Lord, only those whose Wisdom is illimitable
Can completely perceive thy Absolute Body
Which pervades everything knowable
That is infinite like space "[77].

[74] C. regards this sentence as a quotation from some Sūtra. Cf. MPS 41 *a*.

[75] C. regards this verse as a commentary verse and adds one verse in the middle showing the sense that *śrāvaka* cannot see the Buddha. The source of this quotation is unknown.

[76] *chidrâbhra*, T. *sprin-mthon*, C. 薄雲 (thin cloud). T. '*mthon*' is to be changed into '*mthoṅs*', which means 'an open space in a dense forest', hence derivatively, 'slit, small hole', etc.

[77] *nabhas-tala*. For *tala*, T. *dbyiṅs* (*dhātu*). C. 虛空 for the whole. T. seems to have failed to catch the meaning of this verse by omitting one pronoun '*te*' in the third Pada.

XI. THE PURPOSE OF INSTRUCTION[1]

[Someone may ask]: If this Essence [of the Buddha] is thus so difficult to be cognized inasmuch as it is not fully accessible even to the Saints of the Highest rank who are abiding on the Stage characterized as being completely free from any attachment[2], then what is the use of this instruction to the ignorant and ordinary beings? [For replying to this question], we have two *ślokas* summarizing the purpose of instruction[3]. [Of them], one is the question, and the second is the answer[4].

(Kārikās 58–59)

It has been said here and there [in the Scriptures]
That all things are to be known everywhere
As being 'unreal', like clouds, [visions in] a dream, and illusions[5];
Whereas, why has the Buddha declared here
That the Essence of the Buddha[6] 'exists' in every living being?
// 156 //

There are 5 defects [caused by the previous teaching]:
The depressed mind[7], contempt against those who are inferior[8],
Clinging to things unreal[9], speaking ill of Truth[10],

1) C. 爲何義說品第七. Cf. BGŚ 787 *a–b* (Nidāna-parivarta), 811 *b*.

2) C. adds: 'it is accessible only to *sarvajña*'.

3) *deśanā-prayojana*, T. *bstan-paḥi dgos-pa*, C. (爲何義說).

4) *vyākaraṇa* (explanation), T. *lam bstan-pa*, C. om.

5) Especially in the *Prajñāpāramitā*, which is at the same time the basic scripture of the Mādhyamikas. Cf. MK, VII, 35:
yathā māyā yathā svapno gandharva-nagaraṃ yathā /
tathôtpādas tathā sthānaṃ tathā bhaṅga udāhṛtam //

6) *buddha-dhātu*, T. *saṅs-rgyas sñiṅ-po* (= *buddhagarbha*), C. 如來性.

7) *līnaṃ cittaṃ*, T. *sems shum*, C. 怯弱心. See v. 161.

8) *hīnasattveṣu avajñā*, T. *sems-can dman-la bsñas-pa*, C. 輕慢諸衆生. See v. 162.

9) *abhūtagrāha*, T. *yaṅ-dag mi-ḥdsin* (*bhūta-agraha*), C. 執著虚妄法. See v. 163.

10) *bhūtadharmâpavāda*, T. *yaṅ-dag chos-la skur*, C. 謗眞如佛性 (C. regards this *bhūtadharma* as *tathatā* or *buddhadhātu*. See v. 165 *a b*.

And besides [11], affection for one's self".
[The teaching about Essence of the Buddha] has been taught
In order that those who are possessed of these defects [12]
Might get rid of their defects. // 157 //

The meaning of these two *ślokas* is briefly to be known by the following ten verses.

It has been said [in the Scriptures]
All kinds of phenomena, made by causes and conditions
And known in the forms of Defilement, Action and Result [13],
Are, like clouds, etc., deprived of reality [14]. // 158 //
The Defilements are like the clouds,
Undertaking of Actions [15] is like the enjoyment [16] in a dream;
Being the Results made by Defilements and Actions,
The Group of elements are like illusions made by magic [17]. // 159 //
So has it been ascertained 'before';
But now, in this 'ultimate' Doctrine [18],

[11] *adhikaḥ*, T. *lhag-pa* (which is connected to '*sneha*').

[12] *ātmasneha*, T. *bgag-cag*, C. 計身有神我 (= *ātmadṛṣti*, but it is not the case here). See v. 165 *c d*. Of these 5, BGŚ gives the following terms:

1) 下劣心; 2) 慢下品人; 3) 虚妄執; 4) 誹謗真實法; 5) 我執.

[13] *kleśa-karma-vipāka*. '*vipāka*' stands for *janman* or *duḥkha*. These three are the principal factors of *saṃsāra* or *saṃskṛtadharmas*. See Note VIII-132. Also see vv. I, 56 ff., where *vipāka*' is replaced by *skandha-dhātv-āyatana*.

[14] *viviktaṃ bhūtakoṭiṣu*. C. 虚妄 for the whole. T. *dben-pa* (solitary) for *vivikta*, and regards *bhūtakoṭi* as the subject and reads '*bhūtakoṭi* (the reality) is apart from *saṃskṛtam*'. From the context, C. reading seems better, since '*bhūtakoṭiṣu viviktaṃ*' here stands for *śūnyaṃ* in the Kārikā (usually *vivikta* is used for denoting purity of *mokṣa* or *nirvāṇa*, in the sense 'separation from *kleśas*,'). As for the use of *bhūtakoṭi* in the plural, I could not trace it anywhere else.

[15] *kṛtyakriyā*, T. *bya-ba-yi las*, C. 所作業.

[16] C. om. *upabhoga*.

[17] *māyā-nirmita*, T. *sgyu-ma spral-ba*, C. 幻 (om. *nirmita*).

[18] *uttara tantra*, T. *bla-maḥi rgyud*, C. 究竟論. This is the word which gives this work its title. Here the term '*tantra*' (for which C. 論 = *śāstra*) has nothing to do with Tantric Buddhism. The meaning is simply 'doctrine' or 'philosophy'. Significance lies more in the word '*uttara*' than in '*tantra*', since by the term '*uttara*', the author of the *Ratna.* declared his aim and the position of this theory in the currency of Buddhist philosophy. In one sense, this theory is opposite to that of '*pūrva*', by which is meant here clearly the doctrine of the *Prajñāpāramitā* and of the *Mūlamadhyamaka*,

In order to remove the 5 defects [caused by the previous teaching],
It is shown that the Essence of the Buddha[19] exists. // 160 //
Indeed, if [the people] have not heard of this teaching,
Some of them, being possessed of depressed[20] mind,
May have a fault of self-depreciation[21], and hence,
The Will towards the Enlightenment does never arise in them. // 161 //
Even if someone has resolved towards Enlightenment[22],
Then he, being proud of it, saying: I am superior to [others],
Will produce the notion of inferiority for those
Whose mind is not aroused towards Enlightenment. // 162 //
With him who thinks like that[23],
The true knowledge will never arise, and hence,
He clings to unreal things [as if they were real]
And does not cognize the true meaning. // 163 //
[Indeed][24], the defects of living beings are unreal
Because they are non-genuine[25] and accidental

since the 'former' one emphasizes '*śūnyatā*', i.e. unreality of things, while this '*latter*' one emphasizes '*astitva*' of *buddhadhātu*. In another sense, however, this doctrine is not against the former, but a real successor of the former, as being the 'answer'–giver to the problem which has never been explained 'before'; in other words, as we had already known by previous passages, this '*buddhadhātvastivāda*' is a synthetic *śūnyavāda* of *śūnya* and *aśūnya*, and hence it is the '*ultimate*'. T. '*bla-ma*' shows this sense.

[19] *dhātu*, T. *khams*, C. 真如性. For these 3 verses, cf. BGŚ 811 *b* (after the explanation of *buddhakāyatraya*).

[20] *nīca*, T. *shum-pa*, C. 怯弱心 = *līna*.

[21] *ātmâvajñāna*, T. *bdag-la brñas-pa*, C. 欺自身. This self-depreciation is the first defect, and towards those people having this defect, BGŚ says, the Buddha has taught *tathāgatagarbha*-'*asti*'.

[22] For '*bodhicittôdaye 'py asya*', T. reads as '*bodhicittôdaye yasya*' and relates this '*yasya*' to '*tasya*' of the next verse. But in relation to the preceding verse, the word '*api*' is quite necessary, while '*tasya*' of the next verse can stand for that which is described in this v. 162 without any relative pronoun.

This 'self-pride' is the second defect (lack of the notion of 'equality'), for removing it, it is taught that '*sarva*'–*sattvāḥ tathāgatagarbhāḥ*' (BGŚ).

[23] C. 如是憍慢人 (such a man of self-pride). In this 3rd defect, emphasis lies on the ignorance about *tathāgatagarbha*, which causes the affection toward the unreal thing.

[24] This verse expresses the true meaning (*bhūtârtha*). T. as S. but C. puts the word '不知' (does not know) and regards this verse as explaining the 4th defect.

[25] *kṛtrima*, T. *bcos-ma*, C. om. For these two, i.e. *kṛtrimatva* & *āgantukatva*, BGŚ: 本無 & 客.

But the non-substantiality[26] of such defects is real,
That is, the virtues [of living beings], pure by nature. // 164 //
If a man of intelligence[27] perceives [only]
That the defects [of living beings] are unreal,
And depreciates [their] virtues which are real,
He cannot obtain benevolence[28] by which
One regards [other] living beings as equal to oneself. // 165 //
On the contrary[29], if one hears of this teaching,
There arises in him great exertion[30],
Respect [for all living beings] as for the Teacher[31],
Intuition, Wisdom[32], and great Benevolence[33];
These 5 properties having become originated, // 166 //
He, being free from [self-] depreciation[34],
Obtaining equal regard [for every body],

26) *nairātmya*, T. *bdag-med-pa*. '*guṇa*' being opposite to *doṣa*, means the 'emptiness' of *doṣa*, and this is real.

27) *dhīmat*, which represents '*navayānasamprasthita-bodhisattva*'. He is intelligent because he can perceive '*doṣâbhūtatva*', but this knowledge is merely one side of the true knowledge. Consequently, he maintains that there is nothing real, and hence this conception is nothing but the 'depreciation of reality'. This 4th defect seems to be the most important among the 5. It clearly implies the defect caused by certain Mādhyamikas whose position gave rise to the appellation of '*nāstika*' for Buddhists.

28) *maitrī*, T. *byams-pa*, C. 慈. The lack of *maitrī*, which is the 5th defect, is the natural consequence of the 4th defect.

29) Hereafter, referring to the 5 *guṇas* which are the antidotes for the respective 5 *doṣas*. About the 5 *guṇas*, cf. AĀS 469 *b–c*.

30) *prôtsaha*, T. *spro*, C. 大勇猛力 (BGŚ 正勤心) ...(1)

31) *śāstṛ-gaurava*, T. *ston-pa-bshin gus*, C. 恭敬世尊 (BGŚ 恭敬事) ...(2) T. catches the meaning better. But the best explanation is given in AĀS, which runs: 於諸衆生 生尊重心 起大師敬 (having aroused the mind of respect towards living beings, he produces *śāstṛgaurava*.

32) *prajñā* (3) & *jñāna* (4). C. 智 & 慧, (in an opposite order). Here '*prajñā*' represents '*prajñāpāramitā*' of the Mādhyamika or '*avikalpajñāna*' of the Vijñānavāda, and its function is said to be the intuition of '*śūnyaṃ sarvam*', while '*jñāna*', representing '*tatpṛṣṭhalabha-jñāna*' being *laukika jñāna*, has a function of 'manifesting the reality' (BGŚ 由生闍那俗智 能顯實智).

33) *maitrī* (5) = *mahākaruṇā* (C. 悲, BGŚ 大悲). Manifestation of the reality is for the sake of living beings, that is to say, because of '*mahākaruṇā*', hence BGŚ interprets that *prajñā* and *mahākaruṇā* (instead of mentioning of *jñāna*) are the two *upāyas* by means of which one can attain the state of *apratiṣṭhitanirvāṇa*.

34) For *niravajya*, C. 不退轉 (*avivarta*).

Being devoid of defects and possessed of virtues,
Having love, equally for himself and for living beings[35],
Attains the State of Buddha[36] at an early date. // 167 //

Finished is the first Chapter entitled 'the Matrix of the Tathāgata' in the ANALYSIS OF THE GERM OF THE JEWELS, a Treatise on the Ultimate Doctrine of the Great Vehicle, with the commentary [named] 'the Summary of Meaning of the *ślokas*'[37].

[35] For *ātmasattvasamasneha*, C. 取一切衆生如我身無異 (regarding all living beings as not being different from himself).

[36] *buddhatā* (= *buddhatva*, *bodhi*), T. *saṅs-rgyas-ñid*, C. 無上佛菩提 (*anuttarabuddhabodhi*). Cf. BGŚ 菩提, AĀS 菩薩入阿鞞跋致位 (*bodhisattva* can enter the *avivarta* state).

[37] *ślokârthasaṃgraha-vyākhyānataḥ*. T. om. the ablative case-ending. C. has no equivalent term. '*ślokârthasaṃgraha-vyākhyāna*' seems to be the name for the commentary, while '*śloka*' stands for the basic Kārikās.

CHAPTER II.

THE ENLIGHTENMENT [1]

2. NIRMALĀ TATHATĀ

XII. GENERAL CHARACTERISTICS OF THE REALITY FREE FROM POLLUTIONS

We have finished the explanation of 'the Reality mingled with Pollutions'. Hereafter, we shall speak of the undefiled Reality. Now, what is this 'Reality free from Pollutions'? It is that which is called 'the Perfect Manifestation of the Basis (i.e. the Germ of the Buddha)' (*āśrayaparivṛtti*), since, in the Immaculate Sphere of the Buddhas, [this Reality] is [absolutely] freed from all kinds of pollutions [2]. And this undefiled Reality is to be known in brief in the reference to the 8 categories [3] [which show its characteristics]. Then which are the 8 categories ?

[The Buddhahood [4] is] the purity [5], the attainment [6],
The liberation [from obstructions] [7],
The action in behalf of oneself and others [8],
And the foundation [9] of these two kinds of actions ;

1) Cf. AĀS Chapter III (Bodhi-parivarta), 470 *c*–473 *c*.

2) AĀS 470 *c*: 諸佛婆伽婆在無漏界一切障永盡轉依寂靜明淨 ('轉依' for '*āśrayaparivṛtti*').

3) For '*padârtha*', T. simply '*don*' (*artha*).

4) The whole of this verse seems to be merely a row of technical terms. However, as all those terms, *śuddhi* and so forth, show the various aspects of '*buddhatva*', the term Buddhahood may be suplied here as the subject term.

5) *śuddhi*, T. *dag*, C. 淨 ... (1).

6) *prāpti*, T. *thob*, C. 得 ... (2). This reminds us of the '*jñānâpti*' in v. I, 3.

7) *visaṃyoga*, T. *bral-ba*, C. 遠離 ... (3).

8) *svaparârtha*, T. *raṅ-gshan-don*, C. 自他利 ... (4).

9) (*tad-*) *āśraya*, T. (*de-*)*brten*, C. 依止 ... (5). C. adds '相應' (*yoga*) before

Being profound[10], magnificent and magnanimous,
It [manifests itself] as long as the world exists,
In a manner as it is[11]. // 1 //.

Thus, by this verse[12], these 8 subjects are indicated according to order; namely: 1) the own nature (*svabhāva*); 2) the cause (*hetu*); 3) the result (*phala*); 4) the function (*karman*); 5) the union (*yoga*); 6) the manifestation (*vṛtti*); 7) the eternal (*nitya*), and 8) the inconceivable (*acintya*) character [of Manifestation][13].

1) First of all the Essence [of the Buddhahood], which is called by the Lord 'the Matrix of the Tathāgata' when it is unreleased from the sheath of defilements, is to be understood, when it is 'perfectly purifi-

āśraya. The term '相應' has probably no ground in the Ms. used for C. translation. But in the commentary, C. regards it as the term indicating the fifth subject, and reads '依止' in connection with the next subject.

10) The reading should be '*gāmbhīrya*' instead of '*gambhirya*' in the text, and is to be written without separation from the succeeding '*audārya*' (*gāmbhīryaudārya-*). For this 6th category, S. *gāmbhīryaudārya-māhātmya*, T. *zab daṅ rgya-che daṅ bdag-ñid-chen-po*, C. 深快大...(6). Cf. AĀS 472 *c*, 1) 甚深道理; 2) 廣大道理; 3) 萬德道理. BGŚ 811 *a*, 1) 甚深; 2) 廣大. 3) 和善;

11) For these two categories, S. *yāvad kālam, yathā ca tat*; T. *ji-srid-dus, ji-lta-ñid*; C. 如彼所爲義 in the Kārikā text, and 時數如彼法 in the commentary. (The latter matches S. better). T. om. '*tat*'. These two subjects have the same characters as '*yāvadbhāvikatā*' and '*yathāvadbhāvikatā*' used in the characterization of the Jewel of the Community (IV-§ 1).

12) It is quite doubtful whether this verse belongs to the Kārikā-text, though C. includes it within the Kārikā-text. One reason is that this verse is merely a row of certain terms and does not make a sentence by itself. Such is not the case with Kārikā-verses which we have picked up in Chap. I, and also without this verse, we can understand the idea expressed in this Chap. II. Another reason is that these terminologies are not utilized in the following Kārikās at all. With the same probability as for v. 29 in Chap. I, this verse is to be omitted from the line of Kārikā text. See my Introduction.

13) For these 8 subjects, T. & C. give the following terminologies:

1) *ṅo-bo*; 實體, 2) *rgyu*, 因; 3) *ḥbras-bu*, 果; 4) *las*, 業; 5) *ldan*, 相應; 6) *ḥjug-pa*, 行; 7) *rtag-pa*, 常; and 8) *mi khyab-pa*, 不可思議.

Cf. AĀS 470 *c*, which mentions 10 categories, viz. 1) 自性 (*svabhāva*); 2) 因緣 (*hetu*); 3) 惑障 (*paripantha*); 4) 至果 (*phala*); 5) 作事 (*karman*); 6) 相攝 (*yoga*); 7) 行處 (*vṛtti*); 8) 常住 (*nitya*); 9) 不共 (*āveṇika*); 10) 不可思惟 (*acintya*). Of them, the first 4 are identical with the first 3 subjects of 10 categories on '*tathāgatadhātu*' in Chap I, while the latter 6 agree in their contents with those (4)-(8) in this chapter (9th is a part of '*yoga*' here). See Note VIII-8.

ed' (*viśuddhi*)[14], as the 'own nature' of the [Reality] characterized as the 'Perfect Manifestation of the Basis'. It is said[15]:

"O Lord, one who has no doubt about the Matrix of the Tathāgata as it is concealed under the millions of coverings of all defilements, shall likewise have no doubt about the Absolute Body of the Tathāgata which is[16] freed from the coverings of all defilements".

2) There are two kinds of knowledge. One is the 'Supermundane, non-discriminative [Wisdom]' and the other, the Mundane[17] Wisdom which is acquired afterwards [based on the former]'. This supermundane and mundane Wisdom is the 'cause' of the Perfect Manifestation of the Basis[18], and is indicated by the word 'attainment' (*prāpti*). [Here] it is called 'attainment' in the sense 'that by which something is attained'[19].

3) The 'result' [obtained by] these [two kinds of Wisdom] is the 'liberation' (*visaṃyoga*)[20]. There are two kinds of liberation, viz. the liberation from the obstructions of defilement, and the liberation from the obstructions on account of the knowable things, respectively[21].

14) Cf. AAS 470 *c*: 阿難, 是界 (dhātu) 未除煩惱殼, 我說名如來藏, 至極清淨是名轉依法, whereafter, the sūtra mentions 4 characteristics of '*āśrayaparivṛtti*', namely 1) 生起緣故 (*utpattiniśrayadānatvāt*); 2) 滅盡緣故 (*nirodhaniśrayadānatvāt*); 3) 正熟思量所知法果故 (*vipāka-mano-jñeyadharmaphalatvāt*); 4) 最清淨法界體故 (*pariśuddhadharmadhātu-svabhāvataḥ*).

15) ŚMS 221 *b*.

16) The reading should be '... *vinirmukte tathāgatadharmakāye* '*pi*', instead of '... *vinirmuktes tathā-*'.

17) '*laukikaṃ*' is to be insterted after *pṛṣṭhalabdhaṃ*, acc. to T. and Ms. B.

18) For '*āśrayaparivṛtti*', C. 依止行.

19) *prāpyate* '*neneti prāptiḥ*. (*prāpti* means here the means of attainment = *prāptyupāya*, p. 80 l. 1) T. *ḥdis thob-pas na thob-paḥo*, C. 依此得, 得 (this sentence is to be placed immediately after '是名爲因'. See below).

20) The reading, '*tatphalaṃ dvividham* /' is doubtful, although T. completely agrees with S. For this, C. reads as '*jñānâdhigamo eva (tat) phalam* /', and omits '*dvividham*'. What is signified by the term *dvividhaṃ* is quite uncertain. (Acc. to v. III, 2 & 3, it may refer to '*visaṃyoga-phala*' and '*vipāka-phala*', but the term *vipāka* is used nowhere in Chap. II). From the context, therefore, it is preferable to read '*tatphalaṃ visaṃyogaḥ* /', for '... *dvividham* /'.

21) '*yathākramam*' before '*svaparârtha-*' should be connected with the preceding

4) The 'function' is the accomplishment of one's own aim and that of others.

5) [The point that] the foundation (*adhiṣṭhāna*)[22] of this function is 'provided (*samanvāgama*) with' [the inmeasurable properties] is [here called] 'union'.

6)–8) The 'manifestation[23] means that [this Perfect Manifestation of the Basis] manifests itself in the forms of three Bodies of the Buddha which are characterized by profundity, magnificence, and magnanimity, respectively (*gāmbhīrya, audārya, māhātmya*), and [manifests] 'eternally', i.e. 'as long as the world exists', and in an 'inconceivable' manner.

Summary.

The own nature, the cause, and the result,
The function, the union, and the manifestation,
Its eternal and inconceivable character;
By these points, there is the establishment [of the Essence]
In Buddhas' Stages[24]. // 2 //

sentence. (*-visaṃyogaś ca yathākramam / sva-*). So does C. (如是次第故名遠離). (There is no correspondence between each of the two kinds of *visaṃyoga* and of the two kinds of *artha-sampādana*).

Here C. has again confusion in its arrangement. '偈言遠離故, 業者' should be placed after '故名遠離'. The correct arrangement of these passages in C. should be as follows:

...得世間出世間依止行智, 是名爲因。依此得, 得。[偈言, 得故]。果者即證智果, 是名爲果。有二種遠離。一者遠離煩惱障。二者, 遠離智障。如是次第名遠離。[偈言遠離故]。業者, 如是遠離自利利他成就有, 名爲業。

22) T. *rten[-pa]*, C. 住持 (=*āśraya* in the verse). It signifies Buddhahood characterized as *muktikāya* and *dharmakāya* (v. II, 30). For the whole sentence, C. reads: '相應者, 自利利他得無量功德常畢竟住持, 是名相應, 偈言相應故'. It is quite difficult to render this C. translation, but in the light of v. 30, we may interpret it as follows: The union means that the immeasurable qualities which are obtained by *svaparârtha (-sampatti)* are always and ultimately united with the foundation (*yoga iti svaparârthaprāptânumeyaguṇānāṃ nityam acintyam adhiṣṭhāne yogaḥ /*).

23) C. mentions *nitya, acintya* along with *vṛtti*. (行, 常, 不思議者).

24) *buddhabhūmi* (pl.).

XIII. 8 POINTS ON THE UNDEFILED REALITY

(I) SVABHĀVA & (II) HETU

Now, we have one *śloka* on Buddhahood and the means for its attainment [1] referring to the subjects of 'own nature' and 'cause' respectively.

(Kārikā 1)

Buddhahood has been spoken of as being radiant by nature,
[however] as being covered with the net of the multitude of clouds,
In the form of [obstructions on account of] defilements
And knowable things which are of accidental nature,
Just as the sun and the sky [2] [are often interrupted by clouds
Though they are radiant and immaculate, respectively] [3];
This Buddhahood is now eternal, everlasting and constant,
Being endowed with all the the pure properties of the Buddha,
And is attained when the elements [of existence] take resort [4]
To the Non-discriminative and Analytical Wisdom [5]. // 3 //

The meaning of this *śloka* is to be known in brief by the [following] 4 verses.

Buddhahood, which is represented by [6]
The indivisible virtuous properties,

[1] *prāptyupāya*. It stands for '*prāpti*' (= *hetu*) in the preceding passage.

[2] C. says instead 'the sun and the moon'.

[3] Cf. DAŚ 893 *a* (v. 10: 譬如明淨日 爲雲之所翳 煩惱雲若除 法身日明顯).

[4] *dharmāṇām*... *āśrayāt*. But both T. & C. read this *dharma* as connecting with *avikalpa*: T. *chos-la mi-rtog*, C. 無分別諸法. Therefore, the reading '*dharmāṇām*' is somewhat doubtful. Or is it an irregular Skt. style peculiar to the Buddhist text?

[5] *akalpana* & *pravicaya-jñāna*, T. *mi-rtog* & *rnam-ḥbyed ye-śes*. C. for this line, 不分別諸法 得無漏真智 (*dharmeṣv avikalpād, anāsrava-tattvajñānam āpyate*). Here the reference is, however, to the two kinds of *jñāna*, i.e. *avikalpajñāna* and *tatpṛṣṭhalabdha-jñāna*.

[6] *prabhāvita*. C. has no equivalent word for it. T. *rab-dbye-ba* (*prabhinna*).

Has a resemblance to the sun and the sky
In both its characters, knowledge and removal[7]. // 4 //
It is endowed with all the properties of the Buddha,
Which are beyond the sands of the Gaṅgā in number,
And are radiant and of uncreated nature[8],
And whose manifestations are indivisible [from itself][9]. // 5 //
Because of their being unreal by nature[10],
Because of their pervadingness and occasionality,
The obstructions[11] of defilements and of ignorance
Are illustrated as being like clouds. // 6 //
The cause of dissolving[12] these two obstructions is Wisdom,
Which is again considered as[13] of two kinds,
One is the Non-discriminative [Wisdom]
And the other is the knowledge, obtained afterwards[14]. // 7 //

(III) PHALA

It is said that the 'own nature' of the Perfect Manifestation of the Basis is the 'perfect purity'. This purity is here, in short, of two kinds. Namely, 1) the 'innate purity' (*prakṛtiviśuddhi*); and 2) 'the purity, as the result of purification' (*vaimalyaviśuddhi*)[15]. Of them, 1) 'the

7) C. takes '*dvaya*' as '*advaya*' (不二), and reads '智 (*jñāna*) and 離染 (*prahāṇa*) are non-dual'. T. as *prahāṇa-dvaya*, i.e. two kinds of *prahāṇa*.

8) *akṛtaka*, T. *byas-min*, C. 非作法.

9) *avinirbhāgavṛtti* (Bahuvrīhi comp.), T. *dbye-med-par ḥjug-can*, C. 不離彼實體 (om. *vṛtti*).

10) *svabhāvâpariniṣpatti*, T. *raṅ-bshin-gyis ni ma-grub*, C. 實無體.

11) *āvṛti*, T. *sgrib-pa*, C. 障.

12) *viśleṣa*, T. *-daṅ bral-ba*, C. 遠離 (= *visaṃyoga*).

13) For '*iṣyate*', C. 向 (to intend, to be intended).

14) For '*tatpṛṣṭhalabdha*', C. 依彼所得. There is no correspondence between each of the two obstructions and the two kinds of wisdom.

15) T. *raṅ-bshin-gyis rnam-par dag-pa*, & *dri-ma med-paḥi rnam-par dag-pa*: C. 自性清淨 & 離垢清淨, respectively. The former is characterized as '*vimuktir na ca visaṃyogaḥ*', and the latter, '*vimuktir visaṃyogaś ca*' (C. 性解脫 & 得解脫). In this sense, *visaṃyoga* is regarded as '*phala*'. Cf. MSA XII, 15: *svabhāva-śuddhaṃ mala-śuddhitaṃ ca* (自性及無垢, C. *Taisho*, XXXI, p. 620 *b*, and in the commentary, C. distinguishes both purities by the terms '清' & '白'). Also see AĀS 472 *a*: 自性清淨是通相 無垢清淨是別相.

innate purity' represents that which is essentially free [from all stains] but actually associated with them, [i.e. Reality mingled with pollutions]. Indeed, the Innate Mind, though being radiant, is not [always] separated from the accidental pollutions. 2) 'The purity, as the result of purification' represents [that which is] essentially free and actually, too, liberated from [all pollutions][16]. Because, just as water and the like become purified from dirt, impurities, etc., the radiant Innate Mind is completely liberated from the accidental pollutions.

Now we have two *ślokas* about 'the Purity, as the result of purification' with reference to the subject of 'result'[17].

(Kārikās 2–3)

Like a pond, filled with pure water,
Becomes abundant with flowering lotus gradually[18],
Like the full moon delivered from the jaws of Rāhu[19],
Like the sun, whose rays have been released
From the covering of clouds and others[20],
This [Buddhahood], being endowed with pure properties,
Manifests itself as being liberated[21]. // 8 //

16) For *visaṃyoga*, C. reads in negative (不離一切法, *sarvadharmâvisaṃyogaḥ*).

17) Here again C. reads in negative (不離).

18) A simile for the immaculate nature liberated from '*rāga*', see v. 12. But the point of similarity is not clear. Cf. DAŚ 如池無垢濁 (v. 17), 如池水被濁, 貪欲塵土所混雜故 (893 *c*). Rather, lotus is usually said to grow in dirty water.

For the second half of this line, C. 種種雜花樹 周邊常圍遶. It suggests the word '*druma*' as in Ms. B. The last 5 letters are for '*āḍhya*', for which T. *rgyas*.

19) A simile for the immaculate compassion liberated from '*dveṣa*', see v. 13. '*rāhu*' (T. *sgrag-can*, C. 羅睺) is a personification of the phenomenon of eclipse and is counted one of '*nava grahāḥ*', see Mvyut. 164. Cf. DAŚ v. 16: 亦如月盛滿阿修羅所蝕, and 如滿月被蝕 我慢羅睺 所執取故 (893 *b*, comm. on v. 16); v. 18 (893 *c*) 如虛空淸淨.

20) A simile for the immaculate Wisdom, liberated from '*moha*', see v. 14. Cf. DAŚ 893 *c*: 如日未出, 在無明習氣地中故 & 譬如日明現威光徧世間 (v. 91).

21) *bhāti muktaṃ tad eva*, T. *snaṅ-ldan* (*bhāti-yuktaṃ*) *de-ñid-do*, C. 顯現即彼體 (probably as S.).

This Buddhahood[22] is [also] like the Highest of Sages[23],
Like honey, like the kernel [of corns], like gold,
Like a precious store of jewels, like a great fruit-tree,
Like an immaculate precious image of the Buddha,
Like the Highest Lord of the world,
And like a golden statue[24]. // 9 //.

The meaning of these two *ślokas*, in short, is to be known by the following 8 verses:

The result of the Non-discriminative Wisdom
In short, is said to be akin to a pond and others,
Being pure [as the result of the removal] of
Desire and other accidental defilements. // 10 //
[On the other hand], the result of Wisdom,
Attained on the basis of the former, is explained
As the actual sight of the Buddha's state
Possessed of all kinds of excellency[25]. // 11 //
It is like a pond filled with shining water
Because of its rejecting the dirtiness[26] of the dust of Desire,
And because of its sprinkling[27] the water of meditation
On the disciples who are like lotus flowers. // 12 //
It has a resemblance to the immaculate full moon[28],
Since it has been released from the Rāhu of Hatred
And since it pervades all the world
With the rays[29] of Great Love and Compassion. // 13 //

22) *jinatva*, T. *rgyal-ba-ñid*, C. 如來身.

23) *munivṛṣa* (= *munirṣabha*). C. '蜂王' is probably a mistake, it should be 諸佛 (or 法王).

24) As all of these 9 examples are the same as those spoken in Chap. 1, this kārikā cannot be understood by itself unless there is assumed the knowledge of the 9 examples on *tathāgatagarbha*. Such is not a characteristic of the genuine kārikās in this text, and hence the originality of this verse is quite doubtful. See my Introduction.

25) The significance expressed in these two verses is as follows: The *visaṃyoga* of *dhātu* is immediately followed by the manifestation of *buddhatva* accompanied by *buddhaguṇas*, just as *avikalpajñāna* is immediately followed by *tatpṛṣthalabdha-jñāna*.

26) *kāluṣya*, C. 濁水, T. om.

27) *abhiṣyandana*, T. *ḥbab*, C. 習氣潤.

28) *pūrṇavimalêndu* C. 十五日月.

29) For *aṃśu*, C. 水 (*ambu*), but T. *ḥod-zer*.

And this Buddhahood is similar to the immaculate sun,
Because of its being free from the clouds of Ignorance,
And because of its removing the darkness of the world
With the rays of its divine Wisdom. // 14 //
Being possessed of the unequalled [30] properties,
Bringing forth the essence of the Highest Doctrine [31],
And being free from the outer covering [32] [of Defilements],
It is like the Buddha [33], like honey and the kernel [of grains]. // 15 //
Being pure [34], being freed from the poverty
By the richness [35] of its properties,
And being the giver [36] of the fruit of Liberation,
It is like gold, like a treasure, and a tree, [respectively] [37]. // 16 //
By its body's being made of the jewel of the Doctrine [38],
Its being the Highest Lord of the human beings [39],
And its having the appearance of the most precious form [40],
It is like a precious [image], a king and a golden statue. // 17 //

(IV) KARMAN [41]

It has been said that the two kinds of Wisdom, viz. the supermundane Non-discriminative Wisdom and the mundane knowledge, obtained afterwards on the basis of the former [42], are the cause of the Perfect Manifestation of the Basis, which is called 'the result of the liberation', and the

30) *atulyatulya*, T. *mi-mñam mñam*, C. 無等等 (= *asamasama*). This line stands for *adhigamadharma*.

31) It stands for *deśanādharma*.

32) *phalgu*, T. *śun-pa* (= *tvak*), C. 糩障 (Pāli. *pheggu*).

33) C. reads '*sugata*' as the subject. But it is absolutely a mistake.

34) *pavitra*, T. *dag*[-*pa*], C. 妙 (?). C. again misreads this line.

35) *dravya*, T. *rjas*, C. 真實 (?).

36) T. '*smin-byed*' for *dāna* is to be corrected into '*sbyin-byed*'. These three stand for *tathatā*, *prakṛtisthagotra* and *samudānīta-gotra*, respectively.

37) C. om. *nidhi* (a *varia lectio* in *Taisho* edition gives us the reading: 說藏金剛喩. The correct reading is therefore '說金藏樹喩').

38) Indicating *dharmakāya*.

39) *dvipada-agrādhipatya*, T. *rkaṅ-gñis bdag-po mchog*, C. 增上兩足尊. It indicates probably *saṃbhoga-kāya*.

40) Indicating *nirmāṇa-kāya*.

41) Cf. AĀS 472 *c*. . . . (5) 作事 (菩提利益事).

42) For these two *jñānas*, AĀS 無分別智 & 無分別後智.

'function' of the Wisdom is the fulfilment of one's own aim and of that of others. Then, what is the 'fulfilment of one's own aim and of that of others'? That which represents the attainment of the undefiled Absolute Body, as being freed from the obstructions due to Defilements and knowable things along with their potential forces is called the 'fulfilment of one's own aim'. And that which comes after the attainment of the fulfilment of one's own aim, and represents the manifestation, by means of twofold power[43], viz. 1) appearance in the forms of two bodies[44]; and 2) the teaching by means of them, [both of] which continue as long as the world exists, without any effort, it is called the 'fulfilment of the aim of others'.

About this fulfilment of one's own aim and of that of others, with reference to the subject 'function', we have three *ślokas*.

(Kārikās 4–6)

Buddhahood[45], being the foundation[46],
Immaculate and all-pervading,
Of unperishable nature, and everlasting,
Quiescent, constant and unchangeable[47],
Is, like space, the cause[48] for the Intelligent[49]
To experience the objects through 6 sense-organs[50]. // 18 //
It gives always the cause [for enjoyment]
In showing the miraculous apparitional forms,
In the pure audition of its perfect preaching,

43) *vibhutva*, T. *dbaṅ-ḥbyor-ba*, C. 自在力. Two-fold means '*deśanā & darśana-vibhutva*'.

44) From the context, '*kāyadvaya*' here probably means the twofold *rūpakāya*. (C. 二種佛身, AĀS 二種身). The same term is used in v. 28. The correspondence between each of the twofold *jñāna* and of the twofold *arthasampatti* is not clearly observed here. But AĀS regards *svârthasampatti* as caused by *avikalpajñāna*, and *parârthasampatti* as caused by *tatpṛṣṭhalabdha-jñāna*.

45) *tathāgatatva*, C. 諸佛如來身.

46) *pada*, T. *gnas*, C. 處.

47) *acyuta*, T. *ḥpho-ba*, *med-pa*, C. 不退.

48) C. reads '無相' for *kāraṇa* (with a negative, in the sense Buddhahood itself is *animitta*).

49) *sat*, C. 勝智者 (*dhīmat*). T. '*dag-pa*(*śuddha*)' is probably a corruption. This '*satām*' (gen. pl.) is commented on as '*dhīrāṇām*' (v. 28).

50) *ṣaḍindriya-viṣaya*, i.e. *ṣaḍāyatanāni*, namely: *rūpa*, *śabda*, *gandha*, *rasa*, *sparśitavya* and *dharma*, whose account is given in the next verse.

In the pure scent of the Buddhas' morality,
In tasting [51] of the taste of the great, sublime and highest Doctrine, // 19 //
In the enjoyment of the pleasurable touch of meditation,
And in the cognition of doctrine [52], profound by its nature;
[But], being the Highest Truth, the thicket [53] of quite subtle thinking [54],
The Tathāgata himself, like space, is of no visible mark [55]. // 20 //

The meaning of these three *ślokas*, in brief, is to be known by the following 8 verses.

The function of the twofold Wisdom
In short, is to be known as follows:
[One is] the fulfilment of the Body of [innate] liberation,
[The other is] the purification of the Absolute Body [56]. // 21 //
The Body of innate liberation and the Absolute Body,
[Although] being two [in their functions], are to be known as one,

51) *vindana*, T. *myaṅ* (enjoying), C. 與 (giving).

52) *naya*, T. *tshul*, C. 法 (*dharma*).

53) *gahvara*, C. 稠林, for which T. *bde-mdsad* (*śaṃkaraṃ*). C. om. *paramārtha*.

54) '*sūkṣmacintā-paramârtha-gahvaraṃ*' for the whole line.

55) *nimitta-varjitaṃ*, T. *rgyu-mtshan rnams daṅ bral*. C. 佛離虛空相 is a misreading (reading '*tathāgato viyomanimitta-varjitaḥ*). It should be '佛虛空離相'.

56) *muktikāya*, T. *grol-baḥi sku* (*ḥgro-ba* in D. is probably a mistake), C. 解脱身; and *dharmakāya*, C. 真法身, respectively.

These two *kāyas* show the two aspects of the *dharmakāya*, the Absolute itself, in regard to its function. Namely, the *dharmakāya* in its result aspect (III. *phalârtha*) is characterized as '*vimuktir visaṃyogaś ca*'. Here the *muktikāya* seems to represent *vimukti* (as the characteristic common to *samalā tathatā* and *nirmalā tathatā*), and the *dharmakāya*, *visaṃyoga* (as the characteristic unique to *bodhi*). Consequently, these two also correspond to the *prakṛtistha-gotra* and the *samudānīta-gotra*, respectively. From the aspect of '*vimukti*', the function of the *dharmakāya* is characterized as the perfection of Enlightenment, while from the aspect of '*visaṃyoga*', its function is characterized as the purification of itself. As far as this characterization is concerned, these two functions represent *svârthasaṃpatti*. So does the AĀS say (472 *c* 何者自利,圓滿解脱身,持淨法身,滅煩惱障一切智障,是名自利). But if we apply the character of the *samudānītagotra* to the second function, it may be termed *parârthasaṃpatti* because the *dharmakāya* as *samudānītagotra* is the cause of the *rūpakāya* which works for *parârtha*. See my Introduction.

Because they are free from passions and all-pervading,
And are the immaculate substratum [57]. // 22 //
It is 'free from passions'
Since the Defilements are resisted along with impressions;
Wisdom is considered as 'pervading'
Since it has neither attachment nor hindrance. // 23 //
The 'absolute immutability' is caused
By its nature of imperishability [58],
[Here] 'imperishability' is a general statement [59],
Which is explained by the words, 'everlasting', etc. // 24 //
The 'Evanescence' [60] is to be known as of four kinds,
Being the counterparts of 'everlasting' and the rest,
[They are namely]: 'putridity', 'disease',
'Annihilation' and 'death in an inconceivable way' [61]. // 25 //
Because of their absence, it is known to be
'Everlasting', 'quiescent', 'constant' and 'unchangeable',
And this immaculate Wisdom is the 'substratum',
Since it is the support [62] of [all] the pure elements. // 26 //
Just as space, being itself of no cause,
Is the cause of perceiving, hearing and so on
Of form, of sounds, of tastes, of smells,
Of things touchable and of substances respectively, // 27 //
In the same way, the twofold [apparitional] Body [63],
On account of its connection with [64] the undefiled character,

[57] *anāsravatva* (C. 無漏) *vyāpitva* (C. 遍至) and *asaṃskṛtapadatva* (C. 究竟無爲). Cf. AĀS, 自利不相離三功德分 (*svârtha* is *avinirbhāga* from 3 *guṇas*; namely): 一者無漏 二者遍滿 三者無爲.

[58] *avināśitva*, T. *ḥjig-pa med-pa*, C. 不失.

[59] *uddeśa*, C. 根本 (fundamental statement).

[60] *nāśa*, C. 失.

[61] *pūti*, T. *myags*, C. 死; *vikṛti*, T. *rnam-ḥgyur*, C. 無常; *ucchitti*, T. *chad-pa*, C. 轉; and *acintya-namana-cyuta*, T. *bsam mi-khyab-par ḥpho-ba*, C. 不可思議退, respectively.

[62] *āspada*, T. *rten*, C. 體.

[63] For *kāyadvaya*, C. 法身. Does it mean *muktikāya* and *dharmakāya*? But see Note 44. It may be more natural to regard it as the twofold *rūpakāya*. C. interpretation is, however, not untenable, since the Kārikā refers only to *Buddhatva* and the *rūpakāya* is nothing but a term for *buddhatva* or *dharmakāya* when it works for *parârtha*.

[64] *yogataḥ*, T *sbyor-bas* (by means of). C. has no equivalent word. C. shortens this verse omitting many words.

Is the cause for wise men[65] to give rise to
Immaculate virtues in the objects of sense-organs. // 28 //

(V) YOGA[66]

It is said that the Buddha has the character of space[67]. This refers specially[68] to the absolute and exclusive character of the Buddha. So it is said[69]:

"If the Tathāgata could be recognized merely by the 32 marks of a superman, the universal monarch, too, would turn to be a Buddha".

Now, there is one *śloka* about the highest character[70] in reference to the subject of 'union'.

(Kārikā 7)

Being inconceivable, eternal and ever-lasting,
Being quiescent, constant, and perfectly pacified,
Being all-pervading and apart from discrimination,
The pure and immaculate Buddhahood is like space,
It has neither attachment nor hindrance anywhere,
And, being devoid of rough[71] sensation,
It can be neither perceived nor cognized. // 29 //

Now, the meaning of this *śloka* is, in short, to be known by the following 8 verses.

The [fulfilment of] one's own aim and of that of others
Are represented by the Bodies of Liberation and of the Absolute[72];

[65] *dhīra* (= *dhīmat*,) T. *bstan-pa* (*śāstṛ*).

[66] Cf. AĀS 472 *c* . . . (6) 相應.

[67] See above (v. 20): *tathāgata-vyoma*. e.g. JĀA 243 *c*. Also see Chap. III (on the 18 Exclusive Properties).

[68] *abhisaṃdhāya*, T. *dgoṅs-pas*, C. 依 (?).

[69] The *Vajracchedikāsūtra*, Skt. p. 42-43; C. *Taisho*, XII, p. 752 *a*.

[70] *paramārthalakṣaṇa*, T. *don dam-paḥi mtshan-ñid*, C. 第一義相.

[71] *paruṣa*, T. *rtsub*, C. (麤) 澁.

[72] See note XIII-55.

On this foundation [73] of one's own aim and of that of others
There is the 'union' of properties, 'inconceivable' and others.
// 30 //

Buddhahood is accessible only to the Wisdom of the Omniscient,
And is not the object of the 3 [kinds of ordinary] knowledge [74],
Therefore, it is to be known as 'inconceivable'
[Even] for those people of intellect [75]. // 31 //
Being of subtle character, it is not the object of study,
Being the Highest Truth, it is not the object of thought,
And, being the impenetrable Absolute Essence [76],
It is not accessible to the mundane meditation and the like, // 32 //
Because it has never been seen before by ordinary persons,
Like the visible forms [77] for those who are born blind, nor even by the Saints [78],
Like the disk of the sun for infants lying in their mother's bed [79].
// 33 //
It is 'eternal', as it is devoid of birth;
It is 'everlasting', since it does not disappear;
It is 'quiescent', because it is free from dualism,
And is 'constant' because of endurance of Reality [80]. // 34 //
It is 'perfectly pacified' as being the Truth of Extinction,
It is 'all-pervading' since it cognizes everything;
It is 'non-discriminative' as it has no insistence [81];
And 'has no attachment' since it rejects defilements. // 35 //
Being purified from all the obstructions of Ignorance,
It 'has no hindrance' in regard to everything [knowable];

73) *āśraya*, C. 依 (depending upon *svaparârtha*).

74) *trijñāna*, i.e. *śruti–cintā–bhāvanāmaya–jñāna*.

75) *jñānadehin*, (= *dhīmat*), T. *ye–śes–lus–can*, C. om.

76) *dharmatā–gahvaratvataḥ*, T. *chos–ñid zab phyir*, C. 以出世深密 (*lokottara–gahvarataḥ*). For *gahvara*, T. *zab*, C. 深密.

77) So T. *gzugs*, and C. 色. Probably the reading is '*rūpa*' instead of '*kāya*' (or *kāya* in the sense of *rūpakāya*; collective of forms).

78) C. regards this '*ārya*' as those Saints who belong to Śrāvaka- & Pratyekabuddha–*yāna*.

79) *sūtikā–sadma–sthita*, acc. to T. *btsas–paḥi khyim–(g)nas*. The reading is therefore to be '*sadma*' instead of '*madhya*'. C. om. all these words. Cf. ŚMS 222 *a*: 如七日嬰兒不見日輪.

80) As for these 4 epithets, see VIII–(IX C). (vv. I, 80–82).

81) *apratiṣṭhāna*, T. *gnas–pa med*[*–pa*], C. 不住.

Being of soft and light-moving nature [82],
It is 'devoid of rough sensation'. // 36 //
Being immaterial, it cannot be perceived,
And being of no [visible] mark [83], it is 'incognizable';
It is 'pure' since it is pure by nature,
And is 'immaculate' because of its removal of pollutions [84]. // 37 //

(VI) VṚTTI [85]

Now again it should be known that this Buddhahood, due to its possession of properties uncommon to others, manifests itself, though by means of a manifestation which is inseparable from its immutable qualities like space, still in the forms of three [86] immaculate bodies, viz. 'the Body of Absolute Essence (*svābhāvika*)', 'the Body of Enjoyment (*sāṃbhogya*)', and 'the Apparitional Body (*nairmāṇika*) [87], with various inconceivable appliances [88] like the Great skilful means, Great Compassion, and Wisdom, in order to be the support [89] of the welfare and happiness of all living beings, as long as the world exists, without cessation, without interruption, and with no effort.

So, with reference to this subject of 'manifestation', there are 4 *ślokas* about the distinction of [three kinds of] Buddha's Body.

[82] *mṛdu-karmaṇya-bhāvataḥ*, C. 柔軟 (as S.). But for this line, T. *gñis-med las-su ruṅ-baḥi phyir* (*advaya-karmaṇi bhāvataḥ*).

[83] *animitta*, T. *mtshan-ma med*, C. 離相.

[84] AĀS makes 19 *dharmas* possessed by *bodhi* out of this passage. Namely: 1) 不可思量 (*acintya*); 2) 微細 (*sūkṣma*); 3) 真實 (*paramārtha*); 4) 道理甚深 (*gambhīrya-naya*, = *dharmatā-gahvara?*); 5) 不可見 (*adṛśya*); 6) 難通達 (*duṣprativedha*); 7) 常 (*nitya*); 8) 在 (*dhruva?*); 9) 寂 (*praśānta*); 10) 恒 (*śāśvata*); 11) 淸凉 (*śiva*); 12) 遍滿 (*vyāpi*); 13) 無分別 (*avikalpa*); 14) 無著 (*asaṅga* or *asakta*); 15) 無礙 (*apratigha*); 16) 隨順 (*anusāra?*); 17) 不可執 (*agrāhya*); 18) 大淨 (*śubha*); 19) 澄淸 (*amala*). Of them, 6) and 16) have no equivalent in the *Ratna*.

[85] Cf. AĀS 473 *a*, BGŚ 809 *a*–811 *a* (under Avikāra).

[86] '... *amalai stribhiḥ*' should be corrected into '... *amalais tribhiḥ*'. (In Devanāgrī script, they should be written without separation).

[87] For these three, C. 實佛, 受法樂佛 & 化身佛.

[88] *parikarman*, T. *yoṅs-su sbyoṅ-ba*, C. 業. Against J's note, T. (D) has *sñiṅ-rje* between *thabs chen-po* and *śes-rab*.

[89] *ādāna-nimitta*, T. *sgrub-paḥi rgyu*, C. 與...相.

(Kārikās 8–11)

That which has neither beginning, middle nor end,
Is indivisible [90], non-dual, liberated in three ways [91],
Immaculate and non-discriminative, . . .
That represents the nature of the Absolute Essence [92],
And is perceived by the Saints [93],
Who are concentrating their mind, striving after it [94]; // 38 //
This [Absolute Essence] is nothing but the pure Essence [95] of the Tathāgatas,
Which is endowed with properties, inconceivable, unequalled,
Innumerable, and surpassing the sands of the Gaṅgā in number
And has rooted out [96] all the defects along with impressions. // 39 //
One who exerts in concentrating for [97] the liberation of the world,
With the body [98] in the form of different coloured rays of the Highest Doctrine,
Has a resemblance, in his acts, to the king of wish-fulfilling gems,
Appearing in various forms, which, however, have not their own substance [99]. // 40 //
That which is the cause [100], in various worlds,

[90] For *abhinna*, C. 不可壞.

[91] *tridhā vimuktam*. T. as S. And this reading is supported by the commentary verse (v. 45: *kleśa-jñeya-samāpatti-trayāvaraṇa-niḥsritam*). But C. 遠離於三界 (*tridhātu-muktam*), and I guess this was the original reading.

[92] For '*yaṃ dharmadhātu-svabhāvam*', C. 此甚深境界 and adds 非二乘所知 (unknown to *Śrāvaka-* and *Pratyekabuddha-yānikas*).

[93] *yogin*, T. *rnal-ḥbyor-pa*, C. 其勝三昧慧如是人 (connecting with *samāhita*).

[94] For '*tat-prayatnāḥ*', T. *de rtogs-pa* (*tad-adhigacchanti*) (connecting *tad* with '*yaṃ dharmadhātusvabhāvam*'). But S. seems better. C. has no equivalent word.

[95] *dhātu*, T. *dbyiṅs*, C. 體. For '*tathāgatānām amalaḥ . . . dhātuḥ*', C. 如來妙色身清淨無垢體 (insertion of '妙色身' (*rūpakāya*) suggests that C. regards this verse as referring to *saṃbhogakāya*).

[96] *unmūlita*, T. *rnam-spaṅs-pa*, C. 遠離.

[97] For *samāhṛta-udyamaḥ*, T. *grub-la brtson-pa* (*siddhyudyamaḥ*), C. 常無休息.

[98] *vigraha*, T. *sku*, C. 體.

[99] All *bhāvas* are of *niḥsvabhāva*, but are inseparable from the Absolute. See the next verse.

[100] *nidāna*, T. *rgyu*, C. om.

For advancing into the Quiescent Path[101],
For bringing to full development and for giving prophecy,
That is the Apparitional Form [of the Buddha][102],
Which also abides[103] always in the Absolute Essence[104],
As the visible forms in the element of space. // 41 //

The summarized meaning of these 4 *ślokas* are to be known by the following 20 verses:

That which is called Buddhahood
Is the Omniscience of the Self-born,
The highest Nirvāṇa[105], and the inconceivable Arhatship[106],
Which is realized through self-introspection. // 42 //
This [Buddhahood] manifests itself in the variety
Of three Bodies, the Body of the Absolute Essence, etc.,
Represented by the quality of Profundity,
Of Magnificence, and of Magnanimity, [respectively]. // 43 //

a) The Body of the Absolute Essence (*svābhāvika–kāya*)[107].

Here, the Body of the Absolute Essence
Of the Buddha, in short, is to be known
As of five characteristics,
And being possessed of five kinds of properties. // 44 //
It is 'immutable' and 'indivisible',
Is 'devoid of the two extremities',
And is 'delivered from the 3 Obstructions'
Of defilement, ignorance and distraction[108]. // 45 //

101) *śāntipatha* (C. 寂靜處) means *nirvāṇa*.

102) *bimba*, T. *gzugs*, C. 如來鏡像身 (= *nirmāṇakāya*).

103) *avaruddha* (enclosed in), T. *gnas* (*avasthita*, abiding in). But C. 不離.

104) *atra*, in the sense 'in *dharmadhātu–svabhāva*' (v. 38). C. [不離] 本體.

105) *nirvṛtiḥ paramā*, T. *mchog–tu mya–ṅan–ḥdas*. C. takes *paramā* separately and regards it as indicating '*paramârtha*'.

106) For *acintyaprāpti*, both T. & C. read as *acintyârhattva* (T. *bsam–med dgra–bcom*, C. 不思議法應供), which is to be accepted here. Consequently, '*pratyātmaveditā*' is to be corrected into '*pratyātmaveditam*'.

107) Commentary on vv. 39, 40.

108) This is the first appearance of the '*trayâvaraṇa*' theory in the text. The third *āvaraṇa*, i.e. *samāpatty–āvaraṇa* means the obstructions on account of *samādhi*, which is peculiar to the Bodhisattva.

Being free from all stains and thought-construction,
And being accessible to the Saints,
It is 'radiant and pure'
Owing to the nature of the Absolute Essence[109]. // 46 //
Immeasurable', 'innumerable', 'inconceivable', 'incomparable'
And representing 'the highest point of purity';
The Body of the Absolute Essence is endowed
With[110] these [5] kinds of virtuous qualities[111]. // 47 //
Being magnificent[112] and numberless,

[109] These are the 5 *lakṣaṇas*, namely: 1) *asaṃskṛta*; 2) *asaṃbhinna*; 3) *antadvaya-vivarjita*; 4) *trayâvaraṇa-niḥsṛta*; & 5) *prabhāsvaraṃ viśuddhaṃ ca*. For them, AĀS: 1) 無爲; 2) 不相離; 3) 離二邊; 4) 脫一切障; 5) 自性清淨 (473 *a*); and BGŚ: 1) 無爲相; 2) 無一異相 (無別異); 3) 離二邊相; 4) 離障相; 5) 淸淨相 (809 *a*–810 *b*, with a detailed explanation).

The last one is not clear. T. regards '*prabhāsvaraṃ*' as the fifth *lakṣaṇa* and reads '*viśuddha*' in the ablative, and thus makes 5 reasons for these 5 *lakṣaṇas*, but the concordance between each *lakṣaṇa* and its reason is uncertain. C. reads as S., except for the omission of '*avikalpatvād*' (the second *pada*, 故聖人境界, should be '聖人境界故'). BGŚ clearly mentions the 5 reasons in accordance with the 5 *lakṣaṇas*: 1) *asaṃskṛtam, dharmadhātusvabhāvataḥ* (自性故); 2) *abhinnam, avikalpatvāt* (無分別故); 3) *antadvayavivarjitam, yogīnāṃ gocaratvataḥ* (聖智境界故); 4) *āvaraṇaniḥsṛtam, prabhāsvaratayā* (自性淸淨故); 5) *visuddhaṃ, vaimalyād* (究竟淸淨故). (The last two reasons should be interchanged).

There seems to be confusion of the word arrangement in v. 46, but as it is difficult to establish which is the original reading, the present translation is done according to the Skt. text. For the reference, however, I will suggest below the most reasonable rendering of this verse:

And (5) it is 'pure' (*viśuddha*);
Because it is the nature of the Absolute Essence (1),
Because it is non-discriminative (2),
Because it is the acting sphere of the Saints (3),
Because it is free from stains (*vimala*), (4),
And because it is radiant by nature (*prabhāsvara*), (5) respectively.

[110] T. adds '*yaṅ-dag-par*' (*samyak*) before '*yukta*'.

[111] 1) *aprameya*; 2) *asaṃkhya*; 3) *acintya*; 4) *asama*; & 5) *viśuddhipāramiprātpi*, respectively. For these 5 *guṇas*, AĀS, 不可量, 不可數, 難思, 不共, & 究章清淨; BGŚ, 不可量, 不可數, 不可思, 無與等, & 究竟淸淨 (810 *b–c*).

[112] *udāra*, T. *rgya-che*, C. 快.

Being inaccessible to investigation,
Being unique[113] and devoid of the defiling forces,
It is 'immeasurable' and so on, respectively[114]. // 48 //

b) The Body of Enjoyment (*sāṃbhōgika-kāya*)[115].

It manifests itself the Doctrine, owing to its nature[116]
Of enjoying the Doctrine in various forms;
Being the natural outflow[117] of pure Compassion,
It works uninterruptedly for the sake of living beings; // 49 //
It fulfils the aim according to the wish
Without thought-construction and with no effort;
[By these points] the Body of Enjoyment is characterized[118]
Due to its power like that of the wish-fulfilling gems. // 50 //
In teaching, in the visible form, in acting ceaselessly,
And acting with no artificial effort[119],
And in its appearance of illusion[120],
The variety[121] of [its manifestation] is said to be 5-fold. // 51 //
Just as a gem, being dyed with various colours,
Does not make manifest its real essence[122];

113) C. om. *kaivalya* for which T. has *ḥbaḥ-shig*. It means 'being apart from all'.

114) C. adds '不離報' after *kramāt* (次第), whose meaning is not clear to me ('報' = *saṃbhoga* ?).

115) Commentary on v. 40.

116) *rūpa*, T. *raṅ-bshin* (in the sense of '*svarūpa*'?). C. for this line, 受種種法味, 示現諸妙色 (*vicitradharmarasasaṃbhoga-rūpâvabhāsataḥ*).

117) For *niṣyanda*, C. 習氣.

118) *vyavasthiti*, T. *rnam-par gnas*, C. [受樂佛] 如是 (thus is *sāṃbhogya-kāya*). AĀS makes 5 *guṇas*, possessed by *sāṃbhoga-kāya*, out of these two verses, namely: 1) 無分別; 2) 無功用心 (*anābhoga*); 3) 稱衆生意作利益 (*sattvārthakriyā*); 4) 與法身不相離 (*dharmakāyâvinirbhāga*); and 5) 恒遍一時不捨衆生 (*nitya-vyāpi & sattvânupekṣā*)

119) *anabhisaṃskṛti*, T. *mṅon-par ḥdu-byed med-pa*, C. 休息隱沒 (for which the equivalent in S. in uncertain). *deśana* (teaching) in neuter stem is notable.

120) *atatsvabhāvâkhyāna*, T. *de-yi ṅo-bo mi-ston(-pa)*, C. 示現不實體. For these 5 appearances, BGŚ & AĀS offer no reference.

121) *citratā* T. *sna-tshogs*. C. 自在 [*vibhutva* ?].

122) *atatbhāva*, C. [異本生諸相] 一切皆不實. T. adds *bhāsa*(*snaṅ*) in order to make the meaning clear.

Similarly, the Lord [123] never shows its real natuie,
Though it appears in various forms, according to the conditions of the living beings. // 52 //

c) The Apparitional Body (*nairmāṇika-kāya* [124]).

[The Buddha], being the knower of the world [125],
Perceiving fully the world, with Great Compassion,
Manifests himself [126] in various apparitional forms,
Without being separated from his Absolute Body. // 53 //
The [various] previous births [127],
The birth in the Tuṣita-heaven [128], and descent from it [129],
The entrance into the womb [130], and the birth [in this world] [131],
The skilfulness in various arts and works [132], // 54 //
Pleasurable entertainments among ladies in the harem [133],

[123] *vibhu*, T. *khyab-bdag*, C. 如來.

[124] Commentary on v. 41.

[125] *lokavid* (an epithet of the Buddha), T. *ḥjig-rten-mkhyen*. The whole verse is missing in C. O regards this verse as explaining *saṃbhogakāya*.

[126] The word '*darśayati*' is suplied from v. 56. The following (vv. 54–56) are the list of Buddha's '*mahāvastu*' in the world, whose number is counted 14 according to BGŚ (十四事). Hereafter. these 14 will be mentioned in the Note one by one along with their equivalent in BGŚ (810 *c*) and AĀS (473 *a*).

[127] *jātakāni* (1), BGŚ 本生; AĀS 本生之事; T. *skye-ba*, but connecting with next one and reading '*jātakâbhyupapattiṃ* (*skye-ba mṅon-par skye-ba daṅ*). '*jātakāny-upapattiṃ ca*' is missing in C.

[128] *upapattiṃ ca tuṣiteṣu* (2), BGŚ 生於兜率天, AĀS 昇兜率天. T. connects '*tuṣita*' with next one.

[129] *cyutiṃ tataḥ* (= *tuṣitāt*) (3), BGŚ 處於中陰 (abiding midway between Tuṣita and this world), AĀS 從彼天下; T. *dgaḥ-ldan-nas ni ḥpho-ba*, C. 從兜率陀退.

[130] *garbhâvakramaṇa* (4), T. *lhums-su ḥjug*, C. 次第入胎; BGŚ 入胎, AĀS 降神母胎.

[131] *janman* (5), T. *bstams-pa*, C. 生; BGŚ 出胎, AĀS 初生出胎.

[132] *śilpasthānāni kauśalam* (6), T. *gzo-yi gnas-la mkhas-pa*, C. 習學諸伎藝; BGŚ 學技能, AĀS 受學十八明處 (18 *vidyās*). AĀS inserts one more before (6): 俱摩羅位 (*kumārasthāna*). C. (嬰兒) and BGŚ (童子) seem to support this reading. For *śilpasthāna* the Pāli equivalent is *sippaṭṭhāna* (PTS Dic. s. v.), of which the number is often mentioned as 8, 12, or 18.

[133] *antaḥpuraratikrīḍā* (7), T. *btsun-moḥi ḥkhor-gyis dkyes-rol*, C. 嬰兒入王宮; BGŚ 童子遊戲, AĀS 諸戲遊於後園.

The renouncement of the world[134], practice of asceticism[135],
Passage to the Excellent Seat of Enlightenment[136],
The conquest over the army of Evil Demons[137], // 55 //
The [acquisition of] Enlightenment[138],
Setting into motion the wheel of the Doctrine[139],
And the departure into Nirvāṇa[140]; . . . all of them
He shows in the impure worlds[141], as long as they exist. // 56 //
[The Buddha], the knower of means[142], creates an aversion
To the Three Worlds among the living beings
By the words, 'evanescent', 'suffering', 'non-substantial';
And by the word 'quiescent', he leads[143] them into Nirvāṇa.
// 57 //

Those who have entered the way to Quiescence[144],
And who imagine that they have attained Nirvāṇa[145],

[134] *naiṣkramya* (8), T. *ṅes-ḥbyuṅ*, C. 厭離諸欲相出家; BGŚ & AĀS, 出家. C. 厭離諸欲相 (devoid of desires) for *naiṣkramya* shows that this term came out of Pāli *nekkhamma*, which is, in its turn, combined in meaning with *nikkāma* (S. *niṣkāma*). In Pāli, 'renunciation or to become a monk' is often explained as 'to reject the worldly desire, lust, etc.'.

[135] *duḥkhacārikā* (9), T. *dkaḥ-ba spyod-pa*, C. 行苦行: BGŚ & AĀS, 苦行.

[136] *bodhimaṇḍôpasaṃkrānti* (10), T. *byaṅ-chub-sñiṅ-por gśegs-pa*, C. 往詣於道場; BGŚ 詣菩提樹, AĀS 於道場. C. adds '推問諸外道' (asking for the way to various *tīrthikas*) before this. For *bodhimaṇḍa*, T. *byaṅ-chub-sñiṅ-po*, C. 道場. This does not mean the actual obtaining of Enlightenment.

[137] *mārasainyapramadana* (11), T. *bdud sde ḥjoms*, C. 降伏諸魔衆; BGŚ 破魔軍. AĀS om.

[138] *saṃbodhi* (12), T. *rdsogs-par ni byaṅ-chub* (T. seems to have combined this with the next one), C. 成大妙覺尊; BGŚ 成佛, AĀS 成佛道.

[139] *dharmacakra* (13), T. *chos-kyi ḥkhor-lo*, C. 轉無上法輪; BGŚ 轉法輪, AĀS 波羅捺轉妙法輪 (setting *dharmacakra* forth at Varanasi).

[140] *nirvāṇâdhigamakriyā* (14), T. *mya-ṅan-ḥdas-par gśegs-mdsad*, C. 入無餘涅槃; BGŚ 般涅槃, AĀS 堅固林般涅槃那 ('堅固林' = *Sālavana*, indicates Kuṣinagara).

[141] *kṣetra*, T. *shiṅ*, C. 國. For *kṣetra apariśuddha*, AĀS 穢佛土.

[142] *upāyavid*, (used as an epithet of the Buddha), C. 方便智慧力.

[143] *pratārayati*, T. *rab-ḥjug*, C. 入.

[144] *śāntimārga*, T. *shi-baḥi lam*, C. 寂滅道

[145] '*prāpta-nirvāṇa-saṃjñinaḥ*' would be better, since T. & C. agree with it. (T. *mya-*

Them he diverts [146] from their former prejudice,
Through the teaching of the True Doctrines [147]
In the *Saddharmapuṇḍarīka* and other Sūtras,
And, embracing Wisdom and Skilful Means,
Makes them mature in the Ultimate Vehicle [148],
And gives prophecy for them to attain the Highest Enlightenment. // 58–59 //

Being subtle, accomplishing the power [149]
And toiling excessively [150] for the company [151] of ordinary beings, —
In these points [the Buddha] should be known, respectively,
As the Profound, the Magnificent and the Magnanimous. // 60 //
Here, the first Body is the Absolute Body,
And the latter two are the Bodies in visible forms [152],
These latter [153] appear on the basis of the former,
As the visible forms appear in space. // 61 //

(VII) NITYA [154]

Now this threefold Body made manifest in order to be the support for the weal and happiness of the world, has an 'eternal' character [in its manifestation]. With reference to this subject, we have one *śloka*.

ṅan-ḥdas-thob ḥdu-śes-can. C. 言我得涅槃). C. adds '諸聲聞人等有是虛妄相'.

146) *nivartya*, T. *bzlog ste*, C. 廻. For *grāha* C. 虛妄心'.

147) *dharmatattva*, T. *chos-kyi de-ñid*, C. 如實法.

148) Denoting the Mahāyāna. *uttamayāna*, T. *theg-pa mchog*, C. 上乘.

149) *prabhāva*, T. *mthu*, C. 大勢力. T. *sna-tshogs* for *sampatti* is probably a misreading for *phun-tshogs*.

150) *ativāhana*, T. *rab-ḥdren*, C. 過嶮難道 (surpassing the treacherous path).

151) *sārtha*. T. *don-mthun*, C. 衆生 (*sattva*). *sārtha* means a caravan or traders. Therefore, analogically C. interpretation of *ativāhana* seems better.

152) *rūpakāya*, T. *gzugs-kyi sku*, C. 色佛身. C. reads '第二' (the second) for *paciśmau*.

153) *antya*. lit. the last. (C. & T. as S.). From the context, it should be 'the latter two'.

154) Cf. AĀS 473 *a* (無上菩提常住法), BGŚ 811 *a–b*.

(Kārikā 12)

Having infinite causes [for the attainment of his state] [155],
Having an endless number of living beings to convert,
Being endowed with Compassion, Miraculous Powers [156], Wisdom
and Bliss [157],
Governing all the elements, vanquishing the demon of Death,
And representing non-substantiality [158],
The lord of the World [159] is eternal. // 62 //

The summarized meaning of this [*śloka*] is to be known by the following 6 verses.

Casting off his body, life and property,
He has preserved [160] the Highest doctrine;
For the benefits of all living beings,
He fulfills [161] his first vow [162]. // 63 //
In his Buddhahood, there is made manifest
Compassion, pure and immaculate [163],
He shows his [four] bases of Miraculous Powers [164],
By which power he abides in the world [165]; // 64 //

155) *hetv-ānantyāt*, C. 以修無量因.

156) *ṛddhi*, T. *ḥphrul*, C. 如意.

157) *sampatti*, T. *phun-tshogs*, C. 成就. Acc. to the comm., *sampatti* stands for '*sukha-sampatti* through meditation'.

158) *naiḥsvābhāvya*, C. 體寂靜 (*svabhāva-praśānta* ?), which is explained in the comm. as being *asaṃskṛta* and *ādipraśānta*.

159) *lokanātha*, T. *ḥjig-rten-mgon-po*, C. 世尊.

160) *saṃgraha*, T. *ḥdsin*, C. 攝取. This *saddharma-saṃgraha* is the 1st cause standing for *hetv-ānantyāt* in the Kārikā.

161) *uttaraṇa*, T. *mthar-ḥbyin*, C. 究竟滿.

162) *ādipratijñā*, T. *daṅ-poḥi dam-bcas*, C. 本願 (*pūrvapraṇidhi*). Cf. BGŚ: 初發心時 結四弘誓願 起十無盡大願: "若衆生不盡, 我願亦無盡, 衆生若盡, 我願乃盡...".
This stands for (2) *sattvadhātv-akṣayatvāt*.

163) For (3) *kārṇya(-yogāt)*.

164) *ṛddhi-pāda*, T. *rdsu-ḥphrul rkaṅ-ba*, C. 四如意. There are said to be 4, namely: 1) *chanda*; 2) *citta*; 3) *vīrya*; & 4) *mīmāṃsā*. Cf. Mvyut. 40.

165) So C. (以彼力住世). S. *tair avasthitaśaktitaḥ*, T. *de-yis gnas-par spyod-paḥi phyir*. For *śakti*, T. reads as if *caryā*. This is (4) *ṛddhi-(yogāt)*.

Owing to his Wisdom, he is liberated from
The dualistic conception of Saṃsāra and Nirvāṇa[166];
By his constant practice of the inconceivable[167] meditation,
He partakes of the complement of bliss[168], // 65 //
While he is acting in the world,
He is unaffected by the worldly elements[169];
Having attained the state of quiescence and immortality,
He leaves no room for [the activity of] the demon of Death[170];
// 66 //

Being of an immutable nature,
The Lord is perfectly pacified from the outset[171];
And he gives a refuge for those who have no shelter[172],
Because of these [10] points, he is 'eternal'. // 67 //
The first 7 of these motives show
The eternity of the Preceptor[173] in his Apparitional Body,
The latter 3 demonstrate the eternity
From the viewpoint of the Absolute Body. // 68 //

166) For (5) *jñāna(-yogāt)*.

167) For *acintya*, C. reads '*citta-*', but T. *bsam-yas*.

168) This is for (6) *saṃpatti-yogāt*. About *sukhasaṃpatti*, BGŚ: 安樂者,即是金剛心能除無明住地最後念無常苦,以無苦故,故名安樂.

169) *lokadharma*, C. 世法. See Note V-47. This is for (7) *dharmaiśvaryāt*.

170) For (8) *mṛtyumārāvabhaṅgāt*.

171) For (9) *naiḥsvabhāvāt*.

172) This is counted as the 10th cause, but has no correspondent term in the Kārikā. It seems the commentator made this meaning of *śaraṇa*, as the 10th cause, out of *lokanātha*. But BGŚ, though likewise counting 10 causes, omits this last one and counts '*samādhi*' independently out of *sukhasaṃpatti*. The 10 causes acc. to BGŚ are as follows:

1) 因緣無邊 (*hetvānantya*); 2) 衆生界無邊 (*sattvadhātvakṣaya*); 3) 大悲無邊 (*karuṇânantya*); 4) 如意無邊 (*ṛddhyānantya*), 5) 無分別智無邊 (*avikalpajñānânantya*); 6) 恒在禪定無數 (*sadā samādhānânumeya*); 7) 安樂淸凉 (*sukha & śiva*); 8) 行於世間而不染八法 (*loke vicarato aṣṭadharmair anupalepaḥ*); 9) 甘露寂靜遠離死魔 (*amṛta-śama-prāpti & mṛtyumārāvabhaṅga*); & 10) 本生本然無生無滅 (being as it is by nature, it is *anutpādânirodha*).

173) For *śāstṛ*, C. 善逝 (*sugata*).

(VIII) ACINTYA [174]

Now, this method of the attainment [of Buddhahood] by the Buddhas, which represents the 'Perfect Manifestation of the Basis' is to be understood as of inconceivable character. With reference to this 'inconceivability', we have one *śloka*.

(Kārikā 13)

Being unutterable, containing the Highest Truth,
Inaccessible to investigation and incomparable,
Being the supreme, and relating neither
To the Phenomenal World nor to Nirvāṇa [175],
The sphere of Buddha is inconceivable even for the Saints. // 69 //

The summarized meaning of this [*śloka*] is to be understood by the following 4 verses.

It is 'inconceivable' since it is unutterable;
It is 'unutterable' since it is the Highest Truth;
It is 'the Highest Truth', since it cannot be constructed by thought,
It is 'beyond investigation' as it is incomparable [176]; // 70 //
It is 'incomparable' since it is the supreme;
It is 'the supreme' since it is not included
[Either in the Phenomenal World or in Nirvāṇa];
'Not included' means the Buddha abides in neither of the two
And never regards [in a one-sided manner]
That Nirvāṇa is of merit and the other is of defect. // 71 //
Being subtle by the [first] 5 motives [177]
He is inconceivable in his Absolute Body,
And by the 6th, on account of his Apparitional Body,
He is inconceivable because of no identification [178]

[174] Cf. BGŚ 810 c f., AĀS 473 b.

[175] *bhava-śānty-anudgraha*, T. *srid-shis ma bsdus*, C. 不取有涅槃. This idea of 'not relating to both' is the expression of '*apratiṣṭhita-nirvāṇa*'. BGŚ 遠離生死涅槃二執. AĀS mentions these 6 as the causes of inconceivability.

[176] *vyupameya* (acc. to C. 無譬喩知). Though T. & S. agree in their reading '*vyanumeya*', the word '*vyupameya*' is more suitable here, since it is supported by the reading in the Kārikā: *upamā-nivṛttitaḥ*.

[177] From 'unutterable' to 'the supremacy', and the 6th is '*anudgraha*'.

[178] *atattvabhāvitva*, T. *de-yi dṅos-min* [*phyir*] (= *tadbhāvâbhāvāt*). Cf. v. 40: *vici-*

With either Nirvāṇa or Phenomenal World. // 72 //
Being endowed with the Highest Wisdom,
With the Great Compassion and other virtues,
The Buddha, who has attained the ultimate point of virtue,
Is inaccessible to human thought;
Therefore, this final stage of the Buddha
Is unknown even to the Great Sages [179]
Who have attained the stage of Initiation [180]. // 73 //

Finished is the second chapter entitled 'the Enlightenment' in the ANALYSIS OF THE GERM OF THE JEWELS, a Treatise on the Ultimate Doctrine of the Great Vehicle.

trabhāvo na ca tatsvabhāvān. But C. reads '以得自在故' (because of his obtaining *aiśvarya*).

179) *maharṣi.* Here '*maharṣi*', contrary to the common usage of this term for the Buddha, denotes the Bodhisattva of the highest rank.

180) *abhiṣeka*, T. *dbaṅ.* This *abhiṣekatā* or *abhiṣekaprāpta* was regarded in the old *bhūmi*-theory as the 10th and the highest stage of Bodhisattva, next to that of the Buddha, as in the case of the Mahāvastu, &c. On this point, this verse (v. 73) seems to be an old verse and is probably a quotation. The different usage of the term '*ṛṣi*' in this verse is also suggestive. C. om. this verse.

Chapter III.

THE PROPERTIES OF THE BUDDHA

3. BUDDHA-GUṆA [1]

XIV. GENERAL CHARACTERISTICS OF THE BUDDHA'S PROPERTIES

We have finished the explanation of 'the Reality free from Pollutions'. Hereafter, we shall speak of the 'Properties' which are based upon the Reality and are perfectly pure, being indivisible from Reality by nature [2] as the brightness, colour and shape of the jewel are inseparable from the latter. Therefore [3], immediately after [the exposition of the Reality], we have one *śloka* referring to the distinct characteristics [4] of the Buddha's Properties.

(Kārikā 1)

The aim of one's own and that of others,
[Consists in] the Body of the Highest Truth [5]
And the Worldly Emanations [6] based upon it;

1) Cf. AĀS Chap. IV (*Tathāgataguṇa-parivarta*), pp. 473 *c*–475 *c*, in which are mentioned 180 *āveṇikadharmas* including 32 *mahāpuruṣalakṣaṇas*, 80 *anuvyañjanas*, & 68 *dharmas*. Among this last group, 10 *balas*, 4 *vaiśāradyas*, and 18 *āveṇikadharmas* are counted besides 36 other *dharmas*.

2) *abhinna-prakṛtayaḥ* (Bahu. comp. m. pl. N). For this, T. reads as an instrumental case. *dbyer-med-paḥi raṅ-bshin-ñid-kyis.*

3) T. adds '*atas tad*', before '*anantaram*'. C. also adds '*ataḥ*' (以是義故). But, as we have the same construction in the beginning of Chap. IV, it is not necessary to change the Skt. text.

4) *guṇa-vibhāga.* The term '*vibhāga*' corresponds to '*prabheda*' in K 1.

5) From the point of meaning, the reading '*paramarthakāyatā*' of Ms. B. is preferable, though one syllable is in excess by adding '*–tā*'. It is sometimes allowable in such an old-style Kārikā to keep an irregular metre. But T. stands for the present Skt. text.

6) *saṃvṛtikāyatā*, T. *kun-rdsob-sku-ñid*, C. 世俗諦體.

Representing the state of Liberation and Maturation [7],
The result is endowed with Properties,
Which appear in 64 varieties. // 1 //

What is told by this *śloka*?

The Body which represents the Highest Truth
Is the support for the completion of one's own [aim]
And the support for the fulfilment of others' [aim] [8]
Is the Emanational Body [9] of the Buddha [10]. // 2 //
The first Body is endowed with properties,
[10] Powers and so forth, as [the result of] Liberation,
And the second one, with [32] marks of superman,
As the properties [obtained by] the Maturation [which follows after Liberation] [11]. // 3 //

7) *visaṃyoga*, T. *bral[-ba]*, C. 遠離; and *vipāka*, T. *rnam-par smin-pa*, C. 淳熟, respectively.

Here '*visaṃyoga-phala*' means the *dharmakāya* characterized as *āvaraṇadvaya-visaṃyoga* in Chap. II, while '*vipāka-phala*' means the *rūpakāya* characterized as the result obtained by causes (e.g. practices performed in the previous lives as in the case of *saṃbhoga-kāya*).

8) T. translates '*para*' by '*pha-rol*', but it should be '*gshan-gyi*'.

9) *sāṃketikaṃ vapuḥ*, T. *brda-yi sku*, C. 世俗體 (= *saṃvṛtikāya*).

10) *ṛṣi*, T. *draṅ-sroṅ*, C. 如來世尊. Both T. & C. regard '*ṛṣi*' as a plural.

11) *vaipākika*, T. *rnam-smin*, C. 彼受樂報體 (for *vaipākika-guṇa*) (that which represents the enjoyment of bliss as the reward of previous practices). As for the attribution of qualities to each of the two *kāyas*, i.e. *paramārthakāya* and *saṃvṛtikāya*, C. says that to the first body, infinite qualities of the Buddha are attributed, while to the second body, the 10 Powers, etc., are attributed. Attribution of the infinite qualities to the *paramārthakāya* accords with the *dharmakāya*'s 'union' with *paramārthalakṣaṇas* which are indivisible, unthinkable, etc. as told in Chap. II, but as far as the 64 Proerties are concerned, C. attribution does not match the commentary below.

XV. 64 PROPERTIES OF THE BUDDHA

Hereafter, the text refers to which are the [10] Powers and other properties and how they are to be understood [1].

Summary [2].

(Kārikā 2)

The Powers [of the Buddha] are like a thunderbolt,
In [breaking] the hindrance caused by ignorance,
His Intrepidity [3] in the assemblage is like that of a lion,
The Buddha's exclusive properties are like space,
And the two kinds of corporeal forms [4] of the Lord are
Like the moon and its reflection in the water. // 4 //

(I) THE 10 POWERS

It is said that the Buddha is possessed of [10] Powers (*balânvita*) [5].

(Kārikās 3–4)

The knowledge of the proper and improper place [6],
Of the result of former actions [7], and of the faculties [8],

1) The reading should be '*tathā-tad-adhikṛtya*' instead of '*tathatām adhikṛtya*'. T. *de-ltar deḥi dbaṅ-du byas-paḥo.*

2) T. & C. add the word '*uddāna*' before the next Kārikā. (T. *sdom-ni*, C. 畧說二偈.)

3) *viśāradatva*, T. *mi-ḥjigs-pa*, C. 無所畏.

4) *dvidhā-darśana*, T. *bstan-pa rnam gñis*, C. 二種見.

5) Prior to this sentence, C. inserts one sentence showing the following meaning: "Hereafter, the remaining verses in Chap. III expose the 64 properties of the Buddha, 10 Powers and the rest, according to the order mentioned in the previous Kārikā. Its detailed explanation is to be known according to the *Dhāraṇîśvararājasūtra*".

DRS has, however, no explanation about the 32 *mahāpuruṣalakṣaṇas.* Also C. changes the order of verses in the commentary (the Kārikā-text is arranged in the same order as the Skt. text), namely, the verses showing the similes, *vajra, siṃha, ākāśa* & *dakacandra*, are placed among commentary verses.

6) (1) *sthānâsthāna*, T. *gnas daṅ gnas-min*, C. 處非處. About the 10 *balas*, see Mvyut. & DRS 14 *c*–18 *a*, AĀS 475 *b*, RDS 34 *a*–*b*.

7) *vipāke ca karmaṇām* = (2) *karma-vipāka* [*-jñāna-bala*], T. *las rnams-kyi rnam-smin*, C. 果報…業 (reads *vipāka* and *karmaṇām* separately).

8) *indriya* = (3) *indriya-parāpara*[*-jñāna-bala*], T. *dbaṅ-po*, C. 諸根.

Of the component elements[9] and of the faith[10],
Of the path which leads to everywhere[11], // 5 //
Of the impurity and purity in contemplation, etc.[12],
Of the memory of the previous abodes[13],
Of the Divine Eyes[14], and of Quiescence[15],
Such are the ten kinds of Power [of the Buddha]. // 6 //

It is said, [these Powers are] like a thunderbolt[16].

(Kārikā 5)

[Being the power of knowing] about the proper and the improper,
About results, about elements and various faiths of the people,
About the path[17], purity and impurity,
About the complex of faculties, the memory of former abodes,
About the divine eyes, and how to destroy the Evil Influences;
The Powers pierce, break and cut down
The armour, the mountain fortress[18], and the tree of ignorance,
Therefore, they have resemblance to a thunderbolt[19]. // 7 //

(II) THE 4 FORMS OF INTREPIDITY[20]

It is said that [the Buddha] has attained the 4 kinds of intrepidity (*caturvaiśāradyaprāpta*).

(Kārikās 6–7)

[The Buddha's] Intrepidity is of four kinds, namely:
In his perfect Enlightenment of all the elements,

9) *dhātu* = (4) *nānā-dhātu-jñ.-b.*, T. *khams rnams*, C. 性.

10) *adhimukti* = (5) *nānâdhimukti-jñ.-b.*, T. *mos-pa*, C. 信.

11) *mārga sarvatragāmini* = (6) *sarvatragāmini-pratipaj-jñ.-b.*, T. *kun-ḥgroḥi lam*, C. 至處道.

12) *dhyānâdi-kleśa-vaimalya*, T. *bsam-gtan sogs ñon-moṅs dri-ma med-pa*, C. 離垢諸禪定 = *sarvadhyāna-vimokṣa-samādhi-samāpatti-saṃkleśa-vyavadāna-jñ.-b.* (7).

13) *nivāsânusmṛti*, T. *gnas-ni rjes-su dran-pa*, C. 憶念過去世 = (8) *pūrvanivāsânusmṛti-jñ.-b.*

14) *divyā-cakṣus*, T. *lha-yi mig*, C. 天眼 = (9) *cyuty-upapatti-jñ.-b.*

15) *śānti*, T. *shi-ba*, C. 寂靜 = (10) *āsravakṣaya-jñ.-b.*

16) C. puts this verse before v. 29.

17) *naya*. It stands for *mārga*.

18) *acala-prākāra*, T. *go-cha rtsig-brtan*, C. 山牆.

19) About the simile of '*vajra*', see v. I, 4.

20) *catur-vaiśāradya*. Cf. Mvyut. 8, DRS 18 *a*–19 *a*, AĀS 475, RDS 34 *b*.

In rejecting all obstacles,
In preaching the Path, and in acquiring the Extinction [21]. // 8 //
He himself knows [22] and causes others to know
All the things cognizable in all their forms;
He destroy everything to be rejected and causes others to reject them [23];
Serves [himself and lets others serve] in the method [24] to be practised;
And himself attains and causes others to attain
The Highest and Perfectly Pure State which is to be attained;
Thus, teaching the Truth [25] on account of himself and of others,
The Buddha [26], wherever he might be, is not paralyzed by fear [27]. // 9 //

It is said that [the intrepidity of the Buddha] is like [that of] a lion [28].

(Kārikā 8)

Just as the king of beasts in the forest
Has always no fear and acts without fear [29] among beasts,

[21] The 4 *vaiśāradyas* are as follows:

1) *vaiśāradya* in *sarvadharmâbhisaṃbodhi*, T. *chos-kun rdsogs-par byaṅ-chub*, C. 如實覺諸法;

2) *vaiś.* in *vibandha-pratiṣedha*, T. *gegs ni ḥgog-par byed-pa*, C. 遮諸闇道障;

3) *vaiś.* in *mārgâkhyāna*, T. *lam-ston-pa*, C. 說道;

4) *vaiś.* in *nirodhâpti*, T. *ḥgog-thob* (D's *ston* is probably a misreading), C. 得無漏 (*anāsravâpti*).

This order agrees with that in RDS, but Mvyut. and others put the 4th one before *vibandha-pratiṣedha*, under the name of *āsravakṣaya* (*-jñāna*).

[22] '*svayaṃ*' should be connected with '*jñānād*', and hence it is to be written with separation from *jñāpanād*.

[23] *hāni-kāraṇa-kṛti*, in the sense *hāni-* & *hānikāraṇa-kṛti*, T. *spaṅs daṅ spoṅ-mdsad*. C. reading in this and the next phrase is not understandable.

[24] *vidhi*. T. om. it. C. om. the whole phrase of '*sevye vidhau sevanāt*'. About the idea that '*mārga*' is '*sevya*', see Chap. IV, v. 52. Also these 4, i.e. *jñeya*, *heya*, *prāpya* and *sevya* correspond to each of the 4 *satyas*, respectively.

[25] *satya*, which denotes the 4-fold *āryasatya*.

[26] *ārya* (in plural), T. *draṅ-sroṅ* (= *ṛṣi*), C. om.

[27] *astambhita* [*-tva*], T. *thogs-pa med* (= *apratigha*), C. 無畏 (= *abhaya*). (Cf. *astambhin*, adj. not paralyzed by fear, BHS Dic.). For this, BHS & Pāli form is '*acchambhita*', which is parallel to '*abhīta*', '*asaṃtrasta*' or '*asaṃvigna*' (BHS Dic. s. v.) and more or less synonymous with '*viśārada*'. (*chambh* Skt. *stambh*, 'to fix').

[28] C. (in the commentary) puts the following verse before v. 32.

[29] *anuttarasta-gati*, T. *skrag-pa med-par rgyu-ba*, C. 自在 (for *gati*, T. *rgyu-ba* = *carati*).

Similarly, the lion who is the Lord of Sages
Abides among the assembly of attendance,
Independently[30], indifferently[31], with firmness and victory[32]. // 10 //

(III) THE 18 EXCLUSIVE PROPERTIES[33]

It is said that the Buddha is endowed with the 18 Exclusive Properties peculiar only to him (*aṣṭādaśâveṇikabuddhadharmasamanvāgata*).

(Kārikās 9–13)

With the Preceptor,
There is neither error[34] nor rough speech[35],
Neither loss of memory[36] nor distraction of mind[37],
Also, there is no pluralistic conception[38];— // 11 //
He is not indifferent, nor without consideration[39],
He knows no deprivation of his zeal[40], and of his energy[41],
Of his memory[42], of Transcendental Intellect[43], and of Liberation[44],

30) *svastha*, T. *legs-gnas* (= *susthita*), C. 善住 (*su-sthita*).

31) *nirāstha*, T. *ltos-med*, C. 不畏 (without fear).

32) *sthira-vikramastha*. T. regards it as one adjective (*brtan-paḥi rtsal* ...), but acc. to comm. verse (v. 34) and C., it is to be read '*sthirastha* & *vikramastha*'; C. 堅固 & 奮迅, respectively. For these 4 adjectives, see vv. 33–34.

33) For the 18 *āveṇikadharmas*, see Mvyut. 9, DRS 19 *a*–21*b*, AĀS 475 *b*, RDS 34 *b* f.

34) *skhalita*, T. *ḥkhrul*, C. 過 → *nāsti skhalitam* (1).

35) *ravita*, T. *ca-co*, C. 諍 → *n. ravitam* (2).

36) *muṣitā smṛti*, T. *dran-pa nams*, C. 妄念等失 → (3).

37) *asamāhita citta*, T. *mñam-par ma bshag thugs*, C. 不定散心 → (4).

38) *nānātva-saṃjñitā*, T. *ḥdu-śes sna-tshogs*, C. 種種諸想 → (5).

39) *upekṣâpratisaṃkhyā* (*apratisaṃkhyāya* is a BHS form for *-yāyām* (fem. loc.) of Skt.), T. *ma brtags btaṅ-sñoms*, C. 無作意護心 → (6).

40) *chanda*, T. *ḥdun-pa*, C. 欲 ... *nāsti chandasya* (or-*taḥ*) *hāniḥ* (7).

41) *vīrya*, T. *brtson-ḥgrus*, C. 精進 ... *n. vīryataḥ h.* (8).

42) *smṛti*, T. *dran-pa*, C. 念 ... *n. smṛteḥ h.* (9).

43) *prajñā*, T. *śes-rab*, C. 慧 ... *n. prajñayā h.* (10).

44) *vimukti*, T. *rnam-grol*, C. 解脫 ... *n. vimukter h.* (11).

And of the intuition of this liberation [45]; — // 12 //
His [three kinds of] acts [46] are preceded by Wisdom [47],
And his Intuition acts unimpededly in three states of time [48];
These 18 and others [49] are the Properties
Of the Preceptor, which are not common to others. // 13 //
The Sage has neither error [50] nor rough speech,
Neither loses [his memory] nor distracts his mind [51],
Has neither pluralistic views [52] nor indifference [53] to one's own taste,
He is never deprived of his zeal, effort and memory,
Of pure, immaculate Intellect and Liberation,
Of the intuition of freedom [54] and of showing all things knowable; — // 14 //

He makes manifest on the objects the 3 kinds of acts [55],
Which are preceded by [56] all kinds of knowledge,
And brings out the Wisdom, well extensive, without hindrance [57],
Constantly, throughout the 3 states of time;
Thus is Buddhahood [58], endowed with Great Compassion,

45) *vimuktijñānadarśana*, T. *rnam-grol-gyi ye-śes-gzigs-pa*, C. [解脫] 知見 ... (12). Mvyut. & DRS instead have '*nāsti samādher hāniḥ* (C. 定不退).

46) *karman*, T. *las*, C. 業. There are 3 kinds of '*karman*', i.e. *k.* by *kāya*, by *vāk* & by *manas*, and they stand for (13)-(15).

47) *jñāna-pūrvaṃgama*, T. *ye-śes sṅon-ḥgro*, C. 智以本.

48) *try-adhvan*, T. om. *tri* and simply, *dus*. C. 三世. '*jñāna*' acting in each state of time, i.e. *atīta*, *anāgata* & *pratyutpanna*, is counted separately and consists (16)-(18) of the *āveṇikadharma*.

49) *anye ca*, T. ... *daṅ gshan*, C. 及餘不說者. It is uncertain which are counted by this word '*anye*'.

50) *praskhalita* = *skhalita*.

51) The reading should be '*muṣitatâcitte*' (as a Dvandva-comp., dual, nom., i.e. *muṣitatā* & *acitta*) instead of '*muṣitatā citte*' in the text. '*acitta*' here stands for *asamāhita-citta*. (T. *bsñel daṅ thugs-g'yo*).

52) *na saṃbhedataḥ saṃjñā*. (*saṃbhedataḥ* = *nānātva*-)T. *tha-dad-kyi ni ḥdus-śes*.

53) *abhyupekṣaṇa* = *upekṣā*.

54) T. om. *nidarśana* of *muktijñāna-nidarśana* (reading apparently '*vimuktijñānadarśanāt*).

55) In place of '*artheṣu*', T. has '*yasya*'.

56) *purojava*, T. *sṅon-ḥgro* (= *purvaṃgama*), C. ...爲本.

57) *aparāhata*, T. *thogs-med*, C. 無障閡.

58) *jinatā*, T. *rgyal-pa-ñid*, C. 如來體.

And perfectly realized [59] by the Buddha;
And on account of this realization, he sets in motion in the world
The great wheel of the fearless [60] Supreme Doctrine. // 15 //

It is said that [these properties are] like space [61].

(Kārikā 14)

The nature [62] found in the earth and the rest
Is not the nature of space,
And the properties of space represented by
Non-obstruction, etc., are absent in material things [63];
The earth, water, fire, wind and the sky [64], likewise,
Are common to all the [material] worlds,
But the Exclusive Properties of the Buddha
Are not in the least [65] common to those worlds. // 16 //

(IV) THE 32 MARKS OF THE SUPERMAN [66]

It is said that the Buddha is possessed of the corporeal form endowed with the 32 marks of the Superman (*dvātriṃśanmahāpuruṣalakṣaṇarūpa-dhārin*).

59) For '*avabuddhā*', T. *brñes* (*avalabdha*), but C. as in the text.

60) The reading '*abhayadaṃ*' is to be corrected into '*abhayaṃ*' (one syllable is in excess). So T. *ḥjigs-med*, and C. 無畏 [勝妙法] (Lit. it is an adjective to *cakra*). Cf. v. I. 4. (*abhayaṃ mārgaṃ dideśa*).

61) C. (in the commentary) puts the following verse before v. 35.

62) *dharmatā*, T. *chos-ñid*, C. 法.

63) *rūpin*, T. *gzugs*, C. 色 (that which has form).

64) C. om. the word for sky from this line of elements, sothat the sky is to be distinguished from the other elements. Did the author of this Kārikā regard the sky as something material unlike 'space' which, in its turn, is compared to the Buddha's *āveṇikadharma* in the first two lines?

65) *āśv api*. T. *dul phran tsam*, C. 乃至無一法 (even not a single *dharma*). T. om. '*buddha*' of '*buddhāveṇikatā*, for which C. 諸佛如來所有諸功德.

66) Of the 32 *mahāpuruṣalakṣaṇas*, see Mvyut. 17, AĀS 474 *a–b*, RDS 37 *b–c*. Also cf. AA, AAĀ Chap. VIII, The *Prajñāpāramitāśāstra* (大智度論) attributed to Nāgārjuna. Of those in the *Ratna.*, see V. S. Agrawala, *The Thirty-two Marks of the Buddha-Body*, *Journal of the Oriental Institute*, M. S. University of Baroda, vol. I, No. 1. Sept. 1951, Baroda, pp. 20–22.

(Kārikās 15-23)

The feet are firmly placed, marked by circles on the soles,
And with broad insteps and leveled heels which hide the ankles [67],
The fingers are long [68], and those of hands and toes alike
Are connected with each other by a web [69]. // 17 //
His skin is soft and fine like that of youths [70],
His body is round with 7 elevated parts [71],
His shanks are like those of the deer [72], and
The private parts are concealed as with an elephant [73]. // 18 //
The upper part of the body is like that of a lion [74],
The parts between the shoulders are closely set and elevated [75],

67) *supratiṣṭhita-cakrâṅka-vyāyatôtsaṅga-pādatā* (1), which contains actually 4 marks on feet, namely: 1) *supratiṣṭhita-pādatā*), T. *legs-gnas (loṅ)*, C. 足下相平滿 (flat the feet); 2) *cakrâṅka-p.*, T. *ḥkhor los mtshan-pa*, C. 具足千輻輪; 3) *vyāyata-p.*, T. *yaṅs-* (cf. AAĀ, *āyata-pārṣṇitā*); & 4) *utsaṅga-p.*, T. *mi-mṅon* ('not evident', 'hidden'), C. for 3) & 4) 跟脯趺上隆 (but 大智度論; 3) 足跟滿足相 & 4) 足趺高相). For '*utsaṅga*', AAĀ & Mvyut., *ucchaṅka* (or *ucchaṅkha*), which is an equivalent form of Pāli '*ussaṅkha*' and which retains the original meaning of this peculiar mark. T. translation '*mi-mṅon*' matches better '*ucchaṅka*' than '*utsaṅga*'. The form '*utsaṅga*' is, therefore, probably a wrong Sanskritization of Pāli '*ussaṅkha*'. C. traditional interpretation of this mark also supports this sense of 'hidden ankles'.

68) *dīrghâṅgulikatā* (2), T. *sor-mo riṅ*, C. 諸指皆纖長.

69) *jālapānipādâvanaddhatā* (3), T. *phyag-shabs riṅ dra-ba-yis ni ḥbrel-pa*, C. 鵝王網縵指.

70) *tvaṅmṛduśrūtaruṇatā* (4), T. *pags-ḥjam gshon-śa-can legs-ñid*, C. 手足悉柔軟 (instead of '*tvak*', C. has '*hasta-pāda*'. It agrees with AAĀ & Mvyut.). T. *gshon-śa-can* (for *taruṇa*) has the meaning, 'one who has flesh of youth'.

71) *saptôtsada-śarīratā* (5), T. *sku ni bdun-dag mtho-ba*, C. 體相七處滿, 7 *utsadas* are namely: 2 *hastas*, 2 *padas*, 2 *skandhas* & 1 *grīva*.

72) *eneya-jaṅghatā* (6), T. *byin-pa enaya-ḥdra*, C. 伊尼鹿王蹲 [踹].

73) *nāgakośavad-vastiguhyatā* (7), T. *gsaṅ glaṅ-po bshin-du sbubs-su nub*, C. 馬王陰藏相.

74) *siṃhapūrvârdha-kāyatva* (8), T. *ro-stod seṅ-ge ḥdra-ba*, C. 上半如師子.

75) *nirantara-citâṃśatā* (9), T. *thal-goṅ bar-med rgyas-pa*, C. 左右俱圓滿. Cf. AAĀ *citântarâṃśatā*. T. *thal-goṅ* (for *aṃśa*) means the part between shoulder and collar (*goṅ-pa*, collar). C. often interprets it as indicating 'arm-pit' (両腋下滿, AĀS).

And his shoulders are well heaped and round [76];
His arms are fleshy, tender and of no unevenness [77], // 19 //
And are hanging low [down to the knees] [78].
The body has a radiant, pure halo around it [79],
His neck is immaculate like a white conch [80],
And his jaws have a resemblance with those of a lion [81]. // 20 //
He has forty teeth all of which are equal [82],
And are clear and closely set [83], pure and straight [84],
And his eye-teeth are white and of excellent form [85]. // 21 //
His tongue is broad and long [86], [by which he tastes]
The highest taste, infinite and unthinkable [87];
The voice of the Self-Born is like that of the Kalaviṅka [88],
And has the most excellent sound [89]. // 22 //

76) *saṃvṛtta-skandhatā* (10), T. *dpuṅ-pa legs-zlum*, C. 両肩前後平.

77) *vṛttaślakṣṇânunnāma-bāhutā* (11), T. *phyag-ḥjam riṅ zlum-shiṅ mthon dman-med-pa*, C. 臂肘上下臑. This is not mentioned in AAĀ. Mvyut. counts this mark along with the next one saying ' *sthitânavanata-pralamba-bāhutā*.

78) *pralamba-bāhutā* (12), T. *phyag riṅ* C. 立能手過膝.

79) *śuddhaprabhāmaṇḍala-gātratā* (13), T. *yoṅs-su dag-paḥi ḥod-kyi dkyil-ḥkhor dag daṅ ldan* (om. *gātra*), C. 身淨光圓匝.

80) *kambu-grīvatvam amalam* (14), T. *mgrin-pa dri-med duṅ-ḥdra*, C. 項如孔雀王. This is lacking in AAĀ, Mvyut., as well as in RDS.

81) *mṛgêndra-hanutā* (15), T. *ḥgram-pa ri-dags rgyal-po ḥdra*, C. 頤方若師子.

82) *samā catvāriṃśad-daśanatā* (16), T. *tshems ni bshi-bcu mñam-pa*, C. 口含四十齒.

83) *svacchâvirala-dantatā* (17), T. *rab-daṅs tshems thags bzaṅ-ba*, C. 深密内外明.

84) *viśuddhasama-dantatva* (18), T. *rnam-dag tshems mñam-ñid*, C. 上下齒平齊.

85) *śukla-pravara-daṃṣṭratā* (19), T. *mche-ba rab-mchog dkar-ba-ñid*, C. 二牙白踰雪. This is lacking in AAĀ & Mvyut.

86) *prabhūta-jihvatā* (20), T. *ljags riṅ*, C. 細薄廣長舌.

87) *anantâcintya-rasarasâgratā* (21), T. *mthaḥ-med bsam-med-pa ro bro-ba-yi mchog-ñid* (T. seems to regard '*anantâcintya*' as adjectives for the previous one), C. 所食至喉現, 得味中上味.

88) *kalaviṅka-ruta* (22), T. *kalabiṅka-yi sgra*, C. 迦陵頻伽聲. AAĀ, Mvyut., RDS om. it.

89) *brahma-svaratā* (23), T. *tshaṅs-paḥi dbyaṅs-ñid*, C. 妙音深遠聲.

He, the highest of living beings [90], is of beautiful eyes, like a blue-
lotus, with eyelashes like those of a bull [91],
Of handsome face, endowed with the immaculate Ūrṇa-hair [92],
Of a head adorned with the Uṣṇīṣa [93], and of skin,
Purified, subtle and of golden colour [94]; // 23 //
Hairs on the body grow separately from each other,
Soft and subtle, turning upward and to the right [95],
Hairs on his head are of pure blue colour like sapphires [96],
And his figure is fully circular like a Nyagrodha tree [97]. // 24 //
He, the Great Sage, whose body is firm and possessed of
The power of Nārāyaṇa [98], looks sublime and incomparable [99];

90) *agrasattva*, which is a synonym of the Buddha and not one of the 'marks' at all.

91) *nīlôtpalaśrī-vṛṣapakṣma-netra* (24). This actually consists of two marks, namely:

1) *nīlôtpalalaśrī-netra*, T. *spyan-bzaṅs utpala*, C. 二目淳紺色…功德如蓮華;

2) *vṛṣa-pakṣma-netra*, T. *khyu-mchog rdsi-ḥdra[-spyan]*, C. 瞬眼若牛王.

92) *sitâmalôrṇôdita-cāruvaktra* (25), T. *shal-mdses dri-med mdsod spu dkar-bar ldan*, C. 額上白毫相, 通面淨光明;

93) *uṣṇīṣa-śīrṣa* (26), T. *gtsug-tor dbu-ldan*, C. 頂上相高顯.

94) *vyavadātasūkṣma-suvarṇavarṇa-cchaviḥ* (27), T. *dag-ciṅ srab-pa daṅ pags-pa gser-gyi mdog-ḥdra*, C. 身色新淨明, 柔軟金色皮, 淨軟細平密 AAĀ counts this one as two.

95) *ekaikaviśliṣṭa-mṛdu-ūrdhvadeha-pradakṣiṇâvarta-sūkṣma-roma* (28). T. *ba-sphu legs phra, ḥjam shiṅ, re-re-nas, sku-yi gyen-du g'yas phyogs ḥkhil-ba*, C. 一孔一毛生, 毛柔軟上靡, 微細輪右旋. This is originally of 3 marks as C. translation, i.e. 1) *ekaikaviśliṣṭa*; 2) *ūrdhvadehâvarta*; & 3) *pradakṣiṇā-āvarta*.

96) *mahêndra-nīlâmala-ratnakeśa* (29), T. *dbu-skra dri-med rin-chen mthor mthiṅ-bshin*, C. 髮淨金精色, 喻如因陀羅. This is lacking in AAĀ.

97) *nyagrodha-pūrṇadruma-maṇḍalâbha*. (30), T. *ñya-gro rdsogs-paḥi ljon śin dkyil-ḥkhor ḥdra*, C. 身膅相洪雅, 如尼拘樹王.

98) *nārāyaṇasthāma-dṛḍhâtmabhāva* (31), T. *sred-med-bu-yi stobs mṅaḥ* (*sred-med bu* means Viṣṇu), C. 威德勢堅固, 猶如那羅延. AAĀ & Mvyut. have not got this mark.

99) *samantabhadrâpratima* (*-ātmabhāva*) (32), T. *kun-tu bzaṅ-po dpe-med*, C. 皆身不可嫌 (which reads *apratigha* for *apratima*). It is doubtful whether this stands for one of the 32 marks or not. C. does not count it among the marks. T. is not clear. And no other text includes it among the 32 marks.

These 32 features of infinite splendour are taught
By the Preceptor as the marks[100] of the Lord of Men. // 25 //

It is said that [the Buddha, with 32 marks] has a resemblance to the moon and its reflection in the water[101].

(Kārikā 24)

Just as, in autumn, the form[102] of the moon is perceived
In the cloudless sky, as well as in a big pond,
Reflecting this blue sky on its water-surface;
Similarly, the disciples of the Buddha
Can perceive the manifestations of the Omnipresent
On the surface of the pond-like sphere of the Buddha. // 26 //

Thus these 10 Powers of the Buddha, 4 kinds of Intrepidity, 18 Exclusive Properties of the Buddha, as well as the 32 Marks of the Superman, being united under one head, make up the number sixty-four.

These 64 properties are to be understood,
Along with their causes for attainment,
One after the other, according to [the same] order,
Through the investigation of the *Ratna-sūtra*[103]. // 27 //

Now, of these 64 properties of the Buddha, which have been explained above, the detailed exposition is to be known , according to the same order as before, through the investigation of the *Ratnadārikā-sūtra*.

Also, there have been made illustrations of four kinds about these [4] points, respectively, viz. examples of a thunderbolt, a lion, the spaee, and the moon reflected in the water. Of these examples, the summarized meaning will be given in the following 12 verses.

100) *cihna*, T. *mtshan*, C. 相 (= *lakṣaṇa*).

101) *dakacandra*, C. 水中月, T. *chu-zla*.

102) *vibhūti*, T. *gzugs* (= *bimba*, *rūpa*), C. 勢力. C. puts this Kārikā before v. 37.

103) = *Ratnadārikāsūtra*, T. *bu-mo rin-po-cheḥi mdo*, C. 寶女經. There are two translations of this sūtra in C.:

1) 大方等大集經中寶女品第三 (Chap. III of the *Mahāsaṃnipātasūtra*), *Taisho*, XIII, pp. 28 *b*–40 *b*. This one is used here for reference with the abbreviation of RDS;

2) 寶女所問經 (*Ratnadārikā-paripṛcchā*), *Taisho*, No. 399, vol. XIII, pp. 452–472.

Being [respectively] impenetrable[104], with no misery[105],
Perfectly unique[106] and indifferent[107],
[The Buddha's Properties] are illustrated
By the examples of the thunderbolt, the lion, the space
And of the clear moon with her reflection in the water. // 28 //
Of the [10] Powers, six, three, and one,
Taken respectively, remove all [the obscurations]
On account of the knowable, the concentrations,
And of defilements with their potential forces. // 29 //
As if they were piercing an armour,
Breaking a wall, and cutting down a tree,
The Powers of the Sage are like a thunderbolt,
Being heavy, solid, firm and unbreakable[108]. // 30 //
Why are they 'heavy'? Because they are 'solid';
Why are they 'solid'? Because they are 'firm';
Why are they 'firm'? Because they are 'unbreakable'.
And being 'unbreakable', they are like a thunderbolt[109].
// 31 //
Being fearless, being indifferent,
Being firm and accomplishing victory,
The lion of Sages is like a [real] lion,
Has no fear amidst the assembly of audiences[110]. // 32 //

104) *nirvedhikatva*, T. *mi-phyed-pa*, C. 衝過 (breakable, in the sense that the thunderbolt can break everything).

105) *nirdainya*, T. *mi-shan*, C. 無慈心 (without mercy, which is not a proper translation).

106) *niṣkaivalya*, T. *mtshuṅs-pa med*, C. 不共他 (*niḥ*' in the sense of '*atyanta*').

107) *nirīha*, T. *g'yo-med* (immovable), C. 無心 (indifferent). The reflection is *avikalpa* and *nirīhaka* (cf. Chap. IV, v. 19).

108) *guru*, T. *brliṅ* (D. *gliṅ* is a mistake), C. 重; *sāra*, T. *sñiṅ*, C. 堅; *dṛḍha*, T. *brtan*, C. 固; & *abhedya*, T. *mi-byed*, C. 不可破壞, respectively.

109) C. neglects the first 3 *padas* of v. 31.

110) *parṣad-gaṇa* C. adds one more verse before v. 32, indicating the 4-fold *āryasatya*, which makes the analogy quite clear. It runs as follows:

知病苦知因 遠離彼苦因 說聖道妙藥 爲離病證滅.

(The Buddha, having known the *duḥkha* of sickness and its *hetu*, and having been devoid of *duḥkha-hetu*, preaches the *āryamārga*, that is an excellent medicine, in order to cause the people to remove sickness and to realize the *nirodha*).

As he has got all the supernatural faculties,
He abides 'independently'[111] from any fear[112],
He is 'indifferent' [about his superiority],
As he is unequal by nature even to the people of purity[113].
// 33 //

He stands 'firmly' since his mind is always
Concentrated on all the elements of existence,
And he is 'of the highest victory'
Since he has transcended the Dwelling Place of Ignorance. // 34 //
With the worldlings[114], with the Śrāvakas,
With those that act in solitude[115], with the Wise,
And with the Buddha, the Intellect is subtler with one after the
[other;
Therefore, we have illustrations in five kinds[116]. // 35 //
[The first four are] like the earth, water, fire and wind,
Because they sustain all the world,
[But the Buddha] has a resemblance to space,
Because his characters surpass everything mundane and supermun-
dane. // 36 //
These 32 Properties mentioned above
Represent the Body of the Absolute,
Since they are indivisible from it,
As with a gem, the lustre, colour and shape. // 37 //
[On the other hand], the 32 marks are
The properties, visible and causing delight[117] in the body,
And are based on the two Corporeal Bodies
The Apparitional Body and the Body enjoying the Truth. // 38 //
To those who are far from purity and near to it,
The pure manifestation of the Corporeal Body is twofold,

111) *svastha*, T. *rnam-par gnas*, C. 善住.

112) *akutobhaya*, T. *gaṅ-las kyaṅ ḥjigs-med*, C. 一切處不畏.

113) 'Indifference' in the sense that he does not try to see whether he is superior or inferior. For this line, C. 離愚痴凡夫 二乘及清淨 以見我無等 (*ātma-asama-darśanataḥ*). '離' is probably for '*nirāstha*'.

114) C. om. *laukika*.

115) *ekānta-cārin*, T. *mthaḥ-gcig-su spyod*, C. 空行. It denotes the Pratyekabuddha.

116) C. takes '*-pañcadhā tu*' as if '*pañca-dhātu* (五大 = *pañca-mahābhūta*).

117) *ahlādaka*, T. *tshim-byed*, C. 生歡喜.

[One is] in the World, and [the other] in the circle of the Buddha,
Just as the moon shows her form in both the sky and the water [118]**.**
// 39 //

Finished is the third chapter entitled 'the Properties of the Buddha', in the ANALYSIS OF THE GERM OF THE JEWELS, a Treatise on the Ultimate Doctrine of the Great Vehicle.

118) C. adds one verse more after v. 39, whose content is almost the same as v. 37, the difference is only the use of the word '*rūpakāya*' in place of '*dharmakāya*'.

Chapter IV.

THE ACTS OF THE BUDDHA [1]

4. JINAKRIYĀ

XVI. GENERAL CHARACTERISTICS OF THE ACTS OF THE BUDDHA

We have finished the explanation of the 'Immaculate Properties of the Buddha'. Now we shall speak of the functions [associated with those Properties], i. e. 'the Acts of the Buddha'. They are said to be manifested in two modes, i. e. 'without effort' (*anābhogataḥ*), and 'uninterruptedly' (*apraśrabdhitaḥ*). [Therefore] immediately there follow two [2] *ślokas* referring to the Buddha's Acts which are characterized as 'of no effort and interruption' (*anābhogâpraśrabdha*).

(Kārikās 1–2)

The acts of the Lord [3] are always effortless
With regard to the constitution of the converts [4],
The means of conversion, and its [5] functions
[In accordance with the capacity] of the converts,
Working in [proper] place and in [proper] time [6]. // 1 //
Having completely established the Vehicle [7],

[1] AĀS has a chapter of the same title (*Tathāgatakriyā-parivarta*), but it has nothing to associate with RGV in its contents.

[2] T. om. *dvau*.

[3] *vibhu*, T. *khyab-bdag*, C. 諸佛自在人.

[4] *vineyadhātu*, T. *gdul-byaḥi khams*, C. 可化衆生.

[5] T. reads *vineyakriyā* for *vinayakriyā*.

[6] *taddeśakāle gamane ca*. For '*gamana*', T. *gśegs-pa* (going). For the whole phrase, C. 待處待時 (in accordance with proper place and time).

[7] *Par excellence*, it denotes the Mahāyāna. So, C. 大乘. For *niṣpādya*, C. 覺知.

The ocean [8] of knowledge filled with the multitudes of the excellent virtues,
And endowed with the rays of the sun of Merits and Knowledge [9],
And having perceived that Buddhahood [10], like space,
Pervading extensively and of neither limit nor middle,
Exists everywhere [11] in all living beings [12],
As the treasure [13] of the immaculate virtues,
The Buddhas' Compassion, like wind,
Blows away the net of the cloud-like [Obscurations]
Caused by Defilements and Ignorance. // 2 //

The summarized meaning of these two *ślokas* is to be known by the following two and eight verses, respectively.

To whom, by what means, how far [14], and when,
About these matters, there is no rise of discrimination;
Therefore, the Buddha's Act of conversion
Is [working] always 'without effort'. // 3 //
On account of the action of conversion [15],
'Who' means 'the constitution [16] to be converted',
'By what means' [17] denotes 'the manifold means [of conversion]',
And 'where and when', the 'place and time' [of conversion]'. // 4 //
Because, [this act of conversion is] non-discriminative

8) *ratna-svagarbha*, T. *chu-mtsho* (ocean), C. 大海水寶. The Ocean is usually said to be the 'treasure of jewels'.

9) *puṇya* and *jñāna* are called the two *saṃbhāras* (accumulation that brings about the Enlightenment, C. 菩提資糧). The compound should be separated after *raśmi* and before *praviṣṛta*. C. misreads this passage and connects it with the next '*buddhatva*'.

10) For *buddhatva*, C. 菩提.

11) *nirviśiṣṭaṃ*, T. *khyad-med*, C. 遍.

12) *sarvasattva* (*sattva* in a collective sense) = *sattvadhātu*.

13) *nidhi*, T. *gter*, C. 藏. It has a sense similar to '*gotra*' (mine), or '*garbha*'.

14) *yāvat*, which stands for '*yatra*' in the next verse.

15) *vinīti-kriyā*, T. *gdul-byaḥi bya*, C. 能度諸衆生.

16) For *dhātu*, C. 根性 (constitution, faculty).

17) Instead of *upāya*, C. 智慧 (智 in v. 3) (*jñāna*) ...(*yena jñānena*), and om. *bhūriṇā*.

With regard to Deliverance[18] and its support[19],
To the result of [partaking of] this support and the receptacle[20] which accepts this result,
And to the obscurations [which cover] this receptacle and the condition by which these obscurations are removed. // 5 //
[Here] 'Deliverance' means the 10-fold Stage [of Bodhisattvas],
'Its cause' means the 2-fold Accumulation[21],
'The result of this Accumulation' is the Highest Enlightenment,
'[Its] receptacle' means the living beings
Who accept the Enlightenment[22]. // 6 //
The phrase 'The obscurations which cover this receptacle' means
The innumerable Defilements, Sub-defilements and Impressions;
The phrase 'The condition by which the obscurations are removed
And which works for all time' means Compassion. // 7 //
These six points are to be known,
Like the ocean and like the sun,
Like space and like a treasure,
Like clouds and like the wind, respectively. // 8 //
Being [the treasure] of the water of knowledge
And of the jewel of virtuous properties,
The highest Vehicle[23] is like the ocean;
As keeping alive all living beings,
The twofold Accumulation is like the sun; // 9 //
Being extensive and of neither end nor middle,
The Enlightenment has a resemblance to space;
Being of the nature of the Perfect Enlightened One[24],

[18] *niryāṇa*, T. *ṅes-ḥbyin*, C. 進趣 (to enter the path, 出道). It stands for '*yāna*' in the Kārikā.

[19] *upastambha* (in the sense, that which causes '*niryāṇa*'), T. *rton-pa*, C. 功德. Hereafter, the pronoun '*tad*' in each case, denotes the preceding one.

[20] *parigraha*, T. *yoṅs-ḥdsin*, C. 攝取 (攝 in v. 6) '*parigraha*' is here used in the sense of '*nidhi*' (that which contains something).

[21] *saṃbhṛti-dvaya*, viz. *puṇya-saṃbhāra* & *jñāna-s*. The former includes those *pāramitās* of '*dāna, śīla, kṣānti, vīrya* & *dhyāna*', and the latter, that of '*prajñā*'. For *saṃbhṛti*, C. 諦 (*satya*).

[22] *bodheḥ sattvaḥ parigrahaḥ*, T. *byaṅ-chub-sems-can yoṅs-su ḥdsin*, C. 攝菩提眷屬 (眷屬 for *sattva*). Here the living beings are called '*bodhisattva*' in the sense of those who accept (*pari-* √*grah*) the '*bodhi*'.

[23] *agrayāna*. But T. & C. read '*bhūmayaḥ*' (T. *sa-rnams*, C. 諸地).

[24] *samyaksaṃbuddha-dharmatvāt*, T. *yaṅ-dag-rdsogs-saṅs-chos-ñid-phyir*, C. 皆有如來性.

The living beings [25] are akin to a treasure [26]; // 10 //
Being accidental, pervasive, and unreal [27],
Their defilements are like a multitude of clouds;
And, bringing about [28] the dispelling of these,
Compassion is like a strong wind. // 11 //
Performing Deliverance for the sake of others,
Considering the living beings as one's own self [29],
And having works of no termination, [The Buddha]
Acts 'uninterruptedly' as long as the world exists. // 12 //

25) *sattvadhātu.*

26) *nidhāna*, T. *gter*, C. 地中伏藏 (treasure under the ground).

27) *aniṣpatti*, T. *ma-grub*, C. 虛妄. For *vyāpi*, C. 一切, and regards it as an adverb to *aniṣpatti* (unreal everywhere).

28) *pratyupasthāna*, T. *ñer-gnas*, C. 起.

29) Cf. the *Avataṃsakasūtra.* (note VI-28) C. puts these two phrases after v. 10, adding the following phrases before them: '猶如彼大地 體安固不動'.

XVII. 9 ILLUSTRATIONS OF THE BUDDHA'S ACTS

§ 1. Buddha's Magnanimity.

It was said that Buddhahood is characterized[1] as having neither origination nor extinction. Being such, how is it possible that from such an immutable Buddhahood, characterized as of no manifestation[2], the Acts of Buddha manifest in this world, without effort, without discriminination, without interruption, and as long as the world exists ? [To answer this question], in order to produce the faith in the sphere of the Buddha on the part of those people who have misconception and doubt about the Buddha's nature of magnanimity[3], we have one *śloka* with regard to this magnanimous character of the Buddha.

(Kārikā 3)

Like Indra, like the divine drum,
Like clouds, like Brahmā, and like the sun,
Like the wish-fulfilling gem, like an echo,
Like space and like the earth,—
Such is the Buddha [in his acts][4]. // 13 //

[1] *prabhāvita*, T. *rab-tu phye-ba.*

[2] *apravṛtti-lakṣaṇa*, C. 不修行業.

[3] For *māhātmya*, C. 大事 (prob. for *mahākriyā*). In the Kārikā text, C. says '大乘業' (*mahāyāna-kriyā*).

[4] names of the 9 similes in S. T. & C. are as follows:

1) *śakra*, T. *rgya-byin*, C. 帝釋;
2) [*deva*] *dundubhi*, T. [*lhaḥi*] *rṅa*, C. [天中] 妙鼓;
3) *megha*, T. *sprin*, C. 雲;
4) [*mahā*] *brahman*, T. *tshaṅs-pa* [*chen-po*], C. 梵天;
5) *arka* (*sūrya*), T. *ñi-ma*, C. 日;
6) *maṇiratna* (*cintāmaṇi*), T. *nor-bu rin-chen*, C. 摩尼;
7) *pratiśruti* (*pratiśrutka-śabda*), T. *sgra-brñan* C. 響;
8) *ākāśa*, T. *nam-mkhaḥ*, C. 虛空;
9) *pṛthivī*, T. *sa*, C. 地.

§ 2. 9 Illustrations taken from the *Jñānâlokâlaṅkārasūtra*.

Now, of this *śloka* which represents the topics in the Scripture [5], a detailed exposition will be given topic by topic in the remaining part of the text according to the same order.

(I) It is said that [the Buddha has] a resemblance to the form of Indra [6].

(Kārikās 4–20) [7]

Suppose here were a surface
Made of an immaculate Vaiḍūrya stone,
And, owing to its clarity, there were seen on it
The chief of the gods, with the multitude of Apsaras [8], // 14 //
As well as his great place [9] called Vaijayanta,
Other gods [10] and their various dwellings
Along with their divine glories [11]. // 15 //
Suppose then, the multitudes of men and women
Abiding on this surface of the earth,
Would perceive this vision
And make the following prayer : // 16 //
" May we too, at an early date [12],
Become like that chieftain of the gods ! " [13]
And, in order to obtain [14] that state,

5) *sūtrasthānīya* [*śloka*], T. *mdoḥi gnas lta-buḥi* [*tshigs-su-bcad-pa*], C. 修多羅攝取義(偈) (*sūtrârthasaṃgraha-śloka*).

6) Cf. JĀA 240 *b–c*.
Text reading '*-pratibhāsatvād iti*' is to be corrected into '*-pratibhāsavad iti*'.

7) Hereafter, the arrangement of Kārikās varies much between C. & S. (T. agrees with S.). Some Kārikās in each simile are missing in C. while C. has more than three verses which are not available in S. (see my *Introduction*, II-2) Mention will be done in each case about omission and addition in C., and the verse number in C. Kārikā text. (Prior to this passage, in Chap. IV, we have three verses in C. Kārikā text which are equivalent to vv. 1, 2, & 13 in S. Consequently, in the following passages, C. Kārikā number starts with No. 4). C. om. vv. 14–26.

8) For *apsaras*, T. *lhaḥi bu-mo*.

9) *prāsāda*, T. *khaṅ-bzaṅs*. For *Vaijayanta*, T. *rnam-par-rgyal-ba*.

10) *divaukas*, T. *lha-gnas*. (One whose residence is in heaven).

11) *vibhūti*, T. *rnam-maṅ*.

12) The reading should be '*vayam apy acirād*' instead of '*adyaiva na cirād*' in S. T. *ṅed kyaṅ riṅ-por mi-thogs-par* (*riṅ-por mi-thogs-par* = after a little while, in a short time. *Jäschke's Dictionary*, p. 528 s. v.).

13) *tridaśêśvara*, T. *lha-dbaṅ* (*devêndra*).

14) *samādāya*, T. *yaṅ-dag-blaṅs te*.

They would abide adopting the virtues. // 17 //
Though having no notice that this is merely a vision,
They, owing to their virtuous conduct,
Would pass away from the earth [15] and be borne to heaven. // 18 //
After all, it is an illusion,
Of no thought-construction and no activity [16];
Nevertheless, it would appear on the earth,
Being associated with a great benefit. // 19 //
In the same way, the living beings,
If they were pure in their faith and so forth,
And were endowed with [17] virtues, faith and the like,
Would perceive in their own minds the vision of the Buddha, // 20 //
Who is endowed with the visible features and marks [18],
Who acts in manifold actual behavior like
Walking, standing, sitting and sleeping [19], // 21 //
Preaching the Doctrine of Quiescence, being silent,
Abiding in concentration of mind and showing
The various miracles [20], and who has the great glory. // 22 //
Having seen him, the people who are filled with desire,
Undertake the attainment of the Buddhahood,
And, having brought the factors to development
They do attain the desired state [21]. // 23 //
After all, it is an illusion,
Of no thought-construction and no activity;
Nevertheless, it appears in the world,
Being associated with a great benefit. // 24 //
Ordinary people do not notice
That this is merely a reflection of their own mind [22];
Still this manifestation of the Buddha's features

15) *bhū*, T. *sa-steṅ* (for abl. in S., T. reads as loc.).

16) *nirīhaka*, T. *g'yo-ba-med*.

17) For *bhāvita*, T. *sgom-pa* (*bhāvanā*).

18) *vyañjana*, T. *dpe-byad*. '*lakṣaṇa-vyañjana*' signifies 32 *mahāpuruṣalakṣaṇas* and the 80 *anuvyañjanas*.

19) *caṅkramyamāṇa*, *tiṣṭhat*, *niṣa*[illegible] & *śayanasthita*, T. *ḥchag-pa*, *bsheṅs-pa*, *bshugs-pa* & *gzims-pa* (Cf. C. 行住坐臥). These are called '*īryāpatha*' (T. *spyod-lam*, C. 威儀).

20) *prātihārya*, T. *cho-ḥphrul*. There are said to be 3 *prātihāryas*. See below.

21) *īpsitaṃ padam*, T. *ḥdod-paḥi go-ḥphaṅ*, namely '*bodhi*'.

22) This is an expression of the '*cittamātra*' theory. We have a similar expression in Laṅk. (*svacittadṛśyamātra*...).

Is useful for[23] fulfilling their aim. // 25 //
Indeed, those who, having seen this vision,
Have gradually established themselves in this method[24],
Perceive, with the eyes of transcendental wisdom,
The Body of the Highest Truth[25] within themselves[26]. // 26 //
Suppose, the earth, having become completely free from unevenness[27]
And having become pure from within[28], would be as clear and white
As the Vaiḍūrya stone, [because of its] being possessed of
The immaculate qualities of jewel and of pure even surface;
And, owing to its purity, there would appear on its [surface]
The palace of Indra[29] occupied by gods around him[30] as a vision,
But, as this earth would gradually lose its qualities,
The vision [thereof] would subsequently disappear[31]. // 27 //
For obtaining that state, the multitudes of men and women,
Whose mind intends to perform charity and the rest,
Through observing rules regarding fast and conduct[32],
Would scatter flowers with minds full of sublime desire[33].
Similarly, for obtaining the shadow of the Lord of Sages[34]
On their mind which is radiant like the Vaiḍūrya stone,
The sons of the Buddha, with minds full of delight,

23) *avandhya* (not barren), T. *don-yod* [*ḥgyur*] (*sārtha*).

24) For *naya*, T. *theg-pa* (*yāna*). There is not so much difference in its sense. It denotes '*mahāyāna*'.

25) *saddharmakāya*.

26) *madhyastha*, T. *naṅ-gi*.

27) *samanta-vyapagatavişamasthāna*, T. *kun dman-paḥi gnas gshan daṅ bral* (including *antar* by reading *antara* as 'other'), C. 遠離高下. C. puts this verse after v. 30.

28) *antar amalā*. One Avagraha should be inserted between *sthānā* and *antar-*. (*sthānā'ntaramalā*).

29) *surapati*, C. 天主, T. not clear (*lha-dag* is a mistake for *lha-bdag*?

30) *māhendramarutā*. For this passage, T. *lha-dag gnas-tshogs lha-dbaṅ lha-ḥi gzugs-śar te* (which reads *bhavana* in pl. and seems to om. *marutā*), C. 天主鏡像現及莊嚴具生.

31) C., K 6.

32) *upavāsa-vrata-niyamatayā*, T. *bsñen-gnas* (*upavāsa*), *brtul-shugs* (*vrata*), *-ṅes-par*, C. 修行諸善行,持戒.

33) *praṇihita-manas*, T. *smon-paḥi sems*, C. 願?

34) *muni-pati* (= *buddha*), T. *thub-dbaṅ*.

Produce various pictures [35] [showing the Buddha's life, etc.] [36] // 28 //

Just as, on the pure surface of the Vaiḍūrya stone,
There appears the reflection of the body of the highest god;
Similarly, on the pure surface of the mind in the world,
There appears the reflection of the body of the Highest Sage [37]. //29//
The appearance and disappearance of this reflection
Occur due to the condition of one's own mind,
Whether it be pure or impure [38], [respectively],
And, as the feature [of Indra or of the Buddha]
Is seen only as a vision in this world,
So one should not see it as either real or unreal. // 30 // [39]

(II) It is said that [the word of the Buddha] has a resemblance with the celestial drum [40].

(Kārikās 21–25)

Just as, in the heaven of the gods,
Owing to the previous, virtuous experiences,
The divine [41] drum, being apart from efforts,
From a particular place, from forms of mind [42],
And from thought-constructions [43], // 31 //
Alarms all the inattentive gods again and again,
By producing the sounds of 'evanescence', of 'suffering',
Of 'impersonality' and of 'quiescence'; // 32 //
Similarly, in this world, the Buddha who is all-pervading
And free from effort and the rest,
Teaches the Doctrine by his voice

[35] *citra*. T. reads *cittāni* for *citrāṇi*. C. 諸修行.

[36] C. K 7.

[37] C. K 4.

[38] *anāvilata* & *āvilata*, T. *rñog-med* & *rñog-pa*, C. 不濁, 濁.

[39] C. K 5. C. adds 4 verses here with the heading: '*anutpādânirodhas tathāgata iti*', of which 3 are equivalent to vv. 89–91.

[40] Cf. JĀA 241 *a* (In the oldest version of JĀA, this and the following two similes, namely : (II) *devadundubhi*, (III) *megha* & (IV) *brahmā* are lacking).

[41] T. '*dharma*–', instead of '*deva*–'.

[42] *mano–rūpa*, T. *yid–gzugs*. This seems to correspond to '*śarīra*' in v. 34, and probably means '*manomayakāya*'.

[43] C. om. this and the following 2 verses (vv. 31–33).

Towards the worthy [44] without exception. // 33 //
Just as, in the heaven of the gods, the sound
Of the divine drum arises due to their own deeds,
Similarly, in this world, the Doctrine,
Though it is preached by the Buddha, arises [in fact]
Owing to the [previous] own deeds of the people [45];
And just as the [celestial] sound, being devoid of
Effort, place, form and thought-construction [46],
Brings forth quiescence;
Similarly, this Doctrine, devoid of those four [47],
Brings forth Nirvāṇa [48]. // 34 // [49]
At the time of the trouble [50] of battle, in the city of gods,
There is destruction [51] of the victorious play of the Asuras' army [52],
Which is caused by the sound of drum
And gives fearlessness [among the gods];
Similarly, in this world, in preaching the Highest Path,
[Buddha's] speech destroys [53] the defilements
And pacifies the sufferings in the living beings,
Which is due to various practices like contemplations,
Concentrations in the Immaterial Sphere [54] and the rest. // 35 // [55]

(On the superiority of the drum over the other musical instruments) [56].

Now, why has the sound of the drum of Doctrine alone been referred to and not the cymbals [57] and the other kinds of celestial instru-

[44] *bhavya*, T. *skal-ldan*.

[45] *svakarma-udbhava*, C. 衆生自業聞.

[46] *citta*, which corresponds to '*vikalpa*' in v. 31.

[47] Namely: *yatna-sthāna-śarira-citta*.

[48] *śānti*, C. 寂滅道.

[49] C., K 12.

[50] *kleśa*. C. om.

[51] *praṇudana*, T. *sel-ba*, C. 破.

[52] T. uses *g'yul* for *saṃgrāma*, as well as for *bala*.

[53] *pramathana*, T. *rab-ḥjoms*, C. 滅. *kleśa-duḥkha-pramathana-śamana* = *kleśa-pramathana* & *duḥkha-śamana*.

[54] *ārūpya*[-*samāpatti*], T. *gzugs-med*, C. simply 定 (for 無色定).

[55] C. K 13.

[56] C. om. the following prose section along with vv. 36–40, and starts again with v. 41. From the structural viewpoint, this passage (S. p. 102.20–104.12) is no doubt an interpolation of later days.

[57] *tūrya*. T. *sil-sñon*.

ment ? These are likewise produced [58] owing to the previous virtuous deeds made by the gods and make sound agreeable to the ear of deities. [To this, we will answer: They are not referred to] because they have four points of dissimilarity to the Buddha's voice. Then, which are these [four] ? They are, namely, 1) partiality (*prādeśikatva*); 2) lack of benefit (*ahitatva*); 3) unpleasantness (*asukhatva*) [59]; and 4) unconduciveness to Deliverance (*anairyāṇikatva*). [On the other hand] the drum of Doctrine summons the multitudes of inattentive [60] gods without exception and sounds at the right time [61]. For this reason it is explained as being 'not partial'. Owing to its protecting [gods] from the fear of calamity caused by the invasion [62] of Asuras and others, and owing to its enjoining [them] to take heed, its 'beneficiality' is mentioned. Owing to its distinguishing bliss from the pleasure caused by evil enjoyment [63] and to its bringing forth pleasant bliss in taking delight in the Doctrine, it is said to be 'blissful'. [And lastly], owing to its delivering the sounds of 'evanescence', 'suffering', 'non-substantiality' and 'impersonality', and to its pacifying all misfortune and perturbation [64], the drum is explained as being 'conducive to deliverance'. In short, the circle of the Buddha's voice is qualified as being similar to the drum of Doctrine through these four points [65]. In regard to distinguishing the circle of the Buddha's voice, we have one verse.

58) The reading *aghaṭṭitā* should be corrected into *ghaṭṭitā*. For '... *vaśād ghaṭṭitā eva*', T. ...*dbaṅ-gis mod kho-nar* (because of their being from the power)'. *ghaṭṭitā*' in BHS has the same meaning as Skt. *ghaṭita*, i.e. 'produced' 'effected by' or 'made'. (BHS Dic. s.v.)

59) For these 4, T. *ñi-tshe-ba-ñid, phan-pa ma-yin-pa-ñid, bde-ba ma-yin-pa-ñid* & *ṅes-par ḥbyin-pa ma-yin-pa-ñid*, respectively.

60) T. adds *sthāna* after *apramatta*.

61) *kāla-anatikramaṇatā* (lit. not crossing time), T. *dus-la mi-ḥdaḥ-bas*.

62) *paracakra*, T. *pha-rol-gyi tshogs* (*paragaṇa*).

63) *asatkāma*, T. *dam-pa ma-yin-paḥi ḥdod*.

64) *upadrava* & *upāyāsa*, but T. *ñe-bar ḥtshe-baḥi phoṅs-pa*.

65) Throughout the passage, there is some confusion between illustration and illustrated subject. First of all, an analogy was given between *devadundubhi* and *dharmadundubhi*, of which the latter is identical with Buddha's voice. Here, the comparison is made between *dundubhi* and *tūrya* showing the former's superiority to the latter. That is to say, Buddha's voice is said to be compared with *dundubhi* alone, but not with *tūrya*. But reference is actually made only to *dharmadundubhi* and not over *devadundubhi*, though, if logically speaking, we should expect the comparison between *devadundubhi* and *divyā-tūrya*. Furthermore, in the following passage, v. 37 refers to *devadundubhi* as being inferior to Buddha's voice (the reading *tūrya* is quite a comtradiction and is to be corrected. See below). From this point, criticism can be made on this passage to decide that it is a later insertion and not perfectly consistent with the original part. Even

Being universal, bringing benefit and bliss,
And being endowed with the threefold miraculous power [66],
The voice of the Buddha is superior
To [the sound of] the celestial cymbals. // 36 //

Now, of these four points, a brief explanation will be given in the following four verses.

The sounds of drums in heaven, though be great,
Cannot reach the ears of those abiding on the earth;
In this world, however, the sound of the drum [67] of Buddha
Reaches even those in the lowest sphere of Saṃsāra. // 37 //
In heaven, the divine cymbals of a million kinds
Sound only in order to kindle the flame of desire,
But one voice of those full of Compassion
Sounds in order to extinguish the cause [68] of the fire of suffering. // 38 //
The sounds of cymbals in heaven, though they be pure and pleasant,
Are the causes for increasing the elation of mind,
The voice of the great [69] Buddhas, however,
Speaks of the concentration [70] of mind in meditation. // 39 //

verses 31–33, which are lacking in C. are doubtful of its originality, because, in v. 32, the role of *devadundubhi* is said to be that of making the sound of 4 *mudrās*, *anitya*, etc., which is to be attributed to *dharmadundubhi*. On the contrary, v. 35 clearly shows us the role of *devadundubhi* as being that of encouraging gods to take part on the battle-field against *asura*, and this illustration is also given in the basic text, i.e. in JĀA. As far as this illustration of (II) *devadundubhi* is concerned, I am inclined to trust C. arrangement as the original.

66) *prātihārya-traya*, T. *cho-ḥphrul gsum* (Cf. C. 三神變 or 三示導). Explanation is given in detail after v. 40.

67) The reading '*saṃbuddhatūryasya tu*' given by J. is not likely to be accepted. Ms. B. reads '*saṃbuddhabhūmer upayāti*' and T. gives a word for *dundubhi* (*rṅa*). From the context, there is no reason for using *tūrya* to illustrate the Buddha's voice, and rather it is quite a contradiction. There should be a term synonymous with *dundubhi*. From this point, and in the absence of Ms. A, we may accept Ms. B reading by making a slight change from *bhūmer* to *bherer* (*bheri* = *dundubhi*). Here, '*tu*' is not essential for giving contrast between Buddha's voice and that of devadundubhi.

68) T. om. *hetu*. The cause of suffering means '*kleśa*'.

69) Instead of *mahātman*, T. reads *kṛpātman*.

70) *arpaṇabhāva* (the state of fixing upon...), T. *gtoṅ-bsam-pa* (the thought of sending...).

In short, that which is the cause of bliss,
In heaven, on earth, as well as
In all the other numberless worlds [71],
Is the voice [72] [of the Buddha] which manifests
Pervadingly in the world leaving no residue;
And in respect to those [73] points, thus it is illustrated. // 40 //

Now, it is indicated that the all-pervadingness [of the Buddha] through the manifestation [74] of body in all the worlds of the ten directions shows [his] ‘manifestation of miracles by the supernatural power’ (*ṛddhi-prātihārya*) [75]. The illumination of the thicket [76] of mental conduct of living beings, as involved in the mind [77], by knowing the variety of spiritual elements [78], this is called the ‘manifestation of miracle through mind-reading’ (*ādeśānā-prātihārya*) [79]. And, with reference to the Path [80] leading to Deliverance, [the Buddha] preaches and instructs [81] that Path [to the others] by the example of the utterance of his voice. This is called ‘the manifestation of miracle through instruction’ (*anuśāstiprātihārya*) [82].

Thus the circle of Buddha's voice is, like space, unimpeded and acts without interruption, but still this voice cannot be caught everywhere or in its full extent. This is, however, not at all the fault [83] of the circle of the Buddha's voice. In order to explain this point, with reference to the self-fault of those who are not attentive, there is one *śloka* [84].

71) *anantāsu lokadhātuṣu* (f. pl.). T. reads *divi* and *kṣitau* as a genitive and makes them relate to *sukhakāraṇa*.

72) *praghoṣa*, but T. *dbyaṅs-ñid*.

73) For *āgamya*, T. *rab-tu brten-par* (*pratītya*).

74) *vikurvita*, T. *cho-ḥphrul* (= *prātihārya*).

75) T. *rdsu-ḥphrul-gyi cho-ḥphrul*, (C. 神變示導, Mvyut.).

76) *gahana*, T. *zab-mo* (*gambhīra*).

77) *tat-paryāpanna* (*tad* denotes *cetas*). For *paryāpanna*, T. *rtogs-pa*.

78) *cetaḥ-paryāya*, T. *sems-kyi rnam-graṅs*.

79) T. *kun-brjod-paḥi cho-ḥphrul*, (C. 記心示導 Mvyut.).

80) *pratipad*, T. *lam*.

81) *avavāda* & *anuśāsana*, T. *ḥdoms-pa* & *rjes-su bstan-pa*.

82) T. *rjes-su bstan-paḥi cho-ḥphrul*, (C. 教誡示導, Mvyut.).

83) *aparādha*, T. *ñes-pa*, C. 過失.

84) C. starts again with this heading (*atat-prahitānām ātmâparādhe*). For *a[tat]prahita*, T. *ma-gtogs-pa* (= *na prajñāyate*), C. 不覺.

(Kārikā 26)

Just as a deaf person cannot hear a subtle voice,
Or even to a man of divine ears,
Not all sounds become audible [85],
Similarly, being the object of the most [86] subtle Wisdom,
The Doctrine, of subtle character, becomes audible
Only to one whose mind is free from defilements. // 41 // [87]

(III) It is said that [the mind of the Buddha in its activity] is like a cloud [88].

(Kārikās 27–30)

Just as, in the rainy season,
The clouds discharge, without any effort,
The multitudes of water on the earth,
Causing abundance of harvest [89]; // 42 //
In a similar manner, the Buddha
Discharges the rain of the Highest Doctrine
From the clouds of Compassion, with no searching thought,
For [90] [bringing] the crops of virtue among the living beings. // 43 //
Just as the clouds discharge the rain,
Agitated by the wind, upon the earth where
The people behave in the path of virtuous actions [91];
Similarly, the cloud that is the Buddha
Pours the rain of the Highest Doctrine
As the virtues are increased in the world
Owing to the wind of Compassion. // 44 // [92]
Bearing [93] Wisdom and Compassion,

85) The reading should be '...*āyāti nikhilam*', instead of '*āyānti*...' in the text.

86) T. reads *parama* as an indeclinable (*mchog-tu*).

87) C. K 14.

88) Cf. JĀA 241 *b–c*.

89) *sasya*, T. *lo-tog*. C. om. this and the next verse (vv. 42, 43).

90) ...*sasyeṣu* (loc.) in the sense of 'in order to bring harvest'. T. reads '*sasya-hetu*' and regards it as an adjective to *saddharmasalila*.

91) *kuśala-karma-patha* T. om. *karma-*.

92) C. K 16. (interchanging the order with the next one).

93) *avabhṛtka*. C. reads something like '*pravṛtka*' (起). T. has no equivalent word and, has instead '*chen*' (*mahā*). Is it a mistake for '*can*' (*having*)? C. con-

Abiding in the celestial sphere
Without affecting anything, neither perishable nor imperishable [94],
And being the womb of the pure water
Of meditation and mystical formulas [95],
The cloud-like chieftain of sages
Causes the pure crops in various worlds. // 45 // [96]

With reference to the unequality of receptacles in measure [97],

(Kārikā 31)

Cool, sweet, clear, soft, and light [98]
Is the rain descending from the cloud,
But having touched on earth the places filled with salt, etc.,
Becomes of tastes of much variety;
Similar is the rain of the 8-fold Holy Path [99],
Descending from the cloud, the womb abundant with Compassion,
But, owing to the variety of conditions of individuals [100],
It assumes many kinds of taste in the living beings. // 46 // [101]

On the impartial attitude [102],

(Kārikās 32–34)

Those who have faith [103] in the Highest Vehicle,
Those of intermediate nature, and those who resist the Doctrine,

nects '*bhaveṣu*' (in various worlds) with '*saṃvit*' (wisdom, T. *mkhan*) and reads this line as follows:

知有起悲心 (Having known the 'existence', produces the Compassion).

[94] C. om. *kṣarâkṣarâsaṅga*–.

[95] *dhāraṇī*, T. *gzuṅs*, C. 持.

[96] C. K 15.

[97] *vimātratā*, T. *sna–tshogs–ñid* (*vicitratā*), C. 'depending on *bhājanaloka*, the taste of rain changes'.

[98] Of these 5, for *prasanna*, T. *daṅ* = *dvaṅ-ba*; C. says '八功德水' (water endowed with 8 qualities), which seems to be merely an '*alaṅkāra*' in comparison with the 8-fold Holy Path.

[99] *āryâṣṭâṅga*. But C. 八聖道.

[100] *santāna*, T. *rgyud*, C. [衆生] 心處.

[101] C. K 17.

[102] *nirapekṣa-pravṛtti*, T. *ltos–pa med–par ḥjug–pa* C. 無差別心.

[103] *abhiprasanna*, T. *daṅ–ba* (being pure), C. 信.

These are the three kinds of living beings,
And have similarity with men, peacocks [104] and ghosts [105], respectively. // 47 // [106]
Towards the end of the summer, being of no cloud,
Men and those birds who cannot fly in the sky [107]
Experience sufferings [from lack of rain];
In the rainy season, however, because of much rainfall,
The ghosts in the ground experience sufferings;
In the case of the living beings in the world,
Those desirous of the Doctrine [108] and those hostile to it,
The non-arising and the arising of the water of Doctrine
From the clouds of Compassion [cause suffering in each turn];
This is the point of similarity. // 48 // [109]
Discharging the gross drop of rain, hail and lightning [110],
The cloud does not care about the subtle living beings,
Nor about those who are on a trip in the mountains [111];
Similarly, the one who holds the waters of Wisdom and Compassion,
[Discharging them] with various means, methods and rules, subtle or gross,
Does not mind anywhere those who are of Defilements,
Whether [in the burst of] egoistic view or in a dormant state [112].
// 49 // [113]

104) *cātaka*, T. *rma-bya*, C. 遮多鳥. (The peacock is said to be delighted when he sees clouds).

105) *preta*, T. *yi-dags*, C. 鬼 (燒鬼).

106) C., K 18. C. adds one verse before v. 48, explaining the 3 groups of sattvas (正定聚衆生習氣不定聚身見邪定聚邪見流生死).

107) *vyomny-aprâcārāḥ*, *khagā* (= *cātaka*). T. *mkhaḥ mi-rgu-baḥi bya*. C. '空鳥' shows the opposit sense.

108) For *dharma-ākāṅkṣin*, C. 信法器. C. gives a free rendering for this passage.

109) C., K 20.

110) *aśani* & *vajrâgni*, T. *rdo-than* & *rdo-rjeḥi me*, C. 礔礰石 & 金剛爆火.

111) *śaila-deśa-gamika*, T. *ri-yul soṅ-ba*, C. 行人 (*gamika*).

112) The reading should be '*kleśagatâtmadṛṣty-anuśayān*' instead of '*kleśagatān dṛṣty-anuśayān*' (one syllable short). Both T. & C. agree with this reading of '*ātmadṛṣṭi*'; T. *bdag-lta*, C. 我邪見. But the genitive case for *ātmadṛṣṭi* in T. is not correct. C. reads '*kleśagata-anuśaya* (習氣) and *ātmadṛṣṭi*.

113) C. K 21.

On [the function of] calming the fire of Suffering,

(Kārikās 35–37)

The [succession] of birth and death in beginningless time
Is the Saṃsāra, in whose course [114] there are five Paths,
And in these five Paths, there is no happiness,
Just as excretion has no good smell at all;—
Its suffering is constant and as if produced from
The contact with fire, swords, ice, salt and so forth:
But, to pacify it, the cloud of Compassion
Lets fall [115] the great rain of the Highest Doctrine. // 50 // [116]
Having known that the transmigration [from heaven] [117]
Is the suffering among gods, and, for the human beings,
The searching for the objects of desire [118] is the suffering,
The Wise men never seek for the best glory [119] among gods and men;
It is because of their Transcendental Intellect,
Because of their following the faith in the Buddha's words,
And [consequently], because of their realizing analytically,
"This is suffering, this is its cause, and this is its extinction".
// 51 // [120]
Illness is to be cognized, its cause removed,
Health should be attained [121], and a remedy used [122];
Like that, Suffering, its Cause, Extinction and the Path,
Are to be cognized, removed, touched [123] and observed. // 52 // [124].

[114] *saṃsṛti* (course of transmigration), T. *ḥgro-ba*, C. 流轉. On '*anavarâgra*', see Note VIII-242.

[115] *sṛjan* (√ *sṛj*), T. *rab-tu ḥbebs* (*pravarṣate*), C. 降.

[116] C. K 23 (placing after v. 52).

[117] *cyuti-duḥkha*, T. *ḥchi-ḥpho* (om. *duḥkha*), C. 退苦.

[118] *paryeṣṭi-duḥkha*, T. *yoṅs-tshol-sdug-bsṅal*, C. 追求苦 (求不得苦). One of the 8 *duḥkhas*. Cf. Mvyut. 112.

[119] *aiśvaryam uttaram*, T. *dbaṅ-phyug mchog*, C. 自在樂.

[120] C. K 22.

[121] For *prāpya*, C. 取.

[122] For *sevya* (*niṣevya* alike), C. 修 (to be practised).

[123] *sparśitavya*, T. *reg-par-bya* (D's *rig-par-bya* is to be corrected), C. 觸. The term is here used in the sense of 'to be experienced'.

[124] C. K 22.

(IV) It is said that [the Buddha's apparitional form] is like the great Brahmā [125].

(Kārikās 38–41)

Just as Brahmā, without moving from his palace,
Manifests his apparition, without any effort,
In the world of gods everywhere;— // 53 // [126],
Similarly, the Buddha, without moving from the Absolute Body,
Comes to the sight of the worthy [127], without any effort,
With his apparitional form, in all the worlds [128]. // 54 //
Just as with Brahmā, though he never moves from his palace,
His manifestation, always pervading the World of Desire,
Is seen by gods and causes them to remove the desire of objects [129];
Similarly with the Lord, though not moving from the Absolute Body,
His sight is seen by the worthy people, in all the worlds,
And causes them to remove all the stains [130] forever. // 55 // [131]
Because of his own original vow,
And of the pure experiences [132] of the multitudes of gods,
Brahmā manifests his apparition without any effort;
Similar is the Buddha, by means of his Apparitional Body. // 56 // [133]

On the invisibility [134] [of the Apparitional form to some people],

(Kārikā 42)

Descent from [the Tuṣita], entrance in the womb,
Birth, and the arrival at his father's palace,
Merry life [in the harem] [135], wandering in solitude [136],

125) Cf. JĀA 242 *a*.

126) C. om. this and the next verse (vv. 53, 54).

127) *bhavya*, T. *skal-ldan*, C. 衆生 (in v. 55). It denotes here, *par excellence*, the Mahāyānists.

128) *sarvadhātu*. = *sarvaloka* (v. 55).

129) *viṣaya-rati-hara*, T. *yul-la dgaḥ-ba spoṅ-byed*, C. 失五欲境界.

130) For *mala-hara*, C. 不樂諸有樂.

131) C. K 26 (interchanges v. 56 & v. 55).

132) *anubhava*, T. *mthu*, C. 業.

133) C. K 25.

134) *anābhāsa-gamana*, T. *mi-snaṅ-ba* (om. *gamana*), C. 現不現 (*ābhāsânābhāse*).

135) C. inserts '*śilpasthāna-kauśala*' before *rati-krīḍa*. On these *vastus*, see S. p. 87–88 (vv. II, 54–56).

136) C. divides '*āraṇyapravicaraṇa*' into 出家 (*naiṣkramya*) & 行苦行 (*pravicaraṇa* or *duḥkhacariyā*), but T. *dben-par spyod*.

The victory over the Evil One [137],
The attainment of the Supreme Enlightenment,
And the teaching of the Path leading to the city of Peace [138],
The Buddha, though demonstrating such events,
Does not come to the eye-sight of those who are unhappy [139].
// 57 // [140]

(V) It is said that the Buddha [in his Wisdom] is like the sun [141].

(Kārikā 43)

When the sun becomes shining [142], at one and the same time
The lotus flowers awake and the Kumuda [143] folds its flowers;
But the sun has no discrimination in regard to the water-born flowers
Similar is the sun of the Saint [in his acts] in the world
In regard to the awakening of virtues and closing of defects [144].
// 58 // [145]

(On the two kinds of people compared to the two kinds of waterborn flowers) [146].

There are two kinds among the living beings: one is the non-converts and the other is the converts. Of them, with reference to the converts, there are the simile of the sun-lotus and the simile of the receptacle of pure water.

Just as the sun, without thought-construction,
With his own rays, simultaneously everywhere [147],
Lets the lotus flowers come to blossom,

137) C. inserts 現就外道學 (study under the guidance of *tīrthas*) before *mārapramathana*.

138) C. inserts *cakravartin* before this. For *praśamapura*, C. 涅槃, T. *shi-baḥi groṅ-khyer*.

139) For *adhanya*, T. *skal-med* (*abhavya*), but C. 薄福衆生.

140) C. K 27.

141) Cf. JĀA 242 *b*.

142) *tapat* (< √*tap*), T. *gduṅ-ba* (*tapati*), C. 照.

143) A kind of lotus or water-lily, which is said to open its flower at night.

144) For *guṇa* & *doṣa*, C. 有智 & 有罪, respectively.

145) C. K 28.

146) C. om. hereafter up to the prose commentary before v. 63, and this passage seems to be an interpolation.

147) *eka-muktābhir*, T. *ćig-car spros-pa-yis* (*ekatra kālasamaye* = *sakṛt*). '*muktā*' means 'a flash delivered from the sun'.

And lets the other come to ripeness; // 59 //
Similarly, the sun that is the Buddha,
With the rays of the Highest Doctrine,
Appears with no thought-construction,
Upon the converts resembling lotus flowers. // 60 //
With the body of the Absolute and that of Apparition,
Arising in the sky of the Seat of Enlightenment [148],
The sun [149] of Omniscience pervades the world
With the rays of the Transcendental Wisdom; // 61 //
From which, everywhere in the [mind of] converts
Who are like receptacles [150] of pure water,
Appear simultaneously innumerable reflections
Of that sun which is the Lord. // 62 //

Thus the Buddhas, though they are non-discriminative, manifest themselves with visible forms and by teaching among the three categories of living beings according to order. With reference to this order, there is a simile of mountains [151]:

(Kārikās 44–45)

Although the sun of the Buddha pervades [152]
Always and everywhere the sky-like Universe [153],
He casts his rays [154] upon the converts
Who are like mountains, according to their merit [155]. // 63 //
Just as, in this world, the sun [156],
Spreading out his thousands of glorious rays,
Rising and illuminating the whole world,
Shines [157] upon the mountains, high, middle, and low, gradually;

148) *bodhi-maṇḍa*, T. *byaṅ-chub-sñiṅ-po*. (*maṇḍa* = *sāra*).
149) *dinakṛt*.
150) *āśaya*, T. *snod* (= *bhājana*).
151) T. *sūryôpamatā*, instead of '*śailôpamatā*'. C. starts with this heading, saying: '*krame ślokaḥ*'.
152) The readings '*visṛte*' & '*buddhasūrye*' are to be corrected into '*visṛto*' & '*buddhasūryo*', respectively. Also '*vineyâdri*' should be changed into '*vineyâdrau*' (loc.) and be separated from '*tannipāto*'. So T., C. om. this verse.
153) *dharmadhātu*, T. *chos-dbyiṅs*.
154) *tan-nipāta*. (*sūryasya nipāta*). For *nipāta*, T. *ḥbab*.
155) *yathā'rhataḥ*, T. *ji-ltar ḥos-par*.
156) *saptasapti*.
157) *pratapati*. For this, T. *ḥbab* (*prapatati*), but C. 照 (as in the text).

Similar is the sun of the Buddha which shines
Upon the groups of living beings, according to their order. // 64 //[158]

On the superiority of [the Buddha's] light to [that of the sun],—

(Kārikās 46–47)

Of the sun[159], there does not exist the all-pervadingness[160]
In all kinds of lands and in the whole sky,
Nor does he show all things knowable [by removing]
The thicket[161] of the darkness of ignorance;
But those who are of the nature of Compassion,
Illuminate the world with spreading bands[162] of rays,
Produced from each hair[163] and filled with various colours,
And manifest all things knowable[164]. // 65 //[165]
When the Buddhas enter the city,
Those who are of no eyes perceive the object[166],
And, having seen it, cognize how to remove the net of harm[167],
And [likewise] even those blinded by ignorance,
Who have fallen into the sea[168] of the Phenomenal World,
And are obscured by the darkness of false views,
Have their intellect illumined by the light of the sun of the Buddha,
And come to perceive the Truth[169] unseen before. // 66 //[170]

158) C. K 29.

159) *bhānu*.

160) *parispharaṇatā*, T. *ḥphro*, C. 遍照.

161) *gahana*, T. *bkab* (< *ḥgebs*, to cover, spread), C. has no equivalent word and has instead '不破' (not break).

162) *visara*, T. *tshogs*, C. 雲羅網 (*abhrajāla*).

163) T. & C. om. '*ekaikaroma-udbhavair*'.

164) For *jñeyârtha*, C. 真如妙境界.

165) C. K 31. C. adds one verse before this, which runs as follows:

色智身二法 大悲身如空 遍照諸世間 故佛不同日

(The one who is of the nature of compassion,
Manifesting the two bodies, apparitional and of Wisdom,
Pervades, like space, the whole world;
Therefore, the Buddha is not the same as the sun). (C. K 30)

166) For *artha*, C. 大利 (the great benefit).

167) *anarthajāla-vigama*, C. 滅諸惡法. For *jāla*, T. *tshogs*, C. 諸 (several).

168) *arṇava* (BHS) (Pāli *aṇṇava* ?), T. *mtsho*, C. om.

169) *pada*, T. *gnas*, C. 處.

170) C. K 32.

(VI) It is said that [the Buddha's mind in its act] has a resemblance to the wish-fulfilling gem [171].

(Kārikās 48–50)

Just as the wish-fulfilling gem,
Though itself is of no thought-construction,
Fulfills all desires of those
Living in the same region [172], separately; // 67 // [173]
Similarly, those who are of different inclinations,
Having approached [174] the wish-fulfilling gem of the Buddha,
Come to hear the Truth in its various aspects.
But the Buddha has no discrimination regarding them. // 68 // [175]
Just as the precious jewel, having no thought-construction [176],
Produces the desired treasure, without effort, for others;
Similarly, the Lord always benefits others, without effort,
According to their merit, as long as the world exists. // 69 //

It is said that the Buddhas are [177] difficult to obtain.

(Kārikā 51)

Here, in this world, it is quite rare
To obtain the pure gem, even though the people so much
Long for it in the depth of the ocean or under the ground [178];
Similarly, the sight of Buddha should be known as
Not easily achieved in this luckless [179] world
By those whose mind is afflicted by various passions. // 70 //

171) Cf. JĀA 243 *a*.

172) *yugapad-gocara-sthāna*, T. *cig-car-tu spyod-yul gnas-pa*, C. 一時同處住.

173) C. K 33.

174) *sametya*, T. *brten-nas*, C. 同住 (living together) and adds '於悲心' (on the mind of Compassion).

175) C. K. 34.

176) T. om. *avikalpaṃ*, and for *maṇiratna*, *cintāmaṇiratna*; C. om. the whole verse as well as the next one along with its heading.

177) *bhāva*, T. *ḥbyuṅ-ba* (state of being). T. reads as '*durlabhaprāptas tathāgatabhāvaḥ*'.

178) *pātāla-stha*. T. *sa-ḥog gnas*.

179) *durbhaga*, T. *skal-ṅan*.

(VII) It is said that [the Buddha in his voice] is like an echo[180].

(Kārikās 52–53)

Just as the sound of an echo
Arising from the voice[181] of others
Is of no discrimination and of no effort[182],
And has no foundation, either inside or outside; // 71 //[183]
In a similar way, the voice of the Buddha
Arising through the voice of others
Is of no discrimination and of no effort,
And has no foundation, either inside or outside. // 72 //[184]

(VIII) It is said that [the Buddha's body is] like space[185].

(Kārikās 54–55)

Being immaterial[186] and invisible,
Without support[187] and without foundation,
Surpassing the way of eye-sight,
Formless and incapable of being shown, // 73 //[188]
Though being so, the sky is seen as low and high[189],
But, in reality, it is not like that;
Similarly, all kinds of forms are seen in the Buddha,
But, in reality, the Buddha is not like that. // 74 //[190].

(IX) It is said that [the Buddha as the foundation of all activities] is like the earth[191].

(Kārikās 56–57)

Just as all plants[192],

180) Cf. JĀA 243 *b*.
181) *vijñapti*, T. *rnam-rig*. C. om. (but in the next verse, '心').
182) For *anābhoga*, T. *bzo-med*.
183) C. K 35.
184) C., K. 36.
185) Cf. JĀA 243 *c* (after the simile of *pṛthivī*. JĀA puts this simile at the end).
186) *niṣkiṃcana*, T. *cuṅ-zad-med*, C. 無物.
187) *nirālamba*, T. *dmigs-pa med*, C. 無觀.
188) C. K 37.
189) *nimnônnata*, T. *mtho daṅ dmaḥ* (high and low), C. 高下 (as T.).
190) C. K 38.
191) Cf. JĀA 243 *c*.
192) *mahīruha* (= *mahiruh*), T. *sa-las skye-ba*, C. 草木.

Taking resort to the earth
Which has no searching thought,
Come to grow, thrive [193] and expand; // 75 // [194]
Similarly, the roots of virtues in the world,
Taking resort to the ground of the Buddha
Who has no searching thought,
Proceed completely towards growth. // 76 // [195]

§ 3. Summarized Meaning of the Illustrations given by the Commentator.

Summarized meaning of these examples is as follows:

The performance of actions without effort
Connot be seen by us [196]. Therefore,
The ninefold examples have been related
In order to clear the doubts of the converts. // 77 //
Its purpose [of teaching] is explained
By the very name of that Scripture,
Where these nine illustrations
Are demonstrated in detail. // 78 //
Adorned with [197] this light of the great wisdom
Which is the result of study,
The wise men enter rapidly
In the whole region of the Buddha. // 79 //
For this reason [198], there are nine examples
Illustrated by the reflection of Indra
On the surface of Vaiḍūrya stone, and the rest.
In this sense [199], you should know their summarized meaning;—
// 80//

193) *vairūḍhi*, T. *brtan-pa* (become firm), C. om., and for *vaipulya*, 成就 (in the next verse however, C. 增, 廣, 成, 就 for *vṛddhim upayānti*).

194) C. K 39.

195) C. K 40.

196) T. connects '*kaścid*' with '*kriyām*'. C. reads as '*kriyām ṛte*' and om. *prayatnam*.

197) The reading '*ālokâdy-alaṅkṛtāḥ*' had better be changed into '*ālokād alaṅkṛtāḥ*', according to T. which reads '*... ḥdis brgyan-pa*' (*etena alaṅkṛtāḥ*). '*ādi*' gives no sense. This verse stands for the title of the sūtra, namely the *Sarvabuddhaviṣayâvatāra-jñānâlokâlaṅkārasūtra*.

198) *ity artham*, T. *de-don* (*tad-artham*), C. om.

199) *tasmin*, T. *deḥi* (*tasya*), C. om.

[Namely]: appearance, teaching [200], pervasion,
Transformation [201], and emanation of Wisdom,
Secrecy in acts by mind, speech and body,
And acquisition of those whose nature is of Compassion [202]. // 81 //
[The Buddha's] mind [203], being of no thought-construction,
Is such in which all the movements of effort are pacified,
As given in the examples, beginning with the arising
Of the reflection of Indra on the pure Vaiḍūrya stone. // 82 //
The 'proposition' is here the pacification of effort,
The 'logical reason' is the non-discriminativeness of mind,
And, in order to establish the 'subject in discussion' [204],
There are given 'examples', the form of Indra, etc. // 83 //
And here the 'subject in discussion' is that
These nine, 'appearance' and the rest,
Are manifested without any effort
And without birth or death [205] of the Preceptor. // 84 //

§ 4. Summary of examples given in Kārikās [206].

With reference to this meaning (or subject), we have other four *ślokas*, being the summary of all the examples.

(Kārikās 58–61)

The one who acts for the sake of others,
Without effort, as long as the world exists,

200) *darśanādeśanā.* A doubtful reading as J suggested. Shall we accept '*darsanā*' as an irregular form for *darśana*? If so both terms are to be written separately.

201) *vikṛti*, T. *sprul.* C. 以離諸相 gives no suitable sense.

202) *karuṇā-ātmānāṃ prāptiḥ*, T. *thugs-rjeḥi bdag-ñid thob-pa-ñid*, C. 大慈悲者得. I incline to interpret that this '*karuṇâtmānām*', which as a genitive case is connected to all these 9. *Karuṇā-ātmā*, means the Buddha or the Bodhisattva. These 9 meanings are given to each of the 9 illustrations, respectively. Namely: 1) '*darśana*' (*darsanā ?*) for *śakrapratibhāsa*; 2) '*deśanā*' for *devadundubhi*; 3) '*vyāpi*' for *megha*; 4) '*vikṛti*' for *Brahmā*; 5) '*jñāna-niḥsṛti*' for *sūrya*; 6) '*mano-guhyaka*' for *cintāmaṇi*; 7) '*vāg-guhyaka*' for *pratiśrutika*; 8) '*kāya-guhyaka*' for *ākāśa*; & 9) '*prāpti*' for *bhūmi*.

203) *dhī* (text, in pl.), T. *thugs*.

204) *prakṛtârtha*, T. *raṅ-bshin-don* (*prakṛtyartha*), C. as *vicitra-artha*. In the next verse, C. 成...義 (to establish the meaning) (成 is used in the verse for '*susiddha*').

205) *antardhi*, T. *ḥchi*. But C. 離生離神通 (*janmântarddhim ṛte*).

206) C. om. this passage up to v. 87, but mentions v. 88 at the end of the illustration of *pṛthivī*. As for the treatment of this group of verses, see my *Introduction*, II, § 2.

Like Indra, like the divine drum, like clouds,
Like Brahmā, like the sun, like the wish-fulfilling gem,
Like an echo, like the sky and like the earth, . . .
That is [the Buddha] who knows a means [of precept] [207].
// 85 //

The excellent teacher [208] has an appearance
Like the reflection of the chief of gods on the jewel,
His voice is like the [sound of] the divine drum,
Having the great sphere of the clouds of Wisdom and Mercy,
He pervades an unlimited number of living beings,
Up to the highest limit of existence [209]. // 86 //
Like Brahmā, the Buddha
Shows himself variously with the apparitional forms,
Without moving from the immaculate place [210];
Like the sun, he shines always, spreading the light of Wisdom;
And his mind [acts] like the wish-fulfilling gem. // 87 //
Like an echo is the Buddha's voice,
Not being expressed by letters [211];
Like space is his body,
Being all-pervading, formless and eternal;
And like the earth is the State of Buddha [212] in this world,
Being the seat [213] of all virtues, the remedy [214] of the whole world.
// 88 // [215]

[207] *yogavid*, (as an epithet of the Buddha), T. *rnal-ḥbyor-rig*.

[208] *sudaiśika*, T. *legs-par ḥdoms-mdsad*. The Buddha is *sudaiśika*. T. takes *devadundubhi* as relating to this word, and om. '*vibho rutam*'.

[209] *ā bhavāgrataḥ*, T. *srid-rtseḥi bar-du*. The translation is according to T. If we take '*agra*' as 'beginning', the meaning is 'since the very beginning of the world'.

[210] *anāsravāt padād*, which denotes '*anāsravadhātu*', i.e. *dharmakāya*.

[211] *anakṣara-ukta*, T. *yi-ge-min* (om. *ukta*), C. 以名字無說 which gives proper sense.

[212] *buddhabhūmi*, T. *saṅs-rgyas-sa*, C. 佛地.

[213] *āspada*, T. *gshir gyur-pa*, C. 依 . . .

[214] *śukladharma-auṣadhī*, T. *dkar-poḥi chos-kyi sman*, C. 一切諸妙藥 and 自淨妙法藥 (as the earth is *āspada* of *auṣadhi*, the Buddha's *bhūmi* is *āspada* of *śukladharma*, being *auṣadhi*), which shows the proper interpretation of the simile.

[215] C. K 41.

§ 5. Non-origination and Non-extinction of the Buddhahood[216].

Why, then, in this exposition of examples, is the Buddha, who is always of neither origination nor extinction, explained to be seen with appearance and disappearance and as having actions, to work among all living beings, without effort and without interruption? [To answer this question, there are three verses].

Like the Vaiḍūrya stone, the purity in the mind
Is the cause of the Buddha's appearance,
And this purity of mind is intensified
By the irresistible[217] faculty of faith. // 89 //[218]
Owing to the appearance and disappearance of purity,
The forms of the Buddha appear and disappear;
But, in his Body of the Absolute[219] that is like Indra,
The Lord does never appear nor disappear. // 90 //[220]
Thus, his actions, apparition and the rest,
Are manifested without any effort,
From the Absolute Body, which never arises nor disappears,
As long as the world exists[221]. // 91 //[222]

§ 6. The Point of Dissimilarity[223].

This is the summarized meaning of similes
And this very order is told in order to show
That the dissimilarity of the former example

[216] This passage is again doubtful with regard to its position in the text. C. inserts the following 3 verses, along with one additional verse and with the heading '*anutpādânirodhas tathāgata iti*' at the end of the 1st illustration, '*śakrapratibhāsavat*' (after v. 28). As for the treatment of this passage, see my *Introduction*, II, § 2. The verse added in C before v. 89 is as follows: 如毘琉璃滅 彼鏡像亦滅 無可化衆生 如來不出世.

[217] *asaṃhārya*, T. *mi-zlogs-pa*, C. 不壞.

[218] C., K 9.

[219] C. om. *dharmakāya*.

[220] C., K 10.

[221] *ā bhavasthiteḥ*, C. 盡諸際.

[222] C., K 11.

[223] So-called '*vyatirekâlaṅkāra* (O). C. puts v. 92 immediately after v. 84.

[With the Buddha] is removed by the latter one[224]. // 92 //
Buddhahood is like the reflection [of Indra],
But the reflection, being of no voice, is not like that;
[Being endowed with voice, the Buddha] is like
The divine drum, which however does not match him,
Since it is not everywhere making benefits. // 93 //
[Being beneficial everywhere], he is like a big cloud,
Which however, having no seed of virtue[225], is not like him;
[Being the root of virtue][226], he is like great Brahmā,
But, being unable to ripen perfectly, Brahmā is not like him. // 94 //
[As the cause of perfect maturity], he is like the sun,
But the sun cannot remove darkness fully, so it is not like him,
[As the darkness-breaker], he is like the wish-fulfilling gem,
Which, however, is not as difficult to get as he is. // 95 //
The Buddha has a resemblance to an echo[227],
Which however, being a product of causes, is not like him,
[Being of no cause][228] he has a resemblance to space,
Which, not being the basis of virtues, is not like him. // 96 //
The Buddha resembles the region of the earth,
Since he is the ground and foundation[229]
For the achievement of all the virtues
Of living beings, mundane and supermundane[230]. // 97 //

224) '...*kramaḥ punaḥ / pūrvakasyôttareṇôkto vaidharmyaparihārataḥ* /' = *punaḥ, kramo uktaḥ, pūrvakasya vaidharmyasya uttareṇa parihārataḥ*'. T. *rim-pa yaṅ sṅa-ma phyi-mas chos-mi-mthun spaṅs-paḥi sgo-nas brjod-pa yin*. C. 先喻解異後後喻解異前.

225) *sārthabīja*, T. *don-med-paḥi sa-bon spoṅ min* (for '*na sārtha*...'), C. 生種種諸種子. It shows the sense that '*megha*' cannot remove '*anarthabija*', in another word, '*megha*' cannot distinguish either '*sārtha*' or '*anartha*'. After all J's reading seems correct.

226) C. 'being *acala* like *Brahmā*'

227) Here we cannot get the proper similarity of echo to the Buddha by means of the same operation as it is used in former examples. Echo cannot be '*durlabdha*'! Furthermore, '*durlabdhatva*' of *cintāmaṇi* was mentioned previously (v. 70) as a point of similarity to the Buddha.

228) Cf. '*tathāgatavyoma nimittavarjitam*' (II, v. 20).

229) C. reads 不住持, being a dissimilation of '*pṛthivī*' with the Buddha. But it is not the case.

230) In this series of illustrations, the author seems to have had an opinion that the earth is the foundation of everything, and consequently, is the nearest simile for the Buddha. It is, however, quite against the other cases in this text, where '*ākāśa*' is

By resorting to [231] the Buddha's Enlightenment,
There arises the supermundane Path, and hence,
There emerges the Path of virtuous actions,
Consisting of meditation, the immeasurable mind
And the absorption in the Immaterial Sphere [232]. // 98 //

Finished is the fourth chapter entiled 'the Acts of the Buddha', in the ANALYSIS OF THE GERM OF THE JEWELS, a Treatise on the Ultimate Doctrine of the Great Vehicle with the commentary [named] 'the Summary of Meaning of the *ślokas*'. //

used as the most suitable simile for the Buddha. And as this very order was arranged in the Udāharaṇa-kārikās against the order given in JĀA (which puts the simile of '*ākāśa*' at the last), we may be allowed to say that those Udāharaṇa-kārikās in Chap. IV were not composed by the same author as that of the Basic verses in Chapter I.

[231] *āgamya*, T. *brten-nas*, C. 依 (= *āśritya*).

[232] *dhyāna*, *apramāṇa*, *ārūpya*, respectively. '*dhyāna*' stands for the 4 kinds of *dhyāna* (Cf. Mvyut. 67), '*apramāṇa*' stands for those, *maitrī*, *karuṇā* *muditā* & *upekṣa* (Cf. Mvyut. 69), and '*ārūpya*', for the *sampatti* in 4 kinds of *ārūpyadhātu* (Cf. Mvyut. 162).

C. adds one verse more after v. 98, saying:

諸如來自然 常住諸世間 有如是諸業 一時非前後 作如是妙業 (Buddhas perform these actions, without effort, abiding always in [various] worlds, at one and the same time).

Chapter V.

THE MERITS OF FAITH

(ANUŚAMSA)

XVIII. THE MERITS OF HAVING FAITH IN THE DOCTRINE OF THE ESSENCE OF BUDDHAHOOD

§ 1. The Superiority of Faith over Other Virtues in Regard to Their Merits.

Hereafter, with reference to the advantage of faith [1] possessed by those who are believing in these [4] subjects [2] which have been duly described above, we have six *ślokas*.

(Kārikās 1–6)

The Essence of Buddhahood, the Enlightenment of the Buddha,
The Buddha's Properties, and the Buddha's Acts,
They are inconceivable even to those of the pure mind [3],
Being the exclusive sphere of the Leaders [4]. // 1 //
But the wise one, whose intellect [5] accepts the faith
In this exclusive sphere of the Buddha,
Becomes a receptacle of the whole collection of properties,
And, being possessed of the desire [to obtain] [6]
The inconceivable properties [of the Buddha],

1) *adhimukty-anuśaṃsa*, T. *mos-paḥi phan-yon*, C. 信功德.

2) Namely: *Samalā tathatā* (or *tathāgatagarbha*) in Chap. I, *Nirmalā tathatā* in Chap. II, *Buddhaguṇāḥ*, in Chap. III, and *Buddhakriyā* in Chap. IV. T. & C. add '*caturṣu*' before '*sthāneṣu*'.

3) *śuddhasattva*, T. *dag-paḥi sems*, C. [出世] 淨人.

4) *nāyaka*, T. *ḥdren-pa*, C. 佛. The verse corresponds to v. 23 of Chap. I.

5) *buddhi*. But T. as if '*buddha*'. C. has no equivalent word.

6) For *guṇâbhilāṣayogāt*, T. reads *-guṇâbhiḷāṣāt*.

He surpasses the abundance [7] of merits of all living beings. // 2 //
Suppose there were one who, being anxious to obtain the Enlightenment,
Would offer golden lands, constructed [8] by jewels
As innumerable as the sands in the Buddha's lands,
To the Lord of Doctrine, always, day after day;
Another if he hear but one word of this teaching [9],
After hearing of it, would have faith in this Doctrine;
The latter would reap merits far more than the merits [10] of an offering. // 3 //
Suppose a wise man, being desirous of the Highest Enlightenment,
Would keep pure moral conduct by his body, speech and mind,
Without effort, in course of innumerable aeons;
Another, if he hear but one word of this teaching,
After hearing of it, would have faith in this Doctrine;
The latter would reap merits far more than the merits of morality. // 4 //
Suppose one would give himself up to the mystic absorption,
Which suppresses the fire of defilements in the 3 worlds [11],
And, having been transferred [12] to the abode of Brahman in heaven,
Would be irreversible [13] from the means of Enlightenment;
Another, if he hear but one word of this teaching,
After hearing of it, would have faith in this Doctrine;
The latter would reap merits far more than even the merits of the mystic absorption. // 5 //
Charity brings people only to [worldly] enjoyment [14],
Morality leads people to the blissful world [15],
And meditation is conducive to the removal of Defilements,
But the Transcendental Intellect can remove

[7] *prasava*, T. om., C. not clear.
[8] *saṃskṛta*, T. *spros-pa*, C. om.
[9] *itaḥ padam*. '*itas*', from this religion. Cf. *ito-bāhyas* (S. p. 28. 6).
[10] *puṇya*.
[11] *tribhuvana*, T. *srid-pa gsum*, C. 三界.
[12] For *pārami-gata*, C. 過天行彼岸.
[13] For *acyuta*, C. reads 'have no ...(無); T. adds '*bhāvanā*' (*bsgoms*).
[14] For *bhoga*, C. 得富貴報 (to get richness as merits).
[15] *svarga*, T. *mtho-ris*, C. 生人天中.

All [the obscurations of] defilements and ignorance.
Therefore, Intellect is the supreme one [of all virtues]
And its very source is the study of this Doctrine[16]. // 6 //

The summarized meaning of these *ślokas* should be known by the following 9 verses.

The basis [of Buddhahood][17], its transformation[18],
Its properties and the performance of welfare[19],
In these four aspects of the sphere of Buddha's Wisdom,
Which have been explained above, // 7 //
The wise one has become full of faith
With regard to its existence, power and virtue[20],
Therefore, he quickly attains the potentiality[21]
Of acquiring the state[22] of the Tathāgata. // 8 //
Indeed, as he is full of devotion and faith
That there 'exists' this inconceivable sphere,

16) C. adds 3 *padas* explaining: "Therefore, *śruti* is the supreme. Needless to say, about the merit of having faith after hearing of the doctrine (是故聞法勝何況聞法已得能生信心)". This arrangement of the 4 *pāramitās* (which are construed with the 6 *pāramitās* by the commentator) seems to show the previous stage of the '*pāramitā*' doctrine. Of these 4, the first 3 are called '*puṇyakriyā-vastu*' (Cf. Mvyut. 93) and represent '*puṇya-saṃbhāra*'.

17) *āśraya*, T. *gnas*, C. 身. It denotes '*dhātu*' or '*tathāgatagarbha*'.

18) This is the only case where the term '*parāvṛtti*' is used instead of '*parivṛtti*'. (T. *gyur-pa*, C. [彼] 所轉. Probably the original reading was '*-parivṛttau*' as J. suggested. But there is no proof for this suggestion.

19) *artha-sādhana*, C. 成義, T. *don-grub*. This is for '*buddhakriyā*'.

20) *astitva*, *śaktatva* & *guṇavattva*; T. *yod*[*-ñid*], *nus-ñid*, *yon-tan-ldan-pa*; C. 有, 畢竟得, 諸功德, resp. BGŚ makes use of these 3 points in various passages: 794 *b*, 795 *c*–796 *a* (applied to the 3 meanings of *tathāgatagarbha*); 799 *c* (adding '*acintyatva*', counts 4 points of faith); 811 *b* (as the first 3 of the 5 meanings of *garbha* explained through 9 illustrations); 812 *c*–813 *a* (as the 3 fundamental points of discussion of the work).

This theory of '3 points of faith' is often found in the works of Vijñānavāda with the order of '*astivta-guṇavattva-śaktatva*', but the reference is to '*karma-phala*', '*ārya-satya*', and '*triratna*', and not to '*gotra*'. (e. g. VMT *Bhāṣya*, p. 26, ll. 24–30; Hsüang-chuang's tr. of MSbh, *Taisho* 31, p. 350 *b*, etc.). Its application to *gotra* seems to belong only to the *Ratna.* and BGŚ. (Cf. MSbh (P), 194 *b*–200 *c*, where it is applied to '*gotra-astitva*', probably under the influence of the *Ratna.*).

21) *bhavyatā*, T. *skal-ldan* (om. *-tā*) C. 無上道 (*bhavyatā* in the sense of 'excellence' and is regarded as an apposition to '*tathāgata-padâpti*').

22) *pada*, T. *go-ḥphaṅ*, C. 所住處.

That it 'can' be realized by one like him [23],
And this sphere, 'endowed with such virtues', has been attained, // 9 //

So in him the mind intent on Enlightenment [24],
Being a receptacle of virtues like zeal, energy,
Memory, contemplation, Transcendental Intellect, etc.,
Comes to exist always. // 10 //
As this mind constantly exists [25],
The son of the Buddha becomes irreversible,
And he reaches the accomplishment and the perfect purity [26],
With regard to the Highest of Merits [27]. // 11 //
'The [Highest of] Merits' means the [first] 5 Highest virtues,
'Its accomplishment' is owing to his being non-discriminative
With regard to the three aspects [of activity] [28],
And 'the perfect purity' is caused by his removal of the opponents. // 12 //

Charity is the merit consisting of granting gift,
Morality is the merit consisting of moral conduct,
And both Patience and Meditation, is that of practice,
But Exertion is the merit common to all. // 13 //
Discrimination regarding the 3 aspects of activity,
That is the Obscuration of Ignorance;
The opponents [29] [to the 5 Highest Virtues], jealousy, etc.,
They are the Obscurations of Defilements. // 14 //
But, without the Highest Intellect,
The other 5 cannot be the cause of their removal;
Therefore, the Highest Intellect is the supreme one of all,
And, as the source of it [30] is the study [of this Doctrine],
It is this study that is the most important. // 15 //

23) lit. like me. (*mādṛsa*).

24) *bodhicitta*, T. *byaṅ-chub-sems*, C. 無上菩提心.

25) According to T. & C., the reading '*taccittapratyupasthānād*' is to be corrected into '*tannityapratyupasthānād*'.

26) *pūri* & *pariśuddhi*. Both are to be taken as connecting with *puṇyapāramitā*'. For '*pūri*', T. *rdsogs*, C. 畢竟, 畢竟能成就.

27) *puṇya-pāramitā*, which corresponds to '*puṇya-saṃbhāra*'. For '*puṇya*', T. *bsod-nams*, C. 功德.

28) It is explained in v. 14 as '*trimaṇḍala-pariśuddhi*,. 3 are 'giver', 'receiver' and 'gift'.

29) For *vipakṣa*, T. reads *vikalpa*. But it is not the case (see v. 12) C. 所治法.

30) The reading '*câsya*' is to be corrected into '*câsyā*' (being a pronoum for *prajñā*).

§ 2. Authority, Motive, and Characteristics of This Text Being the Correct Doctrine.

[Hereafter we have *ślokas* mentioning on which basis, for what motive, and how this doctrine has been explained and what characteristics it has. First of all, with reference to the basis and motive, there is one *śloka* [31)]].

(Kārikā 7)

Thus, on the basis of the authoritative Scripture and of Logic [32)],
This treatise is expounded by me in order to attain
Perfect purification for myself, exclusively;
At the same time, however, this is in order to assist [33)]
Those intelligent people who are endowed with faith
And accomplishment of virtues [34)]. // 16 //

[Next we have one *śloka* stating how this treatise is explained] [35)].

(Kārikā 8)

Just as, with the aid of a lamp, of lightning,
Of a precious stone, of the moon and the sun [36)],
Those possessed of vision can perceive objects;
Similarly, I have expounded this treatise

31) The headings which are given in brackets are missing in S. Except for this and the last one, i.e. the heading for v. 24, T. retains all the headings, and C., has all of them, including those two. This one is according to C. The topic of each *śloka* is, however, given in the commentary verse.

Emendation: (*ataḥ, paraṃ yataś ca yannimittaṃ ca yathā ca yadudāhṛtaṃ tadārabhya ślokāḥ /) tatra yamāśraye yannimittaṃ côdāhṛtaṃ tadārabhya ślokaḥ /.*

The following passage containing 10 Kārikās (vv. 16–25) and 3 commentary verses (vv. 26–28) along with heading thereon is inserted with exact order and wording in Paramārtha's tr. of MSbh (*Taisho* 31, p. 270 *a–b*).

32) *āptâgama* & *yukti*, T. *yid-ches-luṅ* & *rigs-pa*. But C. seems to divide the first one into '*āpta*' & '*āgama*' and says '諸如來教, 修多羅相應' ('*āpta*' in the sense of '*āptavacana*').

33) *anugraha*, T. *rje-su-gzuṅ*, C. 攝.

34) *kuśalôpasaṃpadā*. C. om. '*kuśalasampad*'.

35) *kathaṃ* (or *yathā*) *udāhṛtaṃ tadārabhya ślokaḥ* /, according to T. C. '*kim artham iti*...'.

36) *bhāskara*.

Relying upon the Lord who is the sun[37]
Manifesting[38] the Doctrine of great welfare. // 17 //

[Then we have one *śloka* stating the characteristics of the correct doctrine][39].

(Kārikā 9)

Whatever the word[40] that is connected with the scriptural texts[41]
It pursues the [ultimate] aim [of living beings][42],
Is conducive to removing the Defilements in the 3 Worlds,
And can demonstrate the advantage of Quiescence,
Such a word is that of the Great Sage[43],
And all others are of perverse character[44]. // 18 //

[Next we have one *śloka* stating by what means this treatise is explained][45].

(Kārikā 10)

Whatever is spoken by those whose mind is not distracted
And who refer to[46] the Lord as the only Preceptor,

37) *prabhākara*. But T. *ḥod-mdsad-pa* (illuminating). C. 光明 (illumination, light) is for either '*prabhākara*' or '*pratibhā*'.

38) *pratibhā*, T. *spobs* (O. flash of idea). For v. 17 *c d*, C. reads:

依佛法光明 聖眼者能見 以法有是利 故我說此法

(Similarly, by the light of the Buddha's doctrine, those possessed of vision of intelligence come to see. As the doctrine has such a benefit, I have expounded this teaching).

39) Acc. to C. (依彼相故). But T. '*yadudāhṛtaṃ tadārabhya ślokaḥ*'. C. gives clearer sense though the original S. was probably as T.

40) *vacas*, T. *gsuṅ*, C. 所說.

41) *dharmapada*, T. *chos* (om. *pada*), C. 法句.

42) *arthavat*, T. *don-ldan*, C. 有義, and separates it from *dharmapada* (有義, 有法句).

43) *ārṣa*, T. *draṅ-sroṅ-gsuṅ*, C. 佛說 [是正經]. This term *ārṣa* is, like *āptâgama*, used originally for the Vedas.

44) *viparīta*, T. *bzlog-pa*, C. 顛倒說. This verse is quoted in the *Bodhicaryâvatāra-pañjikā* (Bibl. Ind. edition, p. 432).

45) Acc. to T., *yenôdāhṛtaṃ tadārabhya ślokaḥ*; C. puts here the heading which is to be put before v. 19. This topic is called '*niṣyandaphala*' in the commentary.

46) *uddiśat*, T. *dbaṅ-byas* (*uddiśya* or *adhikṛtya*). C. reading of this verse is rather

And is favourable to the Path of the [2] Accumulations which lead to Emancipation,
That is also to be accepted with respect [47]
As if it were taught by the Great Sage. // 19 //

§ 3. The Means of Preserving Oneself within the Doctrine.

[Here we have two *ślokas* referring to the means of preserving oneself from becoming deprived (of this Doctrine) [48]]

(Kārikās 11–12)

Indeed in this world there is no one wiser than the Buddha,
No other who is omniscient and knows completely
The highest Truth according to the right method;
Therefore, the Scripture should not be interpolated [49],
Which is discoursed [50] by the Sage himself,
Otherwise, it will do harm [51] to the Highest Doctrine
Because of destroying [52] the teaching [53] of the Buddha. // 20 //

difficult to identify with S. It is as follows:

雖說法句義 斷三界煩惱 無明覆慧眼 貪等諸垢纏
又於佛法中 取少分說者 世典善言說 彼三尙可受
何況諸如來 遠離煩惱苦 無漏眞智人 所說修多羅

(The [word] of one who, although he preaches the *dharmapadârtha* [in order to] remove the *kleśas* in the *tridhātu*, still has vision whose intelligence is covered by *avidyā*, and himself is hindered by the stains, *rāga*, etc., or [the word spoken by] one who accepts a little part of the Buddha's doctrine, or the beneficial words spoken in the worldly books, even those words could be accepted [as the correct teaching]. Needless to say, the doctrine in the *sūtra* which is spoken by the Buddhas who have removed the suffering caused by *kleśas* and are of the immaculate Wisdom is to be accepted.

For v. 19 *b* (*śāstāram ekam jinam uddiśadbhiḥ*), T. *rgyal-paḥi bstan-pa ḥbaḥ-shig-gyis dbaṅ-byas.*

47) *mūrdhnā*, (lit. by the head), T. *spyi-bos.*

48) Acc. to T., ' *ātmarakṣaṇôpāyam ārabhya dvau ślokau* /. C. *dharma-rakṣaṇa*, instead of *ātmarakṣaṇa.*

49) *vicālya* (< *vi-√cal*).

50) *nīta*, which is, *par excellence*, the teaching of the Buddha and is opposite to *neya* [*-artha*]. T. *gshag* (< *ḥjog-pa*, laid down), C. 了義.

51) *pratibādhana*, T. *gnod-pa byed-pa*, C. 謗.

52) *bheda*, T. *gshig* (< *ḥjig-pa*), C. 不識?

53) *nīti*, T. *tshul*, C. 意.

The fact that people abuse [54] the Sages
And blame [55] the doctrine taught by the Sages,
All this is the Defilement of those whose nature is foolish [56]
And is created by a prejudiced conception [57];
Therefore, your mind should not be attached
To the dirt of the prejudiced conception;
Indeed, only clean cloth can be dyed [58]
But not one that is spoiled by oil and dust. // 21 //

§ 4. Causes and Results of the Loss of the Doctrine.

[With reference to the causes of the loss of the Doctrine, there is one *śloka*] [59].

(Kārikā 13)

Want of intelligence, want of faith in the virtuous Doctrine [60],
Indulgence in false pride,
Obscured nature through the rejection [61] of the Highest Doctrine,
Interpretation of the conventional sense [62] as the [ultimate] Truth,
Greediness [63], [adherence to] false conception [64],
Devotion to those who hate the Doctrine,

54) *apa-√vad*, T. *skur-pa*, C. 謗.

55) √ *garh*, T. *brñas*, C. 壞.

56) *vimūḍha*, T. *rmoṅs*, C. 愚癡. T. & C., take *kleśa* together with *vimūḍhâtmānāṃ* and make the sense of 'of or by those whose nature is afflicted by *kleśa* and *vimūḍha*'. But it is not the case.

57) *abhiniveśadarśana*, T., *shen-lta*, C. 邪思惟.

58) *raṅga-vikṛtim upaiti*, T. *tshon-gyis rnam-bsgyur*, C. 受色.

59) Acc. to T, *kṣatihetum ārabhya ślokaḥ* /. C. '*saddharmakṣatim ārabhya*...'.

60) *adhimukta-śukla-viraha*, T. *dkar-mos bral*, C. 不信白法.

61) *vyasana*, T. *phoṅs-pa*, C. 謗. For this defect, C. 過去謗法障 (obscuration caused by the *dharmâpavāda* in the past).

62) *neyârtha*, T. *draṅ-don*, C. 不了義 (imperfect meaning).

63) *lobha-gredhatā*. Both *lobha* & *gredha* have the same sense. Probably it is merely a repetition for arranging syllables. But T. *rñed-la brtam* (*lābha-gredha*, greed of attaining something) and C. 著供養恭敬 (adherence to worship and respecting).

64) *darśana* in the sense of *dṛṣṭi*, i.e. *mithyādṛṣṭi*.

Keeping at distance [65] from those who convey the Doctrine [66],
And delighting in the inferior Doctrine [67],
By all this, one becomes deprived of the Doctrine of the Saint [68].
// 22 //

[With reference to the result of this loss, there are two *ślokas*] [69].

(Kārikās 14–15)

The wise one need not be so much afraid of fire,
Of violent poison of snake, of murder, or of lightning [70],
As he should be afraid of the loss [71] of the profound Doctrine [72],
Because a fire, a snake, an enemy, and lightning,
At most, may deprive one of [this] life
But one will not go, by these causes,
To the most terrible world of Avīci. // 23 //
Even one who, repeatedly serving [73] bad friends [74],
Is hostile to the Buddha [75], and commits the acts [76]
Of killing mother, father, and the Saints [77],

65) *āra* (distance, near or far) T. *bsriṅs*, C. 遠離.

66) *dharmabhṛt*, T. *chos-ḥdsin*, C. 善知識.

67) *hīna*, here, stands for *hīnayāna*. So C. 小乘法.

68) For *arhat*, C. 諸佛. C. adds 不信於大乘 as the general cause.

69) Acc. to T. & C., '*kṣatiphalam ārabhya dvau ślokau* /'.

70) For *aśani*, T. *thog*, C. [因陀羅] 霹靂. C., adds 諸悪獸師子虎狼等.

71) T. '*rnams*' is a mistake for '*ṅams*' (*kṣati*).

72) C. adds 及謗法知識 (blame of those who know the doctrine). It is probably an intentional addition by the C. translator, and this addition corresponds to the Introductory verses in C. and one additional verse after v. 24 referring to the necessity of having respect towards '*dharmabhāṇaka*'. See below.

73) *pratisevya*. About this form, see J's note on this word. C. 近 (to approach).

74) *pāpa-suhṛd*, T. *sdig-grogs*, C. 悪知識.

75) *buddha -duṣṭâśaya*, C. 悪心出佛血 (to injure the Buddha with bad intention.

76) For *ācaraṇakṛt*, T. *bya-ba-min-byed* (to do what is not to be done). *bya-ba-min* = *anācaraṇa* (vice).

77) *arihat* (BHS) = *arhat* (*ari-han*, one who kills the enemy. T. '*dgra-bcom-pa*' for Arhat is according to this etymology).

And breaks the unity of the Highest Community[78],
Even that one can quickly become delivered from that sin
If he meditates upon[79] the meaning[80] of the Doctrine;
But, how would it be possible for the Liberation to arise
In one whose mind is hostile to the Doctrine[81]! // 24 //

§ 5. Conclusion.

[Here, at the end we have one *śloka* in order to turn the merit acquired by the author through this teaching towards the people][82].

(Kārikā 16)

I have thus duly expounded the 7 subjects,
The 3 Jewels, the perfectly pure Essence[83],
The Immaculate Enlightenment, the [Buddha's] Properties and Acts;
By the merit I have acquired through this,
May all living beings come to perceive

[78] These 5 are regarded as the worst sins for the Buddhist. Cf. Mvyut. 122, *pañcânantaryāni*, (C. 五無間業). The first one in this text comes at the end and is called '*tathāgatasyântike duṣṭacitta-rudirôtpādanam*' as C. reads (see Note 75).

[79] *nidhyāna*, T. *ṅes-par bsams-pa*, C. 繫念.

[80] Instead of *dharmârtha*, T. has '*dharmatva*' and C. '*saddharma*'.

[81] C. adds one verse more referring to the necessity of having respect towards the *dharmabhāṇaka*. It runs as follows:

若人令衆生　學信如是法　彼是我父母　亦是善知識
彼人是智者　以如來滅後　廻邪見顚倒　令入正道故

(If one lets the people study this doctrine and teaches how to believe in it, he is as our parents and is a good leader, a wise man, because he lets the people, after the Buddha's *parinirvāṇa*, turn away from the wrong view and enter the right path).

Note that this additional verse is not found in MSbh (P).

[82] This heading is lacking in T. and is reconstructed according to C. (依彼所說法所得功德，以用廻向故，說三偈).

Cf. MSbh (P) 270 *a*:

衆寶界如覺德業　我說句義所生善
因此願悉見彌陀　由得淨眼成正覺

[83] *vyavadānadhātu*, T. *rnam-par-byaṅ-khams*, C. 淸淨性. = *tathāgatagarbha*. These 7 are called '*vajrapada*' by the commentator in the open verse of this treatise. Therefore, the genuine character of this verse as a Kārikā is somewhat doubtful.

The Lord Amitāyus endowed with infinite light [84],
And, having seen him, may they, owing to the arising
Of the immaculate vision of the Doctrine in them,
Obtain the Supreme Enlightenment. // 25 //

The summary of topics discussed in these 10 *ślokas* (vv. 16–25) should be known by the following 3 verses.

Owing to what basis, for what motive,
How and what is expounded [in this treatise],
And what is the natural outflow [of the Buddha's Doctrine],
These topics are explained by the [first] 4 *ślokas* [85]. // 26 //
Two *ślokas* refer to the means of self-protection [86],
And one, to the cause of the loss [of the Doctrine] [87],
And then, the [following] two *ślokas* [88]
Explain the result of this loss. // 27 //
And finally, the acceptance [89] [of the Doctrine]
By those living in the world of Sāṃsāra [90]
And their acquisition of Enlightenment;—
In short, these 2 results of teaching of the meaning
Of the Doctrine [91] are explained by the last *śloka*. // 28 //

Thus is finished the fifth chapter entitled 'the Merits of Faith' in the ANALYSIS OF THE GERM OF THE JEWELS, a Treatise on the Ultimate Doctrine of the Great Vehicle with the commentary [named] 'the Summary of meaning of the *ślokas*'. // 5 //

84) *anantadyuti*, T. *mthaḥ-yas ḥod-mnaḥ*. An epithet of the Lord Amitāyus, for which C. usual translation is '無量光佛'. But here, C. 無量功德身. For Amitāyus, C. 無量壽佛, T. *tshe dpag-med*. This prayer to the Lord Amitāyus is also found in the *Mahāyāna-śraddhôtpāda-śātra*, which is one of the treatises on the *tathāgatagarbha* theory. It seems that there is a certain relationship between the Amitāyus-cult and the *tathāgatagarbha* theory.

85) Of these 5 topics, the first 2 are taught in v. 16, the third, in v. 17, the 4th in v. 18, and the 5th in v. 19, respectively.

86) *ātmasaṃrakṣaṇôpāya*. Instead of *saṃrakṣaṇa*, T. reads *saṃśodhana*. But C. 護[自身方便] as S. This topic, in vv. 20, 21.

87) v. 22.

88) vv. 23, 24.

89) *kṣānti*, T. *bzod-pa*, C. 聞忍受.

90) *saṃsāra-maṇḍala*, T. *ḥkhor-gyi dkyil-ḥkhor*, C. 大衆 (= *sattvāḥ*).

91) *dharmârthavāda*, T. *chos-brjod-pa*, C. om. In accordance with the insertion of one verse after v. 24, C. adds the following summary:

'以二偈示現 於彼說法人 深生敬重心'.

APPENDIXES

APPENDIX I

RATNAGOTRA-VIBHĀGA

(Śloka-grantha)[1]

I

(Śaraṇa-traya)

Yo Buddhatvam anādimadhyanidhanaṃ śāntaṃ vibuddhaḥ svayaṃ
Buddhvā câbudhabodhanârtham abhayaṃ mārgam dideśa dhruvam /
Tasmai jñānakṛpâsivajravaradhṛg-duḥkhâṅkuraîkacchide
Nānādṛggahanôpagūḍha-vimatiprākārabhettre namaḥ // 1 // (v. I, 4)
Yo nâsan na ca san na câpi sadasan nânyaḥ sato nâsato
'śakyas tarkayituṃ niruktyapagataḥ pratyātmavedyaḥ śivaḥ /
Tasmai dharmadivākarāya vimalajñānâvabhāsatviṣe
Śarvârambaṇarāgadoṣatimiravyāghātakartre namaḥ // 2 // (I, 9)
Ye samyak pratividhya sarvajagato nairātmyakoṭiṃ śivāṃ
Taccittaprakṛtiprabhāsvaratayā kleśâsvabhāvêkṣaṇāt /
Sarvatrânugatām anāvṛtadhiyaḥ paśyanti saṃbuddhatāṃ
Tebhyaḥ sattvaviśuddhyanantaviṣayajñānêkṣaṇebhyo namaḥ // 3 // (I, 13)[2]

(Gotra)

Buddhajñānântargamāt sattvarāśes
Tannairmalyasyâdvayatvāt prakṛtyā /
Bauddhe gotre tatphalasyôpacārād
Uktāḥ sarve dehino buddhagarbhāḥ // 4 // (I, 27)[3]
Sadā prakṛtyasaṃkliṣṭaḥ śuddharatnâmbarâmbuvat /
Dharmâdhimuktyadhiprajñāsamādhikaruṇânvayaḥ // 5 // (I,30)

[1] for this selection, see *Introduction*, II, § 3.

[2] In the present text, we have a *śloka* (v. 23) between this and the next one, referring to the 4 aspects of *gotra*.

[3] C. puts verse 29 as a ' Karikā ' after this.

Śubhâtmasukhanityatvaguṇapāramitāphalaḥ [4]
Duḥkhanirvicchamaprāpticchandapraṇidhikarmakaḥ // 6 // (I, 35)
Mahôdadhir ivâmeyaguṇaratnâkṣayâkaraḥ /
Pradīpavad anirbhāgaguṇayuktasvabhāvataḥ // 7 // (I, 42)
Pṛthagjanâryasambuddhatathatâvyatirekataḥ /
Sattveṣu jinagarbho 'yaṃ deśitas tattvadarśibhiḥ // 8 // (I, 45)
Aśuddho 'śuddhaśuddho 'tha suviśuddho yathākramam /
Sattvadhātur iti prôkto bodhisattvas tathāgataḥ // 9 // (I, 47)
Sarvatrânugataṃ yadvan nirvikalpâtmakaṃ nabhaḥ /
Cittaprakṛtivaimalyadhātuḥ sarvatragas tathā // 10 // (I, 49)
Yathā sarvagataṃ saukṣmyād ākāśaṃ nôpalipyate /
Sarvatrâvasthitaḥ sattve [5] tathā 'yaṃ nôpalipyate // 11 // (I, 52)
Yathā sarvatra lokānām ākāśa udayavyayaḥ /
Tathaîvâsaṃskṛte dhātāv indriyāṇāṃ vyayôdayaḥ // 12 // (I, 53)
Yathā nâgnibhir ākāśaṃ dagdhapūrvaṃ kadācana /
Tathā na pradahanty [6] enaṃ mṛtyuvyādhijarāgnayaḥ // 13 // (I, 54)
Pṛthivy ambau jalaṃ vāyau vāyur vyomni pratiṣṭhitaḥ /
Aprathiṣṭhitam ākāśaṃ vāyvambukṣitidhātuṣu // 14 // (I, 55)
Skandhadhātvindriyaṃ tadvat karmakleśapratiṣṭhitam /
Karmakleśāḥ sadā 'yonimanaskārapratiṣṭhitāḥ // 15 // (I, 56)
Ayoniśomanaskāraś cittaśuddhipratiṣṭhitaḥ /
Sarvadharmeṣu cittasya prakṛtis tv apratiṣṭhitā // 16 // (I, 57)
Pṛthivīdhātuvaj jñeyāḥ skandhâyatanadhātavaḥ /
Abdhātusadṛśā jñeyāḥ karmakleśāḥ śarīriṇām // 17 // (I, 58)
Ayoniśomanaskāro vijñeyo vāyudhātuvat /
Tad-amūlâpratiṣṭhānā prakṛtir vyomadhātuvat // 18 // (I, 59)
Cittaprakṛtim ālīnā 'yoniśo manasaḥ kṛtiḥ /
Ayoniśomanaskāraprabhave kleśakarmaṇī // 19 // (I, 60)
Karmakleśâmbusaṃbhūtāḥ skandhâyatanadhātavaḥ /
Utpadyante nirudhyante tatsaṃvartavivartavat // 20 // (I, 61)
Na hetuḥ pratyayo nâpi na sāmagrī na côdayaḥ /
Na vyayo na sthitiś cittaprakṛter vyomadhātuvat // 21 // (I, 62)
Cittasya yā 'sau prakṛtiḥ prabhāsvarā
Na jātu sā dyaur iva yāti vikriyām /
Āgantukai rāgamalâdibhis tv asāv
Upaiti saṃkleśam abhūtakalpajaiḥ // 22 // (I, 63)
Nirvṛttivyuparamarugjarāvimuktām [7]

4) J's Text & T. pāramitā phalam.
5) Ms. B. satvo. T. sarvasattveṣvavastithas tathâyam nôpalipyate.
6) J's text reads pradahati.
7) J's text reads vimuktā.

Asyaîva prakṛtim ananyathâvagamya /
Janmâdivyasanam ṛte 'pi tannidānaṃ
Dhīmanto jagati kṛpôdayād bhajante // 23 // (I, 66)
Ananyathâtmā 'kṣayadharmayogato
Jagaccharaṇyo 'naparântakoṭitaḥ /
Sadā 'dvayo 'sāv avikalpakatvato
'vināśadharmā 'py akṛtasvabhāvataḥ // 24 // (I, 71)
Sa dharmakāyaḥ sa tathāgato yatas
tad āryasatyaṃ paramârthanirvṛtiḥ /
Ato na buddhatvam ṛte 'rkaraśmivad
Guṇâvinirbhāgatayā 'sti nirvṛtiḥ // 25 // (I, 84)

(deśanāprayojana)

Śūnyaṃ sarvaṃ sarvathā tatra tatra
Jñeyaṃ meghasvapnamāyākṛtâbham /
Ity uktvaîvaṃ buddhadhātuḥ punaḥ kiṃ
Sattve sattve 'stîti buddhair ihôktam // 26 // (I, 156)
Līnaṃ cittaṃ hīnasattveṣv avajñā
'bhūtagrāho bhūtadharmâpavādaḥ /
Ātmasnehaś câdhikaḥ pañca doṣā
Yeṣāṃ teṣāṃ tatprahāṇârtham uktam // 27 // (I, 157)
iti ratnagotravibhāga-ślokagranthaḥ samāptaḥ //

APPPENDIX II

CORRECTION & EMENDATION TO THE SANSKRIT TEXT OF THE RATNAGOTRAVIBHĀGA

(This table excludes those errata which were already corrected by the publisher).

Corrigenda

(Page, line)	for	read	(Source)*)
2.9	svaprajñayā draṣṭuṃ vā	svaprajñayā *jñātuṃ vā* draṣṭum	(T)
3.2	bhagavan tathā-	bhagavaṃs tathā- ⌊vā	(grammar)
3.4	-dharmā / avi-	-dharmā'vi-	(cf. S. 39.8)
3.16	-parivartānugatāni	-parivartād anugatāni	(C)
4.14	anyonyaṃ bodhisattva	anyonya-bodhisattva-	(context)
5.1	upa*k*araṇatāṃ	upa*h*araṇatāṃ	(C)
5.10, 12	utkṣālya	unmīlya ?	(Ms.)
9.11	viṭhap*a*ti	viṭhap*e*ti	(cf. S. 49.1-2
10.2	abhāvasvabhāvā*t*	abhāvasvabhāvā*n* (Acc.)	(T)
10.7	-anyatamâv*iśi*ṣta-	-anyatamâv*aśi*ṣṭa-	(T, C)
10.9	abhisam*buddhabodeh*	abhisam*bodhibuddhyā* ?	(T)
11.2	sarvāramvaṇa	sarvāram*b*aṇa	(misprint)
12.2	-dharmā /	-dharm*atayeti*	(cf. S. 44.14)
12.19	-*satya*darśana-	-*tattva*darśana	(T, S. 13.17)
15.4	(after) spṛśanti /	*nâpi cittaṃ saṃkliṣṭam bhavati* /	
15.5	(before) katham	(should be inserted)	(T, C)
15.6	upakle*śâ*rtho	upakl*iṣṭ*ârtho	(cf. S. 22.2)
16.9	-śuddhy*ā*	-śuddhy*aiva* (or śuddhyā *hi*)	(T)
16.10	avaivarty*ād* bha-	avaivarty*ā* bha-	(T, C)
18.2	bodhisattvān	bodhisattv*ayānikān*	(context)
18.5	*pratītya gambhīra*-dh.	*gambhīra-pratītya*dharma	(Ms. B, T, C)
19.9	bhavati syād	bhavati / syād	(context)
19.10	vadhakapuruṣe tasmāt	vadhakapuruṣe / tasmāt	
20.6-7	vyavadānasatyadvaya- virāgadharma-	vyavadānasatyadvaya*lakṣaṇa*- virāgadharma-	(T, S. 11.14)
20.8	pāramārthikamevâtraṇe	pāramārthika*m ekam ev*âtraṇe	(T, C)
20.15	sarvâcāra	sarvâ*k*āra	(T)
22.7	*lakṣaṇa*-	(to be omitted)	(context)
22.15	(before) mahāpṛthivī-	(*mahācakravālapramāṇena mahācakravālaḥ* /)	(T)

*) T. Tibetan Version of the Ratnagotravibhāga (Sde-dge Edition); C. Chinese Version of the Ratnagotravibhāga (Taisho Edition); Ms. A. & B. those Mss. used by Johnston for editing the Sanskrit Text.

Corrigenda

(Page, line)	for	read	(Source)
23.13	tathâśeṣebhyaḥ	tathā śesebhyaḥ	(C)
24.4	-*āryeṇa-mārgô*padeśena	-*āryamārgô*padeśena	(T, C)
24.10	vain*a*yikeṣu	vaineyikeṣu	(vineya)
24.15	nir*nītākāra*ṇaṃ	nir*nānākara*ṇaṃ	(T, C)
24.17	(before) triratnavaṃśa-	*tryadhvânubaddha* (to be inserted)	(T, C)
25.9	bodhan*ā*-padam	bodhan*a*-padam	(grammar)
26.4–5	after v. 27	(*anena kiṃ darśitam*)	(context)
27.14	sattvârth*aṃ* nirapekṣatā	sattvârth*e* nirapekṣatā or sattvâr*thani*rapekṣatā	(T)
28.7	*tri*vidhāḥ	*dvi*vidhāḥ	(C. AĀS, BGŚ)
28.16	-samatâp*atti*	-samatâp*ti*-	(T, context., S. p. 29.4)
29.1	-patitā ihadhārmikā	-patitā*ś ce*hadhārmikā	(C)
29.6	sattvās tadyathā	sattvā*ḥ caturvidhāḥ*/tadyathā	(T, C)
30.4	-pāramitā phala*m*/	-pāramit*āphalaḥ* / (bahuvr.)	(context)
30.9	-hetava eṣāṃ	-hetava *uktā* eṣāṃ	(Ms. B, T, C)
32.4	(before nityapāramitā	insert) *bodhisattvānām*	(T. C)
32.11	sarvatra parama-	*sarvatraparama*	(T)
34.19	-nirvāṇa-samāropa-	nrvāṇâsamāropa-	(C)
36.2–3	*mithyātva-niyata*-	*a*niyata-	(C, BGŚ)
36.5	(after praṇidhim iti /	insert) *tatra cchando 'bhilāṣaḥ* /	(T, C)
36.12	pāp*a*samuccheda-	pāp*â*samuccheda-	(T)
36.17	nipatanti * * * anāgata-	nipatanti *tān upakurvanty* anāgata-	(T, C)
37.13	ki	ki*ṃ*	(misprint)
38.17	-sādharmya	-sādharmya*ṃ*	(misprint)
39.6	avinirbhāgadharmā / avinirmuktaguṇaḥ / yad-	avinirbhāgadharm*ā'vi*-nirmuktaguṇo yad-	(context)
40.17	-upagūḍhaḥ / saṃ-	-upagūḍhaḥ saṃ-	(context)
42.11	pradahati	*pradahanti*	(grammar)
44.13	balī yo	*balīyo* (comparative degree)	
45.9	(before sarvadharmā	insert) *mūlaparicchinnā*	(Mss., T)
46.2	eṣa /	eṣa*ḥ* /	(grammar)
46.6	-vimuktā	-vimuk*tā*-	»
46.7	asyaiva	*ma*syaiva (vimuk*tām* asya-)	(C)
47.17	sreṣṭhiṇo gṛhapater eka-	śreṣṭhiṇo *vā* gṛhapater *vaika*-	(T, C)
47.18	darśanena sa ca	darśanena / sa ca	(context)
48.2–3	ekaputrakâdhyāśāya-premâ*nunīto*	-prem*âlambanataḥ* ?	(T)
48.9	śreṣṭhī gṛhapatir iti	śreṣṭhī *vā* gṛhapatir *v*eti	(T, C)
50.13	āsravakṣay*âbhijñābhi*-mukhy-	āsravakṣayâbhimukhy-	(C)
50.17	dṛḍhay*ā'*dhyāśayaprati-pattyā	dṛ*ḍhâdhyā*śayapratipattyā	(T, C)
51.11	prati*vicy*êmām-	prati*vedhy*emām-	(T)
52.19	bodhisattv*agaṇa*	bodhisattvag*uṇa*-	(T)

Corrigenda

(Page, line)	for	read	(Source)
55.2	tathāgata*garbhasya*	tathāgata*dhātor*	(Ms. B)
55.7	ki	kiṃ	(misprint)
55.19	*sama*dharmatayā	*śama*dharmatayā	(T)
56.3	tathāgato 'nyo	tathāgato *nâ*nyo	(context)
57.2	niṣpatsv–asaṃ–	niṣpa*tty*–asaṃ–	(S. 58.9)
58.13	ekena ca *kāraṇena*	ekena *câkāreṇa*	(T)
61.1	jagat	jagat–	(misprint)
64.21	ujjñitam–	uj*jhi*tam–	(misprint)
67.4	rāgâdidvi*ḍ*moha	rāgâdi*dviṅ*moha	(misprint) (Ms. A)
67.16	aśubhâdi*bhāva*jñāna–	aśubhâdi*bhāvanā*jñāna–	(T, C)
68.6–7	(v. 132	into prose)	(C, context)
68.13	tathāgatagarbh*a* iti	tathāgatagarbh*ā* iti	(context)
69.6	–āvṛ*tā*	–āvṛ*tam*	(T, C, con.)
70.3	d*bi*dhā	*dvi*dhā	(misprint)
70.3	vain*a*yika–	vain*e*yika–	(<vineya)
70.5	dharmadhāt*or* avi–	dharmadhāt*ur* avi–	(T, C)
71.8	vikārā	vikārā–	(misprint)
71.9	sarve	sarve–	(misprint)
71.12	tatra–	tatra	(misprint)
71.14	–advaidhīkāro ti	–advaidhīkā*reti*	(gram.)
72.5	mahādharmâdhir*āja*tvāt	mahādharm*âdhirājy*atvāt	(T)
73.6	iti parikal*pam* asya vacanāyeti	iti parikal*pitam* asya *vacanam iti*	(context)
73.15	vikalpayitavyā'dhimoktavyā	vikalpayitavyā *kevalam tv* adhimoktavyā	(T, C)
74.7	te'tyantasāsrava–	te ' tyan*taṃ* sāsrava–	(T)
74.19		(change the pargraph from ' yathāca sa... ' and connect 'tad yathā'pi nāma...' after ' prasādhitah / 'without changing paragraph.)	(context)
75.11	–*ś*abha–	*ś*ubha	(misprint)
76.11	–*aparyantaṃ* śūnya–	*aviparyastaṃ* śūnya–	(T, C)
79.15	tatphalaṃ dvividham /	tatphalaṃ *visamayogaḥ* /	(context)
79.16	–visaṃyogaś ca / yathākramaṃ	–visaṃyogaś ca yathākrama*m* /	(C, context)
79.7	g*a*mbhīryaudārya–	*gāmbhīryau*dārya	(context)
79.12	–vinirmuk*test*athāgata–	–vinirmuk*te ta*thāgata–	(context)
79.13	(after)–pṛṣṭhalabdhaṃ	(insert) *laukikaṃ*	(T, Ms.B)
84.18	jātyandha*kāya*vat	jātyandha*rūpa*vat	(T, C)
84.19	sūtikā*madhya*sthita	sūtikā*sadma*sthita	(T)
85.8	–amalai stribhiḥ	–amalai*s t*ribhiḥ (to be connected in Devanāgarī)	(context)
86.13	acintya*prāptiḥ* pratyātmavedit*ā*	acintya*ârhattvaṃ* pratyātmavedit*am*	(T, C)
88.7	prā*pya*nirvāṇa–	*prāpta*nirvāṇa–	(T, C)

Corrigenda

(Page, line)	for	read	(Source)
90.5	vy*anu*meyataḥ	*vyupameya*taḥ	(C, context) ... v. 69
90.6	vy*anu*meyo	*vyupameyo*	(C, context) ... v. 69
91.14	*tathatām*adhikṛtya	*tathā–tad*–adhikṛtya	(T)
91.15	(before v. 4)	(add) *uddānam* /	(T, C)
92.11	svayaṃjñāpanā	svayaṃ jñāpanā–	
93.6	apratisaṃkhy*āpa*hānir acc. to J's correction)	apratisaṃkhyāya hānir (as in the text)	(context)
93.10	muṣitatā citte	muṣita*tâ*c*itte*	(T, context)
94.2	abhayadaṃ	*abhayaṃ*	(metre)
98.9	–arkaraśmipravisṛta–	–arkaraśmi pravisṛta– (to be separated)	(context)
100.3	–*tvād* iti	–*vad* iti	
100.10	*adyaiva* na cirād	*vayam apy a*cirād	(T)
101.11	–sthānāntaramalā	–sthân*ā'n*taramalā	(context)
102–21	–vaśād aghaṭṭitā	–vaś*ād gh*aṭṭitā	(T, context)
103.16	saṃbuddha*tūrya tu* yāti	saṃbuddha*bherer upa*yāti	(T, ms. B, context)
104.14	āyā*n*ti nikhilam /	āy*ā*ti nikhilam /	(context)
106.6	kleśagat*ān* dṛṣṭy–	kleśaga*tâtmad*ṛṣṭy–	(T, C)
108.15	visṛt*e*	visṛt*o*	(T)
108.16	buddhasūry*e*	buddhasūry*o*	(T)
108.16	vineyâdr*i*–tannipāto	vine*tâ*dr*au* tannipāto	(T)
111.6	–ālokādy–alaṃkṛtāḥ	–ālokā*d–a*laṃkṛt*āḥ*	(T)
115.1	(before sthāneṣv–)	(insert) *caturṣu*	(T, C)
116.14	tac*citta*pratyupasthānād	ta*nnitya*pratyupasthānād	(T, C)
117.4	câsy*a* mūlaṃ	*câsyā* mūlaṃ	(context)

(The following headings had better be inserted:)

117.5	(before v. 16)	tatra yadāśraye yannimittaṃ côdāhṛtaṃ tadārabhya ślokaḥ /	(C)
117.9	(before v. 17)	yathôdāhṛtam tadārabhya ślokaḥ /	(T)
117.13	(before v. 18)	yadudāhṛtaṃ tadārabhya ślokaḥ /	(T)
117.17	(before v. 19)	yenôdāhṛtaṃ tadārabhya ślokaḥ /	(T)
118.3	(before v. 20)	ātmarakṣanôpāyam ārabhya dvau ślokau /	(T)
118.11	(before v. 22)	kṣatihetum ārabhya ślokaḥ /	(T)
118.15	(before v. 23)	kṣatiphalam ārabhya dvau ślokau /	(T, C)
119.5	(before v. 25)	āptapuṇyapariṇamane ślokaḥ /	(C)

APPENDIX III

DESCRIPTION OF THE ULTIMATE REALITY

by Means of the Six Categories in Mahāyāna Buddhism *)

To describe the characteristics of the *tathāgatagarbha* (the matrix of the Tathāgata, i.e. the Buddha's nature), The Ratnagotravibhāga (RGV) uses in Chap. I the following ten categories: namely, (1) *svabhāva*, (2) *hetu*, (3) *phala*, (4) *karman*, (5) *yoga*, (6) *vṛtti*, (7) *avasthāprabheda*, (8) *sarvatraga*, (9) *avikāra*, & (10) *asaṃbheda*. Similar terms are used in Chap. II as categories for describing the ultimate reality, i.e. the *phala* aspect of the *tathāgatagarbha*. Of its eight categories in all, the first six categories are the same as those used in Chap. I, i.e. (1) *svabhāva* to (6) *vṛtti*, while the remaining two are (7) *nitya* and (8) *acintya*.

As for the ten categories in Chap. I, the RGV says in the commentary that there is a (tenfold) category by which all kinds of explanation of the meaning of the *tathāgatagarbha* exist (i.e. are made) with no variance anywhere in the scripture [1]. After a brief explanation of the threefold meaning of the term *tathāgatagarbha* made on the basis of v. I, 27 [2], the statement mentioned above probably means that these ten categories are commonly used in the scripture for describing the *tathāgatagarbha*, while the threefold meaning belongs only to the RGV.

This statement, however, needs to be corrected to some extent by the following descriptions in the same RGV; namely, after explaining the sixth category, *vṛtti*, the commentary says:

*) This article originally appeared in *The Journal of Indian and Buddhist Studies*, vol. IX, No. 2, 1961 and is reprinted here with the permission of the editor.

1) *yenârthena sarvatrâviśeṣena pravacane sarvâkāraṃ tad* (= *tathāgatagarbha*)*-artha-sūcanaṃ bhavati tad api* ... RGV, p. 26, ll. 10–11.

2) RGV, p. 26, ll. 5–10. The 3 meanings are: *dharmakāyaparispharaṇārtha*, *tathatâvyatirekârtha*, & *gotrasaṃbhavârtha*. About this threefold meaning, see my article: The Tathāgatotpattisaṃbhavanirdeśa of the Avataṃsaka and the Ratngotravibhāga (Uttaratantra), with special reference to the term *tathāgatagotrasaṃbhava*, *Journal of Indian & Buddhist Studies*, Vol. VII, No. 1, 1958, pp. 348–353. Also see *Introduction*, III, § 2.

After this passage, with reference to this very category of *vṛtti*, the other [remaining] four categories are to be known through separate explanations [3].

And also:

All those teachings on the immaculate Ultimate Reality (*anāsravadhātu*) taught by the Lord in detail through various forms of doctrines are contracted in brief into these six categories, i.e. *svabhāva*, *hetu*, *phala*, *karman*, *yoga* and *vṛtti* [4].

What we come to know from these passages is that a set of categories which is commonly used, and hence the basic one, is not the whole of the ten categories, but the first six categories beginning with *svabhāva*, and that the object to which is applied this set of six categories is not the *tathāgatagarbha* alone, but is the Ultimate Reality in every aspect inclusive of the aspect of *tathāgatagarbha*, and thirdly that the RGV added four categories to the regular set in order to explain the mode of manifestation (*vṛtti*) of the *tathāgatagarbha*. This is proved from the use of the same set of categories in Chap. II, where the seventh and the eighth categories are said to be included in the sixth, *vṛtti* [5], as showing special characteristics of the *vṛtti* aspect of the Ultimate Reality characterized as *bodhi* or *āśrayaparivṛtti*.

Then how is this set of six categories used in the scripture (*pravacana*) and what is meant by the term *pravacana* ?

At first, we shall see how it is applied in the basic verses (*śloka*) of the RGV.

sadā prakṛty–asaṃkliṣṭaḥ śuddharatnâṃbarâmbuvat / . . . . (1)
dharmâdhimukty–adhiprajñā-samādhi–karuṇânvayaḥ / (v. I, 30) . . . (2)
śubhâtmasukhanityatva–guṇapārmitā–phalaḥ / [6] . . . . (3)
duḥkhanirvic–chamaprāpticchandapraṇidhi–karmakaḥ // (I, 35) . . . . (4)
mahôdadhir ivā 'meyaguṇaratnâkṣayâkaraḥ /

[3] *ataḥ param etam eva vṛttyartham ārabhya tadanye catvāro 'rthāḥ prabhedanirdeśād eva veditavyāḥ.* RGV, p. 40, ll. 5–6.

[4] *ye kecid anāsravadhātunirdeśe nānādharmaparyāyamukheṣu bhagavatā vistareṇa nirdiṣṭāḥ sarve te ebhir eva samāsataḥ ṣaḍbhiḥ svabhāva–hetu–phala–karma–yoga–vṛttyarthaiḥ* . . . RGV, p. 40, ll. 12–14.

[5] *tribhir gāmbhiryaudāryamāhātmyaprabhāvitair buddhakāyair nityam ā bhavagater acintyena prakāreṇa vartanaṃ vṛttiḥ.* RGV, p. 79, ll. 16–18.

[6] *–tā phalam* / in the text. The reason for the correction will be shown below.

pradīpavad anirbhāgaguṇayukta–svabhāvataḥ // (I, 42) . . . . (5)
pṛthagjanârya–saṃbuddha–tathatâvyatirekataḥ / . . . . (6)
sattveṣu jinagarbho 'yaṃ deśitas tattvadarśibhiḥ // (I, 45)

(Being always undefiled by nature, like the pure [character] of a treasure, the sky and water:
Following after faith in the [Mahāyāna] doctrine, the excellent intellect, Meditation and Compassion:—
Having the climax of qualities with respect to purity, unity, happiness and eternity as its result;
Having aversion from the Suffering and desire for and vow to the attainment of the Quiescence as its functions;—
Being, like an ocean, an imperishable receptacle of treasures of innumerable qualities,
As being by nature united with its properties inseparably, as a lantern [is inseparable from its light and others];—
And as its [various manifestations in the forms of] ordinary beings, the Sages and the Buddhas are not differentiated from the Reality,
[there exists] this Matrix of the Victor (= Tathāgata) among the living beings;—
Thus is it taught by those who perceived the Truth).

These four verses, though they are interrupted by the commentary passages, are no doubt composed in a series, whose subject word is '*jinagarbha*' in the last verse [7] and in which is applied a mode of the set of six categories previously known to the author.

Quite a similar application of the same mode of description in a series of verses is found in the Mahāyānasūtrâlaṃkāra (MSA).

sarvadharmadvayâvara–tathatāviśuddhi–lakṣaṇaḥ /
vastujñāna–tadālamba–vaśitâkṣaya–lakṣaṇaḥ // (v. IX, 56) . . . . . . (1)
sarvatas tathatājñāna–bhāvanā–samudāgamaḥ / . . . . (2)
sarvasatva–dvayâdāna–sarvathâkṣayatā–phalaḥ // [8] (IX, 57) . . . . . (3)
kāyavākcittanirmāṇa–prayogôpāya–karmakaḥ / . . . . (4)
samādhi–dhāraṇī–dvāradvayâmeya–samanvitaḥ // (IX, 58) . . . . . . (5)
svabhāva–dharmasaṃbhoga–nirmāṇair bhinnavṛttikaḥ / . . . . (6)
dharmadhātuviśuddho 'yaṃ buddhānāṃ samudāhṛtaḥ // (IX, 59)

[7] Being appositional to '*jinagarbho 'yam*', the reading '*–pāramitā–phalaḥ*' as a Bahuvrīhi comp. should be accepted. See note 6.

[8] '*. . . tā phalam* /' in the text is corrected for the same reason as above. See also Tib., which has '*ḥbras–bu–can*'.

(Its characteristic is the purification of the two kinds of obscurations with regard to the Reality of all phenomena,
And is the inexhaustible controlling power of the knowledge of the nature and the object of its cognition;—
It is originated from the practices of wisdom with regard to the Reality in all respects;
It is the result of the inexhaustible formation of the two [i.e. benefit and happiness] by all possible means for the sake of all the living;—
Its function is the transformation of body, speech and mind as the means of appliance;
It is endowed with the gates of meditation and mystical formulae and with the immeasurable accumulation of the two [i.e. bliss and wisdom];—
It manifests itself variously by the Body of its own essence, by that of Enjoyment of the doctrine, and by that of incarnation:—
[Thus] is explained this immaculate Ultimate Reality of the Buddhas.)

These four verses in a series are said to be the *ślokas* on the topic of '*dharmadhātuviśuddhi*' which is, at the same time, like '*jinagarbha*' in the example of the RGV, the subject word for the whole sentence.

Thus in the application of the same mode of description, the RGV and the MSA show a close relationship between them, and as the RGV quotes the MSA in the commentary, it was no doubt the RGV which imitated the MSA. It is especially certain about Chap. II of the RGV which, though there is no example of application of the same mode in a series of verses as above, has many traces of the influences of the MSA on its doctrine (e.g. the triple *kāya* theory, *avikalpajñāna* and *tatpṛṣṭalabdha*, etc. [9]).

But the MSA cannot claim its originality of the use of the six categories, because according to Prof. Nishio's information [10], almost the same

[9] The same is possibly said about the commentary passage of Chap. I, but, as for the *ślokas* or basic verses in Chap. I, the influences of the MSA are scarcely observed except for the application of the six categories mentioned above.

[10] Kyōyū Nishio, *Bucchikyōron no kenkyū* (in Jap.) (Studies on the BBS and the Buddhabhūmi-vyākhyāna, studies, translation & the Tib. texts), 2 Vols., Nagoya, 1940. The following is a comparative table of the 4 verses of BBS & MSA in their Tib. versions.

BBS (Nishio's text. p. 23)	MSA (Peking Mdo-ḥgrel, Phi, 12 b, 2-5; Repr. Vol. 108, p. 7)
/chos rnams kun-gyi de-bshin-ñid/	*/chos rnams kun-gyi de-bshin-ñid/*
/sgrib gñis ldan dag mtshan-ñid-can/	*/sgrib-gñis dag-paḥi mtshan-ñid-can/*
/dṅos-po śes-pa de dmigs-pa/	*/dṅos-po śes-pa de-la dmigs/*
/dbaṅ tshad mi-śes mtshan-ñid-can//	*/dbaṅ zad mi-śes mtshan-ñid do//*
/de-bshin-ñid śes thams-cad-nas/	*/de-bshin-ñid śes thams-cad-nas/*

verses as in the MSA mentioned above are found in the Buddhabhūmisūtra (BBS) towards the end of the text as a kind of concluding verses. Also, there are other passages in the MSA where the doctrines taught in the BBS are summarized, and hence the originality seems better to be ascribed to the BBS.

It is however still difficult to regard the BBS as the only source of the set of six categories. Because the Yogācārabhūmi (YB), in which is also found the mention of the same set of categories[11], has not such a clear theory as that found in the BBS on the *buddhakāya* or has no exposition of the four kinds of wisdom (i.e. *ādarśa–ñ.*, *samatā–jñ.*, *pratyavekṣa–jñ.*, *kṛtyânuṣṭhāna–jñ.*), both of which are the central topics of the BBS, and at present we have no objective proof to fix the order of composition between the two treatises. Furthermore, curious enough is the manner of mention of the said categories in the YB. Namely, it is found in the passage where the science of grammar (*śabda–vidyā* or *vyākaraṇa*) is explained as one of the five sciences (*vidyā–sthāna*), but without any detailed comment. There seems to be no use of such a set of terms in Sanskrit grammars although most of the terms used for the six categories are the technical terms of grammar. In this respect, I suppose that the set of terms are put or rather inserted in that passage in connection with the word '*artha*' (meaning) just because there was a traditional usage of those terms as a mode of description among the Vijñāvādins, even in the days of the composition of the YB. What is meant by the term '*pravacana*' in the RGV is, therefore, not necessarily to be affixed to any special scripture or treatise, but is to be understood as 'the word of predecessor'.

Now, we shall proceed to examine the extent of application of the said categories. Besides their application to the *dharmadhātuviśuddhi*, there is another mode of application in the MSA. It is found in a couple of verses

/bsgoms–la yaṅ–dag ḥgrub–pa–can /
/sems–can kun–la gñis bskyed–pa/
/rnam–kun mi–bzad ḥbras–bu–can //
/lus daṅ ṅag daṅ sems sprul–paḥi /
/sbyor–baḥi thabs–kyi las–can yin /
/tiṅ–ṅe–ḥdsin daṅ gzuṅs sgo daṅ /
/dpag–tu med–pa gñis–daṅ ldan //
/raṅ–bshin chos–rdsogs loṅs–spyod daṅ/
/sprul–pas tha–dad ḥjug–pa–can /
/saṅs–rgyas rnams–kyi chos–kyi dbyiṅs/
/rnam dag ḥdi ni yaṅ–dag brjod //

/bsgoms–pa las ni yaṅ–dag ḥbyuṅ /
/sems–can kun–la rnam–kun–tu /
/gñis bskyod mi–zad ḥbras–bu–can //
/sku daṅ gsuṅ daṅ thugs sprul–paḥi //
/ḥbyor–baḥi thabs–kyi las–can te /
/tiṅ–ṅe–ḥdsin daṅ gzuṅs sgo daṅ /
/dpag–tu med–pa gñis–daṅ ldan //
/raṅ–bshin chos–rdsogs loṅs–spyod daṅ /
/sprul de–dag–gi(s) tha–dad–ḥjug/
/ḥdi–ni saṅs–rgyas rnam–dag–gi/
/chos–dbyiṅs rnam–par dag–par bśad //

11) YB (Tib.) Peking Mdo–ḥgrel, Dsi, 230 *a*, 5–6. (Repr. Vol. 109, p. 304); (Ch) *Taisho*, Vol. 30, p. 361 *a*. The six terms in Tib. are as follows: *ṅo–bo–ñid*, *rgyu*, *ḥbras–bu*, *bya–ba* (*kriyā*), [*khyad–par–du*] *sbyor–ba* (*viśeṣa–yoga*), *ḥjug–pa*.

at the end of the work, which are a kind of eulogy on the Buddha. They run as follows:

niṣpanna-paramārtho 'si, sarvabhūmi-viniḥsṛtaḥ / . . . . (1, 2)
sarvasatvâgratāṃ prāptaḥ, sarvasatvavimocakaḥ // (XX–XXI 60) . (3, 4)
akṣayair asamair yukto guṇair, lokeṣu dṛśyase / . . . . (5, 6)
maṇḍaleṣv apy, adṛśyaś ca sarvathā devamānuṣaiḥ // (61) . . . . (6)

(Thou art the one who is perfect-transcendental,
who has come out of [the practices in] all stages,
who has attained the highest point among all living beings, and makes them liberate;—
And who is endowed with virtues, inexhaustible and unequalled;
Thou art perceived in various worlds and in the circles [of the assemble of Bodhisattvas through thy two apparitional Bodies],
However invisible is thy [Body of Essence] by all means to those who belong to the world of gods and human beings).

According to the Commentary, these two verses refer to the characteristics of the Buddha (*buddhalakṣaṇa*), among which we find the triple Body theory under the category of *vṛtti*.

The same verses are quoted in the Mahāyānasaṃgraha (MS) of Asaṅga [12] explaining that they refer to the highest qualities of the Absolute Body (*dharmakāya*), and this is commented upon by Vasubandhu: 'the highest' means 'belonging only to the Mahāyāna, i.e. not common to the Hīnayāna' [13]. It seems to show that the use of this set of categories belougs only to the Mahāyana.

The third mode of application of the six categories is found in the first two of the dedicative verses placed at the head of the Abhidharmasamuccaya–vyākhā, a commentary on the Abhidharmasamuccaya (AS) of Asaṅga. They run as follow [14]:

|rtogs–pa des gnas dri–med don | . . . . (1)
|gaṅ spyod rgya–mtshoḥi pha–rol gśegs | . . . . (2)

12) MS *Taisho*, 31, 111 *a* (No. 1592); 131 *a* (No. 1593); 150 *b* (No. 1594), Tib. Peking Ed. Mdo-ḥgrel, Li, 46 *b* 3–6 (Repr. Vol. 112, p. 334).

13) 於大小乘中不與他共故無有上 (*Taisho*, 31, p. 258 *a*). However, this is found only in Paramārtha's translation (No. 1595), and Vasubandhu's authorship is somehow doubtful.

14) AS.Vyākhyā, Peking Mdo-śgrel, Śi, 143 *b* 3–5 (Repr.Vol. 113, p. 141). Cf. *Taisho*, 31, p. 694 *b*: 諸曾真淨究竟理 超聖行界昇彼岸 證得一切法自在 善權化導不思議 無量希有勝功德 自他並利所依止 敬禮如是大覺尊 無等妙法諸聖衆.

/chos-kun dbaṅ-phyug, bsam mi-khyab / . . . . (3), (4)
/ḥdul-baḥi thabs-kyis ḥdren-pa-can // . . . . (4)
/gshal-med legs gyur yon-tan ni / . . . . (5)
/raṅ daṅ gshan don gñis-la brten / . . . . (6)
/saṅs-rgyas chos daṅ ḥphags-pa-yi /
/tshogs-laḥaṅ de-phyir phyag-ḥtsal-lo //

(I bow to the Buddha, and to the Doctrine and Holy community as well, because—
He is [by nature] the realization and the immaculate truth established by it;
Having reached the other shore of the ocean of practices,
And having [attained] the controlling power over the phenomena,
He leads [the living beings] by skillful means and in an inconceivable manner;—
He is endowed with the immeasurable and marvellous qualities,
And is the foundation of the benefits of his own and of others).

Commenting on these verses by himself, the commentator [15] says that by the first two there are shown the six categories with respect to the excellent qualities of the Buddha, i.e. the categories of *svabāva*, *hetu* etc.[16]. This explanation is exactly on the same line as in the MS.

Thus examining, we have got, I think, a fairly good account of the idea of the six categories and their applications to the Ultimate Reality, however it may be called, in treatises of the Vijñānavada. Before giving a conclusion to this investigation, I must lastly refer to the Abhidharmasamuccaya in which is an explanation of this set of categories as one of the seven methods for interpreting a topic in discussion (*sāṃkathya-viniścaya*) under the name of *artha-viniścaya* [17].

The Abhidharmasamuccaya is a kind of classified lexicon of technical terms of the Mahāyāna Abhidharma, i.e. the works of the Yogācāra school or the Vijñānavādins. It is divided into two parts, one is the collection of terms concerning the phenomena (*lakṣaṇa*), the other is that of terms concerning the interpretation (*viniścaya*), and the Sāṃkathya-

15) According to Chinese tradition, it is ascribed to Sthiramati, while in Tibet, to Jinaputra (Rgyal-baḥi sras).

16) AS Vyākhyā, *ibid.*, p. 144 *a* 2–3.

17) AS (Tib.) Peking, Śi 344 *a* 345 *a* 8 (Vol. 113, No. 5555); (C.) *Taisho*, 31, 693 *b*; (Sthiramati) *ibid.*, 765 *b*-c; (Skt.) ed. by P. Pradhan, Santiniketan, 1950, pp. 102–103 (This passage is restored from Tib. & C.).

viniścaya is the last of the four chapters belonging to the latter part. Being thus situated and in comparison to the other six methods, i.e., commentary (*vyākhyā*), exhibition of difference (*prabhidyasaṃdarśana*), questioning (*saṃpraśna*), summary (*saṃgraha*), dialogue or logic (*vāda*), and implication (*abhisandhi*), this *arthaviniścaya* is clearly a mode of description or interpretation recognized by the authority of the Vijñānavāda.

The explanation of the six categories in the AS is, however, unsatisfactory for us. It shows us merely the terms of three to five kinds of each category [18], but not any example of application of the whole set as examined above.

Rather, it seems difficult to limit the application exclusively to the Ultimate Reality, because the sub-divisions of the six categories include all the varieties, so that by using one of them any kind of subject, *saṃskṛta* or *asaṃskṛta*, of impure or pure character, can be described. It may be natural from the logical point of view as the terminologies used for the six categories do not contain any evaluation in themselves. Actually, however, there is no example of their application to any subject other than the Ultimate Reality, and taking the explanation in the RGV referred to at the beginning of this article into consideration, we may safely say that there was a traditional use of the set of six categories among the Vijñānavādins for describing the Ultimate Reality, and that its latest example available to us is observed in the AS Vyākhyā.

Additionally, I will give a rough observation on the modified use of this set of categories in the works belonging to the so-called *Tathāgatagarbha* theory. The RGV, though it is written by one of the Vijñānavādins (it may be sure at least from his knowledge of the use of the said categories), has established the system of the *Tathāgatagarbha* theory, and to describe its doctrine, it modified the six categories according to its own need but without losing their original character. But the modification was further extended until the character as categories of general use has disappeared by mixing or replacing of the new terms which show the characteristics

18) (1) *svabhāva* ... 1. *parikalpita*, 2. *paratantra*, 3. *pariniṣpanna*.
(2) *hetu* ... 1. *utpatti*–, 2. *pravṛtti*–, 3. *siddhi*–.
(3) *phala* ... 1. *vipāka*–, 2. *niṣyanda*–, 3. *adhipati*–, 4. *puruṣakāra*–, 5. *visaṃyoga*–.
(4) *karman*... 1. *upalabdhi*–, 2. *kāritra*–, 3. *vyāvasāya*–, 4. *pariṇati*–, 5. *prāpti*–.
(5) *yoga* ... 1. *sāmūhiko y.*, 2. *ānubandhiko y.*, 3. *sāṃbandhiko y.*, 4. *āvasthiko y.*, 5. *vaikāriko y.*
(6) *vṛtti* ... 1. *lakṣaṇa*–, 2. *avasthāna*–, 3. *viparyāsa*–, 4. *aviparyāsa*–, 5. *prabheda*–, (Skt. terms are acc. to Pradhan's text).

of the Absolute belonging to the *Tathāgatagarbha* theory. As such examples we have the ten categories of the *tathāgatabodhi* in the Anuttāśrayasūtra (AĀS) , the ten categories of the *tathāgatagarbha* in the Buddhagotraśātra (BGŚ), and the twelve categories of the *bodhicitta* in the Dharmadhātvaviśeṣaśāstra (DAŚ) [19].

19) AĀS, *Taisho*, 16, p. 470 *c*; BGŚ, *Taisho*, 31, p. 796 *b*; DAŚ, *Taisho*, 32, p. 892 *a*. (All of these works are kept only in the Chinese Tripitaka, and their Skt. titles are restored from C.).

INDEXES

INDEX OF SANSKRIT TERMS

1. Terms in brackets refer to those not found in the Ratna.
2. Terms with the mark § refer to the subject matters of the text.
3. Reference is to the pages in the present work or section numbers applied in the present work.
4. Abbreviations:

VP	vajrapada (1–7)
RG	ratnagotra (4 aspects) (I–IV)
TG	tathāgatagarbha (3 meanings) (a–c)
	(10 aspects) (I–X)
	(9 illustrations) (1–9)
B	bodhi (RG II) (8 aspects) (I–VIII)
G	guṇa (RG III) (I–IV)
vaiś.	catur–vaiśāradya (G I)
bala	daśa–bala (G II)
āveṇ.	āveṇika–buddhadharma (G III)
mahāp.	mahāpuruṣalakṣaṇa (G IV)
K	karman (RG IV) (9 illustrations) (I–IX)
s.	simile

A

Ā

GH

C

CH

J

DH

N

PH

B

BH

Ś

Ṣ

S

H

INDEX OF WORKS, AUTHORS & SCHOOLS

(Those with the mark * are the titles restored from C)

PRINTED IN ROME
BY
AZIENDE TIPOGRAFICHE EREDI DOTT. G. BARDI
SALITA DE' CRESCENZI, 16
1966

CORRIGENDA

J. Takasaki

A STUDY ON THE RATNAGOTRAVIBHĀGA (UTTARATANTRA).

S. O. R. XXXIII, Roma, 1966

(References are made with page and line numbers for the main sentences, and note numbers for foot-notes).

(Page)	instead of	read
ix, l. 10	*Orientalia, XI*	*Orientalia, IX*
l. 23	*Abhisamayâlaṅkārâloka*	*Abhisamayâlaṅkārâlokā*
l. 31	*Abhisamayâlaṅkārâloka*	*Abhisamayâlaṅkārâlokā*
l. 33	*Avataṃsakaśūtra*	*Avataṃsakasūtra*
xiii, l. 4	Ratnagotravighāga	Ratnagotravibhāga
l. 8	(before ' Jap. '	insert) (in
7, l. 21	*pao–sing–lun*	*pao–hsing–lun*
7, l. 25	*K'ai–yuan che–chiao mo–lu*	*K'ai–yüan shih–chiao mu–lu*
8, l. 5	*Pao–ch'ung–lu*	*Pao–ch'ang–lu*
l. 10	*nei–t'en–lu*	*nei–t'ien–lu*
l. 26	Hsüang–chuang	Hsüan–chuang
n. 13	*Nai–t'en–lu*	*Nai–t'ien–lu*
9, l. 12	Kien–huei	Chien–hui
l. 38	*Ta–cheng–fa–chieh–wu–ch'a–pieh–lun–chu*	*Ta–cheng–fa–chieh–wu–ch'a–pieh–lun–shu*
21, n. 35	In his opinion	To his opinion
22, l. 9	*buddhadhatu*	*buddhadhātu*
l. 9	*buddhgotra*	*buddhagotra*
31, l. 5	*nityanda*	*niṣyanda*
32, l. 20	*raṇirāja°*	*raṇirāja°*
35, n. 58	*idam yad*	*idaṃ yad*
n. 58	*tasyaîvam*	*tasyaîvaṃ*
38, n. 64	*ekayānaniṣṭhā*	*ekayānaniṣṭhā*

Corrigenda

(Page)	instead of	read
39, n. 66 (l. 7)	thruogh	through
n. 67	*Mahāparinirvaṇasūtra*	*Mahāparinirvāṇasūtra*
41, l. 22	*pariniṣpaṇṇa*	*pariniṣpanna*
n. 70	*nairātmyameva*	*nairātmyam eva*
43, l. 7	*sarvâkarajñāna*	*sarvâkārajñāna*
44, l. 8	*asyâśyayaḥ*	*asyâśrayaḥ*
n. 74 (l. 3)	*chal dog*	*cha ldog*
45, l. 4	WONKS	WORKS
47, l. 32	*satkāyadṛṣṭipatitā*	*satkāyadṛṣṭipatitāḥ*
49, l. 8	*Anūttarâśrayasūtra*	*Anuttarâśrayasūtra*
60, l. 10	*saṃkliṣṭadharma*	*saṃkleśadharma*
67, (Q&R, the last line)	26--b 27 c	26 b–27 c
68, l. 3	budha	buddha
l. 31	svârthasaṃpatti	svârthasaṃpad
70, l. 24	dveśa	dveṣa
71 (BGŠ)	Parāmârtha	Paramârtha
72, l. 4 from the last	*boddhisattva*	*bodhisattva*
76, l. 18	anupraviṣṭaṃ	anupraviṣṭam
80, l. 7	itobāhyā	itobāhyās
l. 2 from the last	samadhi	samādhi
90, l. 7	cittaṃ āgantu°	cittam āgantu°
92, l. 21	3. avivartika	3. avaivartika
95, (Q&R l. 5)	JĀA 341 c	JĀA 241 c
100, l. 21	sattvadhātoḥ	sattvadhātos
l. 28	prakṛteḥ	prakṛter
106, l. 16	līna–cutta	līna–citta
108, l. 3	āśrayaparivṛtter sva°	āśrayaparivṛtteḥ sva°
109 (BCŚ)	311 a	811 a
112, l. 6	avināśadharmi)	avināśadharmin)
l. 12	pāriṇāmikī cyuti	pāriṇāmikī cyutiḥ
l. 25	lakṣana	lakṣaṇa
120, l. 2	ādyam	ādya
l. 2	dvitīyam	dvitīya
l. 3	pāramarthika	pāramārthika
l. 27	(seva &)	(to be omitted)
l. 28	prāpta	prāpti
l. 28	prāpana	prāpaṇa
122, l. 1	vīryataḥ	vīryato
l. 2	smṛteḥ	smṛter
l. 3	darśanāt	darśanād
l. 12	eṇeyajaṇghatā	eṇeyajaṅghatā
l. 14	vṛttaślakṣaṇâ	vṛttaślakṣṇâ
128, l. 29	kāyagubya	kāyaguhya
129 (Q&R l. 2)	cf. JĀA 242 a	JĀA 243 a
130, l. 25	(buddhadhrmâvi°	(buddhadharmâvi°

The Ratnagotravibhāga

(Translation)

	(Page)	instead of	read
I.	144, l. 4	*saṃyaksaṃbodhi*	*saṃyaksaṃbodhiḥ*
	n. 22 (l. 2)	*modo*	*mdo*
	145, l. 3	Mañjuśri	Mañjuśrī
	n. 23 (l. 20)	°*nadivālikā*°	°*nadīvālikā*°
	148, n. 51	*yons-su*	*yoṅs-su*
	149, n. 59	*ne-bar*	*ñe-bar*
	151, n. 73	*klu-pa*	*khu-ba*
	n. 74	*lal-gyi*	*bal-gyi*
II.	156, l. 12	[*supernatural*]	[supernatural]
	157, n. 15	*prapanca*	*prapañca*
	158, n. 25	*mṅon-par śen-pa*	*mṅon-par shen-pa*
	159, n. 28	*go-rims*	*go-rim*
	nn. 29, 30, 32	JAÂ	JÂA
	160, nn. 37, 39	JAÂ	JÂA
	162, l. 10	*svârthasampad*	*svârthasaṃpad*
III.	163, n. 5 (l. 4)	*ārambana*	*ārambaṇa*
	166, n. 15	*ṅe-tshig*	*ṅes-tshig*
	167, n. 22	JAÂ	JÂA
	168, n. 29 (l. 5)	*brol-bar*	*bral-bar*
	170, n. 43 (l. 2)	*mtshan-par*	*mtshan-mar*
IV.	172, l. 7	all the worlds	all the world
	176, n. 25	cig-śes	cig-śos
	l. 12	the superficial	another, superficial
	178, n. 43	(利)	(to be omitted)
	179, n. 49	*gzugs-brñen*	*gzugs-brñan*
V.	181, n. 8 (l. 2)	*rje-su*	*rjes-su*
	n. 8 (l. 4)	Pretyekabuddha	Pratyekabuddha
	183, n. 28	*gśad-maḥi*	*gśed-maḥi*
	184, n. 33 (l. 3)	*mthar-thung-paḥi*	*mthar-thug-paḥi*
	n. 36	*vyavadana*	*vyavadāna*
	185, n. 42 (l. 2)	BGS 808 a	BGŚ 808 b
	n. 49	*bsñan-pa*	*brñan-pa*
VI.	190, n. 33 (l. 7)	*ston-gñis-paḥi*	*stoṅ-gñis-paḥi*
VII.	198, l. 5	*tathātā*	*tathatā*
VIII.	205, l. 7	*aniyaṭaḥ*	*aniyataḥ*
	n. 58	*sṅaṅ-ba*	*sdaṅ-ba*
	206, n. 61	*sṅaṅ-ba*	*sdaṅ-ba*
	209, n. 78	*bshuṅ*	*gshuṅ*
	n. 82	*ston-pa-ñid*	*stoṅ-pa-ñid*
	214, n. 109 (l. 4)	*Laṅkāvatāra*	*Lalitavistara*
	215, n. 112 (l. 14)	*vāsabūmi*	*vāsabhūmi*
	n. 115	*raṅ-bshin-kyi*	*raṅ-bshin-gyi*
	216, n. 123 (twice)	*drir-ba*	*dri ṅa-ba*
	221, n. 162	*pratyupasthāna*	*pratyupasthāpana*
	223, n. 177	JAÂ	JÂA
	224, n. 181	*śukladhamra*	*śukladharma*

Corrigenda

	(Page)	instead of	read
	227, n. 204	*ḥbral-pa*	*ḥbrel-pa*
	228, n. 218	quote	quotes
	234, n. 259	*bsdus-has-paḥi*	*bsdus-paḥi*
	240, n. 305	*kliṣyate*	*kliśyate*
	n. 305 (l. 9)	Taisho XVIIX	Taisho XXVII
	241, n. 308	AAS	AĀS
	242, n. 311	*tha-mal-ba*	*tha-mal-pa*
	246, n. 353	*yid-du hoṅ-ba*	*yid-du ḥoṅ-ba*
	249, n. 382	*thad-tu*	*thad-du*
	250, n. 387	*gzugs-brñan-yid*	*gzugs-brñan*
	254, n. 417	*Catuḥśubha*	*Catuḥstava*
	n. 417	*Minor Buddhist Works*	*Minor Buddhist Texts*
	n. 420	*sbyod-lam*	*spyod-lam*
	256, n. 434	*myur thug*	*mur thug*
	257, l. 1	costant	constant
	n. 439	*hdsin-pa*	*ḥdsin-pa*
IX.	270, n. 28	*khrab-khrig*	*khrag-khrig*
	288, l. 1	Mañjusrī	Mañjuśrī
	n. 159 (l. 3)	*samudānita*	*samudānīta*
	289, l. 8	is	it
	n. 166	*rgyal-srid-du*	*rgyal-srid che*
	n. 167	*sprul-ba*	*sprul-pa*
	290, n. 175 (l. 5)	*Triṃṣikā*	*Triṃśikā*
X.	294, n. 4	*tshas-mar*	*tshad-mar*
	n. 7 (l. 14)	*where*	where
	295, n. 12	*ñe-bar*	*ṅes-par*
	299, n. 42	*gshags-pa*	*gshag-pa*
	300, n. 53 (l. 10)	3) *Sumaṅgala-visāraṇī*	3) *Sumaṅgala-vilāsinī*
	302, n. 63	*ḥphrol*	*ḥphro* (omit the explanation in brackets after '*ḥphrol*', and instead insert) (D) '*ḥphrol*' is to be read as '*ḥphro-la*' [*la* being a conjunction]
XI.	305, n. 4	*lam bstan-pa*	*lan bstan-pa*
	306, n. 12	*bgag-cag*	*bdag-chags*
	n. 17	*spral-ba*	*sprul-pa*
XIII.	314, l. 13	all the the pure	all the pure
	n. 5 (l. 3)	*āpyate*	*āpnoti*
	316, n. 19	*sgrag-can*	*sgra-gcan*
	318, n. 35	*rjas*	*rdsas*
	319, n. 43	*dbaṅ-ḥbyor-ba*	*dbaṅ-ḥbyor-pa*
	n. 47	*ḥpho-ba, med-pa*	*ḥpho-ba med-pa*
	322, n. 67	*tathāgata-vyoma*	*tathāgata-vyoman*
	n. 72	XIII-55	XIII-56
	324, n. 82	(*advaya-karmaṇi bhāvatah*)	(*advaya-karmaṇi bhavyataḥ*)
	326, n. 102	*gzugṣ*	*gzugs*
	327, n. 109 (l. 13)	5) *visuddhaṃ*,	*viśuddhaṃ*,

	(Page)	instead of	read
	328, n. 120	*mi–stoṅ (–pa)*	*mi–ston–pa*
	329, l. 4	*nairṃānika*	*nairmāṇika*
	n. 131	*bstams–pa*	*bltams–pa*
	n. 133	*dkyes–rol*	*dgyes–rol*
XIV.	336, n. 1	*mahāpuruṣalakṣanas*	*mahāpuruṣalakṣaṇas*
XV.	339, n. 18	*go–cha*	(to be omitted)
	341, l. 12	*nor*	(to be omitted)
	n. 36	*nams*	*ñams*
	n. 39	*apratisaṃkhyā*	*apratisaṃkhyāya*
	342, n. 53	*abhyupekṣaṇa*	*adhyupekṣaṇa*
	n. 56	*purvaṃgama*	*pūrvaṃgama*
	346, n. 91	*nīlôtpalaśṛī*	*nīlôtpalaśrī*
	n. 95	*ba–sphu*	*ba–spu*
	n. 96	*mthor*	*mthon*
XVII.	356, l. 11	place	palace
	362, n. 70	*gtoṅ*	*gtod* (and omit:) *bsam–pa* (the thought of ṣending ...)
	363, n. 77	*rtogs–pa*	*gtogs–pa*
	n. 84	(= *na prajñāyate*)	(to be omitted)
	366, n. 107	*mi–rgu–baḥi*	*mi–rgyu–baḥi*
	n. 110	*rdo–than*	*rdo–tshan*
	n. 111	*ri–yul soṅ–ba*	*ri–sul soṅ–ba*
	368, n. 122	*anubhava*	*anubhāva*
	372, l. 7	separately	simultaneously
	n. 172	*yugapad–gocara–sthāna*	(*yugapad*) *gocarastha*
	n. 172	T. *cig–car–tu*	T. *cig–car–du*
	374, l. 12	Connot	Cannot
	375, n. 202	*darsanā*	*darśanā*
XVIII.	384, n. 33	*rje–su–gzuṅ*	*rjes–su gzuṅ*
	n. 35	*kathaṃ*	*katham*
	386, n. 46	*ekam jinam*	*ekaṃ jinam*
	n. 46	*rgyal–paḥi*	*rgyal–baḥi*
	387, n. 62	*dran–don*	*draṅ–don*
	n. 63	*brtam*	*brkam*
	388, n. 71	*ṅams*	*ñams*

(Appendixes)

I.	393, l. 7	mārgam	mārgaṃ
II.	397, l. 18	nrvāṇâsamāropa	nirvāṇâsamāropa
	398, l. 1	taṭhāgatadhātor	tathāgatadhātor
III.	404, l. 10	*ādarša–ñ.*	*ādarśa–jñ.*
	405, l. 23	belougs	belongs
	407, n. 18	*pariniṣpaṇṇa*	*pariniṣpanna*

(Indexes)

412	(after ' adhyāśaya ',	insert) adhyupekṣaṇa, 342
413	anubhava, 368	anubhāva, 359, 368

Corrigenda

(Page)	instead of	read
413	anvâdhana	anvâdhāna
414	*abhyupekṣaṇa, 342*	(to be omitted)
415	*avivartika* (bodhisattva), 92	(to be omitted)
415	(under the entry of 'avaivartika (bodhisattva))	(insert) 92
417	upekṣâpratisaṃkhyā	upekṣâpratisaṃkhyāya [na ~]
419	(after 'gocaraviṣaya'	insert) gocarastha, 372
427	(after 'pratyupasthāna'	insert) *pratyupasthāpana*, 221
	221 (under the entry of 'pratyupasthāna')	(to be omitted)
430	*yugapad-gocara-sthāna*, 372	(to be omitted)
432	vṛtta-ślakṣaṇânunnāma-	vṛttaślakṣṇânunnāma-
437	Catuḥśubha	Catuḥstava
438	Sumaṅgala-visāraṇī	Sumaṅgala-vilāsinī

REVIEW

PHILOLOGISCHE BEMERKUNGEN ZUM RATNAGOTRAVIBHĀGA[1]

Von Lambert Schmithausen, Münster

1. Zur Struktur des RGV

In seinem Buch „A Study on the Ratnagotravibhāga"[2] hat J. Takasaki gezeigt, daß der Ratnagotravibhāgaḥ (RGV) im wesent-

---

[1] In dem vorliegenden Aufsatz finden folgende Abkürzungen Verwendung.

A. = Anmerkung (nie bei Verweisen auf den vorl. Aufsatz).
BCA-I = Friedrich Weller, Tibetisch-Sanskritischer Index zum Bodhicaryāvatāra. Abh. Sächs. Ak. Philol.-hist. Kl. 46, 3 u. 47, 3 (1952—1955).
Bem. = Bemerkung (bezieht sich auf die philologischen Bemerkungen des vorl. Aufsatzes).
BGŚ = *Buddhagotraśāstram (T 1610).
BHSD = Franklin Edgerton, Buddhist Hybrid Sanskrit Dictionary, New Haven 1953.
BHSG = Franklin Edgerton, Buddhist Hybrid Sanskrit Grammar, New Haven 1953.
BoBh = Bodhisattvabhūmiḥ, ed. Wogihara, Tokyo 1930—1936.
C. = Chinesische Übersetzung des RGV (T 1611).
D = Derge-Ed. des tibetischen Tripiṭaka.
de J. = J. W. de Jong, Besprechung von Tak. in IIJ XI/1968, p. 36—54.
F. = Fußnote (nur bei Verweisen auf den vorl. Aufsatz!).
Hs., Hss. = Handschrift, Handschriften.
J. = E. H. Johnstons Ed. des RGV (s. Fußn. 29 des vorl. Aufs.).
Jñ = Jñānaśrīmitranibandhāvaliḥ, ed. A. Thakur, Patna 1959.
MVy = Mahāvyutpattiḥ, ed. Sakaki, Kyoto 1916—1925.
MW = Monier-Williams, A Sanskrit-English Dictionary, Reprint, Oxford 1951.
Nak. = Zuiryū Nakamura, Zōwa-taiyaku Kukyōichijōhōshōron-kenkyū, Tokyo 1967.
NVinSg = Lambert Schmithausen, Der Nirvāṇa-Abschnitt in der Viniścayasaṃgrahaṇī der Yogācārabhūmiḥ. Sb. Öst. Ak. Phil.-hist. Kl. 264/2, Wien 1969.

lichen[3] aus drei Elementen besteht: aus Grundtext-Versen, kommentierenden Versen[4] und kommentierender Prosa (Tak. p. 10). Daß die Grundtext-Verse ursprünglich selbständig — ohne die Kommentar-Verse — existiert haben, ergibt sich aus verschiedenen Tatsachen: Zunächst umfaßt die chinesische Überlieferung des RGV neben der Wiedergabe des aus Versen und Kommentar gemischten Gesamtwerkes[5] auch einen reinen Verstext, der im wesentlichen[6] aus ebendiesen Grundversen besteht (Tak. p. 9f.). Ferner treten durch die Ausschaltung der Kommentarverse drei Namaskāra-Verse (I, 4; I, 9; I, 13) an den Anfang des Textes, wo sie zweifellos ihren natürlichen Platz haben. Weiterhin bilden die Grundverse I, 30, 35, 42 und 45 eine zusammenhängende Satzkonstruktion, woraus mit einiger Sicherheit zu entnehmen ist, daß sie ursprünglich unmittelbar aufeinanderfolgten (Tak. p. 402). Ferner ist die Terminologie von Grundtext-Versen einerseits und Kommentarversen und Prosa andererseits in mancher Hinsicht verschieden: Es

---

p.	= pagina (bezieht sich bei nichtspezifizierter Verwendung auf RGV!)
P	= Peking-Ed. des tibetischen Tripiṭaka.
RGV	= Ratnagotravibhāgaḥ (s. Fußn. 29 des vorl. Aufs.!).
Ru.	= D. SEYFORT RUEGG, La théorie du Tathāgatagarbha et du Gotra (s. Fußn. 33 des vorl. Aufs.!).
S.	= Seite (nur bei Verweisen auf den vorl. Aufsatz!).
SA(Bh)	= (Mahāyāna-)Sūtrālaṅkāra(bhāṣyam), ed. S. LÉVI, Paris 1907—1911.
T	= Taishō-Ausgabe des chinesischen Tripiṭaka.
T.	= Tibetische Übersetzung des RGV (ed. in Nak. [q. v.]).
Tak.	= J. TAKASAKI, A Study on the Ratnagotravibhāga (s. Fußn. 2 des vorl. Aufs.!).
⟨ ⟩	bezeichnet zu ergänzende Textstücke.
[ ]	bezeichnet zu tilgende Textstücke.

Zahlen im Kreis hinter transkribierten chinesischen Wörtern verweisen auf die Zeichenliste auf S. 176.

[2] JIKIDO TAKASAKI, A Study on the Ratnagotravibhāga (Uttaratantra), Being a Treatise on the Tathāgatagarbha Theory of Mahāyāna Buddhism. Rom, Is. M. E. O. 1966 (= Serie Orientale Roma, Bd. XXXIII).

[3] D. h. abgesehen von einigen späteren Zusätzen (vgl. Tak. p. 19).

[4] Vgl. auch Jñ p. 503, 20—22, wo (mit *sāṃvṛtapadaṃ*) auf RGV III, 1 als *mūlam*, auf RGV III, 2—3 hingegen (mit *sāṃketikaśabdaḥ*) als *vivṛtiḥ* (vgl. auch pp. 502, 17; 503, 15; 536, 22) verwiesen wird.

[5] Für längere Grundvers-Reihen wie I, 96—126 wird jedoch in dieser Wiedergabe auf die separate Übersetzung der Grundverse verwiesen (die chin. Wiedergabe des Gesamttextes enthält nur die Inhaltsangabe-Verse I, 96—98).

[6] Nicht zum originalen Grundtext gehören vor allem die ersten 18 Verse (vgl. Tak. p. 10). Unsicher ist in einigen Fällen der ursprüngliche Textbestand von Kap. IV (vgl. Tak. p. 15—17).

fehlen in den Grundversen z. B.: der Terminus *āśrayaparivṛttiḥ*[7] bzw. *-parāvṛttiḥ*[8]; die Lehre von *svābhāvikaḥ* und *sāmbhogikaḥ kāyaḥ* neben dem (auch im Grundtext[9] vorkommenden) *nirmāṇa(kāyaḥ)*[10], die offenbar aus dem Mahāyānasūtrālaṃkāraḥ[11] stammt; oder der dem (schon den Grundversen geläufigen[11a]) *dharmakāyaḥ* gegenübergestellte Begriff des *vimuktikāyaḥ*[12], der offenbar aus Saṃdhinirmocanasūtram X entlehnt ist. Auch andere Termini der Kommentarverse und der Prosa scheinen auf eine in den Grundversen noch nicht feststellbare Beeinflussung durch Terminologien der älteren Yogācāratexte (Yogācārabhūmiḥ, Saṃdhinirmocanasūtram, Mahāyānasūtrālaṅkāraḥ[13]) hinzuweisen, z. B. *prakṛtistham* und *samudānītaṃ gotram*[14] (vgl. BoBh 3, 2ff.), *yathāvadbhāvikatā* und *yāvadbhāvikatā*[15] (vgl. BoBh 37, 1ff.), vielleicht auch *tatpṛṣṭhalabdhaṃ jñānam*[16] (vgl. z. B. BoBh 38, 4; Y_t Zi 302b8; SABh 139, 15).

Angesichts dieser Verwendung von Termini, die offensichtlich aus der älteren Yogācāra-Tradition entlehnt sind, und angesichts der Zitate aus dem Mahāyānasūtrālaṃkāraḥ[17] kann die Abfassung des Kommentars (durch Sāramati, vgl. Tak. pp. 9, 46 u. 62) kaum vor der zweiten Hälfte des 4. Jh. erfolgt sein (Tak. p. 61: Anfang 5. Jh.). Die Frage, ob Vers- und Prosakommentar[18] von ein und demselben Verfasser

---

[7] RGV 21, 9 u. 10; 38, 17; 79, 3f., 10f. u. 14; 80, 15; 82, 5; 89, 16. Offenbar nur in der Prosa!

[8] RGV V, 7 (Kommentar-Vers!). — Ich sehe keinen Grund, anstelle von *parāvṛttau* als ursprüngliche Lesung *parivṛttau* anzusetzen (RGV p. 116, A. 2); der Terminus kann dem Verfasser der Kommentar-Verse des RGV ohne weiteres aus dem SA bekannt gewesen sein, und *parivṛtti-* kommt in den Kommentar-Versen bezeichnenderweise gar nicht vor (s. vorherg. F.!).

[9] RGV IV, 56.

[10] RGV I, 151f.; II, 44/50/53; p. 85, 9.

[11] SA IX, 60ff.

[11a] RGV I, 84; IV, 55.

[12] RGV II, 22 u. 30.

[13] Dieser Text wird ja in der Tat im Prosakommentar des RGV (p. 71) zitiert (vgl. Tak. pp. 33 u. 40).

[14] RGV I, 149.

[15] RGV I, 14—16 u. Prosa dazu.

[16] Z. B. RGV II, 7 u. 11; pp. 79, 13; 82, 5.

[17] S. F. 13.

[18] Einige Kommentar-Verse, die nicht unmittelbar der Erklärung der Grundverse dienen und z. T. im Gegensatz zur großen Masse der Kommentar-Verse nicht im Anuṣṭubh-Metrum abgefaßt sind, gehören offenbar eher in den Rahmen des Prosakommentars: z. B. I, 34, I, 88—92, I, 153—155 und wahrscheinlich auch I, 1—3. Auch I, 39 ist vielleicht hierzu zu rechnen, doch fehlt der Vers nebst der vorausgehenden Prosapartie in der chinesischen

stammen, vermag ich vorerst nicht sicher zu beantworten; einige Einzelbeobachtungen[19] lassen es zum mindesten zweifelhaft erscheinen.

Der von typischen Yogācāra-Termini weitgehend unbeeinflußte Grund-Verstext weist, wie schon Tak. (p. 41) bemerkt hat, lediglich eine gewisse Verwandtschaft zu gewissen Partien des IX. Kap. des Mahāyānasūtrālaṅkāraḥ auf und dürfte ein etwas älterer Text aus dem gleichen oder doch einem verwandten Milieu sein[20]. Ob von demselben Verfasser oder nicht, läßt sich vorerst kaum entscheiden.

Ein zusätzliches Problem ergibt sich daraus, daß — wie Tak. (p. 10ff.) gezeigt hat — auch der Grund-Verstext keine ganz einheitliche Komposition ist. Eine Analyse ergibt folgendes Bild:

(0.) Einleitung:
- *1.* 3 Namaskāra-Verse (I, 4; 9; 13) — A
- *2.* Inhaltsangabe zum Gesamttext (I, 23) — B

I. *samalā tathatā* (= *tathāgatagarbhaḥ*)
- *1.* Drei Bedeutungen des Ausdruckes „*tathāgatagarbhaḥ*" (I, 27) — A
- *2.* Abhandlung des *tathāgatagarbhaḥ* nach 10 Kategorien
  - *a.* Inhaltsangabe (*uddānam*: I, 29)[21] — B
  - *b.* Ausführliche Behandlung (I, 30 etc.) — A
- *3.* Abhandlung des *tathāgatagarbhaḥ* im Anschluß an das Tathāgatagarbhasūtram
  - *a.* Inhaltsangabe (I, 96—98) — B
  - *b.* Ausführliche Behandlung (I, 99ff.) — C
- *4.* Zweck der Lehre vom *tathāgatagarbhaḥ* (I, 156f.) — A

Übersetzung (vgl. Tak. p. 220, Anm. 149 u. 154) und ist vielleicht — ebenso wie I, 69—78 — ein späterer Zusatz, woraus sich dann auch der von Ru. (p. 12) beobachtete terminologische Widerspruch zum folgenden (Kommentar-)Vers I, 40 erklären ließe.

[19] Vgl. Kap. 2, Bem. zu 16, 9f. u. 46, 11f.

[20] Vgl. auch den Umstand, daß das im RGV (z. B. I, 96ff.) häufig angewandte Stilmittel, den gleichen Inhalt doppelt, und zwar das zweite Mal in einem komplizierteren Metrum, auszudrücken, auch in SA IX, 1ff. anzutreffen ist.

[21] Dieser Vers gehört nach Tak. (p. 12f.) zum Kommentar, weil er nicht als *ślokaḥ* bezeichnet wird und überdies die gleichen Kategorien enthält, die in II, 2 der Kommentar in Anwendung bringt. Man könnte sich aber m. E. gut denken, daß I, 29 doch mit C. zum Grundtext gehört und der Kommentar die Kategorien von I, 29 gerade zum Zwecke einer Harmonisierung von I, 29 und II, 1 auch auf Kap. II übertragen hat. Auch metrisch würde der Vers I, 29 schlecht zu den Kommentarversen passen (vgl. F. 18!). Er könnte allenfalls zum Prosa-Kommentar gehören (vgl. F. 18), zumal gegen seine Zugehörigkeit zum Grund-Verstext vielleicht die Tatsache spricht, daß er — im Gegensatz etwa zu den Inhaltsangabeversen I, 23, II, 1 und V, 1 — von den Kommentar-Versen nicht erklärt wird.

II.	*nirmalā tathatā* (= *bodhiḥ*)	
	a. Inhaltsangabe (II, 1)	B
	b. Ausführliche Behandlung (II, 3 etc.)	A
III.	*buddhaguṇāḥ*	
	1. Abhandlung durch einen selbständigen Vers (III, 1)	A
	2. Abhandlung im Anschluß an das Ratnadārikāsūtram	
	a. Inhaltsangabe (III, 4)	B
	b. Ausführliche Behandlung (III, 5ff.)	C
IV.	*jinakriyāḥ*	
	1. Abhandlung durch 2 selbständige Verse (IV, 1—2)	A
	2. Abhandlung im Anschluß an das Jñānālokālaṅkārasūtram	
	a. Inhaltsangabe (*sūtrasthānīyaḥ ślokaḥ*[22]: IV, 13)	B
	b. Ausführliche Behandlung (IV, 27 [od. 14 ?][23] ff.)	C
V.	Schlußwort	
	1. Rückschauende Inhaltsangabe des Gesamtwerkes (V, 1)	B
	2. *śravanaphalam* (V, 2—6)	A
	3. Erkenntnistheoretische Grundlage, Motiv, Legitimation usw. (V, 16—24)	A
	4. Rückschauende Inhaltsangabe und Segenswunsch (V, 25)	(B)

Tak. (p. 18) hat diese verschiedenen Bestandteile des Grundverstextes in drei Klassen eingeteilt: A = selbständige Verse, B = Inhaltsangabe-Verse, und C = Sūtren nachgebildete Vergleiche. Die Gruppe C ist nach seiner Auffassung nachträglich hinzugefügt worden, weil im Falle der 32 *mahāpuruṣalakṣaṇāni* (RGV III, 17ff.) die Aufzählung des RGV (im Anschluß an das Ratnadārikāsūtram) über die des Abhisamayālaṅkāraḥ hinausgeht und Tak. voraussetzt, daß sowohl dieser wie auch der Ur-RGV von „Maitreya" verfaßt seien (Tak. p. 15). Die Aussonderung der dem Ratnadārikāsūtram nachgebildeten Verse über die *buddhaguṇāḥ* impliziert aber angesichts der weitgehend homogenen Struktur aller Verse der C-Klasse, daß auch die dem Tathāgatagarbhasūtram und die dem Jñānālokālaṅkārasūtram nachgebildeten Verse ausscheiden (Tak., ib.). Eine weitere Reduktion des Textes ergibt sich für Tak. daraus, daß Vers II, 9 auf die Illustrationen des Tathāgatagarbhasūtram anspielt und — so Tak. (p. 13) — die zur Klasse C gehörige Versgruppe I, 96ff. unbedingt voraussetzt. Demnach ist entweder II, 9 ein nachträglicher Einschub in Kap. II, oder aber — und das scheint die von Tak. vorgezogene Alternative zu sein — das ganze Kap. II

[22] Tak.s Wiedergabe dieses Terminus („a stanza based upon the scripture") ist unzutreffend. Gemeint ist: „ein Vers, der die Stellung eines Leitfadens einnimmt, als Leitfaden fungiert".

[23] Vgl. F. 6.

ist aus dem Ur-RGV auszuscheiden (Tak. p. 18). Damit fallen aber auch die noch verbliebenen Reste von Kap. III und IV sowie der Inhaltsangabevers I, 23 und wohl, angesichts der in V, 1 und V, 25 enthaltenen Inhaltsangaben, auch Kap. V weg, zumal die Verse I, 156—157 einen idealen Abschluß bilden (Tak., ib.). Es bleibt für Tak. ein Ur-RGV von insgesamt 27 Versen, die er auf S. 393ff. seines Buches zusammengestellt hat.

Dieser in der beschriebenen Weise als Ur-RGV herausgeschälte Text ist, nach Tak., nicht weiter zerlegbar. Eine genauere Untersuchung scheint mir jedoch diese Behauptung zu widerlegen: Vers 24 (= I, 79) sagt über das Absolutum: *ananyathātmā 'kṣayadharmayogato, jagaccharaṇyo 'naparāntakoṭitaḥ | sadā 'dvayo 'sāv avikalpakatvato, 'vināśadharmā 'py akṛtasvabhāvataḥ ||*. Fragt man, welches Substantiv mit dem Pronomen *asau* aufgenommen wird, so gerät man in unerwartete Schwierigkeiten. Der vorhergehende Vers (23 = I, 66)[24] enthält mit *asya* ebenfalls nur ein das in Frage stehende Substantiv repräsentierendes Pronomen. In Vers 22 (= I, 63)[25] scheint sich zunächst das als Genitivattribut von *prakṛtiḥ* auftretende *cittasya* als Bezugspunkt des *asya* von Vers 23, das ja ebenfalls Genitivattribut von *prakṛtiḥ* ist, anzubieten. Aber erstens wäre dieser Bezug durch die dazwischengeschobenen, einen selbständigen Satz bildenden Pādās c—d des Verses 22, in denen überdies das Pronomen *asau* stellvertretend für *prakṛtiḥ* auftritt, gestört. Und darüber hinaus wäre für *asau* in Vers 24 nichts gewonnen, da es sich im Gegensatz zu *asya* in Vers 23 nicht auf das Neutrum *cittam* beziehen kann. Auch die Verse 14—21 (= I, 55—62) helfen nicht weiter: sie alle bezeichnen, wie Vers 22, das Absolute als *cittaprakṛtiḥ* oder *cittaśuddhiḥ*. Erst in Vers 13 (= I, 54)[26] tritt die absolute Wesenheit in Gestalt des maskulinen Pronomens *enaṃ* auf, und in Vers 12 (= I, 53) wird mit *asaṃskṛte dhātau* auch das entsprechende Substantiv ausgesprochen. Es kann kein Zweifel darüber bestehen, daß sich nicht nur das *enaṃ* von Vers 13, sondern auch das (maskuline) *asau* von Vers 24 auf diesen *dhātuḥ* bezieht. Das wäre aber nicht möglich, wenn von Anfang an mehrere Verse dazwischengestanden haben, in

---

[24] *nirvṛttivyuparamarugjarāvimuktām*
asyaiva prakṛtim ananyathāvagamya |
janmādivyasanam ṛte 'pi tannidānaṃ
dhīmanto jagati kṛpodayād bhajante ||

[25] *cittasya yā 'sau prakṛtiḥ prabhāsvarā*
na jātu sā dyaur iva yāti vikriyām |
āgantukai rāgamalādibhis tv asāv
upaiti saṃkleśam abhūtakalpajaiḥ ||

[26] *yathā nāgnibhir ākāśaṃ dagdhapūrvaṃ kadācana |*
tathā na pradahanty enaṃ mṛtyuvyādhijarāgnayaḥ ||

denen nur von der *prakṛtiḥ* des *cittam* die Rede ist. Da von den Versen, in denen dies der Fall ist, die Verse 14—21 (= I, 55—62) inhaltlich eine fest geschlossene Einheit bilden und überdies nachweislich dem Gaganagañjasūtram nachgebildet sind (vgl. RGV p. 44, 8ff.), halte ich es für angebracht, sie als einen nachträglichen Einschub auszuklammern. Auch Vers 22 (= I, 63) ist gewiß an diesen Einschub anzuschließen, nicht nur, weil er das gleiche Subjekt (sc. *cittasya prakṛtiḥ*) hat, sondern auch deshalb, weil er offenbar dazu dient, den Inhalt der den vorhergehenden Versen und ihrer Quelle verwandten Aussagen der Sāgaramatiparipṛcchā (vgl. RGV p. 49, 9ff.) zusammenzufassen[27]. Vers 23 (= I, 66) folgte demnach ursprünglich auf Vers 13 (= I, 54), an dessen zweite Hälfte (. . . *na pradahanty enaṃ mṛtyuvyādhijarāgnayaḥ*) er sich mit *nirvṛtti-vyuparama-rug-jarāvimuktām asyaiva prakṛtim* bestens anschließt. Mit dem Pronomen *asya* in Vers 23b ist somit von Hause aus der *dhātuḥ* gemeint, und es ist vielleicht kein Zufall, daß es noch in der Paraphrase des Prosakommentares in diesem Sinne gedeutet wird: vgl. RGV p. 47, 6: *asyaiva dhātoḥ*.

Mit dieser neuerlichen Verkürzung des Ur-RGV auf insgesamt 18 Verse aber wird das (schon bei Tak.s Text bestehende) Mißverhältnis zwischen den drei wuchtigen Einleitungsstrophen im Śārdūlavikrīḍita-Metrum und dem eigentlichen Körper des Textes — nicht mehr als 15 größtenteils im bescheidenen Anuṣṭubh-Metrum abgefaßten Versen — unübersehbar. Ich glaube daher, daß auch die drei Namaskāra-Verse auszuscheiden sind. Damit aber ist die Bezeichnung „Ur-RGV" für das zurückgebliebene Textstückchen nicht mehr vertretbar. Was uns geblieben ist, ist vielmehr nur einer der Bausteine, aus denen der ursprüngliche RGV zusammengesetzt worden ist, und dieser ursprüngliche RGV ist m. E. im wesentlichen identisch mit dem in der chinesischen Überlieferung separat erhaltenen Verstext, von dem oben ausgegangen wurde.

Dieser Text besteht, wie mir scheint, in einer Zusammenstellung verschiedener Materialien, aus denen sich vor allem ein offenbar vorgegebener kleiner Text über den Tathāgatagarbha und (insgesamt vier) Abschnitte mit dichterischen Neuformulierungen von Teilen einzelner Mahāyānasūtren (sc. die Verse der C-Klasse sowie RGV I, 55—63), die wahrscheinlich vom Verfasser des RGV selbst stammen, herauslösen lassen. Relativ homogen ist auch der Grundvers-Bestand von Kap. II.

[27] Hier werden die *kleśāḥ*, die nach dem Gaganagañjasūtram aus dem *ayoniśomanaskāraḥ* entspringen, auf den *abhūtaparikalpaḥ* zurückgeführt. Außerdem lehren beide Texte die natürliche Reinheit (*prabhāsvaratā*) des Geistes und die Äußerlichkeit (*āgantukatā*) der Verunreinigungen (vgl. RGV pp. 44, 9; 45, 3; 49, 10—12).

Diese verschiedenen Bestandteile sind vom Verfasser des ursprünglichen RGV in dem Schema *samalā tathatā — nirmalā tathatā — buddhaguṇāḥ — jinakriyāḥ* zusammengeordnet sowie mit den einleitenden Namaskāra-Versen und mit einem Schlußwort versehen worden, und auch die eingeschaltenen Inhaltszusammenfassungen dürften bei dieser Gelegenheit entstanden sein[28].

Tak.s Argument, daß die Verse der C-Klasse nicht zum ursprünglichen Textbestand des RGV gehören können, weil die in ihnen enthaltene Darstellung der *mahāpuruṣalakṣaṇāni* nicht zu der des Abhisamayālaṅkāraḥ paßt, kann nicht als schlüssig gelten; denn die legendäre Zuschreibung nicht nur des RGV, sondern auch des Abhisamayālaṅkāraḥ an „Maitreya" reicht angesichts der entscheidenden Unterschiede, die sowohl in formaler wie auch in lehrmäßiger Hinsicht zwischen diesen beiden Texten bestehen, nicht aus, um die Identität ihres Verfassers zu garantieren. Wenn man aber trotz dieser fundamentalen Unterschiede eine solche Verfasseridentität voraussetzt, wird man aus einer ganz nebensächlichen Abweichung im Detail, die sich durch den Anschluß an unterschiedliche Sūtren erklären läßt, erst recht keine literargeschichtlichen Schlüsse ziehen können.

2. Zu Wortlaut und Übersetzung des RGV

Der Sanskrittext des RGV wurde, nach zwei Hss. (A [sehr lückenhaft] und B [fast vollständig])[28a], die R. Sāṅkṛtyāyana in Tibet gefilmt hat, 1950 von E. H. Johnston ediert[29]. Die große Leistung, die hinter dieser Ausgabe steht, wird wohl nur der richtig würdigen können, der den oft miserablen Zustand vor allem der Kopien der Hs. B mit eigenen Augen gesehen hat. Daß bei der Edition solcher Materialien gelegentlich Fehler unterlaufen, ist wohl unvermeidlich. Einige dieser Fehler hat bereits T. Chowdhury, der nach Johnstons Tod den Druck seiner Textausgabe überwachte, im Vorwort (p. IIf.; vgl. auch p. XVI) korrigiert. Eine große Anzahl weiterer und zu einem großen Teil durchaus geglückter Korrekturen steuerte J. Takasaki im Rahmen seiner engli-

[28] Auf diese Weise ließe sich gegebenenfalls auch die Einfügung des Inhaltsangabeverses I, 29 erklären, falls dieser wirklich zum Grund-Verstext gehört (vgl. F. 21).

[28a] In den folgenden Bemerkungen hat in Angaben wie „Hs. (B)" die Klammer syntaktische Funktion, d. h.: „Hs. (B)" = „die Hs., u. zw. Hs. B [während Hs. A zu der betreffenden Stelle fehlt]".

[29] The Ratnagotravibhāga Mahāyānottaratantraśāstra, ed. by E. H, Johnston. Patna 1950.

schen Übersetzung des RGV[30] (p. 396ff.) bei. Weitere wichtige Korrekturen enthält J. W. DE JONGS ausführliche Besprechung von TAKASAKIS Buch[31]. Trotz all dieser Bemühungen ist jedoch noch eine Reihe von Textfehlern unentdeckt geblieben. Einige von ihnen — gewiß nicht alle[32] — möchte ich im folgenden zu berichtigen versuchen. Zur Kontrolle meiner Korrekturvorschläge konnte ich Abzüge der Hss. einsehen, die dank der Großzügigkeit des K. P. Jayaswal Research Institute in Patna im Besitz des Indologischen Seminars der Universität Göttingen sind und mir freundlicherweise zur Verfügung gestellt wurden.

Zu TAKASAKIS Übersetzung des Textes, zu der bereits DE JONG in seiner Besprechung eine Anzahl von Verbesserungen beigesteuert hat, nehme ich, von einigen wenigen besonders problematischen oder wichtigen Stellen abgesehen, nur im Anschluß an Textkorrekturen Stellung. Eine Behandlung aller Stellen, an denen ich anderer Meinung bin als TAKASAKI, war aus Gründen des Raumes und der Zeit nicht möglich. Überdies hat inzwischen D. SEYFORT RUEGG in seiner Studie über *tathāgatagarbhaḥ* und *gotram*[33] zahlreiche Partien des RGV in Übersetzung oder Paraphrase wiedergegeben und dabei oft glücklichere Lösungen gefunden.

1, 6f.[34] *śruticintāmayajñānaduṣprative⟨dhād*[35]⟩. Statt *śruti-* ist mit der Hs. (B) *śruta-* zu lesen (vgl. MVy 1551). Außerdem wäre statt *-duṣprative⟨dhād⟩* vielleicht besser *-duṣprative⟨dhatvād⟩* anzusetzen.

3, 4f. *yo 'yaṃ . . . dharmakāyaḥ, so 'yam avinirbhāgadharmā 'vi*[36]*nirmuktajñānaguṇo yaduta gaṅgānadīvālikāvyatikrāntais tathāgatadharmaiḥ*. Tak. (p. 144): „That which is called the Absolute Body . . . is of indivisible nature, of qualities inseparable from the Wisdom, that is to say [indivisible from or endowed] with the properties of the Buddha which far surpass the particles of sands of the Gaṅgā in number.“ Ru. (p. 360): „. . . le *dharmakāya* . . . a pour qualité d'être inséparable, et il a la propriété du savoir non séparé — [inséparable] des *dharma* de *tathāgata* dépassant [en leur nombre] les sables de la Gaṅgā.“ RUEGG möchte also in diesem Zitat aus dem Anūnatvāpūrṇatvanirdeśaḥ

---

[30] Siehe F. 2.

[31] IIJ XI/1968, p. 36—54.

[32] Eine (von mir nicht durchgeführte!) vollständige Überprüfung beider Hss. würde gewiß noch manche Korrektur ermöglichen.

[33] DAVID SEYFORT RUEGG, La théorie du Tathāgatagarbha et du Gotra. Études sur la Sotériologie et la Gnoséologie du Bouddhisme. Paris 1969.

[34] Die Stellenangaben beziehen sich auf die Seiten und Zeilen von JOHNSTONS Ausgabe des RGV (s. F. 29).

[35] Lücke in der Hs., vgl. RGV p. 1, A. 4.

[36] Vgl. Tak. p. 396.

avinirbhāga- und *avinirmuktajñāna-* als Qualifikationen des *dharmakāyaḥ* verstehen, während im Śrīmālāsūtram *avinirbhāga-* und *amuktajñ(ān)a-* zur Kennzeichnung der *buddhaguṇāḥ* verwendet werden. Hierfür scheint mir aber kein zwingender Grund ersichtlich zu sein. Es ist ohne weiteres möglich, auch an der vorliegenden Anūnatvāpūrṇatvanirdeśa-Stelle zu übersetzen: „Der *dharmakāyaḥ* . . . besitzt unabtrennbare Eigenschaften, und Vorzüge, welche *avinirmuktajñāna-* sind[37], u. zw. in Gestalt von Buddha-Eigenschaften, die zahlreicher sind als Sand der Gaṅgā." — Zu den Termini *(a)vinirmuktajñāna-*, *(a)muktajñāna-* und *(a)muktajña-* (die gewiß gleichbedeutend sind) möchte ich bemerken, daß mir Tak.s Wiedergabe mit „inseparable from the Wisdom" (vgl. auch Tak. p. 144f., A. 23) grammatisch sehr problematisch erscheint. Da der Terminus *(vinir)muktajñ(ān)a-* (bzw. sein Gegenteil) immer dem Ausdruck *vinirbhāga-* (bzw. dessen Gegenteil) folgt — an einer Stelle[37a] geht auch noch *asambaddha-* (bzw. *sambaddha-*) vorher — ist davon auszugehen, daß er eine eng mit dem Begriff „unabtrennbar" (bzw. „abtrennbar") verbundene Bedeutung hat. Das legt auch Bodhirucis chinesische Übersetzung *(pu) t'o* ① („(nicht) losgelöst") nahe[38]. Am günstigsten ist es m. E., den Ausdruck in *(vinir)muktatvena jñānam* (bzw. *jñā*[39]) *yeṣāṃ (na) bhavati* aufzulösen, ihn somit zu verstehen als „bei denen Erkenntnis als losgelöst nicht stattfindet", d. h. „die (niemals) als [von der absoluten Wesenheit] losgelöst oder beseitigt festgestellt werden". Denkbar wäre aber auch eine Zerlegung in *(vinir)muktaṃ jñānaṃ* (bzw. *muktā jñā*) *yeṣāṃ (na) bhavati* = deren Erkenntnis [von der Erkenntnis der absoluten Wesenheit] (nicht) losgelöst [werden kann]", d. h. „ohne deren gleichzeitiges Erkanntwerden die absolute Wesenheit nicht erkannt werden kann".

3, 7 ***na mañjuśrīs tathāgataḥ kalpayati na vikalpayati athavāsyānābhogena . . . iyam evaṃrūpā kriyā pravartate.*** Tak. (p. 145): O Mañjuśrī, the Tathāgata never imagines anything nor distinguishes falsely. That is to say, his acts of this kind flow forth without any effort . . .". *athavā* („oder") ergibt keine sinnvolle Gedankenverknüpfung. Die beiden Sätze stehen vielmehr in einem konzessiven Verhältnis zueinander (vgl. auch T.: . . . *mod kyi* | *de lta na yaṅ* . . .): „Der Tathāgata, o Mañjuśrī, kennt keinerlei reflektive Unruhe. Und dennoch entfaltet sich bei ihm — [auch]

---

[37] D. h. es ist nicht einzusehen, warum *avinirbhāga-* und *avinirmuktajñāna-* im Anūnatvāpūrṇatvanirdeśaḥ Tatpuruṣas und nicht, wie im Śrīmālāsūtram, Bahuvrīhis sein sollen.

[37a] RGV p. 73, 2—4.

[38] Paramārtha (T 669, p. 469b19) hat *pu shê chih* ②.

[39] Wurzel als nomen actionis, vgl. WHITNEY, Sanskrit Grammar § 1147a.

ohne [irgendeine] Anstrengung — eine derartige Wirksamkeit." Statt *athavā* ist infolgedessen *atha ca*, das in der Bedeutung „und doch", „trotzdem" geläufig ist (vgl. z. B. RGV I, 78a), zu lesen.

3, 17: Statt ⟨*tasmā*[40]⟩*d ya*[41]*d uktaṃ* würde ich ⟨**tatra**⟩ *yad uktaṃ* vorziehen. Auch T. (*de las ji skad du . . . źes gsuṅs te*) ist hiermit vereinbar, insofern es *tatra* auf den zuvor genannten Text (Dhāraṇīśvararājasūtram) bezieht und in der Phrase „im (Text) *X* heißt es folgendermaßen" die Ausdrucksweise „*X las* . . ." durchaus üblich ist.

4, 11 *-maṇḍalavyūha-*. Die Hs. (B) erlaubt m. E. durchaus die durch T. nahegelegte[42] und der üblichen Ausdrucksweise entsprechende Lesung *-maṇḍalamāḍa-*[43] (s. BHSD s. v.).

6, 8 *viśuddhagotram*: Hs. (B) *viśuddhigotram*.

6, 16: Nicht nur die Hs. (B), sondern auch T. setzt — gegen J. (RGV p. 6, A. 6) — eindeutig die Lesung *dvātriṃśadākāraṃ* voraus: *de bźin gśegs pa'i phrin las bla na med pa bstan pas* (= *niruttaratathāgatakarmanirdeśena*) *saṅs rgyas kyi phrin las rnam pa sum cu rtsa gñis* (= *buddhakarma dvātriṃśadākāraṃ*) *gsal bar mdzad do*.

7, 2 *saṅghe garbho jñānadhātvāptiniṣṭhaḥ*. DE J. möchte (mit T.) *saṅghād* lesen und übersetzt: „From the Community comes the Matrix which culminates in the obtaining of the Element of Wisdom." Auch diese Übersetzung befriedigt m. E. noch nicht ganz, und ich weiß nicht, ob es notwendig ist, gegen die (hier ganz deutliche) Hs. (B) *saṅghād* zu lesen. Die Gemeinde kann jedenfalls nicht schlechthin die Ursache des (*tathāgata*)*garbhaḥ* an sich selbst sein, sondern nur die Ursache dafür, daß er sich zur aktuellen Buddhaschaft entwickelt. Ich schlage daher vor, *jñānadhātvāptiniṣṭhaḥ* prädikativ zu fassen: „Durch [den Einfluß der] Gemeinde (bzw., wenn man *saṅghe* beibehält: im [Rahmen der] Gemeinde) führt der [den Lebewesen innewohnende Buddha-]Embryo[44] schließlich zur Erlangung der [spirituellen] Stufe des Wissens." — In Pāda d des gleichen Verses — (*agrabodhiḥ*) *dharmair yuktā sarvasattvārthakṛdbhiḥ* — ist *sarvasattvārthakṛdbhiḥ* natürlich ein adjektivisches Upapadasamāsa, das als Attribut zu *dharmaiḥ* fungiert: „(die höchste Erleuchtung) ist verbunden mit Eigenschaften . . ., die das Heil aller Lebewesen bewirken". Tak.s Übersetzung („the Supreme Enlighten-

---

[40] Lücke: s. RGV p. 3, A. 4.

[41] Das Akṣara *dya* ist sehr undeutlich.

[42] Vgl. auch RGV p. 4, A. 7.

[43] Das zweite Akṣara gleicht zwar einem *ha*, aber das erste Akṣara kann kaum als *vyū* gelesen werden.

[44] „*tathāgatagarbhaḥ*" bedeutet, zum mindesten in indischen Texten, nicht „Matrix of the Tathāgata" (Tak.), sondern „Buddha-Embryo" (vgl. Ru. p. 499ff.).

ment, which is endowed with the Qualities ... and accompanied by altruistic Acts ..." ist grammatisch unhaltbar.

8, 1 *anādimadhyanidhanaprakṛtatvād*. Es ist mit der Hs. (B) *-prakṛtitvād* zu lesen.

8, 11—14 *ity asaṃskṛtād apravṛttilakṣaṇād api tathāgatatvād anābhogataḥ sarvasaṃbuddhakṛtyam* ... *pravartate* | (neuer Absatz:) *ity evam atyadbhutācintyaviṣayaṃ* ***buddhatvam*** *aśrutvā parataḥ* ***svayam*** *anācāryakeṇa svayaṃbhūjñānena nirabhilāpyasvabhāvatām* ***abhisaṃbudhya*** ...[45]. Tak. (p. 157): „Thus, as being Tathāgata, though it is immutable and of the characteristic of non-activity, the whole action of the Perfectly Enlightened One proceeds without any effort, ... 4) *Jñāna*, 5) *karuṇā*, & 6) *śakti*: Thus, not having heard the Buddhahood, which is a quite marvellous and unthinkable sphere, from somebody else, but having perfectly cognized its unutterable nature ‚by oneself' ..., i. e. by means of self-born knowledge which needs no teacher, ...". M. E. beginnt mit *ity evam* kein neuer Absatz. Mit dem vorhergehenden *asaṃskṛtaṃ* ... *pravartate* wird vielmehr angegeben, wieso das Buddhatum wunderbar und unbegreiflich ist: „Nachdem [der Buddha] somit[46] das Buddhatum, [das] etwas ganz Wunderbares und Unbegreifliches [ist][47] — weil[48] aus dem Buddhatum, obwohl es unverursacht und nicht durch Aktivität charakterisiert ist, dennoch, ohne [irgendeine] Anstrengung ..., alle Wirkungen des Buddha hervorgehen —, ... vollkommen geschaut hat (*abhisaṃbudhya*), [u. zw.] nicht [erst], nachdem er von anderen [eine Belehrung darüber] vernommen hätte, [sondern] aus sich selbst, [d. h.] vermittels eines selbstgewordenen, [d. h.] nicht durch einen Lehrer hervorgerufenen Wissens, ...". Statt des die Konstruktion etwas störenden *nirabhilāpyasvabhāvatām* ist vielleicht ein prädikativ zu verstehendes *nirabhilāpyasvabhāvam*, oder *nirabhilāpyasvabhāvatayā* („als von Natur als unausdrückbar", „in seiner unausdrückbaren Natur", vgl. T. *brjod du med pa'i raṅ bźin du*) anzusetzen[49].

---

[45] Die gesperrten Wörter nehmen wörtlich oder sinngemäß den Wortlaut des Grundtextes (I, 4a—b) auf. *vibuddhaḥ* (I, 4a) wird in der Paraphrase des Kommentars ausgelassen.

[46] Hiermit wird an die Ausführungen von p. 8, 7—10 angeknüpft.

[47] Wörtl. am besten: „Welches das ganz Wunderbare ... zu seinem Bereich hat". T.: „... welches ein ganz wunderbarer ... Bereich (od. Gegenstand) ist".

[48] Wörtl.: „... in der Weise, daß ...".

[49] In der Hs. ist vor allem das angebliche Akṣaram *-tā-* ganz undeutlich; Doppelschreibung von *-ma-* erscheint nicht ausgeschlossen; *-tayā* statt *-tam a-* ist graphisch weniger wahrscheinlich.

8, 14f. *tadanubodhaṃ praty abudhānām api jātyandhānāṃ pareṣām anubodhāya tadanugāmimārgavyupadeśakaraṇād* ...[50]. Die Hs. (B) liest auf jeden Fall (mit T. *dmus loṅ du* **gyur** *pa*) *jātyandha***bhūtānām** statt *jātyandhānāṃ*, ferner offenbar (in Z. 15) **avabodhāya**[51] und vielleicht eher *tadanu***gama**[52]*mārga-*. Auch das ungebräuchliche *-vyupadeśa-* ist verdächtig[53]. Statt *tadanubodhaṃ praty abudhānām* ... *anu-* (bzw. *ava-*) *bodhāya* („um den bezüglich der Schau des [Buddhatums] Unwissenden ... zu [dieser] Schau zu verhelfen") könnte man auch lesen: *tadanu bodhaṃ praty abudhānām* ... *anu-* (bzw. *ava-*) *bodhāya* („... (erteilt er) anschließend, um auch den bezüglich der Erleuchtung [noch] Unwissenden ... zur Erleuchtung zu verhelfen, (... Belehrungen)").

9, 1: *tacchettṛtve*. Hs. eindeutig *tacchettṛtv***āt**; vgl. Z. 3 *tadbhettṛtvāt* (T. beidemal ... *pa'i phyir*).

9, 10 *evam eva mañjuśrīs tathāgato 'rhan samyaksaṃbuddho neñjate*... Hs. (B) *tathāgato* (')**py** *arhan*: „Genau so ist, o M., auch der Tathāgata unbeweglich ...".

9, 13 *upaśamaprabhedapradeśanirdeśaḥ*. Tak. (p. 160): „explanation of various kinds of aspects of quiescence" (*pradeśa-* = aspect, Tak. p. 160, A. 36). Die Hs. hat *upaśama-***pada***-prabheda-pradeśa-nirdeśaḥ*, vgl. T. *ži ba'i* **tshig** *gi rab tu dbye ba bstan pa*. *pradeśa-* hat in T. keine Entsprechung und fehlt m. E. auch in C. (*ch'a-pieh chih hsiang* ③ dürfte eine interpretierende Wiedergabe von *prabheda-* sein) und ist wahrscheinlich zu tilgen. Zu übersetzen wäre: „die Aufzählung (eines Teiles (*pradeśa-*)) der verschiedenen (*prabheda-*) Ausdrücke (*pada-*) für das Zurruhegekommensein". — Zur Konstruktion des Satzes möchte ich bemerken, daß ich, analog zum vorhergehenden Satz (p. 9, Z. 6—8: *tatra yad uktam* ..., *anena* ... *paridīpitam*) auch im Falle des Textstückes 9, 8—14 gegen T. in *anena* ... *paridīpitam* den Hauptsatz zu dem mit *yat punar* (Z. 8) eingeleiteten Relativsatz sehen möchte. In ‚*evam eva* ... *'vijñapanīya' ity evamādir* ... *-nirdeśaḥ* erblicke ich eine erklärende Parenthese. Also wörtlich: „Mit dem, was dann [das Sūtram] anschließend ... sagt, — [d. h. mit der] Aufzählung (*nirdeśaḥ*) ... in der Form: ‚Genau so, o M., ...' usw. — wird gezeigt, daß ...".

10, 4 *svadharmatāprakṛtinirviśiṣṭatathāgatagarbham*. Hs. (B): *-nirviśiṣṭaṃ tathāgatagarbham*, d. h.: „... das Buddha-Embryo, das seinem

---

[50] S. F. 45.

[51] Vgl. auch T. *rtogs par bya ba'i phyir* (im Gegensatz zu *de rjes su rtogs pa* im Falle von *tadanubodha-* und *tadanugama-*.

[52] Vgl. auch T. *de rjes su rtogs pa'i lam*; zu *rjes su rtogs pa* = *anugama* vgl. RGV p. 18, 8.

[53] Hs. eher *-vyapadeśa-*, doch befriedigt auch das nicht.

eigentlichen Wesen nach von seiner (= des Buddha[54]) eigenen Natur nicht verschieden ist."

10, 8f. *samatayā sarvasattvanimittam abhisaṃbuddhabodheḥ svadharmatādhigamasamprāpaṇāśayatvāt.* Tak. möchte *-buddhyā* statt *-bodheḥ* lesen und übersetzt (p. 161f.): „because [the Buddha], having realized the characteristics of all living beings through equality, has the intention . . .". M. E. ist eine Textänderung nicht notwendig. *abhisaṃbuddhabodheḥ* läßt sich als Genitiv eines Bahuvrīhi *abhisaṃbuddhabodhi-* („die Erleuchtung als eine, zu der man vollkommen erwacht ist, habend") fassen und fungiert syntaktisch als logisches Subjekt des ihm folgenden Abstraktums. *-nimittam* würde ich adverbial verstehen (vgl. auch T. *sems can gyi rgyu mtshan du*). Ich schlage daher folgende Übersetzung vor: „Weil er die Absicht hat, alle Lebewesen dazu zu führen, daß sie seiner [auch ihnen innewohnenden] Natur[55] innewerden (*adhigama*); [denn] er hat die vollkommene Erleuchtung zum [Heile] (*-nimittam*) alle[r] Lebewesen erlangt, da [diese für ihn ihm selbst] gleich sind." — Vgl. auch Ru. p. 288, dessen Übersetzung mir allerdings an dieser Stelle nicht akzeptabel erscheint.

10, 16f. *yo nāsan na ca san na cāpi sadasan nānyaḥ sato nāsato 'śakyas tarkayitum* . . . Tak. (p. 163): „(I bow before the sun of the Doctrine,) which is neither non-being nor being, nor both being and non-being together, and neither different from being nor from non-being; which cannot be speculated upon . . .". J.s Behauptung, T. setze — im Gegensatz zur handschriftlichen Überlieferung *-sataḥ śakyas* (B) — mit C. die Lesart *-sato 'śakyas* voraus, ist unrichtig. T. lautet: *gaṅ źig med min yod min yod med ma yin yod med las gźan du^caṅ || brtag par mi nus.* Dies ist folgendermaßen zu übersetzen: „(Verehrung der Sonne des Dharma,) welche nicht nichtseiend, nicht seiend [und] nicht [zugleich] seiend und nichtseiend ist, [welche] auch nicht als [zugleich] von Seiendem und Nichtseiendem verschieden gedacht werden kann, . . .". T. setzt also eine Interpunktion nach *sadasan* voraus, und die Negation in *mi nus* entspricht dem auf *sadasan* folgenden *na*. T. geht also nicht von *-sato 'sakyaḥ*, sondern mit der Hs. (B) von *-sataḥ śakyaḥ* aus. Andererseits scheint tib. *yod med las gźan* die vom Sinn her naheliegende Korrektur des in der Hs. überlieferten (*na*) *anyaḥ sato nāsataḥ* zu (*na*) *anyaḥ sato cāsataḥ* zu stützen. Die von T. vorausgesetzte Interpunktion nach *sadasan* ist hingegen kaum berechtigt. Man muß hier gewiß dem Kommentar folgen, der alle vier Alternativen mit (*na* . . .) *śakyas tarkayitum* verbindet (p. 11, 19: *asatsatsadasannobhaya-*

[54] Vgl. DE J. zu 10,9!
[55] Vgl. DE J.

prakārais caturbhir api tarkāgocaratvāt). Es ist also (gegen T. und gegen Tak.) zu übersetzen: „(Verehrung der Sonne des Dharma,) welche weder als nichtseiend noch als seiend noch als zugleich seiend und nichtseiend noch als sowohl vom Seienden wie auch vom Nichtseienden verschieden gedacht werden kann, . . .". — In Pāda d von Vers I, 9 würde ich übrigens (trotz 13, 1 ff.) *-rāgadoṣatimiravyāghātakartre* (Tak.: which . . . destroys passion, hatred and darkness . . .) lieber als „welche die Finsternis [in Gestalt] von leidenschaftlicher Zu- und Abneigung vertreibt" wiedergeben (vgl. Pāda c: *-jñānāvabhāsatviṣe* = „die im Licht des Wissens erstrahlt", sowie 12, 19: *tamaḥpratipakṣasādharmyeṇa*).

12, 14 *ayam eva ca bhagavaṃs tathāgatadharmakāyo 'vinirmuktakleśakośas tathāgatagarbhaḥ sūcyate*. Anstelle des m. E. unpassenden *-garbhaḥ sūcyate* ist gewiß *-garbha ity ucyate* zu lesen, vgl. T.: . . . *sñiṅ po źes bgyi*ᶜ*o*. Die Hs. (B) ist zwar undeutlich, hat aber eher *i-* als *-ḥ*.

13, 18 *pravartate*. Hs. (B) *prajñāyate*, vgl. auch T. (D) *rtogs par* ᶜ*gyur ba*).

14, 7 *anuttaraguṇair gaṇaḥ*. T.: *tshogs || bla med yon tan daṅ ldan ñid*. Tak. (p. 173): „. . . the Community . . . [is endowed] with the supreme qualities". Der Instrumental ist unkonstruierbar. M. E. ist die Hs. (B) als *anuttaraguṇo gaṇaḥ* zu lesen.

14, 11 *yathāvat taj jagacchāntadharmatāvagamāt*. T. (ᶜ*gro ba źi ba*ᶜ*i chos ñid du || rtogs phyir ji lta ñid*) setzt, parallel zu Vers I, 16, statt *taj* ein Abstraktsuffix voraus. Die Hs. (B) dürfte in der Tat als *yathāvattvaṃ jagac-* zu lesen sein.

14, 16 — 15, 2 *tatra yā cittasya prakṛtiprabhāsvaratā yaś ca tadupakleśa ity, etad dvayam anāsrave dhātau kuśalākuśalayoś cittayor ekacaratvād dvitīyacittānabhisaṃdhānayogena paramaduṣprativedhyam*. Tak. (p. 174): „Here, these two, i. e. the innate brightness of the mind and the defilement on the mind, are quite difficult to be understood in relation to the fact that, in the immaculate sphere, there is no succession of a second mind because both minds, good and bad, act together as one and the same." Vgl. auch Ru. p. 423. De J. bemerkt mit Recht, daß *ekacara-* gewöhnlich „wandering or living alone" bedeutet (so auch Paramārtha, BGŚ 802 a 24: *tu-tzŭ hsing* ④. De J. bemerkt ferner: „In the immaculate sphere the good and bad thoughts are isolated from each other and therefore there is no relation of a second thought with a first thought, i. e. a bad thought cannot arise from a good thought and vice versa." Ich glaube nicht, daß diese Deutung der Stelle die richtige ist. M. E. will die Stelle zeigen, wieso die Gleichzeitigkeit von (moralisch positiver) Reinheit und (moralisch negativer) Unreinheit von den gewöhnlichen (buddhistischen) Denkkategorien her schwer einleuchtet (vgl. auch p. 21, 17f.: *tatra samalā tathatā yugapad ekakālaṃ* *viśuddhā ca saṃkliṣṭā cety acintyam etat sthānam*). Ich möchte daher folgende Übersetzung vorschlagen: „Die natürliche Leuchtendheit (= Reinheit) des *cittam* und seine [gleichzeitige] Verunreinigung — diese beiden im Falle der makellosen Wesenheit [gegebenen Tatsachen] sind schwer zu begreifen; denn [nach gewöhnlicher buddhistischer Auffassung] treten gutes und böses *cittam* [immer nur] einzeln auf, ohne daß eine Vereinigung [des einen] mit dem zweiten (d. h. dem jeweils anderen) [möglich wäre][56]." Eine gewisse Schwierigkeit bereitet die Interpretation des Ausdruckes *anāsrave dhātau* in diesem Zusammenhang. Er kann hier nur als Bezeichnung des *tathāgatagarbhaḥ*, der *samalā tathatā*, fungieren, wäre also genau genommen als „die [an sich, in ihrem Wesen,] makellose Wesenheit" zu übersetzen. Daß diese Deutung zulässig ist, zeigt RGV I, 122c, wo mit *amalaḥ dhātuḥ* — wie auch der Vergleich (*tadgarbhavat*!) zeigt — eindeutig der *tathāgatagarbhaḥ* (u. zw., nach dem Kommentar [72, 7f.], als *gotram*!) gemeint ist. Eindeutig auf den *tathāgatagarbhaḥ* als *samalā tathatā* bezieht sich der Terminus *anāsravo dhātuḥ* auch RGV 68, 15f.: *tatraiṣām anāsrave dhātau yathākramaṃ caturbhir ekena dvābhyāṃ dvābhyāṃ ca kleśamalābhyām aśuddhiḥ paridipitā*. Tak. übersetzt (p. 281): „Their impurity, on account of [which they cannot identify themselves with] the Immaculate Sphere, is here explained by [the first] four, [the next] one . . . and two . . . and again by two . . . kinds of Pollution, respectively." Diese Wiedergabe von *anāsrave dhātau* scheint mir äußerst unwahrscheinlich. M. E. ist die Stelle wie folgt zu verstehen: „[Durch die neun Vergleiche] ist deutlich gemacht, daß an der [an sich] makellosen Wesenheit bei diesen [vier Kategorien von Personen] respektive durch vier, eine, zwei und zwei [Arten von] Lasterschmutz Unreinheit [haftet]."

15, 4 *na saṃkliṣṭam eva*, Hs. *asaṃkliṣṭam eva*.

15, 4—5: Zwischen *na bhagavan kleśās tac cittaṃ spṛśanti* | und *katham atra* . . . ist, wie auch Tak. festgestellt hat, ein Satz ausgefallen. Er findet sich in der Tat in der Hs. (B) und lautet dort: *nāpi cittaṃ kleśān* |, d. h.: „(Weder berühren die Laster den Geist,) noch [berührt] der Geist die Laster."

16, 5 *tac* (= *avaivartikānāṃ bodhisattvānāṃ lokottarajñānadarśanam*) *ca . . . itaraprādeśikajñānadarśanam upanidhāya suviśuddhir ity ucyate*. Tak. (p. 176): „And this [perception] is called perfectly pure in comparison with the superficial knowledge of everyday life . . .". Man erwartet *tac ca suviśuddham*: das Wissen der Bodhisattvas ist rein,

[56] *dvitīyacittānabhisaṃdhāna-* erscheint bei Paramārtha (BGŚ 802a25) als „Nichtvereinigung der beiden *citta*". Vgl. auch F. Weller, Zum Kāśyapaparivarta, Heft 2 (= Übersetzung), Berlin 1965, p. 120. Anders Ru. p. 423.

nicht Reinheit[57]. In der Tat liest die Hs. (B) nicht *-śuddhir iti*, sondern *-śuddhim iti*, und hätte zu *-śuddham iti* korrigiert werden sollen. — Tak.s Wiedergabe von *itaraprādeśikajñāna-* ist m. E. nicht zutreffend. Es handelt sich gewiß um das partielle, unvollständige Wissen der anderen, d. h. vor allem der Śrāvakas und Pratyekabuddhas (vgl. auch Tak. p. 176, A. 25, u. Mahāyānasaṃgrahaḥ [ed. LAMOTTE] VIII, 22, 2).

16, 9f. *jñānadarśanaśuddhyā* ⏑ *buddhajñānād anuttarāt* | *avaivartyād bhavanty āryāḥ śaraṇaṃ sarvadehinām* ||. Tak.s Auffüllung der Lücke (*-śuddhyā hi* oder *-śuddhyaiva*) ist eine bloße Vermutung, aber seine Korrektur *avaivartyā bhavanty* ist gewiß richtig, auch wenn die Hs. (B) sie nicht zu bestätigen scheint. Konstruktionsmäßig unhaltbar aber ist m. E. Tak.s Übersetzung (p. 176f.): „Through the purity of their perception by wisdom, it is superior as [being the same as] Buddha's Wisdom. Therefore, the Saints abiding in the irreversible state are [worthy of being] the refuge of all living beings." M. E. ist der (offenbar auch von T. mißverstandene) Ablativ *buddhajñānād anuttarāt* von *avaivartyā(ḥ)* abhängig: „Durch die Reinheit ihrer geistigen Schau sind die Heiligen, bei denen die Möglichkeit, sich von dem höchsten Wissen der Buddhas [als dem von ihnen angestrebten Ziel] abzukehren, nicht mehr gegeben ist, die Zuflucht aller Lebewesen." Im Prosakommentar allerdings erscheint *anuttara-* als Attribut der Reinheit der geistigen Schau der Bodhisattvas und der aus ihr resultierenden Reinheit der geistigen Schau der Buddhas — eine Diskrepanz, welche doch vielleicht Zweifel an der Identität des Verfassers von Vers- und Prosakommentar aufkommen lassen könnte.

16, 12 *upaniṣadgatatvād*. Obwohl dieser Wortlaut die Hs. (B) richtig wiedergeben dürfte, scheint mir eine Korrektur von *-gata-* zu *-**bhūta**-* erwägenswert. Tak.s Wiedergabe („because it approached...") ist unzutreffend. *upaniṣad-* (T. hier wörtl. *ñe bar gnas pa*, sonst meist sinngemäß *rgyu*) bedeutet „cause, basis" (s. BHSD s. v. *upaniṣad* 1): „weil sie die Grundlage (od. Vorstufe) . . . ist".

17, 4 *-viśuddhiniṣṭhāgatam āryaśrāvakam*. Die Hs. (B) hat *-viśuddhiniṣṭhāgatam* ***apy*** *āryaśrāvakam*. So auch T.: *ñan thos . . . rnam par dag pa'i mthar phyin par gyur pa* ***yaṅ***.

17, 9 *āryam*. Hs. (B) eher *ary**āḥ***.

18, 1f. *buddhabhāvāyopagatān bodhisattvān*. Tak. emendiert mit T. *bodhisattvān* zu *bodhisattv**ayānik**ān*. Diese Korrektur wird durch die Hs. (B) bestätigt. Aber Tak.s Wiedergabe von *buddhabhāvāyopagatān* mit „who approached to the nature of Buddha" ist nicht korrekt.

---

[57] *tacchuddhir* in Vers I, 17c ist gewiß ein Tatpuruṣa-Kompositum, vgl. auch Tak.: „. . . it is pure . . .".

Richtig wäre: „die für die Buddhaschaft geeignet sind" (vgl. DE J. zu 23, 7).

18, 15 *tatra deśanādharmaḥ sūtrādideśanāyā nāmapadavyañjanakāyasaṃgṛhītaḥ*. Schon J. bemerkt, daß *-deśanāyā* unbefriedigend ist. T. hat *mdo^ci sde la sogs pa bstan pa brjod pa*, woraus sich nach MVy 7084 die Lesung *sūtrādideśanāpāṭhaḥ* gewinnen läßt, die auch von der Hs. (B) bestätigt zu werden scheint.

19, 7 *śaikṣaḥ* bedeutet nicht „learned people" (Tak.), sondern: „einer, der noch zu üben hat", also ungefähr das gleiche wie das folgende *sakaraṇiyaḥ*.

20, 4 *jagaccharaṇam ekatra buddhatvaṃ pāramārthikam*. Tak. (p. 184): „From the ultimate standpoint, Buddhahood is the sole Refuge of the world." *ekatra* paßt nicht. Vielleicht ist ***ekāntaṃ*** anzusetzen, aber die Hs. (B) ist ganz undeutlich, und T. *ñag cig* fehlt in den mir zugänglichen Glossaren mit Skt.-Äquivalenten.

20, 6f.: *anutpādānirodhaprabhāvitasya muner vyavadānasatyadvayavirāgadharmakāyatvād, dharmakāyaviśuddhiniṣṭhādhigamaparyavasānatvāc ca . . . gaṇasya*. Tak.s Hinzufügung von *-lakṣaṇa-* (zwischen *-dvaya-* und *-virāga-*) scheint mir durch seinen Hinweis auf T. und vor allem auf p. 11, 14 gerechtfertigt. Nicht ganz befriedigend hingegen ist seine Übersetzung: „. . . the Sage, represented as neither becoming originated nor disappearing, is endowed with the body of the Doctrine, liberated from passions and [characterized] as the Two Truths of purification (i. e. the Truth of Path and the Truth of Extinction), and in the purity of this Body of the Doctrine . . . the Community . . . sets the ultimate goal of acquisition." Besser wäre m. E., gerade wegen 11, 13—15: „. . . weil der Weise (= der Buddha), der [wesentlich] gekennzeichnet ist durch Nichtentstehen und Nichtvergehen, den [in der] Leidenschaftslosigkeit [bestehenden] Dharma (d. h. den *adhigamadharmaḥ*, vgl. 18, 16f.), der konstituiert ist durch die zwei Wahrheiten der Reinigung (sc. *mārga-* und *nirodhasatyam*), zu seinem ‚Körper' hat[58], und weil die . . . Gemeinde [nichts anderes als] die Erlangung (*adhigama-*) der vollkommenen (*-niṣṭhā*) Reinigung [dieses] *dharmakāyaḥ* zum Ziel (*paryavasāna-*) hat, . . .".

21, 4 *śubharatnatrayasargako yataḥ*. *-sargako* ist unbefriedigend und steht in der Tat auf keinen Fall in der Hs. (B), die vielmehr als ***-sambhavo*** zu lesen sein dürfte.

22, 5: Statt *pūrvamalāsaṃkliṣṭā* (*paścād viśuddhā*) wäre wohl besser

[58] So die grammatische Konstruktion. Gemeint ist aber: „Weil der Dharma (als *adhigamadharmaḥ*) nichts anderes ist als der ‚Körper' des Buddha".

pūrvaṃ malāsaṃkliṣṭā . . . zu lesen. T. *sṅar dri mas kun nas ñon moṅs par ma gyur pa.*

22, 15: Zwischen *bhavet* | und *mahāpṛthivipramāṇena* ist ein Satz der Hs. (der auch in T. vorhanden ist, vgl. Tak. p. 396) ausgefallen: *yaduta mahācakravāḍapramāṇena mahācakravāḍa ālikhito bhavet* |.

23, 5 *tathānyeṣu sarvaparamāṇurajaḥsu*. T. *ma lus pa* entspricht (*a*)*śeṣa*-[59] statt (*a*)*nyeṣu*: eine Korrektur, die von der Hs. (B) bestätigt wird.

23, 6 *utpadyate*. Besser wäre *utpadyeta*, welches sich in der Hs. (B) tatsächlich vorfindet.

23, 16 *sarvāṇi ca tāni sattvacittasaṃtānāny api tathāgatajñānapramāṇāni*. Hs. A liest (wie T.) *-jñānāpramāṇāni*: „Und alle diese Geistesströme der Lebewesen sind [in Wahrheit] unbegrenzt, wie das Wissen des Tathāgata."

24, 9f. *yathāvainayikeṣu sattveṣv akṣūṇam anuguṇaṃ pravartate*. Tak. liest, wohl mit Recht, *yathāvaineyikeṣu* (vgl. Daśabhūmikasūtram, ed. RAHDER, p. 90, 15[59a]). Hs. B hat *yathāvainai-* (od. *-ne-*?) *-keṣu*, Hs. A *yathāvainainayikeṣu* (wie p. 70, A. 4!). — Unrichtig ist m. E. Tak.s Wiedergabe von *anuguṇam*, welches nicht als „in conformance with their merits", sondern einfach als „in der jeweils angemessenen Weise" (vgl. T. *rjes su mthun par*) zu verstehen ist. Und *saṃkṣepamātrakeṇa* in Z. 11 bedeutet wohl kaum „with summarized number", sondern „(um die Lebewesen) mit Hilfe einer [Aussage, die nicht die wirkliche Zahl der Buddha-Taten feststellen soll, sondern] lediglich [eine] Kurzformel [ist], ([provisorisch] einzuführen)".

24, 17 Vor *triratnavaṃśānupacchettṛ* ist, nach T. und Hss. A u. B, *tryadhvānugataṃ* ausgefallen (Tak. hatte *tryadhvānubaddhaṃ* ergänzt).

25, 8 *tritiyaṃ*: Hs. (B) *tṛtīyaṃ*. — *bodhanāpadam* ist wegen *bodhanā* in Vers I, 26b gegen Tak. beizubehalten.

26, 3 *bauddhe gotre tatphalasyopacārāt*. Richtige Übersetzung s. Ru. p. 273.

26, 8 *sarvasattveṣu tathāgatadharmakāyaparispharaṇārthena tathāgatatathatāvyatibhedārthena tathāgatagotrasaṃbhavārthena ca*. Statt *-saṃbhavārthena* ist vielleicht *-sadbhāvārthena* zu lesen (vgl. Bem. zu 72, 8). Tak.s Übersetzung der Stelle („1. the Absolute Body of the Tathāgata penetrates all living beings; 2. the Tathāgata being the Reality is the undifferentiated whole; and 3. there exists the Germ of the Tathāgata

---

[59] *sarva-* ist ohne Entsprechung in T.

[59a] Aber die Aṣṭasāhasrikā Prajñāpāramitā hat *vainayika-* (ed. VAIDYA p. 220, 16).

[in every living being]") ist m. E. nicht ganz korrekt. Im Anschluß an pp. 70, 16—18 u. 71, 8ff. (q. v.) muß es heißen: „. . . in dem Sinne, daß (1.) alle Lebewesen[60] vom *dharmakāyaḥ* des Tathāgata umhüllt-und-durchdrungen werden, (2.) [die Soheit] aller Lebewesen[60] von der Soheit des Tathāgata nicht verschieden ist, und (3.) in allen Lebewesen[60] die Anlage zu[r] Buddha[schaft] vorhanden ist."

28, 1 *mokṣamārgapratihatāśā(ḥ)*. So Hss. A und B (*-tāsāḥ*). T. (*thar pa'i lam daṅ źe 'gras pa*) scheint *-pratihatāś ca* vorauszusetzen (vgl. MVy 2953), was angesichts des parallelen *mahāyānadharmapratihatānām* von p. 31, 8 vielleicht vorzuziehen ist. — In Z. 2 bedeutet übrigens *tadekatyā(ḥ)* nicht „some of these", sondern bloß „some" (vgl. BHSD s. v. *ekatya* 8); der diesem Wort vorhergehende Daṇḍa ist mit Hs. A zu tilgen.

28, 6f. *carakaparivrājakanirgranthiputraprabhṛtayo 'nyatīrthyāḥ*. Die Hinzufügung des in der Hs. fehlenden und durch T. nicht bestätigten *-putra-* (mit C.) erscheint mir unzulässig. Es würde vollkommen genügen, statt *-nirgranthi-* das in den Rahmen der Aufzählung der verschiedenen Arten von nichtbuddhistischen Asketen bestens passende *-nirgrantha-* (BHSD: „a heretical monk") einzusetzen; für eine Verwendung von *nirgranthi-* in diesem Sinne finde ich jedenfalls keinen Beleg.

28, 10f. *yeṣām ihe tadvimokṣamukhe 'pi śūnyatāyāṃ mādyamānānāṃ śūnyataiva dṛṣṭir bhavati*. Die Hs. (B) scheint nicht *mādyamānānāṃ* zu lesen, sondern etwas wie *ādai-* (od. *-de-* ? ?) *-dya*(?)*mānānā*(? ?)*ṃ*, was vielleicht *ādeśyamānāyāṃ* repräsentiert (vgl. C.: „Denn der Erhabene verkündet ihnen[61] die *śūnyatā* als ein Tor zur Befreiung, um ihnen zur Erleuchtung zu verhelfen; aber jene Personen denken [dann], es gebe nur die Leerheit (im Sinne des Nichts) und keine wahre Wirklichkeit"). Ist diese Lesung richtig, so wäre das Skt. folgendermaßen zu übersetzen: „. . . bei denen, wenn ihnen die Leerheit, die doch [eigentlich] ein Tor zur Befreiung ist, gelehrt wird, eben[diese] Leerheit selbst zur falschen Ansicht wird". Tak.s Übersetzung ist auf jeden Fall unhaltbar. Zu T. vgl. DE J.

29, 20 *mātā prajñā buddhadharmaprasūtyai*. Tak.s Übersetzung („on account of the origination of Buddha's Doctrine") ist unmöglich. M. E. muß es heißen: „. . . für die Geburt der Buddha-Eigenschaften." Der Vers scheint also, unvoreingenommen betrachtet, vorauszusetzen, daß die den Buddha charakterisierenden Eigenschaften (*dharmāḥ*) oder Vorzüge (*guṇāḥ*) erzeugt werden müssen, während sie sonst für den

---

[60] Wörtl. m. E.: „. . . daß bei allen Lebewesen ein Eingehüllt-und-Durchdrungensein etc. [besteht]."

[61] *wei* ⑤ verstehe ich im Sinne von *wei chih* ⑥ (vgl. G. VON DER GABELENTZ, Chinesische Grammatik, § 799).

RGV unverursacht (*akṛtaka-*, *asaṃskṛta-*, vgl. z. B. 80, 10 u. 85, 7) sind. Tak.s Ansicht, daß der Vers aus einer fremden Quelle stammt, erscheint somit als nicht unbegründet. Vgl. auch F. 18.

31, 13: Die Hs. B liest hier und auch in Z. 15 *-visaṃvāditatvāt* statt *-visaṃvāditvāt*. Auch die Hs. A (nur zu Z. 15 erhalten) hat *-visaṃvāditatvāt*, wobei aber *-ta-* möglicherweise nachträglich gestrichen ist. — Das handschriftliche *tathāgatavastu ... prāptam* in Z. 13f. (s. RGV p. 31, A. 8) darf, im Sinne von T., als eine Korruptel für *tathāgatas tu ... prāptaḥ* aufgefaßt werden. — Zur Übersetzung des Textstückes vgl. Ru. p. 366.

31, 15f.: Statt *nairātmyam evātmani kṛtvā* ist — wie beide Hss. deutlich bestätigen — *nairātmyam evātmeti kṛtvā* zu lesen: „In dem Gedanken, daß das Selbst (= wahre Wesen) [der Gegebenheiten] eben ihr Kein-Selbst-Haben (= ihre Eigenwesenlosigkeit) ist." Vgl. auch Bem. zu 34, 9.

32, 4 *sattvārthaphaligodhapariśuddhatvād bodhisattvānām*[62]. Hs. B liest (wie T.) *pariśodhapariśuddhatvād*[63], Hs. A hingegen (gegen J.) deutlich *phali-* (statt *pali-*) *-godhapaliguddhatvād*. Das ist gewiß der richtige Text (vgl. Śikṣāsamuccayaḥ [ed. BENDALL] p. 105, 12). Zu übersetzen ist demnach: „Weil die Bodhisattvas vom Verlangen nach dem Heil [aller] Lebewesen besessen sind" o. ä.

33, 2 *acintyā pāriṇāmikī*. Lies *acintyapāriṇāmikī* (Hs. A, Hs. B *(-pari-)* und p. 33, 11).

33, 6f.: s. 34, 9!

34, 9 *paramātmātmanairātmyaprapañcakṣayaśāntitaḥ*. T. (*bdag daṅ bdag med spros pa dag || ñe bar źi bas dam pa'i bdag*) hat keine Entsprechung für *-kṣaya-* und setzt statt dessen *-(vy)upa-* voraus. In der Tat lesen beide Hss. eindeutig *-prapañcavyupaśāntitaḥ*. Übersetzung (vgl. auch Ru. p. 369): „[Der *dharmakāyaḥ*] ist das Selbst [im] höheren [Sinne], weil in ihm [jegliche] Selbst oder Fehlen eines Selbst [setzende] reflektive Aktivität[64] zur Ruhe gekommen ist." — Der Ātman-Begriff hat also hier eine wesentlich ins Spirituelle gewendete Bedeutung erhalten: Er bezeichnet hier die (natürlich irgendwie auch ontologisch fundierte) spirituelle Stufe der Loslösung von allem *prapañcaḥ* als der saṃsāra-konstitutiven reflektiven Aktivität, d. h. aber: das Nirvāṇa, dessen charakteristische Kennzeichnung ja im Madhyamaka gerade die als „*prapañca-(vy)upaśamaḥ*" ist. Vgl. auch RGV p. 33, 6f.: „Weil (*-yogāt*) bei ihnen (= den Śrāvakas etc.), bedingt durch ebendiese

---

[62] Vgl. RGV p. II u. Tak. p. 397.

[63] Vgl. p. 32, A. 1; *spyod* ist in *sbyoṅ* umzuändern.

[64] Zu *prapañcaḥ* vgl. NVinSg p. 137ff.

‚Stufe, auf der man [noch] im Nichtwissen weilt (od.: noch Nichtwissen übrig ist)‘, [noch] eine subtile Erscheinungsbilder-oder-begriffliche-Fixierungen (*nimitta-*) [setzende] reflektive Aktivität (*prapañca-*) auftritt, erreichen sie die ‚Vollkommenheit des Selbst‘, in der es keinerlei reflektiv-voluntative Aktivität (*abhisaṃskāra-*) mehr gibt, nicht“ (*tām eva cāvidyāvāsabhūmiṃ pratītya sūkṣmanimittaprapañcasamudācārayogād atyantam anabhisaṃskārām*[65] *ātmapāramitāṃ nādhigacchanti*). Etwas anders ist die Verwendung des positiv gewerteten Ātman-Begriffes in RGV p. 31, 10ff., wo er sich nur gegen den Ātman-Begriff der Nichtbuddhisten (und nicht, wie p. 34, 14f., auch gegen den Nairātmya-Begriff der Hīnayāna-Anhänger) richtet und dann ganz ontologisch interpretiert wird: Als (positiv gewertetes) ‚Selbst‘ wird hier (Z. 13ff.) das *nairātmyam* bezeichnet — allerdings nicht das hīnayānistische *pudgalanairātmyam*, sondern das *nairātmyam* (d. h. die Eigenwesenlosigkeit) aller Gegebenheiten oder Daseinselemente (*dharmāḥ*) —, u. zw. offensichtlich in dem Sinne, daß dieses *nairātmyam* das wahre Wesen der *dharmāḥ* ist (vgl. BGŚ 798 c 6[66] und SABh 38, 2f.[67]).

34, 17f. *sarvākāraduḥkhanirodhasākṣātkaraṇataś ca manomayaskandhanirodhasākṣātkaraṇāt.* Tak. (p. 219): „and because of the realization of all sufferings as well as the realization of extinction of the Mind-made Aggregates.“ Richtig wäre: „. . . und weil er dadurch, daß er das Aufhören des Leides in jeder Form [spirituell] realisiert hat, auch das Aufhören der [gewissermaßen die subtilste Schicht des *duḥkhasatyam* bildenden] ‚geistgemachten[68] Persönlichkeitskonstituenten‘ realisiert hat.“

35, 10—12: Statt *pratiṣṭhate* (Hs. [B]) in Z. 10 u. 11 ist wohl *pratitiṣṭhate* zu lesen. Statt *śamaikayāna-* in Z. 11 hat die Hs. (B) *śamai-*

[65] So Tak. (vgl. auch RGV p. 33, A. 6). Will man die von beiden Hss. überlieferte Lesung *anabhisaṃskāram* beibehalten, so ist der Ausdruck wohl nicht, wie J. (p. 33, A. 6) will, als Adverb oder Absolutivum, sondern als (substantivisches) Karmadhāraya in Apposition zu *ātmapāramitām* zu verstehen (vgl. auch *nirodham* in Z. 9!). *atyantam* wäre dann natürlich nicht Adverb, sondern Attribut zu *anabhisaṃskāram*.

[66] *wu-wo* ⑦ am Anfang der Zeile dürfte ein Fehler sein; die Negation ist sinnwidrig.

[67] *agraṃ nairātmyaṃ viśuddhā tathatā, sā ca buddhānām ātmā svabhāvārthena* (s. auch Ru. p. 371). Vgl. auch Sūtrālaṅkāraṭīkā (Peking-Tanjur, Sems-tsam Bi) 76b5: „Das Wort ‚*ātman-*‘ kommt im Sinne des fiktiven Selbst (= Ichs) vor (*dṛśyate*), und es kommt im Sinne des Wesens einer Sache vor“ (*bdag ces bya baci sgra cdi ni brtags paci bdag la mthoṅ ṅo || chos kyi ṅo bo ñid la yaṅ mthoṅ ste |*).

[68] D. h. wohl: „dem freien Willen entspringenden“; zum mindesten die Existenzen des Bodhisattva werden ja auch als *saṃcintyabhavopapattiḥ* (vgl. z. B. RGV p. 47, 7ff.) bezeichnet.

kāyana- (vgl. auch Ru. p. 74), und in Z. 12 ist nach *pratiṣṭhānam iti* das Wort *nirdiśati* ausgefallen (Hs. [B] und T. . . . *bstan pa ni* |).

35, 16 *saṃvṛtiṃ nirvṛtiṃ vā*. T. *ᶜkhor ba* empfiehlt die m. E. auch vom Inhaltlichen her nahegelegte Korrektur von *saṃvṛtiṃ* zu *saṃsṛtiṃ*.

36, 1f.: Nach p. 73, 7f. (mit A. 4!) sollte der Text der Hs. (B) mit Ausnahme des *vā* nach *prārthanā* beibehalten und vielleicht folgendermaßen gelesen werden: *na syād duḥkhe 'pi nirvin nirvāṇecchāprārthanāpraṇi⟨dhir ve⟩ti*. Vgl. auch Śrīmālāsūtram (Peking-Kanjur, Dkonbrtsegs Ḥi) 281 a 8f.: . . . *sdug bsṅal la skyo ba daṅ | mya ṅan las ᶜdas pa la ᶜdod ciṅ don du gñer ba daṅ smon pa yaṅ ma mchis par ᶜgyur ro* (nur eine Negation!). — Gegen die handschriftliche Überlieferung *buddhadhātuḥ viśuddhigotram* („die [den Lebewesen innewohnende] buddha[konstitutive] Wesenheit, die die Anlage zur [spirituellen] Läuterung ist") ist m. E., abgesehen vom Sandhi, nichts einzuwenden (vgl. auch p. 6, 8 [u. Bem. dazu]).

36, 9: *agotrāṇāṃ na vidyate* paßt schlecht zu T. *gaṅ phyir de* || *rigs med dag la med phyir ro*. In der Tat ist die Hs. (B) als *agotrāṇāṃ na* ***tad yataḥ*** zu lesen.

36, 11: Zwischen *nāpratyayam iti* und *yadi hi* sind, nach der Hs. (B) und T. (*de ciᶜi phyir źe na*), die Worte ***kiṃ kāraṇam*** ausgefallen.

36, 13—15 *na ca bhavati tāvad, yāvad āgantukamalaviśuddhigotraṃ trayāṇāṃ anyatamadharmādhimuktiṃ na samudānayati satpuruṣasaṃsargādicatuḥśuklasamavadhānayogena*. Statt *satpuruṣasaṃsargādicatuḥśukla-* liest die Hs. *satpuruṣasaṃ****sevādicatuścakra****-*, vgl. T. *skyes bu dam pa la brten* (lies ***bsten***) *pa la sogs pa ᶜ****khor lo*** *bźi*. Die Übersetzung des Satzes bei Tak. ist nicht korrekt [(s. DE J. p. 45)]. Auch DE J.s Vorschlag, *gotram* als Subjekt zu verstehen[60], ist m. E. nicht haltbar. Der Satz soll die vorhergehende Behauptung beweisen, daß die Einsicht in den negativen Charakter des Saṃsāra und in die positiven Qualitäten des Nirvāṇa nicht ohne *gotram* stattfinden kann; denn wenn sie auch ohne *gotram* möglich wäre, müßte sie auch bei den *agotrakāḥ* auftreten. Der vorliegende Satz zeigt nun, daß dies nicht der Fall ist: „[In Wirklichkeit aber kann man beobachten, daß diese Einsicht] nicht auftritt, bevor [das betreffende Lebewesen] vermittels der Ansammlung der vier *cakrāṇi* (s. BHSD s. v.) — Umgang mit tugendhaften Menschen usw. — [das *gotram*] hervorgebracht hat [, u. zw. nicht die in der natürlichen Reinheit bestehende Heilsvoraussetzung (*prakṛtiviśuddhigotram*: p. 37, 3), die bei allen Lebewesen immer schon vorhanden ist (s. p. 37, 1—4), sondern] die Voraussetzung für die Reinigung von den äußerlichen Verschmutzungen (*āgantukamalaviśuddhigotram*), [die in] dem gläubigen-Ver-

---

[60] Müßte es dann in T. nicht *rigs kyis* heißen?

trauen-zu-und-Gefallenfinden-an[70] der Lehre eines der drei [‚Fahrzeuge' besteht]."

36, 16 *yatra hy āha tatra paścād antaśo* ... T. *gaṅ gi phyir de*ᶜ*i* ᶜ*og tu tha na* ... *źes gsuṅs so*. Die Hs. ist sehr undeutlich; auf jeden Fall scheint sie ***yata āha*** zu lesen (vgl. auch Tak. p. 223, A. 178); statt *tatra paścād* ist vielleicht *tata ūrdhvam* anzusetzen.

36, 17 *tathāgatasūryamāṇḍalaraśmayaḥ*. T. setzt statt *-raśmayaḥ* die Lesung *-**jñāna**raśmayaḥ* voraus (vgl. Tak. p. 223, A. 179), welche sich tatsächlich in der Hs. (B) findet.

37, 3 *prakṛtiviśuddhagotra-*: Hs. *prakṛtiviśuddhigotra-*.

37, 11f. *mahodadhir ivāmeyaguṇaratnākṣayākaraḥ | pradīpavad anirbhāgaguṇayuktasvabhāvataḥ* ||. Tak. (p. 225): „Being the inexhaustible storage of jewels of immeasurable virtues, [the Germ of the Buddha is] like the Ocean; it is akin to the lantern, because of its nature of being endowed with properties indivisible [from it]." Die beiden Zeilen enthalten gewiß, in Analogie zu den übrigen Zeilen der als einheitliche Konstruktion aufzufassenden Grundversgruppe I, 30/35/42/45[71] sowie zu SA IX, 56—59[72], je ein Attribut oder Prädikat des *jinagarbhaḥ* (I, 45c). Ich glaube nicht, daß die Vergleiche die Basis der Aussage darstellen; sie sind vielmehr (wie in I, 30a—b) erst sekundär an diese angeschlossen. Für I, 42a—b steht einer solchen Auffassung nichts im Wege: „[Der *jinagarbhaḥ* ist,] dem Ozean vergleichbar, eine unerschöpfliche Quelle unermeßlicher Juwelen in Gestalt vorzüglicher Eigenschaften (*guṇa-*)"; vgl. auch T. *rgya mtsho che bźin dpag med pa || yon tan rin chen mi zad gnas* ||. Auch in der zweiten Zeile ließe sich *-guṇayuktasvabhāvataḥ* (im Sinne eines „predicative ablative": BHSG § 7.47) ohne weiteres als Prädikat des *jinagarbhaḥ* verstehen: „(Der *jinagarbhaḥ* ist gelehrt worden) als, gleich einer Lampe, seinem Wesen nach mit unabtrennbaren vorzüglichen Eigenschaften (*guṇa-*) verbunden." Andernfalls müßte man *-yuktasvabhāvataḥ* in *-yuktasvabhāvakaḥ*[73] umändern — eine Änderung, der sowohl die Hs. (B) wie auch T. (... *ṅo bo ñid phyir*) entgegensteht; vgl. überdies RGV 39, 10 (und Bem. dazu).

38, 7f. *tatsaṃbaddhaḥ samanvāgamaḥ*. Besser, und nach der Hs. (B) wohl auch möglich, wäre *tatsambandhaḥ samanvāgamaḥ*, vgl. auch T. *de daṅ* ᶜ*brel pa daṅ ldan pa ni*.

38, 11 ... *dīpālokoṣṇavarṇasya sādharmyaṃ vimalāśraye*. Die Hs. (B: *dīpāloṣṇatāvarṇṇasya* [od. *-sā-*] *dharmamālāśraye*) spricht eher für

[70] *adhimuktiḥ*, s. NVinSg p. 179f.

[71] Mit Ausnahme von I, 45c—d natürlich; zu I, 45a—b s. Bem. zu 39, 10.

[72] Vgl. Tak. p. 400ff.

[73] Oder *yuktaḥ svabhāvataḥ*.

dīpālo⟨ko⟩ṣṇatāvarṇasādharm⟨y⟩am a⟨ma⟩lāśraye. T. hat *-vara-* statt *-varṇa-* gelesen.

38, 14 *jvālāsādharmyaṃ.* T. *snaṅ ba daṅ chos mtshuṅs pa* = ***āloka**sādharmyaṃ*; so auch die Hs. (B).

39, 2: Statt *tadubhayā-* hat die Hs. (B) *tadubhaya**syā**-.* Ferner ist in Z. 2f. statt *abhijñājñānaprahāṇa-* mit der Hs. und T. (***zag pa med pa***^c^***i*** *mṅon par śes pa daṅ | ye śes daṅ spaṅs pa*) ***anāsrav**ābhijñājñānaprahāṇa-* zu lesen.

39, 4 *dharmadhātusamanvāgamo.* Die Hs. (B) hat *dharmadhātu**samatā**samanvāgamo*, was durch C. und T. (*chos kyi dbyiṅs daṅ* ***mñam pa ñid*** *kyis ldan pa*) bestätigt wird.

39, 7f.: s. 3, 4f.

39, 10 *pṛthagjanāryasaṃbuddhatathatāvyatirekataḥ.* T. *so so'i skye* ^c^*phags rdzogs saṅs kyi || de bžin ñid dbye*^c^*i* ^c^*jug pa las ||* entspräche eine Lesung *tathatā**bhinnavṛttitaḥ***, welche sich in der Tat deutlich und klar in der Hs. (B) vorfindet. Das von der Hs. und T. bestätigte *-bhinnavṛtti**taḥ*** wäre auch an dieser Stelle als „predicative ablative" zu verstehen[74] (vgl. Bem. zu 37, 11f.). Übersetzen würde ich die Zeile folgendermaßen: „(Der *jinagarbhaḥ* ist gelehrt worden) als unterschiedlich auftretend, [insofern er] die Soheit der Weltmenschen, der Heiligen und der vollkommen Erleuchteten [ist]", d. h.: er tritt [trotz seiner wesenhaften Einheit] in verschiedener Gestalt auf, je nachdem er die Soheit der Weltmenschen, der Heiligen (= Śrāvakas, Pratyebuddhas und fortgeschrittenen Bodhisattvas) oder der Buddhas ist[75]." Der Kommentar scheint die Zeile jedoch ganz anders verstanden zu haben; denn er spricht von der unterschiedlichen Einstellung (*pravṛttiḥ*), welche die gewöhnlichen Lebewesen, die Heiligen und die Buddhas im Hinblick auf die *tathatā* haben.

39, 17f. *trayāṇāṃ pudgalānāṃ pṛthagjanasya tattvadarśina āryasya tattvadarśino viśuddhiniṣṭhāgatasya tathāgatasya.* Die Hs. (B) fügt vor *pṛthagjanasya* das durch T. (*de kho na ma mthoṅ ba*^c^*i so so*^c^*i skye bo*) bestätigte Wort *atattvadarśinaḥ* ein und liest *tattvadarśina**viśuddhi**niṣṭhāgatasya*, was gewiß zu *tattvadarś**ana**viśuddhiniṣṭhāgatasya* zu korrigieren ist. Die Stelle ist m. E. folgendermaßen zu übersetzen: „(In der Prajñāpāramitā und anderen [Sūtren] ist, um die Bodhisattvas in das vorstellungsfreie Wissen einzuführen, die [natürliche] Reinheit der ‚Soheit' aller Gegebenheiten als das durchgängige Wesensmerkmal des *tathāgatadhātuḥ* gelehrt worden; zu ihm haben) die drei [Klassen

[74] Andernfalls wäre, mit SA IX, 59b, *-vṛttikaḥ* zu lesen.

[75] Zur Differenzierbarkeit der Soheit nach der Verschiedenheit der Gegebenheiten, denen sie innewohnt, vgl. NVinSg p. 107, Fußn. i, und Dharmadharmatāvibhāgaḥ (ed. NOZAWA, in Festschr. Yamaguchi), p. 46, 14f.

von] Personen — sc. (a) der Weltmensch, der die Wahrheit nicht schaut, (b) der Heilige, der die Wahrheit schaut, und (c) der Tathāgata, der die absolute Reinheit der Schau der Wahrheit erreicht hat — (eine unterschiedliche Einstellung)."

40, 5 *tadanye catvāro 'rthāḥ prabhedanirdeśād eva* (Hs. *-śādveva*) *veditavyāḥ*. T. . . . *dbye ba ston par rig par bya*ᶜ*o*. Besser wäre vielleicht *prabhedanirdeśa***tvena**: „Die übrigen vier Punkte (od. Themen) sind als Darlegungen spezieller Aspekte bezüglich des Punktes (od. Themas) ‚*vṛttiḥ*' zu verstehen".

40, 7f. *aśuddho 'śuddhaśuddho 'tha suviśuddho yathākramam | sattvadhātur iti prokto bodhisattvas tathāgataḥ* ||. Tak. (p. 230f.): „Impure, [partly] pure and [partly] impure, and perfectly pure — these are said of the Ordinary beings, the Bodhisattvas, and the Tathāgata, respectively." Richtiger: „[Je nachdem, ob der *jinagarbhaḥ*] (a) unrein, (b) [teils] unrein und [teils] rein und (c) vollkommen rein ist, wird er respektive ‚*sattvadhātuḥ*'[76], ‚*bodhisattvaḥ*' und ‚*tathāgataḥ*' genannt."

40, 10f. *svabhāvādibhir ity ebhiḥ ṣaḍbhir arthaiḥ samāsataḥ | dhātus tisṛṣv avasthāsu vidito nāmabhis tribhiḥ* ||. Statt *vidito* hat die Hs. (B) ***nirdiṣṭo*** (T. *bstan pa*). Aber auch so ist der Vers schwer zu konstruieren. Tak. (p. 231: „The Essence [of the Buddha], [hitherto briefly explained by these six subjects, beginning with ‚own nature', is, in accordance with its 3 states, designated by 3 different names") hilft sich mit einer Ergänzung. T. (*ṅo bo ñid la sogs pa*ᶜ*i don* || ᶜ*di drug gis ni bsdus pa yi* || *khams ni gnas skabs gsum dag tu* || *miṅ gsum gyis ni bstan pa ñid* (v. l. *yin*) ||) hingegen scheint mir eine Korrektur von *samāsataḥ* (gew. *mdor (bsdu) na* o. ä.!) zu *samāsitaḥ* (vgl. MW s. v.) nahezulegen. Im Prosakommentar wäre dann nicht *samāsataḥ* (p. 40, 13), sondern *saṃgṛhītāḥ* (p. 40, 13f.) die Entsprechung.

41, 9 *anena kiṃ darśitam*. Hs. (B): . . . *darśayati*.

42, 2 *kleśopakleśadoṣayor āgantukayogāt*. In Analogie zu Z. 3 (*-guṇaiḥ prakṛtiyogāt*) erwartet man *-doṣ***air** *āgantukayogāt*. T. *ñon moṅs pa daṅ ñe ba*ᶜ*i ñon moṅs pa glo bur ba daṅ ldan pa*ᶜ*i phyir* setzt anscheinend **kleśopakleśair āgantukaır yogāt* voraus, was aber kaum der ursprüngliche Text sein dürfte.

43, 3 ⟨*manasaḥ kṛtiḥ*⟩[77]. Besser wäre vielleicht ⟨*manasaḥ kriyā*⟩: vgl. Madhyāntavibhāgaḥ V, 7.

44, 1f. *skandhadhātvāyatanaloka-* (Tak.: „the world classified into [5] elementary groups, [18] component elements or [12] bases of cogni-

---

[76] D. h. „Klasse der [gewöhnlichen] Lebewesen", aber auch „[absolute] Wesenheit, [insofern sie] den [gewöhnlichen] Lebewesen [innewohnt]".

[77] In der Hs. (B) eine Lücke, vgl. RGV p. 43, A. 1.

tion") ist, wie *ayoniśomanaskāra-vātamaṇḍala-* und *karmakleśodakarāśi-* („die Wassermasse der Taten und Laster") ein Upamitapūrvapadasamāsa: „die mit der Welt (d. h. dem aus Erde bestehenden *bhājanalokaḥ*) vergleichbaren Taten und Laster".

44, 7 *prakṛtiviśuddhimukhaṃ dharmālokamukham*. Tak. (p. 239) „introduction to the light of doctrine on the Innate Purity [of the mind]". Genauer: „die ‚Einführung in die natürliche Reinheit [des Geistes]' [genannte] Einführung in das Licht der Lehre". Es handelt sich um den Titel eines Kapitels des Gaganagañjasūtram: vgl. T 397, p. 125 a 2f. und T 404, p. 643 c 12.

44, 12f. . . . *vāyudhātor ākāśadhātur eva balī yo*. Tak. will *balīyo* (Komparativ) lesen. Der hier geforderte Nom. Sg. mask. des Komparativs (von *balin-*) lautet aber *balīyān*, und so lesen in der Tat deutlich beide Hss.

45, 3 *upakliśyate*. Nach Tak. (p. 240, A. 305) lautet T. *ñon ma moṅs pa*ᶜ*o* (→ *na kliśyate*). Aber weder bei Nak. noch in P findet sich *ma*.

45, 3f. *tatra paścād yo 'yoniśomanaskāro ye ca karmakleśā yāni ca skandhadhātvāyatanāni, sarva ete dharmā hetupratyayasaṃgṛhītā utpadyante* . . . Tak. (p. 240): „(,. . . defilements.'). After this passage, it is continued as follows: ‚Now, all these phenomena . . .'". Tak.s in A. 306 ausgesprochener Zweifel an der Richtigkeit der Lesung *tatra paścād* sind berechtigt. Hs. B liest nach J. (p. 45, A. 2) *paścād yoniśo*, Hs. A *paścā yoniśo*. Zum mindesten letzteres ist natürlich als ***yaś cāyoniśo-*** zu lesen, und diese Lesung wird auch von T. (*de la tshul bźin ma yin pa*ᶜ*i yid la byed pa gaṅ yin pa daṅ* | . . .) bestätigt. In der Übersetzung ist somit der Einschub „After this passage . . . follows" zu tilgen.

45, 5: Statt (*hetupratyaya*)*visāmagryā* liest Hs. A *-visāmagryāṃ*; vgl. auch T. *daṅ bral* ***na***.

45, 16 *trayas ta upamā jñeyā*[78] *mṛtyuvyādhijarāgnayaḥ*. *ta upamā* ist nicht konstruierbar und, wie Hs. A (und wohl auch Hs. B) bestätigt, zu ***tadu****pamā* zu korrigieren; vgl. auch T. *de* ***daṅ*** ᶜ*dra bar* (nur der Verstext von D hat fälschlich *dag* statt *daṅ*).

46, 6—9 *nirvṛttivyuparamarugjarāvimuktā asyaiva prakṛtim ananyathāvagamya* | *janmādivyasanam ṛte 'pi tannidānaṃ dhīmanto jagati kṛpodayād bhajante* ||. Der Verskommentar (I, 68 c—d: *jātyādivinivṛttāś ca yathābhūtasya darśanāt*) scheint ebenfalls *-vimuktā asyaiva* vorauszusetzen. Wenn jedoch meine auf S. 128f entwickelte These, daß der (Grund-)Vers I, 66 ursprünglich auf I, 54 folgte, stimmt, ist für den ursprünglichen Text der Grundverse gewiß mit Tak. (und C., vgl. RGV p. 46, A. 3) die Lesung *-vimuktām asyaiva* zu postulieren. *asya* nimmt

[78] Siehe RGV p. XVI.

aber dann nicht *citta-* (Tak.: „the Innate mind"), sondern *dhātu-* auf. — Die zweite Hälfte des Verses übersetzt Tak. (p. 243) folgendermaßen: „The Bodhisattvas have no calamity of birth and so forth; still, because of the rising of Compassions towards the world, they assume the cause of calamities." Richtiger wäre m. E. (trotz T.): „. . . nehmen die Bodhisattvas, obwohl [bei ihnen] die [normale] Ursache dafür fehlt, [dennoch] aus Mitleid mit der Welt das Ungemach der Geburt usw. auf." Die logische Verbindung der ersten Vershälfte mit der zweiten besteht darin, daß erstere den Grund für das Fehlen der normalen Ursache der Wiedergeburt angibt.

46, 11f.: *mṛtyuvyādhijarāduḥkhamūlam āryair apoddhṛtam | karmakleśavaśāj jātis, tadabhāvān na teṣu tat ||*. Tak.s Übersetzung der zweiten Vershälfte („There is a birth by the power of Active Force and Defilements; as there is no birth [of such a kind] the saints have no root [of defilements]") ist unzutreffend, zum mindesten unklar. Die nächstliegende Deutung scheint mir folgende zu sein: „[Das Leid] entsteht [nämlich] aus Taten und Lastern; weil diese [Taten und Laster] bei den Bodhisattvas] nicht vorhanden sind, ist auch das [Leid] bei ihnen nicht vorhanden." Der Prosakommentar[79] allerdings faßt *jātiḥ* als „Geburt" (und stellt einen Kausalnexus *karmakleśāḥ* → *jātiḥ* → *duḥkham* auf). Diese Deutung läßt sich aber nur mühsam in den Vers hineininterpretieren (man müßte vor Pāda c den Gedanken „Das Leid beruht auf der Geburt" ergänzen). Wahrscheinlicher ist m. E., daß der Prosakommentar den Verskommentar hier nicht ganz richtig deutet, was vielleicht ein Indiz dafür ist, daß er von einem anderen Verfasser stammt.

47, 3 *kuśalamūlasaṃyojanād dhi bodhisattvāḥ.* Hs. A liest *-saṃyojanā hi*; vgl. auch T. *byaṅ chub sems dpaᶜ rnams ni . . . kun tu sbyor ba can te.*

47, 15 *kuśalamūlabalānvādhānena.* Üblich ist *-balādhānena.* So wohl Hs. B (ziemlich undeutlich). Hs. A deutlich *-balādhādhānena* (Dittographie von *-dhā-*).

47, 19 (u. 48, 7f.) *mātṛjñātayaḥ* (Hs. B, T., T 400 [p. 511 b 17 u. 25] u. viell. auch T 669 [p. 470 a 27][80]). Hs. A hat, wie C., *mātāpitṛjñātayaḥ*: eine Lesung, die zunächst Anstoß erregt, da der Vater erst im folgenden hinzutritt und gerade umgekehrt reagiert[81]. Vielleicht hat aber *mātāpitṛ-* hier die weitere Bedeutung „family, relatives" (vgl. BHSD s. v.), ohne daß der Vater selbst notwendig einbegriffen sein

[79] In Tak.s Übersetzung ist *prajñāyate* (p. 46, 16) falsch konstruiert.

[80] *mu-ch'in* ⑧ = „mother" (MATHEWS' Chinese-English Dictionary, p. 642).

[81] In C. ist der später hinzutretende Vater gegen eine andere Person ausgetauscht worden.

müßte. Ist diese Deutung möglich, so wäre auf jeden Fall der Lesart *mātāpitṛjñātayaḥ* als lectio difficilior der Vorzug zu geben. Ihre Verderbnis zu *mātṛjñātayaḥ* und — nach der tibetischen Übersetzung der Sāgaramatiparipṛcchā[82] — **mātṛmitrajñātayaḥ* wäre leicht erklärbar.

48, 2f. *ekaputrakādhyāśayapremānunīto*. T. *bu gcig po* ᶜ*don par* ᶜ*dod pa*ᶜ*i sred pas byas pa*. Tak. möchte *-adhyālambanataḥ* statt *-anunītaḥ* lesen. Das geht aber auf keinen Fall, zumal auch in der Hs. B die Akṣaras *-nunī-* deutlich lesbar sind. M. E. ist statt *-adhyāśaya-* das graphisch ähnliche *-adhyālamba-* (T. ᶜ*don pa*, vgl. p. 48, 1), eventuell sogar *-adhyālambāya* (od. *-adhyālambe*) anzusetzen. Als Übersetzung würde ich (mit Vorbehalt) vorschlagen: „. . . durch seine [Vater]liebe dazu gebracht, seinen einzigen Sohn zu ergreifen (= zu retten)."

48, 4 *kaḥ prabandho draṣṭavyaḥ*. T. **don** *gaṅ yin par blta že na* = Hs. A *kaḥ* ***punar artho*** *draṣṭavyaḥ* (Hs. B: *purartho*): „Worin ist der [durch den vorhergehenden Vergleich illustrierte] Sachverhalt zu sehen?", d. h.: „Was soll mit diesem Vergleich ausgedrückt werden?".

48, 12: *lipyate* paßt nicht zu T. *gnod*. In der Tat lesen beide Hss. ***hanyate***.

48, 17f. *tatra yadā bodhisattvo yathābhūtājātyanutpattidarśanam āgamya tathāgatadhātor imāṃ bodhisattvadharmatāṃ anuprāpnoti, tathā vistareṇa yathāsūtram anugantavyam*. Tak. (p. 248): „Now, when a Bodhisattva has attained the correct perception of the Essence of the Tathāgata as being of no birth, no origination, then he can obtain this essential quality as a Bodhisattva. This point should be understood in detail according to the [same] Scripture." Statt *yadā* ist (mit T. *ji lta ba*ᶜ*i*[83]) angesichts des den Nachsatz einleitenden *tathā* gewiß — gegen Hs. B, aber mit Hs. A! — ***yathā*** anzusetzen. Übersetzung: „Auf welche Weise der Bodhisattva, gestützt auf die wahrheitsgemäße Einsicht in das Nichtgeborenwerden und Nichtentstehen der [die] Buddha[schaft konstituierenden] Wesenheit (*tathāgatadhātuḥ*), diesen einem Bodhisattva adäquaten [spirituellen] Zustand (*bodhisattvadharmatā*) erlangt, ist ausführlich im Sinne der [folgenden] Sūtren[stelle] zu verstehen."

49, 2 *na cetayanti na prakalpayanti*. Tak.: „they cannot cause [one] to think or to imagin". Eine kausative Bedeutung ist bei *kalpayati* nicht üblich und wohl auch bei *cetayati* nicht notwendig: „[Die *dharmāḥ*] denken nicht, haben keine Vorstellungen".

49, 6: Lies *sāgaramate 'nargham* (Hs. A: *'nar**ghy**am*).

49, 8 *tat sudhautaṃ* . . .: *tat* fehlt in beiden Hss. und auch in T.

[82] Siehe Nak. p. 94, A. 4.

[83] Lies *ji ltar* ?

50, 13—15 *sā punar āsravakṣayābhijñābhimukhy* (Hs. B: *-khyām*) *asaṅgaprajñāpāramitā*[84]*bhāvanayā mahākaruṇābhāvanayā ca sarvasattvadhātuparitrāṇāya tadasākṣātkaraṇād a*[84]*bhimukhyām bodhisattvabhūmau prādhānyena vyavasthāpyate.* M. E. befriedigt weder die Lesart *-ābhimukhy* noch die (von DE J. vorgezogene) Lesart *-ābhimukhyām*, und ich möchte daher eine Korrektur zu *-ābhimukhyād* vorschlagen. Auf diese Weise ergibt sich auch syntaktisch der vom Sinn her geforderte Parallelismus (bzw. Chiasmus): ... *-ābhimukhyād* ... *-bhāvanayā,* ... *-bhāvanayā ca* ... *-asākṣātkaraṇāt.* Auch T. zeigt diesen Parallelismus: *de yaṅ* (a) *thogs pa med pa*ᶜ*i śes rab kyi pha rol tu phyin pa bsgoms pa daṅ* | (b) *sñiṅ rje chen po bsgoms pas* ⟨|⟩ (a) ... *mṅon du phyogs pa daṅ* | (b) ... *mṅon du mi byed pa*ᶜ*i phyir* ... *rnam par bźag pa yin no* || Übersetzung: „Diese (= die *aśuddhaśuddhāvasthā*) wird vornehmlich auf der ‚Abhimukhī' [genannten] Stufe der Bodhisattvas lokalisiert, weil [man in diesem Zustand einerseits] auf Grund der Übung der ungehinderten Vollkommenheit der Einsicht das übernormale Bewußtsein des Geschwundenseins der üblen Einflüsse unmittelbar vor sich hat (*-ābhimukhya-*, d. h. in greifbarer Nähe vorfindet), es [aber andererseits] auf Grund der Übung des Mitleids nicht realisiert (*asākṣātkaraṇa-*), um [auch] alle [anderen] Lebewesen zu retten."

52, 2 *-samāpattipratipannaś.* T. *sñoms par* ᶜ*jug la* ... *sñoms par źugs pa yin* = *-samāpatti***samā***pannaś*; so auch Hs. A (Hs. B: *-pratipannaś*).

52, 6 *deśanyā rūpakāyābhyām.* Die Lesart *deśa***nā***rūpakāyābhyām* bei Amṛtākara (vgl. Tak. p. 254, A. 417 u. 419; DE J. p. 53) ist gewiß besser, da ein Substantiv *deśanī* auch im buddhistischen Sanskrit nicht belegt zu sein scheint. Auch T. (*bstan daṅ gzugs sku dag* ... *gyis*) impliziert nicht notwendig, daß im Original von z w e i materiellen Körpern die Rede war (Tak. p. 254, A. 419); *dag* kann ebensogut die Dualendung des Kompositums wiedergeben: „... vermittels des *deśanā-* (= *dharma-*) und des *rūpakāyaḥ*".

52, 14: Nach *ūrdhvam* ist *ca* ausgefallen (Hs. B; Hs. A fehlt).

52, 18: Nicht das *prathama-* vor *-dvitīyābhyām*, sondern das *prathama-* vor *-lokottara-* hat in T. keine Entsprechung.

53, 2f. *nirantaramahābodhisamudāgamaprayogasamādhiṣu vyavasthitatvāt.* Tak. (p. 256): „because ... he has firmly stood in the meditation as the practice immediately connected with the acquisition of the Great Enlightenment". T. *rgyun mi* ᶜ*chad par byaṅ chub chen po* ᶜ*thob pa*ᶜ*i sbyor ba*ᶜ*i tiṅ ṅe* ᶜ*dzin la* **legs par** *gnas pa*ᶜ*i phyir* impliziert die gewiß bessere Lesung *-samādhi***su***vyavasthitatvāt* und bestätigt überdies, daß *nirantara-* im allgemeinen nicht „unmittelbar danach" (= *ananta-*

---

[84] Siehe RGV p. XVI.

ra-!), sondern „ununterbrochen" bedeutet: „. . . weil er einen festen Stand gefunden hat in der ununterbrochenen [Praxis der] Versenkung, welche die Vorbereitung (*prayoga-*) für die Erlangung der großen Erleuchtung ist".

53, 4f. *sakalasvaparārthasaṃpādanopāyaniṣṭhāgatasya buddhabhūmyekacaramajanmapratibaddhatvād anuttaraparamābhisaṃbodhiprāpter*. Tak. (p. 256): „because [in this last stage] he, having attained the ultimate point of means for fulfilling all the benefits for his own as well as for others, is connected with the Stage of the Buddha by one and the last birth on account of the acquisition of the Supreme Perfect Enlightenment." Ich sehe nicht ein, warum T. *mthar phyin pa* nicht das in der Hs. (B) überlieferte *-niryātasya* (statt *-niṣṭhāgatasya*) wiedergeben soll (vgl. Dictionnaire tibétain-sanscrit par Tse-ring-ouang-gyal, ed. J. Bacot, s. v. *mthar phyin pa*: u. a. = *niryāti*; zur Bedeutung s. BHSD s. v. *niryāta*). In Tak.s Übersetzung ist *pratibaddha-* („verhindert") mißverstanden. Und *anuttaraparamābhisaṃbodhiprāpter* ist gewiß kein begründender Ablativ, sondern ein ablativus separationis: „. . . weil [der Bodhisattva der zehnten Stufe], der alle Mittel für das Zustandebringen des eigenen Heils und des Heiles der anderen vollkommen beherrscht, von der Erlangung der höchsten, vollkommenen Erleuchtung [nur noch] durch eine einzige und letzte Geburt[, nämlich die Geburt] auf der Stufe des Buddha, ferngehalten wird."

54, 3f. *sa khalv eṣa tathāgatadhātur buddhabhūmāv atyantavimalaviśuddhaprabhāsvaratāyāṃ svaprakṛtau sthitaḥ*. Tak. (p. 257): „Indeed, this Essence of the Tathāgata, in case it is abiding on the Stage of the Buddha which is absolutely immaculate, pure and radiant by its own nature, . . .". Statt *-prabhāsvaratāyām* liest die Hs. (B) ***-prabhāsvarāyāṃ*** (vgl. auch T.: *ᶜod gsal ba*). Als Übersetzung würde ich, gegen Tak. und T., aber mit C., vorschlagen: „Wenn diese [die] Buddha-[schaft konstituierende] Wesenheit auf der ‚Stufe des Buddha' in ihrem [nunmehr] absolut makellosen, reinen und leuchtenden (vgl. p. 38, 17ff.) Wesen verharrt (= zu sich selbst gefunden hat), . . .".

54, 10 *tad eṣām asaṃskṛtadhātau*. Hs. (B) teilweise undeutlich, aber wohl eher ***tatraiṣām*** (vgl. T. *de la* . . .) und gewiß ***asaṃskṛte dhātau***.

56, 3f. *nānyo bhagavaṃs tathāgato 'nyo dharmakāyaḥ*. Warum Tak. — seine Übersetzung der Stelle ist richtig — *nānyo* statt *'nyo* lesen will, ist mir unverständlich; die Negation gilt für den ganzen Satz.

56, 12 *mahābhisaṃbodhāt*. Tak. übersetzt „simultaneously with the Perfect Enlightenment", zieht aber nicht die notwendige Konsequenz, den Text zu ***sahābhisaṃbodhāt*** („immediately after . . .", vgl. BHSD s. v. *saha*) zu korrigieren. Auch Hs. A und T. (***lhan cig*** *mṅon par rdzogs par byaṅ chub pas*) bestätigen diese Korrektur.

57, 21 *anutpattikadharmalābhād.* T. *mi skye ba^{c}i chos* ***ñid*** *thob pa^{c}i phyir* = *anutpattikadharmat**ā**lābhāt*; so auch Hss. A und B!

59, 17 *tuṣesu sārāṇy.* Lies *tuṣe**ṣ**u sārāṇy* (so Hs. A) oder allenfalls — mit I, 98c — *tuṣe susārāṇy.*

60, 7f. ... *-avarastrīduḥkhajvalanābhitaptapṛthivīdhātuprakāśā malāḥ.* Tak. (p. 269): „... pollutions are ... like a woman of misery, and like earth tormented by the fire of pains." Letzteres klingt nicht sehr plausibel. Die Lesart *-strī**rū**pa-* der Hs. A ist auf jeden Fall verständlicher: „Die Beschmutzungen sind vergleichbar ... dem Körper einer Frau aus den unteren Schichten, oder dem im Feuer gebrannten Element Erde [einer Gußform]." — In Z. 10 übersetzt Tak. *-ratnabimbavimalaprakhyaḥ sa dhātuḥ paraḥ* als „... and a purified precious statue, the excellent Essence has a resemblance to them". Ich weiß nicht, ob es notwendig ist, hier ein abnormes Kompositum (vgl. WHITNEY § 1314), d. h. ein Karmadhāraya mit nachgestelltem qualifizierendem Adjektiv, anzunehmen. Besser ist es wohl, *vimala-* zu *prakhya-* zu ziehen: „Die höchste Wesenheit hat die reine Erscheinung von (d. h.: ist in ihrer Reinheit vergleichbar mit) einem [Stand]bild aus Gold ...".

62, 16 *suvarṇam asmin navam agraratnam.* Tak.: „There is a piece of gold, fresh and the highest of precious things." *navam* ist vom Sinn her suspekt, da das Gold ja schon seit Jahrhunderten dort liegen soll (v. 108). Hs. A und T. (^{c}*di na yod pa^{c}i gser* || *rin chen mchog* ^{c}***di***) haben *asminn* ***idam*** statt *asmin navam*: „Hier an diesem [übelriechenden Ort voll von Kot (*saṃkarapūtidhāna-*) befindet sich] Gold, eine vorzügliche Kostbarkeit; (reinige [es] ...)."

64, 17f. *sugatāmatmabhāvaṃ | vilokya tiryakṣv api.* Tak. (mit T. *bde gśegs dṅos po ñid*): „... perceives, even among those in the world of animals, the nature of the Buddha". Gewöhnlich bedeutet *ātmabhāvaḥ* aber, wie auch C. (*shen* 身) bestätigt, „Körper" (vgl. BHSD s. v.). Es handelt sich offenbar um ein Überbleibsel der bildlicheren Redeweise des Tathāgatagarbhasūtram. Vgl. Peking-Kanjur, Mdo, Bd. Shu 267a 4f.[85]: „O ihr Söhne aus guter Familie (*kulaputrāḥ*)! [Der Tathāgata] sieht, daß auch in den Lebewesen, die von den Hüllen mannigfacher Laster (*kleśa-*) verhüllt sind — sogar (*antaśaḥ*) dann, wenn sie in eine tierische Existenz geraten sein sollten —, der Körper des Tathāgata, von der gleichen Art wie der meinige[86], vorhanden ist" (*rigs kyi bu dag tha na dud ^{c}gro^{c}i skye gnas su soṅ ba rnams kyaṅ ruṅ ste | sems can ñon moṅs pa sna tshogs kyi dkri bas dkris par gyur pa rnams kyi naṅ na yaṅ de bźin gśegs pa^{c}i lus ṅa ci* (?) ^{c}*dra ba yod pa mthoṅ ṅo* ||).

---

[85] = T 666 p. 458c19—21, = T 667 p. 463b17—19.

[86] Sprecher ist der Buddha.

65, 2 *tiryakṣu vyavalokya*. T. *dud ᶜgro la yaṅ gzigs nas* = *tiryakṣv apy avalokya*, was viel besser ist und durch Hs. A eindeutig bestätigt wird.

66, 2 *saṃcodayed āvaraṇaṃ*; 66, 8 *saṃcodayen mṛttikām*; 66, 10 *saṃcodayaty āvṛtim*. T. hat in allen Fällen für *saṃcodayet* (bzw. *-yati*) *sel bar byed* (bzw. *mdzad*) = „beseitigen (lassen)", was gewiß den richtigen Sinn wiedergibt. Ob *saṃcodayati* diese Bedeutung haben kann, bezweifle ich. Hs. A ist in der Tat in Z. 8 und 10 eindeutig als *saṃ**che***[87]*dayen* bzw. *saṃ**che***[87]*dayaty*, und wahrscheinlich auch in Z. 2 als *saṃ**che**dayed*, zu lesen.

66, 10 *prahāravidhitaḥ*. Hs. A (ganz deutlich!) und wohl auch Hs. B: *prahāravidhi**bhiḥ***.

66, 16f. *sattvadhātor asaṃbaddhaṃ kleśakośeṣv anādiṣu | cittaprakṛtivaimalyam anādimad udāhṛtam* ||. Tak. (p. 276f.): „The Innate Mind of the living beings which is pure from beginningless time, and is not bound by the covering of Defilements, though being within them from the outset is thus illustrated." T. (*ñon moṅs sbubs* || *ma ᶜbrel thog ma med pa na*) zeigt, daß *asaṃbaddha**kleśakośeṣv** anādiṣu* zu lesen ist. In der Tat fehlt der Anusvāra in Hs. B und m. E. auch in Hs. A[88]. Übersetzung: „[In den vorhergehenden Versen] wurde festgestellt, daß das [seit] anfanglose[r Zeit vorhandene] an sich (*prakṛti-*) reine Wesen (*vaimalyam*) des Geistes der Lebewesen, welches in den [ebenfalls] anfanglosen, [aber] nicht [wesenhaft mit dem wahren Wesen des Geistes] verbundenen Hüllen der Laster [steckt], vergleichbar ist mit . . .".

67, 4 *rāgadviḍmoha-*. So wohl Hs. B. Hs. A eher *rāgadviṇmoha-* (wie *viṇmūtra-*, MW p. 995).

67, 13 *āniñjyasaṃskāropacayahetavo* (Tak.: „being the causes of Forces which accumulate the motionless State") bedeutet: „. . . welche Ursache sind für die Ansammlung von ‚unbeweglichen' (d. h. neutralen) karmischen Triebkräften". Analog *puṇyāpuṇyasaṃskāropacayahetavaḥ* in Z. 15.

68, 15: s. 14, 16 — 15, 2.

69, 9f. *hatasatkāyasārāṇām āryamārgānuṣaṅgataḥ | bhāvanājñānaheyānāṃ pūtivastranidarśanam* ||. Tak. (p. 283): „Those who have destroyed the ground of conception of personality are following in the [Practice of the] Saintly Path; therefore, their Defilements which are to be rejected by the Wisdom of Practice are said to be like a tattered garment." M. E. ist die Stelle eher wie folgt zu übersetzen: „[Diejenigen Laster, welche durch das Wissen [auf dem ‚Wege] der Übung (*bhāvanā*)'

---

[87] Genauer: *sañche-*.

[88] Der Schatten über *-ddhakle-* ist kaum als Anusvāra deutbar.

abgestoßen werden müssen, werden, da ihr[89] Kern[90] — die [Ansicht, es gebe] ein reales individuelles Ich — durch die Praxis des heiligen Weges [der Schau] zerstört worden ist, mit einem verfaulten Gewand verglichen."

69, 11: Lies *malāḥ*.

70, 16f. ... *tribhir* ... *-dṛṣṭāntaiḥ tathāgatadharmakāyena niravaśeṣasattvadhātuparispharaṇārtham adhikṛtya tathāgatasyeme garbhāḥ sarvasattvā iti paridīpitam*. Tak. (p. 286): „... by 3 examples ... in reference to the meaning that all living beings, with no exception, are penetrated by the Absolute Body of the Tathāgata, it is explained that ,these, all living beings, are the Matrix (interior) of the Tathāgata, (i. e. the Matrix in which the Tathāgata penetrates[90a])." Zum mindesten in indischen Texten bedeutet aber in dem Kompositum *tathāgatagarbhaḥ* das Wort *garbha-* nicht „Matrix", sondern „Embryo"[91]. Es ist daher zu übersetzen: „Durch die drei Vergleiche ... ist ausgedrückt, daß ,alle diese Lebewesen Embryos des Tathāgata sind', [u. zw.] in dem Sinne, daß alle Lebewesen ohne Ausnahme vom *dharmakāyaḥ* des Tathāgata [wie von einem Mutterleib] umhüllt-und-durchdrungen werden." Vgl. auch den folgenden Satz (*na hi sa kaścit sattvaḥ sattvadhātau saṃvidyate yas tathāgatadharmakāyād bahir*) sowie Ru. pp. 276 u. 507.

71, 7f. *yac cittaṁ aparyantakleśaduḥkhadharmānugatam api prakṛtiprabhāsvaratayā vikārānudāhṛter ataḥ kalyāṇasuvarṇavad ananyathābhāvārthena tathatety ucyate*. Der Satz ist in dieser Form syntaktisch unmöglich. T. *sems gaṅ yin pa de ni ñon moṅs pa daṅ sdug bsṅal mthaᶜ yas pa daṅ rjes su ᶜbrel kyaṅ raṅ bźin gyis ᶜod gsal ba ñid kyis rnam par ᶜgyur ba la mi ston pa deᶜi phyir gser bzaṅ po bźin du gźan du mi ᶜgyur baᶜi don gyis de bźin ñid ces brjod do* || = *yac cittaṃ tad ... vikāraṃ na darśayati* | *ataḥ ... ucyate*. In der Hs. (B) fehlt aber *tad*. Die Akṣaras zwischen *vikāra-* (sic!) und *ataḥ* sind nahezu unleserlich[92]. Eine mögliche Lesung wäre vielleicht *vikāran na bhajate*[93], in welchem Falle in T. wohl (*b*)*sten* statt *ston* zu lesen wäre. Falls *de* = *tad* ein Zusatz des tibetischen Übersetzers ist, wäre dann zu lesen: *yac cittam aparyanta-* ... *vikāraṃ na bhajate* (? ?), *ataḥ* ... *ananyathi*[94]*bhāvārthena tathatety ucyate*, d. h.: „Weil (*yat*) der Geist, obwohl er von zahllosen Gegeben-

---

[89] Wörtl.: „als solche, deren ...".

[90] D. h. das Prinzip ihrer Festigkeit.

[90a] Vgl. aber auch Tak. p. 286, A. 140: „... the compound has the sense of ,one who is within the Tathāgata'".

[91] Siehe F. 44.

[92] Der letzte ist *-tiḥ* oder *-teḥ* (statt *-ti*| od. *te*| ?).

[93] Vgl. SABh p. 16, 19: *vikārābhajana-* = *gźan du gyur pa mi bsten pa*.

[94] So die Hs. (B).

heiten, [die unter die] Laster oder [das] Leid [subsumierbar sind], begleitet wird, dennoch wegen der Reinheit seines eigentlichen Wesens keine Veränderung erleidet, deshalb wird er — in dem Sinne, daß er, wie lauteres Gold, niemals anders wird — als ‚Soheit' bezeichnet."

71, 8—10 *sa ca sarveṣām api mithyātvaniyatasaṃtānānāṃ sattvānāṃ prakṛtinirviśiṣṭānāṃ sarvāgantukamalaviśuddhim āgatas tathāgata iti saṃkhyāṃ gacchati.* Auch dieser Satz ist ganz korrupt. Statt *sa* (Tak.: „this very mind"!) hat die Hs. (B) deutlich *sā*. T.[95] (*de yaṅ log pa ñid du ṅes pa*ᶜ*i rgyu⟨n⟩ can gyi sems can thams cad la yaṅ raṅ bźin khyad par med du zin kyaṅ | glo bur gyi ñon moṅs pa mtha*ᶜ *dag rnam par dag pa las* (?) *gyur pa | de bźin gśegs pa źes bya ba*ᶜ*i graṅs su* ᶜ*gro ste* |) setzt eine dem Z. 16f. zitierten Mahāyānasūtrālaṅkāra-Vers (*sarveṣām aviśiṣṭāpi tathatā śuddhim āgatā tathāgatatvam*) entsprechende Satzstruktur voraus[96]: ***sā** ca s a r v e ṣ ā m api . . . p r a k ṛ t i n i r v i ś i ṣ ṭ **ā p i** s a r v ā g a n t u k a m a l a v i ś u d d h i m ā g a t **ā** t a t h ā g a t a iti saṃkhyāṃ gacchati.* Übersetzung: „Und diese [‚Soheit'] erhält, obgleich sie bei allen[, d. h. auch bei den] Lebewesen, deren [Geistes]strom auf das Falsche festgelegt ist, ohne [irgend]einen — das eigentliche Wesen betreffenden — Unterschied [vorhanden] ist, [dennoch in dem Augenblick, in dem sie] von sämtlichen äußerlichen Verunreinigungen rein geworden [ist], die Bezeichnung ‚Tathāgata'."

71, 11 *tathāgatas tathataiṣāṃ garbhaḥ sarvasattvānām.* T. (*de bźin gśegs pa*ᶜ*i de bźin ñid*) scheint *tathāgatatathatā* gelesen zu haben. Aber angesichts der im vorhergehenden vorgenommenen G l e i c h s e t z u n g der (gereinigten) Soheit mit dem Tathāgata scheint mir die Lesung *tathāgatas tathatā* (Hs. B; A fehlt) die bessere zu sein.

72, 8 *-gotrasvabhāvārtham adhikṛtya.* T. *rigs* **yod** *pa*ᶜ*i* ⟨*don gyi* ?⟩ *dbaṅ du byas te* paßt hierzu nicht. Die Hs. (B) hat offenbar *gotra**sad**bhāvārtham adhikṛtya*, d. h. „in dem Sinne (od.: mit Bezug auf die Tatsache), daß [in allen Lebewesen] die Anlage für . . . vorhanden ist". Vgl. auch p. 26, 9, wo möglicherweise ebenfalls *gotra**sad**bhāvārthena* zu lesen ist.

---

[95] Vgl. auch BGŚ 808b8—10 (Interpunktion nach *ku yüeh ju-ju* ⑩; die Interpunktion in *shih chên ju-ju* ⑪ hingegen ist zu tilgen): „Diese wahre ‚Soheit' ist [zwar] in allen[, auch in den] Lebewesen, die zur Klasse der auf das Falsche Festgelegten (*mithyātvaniyatarāśiḥ*) oder zu den Icchantikas [gehören], ohne irgendeinen das Eigentliche betreffenden (*pên* ⑫) Unterschied vorhanden. Aber wenn es dazu kommt, daß die [sie verhüllenden] äußerlichen Verunreinigungen verschwinden, dann wird sie anschließend ‚Tathāgata' genannt" (*ts'ang* ⑬ nach *ju-lai* ⑭ ist zu tilgen!).

[96] Wörter, die in SA IX, 37 eine wörtliche oder (wie *sā*, *nirviśiṣṭā* und *tathāgata*) sinngemäße Entsprechung haben, sind g e s p e r r t.

73, 6 *saṃsāra iti parikalpam asya vacanāyeti*. So die Hs. (B). Tak.: ... *parikalpitam asya vacanam iti*. Nach dem Text des Śrīmālāsūtram (Peking-Kanjur, Dkon-brtsegs Ḥi, f. 281a2: *tshig de rigs pa lags so* = „... ist das Wort [‚*saṃsāraḥ*'] sinnvoll[97]") erscheint eine solche Konjektur problematisch. Es ist wohl eher an Stellen wie Abhidharmakośabhāṣyam (ed. PRADHAN) p. 470, 2f. zu denken, wo sich in einem Sūtrenzitat die Wendung *akalpam*[98] *syād vacanāya* findet.

73, 8: s. 36, 1f.

73, 9f. *tathāgatagarbho dharmakāyavipralambhas tathatāsaṃbhinnalakṣaṇo niyatagotrasvabhāvaḥ*. M. E. ist die Hs. (B), im Sinne von T. (und wohl auch C.), als *dharmakāyavipulas ta[stata]thatā*- ... zu lesen: „... das Buddha-Embryo, das genau so weit reicht wie der *dharmakāyaḥ*[99], dessen Wesensmerkmale von [denen] der Soheit nicht verschieden sind und das die Natur einer [auf die Buddhaschaft] festgelegten [Heils]-Anlage hat ...".

73, 13f. *paryāyaḥ | evam eva tat syāt | anyathā naiva tat syād*. DE J.s (auf T. gestützte) Korrektur von *paryāyaḥ evam* zu *yayaivam* ist vollkommen überzeugend (in der Hs. ist wohl *ya*- statt *pa*- zu lesen und -*ryā*- in Wirklichkeit vielleicht ein durch zwei darübergesetzte Strichlein getilgtes -*yā*-). Es ist aber nicht einzusehen, warum J. gegen die Hs. zweimal *eva tat* statt *evaitat* angesetzt hat.

74, 8 -*sāsravaskandhādīn dharmān*. T. (*phuṅ po la sogs pa*ᶜ*i chos zag pa daṅ bcas pa*) dürfte -*sāsravān skandhādīn dharmān* voraussetzen.

74, 11f. *nitye tathāgatagarbhe saty uttaribhāvayitavye*. Tak.: „... although the Matrix of the Tathāgata is to be considered as ‚eternal' in its transcendental sense". M. E. ist folgendermaßen zu übersetzen: „... obwohl darüber hinaus [die Betrachtung des] unvergänglichen Tathāgata-Embryos (oder: des Tathāgata-Embryos als [etwas] Unvergänglichem) geübt werden müßte". Vgl. auch Ru. p. 378.

74, 17f. *dharmakāyaprāptividhuramārga*-. *vidhura*- bedeutet „destitute of, wanting" oder „depressed", aber auch „adverse, unfavourable, hostile" (MW). T. hat ... *daṅ* ᶜ*gal ba*, was gewöhnlich *viruddha*- entspricht.

74, 20 *yathā ca sa ... agocaras, tathā vistareṇa Mahāparinirvāṇasūtre bhagavatā ... prasādhitaḥ*. Besser wäre m. E. *prasādhitam* (vgl. auch p. 58, 17 und Bem. dazu).

---

97 Diese Wiedergabe wird dem Sinne nach von den chinesischen Übersetzungen des Śrīmālāsūtram und des RGV bestätigt.

98 Oder *kalyam*? Vgl. Pāli *kallaṃ vacanāya*, z. B. Dīghanikāyo I, 168.

99 Das ist allerdings offenkundig ein anderer Gedanke als der, welcher p. 70, 17 im Hinblick auf das Verhältnis von *tathāgatagarbhaḥ* und *dharmakāyaḥ* ausgesprochen wurde.

75, 3 *pravarteyuḥ*. Die Hs. (B) hat die korrekte Form *pravarttayeyuḥ*.

75, 7: Vor *dharmatattvam ajānadbhis* ist **maṇivad** (Hs. B; Hs. A: *maṇaṇivat*) ausgefallen; vgl. auch T. **nor bu ltar** *chos kyi don de kho na mi śes pa khyed kyis*.

75, 8f. *tasmād bhikṣavo vāpiśarkarakaṭhalyavyavasthitā iva mā bhūtā upāyakuśalā yūyaṃ bhavata*. Tak. (p. 299): „Therefore, o monks ye should become skilful in order not to be determined by this [false conception] like the pebbles and gravels in the pond." Statt *bhūtā* ist (mit Hs. A) ***bhūta*** | zu lesen[100]: „Deshalb, ihr Mönche, seid nicht [so] wie diejenigen, welche auf die Kiesel und Steine des Brunnens fixiert sind (d. h. darauf hereinfallen). Seid ihr [vielmehr diejenigen, welche] geschickt in den Mitteln [sind]!" Hierzu paßt auch T.: ... *rnam par gnas pa ltar mi ᶜgyur bar* (= „ohne ... zu sein", od.: „anstatt ... zu sein") *khyed cag thabs la mkhas par gyis śig*.

75, 11f. *paramadharmatattvavyavasthānam ārabhya viparyāsabhūtanirdeśo*. So Hs. B und wohl auch T. (... *phyin ci log tu gyur pa bstan pa*). Hs. A scheint *viparyā*$\textbf{\textit{sābhi}}$[101]*bhūtanirdeśo* („Ausführung über diejenigen, welche bezüglich ... vom Irrtum überwältigt sind [d. h. über die *viparyāsābhiratāḥ*, vgl. RGV 74, 19]") zu lesen. — Gegen die Wiedergabe von J.s Text bei Ru. (p. 379: „manière d'enseigner à l'envers") habe ich, zumal angesichts der (ein Genitiv-Tatpuruṣa voraussetzenden) syntaktischen Parallele RGV 17, 7f., grammatische, aber auch terminologische Bedenken (*viparyāsaḥ* = die [bezüglich des Absoluten] verkehrte Vorstellung der Śrāvakas etc., alles sei vergänglich usw.; vgl. RGV 74, 11ff. u. 30, 14ff.).

75, 18f. *tathāgatagarbhaśūnyatārthanayavipranaṣṭāḥ*. Tak. (p. 299): „... [since] they are deprived of [the cognition of] the Matrix of the Tathāgata in regard to the true meaning of Non-substantiality". Besser wohl: „... [insofern] sie von der [richtigen] Weise [der Erklärung] dessen, was ‚Leerheit' im Falle des *tathāgatagarbhaḥ* bedeutet, abgefallen sind". Vgl. auch Ru. p. 313.

76, 11 *aparyantaṃ śunyatālakṣaṇam*. Tak.: *aviparyastaṃ*, Jñ p. 488, 1: *aviparita-*. Den richtigen Text gibt Hs. A (und wohl auch Hs. B) mit *aviparītaṃ*.

76, 19 *lokottaradharmaparidīpanāt*. T. (*ᶜjig rten las ᶜdas paᶜi chos* ***kyi sku*** *ni ... bstan paᶜi phyir ro*) und Hss. A und B haben *-dharma-****kāya****-* statt *-dharma-*.

---

100 Hs. B: ... *mā bhūtopāya-*.

101 *-sābhi-* am oberen Rand nachgetragen!

76, 20 *śūnyatāvikṣiptānām*: Hss. A und B[102] sowie T. (*stoṅ pa ñid la* (v. l. *las*) **sems** *rnam par g-yeṅs pa rnams kyi*) lesen (wie pp. 75, 13 u. 76, 13) *śūnyatāvikṣiptacittānām*.

76, 20 — 77, 1 *āgantukamalaśūnyatāprakṛtitvād viśuddhiguṇadharmāṇām*. So Hs. B. Aber T. (**de** *rnam par dag paʾi yon tan gyi chos . . . rnams ni . . .*) entspricht ***tad****viśuddhiguṇadharmāṇām*, welches sich in Hs. A tatsächlich vorfindet.

77, 9 *yady evam . . .*; T. **smras pa** *gal te de ltar . . .* = ***āha*** — *yady evam . . .*; so Hss. A und B.

77, 10 *bāla****pṛthag****janam* (nach T.). Beide Hss. lesen *bālajanam*.

78, 1f. *viviktaṃ saṃskṛtaṃ sarvaprakāraṃ bhūtakoṭiṣu | kleśakarmavipākārthaṃ meghādivad udāhṛtam* ||. Tak., Ui und de J. fassen *bhūtakoṭiṣu* im Anschluß an T. (*yaṅ dag mthaʾ*) als „(absolute) reality". Dabei wird aber der Plural mißachtet. M. E. kann *bhūtakoṭiṣu* nur heißen: „. . . bei den Myriaden von Lebewesen[103]". Dem entspricht die Tatsache, daß mit dem als substanzlos (*viviktam*) bezeichneten Verursachten (*saṃskṛtam*) hier in erster Linie Gegebenheiten gemeint sind, welche die Lebewesen konstituieren, da der Text in der folgenden Zeile sagt, es (= das Verursachte) werde wegen (d. h. zum Zwecke der differenzierenden Charakterisierung von) Lastern, Taten und [den fünf Skandhas als deren] Resultat (*kleśakarmavipākārthaṃ*, T. *ñon moṅs las daṅ rnam smin don*)[104] als [respektive] mit Wolken usw. (s. Vers 156b) vergleichbar bezeichnet. Wichtig für die Interpretation von *bhūtakoṭiṣu* ist ferner die Beobachtung, daß alle übrigen Worte der Zeile 158a—b Worte von Vers 156a aufzunehmen scheinen: *viviktaṃ* entspricht *śūnyam*, *saṃskṛtaṃ* könnte *sarvam* aufgreifen, *sarvaprakāraṃ* gibt *sarvathā* wieder. Es liegt daher nahe, in *bhūtakoṭiṣu* eine Erklärung von *tatra tatra* in 156a zu sehen. Dieses wiederum kann im Sinne des in Vers 156d auftretenden *sattve sattve* verstanden werden. Auf die absolute Wirklichkeit kann sich *tatra tatra* jedenfalls nicht beziehen. Allenfalls wäre es denkbar, daß *tatra tatra* zu *ity uktvaivaṃ* zu ziehen ist und bedeutet: „in manchen [Mahāyānasūtren]". Dieser Auffassung entspricht die chinesische Übersetzung von Vers 158, in der sich statt *bhūtakoṭiṣu* die (von Tak. nicht erwähnte Lesung) ***sūtra****(koṭi)ṣu* (*sūtra*- in Transkription!) findet. Daß bei dieser Deutung die Stellung von *tatra*

---

[102] In Hs. B *citānām* statt *cittānām*.

[103] Diese Verwendung von *bhūta*- scheint zwar in Mahāyānatexten nicht sehr häufig zu sein, ist jedoch auch nicht gänzlich unbelegbar: vgl. z. B. SA(Bh) XX, 40 und Mahāyānasaṃgrahaḥ I, 37.

[104] Ob C. (*fan-nao yeh tĕng* (15)) nur eine verkürzende Wiedergabe ist oder auf einer Lesung *kleśakarmavipākādyaṃ* basiert, ist schwer zu entscheiden.

tatra in Vers 156 etwas ungewöhnlich ist, ist kaum ein entscheidendes Argument gegen sie, da auch in Pāda c—d des Verses 156 *punaḥ kiṃ* aus dem Inhalt des Gesagten herausgelöst und mit *buddhair ihoktam* verbunden werden muß — es sei denn, man wolle *ihoktaḥ* lesen, was aber angesichts des *uktam* in 157d kaum empfehlenswert ist.

78, 9—11 *bodhicittodaye 'py asya . . . hīnasaṃjñā pravartate* || *tasyaivaṃmatinaḥ samyagjñānaṃ notpadyate; tataḥ* | . . . De J. möchte (im Gegensatz zu Tak.) mit T. und gegen beide Hss. *bodhicittodaye yasya* lesen. Der mit *tasya* beginnende Satz gehört aber gedanklich eindeutig bereits zum Folgenden (*abhūtagrāhaḥ* und *bhūtāpavādaḥ*), und es ist m. E. nicht wahrscheinlich, daß der Fehler ‚*hīnasattveṣv avajñā*' nur in einem Nebensatz abgehandelt ist. Den übrigen Fehlern ist jedenfalls jeweils genau ein Vers, der zugleich einen vollständigen Satz bildet, gewidmet (*abhūtagrāhaḥ* und *bhūtāpavadaḥ* werden zusammengefaßt und in insgesamt zwei Versen dargestellt).

78, 14 *bhūtaṃ taddoṣanairātmyaṃ śuddhiprakṛtayo guṇāḥ*. Ich sehe nicht ein, warum das (zum mindesten in Hs. A eindeutig) überlieferte *-nairātmyaśuddhi-* nicht beibehalten werden kann: „Das Wirkliche sind die Vorzüge, die, auf Grund der Wesenlosigkeit jener Fehler, ihrem eigentlichen Wesen nach rein sind".

79, 13f. *dvividhaṃ jñānaṃ lokottaram avikalpaṃ tatpṛṣṭhalabdhaṃ ca* | *laukikalokottarajñānam āśrayaparivṛttihetuḥ prāptiśabdena paridīpitaḥ*. Dies ist der Text der Hs. A, die jedoch den Daṇḍa nach *ca* ausläßt. Tak. folgt Hs. B, die . . . *tatpṛṣṭhalabdhaṃ ca* ***laukikaṃ***[105] | *laukikalokottarajñānam āśrayaparivṛttihetuḥ* . . . liest. Dieser Text wird von T. (D) bestätigt: . . . *daṅ* | *de*ᶜ*i rjes las thob pa*ᶜ*i* ***ᶜjig rten pa*ᶜ*o*** || *ᶜjig rten pa daṅ ᶜjig rten las ᶜdas paᶜi ye śes gnas yoṅs su gyur paᶜi rgyu ni thob paᶜi sgras bstan te*. In T. (P und N) hingegen fehlt *ᶜjig rten pa daṅ*, was aber wohl auf eine (durch das zweimalige *ᶜjig rten* bedingte) Überlieferungsstörung zurückgeführt werden kann. Die chinesische Übersetzung (p. 841a15—17) lautet: . . . *i-ch'u-shih-chien-chih-tê shih-chien ch'u-shih-chien*[106] *i-chih-hsing chih, shih ming wei yin*⑯. Dieser Wiedergabe dürfte ein Original „* . . . *tat*[107]*pṛṣṭhalabdhaṃ ca laukikalokottaraṃ jñānam āśrayapravṛtti* (?) *hetuḥ*" zugrunde liegen. Abgesehen von der Korruptel am Ende der Stelle — das von Skt. und T. bezeugte *āśraya-*

---

[105] So die Hs.; J.s Angabe (nach der *ca* auf *laukikam* folgen müßte) ist ungenau.

[106] *ch'u-shih-chien* fehlt in einem Teil der Überlieferung. Da das ihm entsprechende *lokottara-* aber von beiden Hss. und allen tibetischen Versionen bezeugt wird, dürfte es sich um eine (vielleicht inhaltlich motivierte) sekundäre Auslassung handeln.

[107] In C. paraphrasierend als *lokottarajñāna-* wiedergegeben.

parivṛttihetuḥ ist auf jeden Fall korrekt — hat dieser von C. vorausgesetzte Text m. E. von allen Versionen am ehesten Anspruch darauf, als Repräsentant des ursprünglichen Wortlautes zu gelten. Denn er erlaubt es, die Stelle im Sinne ihrer verkürzten Wiedergabe auf S. 82, 5 (*yat tu „dvividhaṃ lokottaram avikalpaṃ tatpṛṣṭhalabdhaṃ ca jñānam āśrayaparivṛtter hetur* . . .“ *ity uktam, tatra* . . .) als einen Satz zu fassen, in welchem das Subjekt *dvividhaṃ jñānam* durch den gleichsam in Parenthese hinzugefügten Ausdruck *lokottaram avikalpaṃ tatpṛṣṭhalabdhaṃ ca laukikalokottaraṃ jñānam* präzisiert wird (Übers. der Stelle: „Das zweifache Wissen — das vorstellungsfreie überweltliche und das nach diesem erlangte [zugleich] weltliche [und] überweltliche Wissen — ist die Ursache der ‚Neugestaltung der Grundlage‘, die [in Vers II, 1] mit dem Wort ‚Erlangung‘ (im Sinne von: das, wodurch man erlangt) ausgedrückt ist“). Demgegenüber ist der Text der Hs. B syntaktisch schlecht. Zunächst erscheint mir das Kompositum *laukikalokottarajñānam* in dem hier geforderten Sinne „das überweltliche und das weltliche Wissen“ etwas ungewöhnlich. Darüber hinaus wäre aber auch ein an die Definitionen des vorhergehenden Satzes anknüpfendes Demonstrativpronomen (*etad* . . . *jñānam* o. ä.) zu erwarten[108]. Für die von C. vorausgesetzte Lesart spricht ferner die Tatsache, daß die Bezeichnung des *pṛṣṭhalabdhaṃ jñānam* als „weltlich und überweltlich zugleich“ (*laukikalokottaram*) vom Sinn her beurteilt die lectio difficilior ist, da es im allgemeinen nur als „weltlich“ (*laukikam*, z. B. BoBh p. 38, 4; SABh p. 63, 1; Abhidharmakośabhāṣyam [ed. Pradhan] p. 334, 10) oder allenfalls als „rein, [aber doch] weltlich“ (*śuddha-laukikam*, z. B. TrBh 40, 24) bezeichnet wird. Die Charakterisierung des *pṛṣṭhalabdhaṃ jñānam* als *laukikalokottaram* ist aber nicht unbelegbar: Sie findet sich z. B. in der Viniścayasaṃgrahaṇī der Yogācārabhūmiḥ (T 1579, p. 696a6ff., spez. 12f., = Peking-Tanjur Sems-tsam Zi 302b8: *ᶜjig rten las ᶜdas paᶜi śes pa daṅ poᶜi rjes las ᶜthob pa ᶜjig rten pa daṅ ᶜjig rten las ᶜdas pas* [= **prathamalokottarajñānapṛṣṭhalabdhena laukikalokottareṇa*]). Es ist aber leicht verständlich, daß diese Charakterisierung des *pṛṣṭhalabdha-jñānam* als *laukikalokottara-* in der Überlieferung des RGV später nicht mehr verstanden wurde und deshalb der Text geändert wurde. Zu terminologischen Einflüssen der älteren Yogācāratexte auf den Vers- und Prosakommentar des RGV vgl. S. 125.

79, 20: Statt *buddhabhūmiṣv avasthitiḥ* ist *buddhabhūmivyavasthitiḥ* zu lesen; vgl. T. *saṅs rgyas sa ni* **rnam par** *gnas* (v. l. *gźag*).

80, 12: *tasmān* paßt schlecht. T. *der* = *tasmin*; so Hss. A und B.

---

[108] Tak., der Hs. B folgt, übersetzt bezeichnenderweise: „This supermundane and mundane Wisdom“!

80, 18 *vāryādīnām iva rajojalādibhyaḥ*. Das unpassende *-jalā-* ist wohl ein Druckfehler statt *-malā-* (Hs. A und wohl auch Hs. B).

81, 1 *hrada iva vimalāmbuḥ phullapadmakramāḍhyaḥ* (nach T.); Hs. A eher *-drumāḍhyaḥ* (wie C.), aber die Akṣaras *dru* und *kra* sind einander sehr ähnlich. Hs. B (vgl. RGV p. 81, A. 1) ist ziemlich undeutlich. — Ich sehe übrigens keine Schwierigkeiten, dieses Bild auf das (gereinigte) Buddhatum zu übertragen (Tak. p. 316, A. 18): Die Reinheit (wörtl.: Schmutzlosigkeit) des Wassers illustriert das Schwinden der akzidentellen Verschmutzungen, der Reichtum an aufgeblühten Lotussen (und Bäumen) die nunmehr zur Manifestation gelangten zahllosen Vorzüge (*guṇāḥ*) des Buddhatums.

81, 10 *atulyatulyadharmatvāt*. Tak. (p. 318): „Being possessed of the unequalled properties". Richtig wäre: „. . . weil es (= das Buddhatum) nur dem Unvergleichbaren (*atulya-*, sc. dem Tathāgata) vergleichbar ist (*-tulyadharmatvāt* = *-sādharmyāt*)" (vgl. RGV I, 146 und den tib. Kommentar bei Nak. p. 160, A. 8).

83, 8f. *vimuktidharmakāyau ca veditavyau dvir ekadhā | anāsravatvād vyāpitvād asaṃskṛtapatvataḥ ||*. Tak. (p. 320f.): „The Body of innate liberation and the Absolute Body, [although] being two [in their functions], are to be known as one, because they are free from passions and all-pervading, and are the immaculate substratum." Statt *dvir ekadhā* ist aber mit Hss. A und B sowie T. (*rnam gñis rnam gcig*) *dvidhaikadhā* zu lesen. Die Übersetzung muß lauten: „[Diese beiden, sc.] der ‚Körper der Erlösung' und der ‚Körper des Dharma', sind — so muß man wissen — [respektive] auf zwei und auf eine Weise [gekennzeichnet]: [der erstere] als[109] frei von [üblen] Einflüssen und allerfüllend, [der letztere] als die ‚unverursachte Stätte'."

83, 17 *padaṃ tad amalajñānam śukladharmāspadatvataḥ*. Hs. A liest *amalaṃ*, C. („. . . es ist die absolute ‚Stätte', [weil] es reines Wissen [und] ‚weiße' Vorzüge [zum] Wesen (od. ‚Körper') [hat]") anscheinend *amalajñānaśukla-*, was m. E. den besten Sinn ergäbe: „Das [Buddhatum] ist eine ‚Stätte' (II, 18b), weil es die Grundlage makellosen Wissens und [anderer] reiner (wörtl.: weißer) Eigenschaften ist."

85, 7—10 . . . *ākāśavad asaṃskṛtaguṇāvinirbhāgavṛttyāpi tathāgatatvam ā bhavagater . . . jagaddhitasukhādhānanimittam amalais*[110] *tribhiḥ svabhāvikasāṃbhogikanairmāṇikaiḥ ⟨kāyair*[111]*⟩ . . . pravartata iti draṣṭavyam* . . . Die Hs. (B) liest (in Z. 7) *-guṇāvinirbhāgavṛtty api* (vgl. T.

---

[109] Vgl. Speyer, Sanskrit Syntax § 238, und BHSG § 7.47.

[110] Tak. p. 398.

[111] Vgl. RGV p. 85, A. 4. Es ist fraglich, ob die Hinzufügung des Wortes *kāyair* wirklich notwendig ist.

de bźin gśegs pa ñid ᶜ*di*[111a] . . . *rnam par dbye ba med par* ᶜ*jug* ***pa*** *yaṅ*), ferner *svābhāvika-*. Übersetzen würde ich die Stelle folgendermaßen: „Das Buddhatum ist zwar — wie der Raum-Äther — [lediglich] mit unverursachten Eigenschaften untrennbar verbunden; trotzdem tritt es — so muß man es sehen — vermittels seiner drei makellosen ‚Körper', [sc.] wesenhafter, Seligkeits- und Scheinkörper, [in unterschiedlicher Weise] in Erscheinung, um, solange die Welt besteht, . . . das Heil und Wohl der Lebewesen (*jagat*) zu bewirken (*ādhāna-*)."

85, 10f. *tatra* . . . *catvāraḥ ślokāḥ*. Hs. (B) ***tatreme***, vgl. T. *tshigs su bcad pa* ᶜ***di*** *bźi ste*.

85, 13 *vimuktaṃ*. C. (*yüan-li* ⑰) und Hs. (B) eher ***viyuktaṃ***.

86, 4 *jagadvimokṣārthasamāhṛtodyamaḥ*. Ich glaube nicht, daß der Text dieser Stelle korrekt ist. C. („er bewirkt die Erlösung der Lebewesen, ohne [dabei] jemals auszuruhen") und der Kommentar (II, 49d *-sattvārthāsraṃsanatvataḥ* und 51a—b *kṛtyāsraṃsane*) sprechen jedenfalls für einen anderen Text, etwa **jagadvimokṣārtha-sadā-(a)ratodyamaḥ* oder **-ārtham anāratodyamaḥ*, was allerdings durch T. (. . . *don grub la brtson pa*) nicht bestätigt wird.

86, 6 *vicitrabhāvo na ca tatsvabhāvavān* (vgl. auch DE J.!). C. („. . . er zeigt mannigfache Erscheinungsformen . . .") und Kommentar-Vers II, 51c (*atatsvabhāv**ākhyāne***) scheinen für eine (sachlich bessere) Lesung *vicitrabhā**so*** (gegen T. und die Hs. [B]) zu sprechen. Die Lesung *vicitrabhāvo* könnte wohl nur im Sinne von „er hat mannigfache Verhaltensweisen[112]" erklärt werden.

86, 13 *nirvṛtiḥ paramācintyaprāptiḥ pratyātmaveditā*. T. *mchog tu mya ṅan* ᶜ*das bsam med* || ***dgra bcom*** *so so*ᶜ*i bdag* ᶜ*gyur* ***ba*** (v. l. *gyur pa*) ||. Tak. möchte *acintyārhattvaṃ pratyātmaveditam* lesen. Die Hs. (B) hat aber eindeutig . . . *prāptiḥ pratyātmam* ***arhatām***. *acintya-* gehört nach T. nicht zu *prāptiḥ*, so daß wohl *nirvṛtiḥ paramācinty**ā*** *prāptiḥ* (od. viell. *prāpt**ā*** ?)[113] *pratyātmam arhatām* zu lesen ist.

87, 2 *dharmadhātoḥ svabhāvataḥ*. So die Hs. (B). Besser wäre m. E. *dharmadhātu**s**vabhāvataḥ*.

87, 16: Statt *aviralaṃ* ist mit T. (vgl. RGV p. 87, A. 4) und Jñ p. 499, 6 (u. 500, 5) ***avicalan*** zu lesen. Vgl. auch RGV p. 107, 5 (= Jñ p. 499, 12).

87, 18: *śilpasthānāni kauśalam* ist mit T. *bzo yi gnas* ***la*** *mkhas pa*

[111a] Nach D. PN: *ni*.

[112] Vgl. MW s. v. *bhāva*.

[113] T. *so so*ᶜ*i bdag* ᶜ*gyur ba* (bzw. *gyur pa*) für *prāptiḥ* (od. *prāptā* ?) *pratyātmam* ist merkwürdig.

(= **śilpasthāneṣu kauśalam* o. ä.) nicht vereinbar. Vielleicht ist die Hs. als *śilpasthānātikauśalam* zu lesen.

89, 7 *ṛddhipādaprakāśāc ca tair avasthānaśaktitaḥ.* C.: „[Weil] der, welcher die vier *ṛddhipādāḥ* praktiziert, kraft ihrer in der Welt verweilt[114]." T. (*rdzu ᶜphrul rkaṅ pa ston pa ni . . .*) scheint dem handschriftlichen ⟨*ṛddhi*⟩*pāda**praṇetuś** ca* (Hs. B; Hs. A fehlt) zu entsprechen, was mit T. als „weil der Lehrer der *ṛddhipādas* durch diese [in der Welt] zu verweilen vermag" zu übersetzen wäre. *praṇī-* bedeutet aber auch „to perform, to execute" (MW); geht man von dieser Bedeutung aus, so ließe sich das Skt. im Sinne der sachlich näherliegenden Wiedergabe von C. verstehen.

89, 13 *nityam aśaraṇānāṃ* . . . Hs. (B) *nitya**tā**śaraṇānāṃ* . . . De J.s (von J.s Text her gesehen völlig berechtigte) Kritik an Tak.s Übersetzung wird von daher gegenstandslos. T. *rtag pa* (nicht etwa *rtag par*!) ist Prädikat, nicht Adverb.

91, 14 *ataḥ paraṃ ye ca balādayo yathā cānugantavyās tathatām adhikṛtya granthaḥ.* Tak. verbessert *tathatām* zu *tathā tad.* Dem Relativum *ye* würde aber statt *tad* besser ***tān*** entsprechen. Die Hs. (B) hat in der Tat deutlich *tath**ātān**adhi-*.

92, 5: *pūrve nivāsa-* ist natürlich zu einem Wort zusammenzuziehen.

92, 11 *jñānāt svayaṃjñāpanāt* (Tak. *svayaṃ jñāpanāt*). *svayaṃ* ist durch die hier ziemlich undeutliche Hs. (B) schlecht gesichert und in T. ohne Entsprechung. Eine Lesung ***para***- (vgl. Pāda c: *prāpteḥ paraprāpaṇāt*; *para-* in T. auch dort ohne Entsprechung!) scheint nicht ausgeschlossen.

92, 12 *hānikāraṇakṛteḥ* (Tak. p. 340: „. . . he destroys . . . and causes others to reject . . .", = *hāni-* + *hānikāraṇakṛti-* [A. 23]) ist sehr seltsam. Die Hs. hat statt *-kāraṇa-* ein metrisch unmögliches *-karaṇa-* und hilft nicht weiter. M. E. liegt angesichts der parallelen Ausdrücke in Pāda a (*jñānāt . . . jñāpanāt*) und c (*prāpteḥ . . . prāpaṇāt*) eine Korrektur zu *hāni**hāpana**kṛteḥ* nahe. Hierzu paßt auch T. *spaṅs daṅ spoṅ mdzad phyir* (wobei *spoṅ mdzad -hāpana-* entspräche und das metrische Füllsel *-kṛti-* nicht wiedergegeben wäre).

93, 10f. *nāsti . . . muṣitatā citte na saṃbhedataḥ saṃjñā* . . . Es handelt sich um die dritte, vierte und fünfte der eigentümlichen (*āveṇika-*) Eigenschaften des Buddha: *nāsti muṣitasmṛtitā, nāsty asamāhitaṃ cittam, nāsti nānātvasaṃjñā* (MVy Nr. 138—140). Tak. möchte *muṣitatācitte* — dual. Dvandva aus *muṣitatā* (= *muṣitasmṛtitā*) und *acitta-* (= *asamāhitacitta-*) — lesen. Sehr überzeugend ist dieser Änderungs-

---

[114] Zum Sachlichen vgl. NVinSg p. 58—61 (Abs. II, 2).

vorschlag m. E. nicht. T. (. . . *bsñel daṅ thugs* **g-yo** *tha dad kyi ni* ᶜ*du śes daṅ* . . .) empfiehlt die Lesung *muṣitatā cittehitaṃ bhedataḥ saṃjñā* („. . . Unruhe *(īhitam)* des Geistes und Vorstellung [der Dinge] unter [dem Gesichtspunkt der] Unterschiedlichkeit *(*od.: als unterschiedlich*)*"). In der Hs. (B) ist *-taṃ* gut erkennbar, während das vorhergehende Akṣara unleserlich ist.

94, 6 f. *kṣityambujvalanānilāmbarasamā lokeṣu sādhāraṇā buddhāveṇikatā na cāśv api punar lokeṣu sādhāraṇā* ||. Statt *na cāśv api* ist auf jeden Fall das graphisch ganz ähnliche *na cāṇv api* einzusetzen (s. BHSD s. v. *āśu*; vgl. auch RGV p. 94, A. 4). Die Übersetzung der beiden Zeilen bei Tak. (p. 343: „The earth, water, fire, wind and the sky, likewise, are common to all the [material] worlds, but the Exclusive Properties of the Buddha are not in the least common to those worlds") ist grammatisch unhaltbar: *-samā* kann nicht in dieser Weise konstruiert werden. Nach dem zugehörigen Kommentar-Vers (III, 36; s. Bem. zu 97, 5—8) wäre die Stelle wie folgt zu verstehen: „Die eigentümlichen [Eigenschaften] des Buddha[115] sind — [einerseits] Erde, Wasser, Feuer und Wind, [andererseits] dem Raum-Äther [ver]gleich[bar] — [zwar einerseits] aller Welt gemeinsam (indem ihre Wirkungen aller Welt zugute kommen), [andererseits] aber aller Welt nicht im geringsten gemeinsam (indem sie qualitativ von allen weltlichen Eigenschaften[116] totaliter verschieden sind)[117]." Diese Wiedergabe setzt allerdings voraus, daß die in der Hs. (B) in Pāda c überlieferten Lesungen *-samāḥ* und *sādhāraṇāḥ* (so auch in Pāda d!) nachträgliche unkorrekte Auflösungen eines vermeintlichen Saṃdhi sind.

94, 13 *nirantaracitāṃśatā*. Hs. (B) *nirantaracitāṃsatā*: „Er hat Schultern, die [so] füllig (T: breit) sind, [daß] keine Zwischenräume [zwischen ihnen] bestehen."

95, 20 — 96, 2 *vyabhre yathā nabhasi candramaso vibhūtiṃ paśyanti nīlaśaradambumahāhrade ca* | *saṃbuddhamaṇḍalataleṣu vibhor vibhūtiṃ tadvaj jinātmajagaṇā vyavalokayanti* ||. Tak. (p. 347): „Just as, in autumn, the form of the moon is perceived in the cloudless sky, as well as in a big pond, reflecting this blue sky on its water-surface; similarly, the disciples of the Buddha can perceive the manifestations of the

---

115 Ich bin mir nicht darüber im klaren, ob das Abstraktsuffix *-tā* hier in Analogie zu den BHSG § 22.43 aufgezählten Fällen oder in einem kollektiven Sinne (wie etwa in *janatā*) gebraucht ist. Vgl. auch RGV II, 1b u. III, 4.

116 Und — nach Kommentar-Vers III, 36c — auch von den überweltlichen Eigenschaften der Śrāvakas etc.

117 D. h.: Was ihre Wesensbestimmung angeht, sind sie „dem Raum-Äther vergleichbar" (pp. 91, 17 u. 94, 3).

Omnipresent on the surface of the pond-like sphere of the Buddha." Diese Übersetzung ist — in der ersten Vershälfte — auf jeden Fall völlig unhaltbar. Da T. (*ji ltar sprin med nam mkhaʼi zla baʼi gzugs* || *ston kaʼi chu sṅon mtshor ni mthoṅ ba ltar* || . . .) und auch C. („Im Herbst, wenn der Himmel nicht von Wolken verhüllt ist, ist der Mond am Himmel und im Wasser [zu sehen]; alle Menschen in der Welt sehen dann die Majestät des Mondes") *vyabhre nabhasi* als Lokativus absolutus zu fassen scheinen, legt sich etwa folgende Wiedergabe nahe: „Wie man bei wolkenlosem Himmel die majestätische Erscheinung des Mondes auch in einem großen Teich mit seinem dunklen Herbstwasser sieht, so erblicken die Scharen der ‚Buddha-Söhne' die majestätische Erscheinung des Herrn (zugleich: des Allgegenwärtigen) inmitten der [als Spiegel-] Flächen [fungierenden um den] Erleuchteten [gescharten] Versammlungen (*maṇḍala-* steht hier offenbar für *parṣanmaṇḍala-*)." Vielleicht ist aber — trotz C. („. . . am Himmel und im Wasser . . .") — in Pāda b das hypermetrische *-hradeṣu ca* der Hs. (B) nicht (mit J.) zu *-hrade ca*, sondern, in Analogie zu *-taleṣu*[118] in Pāda c, zu *-hradeṣu* zu korrigieren[119]. Auf jeden Fall impliziert der Vers m. E. nur eine Differenzierung zwischen Urbild und Spiegelung, d. h. — im Falle des Buddha — zwischen dem sein eigentliches Sein darstellenden *dharmakāyaḥ* (IV, 55; vgl. auch III, 1) und einem uneigentlichen, IV, 56 als *nirmāṇakāyaḥ*, III, 1 als *saṃvṛtikāyaḥ* bezeichneten ‚Körper', der bloß eine Erscheinungsform für andere ist. In diesem Sinne ist wohl auch das „Zweifach-Sehen" (*dvidhā darśanam*) in Vers III, 4 zu verstehen. Auch die (Grund-) Verse II, 38—41 scheinen mir lediglich eine Differenzierung zwischen *dharma-* und *nirmāṇakāyaḥ* zu beinhalten. Der Vers-Kommentar hingegen interpretiert nicht nur II, 38—41, sondern auch III, 56 im Sinne der Lehre von den drei ‚Körpern' des Buddha und unterscheidet ein zweifaches Sehen der uneigentlichen Erscheinungsform des Buddha (= des *rūpakāyaḥ* [III, 38]): als *nirmāṇakāyaḥ* in der gewöhnlichen Welt, und als *saṃbhogakāyaḥ* in den Buddha-Versammlungen der Bodhisattva-Gefilde, wobei offenbar der *nirmāṇakāyaḥ* mit dem Spiegelbild des Mondes im Wasser, der *saṃbhogakāyaḥ* hingegen mit der urbildlichen Mondscheibe am Himmel verglichen wird (vgl. auch RGV I, 152c—d).

96, 4 *ekenābhisaṃkṣipya* ist ungewöhnlich. Die Hs. hat *ekadhyabhisaṃkṣipya*, was wohl zu *ekadhya⟨m a⟩bhisaṃkṣipya* zu berichtigen ist.

---

[118] Die (durch T. nicht gesicherten!) Akṣaras *-tala-* sind allerdings in der mir vorliegenden Kopie der Hs. sehr undeutlich, desgl. auch die (ebenfalls in T. nicht repräsentierten) Akṣaras *-mahā-* in Pāda b.

[119] T. zeigt weder den Plural noch *ca*. Auch in Pāda c ist der Pl. in T. nicht ausgedrückt.

96, 7f. *eṣāṃ khalu yathoddiṣṭānām eva catuḥṣaṣṭes tathāgataguṇānām api yathānupūrvyā vistaravibhāge nirdeśo.* Die Hs. (B) hat *eṣāṃ khalv* ***api*** und *vistaravibhā**ga**nirdeśo* (vgl. p. 100, 1f.). Statt *-guṇānām api yathānupūrvyā* ist wahrscheinlich mit T. (... *go rim* **ᶜdi ñid** *kyis*) *-guṇānām* ***anayaivā****nupūrvyā* zu lesen (*api* hat keine Entsprechung in T. und würde, bei dieser Lesung, auch in der leider hier ganz undeutlichen Hs. keinen Platz finden).

96, 11—16 *nirvedhikatvanirdainyaniṣkaivalyanirihataḥ | vajrasiṃhāmbarasvacchadakacandranidarśanam || 28 || balādiṣu balaiḥ ṣaḍbhis tribhir ekena ca kramāt | sarvajñeyasamāpattisavāsanamaloddhṛteḥ || 29 || bhedād vikaraṇāc* (besser mit 92, 7: *-kiraṇāc*[120]) *cchedād varmaprākāravṛkṣavat | gurusāradṛḍhābhedyaṃ vajraprakhyam ṛṣer balam || 30 ||*. Die Konstruktion der Verse macht Schwierigkeiten und scheint mir bei Tak. (p. 348) nicht befriedigend gelöst. Ich würde zunächst vorschlagen, *balādiṣu* in 29a mit Vers 28 zu konstruieren, den Rest des Verses 29 aber mit Vers 30 zu einem Satz zu verbinden: „Bei den ‚Kräften' usw. [wird respektive] der Vergleich mit einem Diamant-Donnerkeil, einem Löwen, dem Raum-Äther und dem [Spiegelbild des] Mond[es] im klaren Wasser [zur Anwendung gebracht], weil sie [respektive] durchdringend[121], unverzagt, ausschließlich [dem Buddha] zukommend und ohne Anstrengung [auftretend] sind. (Kommentar zu den ‚Kräften':) Weil durch (a) sechs ‚Kräfte', (b) drei [‚Kräfte'] und (c) eine ‚Kraft' respektive [die Beschmutzung (*mala-*[122], hier offenbar im Sinne von *āvaraṇa-*) bezüglich (a) des] Zuwissende[n, (b) die Beschmutzung bezüglich der] Versenkung [und (c) die in den Leidenschaften bestehende] Beschmutzung samt ihren Residuen ausgetilgt wird, [d. h.] wie ein Panzer, ein Wall [oder] ein Baum gespalten, zerbrochen [bzw.] gefällt wird, gleicht die ‚Kraft' des Weisen (= Buddha), welche gewichtig, fest, stark und unzerbrechlich ist, einem Diamant-Donnerkeil."

· **97, 5—8**: M. E. ist in Z. 6 die von Tak. dem Chinesischen entnommene Lesung *pañcadhātunidarśanam* besser als das von T. vorausgesetzte *pañcadhā tu nidarśanam.* — Der Vers III, 35 bezieht sich offenbar auf Vers III, 16a—b, wo die Verschiedenheit des Raum-Äthers von den vier übrigen Elementen herausgestellt wird; Vers 35 deutet den Raum als Bild für den Buddha, während die vier übrigen Elemente respektive Weltmenschen, Śrāvakas, Pratyekabuddhas und Bodhi-

---

[120] Vgl. auch RGV p. 96, A. 2.

[121] *nir-* ist von Tak. und T. fälschlich als Privativ-Präfix gedeutet worden. Richtig C. („im [Falle des] Aufpralle[s] hindurchdringend").

[122] Fehlt in T. und ist auch in der Hs. undeutlich, findet sich aber in C. — Die Übersetzung der Zeile ist unsicher.

sattvas repräsentieren. — In Vers III, 36 (*sarvalokopajīvyatvād bhūmyambvagnyanilopamāḥ | laukyalokottarātītalakṣaṇatvān nabhonibhāḥ* ||) ergänzt Tak. als Subjekt der ersten Zeile die vier ersten der in Vers 35 genannten Kategorien (also Weltmenschen etc.), als Subjekt der zweiten Zeile den Buddha (Sg.; natürlich kommt nur der Pl. in Frage). Diejenigen, von denen alle Welt lebt (= Nutzen und Heil empfängt), sind aber nicht die Weltmenschen etc., sondern die Bodhisattvas und vor allem die Buddhas, vgl. p. 23, 14f. *tathāgatajñānam . . . sarvasattvopajīvyajñānam* (p. 24, 8: *sarvajagadupajīvyam*) und vor allem p. 17, 10f., wo es — mit Bezug auf den Bodhisattva oder Buddha — heißt: *yaḥ śīlam ādāya paropajīvyaṃ karoti tejo'nilavāribhūvat | kāruṇyam utpādya paraṃ pareṣu* . . . M. E. sind daher Subjekt beider Zeilen des Verses III, 36 die Buddhas oder noch besser vielleicht die in dem zugrunde liegenden Grundvers III, 16c—d (s. Bem. zu 94, 6f.!) behandelten ‚eigentümlichen' (*āveṇika-*) Buddha-Eigenschaften.

97, 11 (s. auch WZKSO XI/1967, p. 213): Statt *-lakṣaṇāḥ kāye* ist mit T. *-lakṣaṇākhyā ye* oder *-lakṣaṇāhvā ye* (so viell. die Hs. [B], die jedenfalls nicht *-ḥ kā-* hat) zu lesen.

97, 14 *dvidhā taddarśanaṃ*[123] *śuddhaṃ vārivyomendubimbavat*. Nicht nur von C. (vgl. RGV p. 97, A. 4), sondern auch von Vers III, 28c—d (*-svacchadakacandra-*) her legt sich die Lesung *śuddhavāri-* nahe, die m. E. auch inhaltlich wesentlich besser ist. Und vielleicht bedeutet auch in T. (*chu daṅ nam mkha*[c] *zla gzugs bźin* || *de mthoṅ ba ni rnam pa gñis* ||) *daṅ* nicht „und", sondern „klar" (= *daṅ ba*). Die Zäsur zwischen *śuddha-* und *vāri-* ist kein Grund für die Nichtzusammengehörigkeit dieser beiden Wörter: vgl. Vers III, 28c—d, wo *svaccha-* und *daka-* zwar auch durch die Zäsur voneinander getrennt sind, aber dennoch unzweifelhaft zusammengehören. — Vgl. auch Bem. zu 95, 20 — 96, 2.

98, 2 *apraśrabdhi-* und 98, 2f. *-apraśrabdhaṃ*. Ich würde in beiden Fällen mit pp. 99, 16 und 21, 8 *apratipra-* vorziehen. Die Hs. (B) hat im ersten Falle *aprapra-*, im zweiten *-aprati-*.

98, 8 *kṛtsnaṃ niṣpādya yānaṃ pravaraguṇagaṇajñānaratnasvagarbhaṃ*. Tak. (p. 351f.): „Having completely established the Vehicle, the ocean of knowledge filled with the multitudes of the excellent virtues, . . .". *-svagarbhaṃ* ist verdächtig. T. (*yon tan rin chen mchog tshogs daṅ ldan ye śes chu mtsho* . . .) legt nahe, *-ratnasvagarbhaṃ* zu *-ratnāmbugarbhaṃ* zu korrigieren. Die Hs. (B) läßt zum mindesten *-tnā-* erkennen, und eine Lesung *-mbu-* statt *-sva-* erscheint zum mindesten nicht unmöglich. In der Übersetzung kann man, ohne eine kaum zulässige Umstellung von *jñāna-* und *ratna-*, T. nicht folgen.

[123] So J. nach T.; Hs. (B): *dvidhā tu darśanaṃ*.

M. E. ist die Stelle folgendermaßen wiederzugeben: „... das ganze [dem Ozean vergleichbare Mahā]yānam, das als Juwelen die vorzüglichen Eigenschaften und als Wasser das Wissen in sich trägt, ...". Für diese Interpretation und auch für die obige Korrektur spricht auch der Kommentar in Vers IV, 9a—b: *jñānāmbuguṇaratnatvād agrayānaṃ samudravat.* — Statt *niṣpādya* (Hs. nach J. *nirmathya*; in der mir vorliegenden Kopie ganz undeutlich) wäre vielleicht *niryāya* („[hindurch und] hinausgegangen seiend, ganz und bis zur vollkommenen Beherrschung durchgemacht habend") passender, sowohl angesichts des *niryāṇam* in Strophe 5 wie auch angesichts der chinesischen Wiedergabe mit „vollständig begriffen habend" (*pien hsüeh-chih* ⑱). Dieser Ausdruck ließe sich (im Gegensatz zu *niṣpādya*) auch mit dem Ozean verbinden.

98, 10: *vimalaguṇanidhiṃ* (als Apposition zu *buddhatvaṃ*) gibt zweifellos einen guten Sinn. Der Kommentar (Vers IV, 10c—d) jedoch verbindet *vimalaguṇanidhi-* mit den Lebewesen, hat also wohl *-nidhau* gelesen. Hs. (B) *-nidhi* (metrisch unkorrekt).

98, 13ff.) *yasya yena ca yāvac ca yadā ca vinayakriyā | tadvikalpodayābhāvād anābhogaḥ sadā muneḥ* ||. Tak. (p. 352): „To whom, by what means, how far, and when, about these matters, there is no rise of discrimination; therefore, the Buddha's Act of conversion is [working] always ‚without effort'." Statt *yāvac ca* hat T. *gaṅ gaṅ du* = ***yā yatra***. Diese Korrektur wird durch den folgenden Vers, der alle Relativa jeweils mit einer Erklärung wiederholt (und von Tak. ebenfalls nicht ganz richtig übersetzt wird), obligatorisch, und auch die Hs. (B) ist m. E. so zu lesen. Die Übersetzung von Vers 3 und 4 müßte m. E. etwa wie folgt lauten: „Bei den Weisen (= Buddhas) gibt es keine Anstrengung, da [bei ihnen] keine Reflexion darüber entsteht, für wen, wodurch, wo und wann welche Bekehrungstat [stattzufinden hat]. ‚Für wen': d. h. [für welche] zu bekehrende Gruppe [von Lebewesen]; ‚wodurch': [d. h.] durch [welche] reichlich [zur Verfügung stehenden] Mittel (o. ä.); ‚welche': [d. h. welche] Bekehrungstat; ‚wo und wann': [d. h.] an [diesem oder] jenem Ort und [zu dieser oder jener] Zeit." — Vers 5 (wo der Kommentar zu Vers 2 beginnt) ist m. E. nur konstruierbar, wenn man *anābhogaḥ sadā muneḥ* aus Vers 3 ergänzt.

100, 1: s. F. 22.

101, 10 *saddharmakāyaṃ madhyasthaṃ paśyanti*. Die Hs. (B) hat *-kāyam* ***adhyātmaṃ***, vgl. auch T. ***nan gi*** *dam paʿi chos sku ni ... mthoṅ bar ʿgyur.*

101, 11 *-vyapagataviṣamasthānāntaramalā*. Tak. möchte diesen Ausdruck als *-vyapagataviṣamasthānā 'ntar-amalā* verstehen. Ich muß gestehen, daß mich dieser Vorschlag nicht überzeugt. Vielleicht ist es besser, von *antara-* in der Bedeutung („Zwischenraum" =) „Loch" auszugehen: „die frei ist von Unebenheiten, Löchern und Schmutz".

101, 13 *śuddhatvāt tatra bimbaṃ surapatibhavanaṃ māhendramarutām utpadyeta. bhavanaṃ* ist syntaktisch verdächtig, und in *māhendra-* ist die Vṛddhi störend. In der Tat ist der Anusvāra über *-na* in der Hs. (B) nicht zu sehen, und das Akṣara *mā-* ist ganz undeutlich. T. lautet *dag phyir der ni lha bdag gnas* **tshogs**[124] *lha dbaṅ lha yi gzugs śar te.* Vielleicht ist *-bhavanavyūhendra-* zu lesen, was jedenfalls metrisch korrekt, graphisch möglich und auch vom Sinn her einleuchtend wäre: „[gesetzt,] in dieser [Bodenfläche] entstünde, weil sie [so] rein ist, ein Spiegelbild des (wohlstrukturierten) Komplexes (*vyūha-*) der Wohnungen des Götterkönigs, des [Götterkönigs] Indra [selbst] und der Maruts . . .".

102, 7 *yatnasthānamanorūpavikalparahitā sati.* Tak. (p. 359): „. . . (the divine drum), being apart from efforts, from a particular place, from forms of mind, and from thought-constructions". De J. (gegen T. und im Anschluß an IV, 34c *yatnasthānaśarīracittarahitaḥ śabdaḥ*): „[the divine drum] which is free from thought-constructions as to effort, place, mind and matter". M. E. ist T.s Wiedergabe (*ᶜbad daṅ gnas daṅ yid gzugs daṅ || rnam par rtog pa med bźin du*) doch die richtige, wobei aber *yid gzugs* als *yid (daṅ) gzugs* zu verstehen ist: „. . . [obwohl sie (= die himmlische Trommel)] frei ist von Anstrengung, Ort, Geist, Materie und Reflexion . . .". Es geht — gerade auch angesichts der Aussage von Vers 34c — nicht darum, daß die himmlische Trommel (oder gar der außenstehende Betrachter) sich nicht denkt (*vikalpa-*), daß ihr Anstrengung usw. zukommen, sondern daß ihr Anstrengung usw. — in Vers 31c—d ist der Vollständigkeit halber die ‚Reflexion', *vikalpa-*, hinzugefügt worden — wirklich nicht zukommen. — *sthāna-* bedeutet übrigens gewiß „Ort": eine Tonhöhe (de J.: „. . . perhaps one must translate *sthāna* by ‚pitch, tone'") werden die Klänge der himmlischen Trommel ja wohl haben müssen. Es geht vielmehr darum, daß sie, ebenso wie der *dharmakāyaḥ* des Buddha, nirgendwo räumlich lokalisierbar ist. C. hat übrigens (in Vers IV, 34; IV, 31 fehlt in C.) für *sthāna-* das übliche *ch'u*⑲; *yung*⑳ („use, function") gehört zu *kung-yung*㉑ = *yatna-*.

102, 20f. *te 'pi hi divaukasāṃ pūrvakṛtakuśalakarmavaśād aghaṭṭitā eva divyaśravaṇamanoharaśabdam anuruvanti.* Tak. will *ghaṭṭitā* statt *aghaṭṭitā* lesen und übersetzt (p. 361): „These are likewise produced owing to the previous virtuous deeds made by the gods and make sound

---

[124] So Tak. nach D. Bei Nak. fehlt *tshogs.* P und N haben irrtümlicherweise *sna tshogs* statt *gnas tshogs.*

agreeable to the ear of deities." Aber *ghaṭṭ-* heißt nicht „to produce", sondern „to touch, to rub, to shake", bezeichnet also hier wohl das Gespieltwerden der Musikinstrumente, und der an der vorliegenden Stelle vom Fragesteller geforderte Vergleich des Hörbarwerdens der Lehre des Buddha mit den himmlischen Instrumenten, die erklingen, ohne gespielt zu werden, findet sich auch SA IX, 18 (wo *aghaṭitebhyaḥ* für *aghaṭṭitebhyaḥ* steht). Es ist also die Lesung *aghaṭṭitā* beizubehalten und zu übersetzen: „Denn auch diese [übrigen himmlischen Instrumente] lassen, ohne daß sie [von jemand] gespielt würden, kraft der früher vollbrachten guten Werke der Himmelsbewohner himmlische, angenehm zu hörende Klänge ertönen."

103, 4 *apramādasaṃniyojanatayā ca.* Hs. (B) *apramāda**pada**saṃniyojanatayā*, vgl. T. *bag yod paʼi* **gnas** *la rab tu sbyor bas na.*

103, 15 *saṃsārapātālagateṣu loke saṃbuddhabherer upayāti*[125] *śabdaḥ.* Statt *-gateṣu* würde besser *-gate* **tu** gelesen; so wohl auch die Hs. (B), die jedenfalls nicht *-ṣu* hat. Übersetzung: „Der Ton der Trommel des Erleuchteten aber ist auch für die Leute, die sich in der niedrigsten Region (Pātāla) des Saṃsāra befinden, hörbar (*upayāti* = *śravaṇam upayāti*, vgl. Pāda b)." T. . . . *ʼkhor ba yi* || *sa ʼog ʼjig rten dag tu* . . . muß nicht unbedingt einen Plural voraussetzen, zumal die Partikel *dag* hinter *ʼjig rten* (*loka-*) und nicht hinter *sa ʼog* (*pātāla-*; *gata-* ohne Entsprechung) steht. Ferner ist *loke* nicht etwa als Entsprechung von *divi* in Pāda a anzusehen; *divi* dient vielmehr zur Spezifizierung der Trommeln (vgl. Vers IV, 34a: *divyadundubhi-*) und entspricht insofern *saṃbuddha-* in Pāda d.

104, 8f. *cetaḥparyāyajñānena tatparyāpannaṃ sarvasattvacittacaritagahanāvabhāsanam ādeśanāprātihāryam.* Tak. gibt *tatparyāpannam* mit „. . . (the illumination of the thicket of mental conduct of living beings,) as involved in the mind, . . ." wieder. Das ist kaum sinnvoll. Die Hs. (B) liest *tatparyāpanna**sarvasattva-***, d. h.: „. . . aller dazu (= zu sämtlichen Weltkomplexen aller Himmelsrichtungen) gehörigen Lebewesen . . .".

104, 11 *sarvaghoṣopalabdhiḥ.* T. **rnam pa** *thams cad kyis dmigs pa(r)* setzt einen anderen Text voraus. In der Tat hat die Hs. deutlich *sarva**thopalabdhiḥ***.

104, 12 *atatprahitānām.* Die Hs. (B) liest m. E. *atatpra**di**nām*, was angesichts C. (*pu hsüeh*㉒) vielleicht zu *atatpra⟨**ve**⟩dinām* ergänzt werden darf. In T. *de ma gtogs pa rnams kyi* ist *gtogs* wahrscheinlich eine Fehlschreibung für ***rtogs***.

104, 19 *sasyasampadaḥ.* Hs. (B) *-saṃpad**āṃ***.

106, 1 *karuṇāmeghābhradharmāmbhaso. -ābhra-* wird durch T. *sñiṅ*

[125] Siehe Tak. p. 362 u. 399!

rje^c^*i sprin* **tshogs** *dag gis* (lies: *gi*) *chos chu* nicht gestützt. Die Hs. (B) scheint *-megh***augha***-* zu lesen (zu *tshogs* = *ogha-* „Menge, Masse" s. BCA-I p. 420).

106, 6 *kleśagatān dṛṣṭyanuśayān nāpekṣate sarvathā.* Tak. verbessert mit Recht im Anschluß an T. und C. *-gatān dṛṣṭy-* zu *-gat***ātma***-dṛṣṭy-* (Hs. versehentlich *-gatādṛṣṭy-*). Aber seine Übersetzung (p. 366: „. . . does not mind anywhere those who are of Defilements, whether [in the burst of] egoistic view or in an dormant state") ist kaum richtig. M. E. muß es heißen: „. . . nimmt in keiner Weise Rücksicht auf die üblen Neigungen zu (od.: bestehend in) den Leidenschaften (*kleśagata-*) und der Ansicht, [es gebe ein individuelles] Selbst." Vgl. auch T.

106, 11 *ca sṛjan* (= Hs.). Besser wäre vielleicht *vyasṛjat.*

110, 3 *durlabhaprāptabhāvās tathāgatā iti.* Hs. A hat *durlabha***prādur***bhāvās* . . .; vgl. T.: *de bźin gśegs pa* ^c^**byuṅ ba** *rñed par dka*^c^ *ba źes bya ba ni.*

111, 6 *-jñānālokādyalaṃkṛtāḥ.* Tak. möchte *-jñānālokād alaṃkṛtāḥ* lesen, was ebenfalls unbefriedigend ist. Hs. A hat m. E. *-jñānālokāsvalaṃkṛtāḥ*, was sich zu *-jñānālokasvalaṃkṛtāḥ* korrigieren läßt. Hs. B ist nicht lesbar.

111, 10 *vikṛtir.* Hs. A und wohl auch Hs. B ***nirmitir*** (= T. *sprul pa*).

112, 7 *sudaiśiko dundubhivad vibho rutam.* T. (*legs par* ^c^*doms mdzad lha yi rṅa daṅ* ^c^*dra*) zeigt an, daß *vibho rutam* eine Fehllesung ist. Hs. A hat in der Tat deutlich ***divaukasāṃ***[126]: „Als derjenige, der [den Dharma] in der rechten Weise verkündet, ist er der Trommel der Himmelsbewohner vergleichbar."

112, 14 *pratirava iva ghoṣo 'nakṣarokto jinānām.* Hs. A (und wohl auch Hs. B) liest ⟨'⟩*nakṣaro* ⟨'⟩**sau**, was durch T. (*rgyal ba rnams kyi gsuṅ* **de** *brag ca bźin du yi ge med*) bestätigt wird.

113, 9 *tadvan na ca no sārthabījavat.* ***sārthabījavat*** ist verdächtig, zumal es nicht mit T. (*don* **med** *pa*^c^*i* || *sa bon* **spoṅ** *min de* ^c^*dra min*) harmoniert. Die Hss. sind m. E. von J. nicht ganz richtig wiedergegeben worden: Hs. A liest *tadvan na ca nāna*[127]*rthabījamut*, Hs. B *tadvan na ca nāna*(?)*rthabījavat*, wobei aber *-vat* ganz undeutlich und unsicher ist. Daraus ergibt sich, angesichts T., als wahrscheinlicher Text *tadvan na ca* ***nā****narthabīja****muk***[128] oder allenfalls *-bīja***hṛt**[129]: „. . . es (= das

---

[126] So wohl auch Hs. B, die hier nicht sehr deutlich ist.

[127] Am unteren Rand des Blattes nachgetragen!

[128] Ein schlecht geschriebenes *k* kann in Hs. A einem *t* ähnlich werden! Zu *spoṅ ba* = Wz. *muc-* vgl. BCA-I p. 325.

[129] Zu *spoṅ ba* = Wz. *hṛ-* vgl. RGV IV, 55b.

Buddhatum) ist aber nicht wie die [Wolke] so beschaffen, daß es nicht von den Samen des Unheils befreite". Daß die soeben vorgeschlagene Rekonstruktion des Textes zutreffen dürfte, läßt sich auch mit einem inhaltlichen Argument begründen: Da in dem vorliegenden Textstück der jeweils folgende Vergleich die Ungleichheit (*vaidharmyam*) des jeweils vorhergehenden wettmachen soll (vgl. IV, 92), müßte der (nach der Wolke als Vergleich herangezogene) Gott Brahmā *anarthabījamuk* oder *-hṛt* sein. In der Tat heißt es in Vers IV, 55b, daß sein Anblick bei den Göttern des *kāmadhātuḥ* das Verlangen nach den Sinnesobjekten (welches gewiß als ‚Same des Unheils' gelten kann) beseitige (*viṣayaratiharaṃ darśanaṃ tac ca teṣām*).

113, 14 *tadvan na ca śuklāspadaṃ ca tat*. T. *dge ba yi | gźi min de daṅ ᶜdra baᶜaṅ min* setzt eine auch vom Sinn geforderte (und in Tak.s Übersetzung vorausgesetzte) zweite Negation voraus. In der Tat liest Hs. A deutlich ***na** tat* statt *ca tat*.

113, 15ff. *pṛthivīmaṇḍalaprakhyaṃ tatpratiṣṭhāśrayatvataḥ | laukyalokottarāśeṣajagatkuśalasaṃpadam* ||. Tak. (p. 378): „The Buddha resembles the region of the earth, since he is the ground and foundation for the achievement of all the virtues of living beings . . .". Diese Wiedergabe setzt die Änderung von *-saṃpadam* zu *-saṃpadām* voraus, welch letzteres sich in der Tat in Hs. A (*-sampadāṃ*) vorfindet. — In Vers IV, 98 (p. 114, 2) ist *śuklakarmapathadhyānāpramāṇārūpya-* im Gegensatz zur Auffassung Tak.s („the Path of virtuous actions consisting of meditation . . .") als viergliedriges Dvandva (*kuśalāḥ karmapathāḥ, dhyānāni, apramāṇāni* und *ārūpyāṇi*) zu fassen: vgl. die Definition der zehn *kuśalāḥ karmapathāḥ* in der Yogācārabhūmiḥ (ed. Bhattacharya), p. 170, 21ff.

115, 18 *divyabrahmavihārapāramigataḥ saṃbodhyupāyācyutaḥ*. Tak. (p. 381): „. . . and, having been transferred to the abode of Brahman in heaven, would be irreversible from the means of Enlightenment". (a.) *divyabrahmavihārapāramigataḥ* ist nach de J. (p. 40, zu 4.3) mit „who has arrived at mastery in the divine brahmic states" zu übersetzen. Das ist richtig, was die Wiedergabe von *-pāramigataḥ* angeht. Aber *divyabrahmavihāra-* ist mit Dīghanikāyo III, p. 220 und Bodhisattvabhūmiḥ (ed. Wogihara) p. 90, 8ff. als „die ‚himmlischen' und die ‚brahmischen' Zustände" zu verstehen (vgl. auch T. *lha daṅ tshaṅs gnas*), wobei mit den *divyā vihārāḥ* die vier Dhyānas und die vier Ārūpyas gemeint sind (Bodhisattvabhūmiḥ p. 90, 11f.). (b.) Statt *saṃbodhyupāyācyutaḥ* liest die Hs. A *saṃbodhyupāyāc cyutaḥ* („wobei er [jedoch] des Mittels für die vollkommene Erleuchtung verlustig gegangen ist"), was dem Sinne nach mit C. („kein⟨e⟩ Mittel für die Erleuchtung habend") übereinstimmt. Hs. B scheint jedoch, mit T.

(*rdzogs paʿi byaṅ chub ʿpho med thabs bsgoms la*), *saṃbodhyupāyācyutaḥ* zu lesen, was J. angesichts des *bodhyarthiko* von Vers 3a und des *bodhim anuttarām abhilaṣan* von Vers 4b wohl mit Recht vorgezogen hat.

116, 8 *astitvaśaktatvaguṇavattvādhimuktitaḥ*. Hss. A und B lesen *-śakyatva-*: „. . . durch das gläubige Vertrauen darauf, daß [die ‚Grundlage'] existiert, [ihre ‚Neugestaltung'] möglich ist und [die Eigenschaften und Wirkungen des Buddhatums] vorzüglich sind" (vgl. auch Ru. p. 422).

117, 4 *śreṣṭhā prajñā*. Hs. A liest *prajñā śreṣṭhā*. — Tak.s Korrektur von *cāsya* zu *cāsyā* in derselben Zeile wird von beiden Hss. bestätigt.

118, 13f. *dharmadviṣāṃ sevanād ārād dharmabhṛtām*. *ārāt* kommt nur als indeklinables Adverb vor; hier aber ist der Ablativ eines Nomens — u. zw. eines Abstraktums oder eines nomen actionis — gefordert (vgl. Tak.: „. . . by . . . keeping at distance from those who convey the Doctrine"). Dies bestätigt auch T. *bsriṅs phyir* („weil sie . . . fernhalten") und C. *yüan-li* ⑰ („weil sie meiden"). Graphisch, metrisch und sachlich befriedigend wäre m. E. die Lesung (*sevanād*) *vārād* (*vāra-* [mask.] bedeutet u. a. „keeping back, restraining" [MW]).

119, 4 *tasmai vimuktiḥ kutaḥ*. Die Hs. (A) hat deutlich ***tasyāsti*** statt *tasmai vi-*.

119, 10f. *yataś ca yannimittaṃ ca yathā ca yad udāhṛtam | yanniṣyandaphalaṃ ślokaiś caturbhiḥ paridīpitam* ||. Die Hs. (A) liest . . . *yanniṣyandaṃ* **ca** ⟨,⟩ ***tac chlokaiḥ*** . . ., was durch T. (. . . *rgyu mthun pa ni gaṅ yin te* (lies: ***de***) || *tshigs su bcad pa bžis bstan to* ||) bestätigt wird.

119, 14f. *saṃsāramaṇḍalakṣantir bodhiprāptiḥ samāsataḥ | dvidhā dharmārthavādasya phalam antyena darśitam* ||. *saṃsāramaṇḍala-* ist nicht gebräuchlich und vor allem im vorliegenden Zusammenhang — es wird doch auf den Anblick des Buddha Amitābha (V, 25c) angespielt! — völlig fehl am Platz. T. *ʿkhor gyi* (und nicht *ʿkhor baʿi*!) *dkyil ʿkhor* entspricht ***parṣanmaṇḍala-***, was tatsächlich in der Hs. (A) steht; m. c. ist allerdings hier *pariṣanmaṇḍala-* anzusetzen. Außerdem sollte *-maṇḍalaṃ kṣāntir* statt *maṇḍalakṣāntir* gelesen werden, da (im Gegensatz zu T. *rnam gñis*) C., Paramārtha (T 1595, p. 270b6) und vielleicht auch die Hs. (A)[130] in Z. 15 ***tridhā*** lesen, was m. E. besser ist, da in Vers V, 25c—d de facto drei Früchte aufgezählt werden: der Anblick Amitābhas (→ *pariṣanmaṇḍalaprāptiḥ*), die Entstehung des *dharmacakṣuḥ* (→ *kṣāntiprāptiḥ*) und die Erlangung der Erleuchtung (→ *bodhiprāptiḥ*).

---

[130] Die Akṣaras *tra* und *dva* unterscheiden sich in dieser Hs. nur geringfügig. An der vorliegenden Stelle ist eine Entscheidung schwierig.

① (不)脱
② 不捨智
③ 差別之相
④ 獨自行
⑤ 爲
⑥ 爲之
⑦ 無我
⑧ 母親
⑨ 身

⑩ 故曰如如
⑪ 是眞如〔同〕如
⑫ 本
⑬ 藏
⑭ 如來
⑮ 煩惱業等
⑯ 依出世間智得世間出世間依止行智是名爲因。

⑰ 遠離
⑱ 遍覺知
⑲ 處
⑳ 用
㉑ 功用
㉒ 不覺

The Ratnagotravibhāga

Summary: The present paper consists of two sections. The first section is concerned with the structure of the Ratnagotravibhāgaḥ (RGV). The starting point is the analysis given by J. TAKASAKI in his book „A Study on the Ratnagotravibhāga“ (Rome 1966). TAKASAKI's distinction between basic verses, commentary verses and prose commentary certainly has to be accepted. His attempt however to recover an original RGV of only 27 verses by declaring most of the basic verses to be later enlargements of the basic text seems open to doubt, because even this pretended original RGV admits of being split up again. Therefore, to my opinion the original RGV is constituted by the totality of basic verses. But this original RGV seems to have made use of several (perhaps only partly remodelled) older materials. — The second section of the present paper is dedicated to suggesting corrections of the Sanskrit text and — in some cases — of the translation of single RGV-passages.

Review
J. W. de Jong

For several reasons the *Ratnagotravibhāga* deserves our attention. It is the only text on the *tathāgatagarbha* which has been preserved in Sanskrit. There are many problems connected with its place in the history of Mahāyāna philosophy and with its authorship.

The Tibetan tradition attributes the verses to Maitreya and the prose commentary to Asaṅga. This text is held in high regard as one of the five treatises composed by Maitreya. However, the Chinese tradition attributes the whole work to Sāramati. This tradition is mentioned by Yüan-ts'e (613-696) in his commentary on the *Saṃdhinirmocanasūtra*[1] and by Fa-tsang (643-712) in his commentary on the *Dharmadhātvaviśeṣaśāstra*[2]. Probably the earliest reference to Sāramati as author of the *Ratnagotravibhāga* is to be found in Chih-i's *Mo-ho chih-kuan* (*Taishō*, Vol. XLVI, Nr. 1911, p. 31b18-26) which has been dictated by him in 594 (cf. p. 125 of Tsukinowa's article mentioned in note 8). The identity of Sāramati raises many problems. Some scholars have identified him with Sthiramati,[3] others have distinguished two Sāramati's.[4] There are also many obscurities in the Chinese traditions concerning the translator of the Chinese version. Chinese catalogues mention two translations, one by Ratnamati and the other by Bodhiruci.

In 1931 E. Obermiller published a translation of the *Ratnagotravibhāga* from the Tibetan: "The Sublime Science of the Great Vehicle to Salvation", *Acta Orientalia*, Vol. IX, Part II.III, pp. 81-306.[5] His interpretation of the text is based upon a commentary by Tsoṅ-kha-pa's pupil and successor rGyal-tshab Dar-ma rin-chen (1364-1432).[6] The Sanskrit text has been edited by E. H. Johnston and published by T. Chowdhury: *The Ratnagotravibhāga Mahāyānottaratantraśāstra* (Patna, 1950). This edition is based upon two manuscripts found in Tibet by Rāhula Sāṁkṛtyāyana. The edition of the Sanskrit text has given a new impulse to the study of the *Ratnagotravibhāga*. Several passages of the *Ratnagotravibhāga* have been translated by E. Conze (*Buddhist Texts through the Ages*, Oxford, 1954, pp. 130-131, 181-184 and 216-217). In *Die Philosophie des Buddhismus* (Berlin, 1956, pp. 255-264) E. Frauwallner has

[1] P. Demiéville, *BEFEO*, XXIV, 1-2 (1924), p. 53.

[2] N. Peri, *BEFEO*, XI (1911), p. 350; Takasaki, p. 9.

[3] Cf. H. W. Bailey and E. H. Johnston, "A Fragment of the Uttaratantra in Sanskrit", *BSOS*, VIII (1935), pp. 77-89 (esp. p. 81) and Johnston's foreword to his edition of the Sanskrit text, pp. x-xii. To this Sthiramati the Tibetan tradition attributes a commentary on the *Kāśyapaparivarta*. The Chinese translation (*Taishō*, 1523) is due to Bodhiruci. According to Chinese catalogues this commentary, just as the *Ratnagotravibhāga*, has been translated by both Bodhiruci and Ratnamati. Cf. A. Staël-Holstein's edition (*A Commentary of the Kāśyapaparivarta*, Peking, 1933) and P. Pelliot's review, *TP*, XXXII (1936), pp. 75-76. According to Chinese traditions both Bodhiruci and Ratnamati have translated also the *Daśabhūmikasūtraśāstra* (*Taishō*, No. 1522), cf. Noël Peri, "A propos de la date de Vasubandhu", *BEFEO*, XI (1911), pp. 352-353; Stanley Weinstein, "The concept of *ālaya-vijñāna* in pre-T'ang Chinese Buddhism". *Essays on the History of Buddhist Thought. Presented to Professor Reimon Yūki* (Tōkyō, 1964), pp. 34-35. On the relations between Bodhiruci and Ratnamati see P. Demiéville, "Sur l'authenticité du *Ta tch'eng k'i sin louen*", *Bulletin de la Maison Franco-Japonaise*, II, 2 (Tōkyō, 1929), pp. 30ff.

[4] See the references given by Ét. Lamotte, *L'Enseignement de Vimalakirti* (Louvain, 1962), pp. 92-93, n. 2. According to Hattori Masaaki, there is only one Sāramati who lived between Nāgārjuna and Asaṅga-Vasubandhu.

[5] Cf. La Vallée Poussin's interesting review, *MCB*, I (1931-1932), pp. 406-409.

[6] Cf. G. Tucci, *Tibetan Painted Scrolls*, I (Roma, 1949), p. 119: *A Catalogue of the Tohoku University Collection of Tibetan Works on Buddhism* (Sendai, 1953), No. 5434. Ogawa Ichijō, "Butsu (Nyorai) to Busshō (Nyoraizō) — Darumarinchen-zō Hōshōron Shakuso o shoe to shite", *IBK*, XIII (1965), pp. 247-250. Id.: "Indo Daijō Bukkyō ni okeru Nyoraizō-Busshō-shisō ni tsuite — Darumarinchen-zō Hōshōron Shakuso no kaidoku o kokoromite —", *Tōhōgaku*, 30 (1965), pp. 102-116. A complete translation of this commentary would be very welcome.

given a summary of the ideas contained in this text and a translation of several verses.[7] In 1959 Ui Hakuju published a detailed study on the *Ratnagotravibhāga* (*Hōshōron Kenkyū*) which contains a complete translation (pp. 471-648), together with a Sanskrit-Japanese glossary (pp. 1-60 with separate pagination).[8] Professor Takasaki's translation was undertaken during his stay in India (1954-1957) and continued afterwards. Apart from this book he has published between 1958 and 1964 ten articles relating to the *Ratnagotravibhāga* (a list is given on pp. xii-xiii).[9]

The translation is preceded by a long introduction (pp. 5-62) and a synopsis (pp. 63-133) which indicates the divisions of the chapters, the main topics, the numbers of the verses, the page numbers in Sanskrit, Tibetan (Derge edition) and in Chinese, quotations and comparisons with passages in the *Buddhagotraśāstra* (*Taishō*, No. 1610), the *Mahāyānadharmadhātvaviśeṣaśāstra* (*Taishō*, No. 1626-1627) and the *Anuttarāśrayasūtra* (*Taishō*, No. 669).

The introduction deals briefly with the Tibetan and Chinese traditions concerning the authorship of the *Ratnagotravibhāga*, but refrains from discussing the theories of modern scholars. The latest discussion of the problems connected with Sāramati is to be found in Ui's book (pp. 89-97), in which the author acrimoniously attacks Johnston's hypothesis of an older Sthiramati, to whom are due the *Ratnagotravibhāga*, the commentary on the *Kāśyapaparivarta*, the *Dharmadhātvaviśeṣaśāstra*, and possibly the *Mahāyānāvatāra* (*Taishō*, No. 1634).[10] In the second section of the introduction Professor Takasaki studies the structure of the text and tries to reconstruct the original text which, according to him, consists of 27 verses of chapter I (cf. pp.

[7] According to Frauwallner Sāramati lived about 250 A.D.

[8] For completeness' sake mention must be made of a synoptic edition of the Sanskrit text in Roman letters and the Chinese translation by Nakamura Zuiryū: *The Ratnagotravibhāga-Mahāyānottaratantra-çāstra. Compared with Sanskrit and Chinese. with introduction and Notes* (Tokyo, 1961) (published originally in *Ōsaki Gakuhō*, 103-110, 1955-1959). More important are the following articles: Tsukinowa Kenryū, "Kukyōichijōhōshōron ni tsuite", *Nihon Bukkyō Kyōkai Nenpō*, VII (1935) pp. 121-139; Takata Ninkaku, "Kukyōichijōhōshōron no johon ni tsuite", *Mikkyō Bunka*, 31 (1955) pp. 9-37; Hattori Masaaki, "'Busshōron' no ichi kōsatsu", *Bukkyō Shigaku*, IV, 3-4 (1955), pp. 16-36 (I have not been able to consult the last two articles); Takata Ninkaku, "Hōshōron ni okeru tenne (āśrayaparivṛtti) ni tsuite", *IBK*, VI (1958), pp. 501-504; Ogawa Ichijō, "'Busshō' to 'buddhatva'", *IBK*, XI (1963), pp. 544-545.

[9] Not mentioned are two articles published in 1953: "Hōshōron ni okeru nyoraizō no igi", *IBK*, I, pp. 368-369; "Nyoraizō to engi — Hōshōron o ṭegakari to shiṭe —", *IBK*, II, pp. 244-247.

[10] Ui dwells at great length on the fact that Johnston gives the Chinese translation of Sāramati's name as Chien I and not as Chien Hui, and insists that Hui and I must be sharply distinguished. However, Tsukinowa quoted as early as 1934 a passage of Chih-i's *Mo-ho chih-kuan* (see above, p. 37) where Sāramati is translated by Chien-i. As far as I can see Ui does not mention anywhere either this passage or Tsukinowa's article. In general, he is very sparing with references to other scholars. Ui's bitter attack on Johnston culminates in the remark that Johnston treats Chinese Buddhism and the history of Chinese Buddhism with too much ease. He adds that without knowledge of Chinese Buddhism, it is impossible to understand Indian Buddhism and Buddhism in general. One could make a similar remark about Ui in respect of Tibetan Buddhism. Although Ui states that the translation of *sāra* by *chien* is quite usual and not limited to personal names, nevertheless Johnston is quite right in remarking that Sāramati is a somewhat unusual form. Usually, personal names ending in *-mati* have as first element an adjective or a participle. The name Sāramati does not seem to occur anywhere else.

393-395 which give the text of these verses). Ui has reconstructed a basic text in 187 verses which he gives in Japanese translation (pp. 38-81). The form of the *Ratnagotravibhāga* is, as Johnston remarks, somewhat unusual. It consists of verses and prose but only part of the verses are *kārikās*. The remaining verses either explain the *kārikās* or illustrate them by similes. Moreover, the Chinese translation consists of two parts. The first contains only verses with occasional captions (*Taishō*, vol. XXXI, pp. 813-820) and the second agrees on the whole with the Sanskrit text but omits many verses which occur in the first part (pp. 820-848). There is a number of omissions and additions in the Sanskrit as compared to the Chinese translation. The main differences between the two texts are listed on page 19 of the introduction and the less important ones are pointed out in the notes to the translation, but not exhaustively (cf. for instance, my remark below apropos of p. 50. 13-15). It would have been helpful to have a synopsis of the two parts of the Chinese translation with the Sanskrit text. In view of the form of the Sanskrit text and the complicated hybrid structure of the Chinese translation, attempts to reconstruct an original text are quite justified, however hypothetical they will always be. Both Ui and Professor Takasaki rely exclusively on internal evidence. For a more reliable reconstruction this should be combined with a detailed comparison of the *Ratnagotravibhāga* with related texts.

Section III of the introduction is devoted to an exposition of the main doctrines of the text and section IV to the genealogy of the *tathāgatagarbha* theory, in which Professor Takasaki discusses the main texts quoted in the *Ratnagotravibhāga*.[11] In the following section it is proved that the *Mahāyānadharmadhātvaviśeṣaśāstra*, the *Buddhagotraśāstra* and the *Anuttarāśrayasūtra* depend on the *Ratnagotravibhāga*.[12] In the last section Professor Takasaki considers the place of the *Ratnagotravibhāga* in Mahāyāna Buddhism. As to the date and the authorship he arrives at the following conclusions: (1) The original verses were composed before Asaṅga. Most probably they are to be attributed to Maitreya. (2) The present form of the text dates from the early 5th century A. D. and after Asaṅga and Vasubandhu. Sāramati is the author of the commentary and the systematizer of the *garbha* theory.

Many problems relating to the *Ratnagotravibhāga* are also discussed in the articles mentioned above. These articles as well as the introduction and the notes to the text contain a wealth of information. We may expect that they form the prelude to a systematic treatment of the *garbha* theory and its history. With his profound knowledge of the Sanskrit, Chinese and Tibetan texts and of the results of Japanese scholarship, Professor Takasaki is eminently qualified to give us an exhaustive study of this important chapter of Mahāyāna philosophy.

The translation of the *Ratnagotravibhāga* by Professor Takasaki is the first to be based on the Sanskrit text and the Chinese and Tibetan translations. Obermiller utilized only the Tibetan version and his translation, excellent as it is, contains a number of mistakes which are obvious in the light of the Sanskrit text. Ui utilized both the Sanskrit text and the Chinese translation, but he was unable to consult the Tibetan translation directly. His knowledge of it was based upon a Japanese translation, made for him by Tada Tōkan, and upon Obermiller's English translation. It is clear from many indications that the Chinese translation is closer to the original than both the Sanskrit text and the Tibetan translation. However, as concerns the interpretation of the text, the Chinese translation is now always a reliable guide. There

[11] Ui has studied in great detail the texts quoted (pp. 272-353) and has devoted a special chapter to the *Śrīmālādevīsiṃhanādasūtra* (pp. 435-469).

[12] In chapter four of his book entitled "The relations with other sūtras and śāstras" (pp. 354-429) Ui has examined the *Anuttarāśrayasūtra* (pp. 354-366), the *Buddhagotraśāstra* (pp. 366-389), the *Mahāyānadharmadhātvaviśeṣaśāstra* (pp. 389-407) and the *Mahāyānāvatāra* (pp. 407-423).

are several places where Professor Takasaki has been too much influenced by it but in general he indicates very well the wrong interpretations which are to be found in the Chinese translation. For the Tibetan translation Professor Takasaki has consulted only the Derge edition. A comparison of the passages quoted in the notes with the corresponding passages in the Peking edition (the only one at my disposal) shows that the Derge edition does not always give a satisfactory text. An edition of the Tibetan translation based on the Derge, Peking and Narthang editons would be highly desirable. In view of the importance of the vocabulary of the *Ratnagotravibhāga* for both Buddhist Sanskrit and Mahāyāna terminology, it would also be very useful to have indexes on the lines of those compiled by Professor Nagao for the *Mahāyānasūtrālaṃkāra*.

The *Ratnagotravibhāga* is not always easy to interpret. While reading the translation, I have made a number of notes with regard to the interpretation, the edition of the text and similar matters. I venture to publish them in the conviction that any contribution, however, insignificant, may be of some help in the study of this very important text. At the same time my remarks are meant as a tribute to Professor Takasaki's scholarship for which I have the greatest respect. I have used the following abbreviations: T. = Tibetan translation (my quotations of T. are taken from the Peking edition. Whenever necessary, I refer to the Derge, Peking and Narthang editions by the initials D., P. and N.); J. = Johnston's edition of the Sanskrit text; O. = Obermiller's translation of the Tibetan translation; *BHSD* = Edgerton's *Buddhist Hybrid Sanskrit Dictionary* (New Haven, 1953); *CPD* = *A Critical Pāli Dictionary* (Copenhagen, 1924-1965).

2.8-10 *sarvaśrāvakapratyekabuddhair api tāvac chāriputrāyam artho na śakyaḥ samyak svaprajñayā jñātuṃ vā draṣṭuṃ vā pratyavekṣituṃ vā / prāg eva bālapṛthagjanair anyatra tathāgataśraddhāgamanataḥ* / Tak. "This meaning, O Śāriputra, can neither be known nor be seen, nor be examined correctly through the knowledge of the Śrāvakas and the Pratyekabuddhas. Needless to say, this applies to the case of ignorant and ordinary beings, except when they have faith in the Tathāgata." Tak. has followed the punctuation of the Sanskrit text which is wrong. The *daṇḍa* after *vā* must be deleted, because those who are able to understand through faith (*śraddhāgamana*; T. *dad-pas rtogs-pa*) in the Tathāgata are to be found among the Śrāvakas and Pratyekabuddhas, cf. 22.3-4: *śeṣāṇāṃ devi sarvaśrāvakapratyekabuddhānāṃ tathāgataśraddhāgamanīyāv evaitau dharmāv iti*. The Tibetan translation puts a double stroke (*ñis-śad*) before *sarvaśrāvaka*° and after *tathāgataśraddhāgamanataḥ*. Ui is right in translating *anyatra* ... as a new sentence, cf. p. 484: *shikashi, nyorai ni taisuru shin ni yotte nomi tsūzuru koto o nozoku*.

4.3 *indriyaparamapāramitāprāptaḥ*; Tak. "brings all faculties [of living beings] to the highest perfection"; T. *dbaṅ-po mchog-gi pha-rol-tu phyin-pa*. See Edgerton, *BHSD* s.v. *pāramitā* (1). It is not possible to give a causative meaning to *prāpta*. One must translate: "has obtained the supreme perfection of [his] faculties", cf. 31.14 *sarvadharmanairātmyaparapāramiprāptaḥ* (°*parapāram abhiprāptaḥ* has been corrected on p. xvi; T. *dam-pa'i pha-rol-tu phyin-pa brñes*); Tak. "has attained the highest supremacy, [knowing] non-substantiality of all the phenomena"; 87.3-4 *guṇaiḥ / viśuddhipāramiprāptair*; 115.18 *divyabrahmavihārapāramigataḥ*; Tak. "having been transferred to the abode of Brahman in heaven"; T. *lha tshaṅs-gnas mthar-soṅ*. This passage deals with meditation (115.17 *dhyāyed dhyānam* ...) and must be translated accordingly: "who has arrived at mastery in the divine brahmic states", cf. Ui. p. 643: *Tenteki no shibonjū no higan ni tōtatsu-shi*.

4.5-6 *anābhogabuddhakāryāpratipraśrabdho*; Tak. "calmed in the Buddha's effortless acts uninterruptedly". Edgerton gives a more understandable translation, cf. *BHSD* s.v. *apratipraśrabdha*: "unceasing in the effortless activities of a Buddha". This passage must be added to those quoted by Edgerton.

5.6-7 *imaṃ cārthavaśam upādāya*; Tak. "and because of the effect of this meaning". See Edgerton, *BHSD* s.v. *artha-vaśa* and Ui, p. 488: *soshite, kakaru riyū ni motozuite.*

7.2 *saṃghe garbho jñānadhātvāptiniṣṭhaḥ*; Tak. "In the Community exists the Matrix, which is The element of Wisdom, aiming at its acquisition". Both T. (*tshogs-las*) and C. have read *saṃghād*. Johnston prefers the MS. reading *saṃghe* "as the Tathāgatagarbha is in each member of the community and by its working leads to the acquisition of knowledge and realisation of the *dhātu*". Ui remarks that the *tathāgatagarbha* exists in all men and is not restricted to the *saṃgha*. I believe that the reading *saṃghād* is preferable also, because it corresponds to the ablatives in the first pāda: *buddhād dharmo dharmataś cāryasaṃghaḥ*. According to Tak. *taj* in the third pāda (*tajjñānāptiś cāgrabodhir*) refers to *garbha* in the second pāda: "Its acquisition of the Wisdom is the Supreme Enlightenment". T. (*ye-śes de thob byaṅ-chub mchog*) does not bear out this interpretation. I suggest that these two pādas be translated as follows: "From the Community comes the Matrix which culminates in the obtaining of the Element of Wisdom. The obtaining of that Wisdom is the Supreme Awakening", see Ui's translation, p. 490: *sō kara zō ga ari, chiekai no shōtoku o kukyō to shi, soshite, sono chie no shōtoku wa saijō bodai de ari.*

8.2 *iti smṛtam*; Tak. "Thus remembered by tradition". Better "thus it is taught (or declared)".

8.10 *udayo 'trābhisaṃbodho 'bhipretotpādaḥ*; "Here the word '*udaya*' means 'perfect enlightenment' (*abhisaṃbodha*), in which the sense 'origination' is implied". T. (P.; D. is quoted by Tak., p. 157, n. 17) *o-ta-ya ni 'dir mṅon-par rtogs-pa la 'dod-kyi skye-ba ni ma yin-no*: O. "Here the word '*udaya*' is to be understood in the sense of 'thorough cognition', but not in that of 'origination'". One must certainly correct the Sanskrit text according to T., which has been misunderstood by Johnston, and add the syllable *no*: *'bhipreto notpādaḥ*; *no* and *to* are almost similar in the script used in the MS. B, so that the omission of *no* is practically a case of haplology. That Ui follows Johnston's text is certainly due to his ignorance of Tibetan, p. 493: *kokoni kaku o eta to yū no wa, shōgaku shita koto de atte, nozomareta mono o eta koto de aru.*

8.18-19 *tatra duḥkhamūlaṃ samāsato yā kācid bhaveṣu nāmarūpābhinirvṛttiḥ*; Tak. "Of these, the root of Suffering is, in short, one kind of origination of Individuality (*nāmarūpa*) on the [three] existences"; *yā kācid* means "any whatsoever", cf. Ui's translation, p. 494: *issai.*

10.7-8 *vikrīḍitā vividhā saṃpannavinayopāyamukheṣu supraviṣṭatvāt*; Tak. "[The Compassion is 'named] mastery (*vikrīḍitā*)', because it enters well into the gates of accomplished means of training in various ways (*vividhā*)". Ui also translates *vividhā* as an adverb: p. 496: *shuju ni*, but no such adverb exists. As Johnston remarks, T. corresponds to *vividheṣu sampannavineyopāyamukheṣu* (p. 10, n. 2). The simplest solution would be to read *vividhasaṃpanna*°.

10.9 *svadharmatādhigamasaṃprāpaṇāśayatvāt*; Tak. "because [the Buddha] ... has the intention to lead [the living beings] to the acquisition of their own nature". In note 50 Tak. remarks "it seems C. takes '*svadharmatā*' as 'Buddha's own nature'". Here *svadharmatā* has indeed the same meaning as in 10.4: *svadharmatāprakṛtinirviśiṣṭatathāgatagarbham* and in verse 100 (60.16-17) *vilokya tadvat sugataḥ svadharmatām avīcisaṃstheṣv api buddhacakṣuṣā*. Ui gives the same interpretation, p. 496: *jiko no hosshō no shōtoku ni tasseshimen to yū igyō taru ga yue de aru.*

10.12-13 *api khalu jñānena paramanityopaśāntipadasvābhisaṃbodhisthānaguṇāt svārthasaṃpat paridīpitā*; Tak. "Besides [there is another meaning]. By the word 'Wisdom', the fulfilment of self-benefit is designated, in so far as the highest, eternal and quiescent place has the character of being the basis of his own perfect enlightenment". T. *yaṅ-na ye-śes-kyis ni mchog-tu rtag-pa daṅ / ñe-bar źi-ba'i gnas raṅ-ñid mṅon-par byaṅ-chub-la gnas-pa'i yon-tan-gyis na raṅ-gi-don phun-sum-tshogs-pa bstan-pa.* T. suggests the following translation of the Sanskrit text: "On the other hand, 'Wisdom' elucidates the accomplishment of one's own purpose, because it has the property of being the basis for the self-realisation of the supreme and eternal place of Quiescence".

12.4 *dvayavikalpāsamudācārayogena*. Tak. translates *samudācāra* by 'origination' just as *samudaya* in 12.3 Elsewhere he translates *samudācāra* by 'takes place' (13.6), 'produce' (13.9) and 'arising' (33.8). Better is the translation 'manifestation' in 50.12. Everywhere T. has *kun-tu spyod-pa* and Ui, p. 499, etc.: *gengyō*. In 13.9 T. (*kun-'byuṅ-ba las*) and the context (*ayoniśomanasikārasamudācārāt kleśasamudayaḥ / kleśasamudayāt karmasamudayaḥ*) suggest a reading °*samudayāt*.

13.1-4 *vibandhaḥ punar abhūtavastunimittārambaṇamanasikārapūrvikā rāgadveṣamohotpattir anuśayaparyutthānayogāt / anuśayato hi bālānāṃ abhūtaṃ atatsvabhāvaṃ vastu śubhākāreṇa vā nimittaṃ bhavati rāgotpattitaḥ / pratighākāreṇa vā dveṣotpattitaḥ / avidyākāreṇa vā mohotpattitaḥ*; Tak. "And 'bondage' (*vibandha*) means the origination of Desire, Hatred and Ignorance preceded by the thought which takes its basis of cognition upon the characteristic of unreal things. It is due to the union of the state of tendency (*anuśaya*) with manifested state (*paryutthāna*) [of defilement]. Indeed, people regard the unreal, i.e. 'not of its nature (*atatsvabhāva*)' thing as the [real] characteristic because of its desirable looks (*śubhākāra*) when Desire comes forth from its state of tendency; when Hatred comes forth [from its state of tendency], [they regard the unreal thing as the real characteristic] because of its detestable looks (*pratighākāreṇa*); and when Ignorance comes forth, then it is the same because of its obscure looks (*avidyākāreṇa*)". This difficult passage becomes clearer when compared with chapter XXIII of the *Prasannapadā* which is devoted to the *viparyāsas*, see kārikā 1: *saṃkalpaprabhavo rāgo dveṣo mohaś ca kathyate / śubhāśubhaviparyāsān saṃbhavanti pratītya hi /* and the commentary (p. 452.4-5): *tatra hi śubhaṃ ākāraṃ pratītya rāga utpadyate / aśubhaṃ pratītya dveṣaḥ / viparyāsān pratītya moha utpadyate / saṃkalpas tv eṣāṃ trayāṇāṃ api sādhāraṇakāraṇam utpattau /*. The commentary explains that the beautiful aspect (*śubhākāra*), the ugly aspect (*aśubhākāra*), the permanent, the self etc. (*nityātmādi*) have been superimposed (*adhyāropa*), see p. 457.6-8. The *Ratnagotravibhāga* explains that an unreal object (*abhūtaṃ vastu*) becomes something which appears (*nimitta*) as having a beautiful, repulsive or wrongly understood aspect, although it has not the nature of those [three characteristics] because desire, repulsion or delusion arise out of their latent state. For *nimitta* see *BHSD nimitta* (I): "external aspect or feature, appearance"; Jacques May, *Candrakīrti, Prasannapadā madhyamakavṛtti* (Paris, 1959), p. 510: "indice de détermination, détermination, cause déterminante", and Haribhadra's *Abhisamayālaṃkārālokā* (Wogihara's ed.), p. 333: *sāmānyarūpaparicchedān nimittikuryāt* (transl. by Edward Conze, *Oriens Extremus*, IX, 1962, p. 36, n. 15 by "[treat as a sign] by defining their general marks"). Tak. has wrongly rendered *atatsvabhāvaṃ* at other places too, see 31.12: *sarve hy anyatīrthyā rūpādikaṃ atatsvabhāvaṃ vastv ātmety upagatāḥ*; Tak. "Indeed, all the other Heretics consider the things consisting of form, etc. as the Ego though they are of the unreal nature". One must understand: "For all other heretics consider the object, consisting of matter, etc. as the Self, although it has not the nature of it." See also 86.5-6 (verse 40 c-d): *kriyāsu cintāmaṇirājaratnavad vicitrabhāvo na ca tatsvabhāvavān*; Tak. "He has a resemblance, in his acts, to the king of wish-fulfilling gems, appearing in various forms, which, however, have not their own substance." This passage refers to the *saṃbhogakāya* which appears as different beings but without possessing the nature of those [different beings] (T. *sna-tshogs-dṅos daṅ de-yi raṅ-bźin min*). In the verses 51 and 52 (87.11-14) which explain verse 40 *atatsvabhāva* occurs once and *atadbhāva* twice: *deśane darśane kṛtyāsraṃsane 'nabhisaṃskṛtau / atatsvabhāvākhyāne ca citratoktā ca pañcadhā / (51) raṅgapratyayavaicitryād atadbhāvo yathā maṇeḥ / sattvapratyayavaicitryād atadbhāvas tathā vibhoḥ / (52)*; Tak. "In teaching, in the visible form, in acting ceaselessly, and acting with no artificial effort, and in its appearance of illusion, the variety of [its manifestation] is said to be five-fold (51). Just as a gem, being dyed with various colours, does not make manifest its real essence; similarly, the Lord never shows its real nature, though it appears in various forms, according to the conditions of the living beings (52)". Here *atatsvabhāvākhyāne* means "in the manifestation of what is not its nature" (T. *de-yi ṅo-bo mi-ston-la* = "in the non-manifestation of its nature"). See also Nyāyabindu (ed. Stcherbatsky), 27.3: *yady atatsvabhāve 'nutpādake ca kaścit pratibaddhasvabhāvo*; Stcherbatsky, *Buddhist Logic*, II, p. 75: "If the existence of something could be necessarily conditioned by something else, something that would neither be its cause, not essentially the same reality." Tak.'s translation of *anuśayaparyutthānayogāt* (13.2) has to be corrected; *yogāt* (T. *dan-ldan-pas*) does not indicate the union of *anuśaya* with *paryutthāna*, but the union with both.

13.15-17 *ya evam asataś ca nimittārambaṇasyādarśanāt sataś ca yathābhūtasya paramārthasatyasya darśanāt tadubhayor anutkṣepāprakṣepasamatājñānena sarvadharmasamatābhisambodhaḥ*: Tak. "And thus, this realization of all natures by Wisdom, as being equal without any addition nor diminution because of these two facts, i.e. because we cannot see any characteristic nor basis of non-being, and we can see the real character of being as the absolute truth." This passage explains that the realization of the sameness of all dharmas is due to the knowledge of the sameness which does neither reject (*utkṣepa*, T. *bsal-ba*) the non-existing support of the appearance (*asan nimittārambaṇam*) nor establish (*prakṣepa*, T. *bźag-pa*) the existing absolute in its true reality (*sad yathābhūtaṃ paramārthasatyam*) because the first is not seen and the second is seen.

15.1-2 *anāsrave dhātau kuśalākuśalayoś cittayor ekacaratvād dvitīyacittānabhisaṃdhānayogena*; Tak. "In the immaculate sphere there is no succession of a second mind because both minds, good and bad, act together as one and the same." T. *dge-ba dan mi-dge-ba'i sems-dag las gcig rgyu-bas sems-gñis-pa mtshams-sbyor-ba med-pa'i tshul-gyi*. O. "when one of the two forms of the Spirit, either the defiled or the undefiled, manifests itself, it has no (real) contact with the other (its counterpart)." Tak. understands *ekacara* as "acting together", T. as "acting of one". The usual meaning, however, of *ekacara* is "wandering or living alone". In the immaculate sphere the good and bad thoughts are isolated from each other and therefore there is no relation of a second thought with a first thought, i.e. a bad thought cannot arise from a good thought and vice versa. Ui seems to understand it in this way: p. 503: *muro no kai ni oitewa, zen to fuzen to wa tandoku no mono de aru kara, dainishin to no ketsugō ni tekishinai node*.

16.17 and 17.2 °*avabhāsapratyupasthitam*; Tak. "standing in the illumination"; *pratyupasthita* means here "engaged in", cf. *BHSD* s.v. *pratyupasthāna, pratyupasthita*. In 36.3 Tak. has misunderstood *pratyupasthāpanam*: *buddhadhātuviśuddhigotraṃ* ... *dvividhakāryapratyupasthāpanaṃ bhavati*; Tak. "the Essence of the Buddha, the perfectly pure Germ, ... has the two kinds of foundation of its actions." The meaning is: "The Germ brings about two kinds of effect", cf. *Daśabhūmika* 49.18: *avidyā dvividhakāryapratyupasthānā* which is quoted by Edgerton.

17.4 *ananyapoṣiganyam* ... *āryaśrāvakam*; Tak. "the holy Śrāvakas ... indifferent to the nourishment of others"; J. notes that *poṣin* is recorded by the *PW* only from the *Kathāsaritsāgara* and Tak. that C. probably has misread *poṣa* for *poṣin*. There is no doubt about the meaning of *ananyapoṣin*, cf. Pāli *anaññaposin*, *CPD*: "not supporting others, said of the houseless ascetic, who maintains no family and fosters no passion"; °*ganya* probably has to be interpreted as "belonging to a class" but T. (*gźan rgyas-par byed-pa mi-ldan-pa* according to D.; P. ... *dan-ldan-pa*, which is certainly wrong) has no word corresponding to it.

20.17 *sarvajagadāśayaśobhānimittatvāt*; Tak. "because they are the cause of beauty intended by the whole world." T. *'gro-ba thams-cad-kyi bsam-pa dge-ba'i rgyu yin-pa'i phyir*, O. "as they are the cause of the virtuous thoughts of all living beings." The interpretation given by the Tibetan translator is correct; *āśayaśobhā* is litterally "the splendour of the thoughts". cf. also Ui's translation, p. 512: *issai seken no kesshutsuseru igyō no in taru ga yue de aru.*

21.11-12 *teṣām eva daśabalādīnāṃ buddhadharmāṇāṃ pratisvam anuttaraṃ karma*: Tak. "the automatic, highest act of these Qualities of the Buddha — 10 Powers, etc." The meaning of *pratisvam* is "one by one", not "automatic" as given by Tak. in accordance with C. One must translate: "the single supreme acts of these qualities of the Buddhas as the ten powers, etc", cf. Ui's translation, p. 513: *sorera jūriki-tō no buppō no ichi-ichi no mujō no gō de atte.*

23.7 *tatropagamikayā mīmāṃsayā samanvāgataḥ*: Tak. "possessed of the skill to approach there (i.e. to the big cloth)." Here *upagamika* has the same meaning as *-upaga* and *-upaka* in Buddhist Hybrid Sanskrit, cf. *BHSD* s.v. *-upaka*: "pertaining, belonging to; suitable, appropriate". The same expression occurs in the *Daśabhūmikasūtra* (p. 61.15) which has *upagatayā* instead of *upagamikayā*: *tatropagatayā mīmāṃsayā samanvāgato.* In *Vinaya* IV.211: *tatrupāyāya vīmaṃsāya samannāgatā* (quoted by The Pali Text Society's *Pali-English Dictionary* s.v. *tatra*) one must probably read *tatrupayāya*. Kern's explanation has to be rejected (*Toevoegselen op 't woordenboek van Childers*, II, Amsterdam, 1916, p. 90: *tatrupāya* = *tadūpiya*, suitable, corresponding, SVibh.II,211. Misschien vervorming van *tadrūpiya*).

26.10-11 *pūrvataraṃ tu yenārthena sarvatrāviśeṣeṇa pravacane sarvākāraṃ tadarthasūcanaṃ bhavati tad apy adhikṛtya nirdekṣyāmi.* Tak. notes that T. reads *pravacana* (*gsuṅ-rab*) as the subject. However, T. has *gsuṅ* (omitted by P.) *-rab thams-cad-du* which corresponds to *sarvatra pravacane*, O. "throughout the whole of Scripture". I do not believe that Tak.'s translation and explanation (p. 198, n. 13) of this sentence are correct, but the text (26.1-11) is clearly in disorder as noted by J. and Tak.

28.10-11 *śūnyatādṛṣṭayaś cābhimānikā yeṣām iha tadvimokṣamukhe 'pi śūnyatāyāṃ mādyamānānāṃ śūnyataiva dṛṣṭir bhavati*; T. *mṅon-pa'i ṅa-rgyal-can stoṅ-pa-ñid-du lta-ba ste / 'di-la stoṅ-pa ñid-du lta-ba gaṅ-dag de'i rnam-par thar-pa'i sgo-la yaṅ stoṅ-pa-ñid-du lta-ba 'gyur-ba.* Probably the text at the basis of T. had *śunyatādṛṣṭīnāṃ* instead of *śūnyatāyāṃ mādyamānānāṃ* which is not represented in C., too.

32.10 *ākāśopamasattvabhājanalokanairātmyaniṣṭhāgamanād*; Tak. "[the Tathāgata] has realized perfectly the non-substantiality of living beings and of the material world, just as the sky [reaches up to the limit of the world]." In a note Tak. remarks that *akāśopama* (T. *nam-mkha' ltar*) is relating to *niṣṭhāgamana*. However, T. relates it to *nairātmya*: *sems-can daṅ snod-kyi 'jig-rten nam-mkha'-ltar bdag-med-pa'i mthar-thug-pa ñid-du rtogs-pa'i phyir* = "because the Tathāgata has realized completely the sky-like non-substantiality of the world of the living beings and the material world." This interpretation seems more obvious, although Tak's interpretation is not precluded. Ui's translation is ambiguous, p. 530: *kokū no gotoki, shujō-seken to kiseken to no muga no kukyō ni tasshita kara to.*

32.15 *vaśitāprāptānāṃ ca bodhisattvānām.* In note 109 Tak. remarks that it is not necessary to limit this qualification to those Bodhisattvas who abide on the 10th *bhūmi* as mentioned in the Tibetan commentary and that we can regard this '*vaśitāprāpta*' as an epithet for Bodhisattvas in general. Tak. refers to *Laṅkāvatāra*, p. 274.21: *sarvabodhisattvabhūmiṣu vaśitāprāptaḥ*, but this quotation is from the *Lalitavistara*. The Tibetan commentary (O., p. 170, n. 1) does not limit this qualification to bodhisattvas on the 10th *bhūmi*, but to bodhisattvas who abide in the last three *bhūmis*. The ten *vaśitās* are obtained on the 8th *bhūmi*, cf. *Daśabhūmikasūtra* (ed. J. Rahder), p. 70 and *Mahāyānasūtrālaṃkāra* 26.2-3: *daśavaśitālābhāt / yathā daśabhūmike 'ṣṭamyāṃ bhūmau nirdiṣṭāḥ.*

33.5-6 *sarvakleśamaladaurgandhyavāsanāpakarṣaparyantaśubhapāramitāṃ*; J. notes: "Text as in A; °*vāsanāprakarṣa*ᶜ, B, which does not make sense; T. seems to have read ᶜ*vāsanāyogāt* (*bag-chags* ... *daṅ-ldan-pa'i phyir*), which would bring the sentence into the same form as the following ones." According to Tak. (p. 216, n. 122) both T and C. take *'paryanta'* as *'atyanta'* and attach it to *śubhāpāramitā* as an attribute and instead of *apakarṣa* T. has *dan-ldan-pa'i phyir*. However, *prakarṣa* makes good sense and corresponds to T. *rab*; T. *mthar-thug-pa* corresponds to *paryanta* and not to *atyanta* which is rendered in T. by *śin-tu* (cf. 32.9, 33.8,9). T. *ñon-moṅs-pa'i dri-ma dri-ṅa-ba'i bag-chags thams-cad daṅ-ldan-pa'i phyir gtsaṅ* (P. *gsaṅ*) *-ba'i pha-rol-tu phyin-pa rab-kyi mthar-thug-pa* = *sarvakleśamaladaurgandhyavāsanāyogāt prakarṣaparyantaśubhapāramitām* / T. confirms the reading of MS. B. but adds *yogāt*. Tak. translates *kleśamaladaurgandhyavāsanā* by the "dusts of defilements with their bad-smelling impressions". In this case, too, the Tibetan interpretation is to be preferred: "the traces of the bad smell of the impurities of the defilements".

34.18-19 *anityasaṃsārānapakarṣaṇataś cocchedāntāpatanān nityanirvāṇāsamāropaṇataś ca śāśvatāntāpatanāt*; Tak. "Because he does not fall into the Nihilistic Extremity through his not diminishing, neglecting the non-eternal Phenomenal Life; nor does he fall into the Eternalistic Extremity through his not intensifying the eternal Nirvāṇa." In T. (P., D. and N.) *apakarṣaṇa* is rendered by *'brid-pa* which has misled both J. and Tak.; it must be corrected into *'bri-ba* which corresponds exactly to *apakarṣaṇa*. The terms *apakarṣaṇa* and *samāropaṇa* are synonymous with the more usual terms *apavāda* and *samāropa*, cf. 76.11. *Samāropa* is the superimposition of non-existing ideas and entities upon the absolute reality; *apavāda* is the opposite of it. For these two terms see Jacques May, *op.cit.*, p. 187, n. 609.

36.13-15 *na ca bhavati tāvad yāvad āgantukamalaviśuddhigotram trayāṇām anyatamadharmādhimuktiṃ na sa samudānayati satpuruṣasaṃsargādicatuḥśuklasamavadhānayogena*; Tak. "Really, it cannot take place unless they bring about the Germ which is purified from accidental pollutions and the faith in any one of th.ee Vehicles through being endowed with the four kinds of good actions, beginning with having contact with a personage of high virtue." The subject is the *gotra* which brings about the *adhimukti* by means of the *catuḥśukla*. The preceding lines explain that without the *gotra* the *duḥkhadoṣadarśanam* and the *sukhānusaṃśadarśanam* are impossible. T. *ji-srid-du blo-bur-gyi dri-ma rnam-par dag-pa'i rigs skyes-bu dam-pa la brten-pa la sogs-pa 'khor-lo bźi yaṅ-dag-par 'byor-ba'i tsul-gyis / gsum-las gaṅ-yaṅ-ruṅ-ba'i chos-la mos-pa / skyed-par byed-par ma-yin-pa de-srid-du ni 'gyur-ba yaṅ ma-yin-no /*.

38.5-7 *bodhisattvakaruṇābhāvanāyā vārisādharmyaṃ tasyāḥ sarvajagati paramasnigdhabhāvaikarasalakṣaṇaprayogād iti*; J. remarks: "T. om. *lakṣaṇapra*; C either as in text or reading *lakṣaṇayogad*, which is perhaps preferable." Both Tak. (p. 226, n. 203) and Ui (p. 538, n. 2) point out that C. corresponds to *lakṣaṇaprayogād*. T. *de ni' gro-ba thams-cad-la mchog-tu brlan-pa'i raṅ-bźin-gyi ro-gcig-pa daṅ-ldan-pa'i phyir-ro*. Tak. renders T. as follows: "its nature of the highest moisture in all the world is endowed with one taste", but the meaning is: "because it [*bodhisattvakaruṇābhāvanā*] possesses the unique savour of extreme moisture in regard to all living beings."

39.2 *prabhāsvaras tadubhayāgantukatāprakṛtitaḥ*: Tak. "It (*āśravakṣaya*) is 'radiant' by nature because these two Obstructions are merely of an occasional nature." In note 214 Tak. remarks: "T. reads as *'tad-ubhaya-āgantukatā-aprakṛtitaḥ'* (*glo-bur-pa-ñid-kyi raṅ-bźin ma yin-pa'i phyir-ro*, being *āgantukatā*, they are not the innate character)." The Sanskrit text must be interpreted in conformity with the Tibetan translation: "It is radiant because these two, being accidental, do not constitute its nature." The compound *āgantukatāprakṛtitaḥ* is analysed by T. as *āgantukatayā-aprakṛtitaḥ*, cf. P. *'od-gsal-ba ni de gñi-ga glo-bur-ba ñid-kyis raṅ-bźin ma-yin-pa'i phyir-ro* (P. adds *raṅ-ñid-kyis* after *ñid-kyis*). See Ui's translation, p. 539: *myōjō towa kono ryōsha no kyakujin taru mono o jishō to nasanai kara de aru.*

50.13-15 *sā punar āsravakṣayābhijñābhimukhyasaṅgaprajñāpāramitābhāvanayā mahākaruṇābhāvanayā ca sarvasattvadhātuparitrāṇāya tadasākṣātkaraṇād abhimukhyām bodhisattvabhūmau pradhānyena vyavasthāpyate*; Tak. "And this state is predominantly established in the 6th stage of Bodhisattva called Abhimukhī. Because, [in this Stage], the Bodhisattva, facing the acquisition of the Extinction of Evil Influences through his practices of unobstructed Highest Intellect and Great Compassion, still does never realize that acquisition in order to protect all living beings." Tak. has omitted the word *abhijñā*, which is missing in C., although both T. and S. give it. I would prefer to follow T. and S. The MS. B has the reading *āsravakṣayābhijñābhimukhyāṃ asaṅga*° which seems preferable: "And this [pure and impure state (*śuddhāśuddhāvasthā*)] is mainly established on the Stage of the Bodhisattva, called Abhimukhī, which approaches the superknowledge of the extinction of the defilements on account of the practice of the unobstructed perfection of wisdom [but does not obtain it] because [the Bodhisattva] on account of the practice of the great compassion has not realized it in order to protect all living beings." T. gives no clue which would allow to choose between the readings of the MSS. A and B but palaeographically it is more likely that the reading of MS. A is corrupt as against that of MS. B. It is necessary to connect *asaṅgaprajñāpāramitābhāvanayā* with *āsravakṣayābhijñābhimukhyām* and *mahākaruṇābhāvanayā* with *asākṣātkaraṇād*, see the commentary (50.16-51.9) which explains that on the sixth stage the Bodhisattva approaches the extinction of the defilements because he has produced the unobstructed wisdom, but that, out of compassion, he is born in the Kāmadhatu, thus being at the same time in the pure and impure state. In his translation Tak. has followed T., whereas C. gives the right interpretation (Tak., p. 251, n. 395). In the Chinese translation the passage between *sarvasattvaparitrāṇāya* (50.19) and *ṣaṣṭhyām* (51.1) is missing. In its place there is a different passage (834c27-835a3) which has been translated by Ui (pp. 554-555) who combines both S. and C.

51.5-7 *śamasukhānāsvādanatayā tadupāyakṛtaparijayasya saṃsārābhimukhasattvāpekṣayā nirvāṇavimukhasya bodhyaṅgaparipūraṇāya dhyānair vihṛtya punaḥ kāmadhātau saṃcintyopapattiparigrahaṇato*; Tak. "While cultivating the means for the bliss of the Quiescence, but not in order to taste it [by himself] he turns his face away from Nirvāṇa, for the sake of the living beings who are facing the world of transmigration. Though abiding [in the desireless World of Form] with [4 kinds of] contemplations in order to accomplish the factors for the acquisition of Enlightenment, he voluntarily assumes again existence in the World of Desire." Instead of *nirvāṇavimukhasya* both T. and C. have *nirvāṇābhimukhasya* (Tak., p. 252, n. 407). This reading is to be preferred: "Although he has cultivated the means for the bliss of Quiescence without tasting it, [nevertheless] for the sake of the living beings who are turned towards transmigration, he, who is turned towards Nirvāṇa, after having dwelt in meditations in order to obtain fully the factors of Awakening, again voluntarily assumes existence in the sphere of desire." T. *ži-ba'i bde-ba'i ro mi-myaṅ-bar-de'i thabs-la byaṅ-bar byas-pa'i 'khor-ba-la mṅon-du phyogs-pa'i sems-can-la bltos-te / mya-ṅan-las-'das-pa la mṅon-du phyogs-pa / byaṅ-chub-kyi yan-lag yoṅs-su rdzogs-par bya-ba'i phyir bsam-gtan dag-gi gnas-nas slar 'dod-pa'i khams-su bsams-bžin-du skye-ba yoṅs-su 'dzin-pas /*. It is exactly the opposition between *saṃsārābhimukhasattva* and *nirvāṇābhimukha-[bodhisattva]* which brings fully into relief the great compassion of the Bodhisattva.

51.13-14 *ata eva jagadbandhor upāyakaruṇe pare / yad āryagotraprāpto dṛśyate bālagocare //* (70): Tak. "Having attained the position of the Saints, he is nevertheless seen amongst ordinary beings; therefore, he is, for the friends of all the world, the Highest means and Compassion." Tak. had misunderstood *jagadbandhu* "the friend of mankind", i.e. the bodhisattva. 70a-b = "therefore the means and the compassion of the friend of mankind are supreme". T. *de-ñid-phyir ni 'gro-ba-yi // gñen-gyi thabs daṅ sñiṅ-rje mchog //*. Ui's translation is correct, p. 555: *seken no shitashiki mono no, saikō no hōben to daihi to no ni o*.

52 8 *jagaty ākāśaparyante*; Tak. "among the world, limitless like the sky". In note

421 Tak. remarks that for *paryanta* T. has *mtha'-klas* (*ananta*) but *mtha'-klas-pa* occurs more often for *paryanta* and *paryavasāna*, cf. G. M. Nagao, *Index to the Mahāyāna-sūtrālaṃkāra*, part I (Tokyo, 1958), p. 150 (*samudraparyantamahāpṛthivī*°), Friedrich Weller, *Tibetisch-sanskritischer Index zum Bodhicaryāvatāra*, I (Berlin, 1952), p. 182 (*aśeṣākāśaparyantavāsināṃ kimu dehinām*), *Mahāvyutpatti*, No. 371 : *ākāśadhātuparyavasānaḥ*. H. A. Jäschke has already noted a case in which *mthas-klas* corresponds to *paryanta*, cf. A *Tibetan-English Dictionary* (London, 1881), p. 240b. Therefore one must translate "in the world bounded by the sky", cf. Ui, p. 556: *kokū o henzai to suru seken ni oite*.

60.20 *jalaruhaṃ saṃmiñjitaṃ*; Tak. "a faded ... lotus flower"; T. *padma zum*; O. "a lotus flower with folded leaves". Tak.'s wrong translation is due to the fact that the lotus is described above (60.12) as *vivarṇa*.

61.4-9 *yathā madhu prāṇigaṇopagūḍhaṃ vilokya vidvān puruṣas tadarthī / samantataḥ prāṇigaṇasya tasmād upāyato 'pakramaṇaṃ prakuryāt // (102) sarvajñacakṣurviditaṃ maharṣir madhūpamaṃ dhātum imaṃ vilokya /* Tak. "Suppose a clever person, having seen honey surrounded by cloudy bees, and wishing to get it, with skillful means, would deprive the bees completely of it; — (102) Similarly, the Great Sage, possessed of the eyes of the Omniscience, perceiving this Essence known as akin to honey." T. ... *de-dan thabs-kyis srog-chags tshogs* (P. *sogs*) *// kun-nas bral-bar rab-tu byed-pa bźin // (102) draṅ-sroṅ chen-pos kun-mkhyen-spyan-gyis ni // rigs khams sbraṅ-rtsi ḍaṅ-'dra 'di gzigs-nas //* = "with the help of a strategem he would completely remove the swarm of bees from it. (102). The Great Seer, having seen that this Essence, which he has perceived with his omniscient eye, is like honey ..."

61.13-14 *madhvā ... kuryāt kāryam*; J. notes: "*kuryāt tatvam*, A and B (reading doubtful in both); *bya byed-pa* T." Perhaps one must read *kuryāt kṛtyam*.

61.19 *bhavanti ye 'nnādibhir arthinas tu*: Tak. "Those who wish to utilize it as food and the like." In a note Tak. remarks that *annādibhir* (instr.) is grammatically peculiar (usually in loc.). However, in classical Sanskrit the instrumental is normal and in Buddhist Hybrid Sanskrit *arthika* also is constructed with the instrumental, cf. *BHSD* s.v. The meaning of this *pāda* is: "those who want food, etc."; T. *zas-sogs don-du gñer-ba gaṅ yin-pa*.

69.4 *kāmasevānimittatvāt paryutthānāny amedhyavat* / Tak. "Being characterized as devoted to [such] Passion, the outburst of Passions is repulsive like impurities." Tak.'s translation is based upon C. which has misunderstood *nimitta*. T. *'dod-pa bsten-pa'i rgyu yin-phyir // kun-nas ldaṅ-pa mi-gtsaṅ 'dra //* ; O. "The outburst of their passions, being the cause for giving way to the desires, is abhorrent like impurities." See also Ui's translation, p. 580: *yoku ni fukeru koto o in to nasu node, ten wa fun no gotoku de aru*.

69.12 *vikośagarbhavaj jñānam avikalpaṃ vipākavat*; Tak. "And the non-discriminative Wisdom has a resemblance to the matured form of an embryo delivered from its covering." It is impossible to relate *vipākavat* to *vikośagarbha*. Ui (p. 580: *mufunbetsu no chi wa taizō o hanareta mono no gotoku, jukushita mono no gotoku de aru*) takes both *vikośagarbhavat* and *vipākavat* as comparisons. The same interpretation is given by T.: *mṅal-sbubs bral-'dra mi-rtog-pa'i // ye-śes rnam-par smin-pa bźin /*, but this does not make sense. One has to take *vipākavat* as a possessive adjective relating to *jñāna* "the ripened knowledge", i.e. the knowledge obtained in the last three stages of the bodhisattva.

71.3 *rūpagateṣu sarvagaṃ*; Tak. remarks that *Mahāyānasūtrālaṃkāra* IX, 15, the source of this quotation, has *rūpagaṇeṣu* instead of *rūpagateṣu*. One must certainly correct *rūpagaṇeṣu* into *rūpagateṣu*; T. has *gzugs-gyur kun-tu*, cf. Nagao, *op.cit.*, I, p. 208. This correction is not listed in Nagao's corrigenda to Lévi's edition. Ui (p. 582) has changed the reading of the *Ratnagotravibhāga* according to the *Mahāyānasūtrālaṃkāra*!

73.10 *sattvadhātāv iti*; Johnston's correction of the reading of the MS. (*saṁrvadyatanatija*) is based upon C. However, T. has *yod-do || źes-bya ba'i bar ni |* = *saṃvidyata iti yāvat*.

73.12-14 *yaiva cāsau dharmatā saivātra yuktir yoga upāyaḥ paryāyaḥ | evam eva tat syāt | anyathā naiva tat syād iti |*. J. remarks: "Reading uncertain. *paryāya eva vai tat syāt*, B." and Tak. notes that both T. and C. do not translate *paryāya*. T. *chos-ñid gaṅ-yin-pa de-ñid ni 'dir gaṅ-gis de-lta-bu kho-nar 'gyur-gyi gźan-du mi 'gyur-ro źes-bya-ba'i rigs-pa daṅ sbyor-ba daṅ thabs yin-te |* = *yaiva cāsau dharmatā saivatra yuktir yoga upāyaḥ | yayaivam eva tat syāt | anyathā naiva tat syād iti |*.

74.10 *nedaṃ sthānaṃ vidyate*; Tak. "There is [absolutely] no room for it." The meaning is: "This is impossible", cf. *BHSD* s.v. *sthāna* (5).

75.14-15 *sata eva dharmasyottārakālam ucchedo vināśaḥ parinirvāṇam iti*; Tak. "thinking that the perfect Nirvāṇa means the Extinction, i.e. the destruction of the elements [for the Phenomenal Existence] in future." Tak. has omitted *sata eva*, T. *yod-pa'i*; O. "... the destruction of elements which did really exist." Cf. Ui, p. 588: *jitsuu no hō ga goji ni danmetsu-shi metsue-suru no ga sunawachi nehan de aru to kangaeru mono*.

77.18 *ātmasnehaś cādhikaḥ*; Tak. "and besides, affection for one's self." T. *bdag-chags lhag-pa['i]* = "excessive self-love." The Tibetan translation is correct. See Ui's translation, p. 591: *tsuyoi jitsuga no aijaku ga*.

78.1 *viviktaṃ saṃskṛtaṃ sarvaprakāraṃ bhūtakoṭiṣu*; Tak. "all kinds of phenomena, made by causes and conditions ... are ... deprived of reality." In Mahāyāna philosophy *vivikta*, litt. "separated, free from", means "without substance", cf. *Prasannapadā*, p. 349,4: *skandha sabhāvatu śūnya vivikta*. Therefore the translation is as follows: "In the absolute reality everything which is produced by causes is isolated (without substance)." See Ui's translation, p. 591: *shinjitsuzai ni oitewa, issai no shurui no ui wa onri-serarete iru*.

78.9 *bodhicittodaye 'py asya*; Tak. remarks that T. has *bodhicittodaye yasya* and relates *yasya* to *tasya* in the next verse, but he prefers the reading of the MSS. because in relation to the preceding verse *api* is quite necessary. I am not convinced by this argument and would prefer to follow T.

78.21-22 *tathāgatagarbhādhikāraḥ prathamaḥ paricchedaḥ ślokārthasaṃgrahavyākhyānataḥ samāptaḥ*; T. *de-bźin-gśegs-pa'i sñiṅ-po'i skabs-te tshigs-su bcad-pa daṅ-po'i don-gyi bsdus-pa'i bśad-pa rdzogs-so ||* = *tathāgatagarbhādhikāraḥ prathamaślokārthasaṃgrahavyākhyānaṃ samāptam*. MS. B has *°ādhikāraprathamaśloka°*. Chapter II ends with *bodhyadhikāro nāma dvitīyaḥ paricchedaḥ* which corresponds to T. *byaṅ-chub-kyi skabs źes-bya-ba ste le'u gñis-pa'o*, chapter III with *guṇādhikāro nāma tritīyaḥ paricchedaḥ*; T. omits *nāma*: *yon-tan-gyi skabs-te le'u gsum-pa'o*. Chapter IV ends with *tathāgatakṛtyakriyādhikāraś caturthaḥ paricchedaḥ ślokārthasaṃgrahavyākhyānataḥ samāptaḥ*; T. *de-bźin-gśegs-pa'i phrin-las mdzad-pa'i skabs-te le'u bźi-pa'o || || tshigs-su bcad-pa'i don-gyi bśad-pa rdzogs-so ||* = ... *caturthaḥ paricchedaḥ | ślokārthasaṃgrahavyākhyānaṃ samāptam*. Finally, chapter V ends with *anuśaṃsādhikāro nāma pañcamaḥ paricchedaḥ ślokārthasaṃgrahavyākhyānataḥ samāptaḥ*; T. *phan-yon-gyi le'u-ste lṅa-pa'o || || tshigs-su bcad-pa'i don-gyi bsdus-pa'i bśad-pa rdzogs-so ||* = ... *pañcamaḥ paricchedaḥ | ślokārthasaṃgrahavyākhyānaṃ samāptam*.

80.5 *dharmāṇāṃ tad akalpanapravicayajñānāśrayād āpyate*; Tak. "and is attained when the elements [of existence] take resort to the non-discriminative and Analytical Wisdom." Tak. considers the reading *dharmāṇāṃ* as doubtful because both T. and C. connect *dharma* with *avikalpa*. However, T. corresponds quite well to S.: *de ni chos-la mi-rtog rnam-'byed ye-śes-la brten-nas 'thob* = "it (Buddhahood) is obtained by having recourse to non-discriminative and analytical knowledge in regard to the dharmas." See Ui's translation, p. 595: *shohō ni taisuru mufunbetsu to kenchaku to no chi ni eshi-suru koto ni yotte, tasserareru no de aru*.

85.14 *tatprayatnāḥ*: T. *de rtogs-pa* = *tatprapannāḥ*?

88.11 *bālasārthātivāhanāt*: Tak. "toiling excessively for the company of ordinary beings." It is better to render *ativāhana* by "leading, guiding", cf. *BHSD* s.v. *ativāha*. Ui's translation is too literal and he has gone wrong in his interpretation of *sārtha*, p. 606: *bonbu o mokuteki kansei ni hakobu ga yue ni*.

89.13 *nityam aśaraṇānāṃ ca śaraṇābhyupapattitaḥ*; Tak. "and he gives a refuge for those who have no shelter, because of these [10] points, he is 'eternal'." Ui interprets *nityam* in the same way, cf. p. 607: *soshite kiesho no nai hito-bito ni kie o keiyo-suru kara, butsu wa jōjū de aru*. It seems to me impossible to relate *nityam* n. to *lokanāthaḥ* in verse 62 (89.2). The eternity of the Buddha is explained by verse 68 (89.14-15). Both C. and T. relate *nityaṃ* to *aśaraṇānām*, etc. T. *rtag-pa skyabs-med rnams-kyi ni || skyabs-la sogs-pa 'thad phyir-ro |*.

89.19 *upamānivṛttitaḥ*: T. has read *upamātivṛttitaḥ* (*dpe-las 'das-pa'i phyir*). This reading seems preferable.

92.11 *jñeye vastuni sarvathātmaparayor jñānāt svayaṃ jñāpanād*; Tak. "He himself knows and causes others to know all the things cognizable in all their forms." Tak. seems to relate *ātman* to *jñāna* and *para* to *jñāpana*. Also Ui has the same interpretation, p. 613: *ji to ta to no ni ni oite, mizukara shiru kara, ta ni shirashimeru kara*. However, T. relates *ātmaparayor* to *jñeye vastuni*: *bdag-gźan śes-bya'i dṅos-po rnam-kun śes daṅ śes-mdzad phyir*. Obermiller's translation ("He knows himself and makes known to others all the things cognizable in their forms") is improbable on account of the position of *bdag-gźan*. It is impossible to translate the Sanskrit text in this way because *svayaṃ* would duplicate *ātman*. Moreover, the caesura after *ātmaparayor* shows also that it is related to *jñeye vastuni*: "In regard to the things to be known completely by himself and others he himself knows and causes others to know."

93.6 *nopekṣāpratisaṃkhyāya*; Tak. "He is not indifferent, nor without consideration." Of course, one must understand: "He has no *apratisaṃkhyāyopekṣā*", cf. T *ma-brtags btaṅ-sñoms mi-mṅa'-ste*. *Apratisaṃkhyāya* is a gerund and not a BHS form for *-yāyām* (fem-loc.) as stated by Tak. See Ui's note (p. 615, n. 1) and his translation p. 615: *shichaku-sezu shite no sha no nai to*.

93.11 *svarasādhyupekṣaṇam*; Tak. "indifference to one's own taste". *Svarasādhyupekṣaṇam* (T. *ṅaṅ-gis gtaṅ-sñoms*), litterally "natural indifference", is a synonym of *apratisaṃkhyāyopekṣā*. See Ui's note (p. 615, n. 2) and his translation p. 615: *jinen no sha*. Tak.'s renderings of *svarasa* are not very adequate, cf. 44.13 *svarasayogena*, T. *raṅ-gi ṅaṅ-gis*, Tak. "with its own essence"; 58.1 °*svarasavāhimārgajñāna*° (*svarasavāhin*, T. *raṅ-gi ṅaṅ-gis 'jug-pa*). Tak. "the knowledge of the Path ... bearing its own taste". In both places C. translates well by "natural" (*tzŭ-jan*). *Svarasayogena* means "in its nature" and *svarasavāhimārgajñāna* "the knowledge of the path which proceeds naturally".

93.13 *muktijñānanidarśanāc ca*; Tak. "of the intuition of freedom". In a note Tak. remarks that T. om. *nidarśana* of *muktijñānanidarśana* (reading apparently '*vimuktijñānadarśanāt*'). However, T. has *grol-ba'i ye-śes las* (*muktijñānāt*). Both the Sanskrit text and the Tibetan translation are imperfect renderings of *vimuktijñānadarśanāt* (cf. 93.7) Metrical exigencies made it impossible for the Sanskrit text to repeat *vimuktijñānadarśanāt* and for T. to translate *darśana*. As one of the *āveṇikabuddhadharmas* '*nāsti vimuktijñānadarśanaparihāṇiḥ*' is mentioned in the *Dharmasaṃgraha*. However, it does not occur in other lists, cf. *Mahāvyutpatti*, 136-153; *Mahāyānasūtrālaṃkāra*, pp. 187-188. Its authencity is guaranteed by the fact that it is listed in the *Daśasāhasrikā Prajñāpāramitā*, cf. Sten Konow, *The two first chapters of the Daśasāhasrikā Prajñāpāramitā* (Oslo, 1941), p. 43. As far as I know, there is no detailed study of these lists. References are given by L. de La Vallée Poussin, *L'Abhidharmakośa de Vasubandhu*, VII (Paris-Louvain, 1923), p. 67; Har Dayal, *The Bodhisattva Doctrine in Buddhist Sanskrit Literature* (London, 1932), p. 326, n. 81; Ét. Lamotte, *La somme* *du grand Véhicule*, Tome II (Louvain, 1939), p. 61*; *BHSD* s.v. *āveṇika*; *Mochizuki Shinkō's Bukkyō daijiten*, s.v. *jūhachi fuguhō*, pp. 2361c-2366a.

97.11 *dvātriṃśal lakṣaṇāḥ kāye darśanāhlādakā guṇāḥ*; Tak. "the 32 marks are the properties, visible and causing delight in the body." T. *mthoṅ-na tshim-byed yon-tan gaṅ // sum-cu-rtsa-gñis źes bya-ba //* O. "The other 32 distinctive features, which, being perceived, arouse delight." T. 's translation of *darśanāhlādaka* is correct. See also Ui's translation, p. 619: *shin ni sonsuru sanjūnisō wa, kore o mireba kangi o ataeru shokudoku de atte.*

98.8-10 *kṛtsnaṃ niṣpādya yānaṃ pravaraguṇagaṇajñānaratnasvagarbhaṃ puṇyajñānārkaraśmipravisṛtavipulānantamadhyāmbarābham / buddhatvaṃ ... vilokya*; Tak. "Having completely established the Vehicle, the ocean of knowledge filled with the multitudes of the excellent virtues and endowed with the rays of the sun of Merit and Knowledge, and having perceived that Buddhahood, like space, pervading extensively and of neither limit nor middle ..." Tak. follows T. in making a break after °*raśmi* and in relating *puṇyajñānārkaraśmi* to *yānaṃ* and *pravisṛta*° to *buddhatvaṃ*. T. *yon-tan rin-chen mchog tshogs daṅ-ldan ye-śes chu-mtsho bsod-nams ye-śes ñi-'od can // theg-pa ma-lus ṅes-par bsgrubs-te mtha'-daṅ-dbus med rgya-cheṅ nam-mkha' ltar khyab-pa // saṅs-rgyas-ñid* ... C. relates *puṇya*°...°*bham* to *buddhatvaṃ*. I prefer to follow this interpretation and to translate: "Buddhahood, which is like the sky without end and middle and pervaded by the rays of the sun of merit and knowledge." Ui, also, does not split up *puṇya*°...°*bham* but relates it to *yānaṃ* p. 620: *fukutoku to chie to no hi no hikari o sosogi, kōdai de, hen mo chū mo naki kokū no gotoki jō no subete o jōju-shita no de,* ... The impossibility of this interpretation is clearly shown by 99.9 *vipulānantamadhyatvād bodhir ākāśadhātuvat.* A break after °*raśmi* is impossible because the rays of the sun of merit and wisdom cannot illuminate the Vehicle which is compared to an ocean but only the Buddhahood which is likened to the sky.

101.7-8 *svacittapratibhāso 'yam iti naivaṃ pṛthagjanāḥ / jānanty atha ca tat teṣām avandhyaṃ bimbadarśanam //* Tak. "Ordinary people do not notice that this is merely a reflection of their mind; still this manifestation of the Buddha's features is useful for fulfilling their aim." A preceding verse (100.16-17) explains that one sees the Buddha appear in one's own mind (*svacetasi*) when it is pure through faith etc. (*śraddhādivimale*) and developed by the virtues of faith, etc. (*śraddhādiguṇabhāvite*). [Tak.'s translation of this verse is rather too free.] Therefore, I think that it is better to translate *svacittapratibhāsa* by "an appearance in their own mind" and *bimdadarśanam* by "the vision of the image (of the Buddha)". *Bimba* refers to the *nirmāṇakāya*, cf. 86.9.

101.17-18 *vaiḍūryasvacchabhūte manasi munipaticchāyādhigamane, citrāṇy utpādayanti pramuditamanasas tadvaj jinasutāḥ //* Tak. "Similarly, for obtaining the shadow of the Lord of Sages on their mind which is radiant like the Vaiḍūrya stone, the sons of the Buddha, with minds full of delight, produce various pictures showing the Buddha's life, etc." The reading *citrāṇy utpādayanti* gives no good sense. T. has *sems rab-skyed-par byed* (D.; P. *gśegs* instead of *sems*, a mistake due to the preceding *de-bźin*) and C. "they make vows to carry out different acts." Johnston himself had read *cittān vyutpādayanti* which was "corrected" by T. Chowdhury (p. ii). I propose to read *cittāny utpādayanti* which corresponds well to both C. and T.

102.6 *pūrvaśuklānubhāvataḥ*; Tak. "owing to the previous, virtuous experiences". Here as well as in 107.10 (*śubhānubhāvāt*; Tak. "of the pure experiences") Tak. has mistaken *anubhāva* for *anubhava*.

102.7 *yatnasthānamanorūpavikalparahitā sati*; Tak. "[the divine drum], being apart from efforts, from a particular place, from forms of mind, and from thought-constructions." Tak.'s translation is probably the result of the wrong interpretation by T.: *'bad daṅ gnas daṅ yid-gzugs daṅ // rnam-par rtog-pa med.* It is clear from 102.14 (*yatnasthānaśarīracittarahitaḥ śabdaḥ*; P. *'bad gnas lus daṅ sems bral-ba'i // sgra*) that one has to translate as follows: "[the divine drum] which is free from thought-constructions as to effort, place, mind and matter". Tak. equates *manorūpa* and *vikalpa* in 102.7 with *śarīra* and *citta* in 102.14, but *manas* and *rūpa* correspond to *citta* and *śarīra*. Perhaps one must translate *sthāna* by "pitch, tone"; C. (818b29) has "use, function" (*yung*).

102.10-11 *vyāpya buddhasvareṇaivaṃ vibhur jagad aśeṣataḥ / dharmaṃ diśati bhavyebhyo yatnādirahito 'pi san //* Tak. "Similarly in this world, the Buddha who is all-pervading and free from effort and the rest, reaches the Doctrine by his voice towards the worthy without exceptions." I prefer T.'s interpretation: *de-bźin khyab-bdag 'bad-sogs-daṅ // bral-daṅ 'gro-ba ma-lus-pa // saṅs-rgyas gsuṅ-gis khyab-mdzad-de // skal-ldan rnams-la chos ston-to //* = "In the same way, the Lord who pervades the world entirely with his Buddha-voice teaches without effort etc. the Law to the worthy." See Ui's translation, p. 626: *butsu no koe no hibiki mo, hiroku, amasu tokoro mo naku, seken ni shūhen-shite, doryoku-nado o hanarete itemo, butsu ni narubeki mono-tō ni hō o shisetsu-suru no de aru.*

103.4 *asurādiparacakra*°; Tak. "the invasion of Asuras and others." One must follow T.: *lha-ma-yin la-sogs-pa pha-rol-ghi tshogs*, O. "the Asuras and the other hosts of adversaries." Ui translates *cakra* with "weapon" which is possible but less probable, p. 627: *ashura-tō no teki no buki.*

103.5 *asatkāmaratisukhavivecanatayā*; Tak. "owing to its distinguishing bliss from the pleasure caused by evil enjoyment." See *BHSD* s.v. *vivecayati*: "causes to abandon, dissuades from". See Ui's translation, p. 627: *fujitsunaru gokan no yokubō kiraku no raku kara hanareshimeru koto ni yori.*

104.2 *samādhicittārpaṇabhāvavācakam*: T. *tiṅ-'dzin sems-gtod bsam-pa skul-byed ñid //* = *samādhicittārpaṇabhāvacodakam*. This latter reading seems preferable.

104.3-6 *samāsato yat sukhakāraṇaṃ divi kṣitāv anantāsv api lokadhātuṣu / aśeṣalokaspharaṇāvabhāsanaṃ praghoṣam āgamya tad apy udāhṛtam //* Tak. "In short, that which is the cause of bliss, in heaven, on earth, as well as in all the other numberless worlds, is the voice [of the Buddha] which manifests pervadingly in the world leaving no residue; and in respect to those points, thus it is illustrated." T. *mdor-na ma-lus 'jig-rten khams-su yaṅ // lha daṅ sa-gnas bde-ba'i rgyu gaṅ-yin // de ni ma-lus 'jig-rten khyab snaṅ-ba // dbyaṅs-ñid la ni rab-tu brten-par brjod //*; O. "In short, that which is the cause of bliss, in all the regions of the world, the celestial and the earthly is said to have its foundation in the unique voice which pervades the whole of the world without exception." Obermiller's translation corresponds well to the Sanskrit text. For *āgamya* see *BHSD* s.v.: "with reference to, owing to, because of, on account of, thanks to", "that which is the cause of bliss is said to be due to the voice [of the Buddha]".

104.10 *aparicchinna*°; Tak. "without interruption"; rather "without limitation".

106.14 °*śraddhānumānyād*; Tak. "because of their following the faith". Tak.'s translation corresponds to T.: *dad-pa'i rjes-'braṅs-nas*. Perhaps one must read °*śraddhānusārād*.

108.15-16 *sadā sarvatra visṛte dharmadhātunabhastale / buddhasūrye vineyādritannipāto yathārhataḥ //* Tak. remarks: "The readings '*visṛte*' and '*buddhasūrye*' are to be corrected into '*visṛto*' and '*buddhasūryo*', respectively. Also '*vineyādri*' should be changed into '*vineyādrau*' (loc.) and be separated from '*tannipāto*'. So T., C. omit this verse." There is no need to change this verse in this drastic way. T. corresponds to S.: *rtag-tu thams-cad-la khyab-pa // chos-dbyiṅs nam-mkha'i dkyil-du ni // saṅs-rgyas ñi-ma gdul-bya-yi // ri-la ji-ltar 'os-par 'bab //* The fact that T. does not render the locative absolute and has *ri-la* does not mean that the Tibetan translator has made use of a different Sanskrit text.

109.15-16 *yugapad gocarasthānāṃ sarvābhiprāyapūraṇam / kurute nirvikalpo 'pi pṛthak cintāmaṇir yathā //* Tak. "Just as the wishfulfilling gem, though itself is of no thought-construction, fulfills all desires of those living in the same region, separately".

Tak. considers *yugapadgocarastha* as a compound. It seems preferable to relate *yugapad* to *kurute*: "Just as the wishing gem, without discriminations, fulfills simultaneously and separately the wishes of all who are in its reach". T. *ji-ltar yid-bźin nor-bu ni || rtog-pa med-kyaṅ cig-car-du || spyod-yul-gnas-pa rnams-kyi ni || bsam-kun so-sor rdzogs-byed ltar ||.*

115.9 *maṇisaṃskṛtāni kanakakṣetrāṇi*; Tak. "golden lands, constructed by jewels"; preferable "adorned with jewels". T. renders *saṃskṛta* by *spras-pa*, not *spros-pa* as given by Tak. See Ui's translation, p. 642: *manishu ni kazarareta ōgon no kokudo o.*

116.10-11 *asty asau viṣayo 'cintyaḥ śakyaḥ prāptuṃ sa mādṛśaiḥ / prāpta evaṃguṇaś cāsāv iti śraddhādhimuktitaḥ ||* Tak. "Indeed, as he is full of devotion and faith that there 'exists' this inconceivable sphere, that it 'can' be realized by one like him, and this sphere, 'endowed with such virtues', has been attained." The context shows that it is impossible to translate *prāpta* by 'has been attained'. I suggest to translate:"that it (this sphere), when attained, has such good qualities." This interpretation agrees with C: "that it has such good qualities." T. *bsam mi-khyab-pa'i yul 'di ni || yod-pa* (P. *yon-tan*) *bdag-'dras thob* (P. *thos*)*-nus daṅ || thob-pa 'di-'dra'i yon-tan daṅ || ldan żes dad-pas mos-pa'i phyir ||* O. "Indeed, he is full of devotion and faith that this inconceivable sphere exists that one like himself can realize it, and, having once attained it, becomes endowed with such properties." Also Ui relates *prāpta* to the wise man mentioned in the preceding verse; cf. p. 643: *soshite tasshita toki ni wa, kare wa kakuno gotoki moromoro no kudoku o uru to.* This translation is not possible because *asau* (which is not rendered in T.) can only refer to *viṣaya.*

117.7-8 *dhiyādhimuktyā kuśalopasaṃpadā samanvitā ye* ...; Tak. "Those intelligent people who are endowed with faith and accomplishment of virtues." Tak.'s interpretation corresponds to C. and T.: *gaṅ-dag mos dge phun-sum-tshogs ldan blo ||* but, nevertheless, one must understand *dhiyā-adhimuktyā*: "Those who are endowed with intelligence, faith and the attainment of virtue." See Ui's translation, p. 645: *chi to shinge to o gushi, shuzen bugyō o guseru mono.*

117.18 *śāstaram ekaṃ jinam uddiśadbhiḥ.* Tak. "who refer to the Lord as only Preceptor." See *BHSD* s.v. *uddiśyati*: "*uddiśyati* (= *uddiśati*; not recorded in this sense), recognizes: *Divy.* 191.3 (*māṃ* ...) *śāstaram uddiśyadbhir* ..., those who recognize me as teacher ..."

118.5 *yat svayam eva nītam ṛṣiṇā sūtraṃ vicālyaṃ na tat*; Tak. "the Scripture should not be interpolated, which is discoursed by the Sage himself." *Vi-cal-* means "to depart or deviate from". Therefore, it would be better to translate: "One must not deviate from the discourse taught as final doctrine by the Sage himself."

118.9 *tasmān nābhiniveśadṛṣṭimaline tasmin niveśyā matiḥ*; Tak. "Therefore, your mind should not be attached to the dirt of the prejudiced conception." More precisely: "to that which is soiled by a prejudiced conception".

118.13 *lobhagredhatayā*; Tak. notes that T. has *lābhagredhatayā* (P. *rñed-la brkam*). This reading must be adopted.

In the notes there are many references to the Tibetan text. Tak. has used only the Derge edition. In several cases P. gives a better reading. In some cases the interpretation of the Tibetan translation is not correct. Also quite a few misprints must be corrected. P. 146, n. 27: "For '*svalakṣaṇenānugatāni*', T. as if '*svalakṣaṇasyānugatāni*'". P. *raṅ-mtshan-ñid-kyis rjes-'brel-ba* corresponds to S. p. 148, n. 51: correct *yoṅs-su* to *yoṅs-su.* P. 149, n. 59: correct *ne-bar* to *ñe-bar.* P. 151, n. 74: correct *lal* to *bal.* P. 158. n. 25: correct *śen* to *żen.* P. 166, n. 15: correct *ṅe-tshig* to *ṅes-tshig.* P. 168, n. 29: correct *brol* to *bral.* P. 170, n. 43: correct *mtshan-par* to *mtshan-mar.* P. 176, n. 25: correct *cig-śes* to *cig-śos.* P. 179, n. 49: correct *gzugs-brñen* to *gzugs-brñan.* P. 183, n. 28: correct *gśad* to *gśed.* P. 184, n. 33: correct *thung* to *thug.* P. 185, n. 49: correct *bsñan to brñan.* P. 203, n. 31: read with P. *mun-pa bas kyaṅ ches mun-pa /*

mun-pa nas mun-pa chen-por instead of *mun-pa-las kyaṅ ches, mun-pa chen-por*. P. 209, n. 78: read with P. *gźuṅ* instead of *bźuṅ*; n. 82: correct *ston* to *stoṅ*. P. 216, n. 123: correct *drir* to *dri-ṅa*. P. 221, n. 162: *pratyupasthāpana* (not *pratyupasthāna*) corresponds exactly to T. *ñe-bar gnas-par byed-de*. P. 229, n. 225: read with P. *sgo-nas* instead of *sgo-la*. P. 241, n. 310: read with P. *'go-nad* instead of *mgo'i nad*. P. 254, n. 420: correct *sbyod* to *spyod*. P. 264, n. 491: T. does not omit *ākāra*; P. has *de-rnams* which has to be corrected to *de-rnam*. P. 270, n. 21: read with P. *zum* instead of *thum*. P. 272, n. 40: P. has *kun-tu dag-par*. P. 283, n. 115: correct *sniṅ* to *sñiṅ*. P. 294, n. 4: correct *tshas* to *tshad*. P. 295, n. 12: read with P. *ṅes-par* instead of *ñe-bar*. P. 299, n. 42: *ñe-bar bźag* (D. *gźags*)-*pa* corresponds to *upasthāpita*, not to *upasthita*. P. 302, n. 63: correct *'phrol* to *'phro-la*. P. 304, n. 76: P. has *mthoṅs*. P. 305, n. 4: correct *lam* to *lan*. P. 306, n. 12.: correct *bgag-cag* to *bdag-chags*; n. 17: correct *spral-ba* to *sprul-pa*. P. 318, n. 35: correct *rjas* to *rdzas*. P. 319, n. 49: read with P. *dam-pa* instead of *dag-pa*. P. 322, n. 65: correct *bstan* to *brtan*. P. 326, n. 102: correct *gzugz* to *gzugs*. P. 328, n. 120: correct *stoṅ* to *ston*. P. 329, n. 133: read with P. *'khor dgyes-rol-pa* instead of *'khor-gyis dkyes-rol*. P. 339, n. 18: delete *go-cha*. P. 341, n. 36: correct *nams* to *ñams*. P. 344, n. 69: read with P. *ni* instead of *riṅ*. P. 346, n. 95: correct *sphu* to *spu*; n; 96: correct *mthor* to *mthon*. P. 357, n. 17: *sgom-pa* renders *bhāvita* P. 358, n. 30: read with P. *lha-bdag* instead of *lha-dag*; T. does not omit *marutām* which is rendered by *lha'i*. P. 362, n. 70: correct *gtoṅ* to *gtod*. P. 363, n. 77: correct *rtogs* to *gtogs*. P. 366, n. 110: read with P. *rdo-tshan* instead of *rdo-than*; n. 111: read with P. *sul* instead of *yul* (cf. Mahāvyutpatti 5260). P. 381, n. 8: read with P. *spras* instead of *spros*; n. 13: *bsgoms* renders *dhyāyed* (115.17). P. 384, n. 33: correct *rje* to *rjes*. P. 386, n. 46: read with P. *rgyal-ba ston-pa* instead of *rgyal-pa'i bstan-pa*. P. 387, n. 63: correct *brtam* to *brkam*. P. 388, n. 71: correct *ṅams* to *ñams* (so P.); n. 76: *bya-ba min* renders *acaraṇa*; *vadhācaraṇa* "the bad act of killing".

Due to a slip of the pen is the remark that *abudha* is Buddhist Hybrid Sanskrit for Sanskrit *abuddha* (p. 155, n. 5; p. 158, n. 20). In note 417 (p. 254) *Catuḥśubha* must be corrected to *Catuḥstava* and *Minor Buddhist Works*, II, etc. to *Minor Buddhist Texts*, II, pp. 235-246, Roma, 1956. Misprints are rather numerous, especially in Sanskrit words. They will give no difficulties to specialists and it is superfluous to list them here.

The translation does not indicate the pages of the Sanskrit text. For this reason a concordance of the page numbers of the text and the translation may be helpful. The first number refers to the text, the second to the translation.

1 – 141	18 – 180	35 – 219	52 – 253	69 – 282
2 – 142	19 – 182	36 – 221	53 – 255	70 – 284
3 – 144	20 – 183	37 – 224	54 – 257	71 – 286
4 – 147	21 – 186	38 – 226	55 – 258	72 – 288
5 – 149	22 – 188	39 – 228	56 – 261	73 – 291
6 – 151	23 – 190	40 – 230	57 – 262	74 – 296
7 – 153	24 – 191	41 – 232	58 – 264	75 – 298
8 – 156	25 – 193	42 – 234	59 – 266	76 – 300
9 – 158	26 – 197	43 – 237	60 – 269	77 – 303
10 – 160	27 – 200	44 – 238	61 – 270	78 – 306
11 – 163	28 – 202	45 – 240	62 – 271	79 – 310
12 – 166	29 – 205	46 – 242	63 – 272	80 – 314
13 – 169	30 – 207	47 – 244	64 – 273	81 – 316
14 – 172	31 – 209	48 – 246	65 – 274	82 – 318
15 – 174	32 – 212	49 – 248	66 – 276	83 – 320
16 – 176	33 – 215	50 – 249	67 – 277	84 – 321
17 – 178	34 – 217	51 – 252	68 – 280	85 – 323

The Ratnagotravibhāga

86 – 325	93 – 341	100 – 356	107 – 368	114 – 379
87 – 327	94 – 342	101 – 357	108 – 369	115 – 380
88 – 329	95 – 345	102 – 359	109 – 370	116 – 381
89 – 332	96 – 347	103 – 361	110 – 372	117 – 383
90 – 334	97 – 347	104 – 362	111 – 374	118 – 386
91 – 336	98 – 351	105 – 364	112 – 375	119 – 388
92 – 339	99 – 353	106 – 366	113 – 377	

A. N. U., Canberra

J. W. de Jong